HOUGHTON MIFFLIN HARCOURT

On Core
Mathematics

Algebra 2

TEACHER ED

Contents

Unit 3 Polynomial Functions

Unit 4 Rational Functions

Unit 5 Radical Functions

Unit 6 Exponential Functions

Unit 9   Sequences and Series

Unit 10   Statistics

© Houghton Mifflin Harcourt Publishing Company

Learning the Common Core State Standards

Has your state adopted the Common Core standards? If so, then students will be learning both mathematical content standards and the mathematical practice standards that underlie them. The supplementary material found in *On Core Mathematics Algebra 2* will help students succeed with both.

Here are some of the special features you'll find in *On Core Mathematics Algebra 2*

INTERACTIVE LESSONS

Students actively participate in every aspect of a lesson. They read the mathematical concepts in an Engage, carry out an activity in an Explore, and complete the solution of an Example. This interactivity promotes a deeper understanding of the mathematics.

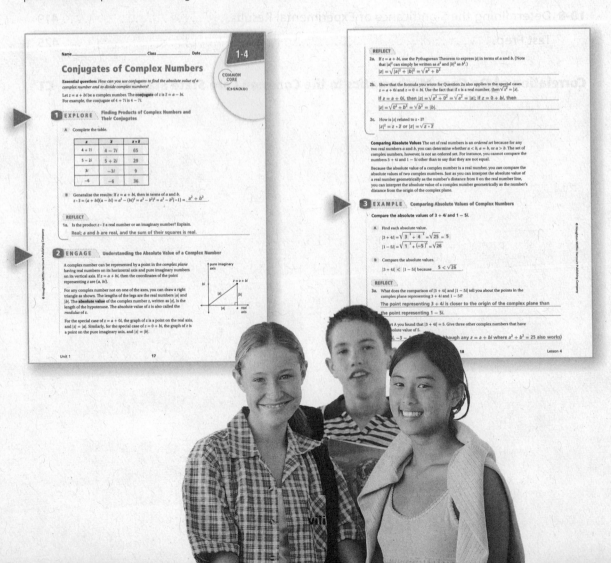

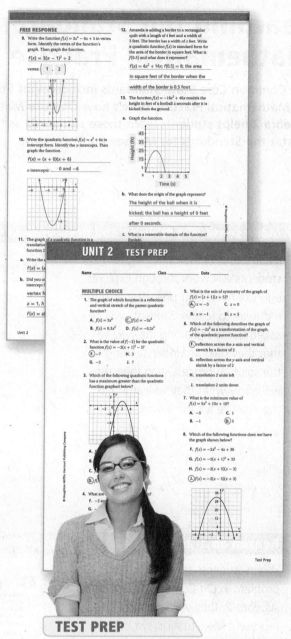

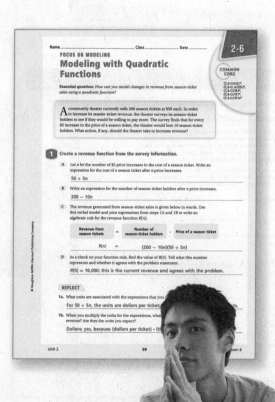

REFLECTIVE LEARNING

Students learn to be reflective thinkers through the follow-up questions after each Engage, Explore, and Example in a lesson. The Reflect questions challenge students to really think about the mathematics they have just encountered and to share their understanding with the class.

TEST PREP

At the end of a unit, students have an opportunity to practice the material in multiple choice and free response formats used on standardized tests.

FOCUS ON MODELING

Special lessons that focus on modeling occur near the ends of units. These features help students pull together the mathematical concepts and skills taught in a unit and apply them to real-world situations.

Learning the Standards for Mathematical Practice

The Common Core State Standards include eight Standards for Mathematical Practice. Here's how *On Core Mathematics Algebra 2* helps students learn those standards as they master the Standards for Mathematical Content.

① Make sense of problems and persevere in solving them.

In *On Core Mathematics Algebra 2*, students will work through Explores and Examples that present a solution pathway to follow. Students will be asked questions along the way so that they gain an understanding of the solution process, and then they will apply what they've learned in the Practice for the lesson.

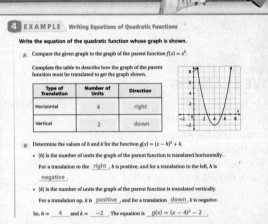

4 EXAMPLE Writing Equations of Quadratic Functions

Write the equation of the quadratic function whose graph is shown.

A Compare the given graph to the graph of the parent function $f(x) = x^2$.

Complete the table to describe how the graph of the parent function must be translated to get the graph shown.

Type of Translation	Number of Units	Direction
Horizontal	4	right
Vertical	2	down

B Determine the values of h and k for the function $g(x) = (x - h)^2 + k$.

- $|h|$ is the number of units the graph of the parent function is translated horizontally.
  For a translation to the right, h is positive, and for a translation to the left, h is negative.
- $|k|$ is the number of units the graph of the parent function is translated vertically.
  For a translation up, k is positive, and for a translation down, k is negative.

So, $h =$ 4 and $k =$ −2 . The equation is $g(x) = (x - 4)^2 - 2$.

② Reason abstractly and quantitatively.

When students solve a real-world problem in *On Core Mathematics Algebra 2*, they will learn to represent the situation symbolically by translating the problem into a mathematical expression or equation. Students will use these mathematical models to solve the problem and then state the answer in terms of the problem context. Students will reflect on the solution process in order to check their answers for reasonableness and to draw conclusions.

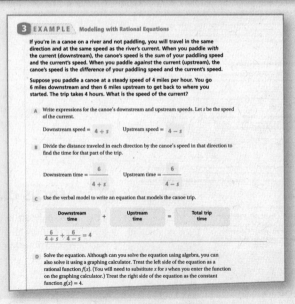

3 EXAMPLE Modeling with Rational Equations

If you're in a canoe on a river and not paddling, you will travel in the same direction and at the same speed as the river's current. When you paddle *with* the current (downstream), the canoe's speed is the *sum* of your paddling speed and the current's speed. When you paddle *against* the current (upstream), the canoe's speed is the *difference* of your paddling speed and the current's speed.

Suppose you paddle a canoe at a steady speed of 4 miles per hour. You go 6 miles downstream and then 6 miles upstream to get back to where you started. The trip takes 4 hours. What is the speed of the current?

A Write expressions for the canoe's downstream and upstream speeds. Let s be the speed of the current.

Downstream speed = 4 + s   Upstream speed = 4 − s

B Divide the distance traveled in each direction by the canoe's speed in that direction to find the time for that part of the trip.

Downstream time = $\dfrac{6}{4 + s}$ Upstream time = $\dfrac{6}{4 - s}$

C Use the verbal model to write an equation that models the canoe trip.

Downstream time	+	Upstream time	=	Total trip time

$\dfrac{6}{4 + s} + \dfrac{6}{4 - s} = 4$

D Solve the equation. Although can you solve the equation using algebra, you can also solve it using a graphing calculator. Treat the left side of the equation as a rational function $f(x)$. (You will need to substitute x for s when you enter the function on the graphing calculator.) Treat the right side of the equation as the constant function $g(x) = 4$.

③ Construct viable arguments and critique the reasoning of others.

Throughout *On Core Mathematics Algebra 2*, students will be asked to make conjectures, construct a mathematical arguments, explain their reasoning, and justify their conclusions. Reflect questions offer opportunities for cooperative learning and class discussion. Students will have additional opportunities to critique reasoning in Error Analysis problems.

---

③ EXAMPLE   Proving That the Sum of a Rational Number and an Irrational Number Is Irrational

Given that the set of rational numbers is closed under addition, prove that the sum of a rational number and an irrational number is an irrational number.

Let a be a rational number, let b be an irrational number, and let $a + b = c$. Assume that c is rational.

Rewrite $a + b = c$ as $b = -a + c$ by adding $-a$ to both sides. Because $-a$ and c are both __rational__ and the set of rational numbers is closed under addition, $-a + c$ must be __rational__, which means that b is __rational__.

This contradicts the condition that b be irrational. So, the assumption that c is rational must be false, which means that c, the sum of a rational number and an irrational number, is __irrational__.

REFLECT

3a. Indirect proof is also called *proof by contradiction*. What is the contradiction in the preceding proof?

The number b cannot be both rational and irrational.

---

22. **Error Analysis** A student simplified the expression $\sqrt[3]{x^2} \cdot \sqrt{x}$ by writing $\sqrt[3]{x^2} \cdot \sqrt{x} = x^{\frac{2}{3}} \cdot x^{\frac{1}{3}} = x^{\frac{2}{3} + \frac{1}{3}} = x^{\frac{3}{3}} = x^2$. Describe and correct the student's error.

$\sqrt[3]{x^2} = x^{\frac{2}{3}}$, not $x^{\frac{1}{3}}$; $\sqrt[3]{x^2} \cdot \sqrt{x} = x^{\frac{2}{3}} \cdot x^{\frac{1}{2}} = x^{\frac{2}{3} + \frac{1}{2}} = x^{\frac{7}{6}} = x^{1 + \frac{1}{6}} = x^1 \cdot x^{\frac{1}{6}} = x\sqrt[6]{x}$

---

④ Model with mathematics.

On *Core Mathematics Algebra 2* presents problems in a variety of contexts such as science, business, and everyday life. Students will use mathematical models such as expressions, equations, tables, and graphs to represent the information in the problem and to solve the problem. Then students will interpret their results in context.

---

④ EXAMPLE   Modeling Quadratic Functions in Vertex Form

The shape of a bridge support can be modeled by $f(x) = -\frac{1}{600}(x - 300)^2 + 150$, where x is the horizontal distance in feet from the left end of the bridge and $f(x)$ is the height in feet above the bridge deck. Sketch a graph of the support. Then determine the maximum height of the support above the bridge deck and the width of the support at the level of the bridge deck.

A   Graph the function.

- The vertex of the graph is __(300, 150)__.
- Find the point at the left end of the support ($x = 0$).

   Since $f(0) =$ __0__, the point __(0, 0)__ represents the left end.

- Use symmetry to find the point at the right end of the support.

   Since the left end is 300 feet to the left of the vertex, the right end will be 300 feet to the right of the vertex.

   The point __(600, 0)__ represents the right end.

- Find two other points on the support.

   $\left(120, \boxed{96}\right)$ and $\left(480, \boxed{96}\right)$

- Sketch the graph.

B   Determine the maximum height of the support.

   The maximum of the function is __150__.

   So, the maximum height of the bridge support is __150__ feet.

C   Determine the width of the bridge support at the level of the bridge deck.

   The distance from the left end to the right end is __600__ feet.

   So, the width is __600__ feet at the level of the bridge deck.

REFLECT

4a. Explain how you know that the *y*-coordinate of the right end of the support is 0.

The support has the shape of a parabola, so it is symmetric. The left end has a *y*-coordinate of 0, so the right end must also have a *y*-coordinate of 0.

4b. What does the vertex represent in this situation?

the point on the support above the midpoint of the bridge deck and at the greatest height above the bridge deck

⑤ Use appropriate tools strategically.

Students will use a variety of tools in *On Core Mathematics Algebra 2*, including manipulatives, paper and pencil, and technology. Students might use manipulatives to develop concepts, paper and pencil to practice skills, and technology (such as graphing calculators, spreadsheets, or geometry software) to investigate more complicated mathematical ideas.

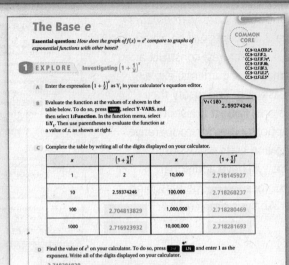

⑥ Attend to precision.

Precision refers not only to the correctness of arithmetic calculations, algebraic manipulations, and geometric reasoning but also to the proper use of mathematical language, symbols, and units to communicate mathematical ideas. Throughout *On Core Mathematics Algebra 2* students will demonstrate their skills in these areas when asked to calculate, describe, show, explain, prove, and predict.

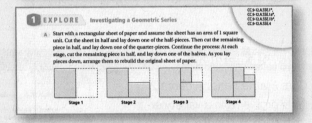

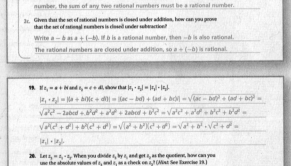

7 Look for and make use of structure.

In *On Core Mathematics Algebra 2*, students will look for patterns or regularity in mathematical structures such as expressions, equations, geometric figures, and graphs. Becoming familiar with underlying structures will help students build their understanding of more complicated mathematical ideas.

Value of Discriminant	Number of Real Solutions
$b^2 - 4ac > 0$	Two real solutions: $x = \frac{-b + \sqrt{b^2 - 4ac}}{2a}$ and $x = \frac{-b - \sqrt{b^2 - 4ac}}{2a}$
$b^2 - 4ac = 0$	One real solution: $x = -\frac{b}{2a}$
$b^2 - 4ac < 0$	No real solutions

Value of Discriminant	Number of Complex Solutions
$b^2 - 4ac > 0$	Two real solutions
$b^2 - 4ac = 0$	One real solution
$b^2 - 4ac < 0$	Two imaginary solutions

8 Look for and express regularity in repeated reasoning.

In *On Core Mathematics Algebra 2*, students will have the opportunity to explore and reflect on mathematical processes in order to come up with general methods for performing calculations and solving problems.

Name _____ Class _____ Date _____

2-2

Stretching, Shrinking, and Reflecting the Graph of $f(x) = x^2$

COMMON CORE

CC-9-12.F.IF.2,
CC-9-12.F.IF.7*,
CC-9-12.F.IF.7a*,
CC-9-12.F.BF.3

Essential question: *How does the graph of $g(x) = ax^2$ differ from the graph of $f(x) = x^2$?*

In this lesson, you will investigate stretches, shrinks, and reflections of the graph of the parent quadratic function.

1 EXAMPLE Graphing $f(x) = ax^2$ when $|a| > 1$

Graph each quadratic function using the same coordinate plane. (The graph of the parent function is shown.)

A $g(x) = 2x^2$

x	−3	−2	−1	0	1	2	3
$g(x) = 2x^2$	18	8	2	0	2	8	18

B $g(x) = -2x^2$

x	−3	−2	−1	0	1	2	3
$g(x) = -2x^2$	−18	−8	−2	0	−2	−8	−18

REFLECT

1a. In general, how does the y-coordinate of a point on the graph of $g(x) = 2x^2$ compare with the y-coordinate of a point on the graph of $f(x) = x^2$ when the points have the same x-coordinate?

The y-coordinate of a point on the graph of $g(x)$ is 2 times the y-coordinate of a point on the graph of $f(x)$.

1b. Describe the graph of $g(x) = 2x^2$ as a transformation of the graph of $f(x) = x^2$. Use the word *stretch* in your description.

The graph of $g(x)$ is a vertical stretch of the graph of $f(x)$ by a factor of 2.

1c. What transformation occurs when the value of a in $g(x) = ax^2$ is negative?

Reflection across the x-axis

UNIT 1

Real and Complex Numbers

Unit Vocabulary

absolute value	(1-4)
closed	(1-1)
complex number	(1-3)
conjugate	(1-4)
imaginary number	(1-3)
imaginary unit	(1-3)
indirect proof	(1-1)
pure imaginary number	(1-3)
radical expression	(1-2)

UNIT 1

Real and Complex Numbers

Unit Focus

In Algebra 1, the numbers that you worked with were real numbers. In this unit, you will take a closer look at the set of real numbers by investigating closure properties of its two subsets, rational and irrational numbers. You will also learn different ways to express irrational numbers using radical notation and rational exponents. By defining $\sqrt{-1}$ as a new type of number called the imaginary unit, you will create a new set of numbers called imaginary numbers. Just as rational and irrational numbers together form the set of real numbers, imaginary numbers and real numbers together form a new set called the set of complex numbers. You will learn to perform operations with complex numbers, and you will see how complex numbers allow you to solve quadratic equations that you weren't able to solve in Algebra 1.

Unit at a Glance

COMMON CORE

Lesson		Standards for Mathematical Content
1-1	Real Numbers	CC.9-12.N.RN.3
1-2	Radicals and Rational Exponents	CC.9-12.N.RN.1, CC.9-12.N.RN.2
1-3	Adding, Subtracting, and Multiplying Complex Numbers	CC.9-12.N.CN.1, CC.9-12.N.CN.2
1-4	Conjugates of Complex Numbers	CC.9-12.N.CN.3(+)
1-5	Complex Solutions of Quadratic Equations	CC.9-12.N.CN.7, CC.9-12.A.REI.4, CC.9-12.A.REI.4b
	Test Prep	

Unpacking the Common Core State Standards

Use the table to help you understand the Standards for Mathematical Content that are taught in this unit. Refer to the lessons listed after each standard for exploration and practice.

COMMON CORE Standards for Mathematical Content	What It Means For You
CC.9-12.N.RN.1 Explain how the definition of the meaning of rational exponents follows from extending the properties of integer exponents to those values, allowing for a notation for radicals in terms of rational exponents. Lesson 1-2	Although you're accustomed to writing a radical using a radical symbol, such as writing $\sqrt{2}$ for the positive square root of 2, you will learn that radicals can also be written using rational exponents. For instance, you can write $\sqrt{2}$ as $2^{\frac{1}{2}}$.
CC.9-12.N.RN.2 Rewrite expressions involving radicals and rational exponents using the properties of exponents. Lesson 1-2	By writing a radical expression using rational exponents, you can apply the properties of exponents to simplify the expression.
CC.9-12.N.CN.3 Explain why the sum or product of two rational numbers is rational; that the sum of a rational number and an irrational number is irrational; and that the product of a nonzero rational number and an irrational number is irrational. Lesson 1-1	You will investigate and prove closure properties for the sets of rational and irrational numbers.
CC.9-12.N.CN.1 Know there is a complex number i such that $i^2 = -1$, and every complex number has the form $a + bi$ with a and b real. Lesson 1-3 (Also 1-4, 1-5)	Defining the imaginary unit $i = \sqrt{-1}$ as the number whose square equals -1 allows you to create new numbers of the form $a + bi$ where a and b are real. Such numbers are called complex numbers.
CC.9-12.N.CN.2 Use the relation $i^2 = -1$ and the commutative, associative, and distributive properties to add, subtract, and multiply complex numbers. Lesson 1-3 (Also 1-4, 1-5)	You will learn to perform operations with complex numbers of the form $a + bi$ by thinking of them as binomials with a real term, a, and an imaginary term, bi.
CC.9-12.N.CN.3(+) Find the conjugate of a complex number; use conjugates to find moduli and quotients of complex numbers. Lesson 1-4	The conjugate of $a + bi$ is $a - bi$. You will learn how the conjugate of a complex number is related to its absolute value, or modulus, and you will see how conjugates are used when dividing complex numbers.
CC.9-12.N.CN.7 Solve quadratic equations with real coefficients that have complex solutions. Lesson 1-5	Although not all quadratic equations have solutions in the real number system, you can solve any quadratic equation in the complex number system.

Unpacking the Common Core State Standards

This page lists and explains the Standards for Mathematical Content that are addressed in this unit. For information about the Standards for Mathematical Practice, which are integrated throughout the text, see Teacher Edition pages x–xiii.

Additional Standards in this Unit

CC.9-12.N.CN.8(+) Extend polynomial identities to the complex numbers. Lesson 1-5

UNIT 1

Notes

COMMON CORE Standards for Mathematical Content	What It Means For You
CC.9-12.A.REI.4 Solve quadratic equations in one variable. **CC.9-12.A.REI.4b** Solve quadratic equations by inspection (e.g., $x^2 = 49$), taking square roots, completing the square, the quadratic formula and factoring, as appropriate to the initial form of the equation. Recognize when the quadratic formula gives complex solutions and write them as $a \pm bi$ for real numbers a and b. Lesson 1-5	You will learn to recognize, using the discriminant from the quadratic formula, when a quadratic equation has imaginary solutions, and you will be able to use the quadratic formula to find them.

Notes

_____

_____

_____

_____

_____

_____

_____

_____

_____

Notes

Real Numbers

Essential question: *In which subset of real numbers does the sum or product of a rational number and an irrational number belong?*

COMMON **Standards for**
CORE **Mathematical Content**

CC.9-12.N.RN.3 Explain why the sum or product of two rational numbers is rational; that the sum of a rational number and an irrational number is irrational; and that the product of a nonzero rational number and an irrational number is irrational.

Vocabulary

closed

indirect proof

Prerequisites

Subsets of real numbers, Grade 8

Math Background

A set of numbers is closed under an operation if the result of the operation on any two numbers in the set is another number in the set. For example, the set $\{0, 1\}$ is closed under multiplication because $0 \times 0 = 0$, $1 \times 0 = 0$, $0 \times 1 = 0$, and $1 \times 1 = 1$. The products 0 and 1 are both in the original set, and they represent all possible products of the original numbers in the set. The set $\{0, 1\}$ is not closed under addition, however, because $1 + 1 = 2$, and the sum 2 is a number that is not in the original set. Finding one counterexample (the sum 2) is sufficient to prove that a set is not closed under an operation (addition in this case).

INTRODUCE

Students will already be familiar with real numbers and subsets of real numbers. Ask them to think about how important numbers are in banking. Discuss the repercussions that may occur when a bank lists a balance as a negative integer rather than as a positive integer.

TEACH

1 ENGAGE

Questioning Strategies

- In the Venn diagram on page 5, why is the circle for whole numbers completely contained in the circle for integers? Can the circles be interchanged? Every whole number is an integer. No, not every integer is a whole number.

- Is the sum or difference of two irrational numbers always irrational? If not, give a counterexample. No; $\sqrt{2} + (-\sqrt{2}) = 0$ and $\sqrt{3} - \sqrt{3} = 0$, and 0 is not irrational.

2 EXAMPLE

Questioning Strategies

- In the first step, why is $a + b$ expressed as $\frac{p}{q} + \frac{r}{s}$? A rational number can be expressed as the quotient of two integers. Since a and b are rational numbers and p, q, r, and s are integers, you can rewrite $a + b$ as $\frac{p}{q} + \frac{r}{s}$.

EXTRA EXAMPLE

Given that the set of integers is closed under addition and multiplication, prove that the set of even integers is closed under addition. Use the fact that an even integer a can be written as $2m$ where m is an integer. For instance, 6 is an even integer because you can write –6 as $2(-3)$.

Let a and b be even integers.
$a + b = 2m + 2n$ m and n are integers.
      $= 2(m + n)$ Factor out the 2.
Because the set of integers is closed under addition, $m + n$ is an integer, so $a + b$ is an even integer.

Name_____ Class_____ Date_____

1-1

COMMON CORE
CC.9-12.N.RN.3

Real Numbers

Essential question: *In which subset of real numbers does the sum or product of a rational number and an irrational number belong?*

1 ENGAGE Understanding Real Numbers and Their Properties

The Venn diagram shows the relationship between the set of real numbers and its subsets.

| Real Numbers |
| Rational Numbers ... Integers ... Irrational Numbers |

A rational number can be expressed in the form $\frac{p}{q}$ where p and q are integers and $q \neq 0$. The decimal form a rational number either terminates or repeats. For instance, $\frac{3}{4} = 0.75$ and $-\frac{5}{6} = -0.8333\ldots$.

An irrational number cannot be written as the quotient of two integers, and its decimal form is nonrepeating and nonterminating. For instance, the decimal form of $\sqrt{3}$, $1.7320508\ldots$, neither repeats nor terminates.

Real numbers, regardless of whether they are rational or irrational, have the following properties with respect to addition and multiplication.

Properties of Real Numbers	
Commutative Property of Addition	$a + b = b + a$
Associative Property of Addition	$(a + b) + c = a + (b + c)$
Additive Identity	The additive identity is 0, because $a + 0 = a$.
Additive Inverse	The additive inverse of a is $-a$, because $a + (-a) = 0$.
Commutative Property of Multiplication	$a \cdot b = b \cdot a$
Associative Property of Multiplication	$(a \cdot b) \cdot c = a \cdot (b \cdot c)$
Multiplicative Identity	The multiplicative identity is 1, because $1(a) = a$.
Multiplicative Inverse	The multiplicative inverse of a for $a \neq 0$ is $\frac{1}{a}$, because $a\left(\frac{1}{a}\right) = 1$.
Distributive Property	$a(b + c) = ab + ac$

A set of numbers is **closed** under an operation if the result of the operation on any two numbers in the set (provided the operation is defined for those two numbers) is another number in that set. To prove that a set is not closed under an operation, you need to find only one counterexample.

Closure of Sets Under the Four Basic Operations				
Set	Addition	Subtraction	Multiplication	Division
Real numbers	Yes	Yes	Yes	Yes
Irrational numbers	No	No	No	No
Rational numbers	Yes	Yes	Yes	Yes
Integers	Yes	Yes	Yes	No

REFLECT

1a. Give a counterexample to show why the set of integers is not closed under division.

$\frac{-5}{2} = -2.5$, which is not an integer.

1b. Give a counterexample to show why the set of irrational numbers is not closed under multiplication.

$\sqrt{2} \cdot \sqrt{2} = 2$, which is not an irrational number.

1c. State the operations under which the set of whole numbers is closed. Then state the operations under which the set of whole numbers is not closed, and give counterexamples to show why.

Closed: addition, multiplication; not closed: subtraction, division; counterexamples:

$1 - 2 = -1$, which is not a whole number, and $\frac{1}{2} = 0.5$, which is not a whole number

2 EXAMPLE Proving That a Set Is Closed

Given that the set of integers is closed under addition and multiplication, prove that the set of rational numbers is closed under addition.

Let a and b be rational numbers.

$a + b = \frac{p}{q} + \frac{r}{s}$ $p, q, r,$ and s are integers with q and s nonzero.

$= \frac{s}{s}\left(\frac{p}{q}\right) + \frac{q}{q}\left(\frac{r}{s}\right)$ Find a common denominator.

$= \frac{ps}{qs} + \frac{qr}{qs}$ Multiply.

$= \frac{ps + qr}{qs}$ Add the numerators.

Because $ps + qr$ and qs are integers, $\frac{ps + qr}{qs}$ is a rational number.

Avoid Common Errors

When students do the proof in **2 EXAMPLE**, they may inadvertently assume what they are trying to prove. Remind them that their goal is to start with two rational numbers and then derive a rational expression whose numerator and denominator are integers. Since the expression $\frac{ps + qr}{qs}$ is composed of sums and products of integers and the set of integers is closed under addition and multiplication, the expression is a rational number.

3 EXAMPLE

Questioning Strategies

- In the beginning of the proof, why is c assumed to be rational? An indirect proof starts by assuming that what you want to prove is *not* true.

- If the statement that the sum of a rational and irrational number is irrational is false, why does it follow that the sum of a rational and irrational number is rational is true? Can't both statements be false? Since the set of real numbers is closed under addition and all real numbers are either rational or irrational, both statements cannot be false.

EXTRA EXAMPLE

Given that the set of rational numbers is closed under addition, prove that the difference of an irrational number and a rational number is an irrational number.

Let a be an irrational number, let b be a rational number, and let $a - b = c$. Assume that c is rational. Rewrite $a - b = c$ as $a = c + b$ by adding b to both sides. Because c and b are both rational, and the set of rational numbers is closed under addition, $c + b$ must be rational, which means that a is rational. This contradicts the condition that a be irrational. So, the assumption that c is rational must be false, which means that c must be irrational.

CLOSE

Essential Question

In which subset of real numbers does the sum or product of a rational number and an irrational number belong?

The sum of an irrational number and a rational number is irrational, and the product of an irrational number and a rational number is irrational.

Summarize

Have students write a journal entry in which they describe how to prove a statement about real numbers by using an indirect proof.

MATHEMATICAL PRACTICE   **Highlighting the Standards**

As students work through the proofs in this lesson, ask them to think about how the format of each proof makes it easier to understand the underlying structure of the argument. This addresses Mathematical Practice Standard 3 (Construct viable arguments and critique the reasoning of others). Students should recognize that an indirect proof starts by assuming that what you want to prove is not true. Then, you need to show that the assumption leads to a contradiction, which makes the original assumption false and the original statement true. Have pairs of students exchange their journal entries and comment on the clarity and completeness of the journal entry by using their partner's steps to do a proof of their own.

PRACTICE

Where skills are taught	Where skills are practiced
2 EXAMPLE	EXS. 1, 2
3 EXAMPLE	EXS. 3, 4

© Houghton Mifflin Harcourt Publishing Company

REFLECT

2a. How do you know that $ps + qr$ and qs are integers?

The set of integers is closed under addition and multiplication, so both expressions

represent integers.

2b. Why does $a + b = \frac{ps + qr}{qs}$ prove that the set of rational numbers is closed under addition?

Because a and b are any two rational numbers and $a + b$ is also a rational

number, the sum of any two rational numbers must be a rational number.

2c. Given that the set of rational numbers is closed under addition, how can you prove that the set of rational numbers is closed under subtraction?

Write $a - b$ as $a + (-b)$. If b is a rational number, then $-b$ is also rational.

The rational numbers are closed under addition, so $a + (-b)$ is rational.

An **indirect proof** starts by assuming that what you want to prove is *not* true. If the assumption leads to a contradiction, then the original statement must be true.

3 EXAMPLE Proving That the Sum of a Rational Number and an Irrational Number Is Irrational

Given that the set of rational numbers is closed under addition, prove that the sum of a rational number and an irrational number is an irrational number.

Let a be a rational number, let b be an irrational number, and let $a + b = c$. Assume that c is rational.

Rewrite $a + b = c$ as $b = -a + c$ by adding $-a$ to both sides. Because $-a$ and c are both

____rational____ and the set of rational numbers is closed under addition, $-a + c$ must

be ____rational____, which means that b is ____rational____.

This contradicts the condition that b be irrational. So, the assumption that c is rational must be false, which means that c, the sum of a rational number and an irrational

number, is ____irrational____.

REFLECT

3a. Indirect proof is also called *proof by contradiction*. What is the contradiction in the preceding proof?

The number b cannot be both rational and irrational.

3b. Compare an indirect proof to a counterexample.

A counterexample shows that a statement is false by finding an example that

contradicts it. An indirect proof shows that a statement is true by proving that a

contrary statement is false.

© Houghton Mifflin Harcourt Publishing Company

Unit 1   7   Lesson 1

PRACTICE

1. Given that the set of integers is closed under multiplication, prove that the set of rational numbers is closed under multiplication.

Let a and b be rational numbers, $a = \frac{p}{q}$ and $b = \frac{r}{s}$ where p, q, r and s are integers,

$q \neq 0$, and $s \neq 0$. Then $ab = \frac{p}{q} \cdot \frac{r}{s} = \frac{pr}{qs}$. The set of integers is closed under

multiplication, so pr and qs are integers, and $q \neq 0$ and $s \neq 0$, so $qs \neq 0$. Therefore,

ab is rational, so the set of rational numbers is also closed under multiplication.

2. Given that the set of rational numbers is closed under multiplication, how can you prove that the set of rational numbers is closed under division?

Let a and b be rational numbers where $b \neq 0$. Write $a \div b$ as $a \cdot \frac{1}{b}$. If b is a

rational number, then $\frac{1}{b}$ is also rational. The rational numbers are closed under

multiplication, so $a \cdot \frac{1}{b}$ is rational.

3. Given that the set of rational numbers is closed under multiplication, prove that the product of a nonzero rational number and an irrational number is an irrational number.

Let $a \neq 0$ be rational, let b be irrational, and let $a \cdot b = c$. Assume that c is rational.

Rewrite $a \cdot b = c$ as $b = \frac{1}{a} \cdot c$ by multiplying both sides by $\frac{1}{a}$. Because both $\frac{1}{a}$ and c are

rational numbers and the set of rational numbers is closed under multiplication, $\frac{1}{a} \cdot c$

must be rational. This contradicts the condition that b be irrational. So, the assumption

that c is rational must be false, which means that c, the product of a rational number

and an irrational number, must be an irrational number.

4. Given that 3 is a rational number and $\sqrt{3}$ is an irrational number, classify each number below as either rational or irrational. Explain your reasoning.

a. $3 + \sqrt{3}$

Irrational because this is the sum of a rational number and an irrational number

(see the Example on page 7)

b. $3 - \sqrt{3}$

Irrational because you can write this as $3 + (-\sqrt{3})$, which is again the sum of a

rational number and an irrational number

c. $(3 + \sqrt{3})(3 - \sqrt{3})$

Hint: Use the distributive property to carry out the multiplication.

Rational because $(3 + \sqrt{3})(3 - \sqrt{3}) = 9 + 3\sqrt{3} - 3\sqrt{3} - 3 = 6$

© Houghton Mifflin Harcourt Publishing Company

Unit 1   8   Lesson 1

© Houghton Mifflin Harcourt Publishing Company

Radicals and Rational Exponents

Essential question: *How are radicals and rational exponents related?*

COMMON CORE Standards for Mathematical Content

CC.9-12.N.RN.1 Explain how the definition of the meaning of rational exponents follows from extending the properties of integer exponents to those values, allowing for a notation for radicals in terms of rational exponents.

CC.9-12.N.RN.2 Rewrite expressions involving radicals and rational exponents using the properties of exponents.

Vocabulary
radical expression

Prerequisites
Square roots and cube roots, Grade 8

Properties of integer exponents, Grade 8

Math Background
In Grade 8, students learned that the properties of exponents apply to real numbers with integer exponents. In this lesson, students will apply the properties of exponents to real numbers with rational exponents and then use them to simplify expressions that contain radicals or rational exponents.

INTRODUCE

Review the properties of integer exponents with students. Make sure students understand that x is the same as x^1, $x^2 \cdot x^3 = x^5$, and $\frac{x^2}{x^3} = x^{-1}$. Students should also understand that $x^2 + x^2 = 2x^2$ (by the distributive property, not by a property of exponents) and that $x^2 + x^3$ cannot be simplified.

TEACH

1 ENGAGE

Questioning Strategies
- When you convert between radical form and rational exponent form, what are the restrictions on the radicand and index? Conversions are done for all real numbers for which the radical is defined. The index must be a positive integer and the power of the radicand must be an integer.

- After converting a radical expression to rational exponent form, what is another way to describe the rational exponent? The rational exponent is the ratio of integers such that the numerator is the power of the radicand and the denominator is the index of the radical.

Differentiated Instruction
To help students learn the properties of rational exponents, you may want to have students add a column to the table that includes examples of each property.

2 EXAMPLE

Questioning Strategies
- When you simplify the rational exponent, what does it mean if the simplified form is an integer? if it is a fraction? If the exponent is an integer, the final form will not contain a radical sign. If the exponent is a fraction, the final form will contain a radical sign.

EXTRA EXAMPLE
Simplify each expression. Assume all variables are positive.

A. $\sqrt[4]{(xy)^{12}}$ $\quad x^3y^3$

B. $\dfrac{\sqrt[3]{a}}{\sqrt[6]{a}}$ $\quad \sqrt[6]{a}$

Name_____ Class_____ Date_____

1-2

COMMON CORE
CC.9-12.N.RN.1,
CC.9-12.N.RN.2

Radicals and Rational Exponents

Essential question: *How are radicals and rational exponents related?*

1 ENGAGE — Understanding Radicals and Rational Exponents

A **radical expression** is an expression that is written using the radical sign, $\sqrt{}$. A radical expression has an *index* and a *radicand* as identified below.

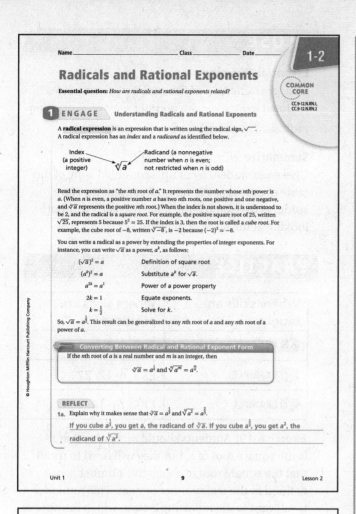

Index (a positive integer) → $\sqrt[n]{a}$ ← Radicand (a nonnegative number when n is even; not restricted when n is odd)

Read the expression as "the nth root of a." It represents the number whose nth power is a. (When n is even, a positive number a has two nth roots, one positive and one negative, and $\sqrt[n]{a}$ represents the positive nth root.) When the index is not shown, it is understood to be 2, and the radical is a *square root*. For example, the positive square root of 25, written $\sqrt{25}$, represents 5 because $5^2 = 25$. If the index is 3, then the root is called a *cube root*. For example, the cube root of −8, written $\sqrt[3]{-8}$, is −2 because $(-2)^3 = -8$.

You can write a radical as a power by extending the properties of integer exponents. For instance, you can write $\sqrt{a}$ as a power, a^k, as follows:

$(\sqrt{a})^2 = a$	Definition of square root
$(a^k)^2 = a$	Substitute a^k for $\sqrt{a}$.
$a^{2k} = a^1$	Power of a power property
$2k = 1$	Equate exponents.
$k = \frac{1}{2}$	Solve for k.

So, $\sqrt{a} = a^{\frac{1}{2}}$. This result can be generalized to any nth root of a and any nth root of a power of a.

Converting Between Radical and Rational Exponent Form

If the nth root of a is a real number and m is an integer, then
$$\sqrt[n]{a} = a^{\frac{1}{n}} \text{ and } \sqrt[n]{a^m} = a^{\frac{m}{n}}.$$

REFLECT

1a. Explain why it makes sense that $\sqrt[3]{a} = a^{\frac{1}{3}}$ and $\sqrt[3]{a^2} = a^{\frac{2}{3}}$.

If you cube $a^{\frac{1}{3}}$, you get a, the radicand of $\sqrt[3]{a}$. If you cube $a^{\frac{2}{3}}$, you get a^2, the

radicand of $\sqrt[3]{a^2}$.

Unit 1   9   Lesson 2

If radical expressions are rewritten in rational exponent form, you can then apply the following properties to simplify them.

Properties of Rational Exponents	
Let a and b be real numbers and m and n be integers.	
Product of Powers Property	$a^m \cdot a^n = a^{m+n}$
Quotient of Powers Property	$\frac{a^m}{a^n} = a^{m-n}, a \neq 0$
Power of a Product Property	$(a \cdot b)^n = a^n \cdot b^n$
Power of a Quotient Property	$\left(\frac{a}{b}\right)^n = \frac{a^n}{b^n}, b \neq 0$
Power of a Power Property	$(a^m)^n = a^{mn}$
Negative Exponent Property	$a^{-n} = \frac{1}{a^n}, a \neq 0$

2 EXAMPLE — Using Exponent Properties to Simplify Radical Expressions

Simplify each expression. Assume all variables are positive.

A $\sqrt[3]{(xy)^6} = (xy)^{\frac{6}{3}}$ Rewrite using a rational exponent.

     $= (xy)^2$ Simplify the exponent.

     $= x^2 y^2$ Power of a product property

B $\sqrt{x} \cdot \sqrt[3]{x} = x^{\frac{1}{2}} \cdot x^{\frac{1}{3}}$ Rewrite using rational exponents.

     $= x^{\frac{1}{2} + \frac{1}{3}}$ Product of powers property

     $= x^{\frac{5}{6}}$ Simplify the exponent.

     $= \sqrt[6]{x^5}$ Rewrite the expression in radical form.

C $\frac{\sqrt{x}}{\sqrt[4]{x}} = \frac{x^{\frac{1}{2}}}{x^{\frac{1}{4}}}$ Rewrite using rational exponents.

     $= x^{\frac{1}{2} - \frac{1}{4}}$ Quotient of powers property

     $= x^{\frac{1}{4}}$ Simplify the exponent.

     $= \sqrt[4]{x}$ Rewrite the expression in radical form.

Unit 1   10   Lesson 2

Highlighting the Standards

2 EXAMPLE provides an opportunity to address Mathematical Practice Standard 7 (Look for and make use of structure). Students should review the properties of rational exponents to find structure in the samples and then apply the structure in each step of the simplifying process. Make sure students can justify the appropriate steps using the properties.

3 EXAMPLE

Questioning Strategies

- How would the example be different if the expression were $27(x^9)^{\frac{2}{3}}$? What would the answer be in this case? The rational exponent would apply only to the variable part, x^9. The final answer would be $27x^6$.

EXTRA EXAMPLE

Simplify $(81x^8)^{\frac{3}{4}}$. $27x^6$

Technology

Encourage the use of graphing calculators to check the results of simplifying numerical radical expressions and numerical expressions with rational exponents. Ask students to use the following sample problems to practice entering expressions correctly into their calculators: Enter $\sqrt[3]{6^2}$ as 6 ^ (2/3); enter $32^{\frac{3}{2}}$ as 32 ^ (3/2); enter $25^{-\frac{1}{2}}$ as 25 ^ (−1/2). Make sure students understand the importance of including parentheses.

CLOSE

Essential Question

How are radicals and rational exponents related? Rational exponents are another way of expressing radicals. The radical $\sqrt[n]{a^m}$ is the same as $a^{\frac{m}{n}}$.

Summarize

Give each student a cut up, scrambled copy of the table of properties of rational exponents. Have students reassemble the table correctly without looking at the table on page 10.

PRACTICE

Where skills are taught	Where skills are practiced
1 ENGAGE	EXS. 1–3
2 EXAMPLE	EXS. 4–12, 22
3 EXAMPLE	EXS. 13–18

Exercise 19: Students should recognize that $x^{\frac{1}{2}}$ is the square root of x, but they will need to recall that the square root of a negative number is not defined in the real number system. This reminder is relevant to the following lesson, which introduces imaginary numbers.

Exercises 20–21, 23: Students extend what they learned in **1 ENGAGE** and **2 EXAMPLE** to writing proofs involving radicals, which is facilitated by rewriting them in rational exponent form. Students should realize that the properties of rational exponents are necessary to justify how to convert from rational exponent form back to radical form.

REFLECT

2a. In parts B and C, you started with an expression in radical form, converted to rational exponent form, and then converted back to radical form to record the answer. Explain the purpose of each conversion.

The first conversion made it possible to apply the properties of rational exponents to simplify the expression. The second conversion let you write the simplified expression is in its original radical form.

2b. Can $\sqrt{a} \cdot \sqrt[3]{b}$ be simplified? Refer to the properties of exponents to support your answer.

No, it cannot. In rational exponent form, the expression is $a^{\frac{1}{2}} \cdot b^{\frac{1}{3}}$. Because the bases are different, the product of powers property does not apply, and the expression cannot be simplified.

2c. Use the properties of exponents to prove that $\sqrt[n]{a} \cdot \sqrt[n]{b} = \sqrt[n]{ab}$.

$\sqrt[n]{a} \cdot \sqrt[n]{b}$ in rational exponent form is $a^{\frac{1}{n}} \cdot b^{\frac{1}{n}}$. Use the power of a product property to write this as $(ab)^{\frac{1}{n}}$. Convert back to radical form to get $\sqrt[n]{ab}$.

3 EXAMPLE Simplifying Expressions Involving Rational Exponents

$(27x^9)^{\frac{2}{3}} = (3^3)^{\frac{2}{3}} (x^9)^{\frac{2}{3}}$ Power of a product property

$= 3^{3 \cdot \frac{2}{3}} x^{9 \cdot \frac{2}{3}}$ Power of a power property

$= 3^2 x^6$ Simplify exponents.

$= 9 x^6$ Evaluate the numerical power.

REFLECT

3a. Show that you get the same simplified form of $(27x^9)^{\frac{2}{3}}$ if you simplify $[(27x^9)^2]^{\frac{1}{3}}$. That is, square $27x^9$ and then raise to the $\frac{1}{3}$ power.

$[(27x^9)^2]^{\frac{1}{3}} = [(3^3)^2(x^9)^2]^{\frac{1}{3}} = [3^6 x^{18}]^{\frac{1}{3}} = (3^6)^{\frac{1}{3}}(x^{18})^{\frac{1}{3}} = 3^{6 \cdot \frac{1}{3}} x^{18 \cdot \frac{1}{3}} = 3^2 x^6 = 9x^6$

3b. What is the simplified form of $(27x^9)^{-\frac{2}{3}}$? How is it related to the simplified form of $(27x^9)^{\frac{2}{3}}$?

$\frac{1}{9x^6}$; they are reciprocals.

© Houghton Mifflin Harcourt Publishing Company

PRACTICE

Write each radical expression in rational exponent form. Assume all variables are positive.

1. $\sqrt[5]{d}$ $d^{\frac{1}{5}}$

2. $\sqrt[3]{b^2}$ $b^{\frac{2}{3}}$

3. $\sqrt[4]{m^3}$ $m^{\frac{3}{4}}$

Simplify each expression. Assume all variables are positive.

4. $\sqrt[3]{y^3 z}$ $y\sqrt[3]{z}$

5. $\sqrt{x^4 y}$ $x^2\sqrt{y}$

6. $\sqrt{49x^2 y^4}$ $7xy^2$

7. $\sqrt[3]{x} \cdot \sqrt[4]{x}$ $\sqrt[12]{x^7}$

8. $\sqrt{(3x)(12x^3)}$ $6x^2$

9. $\sqrt{xy} \cdot \sqrt{x^3 y^5}$ $x^2 y^3$

10. $\frac{\sqrt[3]{x}}{\sqrt[5]{x}}$ $\sqrt[15]{x^2}$

11. $\sqrt[3]{\frac{8x^6}{y^3}}$ $\frac{2x^2}{y}$

12. $\sqrt{\frac{x}{y^8}}$ $\frac{\sqrt{x}}{y^4}$

13. $(8x^3)^{\frac{2}{3}}$ $4x^2$

14. $\left(\frac{x^3}{y^{-1}}\right)^{12}$ $x^9 y^3$

15. $\left(\frac{4x^2}{y^8}\right)^{\frac{1}{2}}$ $\frac{2x}{y^4}$

16. $(216a^9)^{\frac{1}{3}}$ $6a^3$

17. $(a^4 b^{-8})^{-\frac{3}{4}}$ $\frac{b^6}{a^3}$

18. $(16b^{-2})^{-\frac{1}{2}}$ $\frac{b}{4}$

19. Explain why the expression $x^{\frac{1}{2}}$ is undefined when $x < 0$.

In radical form, $x^{\frac{1}{2}} = \sqrt{x}$ and the square root of a negative number is undefined in the real number system.

20. Use the properties of exponents to show that $\sqrt[n]{\frac{a}{b}} = \frac{\sqrt[n]{a}}{\sqrt[n]{b}}$.

In rational exponent form, $\sqrt[n]{\frac{a}{b}} = \left(\frac{a}{b}\right)^{\frac{1}{n}}$. Use the power of a quotient property to write $\left(\frac{a}{b}\right)^{\frac{1}{n}}$ as $\frac{a^{\frac{1}{n}}}{b^{\frac{1}{n}}}$. Convert back to radical form to get $\frac{\sqrt[n]{a}}{\sqrt[n]{b}}$.

21. Show that $\sqrt[n]{a^m} = (\sqrt[n]{a})^m$.

$\sqrt[n]{a^m} = a^{\frac{m}{n}} = a^{\frac{1}{n} \cdot m} = \left(a^{\frac{1}{n}}\right)^m = (\sqrt[n]{a})^m$

22. Error Analysis A student simplified the expression $\sqrt[3]{x^2} \cdot \sqrt{x}$ by writing $\sqrt[3]{x^2} \cdot \sqrt{x} = x^{\frac{3}{2}} \cdot x^{\frac{1}{2}} = x^{\frac{3}{2} + \frac{1}{2}} = x^2 = x^2$. Describe and correct the student's error.

$\sqrt[3]{x^2} = x^{\frac{2}{3}}$, not $x^{\frac{3}{2}}$; $\sqrt[3]{x^2} \cdot \sqrt{x} = x^{\frac{2}{3}} \cdot x^{\frac{1}{2}} = x^{\frac{2}{3} + \frac{1}{2}} = x^{\frac{7}{6}} = x^{1 + \frac{1}{6}} = x^1 \cdot x^{\frac{1}{6}} = x\sqrt[6]{x}$

23. In the expression $\sqrt[n]{a^m}$, suppose m is a multiple of n. That is, $m = kn$ where k is an integer. Show how to obtain the simplified form of $\sqrt[n]{a^m}$. If a is a nonzero rational number, is $\sqrt[n]{a^m}$ rational or irrational? Explain.

$\sqrt[n]{a^m} = \sqrt[n]{a^{kn}} = a^{\frac{kn}{n}} = a^k$; rational because raising a nonzero rational number a to the kth power is equivalent to the product consisting of k factors of a (if $k > 0$) or k factors of $\frac{1}{a}$ (if $k < 0$), and the set of rational numbers is closed under multiplication.

© Houghton Mifflin Harcourt Publishing Company

Adding, Subtracting, and Multiplying Complex Numbers

Essential question: *How do you add, subtract, and multiply complex numbers?*

CC.9-12.N.CN.1 Know there is a complex number i such that $i^2 = -1$, and every complex number has the form $a + bi$ with a and b real.

CC.9-12.N.CN.2 Use the relation $i^2 = -1$ and the commutative, associative, and distributive properties to add, subtract, and multiply complex numbers.

Vocabulary

imaginary unit

complex number

imaginary number

pure imaginary number

Prerequisites

Solving quadratic equations, Algebra 1

Adding and multiplying binomials, Algebra 1

Real numbers, Lesson 1-1

Math Background

Solving some quadratic equations requires taking square roots of negative numbers. Such equations have no real solutions. However, the solutions can be expressed using complex numbers. A complex number is of the form $a + bi$, where a and b are real numbers and $i = \sqrt{-1}$. If $b = 0$, the complex number is a real number. Otherwise, it is an imaginary number.

INTRODUCE

Review the discriminant $b^2 - 4ac$ from the quadratic formula in Algebra 1. Remind students that if the discriminant is negative, a quadratic equation has no real solutions. This is because solving the quadratic formula when the discriminant is negative requires taking the square root of a negative number. In this lesson, students will learn how to express such solutions using complex numbers.

TEACH

1 ENGAGE

Questioning Strategies

- When you graph the quadratic function $y = x^2 + 1$, why are there no x-intercepts? The sum of the square of a number and 1 is always positive, so the graph does not cross the x-axis.

- How does using the number i to represent $\sqrt{-1}$ make it possible to solve all quadratic equations? Quadratic equations with no real solutions have solutions that can be expressed as complex numbers of the form $a + bi$ where $b \neq 0$.

Differentiated Instruction

To help visual learners see the relationships among the various types of numbers, show them the following diagram. Ask them to give examples of each type of number.

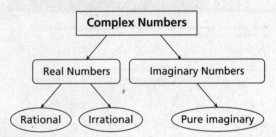

2 EXAMPLE

Questioning Strategies

- Can the sum of two imaginary numbers be 0? Yes, if both the real parts and the imaginary parts are opposites of each other

- When is the sum of two imaginary numbers a pure imaginary number? Give an example. when the real parts are opposites; sample: $(6 + 4i) + (-6 - 8i) = -4i$

EXTRA EXAMPLE

Add or subtract.

A. $(6 + 3i) + (-2 + 5i)$ $4 + 8i$

B. $(-2 + 7i) - (3 + i)$ $-5 + 6i$

Name _____ Class _____ Date _____

1-3

Adding, Subtracting, and Multiplying Complex Numbers

COMMON CORE

CC.9-12.N.CN.1,
CC.9-12.N.CN.2

Essential question: *How do you add, subtract, and multiply complex numbers?*

1 ENGAGE Understanding Complex Numbers

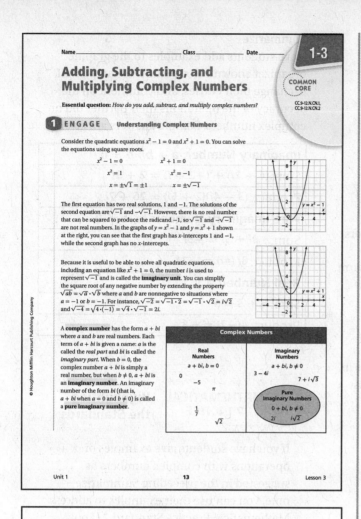

Consider the quadratic equations $x^2 - 1 = 0$ and $x^2 + 1 = 0$. You can solve the equations using square roots.

$$x^2 - 1 = 0 \qquad\qquad x^2 + 1 = 0$$
$$x^2 = 1 \qquad\qquad x^2 = -1$$
$$x = \pm\sqrt{1} = \pm 1 \qquad x = \pm\sqrt{-1}$$

The first equation has two real solutions, 1 and -1. The solutions of the second equation are $\sqrt{-1}$ and $-\sqrt{-1}$. However, there is no real number that can be squared to produce the radicand -1, so $\sqrt{-1}$ and $-\sqrt{-1}$ are not real numbers. In the graphs of $y = x^2 - 1$ and $y = x^2 + 1$ shown at the right, you can see that the first graph has x-intercepts 1 and -1, while the second graph has no x-intercepts.

Because it is useful to be able to solve all quadratic equations, including an equation like $x^2 + 1 = 0$, the number i is used to represent $\sqrt{-1}$ and is called the **imaginary unit**. You can simplify the square root of any negative number by extending the property $\sqrt{ab} = \sqrt{a} \cdot \sqrt{b}$ where a and b are nonnegative to situations where $a = -1$ or $b = -1$. For instance, $\sqrt{-2} = \sqrt{-1 \cdot 2} = \sqrt{-1} \cdot \sqrt{2} = i\sqrt{2}$ and $\sqrt{-4} = \sqrt{4 \cdot (-1)} = \sqrt{4} \cdot \sqrt{-1} = 2i$.

A **complex number** has the form $a + bi$ where a and b are real numbers. Each term of $a + bi$ is given a name: a is the called the *real part* and bi is called the *imaginary part*. When $b = 0$, the complex number $a + bi$ is simply a real number, but when $b \neq 0$, $a + bi$ is an **imaginary number**. An imaginary number of the form bi (that is, $a + bi$ when $a = 0$ and $b \neq 0$) is called a **pure imaginary number**.

Complex Numbers	
Real Numbers $a + bi, b = 0$	**Imaginary Numbers** $a + bi, b \neq 0$
0	$3 - 4i$
-5	$7 + i\sqrt{3}$
π	**Pure Imaginary Numbers** $0 + bi, b \neq 0$
$\frac{1}{7}$	$2i \qquad i\sqrt{2}$
$\sqrt{2}$	

REFLECT

1a. How many real solutions does $x^2 + 4 = 0$ have? How many imaginary solutions? Explain.

0; 2; $x = \pm\sqrt{-4} = \pm 2i$, which are imaginary numbers.

1b. What is the value of i^2? Explain.

Since $i = \sqrt{-1}$, $i^2 = (\sqrt{-1})^2 = -1$.

1c. Using the Venn diagram on the previous page, name all sets to which each of the following numbers belongs.

$1 - 2i$ ___Complex numbers, imaginary numbers___

$-2i$ ___Complex numbers, imaginary numbers, pure imaginary numbers___

-2 ___Complex numbers, real numbers___

To add or subtract complex numbers, add or subtract their real parts and add or subtract their imaginary parts. You can use the distributive property to add or subtract the imaginary parts. For instance, $3i + 2i = (3 + 2)i = 5i$.

2 EXAMPLE Adding and Subtracting Complex Numbers

A $(8 + 3i) + (7 + 5i) = \left(\boxed{8} + \boxed{7}\right) + \left(\boxed{3i} + \boxed{5i}\right)$ Collect real parts, and collect imaginary parts.

   $= \boxed{15} + \boxed{8i}$ Add real parts, and add imaginary parts.

B $(8 + 3i) - (7 + 3i) = \left(\boxed{8} - \boxed{7}\right) + \left(\boxed{3i} - \boxed{5i}\right)$ Collect real parts, and collect imaginary parts.

   $= \boxed{1} + \left(\boxed{-2i}\right)$ Subtract real parts, and subtract imaginary parts.

   $= \boxed{1} - \boxed{2i}$ Write the number without parentheses.

REFLECT

2a. Give an example of two imaginary numbers whose sum is a real number. Find the sum of the numbers.

Sample answer: $2 + 3i$ and $2 - 3i$; $(2 + 3i) + (2 - 3i) = 4$

2b. What properties (extended to imaginary numbers) allow you to collect the real parts and imaginary parts of two complex numbers being added?

Commutative and associative properties of addition

Questioning Strategies

- How is multiplying two imaginary numbers similar to the FOIL method? The same steps are used when multiplying two imaginary numbers as when multiplying two binomials.

- If you use the FOIL method to multiply two imaginary numbers, which of the F, O, I, or L products are real? Which are pure imaginary? F and L; O and I

- Why isn't the product of two imaginary numbers a trinomial? The product of two imaginary numbers has an i^2-term. Since $i^2 = -1$, the i^2-term is real and can be added to the other real term.

Avoid Common Errors

Remind students that after they use FOIL to multiply two imaginary numbers, they are not finished simplifying the result until the answer is in the form $a + bi$. That means that the i^2-term must be simplified and added to the other real term.

Teaching Strategy

Reinforce how FOIL is used to multiply two binomials, such as the product of $2 + 3x$ and $1 - 4x$, before asking students to use FOIL to multiply two imaginary numbers, such as the product of $2 + 3i$ and $1 - 4i$. Show the work for the binomials and for the imaginary numbers side-by-side and ask students to point out the similarities and differences in the steps.

EXTRA EXAMPLE

Multiply.

A. $(4 + 2i)(3 + 5i)$ $2 + 26i$

B. $(-2 + 5i)(3 - 4i)$ $14 + 23i$

CLOSE

Essential Question

How do you add, subtract, and multiply complex numbers?
Adding and subtracting complex numbers is similar to adding and subtracting binomial expressions with variables. You can use FOIL to multiply complex numbers; then, simplify so the answer is expressed as $a + bi$.

Summarize

Have students add examples to the graphic organizer shown below. Students can pair off, exchange their entries, and comment on the accuracy of the operations their partner did on complex numbers. Sample answers are given.

Imaginary Number: $a + bi$, $b \neq 0$
Sum: $(4 + 2i) + (-2 + i) = 2 + 3i$
Product: $(3 - 4i)(2 + 5i) = 26 + 7i$
Pure Imaginary Number: bi, $b \neq 0$
Sum: $-8i + 3i = -5i$
Product: $6i\,(4i) = -24$
Real Number: a
Sum: $6 + 3 = 9$
Product: $4(-2) = -8$

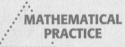

MATHEMATICAL PRACTICE   **Highlighting the Standards**

If you have students give examples of operations with complex numbers as suggested in the preceding Summarize note, you can use their examples to address Mathematical Practice Standard 7 (Look for and make use of structure). Be sure students understand the structure of complex numbers. An imaginary number has the form $a + bi$ where a and b are real and $b \neq 0$, a pure imaginary number has the form bi where b is real and $b \neq 0$, and a real number simply has the form a where a is real.

PRACTICE

Where skills are taught	Where skills are practiced
2 EXAMPLE	EXS. 1–10
3 EXAMPLE	EXS. 11–20

Exercise 21: Students look for a pattern in powers of the imaginary unit i, going beyond i^2, the highest power used in the lesson. Students will need to deduce that the higher powers can all be simplified by repeatedly dividing out $i^4 = 1$.

Exercise 22: Students use the results of Exercise 21 to simply $i^{18} \cdot i^{23}$ in two ways.

To multiply two complex numbers, use the distributive property to multiply each part of one of the numbers with each part of the other. Then simplify by using the fact that $i^2 = -1$ and combining like terms. The general multiplication pattern is shown below.

$$(a + bi)(c + di) = ac + adi + bci + bdi^2$$

3 EXAMPLE Multiplying Complex Numbers

A $(5 + 3i)(9 + 8i) = 45 + 40i + 27i + 24i^2$ Multiply.

$= 45 + 40i + 27i + 24(-1)$ $i^2 = -1$

$= 21 + 67i$ Combine like terms.

B $(8 + 12i)(4 - 2i) = 32 - 16i + 48i + \left(-24i^2\right)$ Multiply.

$= 32 + 32i + 24$ $i^2 = -1$

$= 56 + 32i$ Combine like terms.

REFLECT

3a. How is multiplying $(5 + 3i)(9 + 8i)$ like multiplying $(5 + 3x)(9 + 8x)$? How is it different?

The distributive property is used to multiply both expressions. For the first

expression, you need to replace i^2 with -1 and combine the like terms. For the

second expression, you only combine the like terms.

3b. What is the product of $a + bi$ and $a - bi$ where a and b are real numbers, $a \neq 0$, and $b \neq 0$? Classify the product as a real number or an imaginary number. Explain.

$(a + bi)(a - bi) = a^2 - abi + abi - (bi)^2 = a^2 + b^2$; because a and b are real

numbers, the product is a real number.

3c. What is the square of $a + bi$ where a and b are real numbers, $a \neq 0$, and $b \neq 0$? Classify the square as a real number or an imaginary number.

$(a + bi)^2 = a^2 + 2abi + (bi)^2 = (a^2 - b^2) + 2abi$; because $a \neq 0$ and $b \neq 0$, $2ab \neq 0$, so

the square is an imaginary number.

3d. If you multiply a nonzero real number and an imaginary number, is the product real or imaginary? Explain.

Imaginary; $a(b + ci) = ab + aci$, which is imaginary since ab and ac are real and $ac \neq 0$.

PRACTICE

Add or subtract.

1. $3i + 7i$ $10i$

2. $10i - 2i$ $8i$

3. $8 + (-4 + 2i)$ $4 + 2i$

4. $9i - (13 + 7i)$ $-13 + 2i$

5. $(4 + 2i) + (9 + 8i)$ $13 + 10i$

6. $(5 - 6i) + (11 + 4i)$ $16 - 2i$

7. $(14 + i) - (4 + 6i)$ $10 - 5i$

8. $(9 - 8i) - (6 - 4i)$ $3 - 4i$

9. $(6 - 4i) + (17 - 2i)$ $23 - 6i$

10. $(3 + 15i) - (-5 + i)$ $8 + 14i$

Multiply.

11. $-2(1 - 3i)$ $-2 + 6i$

12. $5i(-5 + 2i)$ $-10 - 25i$

13. $(3 + 7i)(6 + i)$ $11 + 45i$

14. $(3 - 2i)(10 + 4i)$ $38 - 8i$

15. $(-4 + 6i)(5 + 9i)$ $-74 - 6i$

16. $(1 + 7i)(12 - 2i)$ $26 + 82i$

17. $(4 - 8i)(5 - 6i)$ $-28 - 64i$

18. $(5 + 4i)(3 + 9i)$ $-21 + 57i$

19. $(1 + 2i)^2$ $-3 + 4i$

20. $(2 - i)^2$ $3 - 4i$

21. Complete the table. To the right of the table, generalize the pattern that you see.

Power of i	Value
i^1	i
i^2	-1
i^3	$-i$
i^4	1
i^5	i
i^6	-1
i^7	$-i$
i^8	1

Given i^n, divide n by 4 and note the

remainder r.

If $r = 0$, then $i^n = 1$.

If $r = 1$, then $i^n = i$.

If $r = 2$, then $i^n = -1$.

If $r = 3$, then $i^n = -i$.

22. Using what you learned about powers of i in Exercise 21, find the product $i^{18} \cdot i^{23}$ two ways: (1) by simplifying each power before multiplying, and (2) by using the product of powers property and then simplifying.

$i^{18} = -1$ and $i^{23} = -i$, so $i^{18} \cdot i^{23} = (-1)(-i) = i$; $i^{18} \cdot i^{23} = i^{41} = i$

Conjugates of Complex Numbers

Essential question: *How can you use conjugates to find the absolute value of a complex number and to divide complex numbers?*

© Houghton Mifflin Harcourt Publishing Company

COMMON Standards for
CORE Mathematical Content

CC.9-12.N.CN.3(+) Find the conjugate of a complex number; use conjugates to find moduli and quotients of complex numbers.
Also: CC.9-12.N.CN.1, CC.9-12.N.CN.2

Vocabulary
conjugate
absolute value

Prerequisites
Absolute value, Algebra 1
Multiplying complex numbers, Lesson 1-3
Pythagorean Theorem, Geometry

Math Background
This lesson presents three mathematical concepts: (1) what the conjugate of a complex number is, (2) what the absolute value (modulus) of a complex number is and how conjugates are related to absolute value, and (3) what it means to divide complex numbers and the role that conjugates play in the division process.

Although the definition of a conjugate (i.e., that the conjugate of a complex number $z = a + bi$ is $\bar{z} = a - bi$) is simple, students need to understand that it is essentially three definitions rolled into one: (1) for a real number a, the conjugate is just a; (2) for a pure imaginary number bi, the conjugate is $-bi$; and (3) for an imaginary number $a + bi$, the conjugate is $a - bi$.

The definition of the absolute value of a complex number is most easily understood from a geometric point of view by plotting the complex number in the complex plane. The absolute value of $z = a + bi$ can then be interpreted as the distance of the point (a, bi) from the origin.

The idea of distance is an extension of the geometric interpretation of the absolute value of a real number: If a is a real number plotted on the real number line, then $|a|$ is the distance of a from 0. Students should understand the connection between these two notions of absolute value: Given that $|z|$ is defined to be $\sqrt{a^2 + b^2}$, you can write the real number a in the complex form $a + 0i$ so that $|a| = \sqrt{a^2 + 0^2} = \sqrt{a^2}$. Taking the square root of the square of the real number a always results in either a if $a \geq 0$ or $-a$ if $a < 0$, which is exactly the definition of absolute value that students learned in Algebra 1. Returning to the geometric interpretation of absolute value, you know that on the real number line, every nonzero real number and its opposite have the same absolute value. The analogue to this fact in the complex plane is that all complex numbers that lie on the circle centered at the origin with radius $\sqrt{a^2 + b^2}$ have the same absolute value. Among these points are $z = a + bi$, $\bar{z} = a - bi$, $-z = -a - bi$, and $-\bar{z} = -a + bi$.

INTRODUCE

Remind students that the product of two complex numbers can be found using the FOIL method. Make sure students understand that i^2 is -1 so that they can simplify the results of the FOIL method.

TEACH

 EXPLORE

Questioning Strategies
• Why is the product of a complex number and its conjugate always a real number? If you use FOIL, the middle terms containing *i* add to zero. Since the coefficient of the *i*-term is zero, the number is real.

Name_____ Class_____ Date_____

1-4

Conjugates of Complex Numbers

COMMON CORE

CC.9-12.N.CN.3(+)

Essential question: *How can you use conjugates to find the absolute value of a complex number and to divide complex numbers?*

Let $z = a + bi$ be a complex number. The **conjugate** of z is $\bar{z} = a - bi$. For example, the conjugate of $4 + 7i$ is $4 - 7i$.

1 EXPLORE Finding Products of Complex Numbers and Their Conjugates

A Complete the table.

z	$\bar{z}$	$z \cdot \bar{z}$
$4 + 7i$	$4 - 7i$	65
$5 - 2i$	$5 + 2i$	29
$3i$	$-3i$	9
-6	-6	36

B Generalize the results: If $z = a + bi$, then in terms of a and b,
$z \cdot \bar{z} = (a + bi)(a - bi) = a^2 - (bi)^2 = a^2 - b^2 i^2 = a^2 - b^2(-1) = \underline{a^2 + b^2}$.

REFLECT

1a. Is the product $z \cdot \bar{z}$ a real number or an imaginary number? Explain.

Real; a and b are real, and the sum of their squares is real.

2 ENGAGE Understanding the Absolute Value of a Complex Number

A complex number can be represented by a point in the *complex plane* having real numbers on its horizontal axis and pure imaginary numbers on its vertical axis. If $z = a + bi$, then the coordinates of the point representing z are (a, bi).

For any complex number not on one of the axes, you can draw a right triangle as shown. The lengths of the legs are the real numbers $|a|$ and $|b|$. The **absolute value** of the complex number z, written as $|z|$, is the length of the hypotenuse. The absolute value of z is also called the *modulus* of z.

For the special case of $z = a + 0i$, the graph of z is a point on the real axis, and $|z| = |a|$. Similarly, for the special case of $z = 0 + bi$, the graph of z is a point on the pure imaginary axis, and $|z| = |b|$.

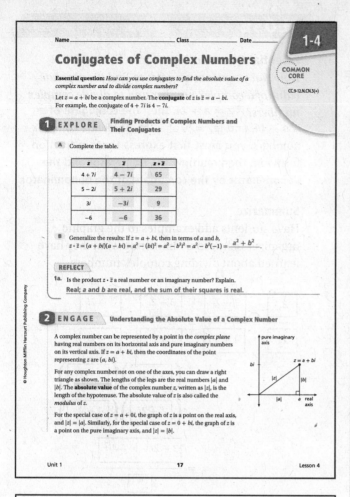

Unit 1   17   Lesson 4

© Houghton Mifflin Harcourt Publishing Company

REFLECT

2a. If $z = a + bi$, use the Pythagorean Theorem to express $|z|$ in terms of a and b. (Note that $|a|^2$ can simply be written as a^2 and $|b|^2$ as b^2.)
$|z| = \sqrt{|a|^2 + |b|^2} = \sqrt{a^2 + b^2}$

2b. Show that the formula you wrote for Question 2a also applies to the special cases $z = a + 0i$ and $z = 0 + bi$. Use the fact that if x is a real number, then $\sqrt{x^2} = |x|$.
If $z = a + 0i$, then $|z| = \sqrt{a^2 + 0^2} = \sqrt{a^2} = |a|$; if $z = 0 + bi$, then
$|z| = \sqrt{0^2 + b^2} = \sqrt{b^2} = |b|$.

2c. How is $|z|$ related to $z \cdot \bar{z}$?
$|z|^2 = z \cdot \bar{z}$ or $|z| = \sqrt{z \cdot \bar{z}}$

Comparing Absolute Values The set of real numbers is an *ordered set* because for any two real numbers a and b, you can determine whether $a < b$, $a = b$, or $a > b$. The set of complex numbers, however, is not an ordered set. For instance, you cannot compare the numbers $3 + 4i$ and $1 - 5i$ other than to say that they are not equal.

Because the absolute value of a complex number is a real number, you *can* compare the absolute values of two complex numbers. Just as you can interpret the absolute value of a real number geometrically as the number's distance from 0 on the real number line, you can interpret the absolute value of a complex number geometrically as the number's distance from the origin of the complex plane.

3 EXAMPLE Comparing Absolute Values of Complex Numbers

Compare the absolute values of $3 + 4i$ and $1 - 5i$.

A Find each absolute value.
$|3 + 4i| = \sqrt{3^2 + 4^2} = \sqrt{25} = 5$
$|1 - 5i| = \sqrt{1^2 + (-5)^2} = \sqrt{26}$

B Compare the absolute values.
$|3 + 4i| < |1 - 5i|$ because $5 < \sqrt{26}$

REFLECT

3a. What does the comparison of $|3 + 4i|$ and $|1 - 5i|$ tell you about the points in the complex plane representing $3 + 4i$ and $1 - 5i$?
The point representing $3 + 4i$ is closer to the origin of the complex plane than the point representing $1 - 5i$.

3b. In part A you found that $|3 + 4i| = 5$. Give three other complex numbers that have an absolute value of 5.
$-3 + 4i$, $-3 - 4i$, and $3 - 4i$ (although any $z = a + bi$ where $a^2 + b^2 = 25$ also works)

Unit 1   18   Lesson 4

© Houghton Mifflin Harcourt Publishing Company

Questioning Strategies

- Why is the absolute value of a complex number always a real number? $|a + bi| = \sqrt{a^2 + b^2}$; since a^2 and b^2 are both positive, $\sqrt{a^2 + b^2}$ is a real number.

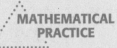

Highlighting the Standards

In **2** ENGAGE and its Reflect questions, students address Mathematical Practice Standard 7 (Look for and make use of structure). By analyzing the graph and applying the Pythagorean Theorem, students find the relationship between the absolute value of a complex number and the coordinates of the complex number when graphed in the complex plane.

 EXAMPLE

Questioning Strategies

- How is the absolute value of a complex number similar to the absolute value of a real number? Both are real numbers indicating the distance of the number from the origin.

EXTRA EXAMPLE

Compare the absolute values of $2 - i$ and $4 + 3i$. $|2 - i| < |4 + 3i|$ because $\sqrt{5} < 5$.

 EXAMPLE

Questioning Strategies

- How is the conjugate of the denominator used to divide two complex numbers? The numerator and denominator are both multiplied by the conjugate of the denominator to give an expression with a real number in the denominator.

EXTRA EXAMPLE

Divide.

A. $\dfrac{9 + 3i}{3i}$ $1 - 3i$

B. $\dfrac{10 - 10i}{2 + i}$ $2 - 6i$

C. $\dfrac{4 + 2i}{3 + 3i}$ $1 - \frac{1}{3}i$

CLOSE

Essential Question

How can you use conjugates to find the absolute value of a complex number and to divide complex numbers? If $z = a + bi$, then the conjugate of z is $a - bi$, and $|z| = \sqrt{a^2 + b^2}$. To divide complex numbers, you must first express them in fraction form and then multiply the numerator and the denominator by the conjugate of the denominator.

Summarize

Have students add examples to the graphic organizer below to demonstrate what they have learned about dividing complex numbers.

$$\frac{\boxed{z_1}}{\boxed{z_2}} = \frac{\boxed{3 + 2i}}{\boxed{1 + 2i}} = \frac{\boxed{3 + 2i}}{\boxed{1 + 2i}} \cdot \frac{\boxed{1 - 2i}}{\boxed{1 - 2i}}$$

$$= \frac{\left(\boxed{3 + 2i}\right)\left(\boxed{1 - 2i}\right)}{\left(\boxed{1 + 2i}\right)\left(\boxed{1 - 2i}\right)}$$

$$= \frac{\boxed{3 + 2i - 6i - 4i^2}}{\boxed{5}}$$

$$= \boxed{\tfrac{7}{5}} - \boxed{\tfrac{4}{5}}i$$

PRACTICE

Where skills are taught	Where skills are practiced
2 ENGAGE	EXS. 1–6
3 EXAMPLE	EXS. 7–10
4 EXAMPLE	EXS. 11–16

Exercises 17–20: Students explore properties of the absolute value of complex numbers.

Dividing Complex Numbers To divide two complex numbers $a + bi$ and $c + di$, express the quotient as $\frac{a+bi}{c+di}$. You can write this fraction as a single complex number by multiplying the numerator and denominator by the conjugate of the denominator and then simplifying.

4 EXAMPLE Dividing Complex Numbers

Divide.

A $\dfrac{6-4i}{2i} = \dfrac{6-4i}{2i} \cdot \dfrac{-2i}{-2i}$ Multiply the numerator and denominator by the conjugate of the denominator.

$= \dfrac{-8-12i}{4}$ Multiply the numerators, and multiply the denominators. Simplify each product.

$= -2 - 3i$ Write in the form $a + bi$.

B $\dfrac{10-15i}{2+i} = \dfrac{10-15i}{2+i} \cdot \dfrac{2-i}{2-i}$ Multiply the numerator and denominator by the conjugate of the denominator.

$= \dfrac{5-40i}{5}$ Multiply the numerators, and multiply the denominators. Simplify each product.

$= 1 - 8i$ Write in the form $a + bi$.

C $\dfrac{1}{2+2i} = \dfrac{1}{2+2i} \cdot \dfrac{2-2i}{2-2i}$ Multiply the numerator and denominator by the conjugate of the denominator.

$= \dfrac{2-2i}{8}$ Multiply the numerators, and multiply the denominators. Simplify each product.

$= \dfrac{1}{4} - \dfrac{1}{4}i$ Write in the form $a + bi$.

REFLECT

4a. How can you use multiplication to check the quotient that you obtain when you divide one complex number by another? Illustrate this procedure using the quotient from part A.

Multiply the quotient by the divisor to see if you get the dividend;

$(-2 - 3i)(2i) = -4i - 6i^2 = -4i - 6(-1) = 6 - 4i.$

4b. Find the absolute values of the dividend, the divisor, and the quotient in part A. How are these absolute values related?

$|6 - 4i| = \sqrt{52} = 2\sqrt{13}$, $|2i| = \sqrt{4} = 2$, and $|-2 - 3i| = \sqrt{13}$; the absolute value

of the dividend divided by the absolute value of the divisor gives the absolute

value of the quotient.

PRACTICE

Find the absolute value of each complex number.

1. $4 + 3i$ 5

2. $6 - 2i$ $2\sqrt{10}$

3. $1 + i$ $\sqrt{2}$

4. $5i$ 5

5. $7 - 9i$ $\sqrt{130}$

6. $-3 - 2i$ $\sqrt{13}$

Compare the absolute values of each pair of complex numbers.

7. $1 + 2i, 2 - i$ $|1 + 2i| = |2 - i|$

8. $4i, 3 + 2i$ $|4i| > |3 + 2i|$

9. $5 + 3i, -1 + 6i$ $|5 + 3i| < |-1 + 6i|$

10. $7 - 2i, 6 + 4i$ $|7 - 2i| > |6 + 4i|$

Divide.

11. $\dfrac{4-6i}{1-i}$ $5 - i$

12. $\dfrac{3+4i}{2-i}$ $\dfrac{2}{5} + \dfrac{11}{5}i$

13. $\dfrac{3}{1+3i}$ $\dfrac{3}{10} - \dfrac{9}{10}i$

14. $\dfrac{-3-2i}{i}$ $-2 + 3i$

15. $\dfrac{8-12i}{5+3i}$ $\dfrac{2}{17} - \dfrac{42}{17}i$

16. $\dfrac{5+2i}{3+6i}$ $\dfrac{3}{5} - \dfrac{8}{15}i$

17. For a complex number z, compare $|z|$ and $|\overline{z}|$. Explain the relationship two ways: using algebra and using a geometric interpretation.

$|z| = |\overline{z}|$; if $z = a + bi$, then $\overline{z} = a - bi$, $|z| = \sqrt{a^2 + b^2}$, and $|\overline{z}| = \sqrt{a^2 + (-b)^2} =$

$\sqrt{a^2 + b^2}$; $\overline{z}$ can be represented by the point $(a, -bi)$, which is the reflection in

the x-axis of the point (a, bi) representing z, so $\overline{z}$ is the same distance as z from

the origin.

18. For a real number a, $|a| = |-a|$. Show that this property also applies to a complex number and its opposite.

If $z = a + bi$, then $-z = -a - bi$ and $|-z| = |-a - bi| = \sqrt{(-a)^2 + (-b)^2} =$

$\sqrt{a^2 + b^2} = |z|.$

19. If $z_1 = a + bi$ and $z_2 = c + di$, show that $|z_1 \cdot z_2| = |z_1| \cdot |z_2|$.

$|z_1 \cdot z_2| = |(a + bi)(c + di)| = |(ac - bd) + (ad + bc)i| = \sqrt{(ac - bd)^2 + (ad + bc)^2} =$

$\sqrt{a^2c^2 - 2abcd + b^2d^2 + a^2d^2 + 2abcd + b^2c^2} = \sqrt{a^2c^2 + a^2d^2 + b^2c^2 + b^2d^2} =$

$\sqrt{a^2(c^2 + d^2) + b^2(c^2 + d^2)} = \sqrt{(a^2 + b^2)(c^2 + d^2)} = \sqrt{a^2 + b^2} \cdot \sqrt{c^2 + d^2} =$

$|z_1| \cdot |z_2|.$

20. Let $z_3 = z_1 \cdot z_2$. When you divide z_3 by z_1 and get z_2 as the quotient, how can you use the absolute values of z_3 and z_1 as a check on z_2? (*Hint:* See Exercise 19.)

Divide $|z_3|$ by $|z_1|$; the result should equal $|z_2|$ because $\dfrac{|z_3|}{|z_1|} = \dfrac{|z_1 \cdot z_2|}{|z_1|} = \dfrac{|z_1| \cdot |z_2|}{|z_1|} = |z_2|.$

Complex Solutions of Quadratic Equations

Essential question: *When does a quadratic equation have imaginary solutions, and how do you find them?*

© Houghton Mifflin Harcourt Publishing Company

COMMON CORE Standards for Mathematical Content

CC.9-12.N.CN.7 Solve quadratic equations with real coefficients that have complex solutions.

CC.9-12.A.REI.4 Solve quadratic equations in one variable.

CC.9-12.A.REI.4b Solve quadratic equations by … the quadratic formula … Recognize when the quadratic formula gives complex solutions and write them as $a \pm bi$ for real numbers a and b.

Also: CC.9-12.N.CN.1, CC.9-12.N.CN.2, CC.9-12.N.CN.8(+)

Prerequisites

Quadratic formula, Algebra 1

Multiplying binomials, Algebra 1

Multiplying complex numbers, Lesson 1-3

Math Background

In Algebra 1, students used the quadratic formula to find the solutions to a quadratic equation. If the expression $b^2 - 4ac$ (the discriminant) in the quadratic formula was negative, students learned there were no real solutions. In this lesson, students will find the non-real solutions to quadratic equations. When the discriminant is negative, then $\sqrt{b^2 - 4ac}$ is rewritten as $\sqrt{(-1) \cdot (4ac - b^2)}$, or $\sqrt{-1} \cdot \sqrt{4ac - b^2}$. This simplifies to $\left(\sqrt{4ac - b^2}\right)i$. The solutions are then expressed as imaginary numbers. By examining the discriminant, the number and type of solutions to a quadratic equation can be summarized as follows:

Value of Discriminant	Number and type of solutions
$b^2 - 4ac > 0$	two real solutions
$b^2 - 4ac = 0$	one real solution
$b^2 - 4ac < 0$	two imaginary solutions

INTRODUCE

Draw the following parabolas on the board.

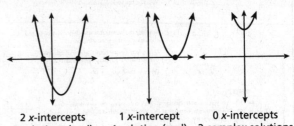

2 *x*-intercepts   1 *x*-intercept   0 *x*-intercepts
2 solutions (real)   1 solution (real)   2 complex solutions

Remind students that if $f(x)$ is a quadratic function, then the solutions of the equation $f(x) = 0$ give the *x*-intercepts of the function's graph. If the graph of $f(x)$ does not cross the *x*-axis, then there are no *x*-intercepts and the equation $f(x) = 0$ has no real solutions. Tell students they will now learn how to find imaginary solutions of quadratic equations.

TEACH

1 ENGAGE

Questioning Strategies

- Why are there two solutions if $b^2 - 4ac > 0$ in the quadratic formula $x = \dfrac{-b \pm \sqrt{b^2 - 4ac}}{2a}$?

  The radical expression is preceded by $\pm$. In one case the radical is added to $-b$, and in the other the radical is subtracted from $-b$, resulting in two solutions.

- Why are there always two solutions to a quadratic equation that has imaginary solutions? How are they related? Since $\sqrt{b^2 - 4ac}$ is not zero, its value will be both added to and subtracted from $-b$ in the numerator, resulting in two solutions; they are complex conjugates.

- What is the general solution of a quadratic equation with only one solution? $-\dfrac{b}{2a}$

Name_____ Class_____ Date_____

1-5

Complex Solutions of Quadratic Equations

Essential question: *When does a quadratic equation have imaginary solutions, and how do you find them?*

COMMON CORE

CC.9-12.N.CN.7,
CC.9-12.A.REI.4,
CC.9-12.A.REI.4b

1 ENGAGE   Revisiting the Quadratic Formula

In Algebra 1, you solved quadratic equations of the form $ax^2 + bx + c = 0$, where the coefficients a, b, and c are real numbers and $a \neq 0$, in several ways. One way was by using the *quadratic formula*:

$$x = \frac{-b \pm \sqrt{b^2 - 4ac}}{2a}$$

The radical $\sqrt{b^2 - 4ac}$ has meaning in the real number system only if the radicand $b^2 - 4ac$ is nonnegative. The radicand determines the number of real solutions and for this reason is called the *discriminant* for the quadratic equation. The table below summarizes the possible numbers of real solutions of a quadratic equation.

Value of Discriminant	Number of Real Solutions
$b^2 - 4ac > 0$	Two real solutions: $x = \frac{-b + \sqrt{b^2 - 4ac}}{2a}$ and $x = \frac{-b - \sqrt{b^2 - 4ac}}{2a}$
$b^2 - 4ac = 0$	One real solution: $x = -\frac{b}{2a}$
$b^2 - 4ac < 0$	No real solutions

When you solve a quadratic equation in the complex number system, where the radical $\sqrt{b^2 - 4ac}$ has meaning no matter what the value of the radicand is, the equation always has solutions. The table below summarizes the possible numbers of complex solutions of a quadratic equation.

Value of Discriminant	Number of Complex Solutions
$b^2 - 4ac > 0$	Two real solutions
$b^2 - 4ac = 0$	One real solution
$b^2 - 4ac < 0$	Two imaginary solutions

The table below gives three simple quadratic equations having different numbers and types of complex solutions.

Equation	Value of Discriminant	Solutions
$x^2 - 1 = 0$	$0^2 - 4(1)(-1) = 4$	$x = \pm 1$ (two real solutions)
$x^2 = 0$	$0^2 - 4(1)(0) = 0$	$x = 0$ (one real solution)
$x^2 + 1 = 0$	$0^2 - 4(1)(1) = -4$	$x = \pm i$ (two imaginary solutions)

REFLECT

1a. Use the discriminant to explain why the equation $x^2 + 2x - 3 = 0$ has two real solutions while the equation $x^2 + 2x + 3 = 0$ has no real solutions.

For the first equation, $b^2 - 4ac = 2^2 - 4(1)(-3) = 4 + 12 = 16 > 0$; for the second

equation, $b^2 - 4ac = 2^2 - 4(1)(3) = 4 - 12 = -8 < 0$

1b. For what value of c does the equation $x^2 + 2x + c = 0$ have exactly one real solution? Explain.

$c = 1$ because then $b^2 - 4ac = 2^2 - 4(1)(1) = 4 - 4 = 0$

2 EXAMPLE   Finding the Complex Solutions of a Quadratic Equation

Tell whether the solutions of $x^2 + 4 = 0$ are real or imaginary. Then find the solutions.

A Use the discriminant to determine the number and type of solutions.

$b^2 - 4ac = \ 0\ ^2 - 4(\ 1\ )(\ 4\ ) = \ -16$

Because $b^2 - 4ac\ <\ 0$, there are two ___imaginary___ solutions.

B Use the quadratic formula to solve the equation.

$x = \frac{-b \pm \sqrt{b^2 - 4ac}}{2a}$ Write the quadratic formula.

$= \frac{-\ 0\ \pm \sqrt{-16}}{2(\ 1\ )}$ Substitute values. For the radicand $b^2 - 4ac$, use the value from part A.

$= \frac{\pm 4i}{2}$ Simplify the numerator, and simplify the denominator.

$= \pm 2i$ Simplify the fraction.

REFLECT

2a. Describe how you can check the solutions of a quadratic equation. Use the method to check the solutions of $x^2 + 4 = 0$.

Substitute the solutions into the equation to see if they produce a true statement;

$(\pm 2i)^2 + 4 = -4 + 4 = 0$, so the solutions check.

2b. Why is it important to write a quadratic equation in the form $ax^2 + bx + c = 0$ before identifying the values of a, b, and c? For instance, why should you write $x^2 = -4$ as $x^2 + 4 = 0$ before using the quadratic formula to solve the equation?

You need to know the correct signs of a, b, and c; for instance, if you use

$c = -4$ when solving $x^2 = -4$, you will get two real solutions rather than

two imaginary solutions.

2 EXAMPLE

Questioning Strategies

- In part A, is the discriminant the solution to the quadratic equation? No; it gives only the type and number of solutions.

- In part B, why does a discriminant of -16 give you two imaginary solutions? There are two solutions because the quadratic formula uses a $\pm$ symbol. The solutions are imaginary because evaluating the formula requires finding the square root of a negative number.

EXTRA EXAMPLE

Tell whether the solutions of $x^2 + 25 = 0$ are real or imaginary. Then find the solutions.

imaginary solutions; $\pm 5i$

| MATHEMATICAL PRACTICE | Highlighting the Standards |

If students have difficulty evaluating $b^2 - 4ac$, you can provide a connection to Mathematical Practice Standard 6 (Attend to precision). Have them organize the variables as shown in the table below. Have them fill in the table for $3x^2 + 2x + 5 = 0$ and then predict the number and type of solutions.

a	b	c	b^2	$4ac$	$b^2 - 4ac$	number/type of solutions
3	2	5	4	60	-56	2 imaginary

Avoid Common Errors

Make sure that students do not leave the i under the radical sign when solving quadratic equations: $\sqrt{-5} \neq \sqrt{5i}$; $\sqrt{-5} = i\sqrt{5}$. If students have trouble with this, have them rewrite the radical first: $\sqrt{-5} = \sqrt{-1} \cdot \sqrt{5} = i\sqrt{5}$

3 EXAMPLE

Questioning Strategies

- Why can $(x - (2 + 3i))(x - (2 - 3i))$ be called a factorization of $x^2 - 4x + 13$? The product equals $x^2 - 4x + 13$.

- You are given that $(1 + 3i)$ is a solution to a quadratic equation. What is another solution? Why? $(1 - 3i)$; imaginary solutions to quadratic equations come in pairs and are conjugates of one another.

Teaching Strategy

Encourage students to check their solutions as shown in part C. Remind students that imaginary solutions always come in pairs—an imaginary number and its conjugate—so a complete check involves checking both.

EXTRA EXAMPLE

Tell whether the solutions of $x^2 + 4x + 5 = 0$ are real or imaginary. Then find the solutions.

imaginary solutions; $-2 \pm i$

CLOSE

Essential Question

When does a quadratic equation have imaginary solutions, and how do you find them?

When the value of the discriminant is negative, the quadratic equation will have two imaginary solutions. You find the solutions by using the quadratic formula to solve the equation, writing the solutions as a pair of complex conjugates of the form $a \pm bi$.

Summarize

Have students summarize how to use the discriminant to help solve any quadratic equation. Have them include examples of quadratic equations with one or two real solutions and with two imaginary solutions.

PRACTICE

Where skills are taught	Where skills are practiced
1 ENGAGE	EXS. 1–9
2 EXAMPLE	EXS. 10–12
3 EXAMPLE	EXS. 13–18

Exercise 19: Students extend what they learned in **3** EXAMPLE to finding a quick way to check the solutions of a quadratic equation.

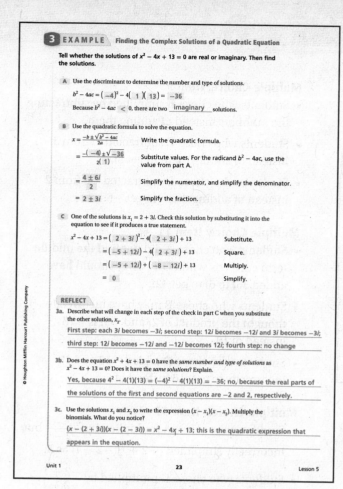

3 EXAMPLE Finding the Complex Solutions of a Quadratic Equation

Tell whether the solutions of $x^2 - 4x + 13 = 0$ are real or imaginary. Then find the solutions.

A Use the discriminant to determine the number and type of solutions.

$b^2 - 4ac = (\underline{-4})^2 - 4(\underline{1})(\underline{13}) = \underline{-36}$

Because $b^2 - 4ac < 0$, there are two __imaginary__ solutions.

B Use the quadratic formula to solve the equation.

$x = \dfrac{-b \pm \sqrt{b^2 - 4ac}}{2a}$ Write the quadratic formula.

$= \dfrac{-(\underline{-4}) \pm \sqrt{\underline{-36}}}{2(\underline{1})}$ Substitute values. For the radicand $b^2 - 4ac$, use the value from part A.

$= \dfrac{4 \pm 6i}{2}$ Simplify the numerator, and simplify the denominator.

$= 2 \pm 3i$ Simplify the fraction.

C One of the solutions is $x_1 = 2 + 3i$. Check this solution by substituting it into the equation to see if it produces a true statement.

$x^2 - 4x + 13 = (\underline{2 + 3i})^2 - 4(\underline{2 + 3i}) + 13$ Substitute.

$= (\underline{-5 + 12i}) - 4(\underline{2 + 3i}) + 13$ Square.

$= (\underline{-5 + 12i}) + (\underline{-8 - 12i}) + 13$ Multiply.

$= \underline{0}$ Simplify.

REFLECT

3a. Describe what will change in each step of the check in part C when you substitute the other solution, x_2.

First step: each $3i$ becomes $-3i$; second step: $12i$ becomes $-12i$ and $3i$ becomes $-3i$;

third step: $12i$ becomes $-12i$ and $-12i$ becomes $12i$; fourth step: no change

3b. Does the equation $x^2 + 4x + 13 = 0$ have the *same number and type of solutions* as $x^2 - 4x + 13 = 0$? Does it have the *same solutions*? Explain.

Yes, because $4^2 - 4(1)(13) = (-4)^2 - 4(1)(13) = -36$; no, because the real parts of

the solutions of the first and second equations are -2 and 2, respectively.

3c. Use the solutions x_1 and x_2 to write the expression $(x - x_1)(x - x_2)$. Multiply the binomials. What do you notice?

$(x - (2 + 3i))(x - (2 - 3i)) = x^2 - 4x + 13$; this is the quadratic expression that

appears in the equation.

PRACTICE

Find the number and type of solutions of each equation.

1. $x^2 - 9 = 0$ **2.** $x^2 + 16 = 0$ **3.** $x^2 = 0$

    2 real solutions   2 imaginary solutions   1 real solution

4. $x^2 - 2x + 4 = 0$ **5.** $x^2 - 10x + 25 = 0$ **6.** $x^2 - 3x - 10 = 0$

    2 imaginary solutions   1 real solution   2 real solutions

7. $x^2 + 12x = -36$ **8.** $2x^2 + 5 = -3x$ **9.** $3x^2 = 7 - 4x$

    1 real solution   2 imaginary solutions   2 real solutions

Find the complex solutions of each equation.

10. $x^2 + 49 = 0$ **11.** $x^2 + 5 = 0$ **12.** $4x^2 + 9 = 0$

    $\pm 7i$ $\pm i\sqrt{5}$ $\pm \dfrac{3}{2}i$

13. $x^2 - 2x + 2 = 0$ **14.** $x^2 - 6x + 13 = 0$ **15.** $x^2 + 10x + 29 = 0$

    $1 \pm i$ $3 \pm 2i$ $-5 \pm 2i$

16. $5x^2 - 2x + 1 = 0$ **17.** $9x^2 + 12x + 5 = 0$ **18.** $2x^2 - 6x + 7 = 0$

    $\dfrac{1}{5} \pm \dfrac{2}{5}i$ $-\dfrac{2}{3} \pm \dfrac{1}{3}i$ $\dfrac{3}{2} \pm \dfrac{\sqrt{5}}{2}i$

19. Multiplying the binomials in $(x - x_1)(x - x_2)$ gives $x^2 - (x_1 + x_2)x + x_1 x_2$.

a. Explain why x_1 and x_2 are solutions of the equation $(x - x_1)(x - x_2) = 0$ as well as the equation $x^2 - (x_1 + x_2)x + x_1 x_2 = 0$.

Substituting x_1 or x_2 into either equation produces a true statement.

b. For the equation $x^2 - (x_1 + x_2)x + x_1 x_2 = 0$, how is the coefficient of the x-term related to the equation's solutions? How is the constant term related to the solutions?

The opposite of the sum of the solutions; the product of the solutions

c. Describe a quick way to check the solutions x_1 and x_2 of an equation in the form $x^2 + bx + c = 0$. Then check to see if $x_1 = 2 + i$ and $x_2 = 2 - i$ are solutions of the equation $x^2 - 4x + 5 = 0$.

Check to see if $-(x_1 + x_2) = b$ and $x_1 x_2 = c$; $-[(2 + i) + (2 - i)] = -4$ and

$(2 + i)(2 - i) = 5$.

⋯ COMMON
CORE CORRELATION

Standard	Items
CC.9-12.N.RN.1	17
CC.9-12.N.RN.2	4, 5, 6, 17
CC.9-12.N.RN.3	1, 2, 3
CC.9-12.N.CN.1	7, 8
CC.9-12.N.CN.2	9, 10, 11, 18
CC.9-12.N.CN.3(+)	12, 13, 14
CC.9-12.N.CN.7	16, 18
CC.9-12.A.REI.4b	15, 16, 18

TEST PREP DOCTOR ⊕

Multiple Choice: Item 3
- Students who chose **A** may have read the question incorrectly and chose an example that seems to show closure.
- Students who chose **C** or **D** did not realize that the radicals being used are rational numbers instead of irrational numbers.

Multiple Choice: Item 4
- Students who chose **G** or **J** were raising 8 to the third power instead of taking its cube root.
- Students who chose **H** or **J** thought the negative exponent made the number negative.

Multiple Choice: Item 8
- Students who chose **G** gave the definition of a pure imaginary number and allowed for the possibility of 0.
- Students who chose **H** gave the definition of a real number.
- Students who chose **J** gave the definition of a pure imaginary number.

Multiple Choice: Item 9
- Students who chose **B** simplified by subtracting the numbers instead of adding them.
- Students who chose **C** subtracted $2i$ from $3i$ instead of adding them to get $5i$.
- Students who chose **D** subtracted -8 from 2 instead of adding them to get -6.

Multiple Choice: Item 11
- Students who chose **A** did not find the middle term correctly with FOIL. They should have added $36i$ to $6i$ to get $42i$.
- Students who chose **B** may have incorrectly thought the product of $2i$ and $-9i$ is -18 instead of 18.
- Students who chose **D** added -12 and 18 incorrectly to get -6 instead of 6.

Multiple Choice: Item 13
- Students who chose **A** multiplied by $\frac{-2-i}{-2-i}$ but incorrectly simplified $(-2+i)(-2-i)$ as 3.
- Students who chose **D** multiplied by $\frac{-2+i}{-2-i}$.
- Students who chose **C** multiplied by $\frac{-2+i}{-2-i}$ and incorrectly simplified $(-2+i)(-2-i)$ as 3.

Multiple Choice: Item 15
- Students who chose **A**, **B**, or **D** did not find the discriminant correctly or did not interpret the value of the discriminant properly.

Free Response: Item 17b
- Students who gave $\sqrt[8]{a}$ as the final answer probably added the fractional exponents incorrectly.
- Students who gave $\sqrt[12]{a}$ as the final answer may have converted to rational exponent form, but they multiplied the exponents.
- Students who gave $\sqrt[2]{a^3}$ as the final answer did not convert an expression with a rational exponent into a radical expression correctly.

Free Response: Item 18b
- Students who answered $6 \pm i$ got -16 instead of 16 when they squared -4.
- Students who answered $-2 \pm i$ found the solutions to the equation $x^2 + 4x + 5 = 0$.

© Houghton Mifflin Harcourt Publishing Company

Name _____ Class _____ Date _____

MULTIPLE CHOICE

1. Which set of numbers is *not* closed under multiplication?

A. Real numbers

B. Rational numbers

C. Integers

D. Irrational numbers ●

2. If a, b, c, and d are integers with $b \neq 0$ and $d \neq 0$, what conclusion can you draw from the statement $\frac{a}{b} + \frac{c}{d} = \frac{ad + bc}{bd}$ given that the set of integers is closed under addition and multiplication?

F. The set of rational numbers is closed under multiplication.

G. The set of irrational numbers is closed under multiplication.

H. The set of rational numbers is closed under addition. ●

J. The set of irrational numbers is closed under addition.

3. Which of the following statements shows that the set of irrational numbers is *not* closed under addition?

A. $\sqrt{2} + \sqrt{2} = 2\sqrt{2}$

B. $-\sqrt{2} + \sqrt{2} = 0$ ●

C. $\sqrt{4} + \sqrt{1} = 3$

D. $1 + \sqrt{1} = 2$

4. What is the simplified form of $8^{-\frac{1}{3}}$?

F. $\frac{1}{2}$ ●

G. $\frac{1}{512}$

H. -2

J. -512

5. What is $\sqrt[3]{a^2}$ in rational exponent form?

A. $a^{\frac{3}{2}}$

B. $a^{\frac{2}{3}}$ ●

C. a^6

D. a^5

6. Sue began simplifying the expression $\sqrt{x} \cdot \sqrt[4]{x}$ by writing $\sqrt{x} \cdot \sqrt[4]{x} = x^{\frac{1}{2}} \cdot x^{\frac{1}{4}}$. What is the next step that she should take?

F. Write $x^{\frac{1}{2}} \cdot x^{\frac{1}{4}}$ as $x^{\frac{1}{2} \cdot \frac{1}{4}}$.

G. Write $x^{\frac{1}{2}} \cdot x^{\frac{1}{4}}$ as $\frac{1}{x^{\frac{1}{2} \cdot \frac{1}{4}}}$.

H. Write as $x^{\frac{1}{2}} \cdot x^{\frac{1}{4}}$ as $x^{\frac{1}{2} + \frac{1}{4}}$. ●

J. Write $x^{\frac{1}{2}} \cdot x^{\frac{1}{4}}$ as $\frac{1}{x^{\frac{1}{2} + \frac{1}{4}}}$.

7. What is the value of i^6?

A. i

B. $-i$

C. -1 ●

D. 1

8. What is the definition of a complex number?

F. A number of the form $a + bi$ where a and b are real ●

G. A number of the form $a + bi$ where $a = 0$ and b is real

H. A number of the form $a + bi$ where a is real and $b = 0$

J. A number of the form $a + bi$ where $a = 0$, b is real, and $b \neq 0$

9. What is the simplified form of the sum $(2 + 3i) + (-8 + 2i)$?

A. $-6 + 5i$ ●

B. $10 + i$

C. $-6 + i$

D. $10 + 5i$

10. What is the simplified form of the difference $(5 - 7i) - (-4 + 6i)$?

F. $1 - i$

G. $9 - i$

H. $9 - 13i$ ●

J. $1 - 13i$

11. What is the simplified form of the product $(-4 + 2i)(3 - 9i)$?

A. $6 - 42i$

B. $-30 - 42i$

C. $6 + 42i$ ●

D. $-6 + 42i$

12. What is the conjugate of $2 - 3i$?

F. $-2 - 3i$

G. $2 + 3i$ ●

H. $3 + 2i$

J. $3 - 2i$

13. What is the simplified form of the quotient $\frac{1 - 4i}{-2 + i}$?

A. $-2 + \frac{7}{3}i$

B. $-\frac{6}{5} + \frac{7}{5}i$ ●

C. $\frac{2}{5} + 3i$

D. $\frac{2}{5} + \frac{9}{5}i$

14. What is $|-1 - i|$?

F. $1 + i$

G. 1

H. $\sqrt{2}$ ●

J. 0

15. Which quadratic equation has imaginary solutions?

A. $x^2 + 3x - 4 = 0$

B. $x^2 + 4x + 4 = 0$

C. $x^2 + 3x + 4 = 0$ ●

D. $x^2 - 4x - 4 = 0$

16. What are the solutions of $x^2 + 2x + 5 = 0$?

F. $2 + 4i, 2 - 4i$

G. $-2 + 4i, -2 - 4i$

H. $1 + 2i, 1 - 2i$

J. $-1 + 2i, -1 - 2i$ ●

FREE RESPONSE

17. a. Explain why you can write $\sqrt{a}$ as $a^{\frac{1}{2}}$.

> The definition of $\sqrt{a}$ says that $(\sqrt{a})^2 = a$; $a^{\frac{1}{2}}$ satisfies this definition because $\left(a^{\frac{1}{2}}\right)^2 = a^1 = a$.

b. Complete the simplification of the product $\sqrt{a} \cdot \sqrt[3]{a}$.

$\sqrt{a} \cdot \sqrt[3]{a} = a^{\frac{1}{2}} \cdot a^{\frac{1}{6}}$	Rational exponent form
$= a^{\frac{1}{2} + \frac{1}{6}}$	Product of powers property
$= a^{\frac{2}{3}}$	Simplify the exponent.
$= \sqrt[3]{a^2}$	Radical form

18. Consider the equation $x^2 - 4x + 5 = 0$.

a. Without solving the equation, tell whether it has real or imaginary solutions. Explain how you know.

> Imaginary; the discriminant
> $b^2 - 4ac = (-4)^2 - 4(1)(5) =$
> $16 - 20 = -4 < 0$

b. What are the solutions of the equation?

> $2 \pm i$

c. Evaluate $x^2 - 4x + 5$ for each solution. Show your results each time you perform an operation (squaring, multiplying, subtracting, and adding). What can you conclude?

> $(2 + i)^2 - 4(2 + i) + 5 = (3 + 4i) -$
> $4(2 + i) + 5 = (3 + 4i) - (8 + 4i) +$
> $5 = -5 + 5 = 0; (2 - i)^2 - 4(2 - i)$
> $+ 5 = (3 - 4i) - 4(2 - i) + 5 =$
> $(3 - 4i) - (8 - 4i) + 5 = -5 + 5 =$
> $0;$ because the value is 0 in each
> case, both solutions check.

UNIT 2

Quadratic Functions

Unit Vocabulary

UNIT 2

UNIT 2

Quadratic Functions

Unit Focus

In this unit, you will learn how to recognize and graph quadratic functions. You will learn how to write quadratic functions in standard form, vertex form, and intercept form and to identify the vertex and the intercepts of the graphs of quadratic functions. You will also use quadratic functions to model and solve real-world problems.

Unit at a Glance

COMMON CORE

Lesson		Standards for Mathematical Content
2-1	Translating the Graph of $f(x) = x^2$	CC.9-12.F.IF.2, CC.9-12.F.IF.7*, CC.9-12.F.IF.7a*, CC.9-12.F.BF.3
2-2	Stretching, Shrinking, and Reflecting the Graph of $f(x) = x^2$	CC.9-12.F.IF.2, CC.9-12.F.IF.7*, CC.9-12.F.IF.7a*, CC.9-12.F.BF.3
2-3	Graphing Quadratic Functions in Vertex Form	CC.9-12.A.CED.2*, CC.9-12.F.IF.2, CC.9-12.F.IF.7*, CC.9-12.F.IF.7a*, CC.9-12.F.BF.3
2-4	Writing Quadratic Functions in Vertex Form	CC.9-12.A.SSE.3b*, CC.9-12.A.CED.2*, CC.9-12.F.IF.2, CC.9-12.F.IF.7*, CC.9-12.F.IF.7a*, CC.9-12.F.IF.8a
2-5	Writing Quadratic Functions in Intercept Form	CC.9-12.A.SSE.3a*, CC.9-12.A.CED.2*, CC.9-12.F.IF.2, CC.9-12.F.IF.7a*, CC.9-12.F.IF.8, CC.9-12.F.IF.8a
2-6	Modeling with Quadratic Functions	CC.9-12.N.Q.1*, CC.9-12.A.SSE.1*, CC.9-12.A.CED.2*, CC.9-12.A.CED.3*, CC.9-12.F.IF.4*, CC.9-12.F.IF.7a*
	Test Prep	

UNIT 2

Unpacking the Common Core State Standards

Use the table to help you understand the Standards for Mathematical Content that are taught in this unit. Refer to the lessons listed after each standard for exploration and practice.

COMMON CORE Standards for Mathematical Content	What It Means For You
CC.9-12.N.Q.1 Use units as a way to understand problems and to guide the solution of multi-step problems; choose and interpret units consistently in formulas; choose and interpret the scale and the origin in graphs and data displays.* Lesson 2-6	You will use the units of quantities in real-world situations to help you write quadratic functions that model the situations. You will also interpret the scale and the origin in graphs of quadratic functions that represent real-world situations.
CC.9-12.A.SSE.1 Interpret expressions that represent a quantity in terms of its context.* **CC.9-12.A.SSE.1a** Interpret parts of an expression, such as terms, factors, and coefficients.* **CC.9-12.A.SSE.1b** Interpret complicated expressions by viewing one or more of their parts as a single entity.* Lesson 2-6	To model real-world situations, you need to be able to interpret the verbal description and form algebraic expressions that represent relationships between quantities. You also need to be able to interpret algebraic expressions and recognize what they mean.
CC.9-12.A.SSE.3 Choose and produce an equivalent form of an expression to reveal and explain properties of the quantity represented by the expression. **CC.9-12.A.SSE.3a** Factor a quadratic expression to reveal the zeros of the function it defines. **CC.9-12.A.SSE.3b** Complete the square in a quadratic expression to reveal the maximum or minimum value of the function it defines. Lessons 2-4, 2-5	You will factor a quadratic function in standard form to write it in intercept form. The intercept form allows you to identify the zeros of the function. You will also complete the square for a quadratic function in standard form to convert it to vertex form. The vertex form allows you to identify the maximum or minimum value of the function.
CC.9-12.A.CED.2 Create equations in two or more variables to represent relationships between quantities; graph equations on coordinate axes with labels and scales.* Lessons 2-3, 2-4, 2-5, 2-6	You will write equations to represent quadratic functions modeling real-world situations, and you will graph quadratic functions.
CC.9-12.A.CED.3 Represent constraints by equations or inequalities, and by systems of equations and/or inequalities, and interpret solutions as viable or non-viable options in a modeling context.* Lesson 2-6	You will use equations and inequalities to represent conditions in a real-world problem, and use them to determine a reasonable domain or range of a function in a real-world situation.
CC.9-12.F.IF.2 Use function notation, evaluate functions for inputs in their domains, and interpret statements that use function notation in terms of a context. Lessons 2-1, 2-2, 2-3, 2-4, 2-5, 2-6	You will use function notation to represent, evaluate, and interpret quadratic functions, including functions that represent real-world situations.

Unpacking the Common Core State Standards

This page lists and explains the Standards for Mathematical Content that are addressed in this unit. For information about the Standards for Mathematical Practice, which are integrated throughout the text, see Teacher Edition pages x–xiii.

Notes

UNIT 2

Additional Standards in This Unit

CC.9-12.N.Q.2 Define appropriate quantities for the purposes of descriptive modeling.* Lesson 2-6

CC.9-12.A.APR.1 ... multiply polynomials. Lesson 2-6

CC.9-12.A.CED.1 Create equations and inequalities in one variable and use them to solve problems.* Lesson 2-6

CC.9-12.A.REI.3 Solve linear ... inequalities in one variable ... Lesson 2-6

CC.9-12.A.REI.4 Solve quadratic equations in one variable. Lesson 2-6

CC.9-12.F.IF.9 Compare properties of two functions each represented in a different way (algebraically, graphically, numerically in tables, or by verbal descriptions). Lessons 2-1, 2-3

COMMON CORE **Standards for Mathematical Content**	**What It Means For You**
CC.9-12.F.IF.4 For a function that models a relationship between two quantities, interpret key features of graphs and tables in terms of the quantities, and sketch graphs showing key features given a verbal description of the relationship.* Lesson 2-6	You will learn to determine the vertex of the graph of a quadratic function that models a real-world situation. You will determine whether the function has a minimum or a maximum and identify the x-intercepts of the function.
CC.9-12.F.IF.5 Relate the domain of a function to its graph and, where applicable, to the quantitative relationship it describes.* Lesson 2-6	The domain of a quadratic function may be restricted in real-world applications. You will use the context of the situation to determine which values are in the domain of the function.
CC.9-12.F.IF.6 Calculate and interpret the average rate of change of a function (presented symbolically or as a table) over a specified interval. Estimate the rate of change from a graph.* Lesson 2-6	Using tables of values, you will examine the rate of change of a quadratic function.
CC.9-12.F.IF.7 Graph functions expressed symbolically and show key features of the graph, by hand in simple cases and using technology for more complicated cases.* **CC.9-12.F.IF.7a** Graph linear and quadratic functions and show intercepts, maxima, and minima.* Lessons 2-1, 2-2, 2-3, 2-4, 2-5, 2-6	You will graph quadratic functions and identify the intercepts and maximum or minimum value of the functions.
CC.9-12.F.IF.8 Write a function defined by an expression in different but equivalent forms to reveal and explain different properties of the function. **CC.9-12.F.IF.8a** Use the process of factoring and completing the square in a quadratic function to show zeros, extreme values, and symmetry of the graph, and interpret these in terms of a context. Lessons 2-4, 2-5 (Also 2-6)	You will learn how to convert a quadratic function in standard form to forms that make it easier to identify the vertex or the intercepts. You will also describe and apply the symmetry of the graphs of quadratic functions.
CC.9-12.F.BF.1 Write a function that describes a relationship between two quantities.* **CC.9-12.F.BF.1a** Determine an explicit expression, a recursive process, or steps for calculation from a context. Lesson 2-6	You will write a quadratic function that models revenue from ticket sales.
CC.9-12.F.BF.3 Identify the effect on the graph of replacing $f(x)$ by $f(x) + k$, $k\,f(x)$, $f(kx)$, and $f(x + k)$ for specific values of k (both positive and negative); find the value of k given the graphs. Experiment with cases and illustrate an explanation of the effects on the graph using technology. Lessons 2-1, 2-2, 2-3	You will examine parabolas and the effects of changing the constants in the equations that describe them.

Notes

_____

_____

_____

_____

_____

_____

_____

_____

_____

_____

Notes

Translating the Graph of $f(x) = x^2$

Essential question: *How does the graph of $g(x) = (x - h)^2 + k$ compare with the graph of $f(x) = x^2$?*

COMMON **Standards for**
CORE **Mathematical Content**

CC.9-12.F.IF.2 Use function notation, evaluate functions for inputs in their domains ...

CC.9-12.F.IF.7 Graph functions expressed symbolically and show key features of the graph ...*

CC.9-12.F.IF.7a Graph ... quadratic functions and show intercepts, maxima, and minima.*

CC.9-12.F.BF.3 Identify the effect on the graph of replacing $f(x)$ by $f(x) + k$, ... and $f(x + k)$ for specific values of k (both positive and negative); find the value of k given the graphs ...

Also: CC.9-12.F.IF.9

Vocabulary

quadratic function
parent quadratic function
parabola
vertex
axis of symmetry
minimum
maximum

Prerequisites

Transformations, Grade 8

Math Background

An even function $f(x)$ has the property that $f(-x) = f(x)$ for all values x in the domain of f, and the graph of an even function is symmetric about the y-axis.

The function $f(x) = x^2$ is the parent quadratic function; it is the simplest form of a quadratic function, and it is even. Important points about the graph of the function $f(x) = x^2$ include its shape (it is a U-shaped curve called a parabola), the direction the parabola opens (up in this case), and the location of the vertex (the turning point of the parabola), which is the point $(0, 0)$.

Since $f(-x) = f(x)$, the function can be graphed quickly by plotting points on one side of the y-axis (the axis of symmetry) and then using symmetry to find points on the other side of the y-axis.

INTRODUCE

Students are familiar with linear functions and their graphs. Ask students to give the general equation of a linear function. $f(x) = mx + b$ Have them describe the graph when $m > 0$ and when $m < 0$. Line rises; line falls. Ask them what happens to the graph as the value of b changes. The y-intercept changes.

In this lesson, students will graph the parent quadratic function, $f(x) = x^2$. Just as they saw how changing the value of b in $f(x) = mx + b$ changes the y-intercept of the function's graph, they will investigate how adding or subtracting a number outside the squared term and then inside the squared term affects the graph of the parent quadratic function.

TEACH

1 ENGAGE

Questioning Strategies

• Look at the table. Describe how the values of $f(x)$ change. They decrease down to 0 and then increase again. Also, $f(1) = f(-1)$, $f(2) = f(-2)$, and so on.

• About what line is the graph of the function symmetric? the y-axis Is the function an even function? Explain. yes; $f(x) = f(-x)$

• Each point (x, y) on the graph of $f(x) = x^2$ has a "mirror image." What are the coordinates of the mirror image? $(-x, y)$

2 EXAMPLE

Questioning Strategies

• How is the graph of $g(x) = x^2 + 1$ related to the graph of $f(x) = x^2$? It is the graph of the parent function $f(x) = x^2$ translated up 1 unit.

• Is the function $g(x) = x^2 + 1$ symmetric about the y-axis? yes Is the function $g(x) = x^2 + 1$ an even function? Explain. Yes; $g(1) = g(-1)$, $g(2) = g(-2)$, and so on.

continued

Name_____ Class_____ Date_____

2-1

Translating the Graph of $f(x) = x^2$

Essential question: *How does the graph of $g(x) = (x - h)^2 + k$ compare with the graph of $f(x) = x^2$?*

COMMON CORE

CC.9-12.F.IF.2
CC.9-12.F.IF.7*
CC.9-12.F.IF.7a*
CC.9-12.F.BF.3

1 ENGAGE Understanding the Parent Quadratic Function

A **quadratic function** is a function that can be written in the form $f(x) = ax^2 + bx + c$ where $a \neq 0$. The most basic quadratic function is $f(x) = x^2$. This function is often called the **parent quadratic function**. Once you understand the graph of the parent function, you can understand the graphs of other quadratic functions. To graph $f(x) = x^2$, make a table of values, plot the ordered pairs, and draw the graph.

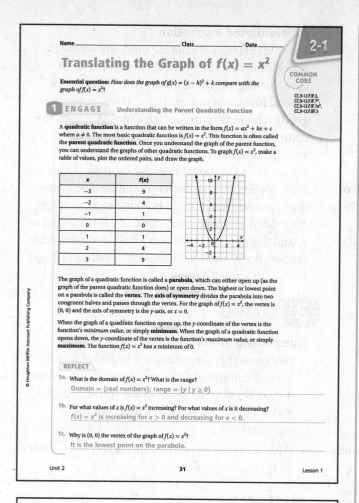

x	f(x)
−3	9
−2	4
−1	1
0	0
1	1
2	4
3	9

The graph of a quadratic function is called a **parabola**, which can either open up (as the graph of the parent quadratic function does) or open down. The highest or lowest point on a parabola is called the **vertex**. The **axis of symmetry** divides the parabola into two congruent halves and passes through the vertex. For the graph of $f(x) = x^2$, the vertex is $(0, 0)$ and the axis of symmetry is the y-axis, or $x = 0$.

When the graph of a quadratic function opens up, the y-coordinate of the vertex is the function's *minimum value*, or simply **minimum**. When the graph of a quadratic function opens down, the y-coordinate of the vertex is the function's *maximum value*, or simply **maximum**. The function $f(x) = x^2$ has a minimum of 0.

REFLECT

1a. What is the domain of $f(x) = x^2$? What is the range?

Domain = {real numbers}; range = $\{y \mid y \geq 0\}$

1b. For what values of x is $f(x) = x^2$ increasing? For what values of x is it decreasing?

$f(x) = x^2$ is increasing for $x > 0$ and decreasing for $x < 0$.

1c. Why is $(0, 0)$ the vertex of the graph of $f(x) = x^2$?

It is the lowest point on the parabola.

Unit 2   31   Lesson 1

© Houghton Mifflin Harcourt Publishing Company

---

2 EXAMPLE Graphing Quadratic Functions

Graph each quadratic function. (The graph of the parent function is shown.)

A $g(x) = x^2 + 1$

x	$g(x) = x^2 + 1$
−3	10
−2	5
−1	2
0	1
1	2
2	5
3	10

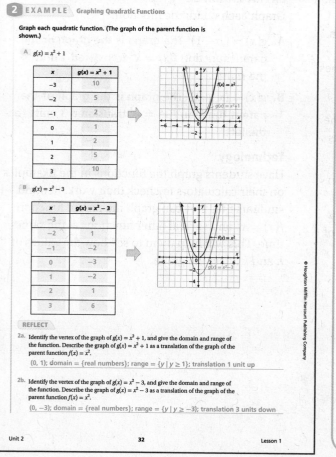

B $g(x) = x^2 - 3$

x	$g(x) = x^2 - 3$
−3	6
−2	1
−1	−2
0	−3
1	−2
2	1
3	6

REFLECT

2a. Identify the vertex of the graph of $g(x) = x^2 + 1$, and give the domain and range of the function. Describe the graph of $g(x) = x^2 + 1$ as a translation of the graph of the parent function $f(x) = x^2$.

$(0, 1)$; domain = {real numbers}; range = $\{y \mid y \geq 1\}$; translation 1 unit up

2b. Identify the vertex of the graph of $g(x) = x^2 - 3$, and give the domain and range of the function. Describe the graph of $g(x) = x^2 - 3$ as a translation of the graph of the parent function $f(x) = x^2$.

$(0, -3)$; domain = {real numbers}; range = $\{y \mid y \geq -3\}$; translation 3 units down

Unit 2   32   Lesson 1

© Houghton Mifflin Harcourt Publishing Company

- How is the graph of $g(x) = x^2 - 3$ related to the graph of $f(x) = x^2$? **It is the graph of the parent function $f(x) = x^2$ translated down 3 units.**

- Is the function $g(x) = x^2 - 3$ symmetric about the y-axis? **yes** Is the function $g(x) = x^2 - 3$ an even function? Explain. **Yes; $g(1) = g(-1)$, $g(2) = g(-2)$, and so on.**

- Describe the effect of the constant k on the graph of $g(x) = x^2 + k$. Address symmetry and evenness. **The graph of $g(x)$ is the graph of $f(x) = x^2$ translated k units vertically. The y-axis is still the graph's axis of symmetry, and the function is still even.**

EXTRA EXAMPLE

Graph each quadratic function.

A. $g(x) = x^2 + 3$ **The graph is the graph of the parent function $f(x) = x^2$ translated 3 units *up*.**

B. $g(x) = x^2 - 1$ **The graph is the graph of the parent function $f(x) = x^2$ translated 1 unit *down*.**

Teaching Strategy

Have students build on their knowledge of graphing lines. Students should start by constructing a table of values for the parent function $f(x) = x$. They should find the coordinates of at least three points. Then, students can graph the line and examine whether or not it is symmetric. (It's not.) They can also determine whether it is an even function. (It's not.) Then, have students graph two other lines on the same axes: $g(x) = x + 3$ and $h(x) = x - 4$. Students should determine how the graph of $g(x) = x + k$ is related to the graph of $f(x) = x$. (The graph of $g(x)$ is the graph of $f(x)$ translated k units vertically.)

Once students have summarized the effect of k on the graph of $g(x) = x + k$, they should extend that knowledge to quadratic functions, explaining how the graph of $g(x) = x^2 + 4$ is related to the graph of $f(x) = x^2$.

Differentiated Instruction

For students who are having difficulty seeing in which direction the parabola moves (up or down), constructing a table of values with columns for several functions can be useful. Have students create a table for part A of **2 EXAMPLE**, with the columns x, x^2, and $x^2 + 1$, which is $g(x)$. They should complete the columns using the same values of x as in the table in the Example. Once the table is complete, students should be able to see that, for each value of x, 1 is added to x^2 to obtain $g(x)$. Consequently, each value of y is increased by 1, and the parabola shifts *up* 1 unit. A similar table for part B will show a decrease in y-values of 3 and thus a shift *down* 3 units.

3 EXAMPLE

Questioning Strategies

- You know that the constant k in $g(x) = x^2 + k$ shifts the graph of $f(x) = x^2$ up and down. What do you think is the effect of the constant h in $g(x) = (x - h)^2$? **It shifts the graph of $f(x) = x^2$ right and left.**

- What is the vertex of the graph of $g(x) = (x - h)^2$? **$(h, 0)$**

EXTRA EXAMPLE

Graph each quadratic function.

A. $g(x) = (x - 1)^2$ **The graph is the graph of the parent function $f(x) = x^2$ translated 1 unit to the right.**

B. $g(x) = (x + 3)^2$ **The graph is the graph of the parent function $f(x) = x^2$ translated 3 units to the left.**

Technology

Have students graph the functions in the Examples on their calculators to check their work. Remind students that they can graph the parent function $f(x) = x^2$ and several other functions at the same time. This will help them to see how the values of h and k affect the graph.

2c. Describe the graph of $g(x) = x^2 + 5$ as a translation of the graph of the parent function. Identify the vertex of the graph of $g(x) = x^2 + 5$, and give the domain and range of the function.

translation 5 units up; (0, 5), domain = {real numbers}, range = {$y \mid y \geq 5$}

2d. Write a general statement describing how the graph of $g(x) = x^2 + k$ is related to the graph of the parent function $f(x) = x^2$. Identify the vertex of the graph of $g(x) = x^2 + k$, and give the domain and range of the function.

The graph of $g(x) = x^2 + k$ is a translation of $f(x) = x^2$ either k units up if $k > 0$ or

$|k|$ units down if $k < 0$. Vertex: (0, k); domain = {real numbers}; range = {$y \mid y \geq k$}

3 EXAMPLE Graphing Quadratic Functions

Graph each quadratic function. (The graph of the parent function is shown.)

A $g(x) = (x + 1)^2$

x	$g(x) = (x + 1)^2$
−3	4
−2	1
−1	0
0	1
1	4
2	9
3	16

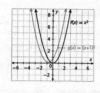

B $g(x) = (x − 3)^2$

x	$g(x) = (x − 3)^2$
6	9
5	4
4	1
3	0
2	1
1	4
0	9

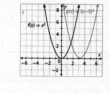

REFLECT

3a. Identify the vertex of the graph of $g(x) = (x + 1)^2$, and give the domain and range of the function. Describe the graph of $g(x) = (x + 1)^2$ as a translation of the graph of the parent function $f(x) = x^2$.

(−1, 0); domain = {real numbers}; range = {$y \mid y \geq 0$}; translation 1 unit left

3b. Identify the vertex of the graph of $g(x) = (x − 3)^2$, and give the domain and range of the function. Describe the graph of $g(x) = (x − 3)^2$ as a translation of the graph of the parent function $f(x) = x^2$.

(3, 0); domain = {real numbers}; range = {$y \mid y \geq 0$}; translation 3 units right

3c. Write a general statement describing how the graph of $g(x) = (x − h)^2$ is related to the graph of the parent function $f(x) = x^2$. Identify the vertex of the graph of $g(x) = (x − h)^2$, and give the domain and range of the function.

The graph of $g(x) = (x − h)^2$ is a translation of $f(x) = x^2$ either h units right if $h > 0$ or

$|h|$ units left if $h < 0$. Vertex: (h, 0); domain = {real numbers}; range = {$y \mid y \geq 0$}

4 EXAMPLE Writing Equations of Quadratic Functions

Write the equation of the quadratic function whose graph is shown.

A Compare the given graph to the graph of the parent function $f(x) = x^2$.

Complete the table to describe how the graph of the parent function must be translated to get the graph shown.

Type of Translation	Number of Units	Direction
Horizontal	4	right
Vertical	2	down

B Determine the values of h and k for the function $g(x) = (x − h)^2 + k$.

• $|h|$ is the number of units the graph of the parent function is translated horizontally.

For a translation to the ___right___, h is positive, and for a translation to the left, h is ___negative___

• $|k|$ is the number of units the graph of the parent function is translated vertically.

For a translation up, k is ___positive___, and for a translation ___down___, k is negative.

So, $h =$ ___4___ and $k =$ ___−2___. The equation is ___$g(x) = (x − 4)^2 − 2$___

Questioning Strategies

- How is the graph of $g(x) = (x - h)^2 + k$ related to the graph of $f(x) = x^2$? The graph of $g(x) = (x - h)^2 + k$ is the graph of $f(x) = x^2$ translated k units vertically and h units horizontally.

- Is the vertex of the graph of $g(x) = (x - h)^2 + k$ the same as the vertex of the graph of $f(x) = x^2$? No; the graph of $f(x) = x^2$ has vertex (0, 0), while the graph of $g(x) = (x - h)^2 + k$ has vertex (h, k).

EXTRA EXAMPLE

Write the equation of the quadratic function whose the graph is shown.

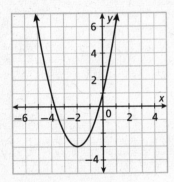

$f(x) = (x + 2)^2 - 3$

MATHEMATICAL PRACTICE — Highlighting the Standards

The Examples in this lesson provide opportunities to address Mathematical Practice Standard 7 (Look for and make use of structure). Draw students' attention to the multiple representations for the quadratic functions. Specifically, emphasize to students how using a table or graph may be helpful in understanding the symmetry of a parabola and how symmetry can be used to locate points on the graph of a quadratic function.

CLOSE

Essential Question

How does the graph of $g(x) = (x - h)^2 + k$ compare with the graph of $f(x) = x^2$?
The graph of $g(x) = (x - h)^2 + k$ is the graph of the parent function $f(x) = x^2$ translation h units horizontally and k units vertically. In particular, the vertex of the graph of $f(x)$ is (0, 0), so the vertex of the graph of $g(x)$ is (h, k).

Summarize

Students should write a journal entry that discusses and illustrates the effects of the constants h and k on the graph of $g(x) = (x - h)^2 + k$.

PRACTICE

Where skills are taught	Where skills are practiced
2 EXAMPLE	EXS. 1–3
3 EXAMPLE	EXS. 4–6
4 EXAMPLE	EXS. 10–12

Exercises 7–9: Students extend what they learned in **2** EXAMPLE and **3** EXAMPLE to graph a quadratic function of the form $g(x) = (x - h)^2 + k$.

Exercises 13–14: Students compare the minimums of quadratic functions represented in different ways (equation versus graph).

Exercises 15–20: Students use their knowledge from **1** ENGAGE to find the vertex, domain, and range of a variety of quadratic functions.

Exercise 21: Students extend what they learned in **4** EXAMPLE and write the new function from a verbal description of a translation of a given quadratic function.

REFLECT

4a. How can you check that the equation you wrote is correct?

Graph the equation and check whether its graph is identical to the given graph.

4b. The graph of a quadratic function is a translation of the graph of the parent function. How can you use the vertex of the translated graph to determine the equation of the function?

If the vertex has coordinates (h, k), the equation of the translated function is

$g(x) = (x - h)^2 + k.$

PRACTICE

Graph the quadratic function.

1. $g(x) = x^2 + 3$

2. $g(x) = x^2 - 4$

3. $f(x) = 5 + x^2$

4. $g(x) = (x - 1)^2$

5. $g(x) = (x + 1)^2$

6. $g(x) = (2 + x)^2$

7. $g(x) = (x - 1)^2 + 1$

8. $g(x) = (x + 4)^2 + 4$

9. $g(x) = (x - 2)^2 + 3$

Write the equation of the quadratic function whose graph is shown.

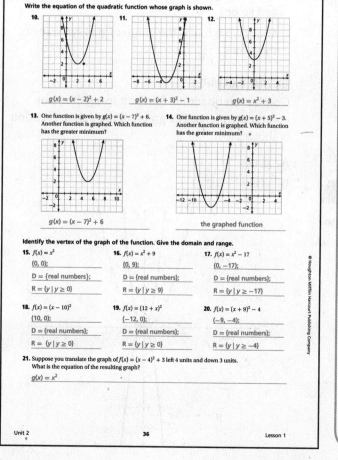

10.

$g(x) = (x - 2)^2 + 2$

11.

$g(x) = (x + 3)^2 - 1$

12.

$g(x) = x^2 + 3$

13. One function is given by $g(x) = (x - 7)^2 + 6$. Another function is graphed. Which function has the greater minimum?

$g(x) = (x - 7)^2 + 6$

14. One function is given by $g(x) = (x + 5)^2 - 3$. Another function is graphed. Which function has the greater minimum?

the graphed function

Identify the vertex of the graph of the function. Give the domain and range.

15. $f(x) = x^2$

(0, 0);

D = {real numbers};

R = {y | y ≥ 0}

16. $f(x) = x^2 + 9$

(0, 9);

D = {real numbers);

R = {y | y ≥ 9}

17. $f(x) = x^2 - 17$

(0, −17);

D = {real numbers);

R = {y | y ≥ −17}

18. $f(x) = (x - 10)^2$

(10, 0);

D = {real numbers);

R = {y | y ≥ 0}

19. $f(x) = (12 + x)^2$

(−12, 0);

D = {real numbers);

R = {y | y ≥ 0}

20. $f(x) = (x + 9)^2 - 4$

(−9, −4);

D = {real numbers);

R = {y | y ≥ −4}

21. Suppose you translate the graph of $f(x) = (x - 4)^2 + 3$ left 4 units and down 3 units. What is the equation of the resulting graph?

$g(x) = x^2$

Stretching, Shrinking, and Reflecting the Graph of $f(x) = x^2$

Essential question: *How does the graph of $g(x) = ax^2$ differ from the graph of $f(x) = x^2$?*

CC.9-12.F.IF.2 Use function notation, evaluate functions for inputs in their domains ...

CC.9-12.F.IF.7 Graph functions expressed symbolically and show key features of the graph ...*

CC.9-12.F.IF.7a Graph ... quadratic functions and show intercepts, maxima, and minima.*

CC.9-12.F.BF.3 Identify the effect on the graph of replacing $f(x)$ by ... $kf(x)$ ... for specific values of k (both positive and negative); find the value of k given the graphs ...

Prerequisites

Translating the graph of $f(x) = x^2$, Lesson 2-1

Math Background

To motivate a discussion of the effect of a on the graph of $g(x) = ax^2$, you might introduce the function $d(t) = 16t^2$, which gives the distance (in feet) that a falling object travels in time t (in seconds). Have students compare this function with the parent function $f(t) = t^2$. They should see that $d(t) = 16 \cdot f(t)$, which means that every point on the graph of $d(t)$ has a y-coordinate that is 16 times the y-coordinate of the corresponding point on the graph of $f(t)$. In other words, the graph of $f(t)$ must be stretched vertically by a factor of 16 to obtain the graph of $d(t)$.

INTRODUCE

Discuss the transformation given by the coordinate notation $(x, y) \rightarrow (x, ay)$. Give students the coordinates of the vertices of a triangle with one of its sides on the x-axis, and have students apply the transformation to those coordinates in order to obtain the coordinates of the vertices of the transformed triangle. Then have students draw the transformed triangle. They should observe that the new triangle is a vertical stretch of the original triangle and that the side of the original triangle that is on the x-axis is not affected by the transformation.

TEACH

1 EXAMPLE

Questioning Strategies

- Look at the table in part A. Describe how the values of $g(x)$ change. **They decrease to 0 and then increase again. Also, $g(1) = g(-1)$, $g(2) = g(-2)$, and so on.**

- Compare in general, not number by number, the values of $g(x)$ to the values of the parent function $f(x)$ for the same values of x. **Except for $x = 0$, the values for $g(x)$ are greater than the corresponding values of $f(x)$.**

- About what line is the graph of $g(x)$ symmetric? **the y-axis**

- Look at the table in part B. Describe how the values of $g(x)$ change. **They increase to 0 and then decrease again. Also, $g(1) = g(-1)$, $g(2) = g(-2)$, and so on.**

- About what line is the graph of $g(x)$ symmetric? **the y-axis**

EXTRA EXAMPLE

Graph each quadratic function using the same coordinate plane. The graph of the parent function is shown.

A. $g(x) = 5x^2$

B. $g(x) = -5x^2$

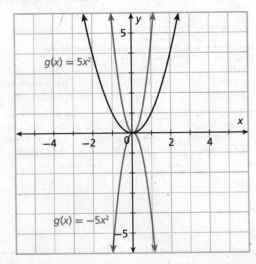

Name_____ Class_____ Date_____

2-2

Stretching, Shrinking, and Reflecting the Graph of $f(x) = x^2$

COMMON CORE

CC.9-12.F.IF.2,
CC.9-12.F.IF.7*,
CC.9-12.F.IF.7a*,
CC.9-12.F.BF.3

Essential question: *How does the graph of $g(x) = ax^2$ differ from the graph of $f(x) = x^2$?*

In this lesson, you will investigate stretches, shrinks, and reflections of the graph of the parent quadratic function.

1 EXAMPLE Graphing $f(x) = ax^2$ when $|a| > 1$

Graph each quadratic function using the same coordinate plane. (The graph of the parent function is shown.)

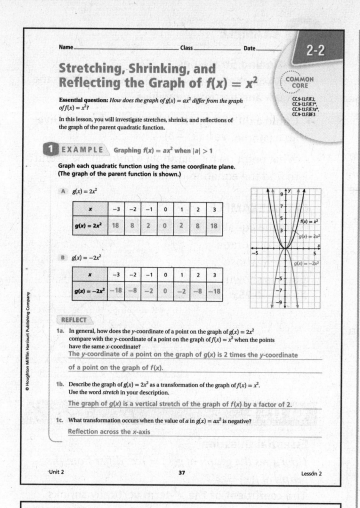

A $g(x) = 2x^2$

x	−3	−2	−1	0	1	2	3
$g(x) = 2x^2$	18	8	2	0	2	8	18

B $g(x) = -2x^2$

x	−3	−2	−1	0	1	2	3
$g(x) = -2x^2$	−18	−8	−2	0	−2	−8	−18

REFLECT

1a. In general, how does the y-coordinate of a point on the graph of $g(x) = 2x^2$ compare with the y-coordinate of a point on the graph of $f(x) = x^2$ when the points have the same x-coordinate?

The y-coordinate of a point on the graph of $g(x)$ is 2 times the y-coordinate

of a point on the graph of $f(x)$.

1b. Describe the graph of $g(x) = 2x^2$ as a transformation of the graph of $f(x) = x^2$. Use the word *stretch* in your description.

The graph of $g(x)$ is a vertical stretch of the graph of $f(x)$ by a factor of 2.

1c. What transformation occurs when the value of a in $g(x) = ax^2$ is negative?

Reflection across the x-axis

2 EXAMPLE Graphing $f(x) = ax^2$ when $|a| < 1$

Graph each quadratic function using the same coordinate plane. (The graph of the parent function is shown.)

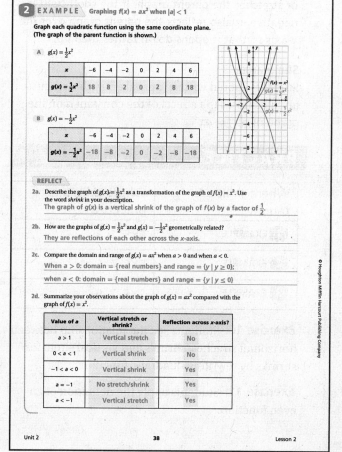

A $g(x) = \frac{1}{2}x^2$

x	−6	−4	−2	0	2	4	6
$g(x) = \frac{1}{2}x^2$	18	8	2	0	2	8	18

B $g(x) = -\frac{1}{2}x^2$

x	−6	−4	−2	0	2	4	6
$g(x) = -\frac{1}{2}x^2$	−18	−8	−2	0	−2	−8	−18

REFLECT

2a. Describe the graph of $g(x) = \frac{1}{2}x^2$ as a transformation of the graph of $f(x) = x^2$. Use the word *shrink* in your description.

The graph of $g(x)$ is a vertical shrink of the graph of $f(x)$ by a factor of $\frac{1}{2}$.

2b. How are the graphs of $g(x) = \frac{1}{2}x^2$ and $g(x) = -\frac{1}{2}x^2$ geometrically related?

They are reflections of each other across the x-axis.

2c. Compare the domain and range of $g(x) = ax^2$ when $a > 0$ and when $a < 0$.

When $a > 0$: domain = {real numbers} and range = {$y \mid y \geq 0$};

when $a < 0$: domain = {real numbers} and range = {$y \mid y \leq 0$}

2d. Summarize your observations about the graph of $g(x) = ax^2$ compared with the graph of $f(x) = x^2$.

Value of a	Vertical stretch or shrink?	Reflection across x-axis?
$a > 1$	Vertical stretch	No
$0 < a < 1$	Vertical shrink	No
$−1 < a < 0$	Vertical shrink	Yes
$a = −1$	No stretch/shrink	Yes
$a < −1$	Vertical stretch	Yes

2 EXAMPLE

Questioning Strategies

- Look at the table in part A. Describe how the values of $g(x)$ change. **They decrease to 0 and then increase again. Also, $g(1) = g(-1)$, $g(2) = g(-2)$, and so on.**

- Compare in general, not number by number, the values of $g(x)$ to the values of the parent function $f(x)$ for the same value of x. **Except for $x = 0$, the values for $g(x)$ are less than the corresponding values of $f(x)$.**

- About what line is the graph of $g(x)$ symmetric? **the y-axis**

EXTRA EXAMPLE

Graph each quadratic function using the same coordinate plane. The graph of the parent function is shown.

A. $g(x) = \frac{1}{3}x^2$

B. $g(x) = -\frac{1}{3}x^2$

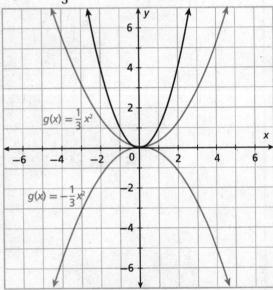

3 EXAMPLE

Questioning Strategies

- Why was the point $(-3, -3)$ chosen? **It is on the graph and has integer values.**

- Could a different point have been chosen? Give an example. **yes; $(3, -3)$**

- What point on the parabola would *not* be useful to find the equation of the function? **$(0, 0)$**

EXTRA EXAMPLE

Write the equation for the quadratic function whose graph is shown. $f(x) = -0.25x^2$

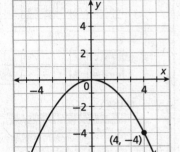

(4, −4)

CLOSE

Essential Question

How does the graph of $g(x) = ax^2$ differ from the graph of $f(x) = x^2$?

The coefficient of the x^2-term vertically shrinks or stretches the parent graph. If the coefficient is negative, it also reflects the parent graph over the x-axis so that it opens down rather than up.

Summarize

Students should write a journal entry that discusses and illustrates the effects of the constant a on the graph of $g(x) = ax^2$.

PRACTICE

Where skills are taught	Where skills are practiced
1 EXAMPLE	EXS. 1–3
2 EXAMPLE	EXS. 4–6
3 EXAMPLE	EXS. 7–9

Exercise 10: Students see the relationship between horizontal streches/shrinks and vertical stretches/shrinks by rewriting quadratic functions.

Exercise 11: Students apply the definition of an even function.

3 EXAMPLE Writing Equations of Quadratic Functions

Write the equation for the quadratic function whose graph is shown.

Use the point $(-3, -3)$ to find the value of a in the general form $g(x) = ax^2$.

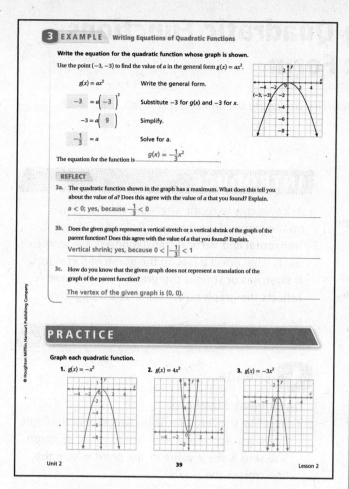

$g(x) = ax^2$ Write the general form.

$-3 = a(-3)^2$ Substitute -3 for $g(x)$ and -3 for x.

$-3 = a(9)$ Simplify.

$-\dfrac{1}{3} = a$ Solve for a.

The equation for the function is $g(x) = -\dfrac{1}{3}x^2$.

REFLECT

3a. The quadratic function shown in the graph has a maximum. What does this tell you about the value of a? Does this agree with the value of a that you found? Explain.

$a < 0$; yes, because $-\dfrac{1}{3} < 0$

3b. Does the given graph represent a vertical stretch or a vertical shrink of the graph of the parent function? Does this agree with the value of a that you found? Explain.

Vertical shrink; yes, because $0 < \left|-\dfrac{1}{3}\right| < 1$

3c. How do you know that the given graph does not represent a translation of the graph of the parent function?

The vertex of the given graph is $(0, 0)$.

PRACTICE

Graph each quadratic function.

1. $g(x) = -x^2$ **2.** $g(x) = 4x^2$ **3.** $g(x) = -3x^2$

Graph each quadratic function.

4. $g(x) = \dfrac{1}{4}x^2$ **5.** $g(x) = -\dfrac{3}{4}x^2$ **6.** $g(x) = \dfrac{1}{3}x^2$

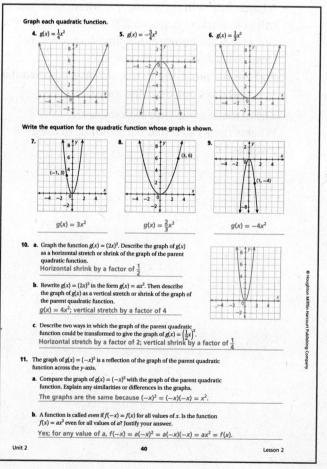

Write the equation for the quadratic function whose graph is shown.

7. $(-1, 3)$ **8.** $(3, 6)$ **9.** $(1, -4)$

$g(x) = 3x^2$ $g(x) = \dfrac{2}{3}x^2$ $g(x) = -4x^2$

10. a. Graph the function $g(x) = (2x)^2$. Describe the graph of $g(x)$ as a horizontal stretch or shrink of the graph of the parent quadratic function.

Horizontal shrink by a factor of $\dfrac{1}{2}$

b. Rewrite $g(x) = (2x)^2$ in the form $g(x) = ax^2$. Then describe the graph of $g(x)$ as a vertical stretch or shrink of the graph of the parent quadratic function.

$g(x) = 4x^2$; vertical stretch by a factor of 4

c. Describe two ways in which the graph of the parent quadratic function could be transformed to give the graph of $g(x) = \left(\dfrac{1}{2}x\right)^2$.

Horizontal stretch by a factor of 2; vertical shrink by a factor of $\dfrac{1}{4}$

11. The graph of $g(x) = (-x)^2$ is a reflection of the graph of the parent quadratic function across the y-axis.

a. Compare the graph of $g(x) = (-x)^2$ with the graph of the parent quadratic function. Explain any similarities or differences in the graphs.

The graphs are the same because $(-x)^2 = (-x)(-x) = x^2$.

b. A function is called *even* if $f(-x) = f(x)$ for all values of x. Is the function $f(x) = ax^2$ even for all values of a? Justify your answer.

Yes; for any value of a, $f(-x) = a(-x)^2 = a(-x)(-x) = ax^2 = f(x)$.

Graphing Quadratic Functions in Vertex Form

Essential question: *How can you graph the function $f(x) = a(x - h)^2 + k$?*

© Houghton Mifflin Harcourt Publishing Company

COMMON CORE Standards for Mathematical Content

CC.9-12.A.CED.2 … graph equations on coordinate axes with labels and scales.*

CC.9-12.F.IF.2 Use function notation, evaluate functions for inputs in their domains, and interpret statements that use function notation in terms of a context.

CC.9-12.F.IF.7 Graph functions expressed symbolically and show key features of the graph …*

CC.9-12.F.IF.7a Graph … quadratic functions and show intercepts, maxima, and minima.*

CC.9-12.F.BF.3 Identify the effect on the graph of replacing $f(x)$ by $f(x) + k$, $kf(x)$, … and $f(x + k)$ for specific values of k (both positive and negative); find the value of k given the graphs.

Also: CC.9-12.F.IF.9

Vocabulary
vertex form

zero of a function

Prerequisites
Graphing functions of the form $f(x) = (x - h)^2 + k$ and of the form $f(x) = ax^2$, Lessons 2-1 and 2-2

Math Background
Quadratic functions are used in a variety of real-world applications. In this lesson, students will use them to model the shape of a curved bridge support.

INTRODUCE

Ask students to recall what effect h and k have on the graph of the function $f(x) = (x - h)^2 + k$. **horizontal and vertical translation** Ask students to recall what effect a has on the graph of $f(x) = ax^2$. **It stretches or shrinks the graph vertically, and it reflects the graph across the x-axis if negative.**

TEACH

1 ENGAGE

Questioning Strategies

- Describe the zero of a linear function of the form $f(x) = mx + b$ where $m \neq 0$ in terms of its graph. **The zero is the x-value of the point where the line crosses the x-axis.**

- A linear function $f(x) = mx + b$ where $m = 0$ is called a *constant function*. If $b \neq 0$, how many zeros does the constant function $f(x) = b$ have? How is this evident from the graph of $f(x)$? **$f(x)$ has no zeros; the graph of $f(x)$ is a horizontal line that does not cross the x-axis.**

- The zeros of a function are x-values. What is the y-value that corresponds to these x-values? **0**

Name_____ Class_____ Date_____

2-3

Graphing Quadratic Functions in Vertex Form

COMMON CORE

CC.9-12.A.CED.2*,
CC.9-12.F.IF.2,
CC.9-12.F.IF.7*,
CC.9-12.F.IF.7a*,
CC.9-12.F.BF.3

Essential question: *How can you graph the function* $f(x) = a(x - h)^2 + k$?

1 ENGAGE   Understanding Vertex Form

The **vertex form** of a quadratic function is $f(x) = a(x - h)^2 + k$. The vertex of the graph of a quadratic function in vertex form is (h, k).

$$f(x) = a(x - h)^2 + k$$

| *a* indicates a vertical stretch or shrink and/or a reflection across the *x*-axis. | *h* indicates a horizontal translation. | *k* indicates a vertical translation. |

A **zero of a function** is an input value *x* that makes the output value $f(x)$ equal 0. You can estimate the zeros of a quadratic function by observing where the graph crosses the *x*-axis.

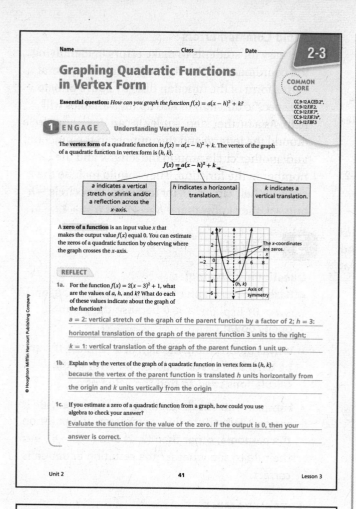

The *x*-coordinates are zeros.

(h, k) Axis of symmetry

REFLECT

1a. For the function $f(x) = 2(x - 3)^2 + 1$, what are the values of *a*, *h*, and *k*? What do each of these values indicate about the graph of the function?

a = 2: vertical stretch of the graph of the parent function by a factor of 2; *h* = 3: horizontal translation of the graph of the parent function 3 units to the right; *k* = 1: vertical translation of the graph of the parent function 1 unit up.

1b. Explain why the vertex of the graph of a quadratic function in vertex form is (h, k).

because the vertex of the parent function is translated *h* units horizontally from the origin and *k* units vertically from the origin

1c. If you estimate a zero of a quadratic function from a graph, how could you use algebra to check your answer?

Evaluate the function for the value of the zero. If the output is 0, then your answer is correct.

Unit 2   41   Lesson 3

---

2 EXAMPLE   Graphing $f(x) = a(x - h)^2 + k$

Graph the function $f(x) = 2(x + 1)^2 - 2$. Identify the vertex, minimum or maximum, axis of symmetry, and zeros of the function.

A Identify and graph the vertex.

$h = \underline{-1}$

$k = \underline{-2}$

The vertex of the graph is $\underline{(-1, -2)}$.

B Identify the coordinates of points to the left and right of the vertex.

x	−3	−2	0	1
f(x)	6	0	0	6

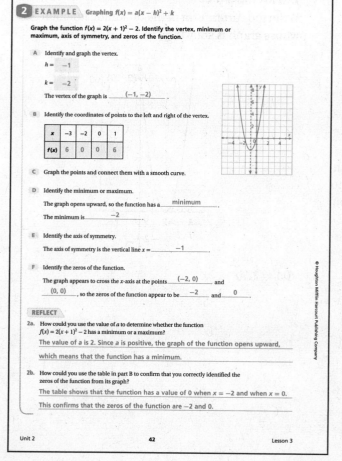

C Graph the points and connect them with a smooth curve.

D Identify the minimum or maximum.

The graph opens upward, so the function has a $\underline{\text{minimum}}$.

The minimum is $\underline{-2}$.

E Identify the axis of symmetry.

The axis of symmetry is the vertical line $x = \underline{-1}$.

F Identify the zeros of the function.

The graph appears to cross the *x*-axis at the points $\underline{(-2, 0)}$ and $\underline{(0, 0)}$, so the zeros of the function appear to be $\underline{-2}$ and $\underline{0}$.

REFLECT

2a. How could you use the value of *a* to determine whether the function $f(x) = 2(x + 1)^2 - 2$ has a minimum or a maximum?

The value of *a* is 2. Since *a* is positive, the graph of the function opens upward, which means that the function has a minimum.

2b. How could you use the table in part B to confirm that you correctly identified the zeros of the function from its graph?

The table shows that the function has a value of 0 when $x = -2$ and when $x = 0$. This confirms that the zeros of the function are −2 and 0.

Unit 2   42   Lesson 3

Questioning Strategies

- How would the graph be different if $a = -2$ rather than $a = 2$? Describe the vertex and the direction in which the parabola opens. The vertex is unchanged. The graph opens down.

- Make a table of values for $g(x) = -2(x + 1)^2 - 2$ for $x = -3, -2, -1, 0$, and 1. $g(x) = -10, -4, -2, -4, -10$

- Explain why the vertex of the graph of $g(x) = -2(x + 1)^2 - 2$ stays the same as the vertex of the graph of $f(x)$. The value of h is still -1, and the value of k is still -2, so the vertex remains at $(-1, -2)$.

- What are the zeros of $g(x) = -2(x + 1)^2 - 2$? There are no zeros.

EXTRA EXAMPLE

Graph the function $f(x) = -3(x - 4)^2 - 1$. Identify the vertex, minimum or maximum, axis of symmetry, and zeros of the function.

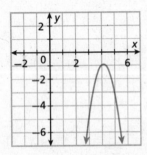

The vertex is $(4, -1)$; the maximum is -1; the axis of symmetry is $x = 4$; there are no zeros.

Technology

Students can graph the quadratic function in the Example using a calculator and compare this graph to the one they drew by hand. However, reinforce to students that prior to graphing a quadratic function in vertex form on a graphing calculator, they should identify the vertex and know which way the parabola opens.

Avoid Common Errors

It is easy for students to make errors in identifying the coordinates of the vertex. Writing the general vertex form of the function directly above or below the specific function to line up the variables will help. As a further step, students can draw one circle around the letter h and the number in the function, and another circle around the letter k and the number in the function. They should include the signs in their circles. If, for instance, they circle $-h$ and $+4$, they know that $-h = +4$, or $h = -4$.

Questioning Strategies

- Based on the graph of the function, is $a < 0$, or is $a > 0$? Explain. $a < 0$ because the parabola opens down.

- Why is determining the sign of a helpful? It can be used as a check to detect an error in the calculations used to find the value of a.

- How can you check whether your function rule is correct? Substitute the coordinates of a point on the parabola, other than $(2, 2)$ and $(-2, -6)$, into the rule to see whether the resulting equation is correct.

EXTRA EXAMPLE

Write the vertex form of the quadratic function whose graph is shown.

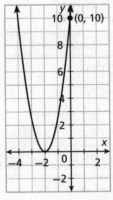

$f(x) = 2.5(x + 2)^2$

3 **EXAMPLE** Writing Equations in Vertex Form

Write the vertex form of the quadratic function whose graph is shown.

A Use the vertex of the graph to identify the values of h and k.

The vertex of the graph is (2, 2) .

$h = 2$

$k = 2$

Substitute the values of h and k into the vertex form:

$f(x) = a\left(x - 2\right)^2 + 2$

B Use the point $(-2, -6)$ to identify the value of a.

$f(x) = a(x - 2)^2 + 2$ Vertex form

$-6 = a\left(-2 - 2\right)^2 + 2$ Substitute -6 for $f(x)$ and -2 for x.

$-6 = a\left(16\right) + 2$ Simplify.

$-8 = a(16)$ Subtract 2 from both sides.

$-\dfrac{1}{2} = a$ Divide both sides by 16.

Substitute the value of a into the vertex form:

$f(x) = -\dfrac{1}{2}(x - 2)^2 + 2$

So, the vertex form of the function shown in the graph is

$f(x) = -\dfrac{1}{2}(x - 2)^2 + 2$

REFLECT

3a. How can you tell by looking at the graph that the value of a is negative?

The graph opens downward, which indicates a reflection of the graph of the

parent function across the x-axis. A reflection across the x-axis results in a

negative value of a.

3b. Describe the graph of the given function as a transformation of the parent quadratic function.

Reflection across the x-axis, vertical shrink by a factor of $\frac{1}{2}$, and translation

2 units to the right and 2 units up

© Houghton Mifflin Harcourt Publishing Company

4 **EXAMPLE** Modeling Quadratic Functions in Vertex Form

The shape of a bridge support can be modeled by $f(x) = -\dfrac{1}{600}(x - 300)^2 + 150$, where x is the horizontal distance in feet from the left end of the bridge and $f(x)$ is the height in feet above the bridge deck. Sketch a graph of the support. Then determine the maximum height of the support above the bridge deck and the width of the support at the level of the bridge deck.

A Graph the function.

• The vertex of the graph is (300, 150) .

• Find the point at the left end of the support ($x = 0$).

Since $f(0) = \underline{\quad 0 \quad}$, the point (0, 0) represents the left end.

• Use symmetry to find the point at the right end of the support.

Since the left end is 300 feet to the left of the vertex, the right end will be 300 feet to the right of the vertex.

The point (600, 0) represents the right end.

• Find two other points on the support.

$\left(120, 96\right)$ and $\left(480, 96\right)$

• Sketch the graph.

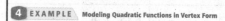

B Determine the maximum height of the support.

The maximum of the function is 150 .

So, the maximum height of the bridge support is 150 feet.

C Determine the width of the bridge support at the level of the bridge deck.

The distance from the left end to the right end is 600 feet.

So, the width is 600 feet at the level of the bridge deck.

REFLECT

4a. Explain how you know that the y-coordinate of the right end of the support is 0.

The support has the shape of a parabola, so it is symmetric. The left end has a

y-coordinate of 0, so the right end must also have a y-coordinate of 0.

4b. What does the vertex represent in this situation?

the point on the support above the midpoint of the bridge deck and at the

greatest height above the bridge deck

© Houghton Mifflin Harcourt Publishing Company

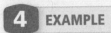

Questioning Strategies

- What shape does the bridge support have? How do you know? Parabola; it is represented by a quadratic function.

- Why is the graph only in the first quadrant? In this situation, the values of x and $f(x)$ represent distance and height. Distance and height cannot be negative.

MATHEMATICAL PRACTICE | **Highlighting the Standards**

4 EXAMPLE is an opportunity to address Mathematical Practice Standard 4 (Model with mathematics). Students will describe the quadratic relationship between the height of a bridge support and the horizontal distance from the base of the support. They will sketch a graph of the quadratic function (which is the shape of the bridge support) and identify and use the zeros and the vertex of the function to determine physical quantities.

EXTRA EXAMPLE

The shape of a highway tunnel through a mountain can be modeled by $f(x) = -\frac{1}{15}(x - 20)^2 + 27$, where x is the horizontal distance in feet from the left edge of the tunnel and $f(x)$ is the height in feet above the highway. Sketch a graph of the function. Determine the maximum height of the tunnel and the width of the tunnel.

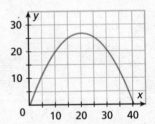

height = 27 ft; width = 40 ft

CLOSE

Essential Question

How can you graph the function $f(x) = a(x - h)^2 + k$?
To graph the function $f(x) = a(x - h)^2 + k$, first identify the vertex as (h, k). Determine whether the parabola will open up or down by examining whether $a > 0$ or $a < 0$. Then, choose two x-values on one side of the vertex and calculate their y-values. Using symmetry, find two points on the other side of the vertex. Finally, graph the function.

Summarize

Students should write a journal entry to describe how to graph the vertex form of a quadratic function by hand. They should mention the value of a, the vertex, and how they will use symmetry to help them graph the function. Next, they should address how they would check the graph of a quadratic function obtained from a calculator.

PRACTICE

Where skills are taught	Where skills are practiced
2 EXAMPLE	EXS. 1–4
3 EXAMPLE	EXS. 5, 6
4 EXAMPLE	EXS. 7, 8

Exercises 9 and 10: Students extend what they learned in **2 EXAMPLE** and **3 EXAMPLE** to compare the maximum or minimum of two quadratic functions—one given as an equation and the other as a graph.

PRACTICE

Graph each quadratic function. Identify the vertex, minimum or maximum, axis of symmetry, and zeros of the function.

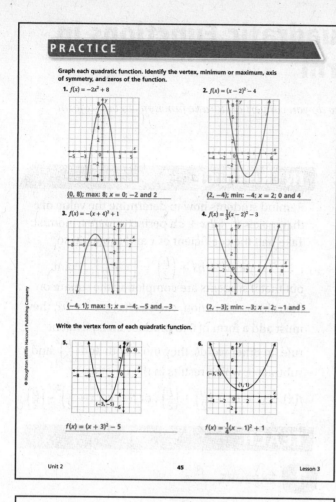

1. $f(x) = -2x^2 + 8$

(0, 8); max: 8; $x = 0$; −2 and 2

2. $f(x) = (x - 2)^2 - 4$

(2, −4); min: −4; $x = 2$; 0 and 4

3. $f(x) = -(x + 4)^2 + 1$

(−4, 1); max: 1; $x = -4$; −5 and −3

4. $f(x) = \frac{1}{3}(x - 2)^2 - 3$

(2, −3); min: −3; $x = 2$; −1 and 5

Write the vertex form of each quadratic function.

5.

(0, 4)

(−3, −5)

$f(x) = (x + 3)^2 - 5$

6.

(−3, 5)

(1, 1)

$f(x) = \frac{1}{4}(x - 1)^2 + 1$

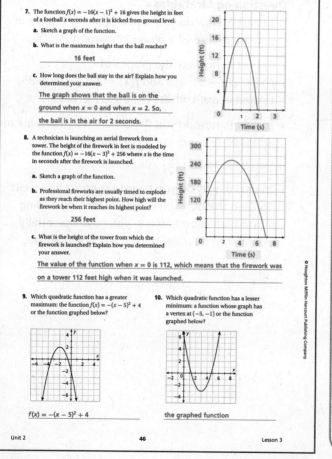

7. The function $f(x) = -16(x - 1)^2 + 16$ gives the height in feet of a football x seconds after it is kicked from ground level.

a. Sketch a graph of the function.

b. What is the maximum height that the ball reaches?

16 feet

c. How long does the ball stay in the air? Explain how you determined your answer.

The graph shows that the ball is on the

ground when $x = 0$ and when $x = 2$. So,

the ball is in the air for 2 seconds.

8. A technician is launching an aerial firework from a tower. The height of the firework in feet is modeled by the function $f(x) = -16(x - 3)^2 + 256$ where x is the time in seconds after the firework is launched.

a. Sketch a graph of the function.

b. Professional fireworks are usually timed to explode as they reach their highest point. How high will the firework be when it reaches its highest point?

256 feet

c. What is the height of the tower from which the firework is launched? Explain how you determined your answer.

The value of the function when $x = 0$ is 112, which means that the firework was

on a tower 112 feet high when it was launched.

9. Which quadratic function has a greater maximum: the function $f(x) = -(x - 5)^2 + 4$ or the function graphed below?

$f(x) = -(x - 5)^2 + 4$

10. Which quadratic function has a lesser minimum: a function whose graph has a vertex at (−5, −1) or the function graphed below?

the graphed function

Writing Quadratic Functions in Vertex Form

Essential question: *How do you convert quadratic functions to vertex form* $f(x) = a(x - h)^2 + k?$

COMMON
CORE **Standards for Mathematical Content**

CC.9-12.A.SSE.3 Choose and produce an equivalent form of an expression to reveal and explain properties of the quantity represented by the expression.*

CC.9-12.A.SSE.3b Complete the square in a quadratic expression to reveal the maximum or minimum value of the function it defines.*

CC.9-12.A.CED.2 ... graph equations on coordinate axes with labels and scales.*

CC.9-12.F.IF.2 Use function notation, evaluate functions for inputs in their domains ...

CC.9-12.A.F.IF.7 Graph functions expressed symbolically and show key features of the graph ...*

CC.9-12.F.IF.7a Graph ... quadratic functions and show intercepts, maxima, and minima.*

CC.9-12.F.IF.8 Write a function defined by an expression in different but equivalent forms to reveal and explain different properties of the function.

CC.9-12.F.IF.8a Use the process of factoring and completing the square in a quadratic function to show zeros, extreme values, and symmetry of the graph, and interpret these in terms of a context.

Vocabulary

standard form

Prerequisites

Completing the square, Algebra 1

Graphing quadratic functions in vertex form, Lesson 2-3

Math Background

Quadratic functions can be written in a variety of forms: standard form, $f(x) = ax^2 + bx + c$; vertex form, $f(x) = a(x - h)^2 + k$; and intercept form, $f(x) = a(x - p)(x - q)$. Since they are all equivalent, it is possible to convert from one form to another.

INTRODUCE

Remind students how to determine the value of c that makes $x^2 + bx + c$ a perfect square trinomial: Take half the coefficient of x and square it, so $c = \left(\frac{b}{2}\right)^2$ and $x^2 + bx + \left(\frac{b}{2}\right)^2 = \left(x + \frac{b}{2}\right)^2$. Point out that if students are completing the square on the rule for a function, such as $f(x) = x^2 + bx$, they must add a form of 0 to produce an equivalent rule. In other words, they must both add $\left(\frac{b}{2}\right)^2$ and subtract it, which results in the function $f(x) = x^2 + bx + \left(\frac{b}{2}\right)^2 - \left(\frac{b}{2}\right)^2$, or $f(x) = \left(x + \frac{b}{2}\right)^2 - \left(\frac{b}{2}\right)^2$.

TEACH

1 EXPLORE

Questioning Strategies

- In part A, how do you expand $(x - 4)^2$? You can use the square of a binomial pattern or FOIL.

- In part A, how are the graphs of $f(x) = 2(x - 4)^2 + 3$ and $f(x) = 2x^2 - 16x + 35$ related to each other? They are the same.

- In part B, how do you determine that the value to add is 9? To complete the square on $x^2 + 6x$, you have to add $\left(\frac{6}{2}\right)^2$, or 9.

- In part B, why do you have to subtract 9 as well? To keep the function rule the same; by adding 9 and then subtracting 9, you have essentially added 0 to the rule; thus, it has not changed.

© Houghton Mifflin Harcourt Publishing Company

Name_____ Class_____ Date_____

2-4

Writing Quadratic Functions in Vertex Form

COMMON CORE
CC.9-12.A.SSE.3b*,
CC.9-12.A.CED.2*,
CC.9-12.F.IF.2,
CC.9-12.F.IF.7*,
CC.9-12.F.IF.7a*,
CC.9-12.F.IF.8a

Essential question: *How do you convert quadratic functions to vertex form* $f(x) = a(x - h)^2 + k?$

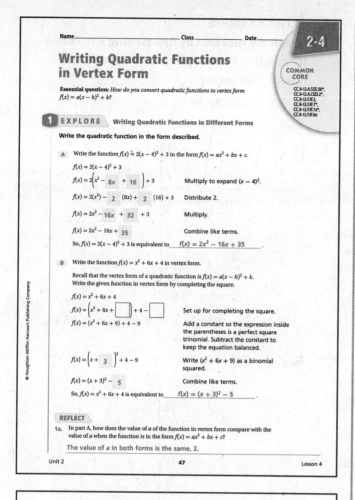

1 EXPLORE Writing Quadratic Functions in Different Forms

Write the quadratic function in the form described.

A Write the function $f(x) = 2(x - 4)^2 + 3$ in the form $f(x) = ax^2 + bx + c$.

$f(x) = 2(x - 4)^2 + 3$

$f(x) = 2\left(x^2 - \boxed{8x} + \boxed{16}\right) + 3$ Multiply to expand $(x - 4)^2$.

$f(x) = 2(x^2) - \boxed{2}(8x) + \boxed{2}(16) + 3$ Distribute 2.

$f(x) = 2x^2 - \boxed{16x} + \boxed{32} + 3$ Multiply.

$f(x) = 2x^2 - 16x + \boxed{35}$ Combine like terms.

So, $f(x) = 2(x - 4)^2 + 3$ is equivalent to $\underline{f(x) = 2x^2 - 16x + 35}$.

B Write the function $f(x) = x^2 + 6x + 4$ in vertex form.

Recall that the vertex form of a quadratic function is $f(x) = a(x - h)^2 + k$. Write the given function in vertex form by completing the square.

$f(x) = x^2 + 6x + 4$

$f(x) = \left(x^2 + 6x + \boxed{}\right) + 4 - \boxed{}$ Set up for completing the square.

$f(x) = (x^2 + 6x + 9) + 4 - 9$ Add a constant so the expression inside the parentheses is a perfect square trinomial. Subtract the constant to keep the equation balanced.

$f(x) = \left(x + \boxed{3}\right)^2 + 4 - 9$ Write $(x^2 + 6x + 9)$ as a binomial squared.

$f(x) = (x + 3)^2 - \boxed{5}$ Combine like terms.

So, $f(x) = x^2 + 6x + 4$ is equivalent to $\underline{f(x) = (x + 3)^2 - 5}$.

REFLECT

1a. In part A, how does the value of a of the function in vertex form compare with the value of a when the function is in the form $f(x) = ax^2 + bx + c$?

The value of a in both forms is the same, 2.

1b. In part B, how could you check that you found the vertex form of the quadratic equation correctly?

Use the vertex form to write the equation in the form $f(x) = ax^2 + bx + c$. Then

check that the values of a, b, and c match those given in the original equation.

1c. Describe how to complete the square for the quadratic expression

$x^2 + 8x + \boxed{}$

Divide the coefficient of x by 2, and square the quotient: $\left(\frac{8}{2}\right)^2 = 16$.

Add the result to the quadratic expression: $x^2 + 8x + 16$.

The **standard form** of a quadratic equation is $f(x) = ax^2 + bx + c$. Any quadratic function in standard form can be written in vertex form, and any quadratic function in vertex form can be written in standard form.

2 EXAMPLE Graphing by Completing the Square

Graph the function by first writing it in vertex form. Then give the maximum or minimum of the function and identify its zeros.

A $f(x) = x^2 - 8x + 12$

• Write the function in vertex form.

$f(x) = \left(x^2 - 8x + \boxed{}\right) + 12 - \boxed{}$ Set up for completing the square.

$f(x) = \left(x^2 - 8x + \boxed{16}\right) + 12 - \boxed{16}$ Add a constant to complete the square. Subtract the constant to keep the equation balanced.

$f(x) = \left(x - \boxed{4}\right)^2 + 12 - 16$ Write the expression in parentheses as a binomial squared.

$f(x) = (x - 4)^2 - \boxed{4}$ Combine like terms.

• Sketch a graph of the function.

The vertex is $\underline{(4, -4)}$.

Two points to the left of the vertex are

$\left(2, \boxed{0}\right)$ and $\left(3, \boxed{-3}\right)$.

Two points to the right of the vertex are

$\left(5, \boxed{-3}\right)$ and $\left(6, \boxed{0}\right)$.

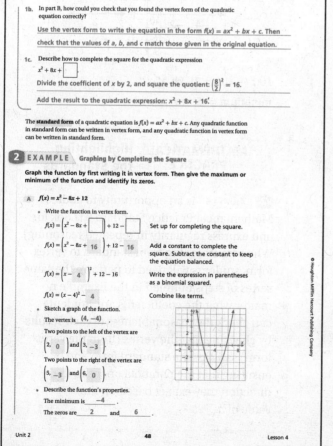

• Describe the function's properties.

The minimum is $\underline{-4}$.

The zeros are $\underline{2}$ and $\underline{6}$.

Differentiated Instruction

Students who are having difficulty completing the square in part B can work with algebra tiles. They should model $x^2 + 6x + 4$ using tiles, with 3 x-tiles to the right of the x^2-tile and 3 x-tiles below the x^2-tile. Once they have the tiles laid out, they should move the 1-tiles, as a group, off to the side. Students should then add enough positive 1-tiles to the x^2-tile and six x-tiles to complete the square (9 tiles). They add an equal number of negative 1-tiles to their separated group of four 1-tiles so that the net amount added is 0. Combining the 1-tiles off to the side gives 5 negative 1-tiles, or –5. Students then write the expression as a square of a binomial, $(x + 3)^2$, plus the number of 1-tiles off to the side. The final expression, $(x + 3)^2 - 5$, is equal to the original one, since students have simply added a form of 0 to the original.

2 EXAMPLE

- In part A, how do you determine what number to add (and subtract) to complete the square? Take half of the coefficient of x and square it;
$$\left(\frac{b}{2}\right)^2 = \left(\frac{8}{2}\right)^2 = 16$$

- In part B, why do you multiply 9 by -2 before you subtract it? The 9 being added to complete the square on $x^2 + 6x$ is being multiplied by -2, the number that was originally factored out of the variable terms of the function rule. Essentially, you are adding -18 to the function rule, so you have to subtract -18 to keep the equation balanced.

Graph the function by first writing it in vertex form. Give the maximum or minimum and identify the zeros.

A. $f(x) = x^2 + x - 6$

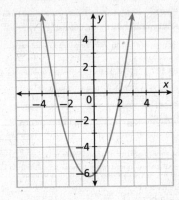

$f(x) = (x + 0.5)^2 - 6.25$; minimum $= -6.25$; The zeros are -3 and 2.

B. $f(x) = 3x^2 - 6x + 8$

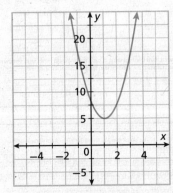

$f(x) = 3(x - 1)^2 + 5$;

minimum $= 5$; no zeros

MATHEMATICAL PRACTICE   Highlighting the Standards

2 EXAMPLE is an opportunity to address Mathematical Practice Standard 8 (Look for and express regularity in repeated reasoning). When transitioning from standard to vertex form, students will need to perform the same series of steps outlined in the Example no matter what the coefficients are. Students can check the reasonableness of their results by checking that the vertex (from the vertex form) satisfies the standard form and by ensuring that the parabola opens in the direction they expect based on the value of a.

B $f(x) = -2x^2 - 12x - 16$

• Write the function in vertex form.

$f(x) = \boxed{-2}\ (x^2 + 6x) - 16$ Factor the variable terms so that the coefficient of x^2 is 1.

$f(x) = -2\left(x^2 + 6x + \boxed{}\right) - 16 - \boxed{}$ Set up for completing the square.

$f(x) = -2\left(x^2 + 6x + \boxed{9}\right) - 16 - (-2)\ \boxed{9}$ Complete the square. Since the constant is multiplied by -2, subtract the product of -2 and the constant to keep the equation balanced.

$f(x) = -2\left(x + \boxed{3}\right)^2 - 16 - (-2)9$ Write the expression in parentheses as a binomial squared.

$f(x) = -2(x + 3)^2 - 16 - \left(\boxed{-18}\right)$ Simplify $(-2)9$.

$f(x) = -2(x + 3)^2 + \boxed{2}$ Combine like terms.

• Sketch a graph of the function.

The vertex is $\underline{(-3,\ 2)}$.

Two points to the left of the vertex are

$\left(-5,\ \boxed{-6}\right)$ and $\left(-4,\ \boxed{0}\right)$.

Two points to the right of the vertex are

$\left(-2,\ \boxed{0}\right)$ and $\left(-1,\ \boxed{-6}\right)$.

• Describe the function's properties.

The maximum is $\underline{\boxed{2}}$.

The zeros are $\underline{\boxed{-4}}$ and $\underline{\boxed{-2}}$.

REFLECT

2a. How do you keep the equation of a quadratic function balanced when completing the square?

Subtract the constant that you add to complete the square. If the constant is multiplied by a number, subtract the product of the constant and the number.

2b. In part B, why do you factor out -2 from the variable terms before completing the square?

-2 is the coefficient of x^2, and it is easier to complete the square when the coefficient of x^2 is 1.

© Houghton Mifflin Harcourt Publishing Company

2c. Why might the vertex form of a quadratic equation be more useful in some situations than the standard form?

In vertex form, you can use the values of a, h, and k to easily identify the vertex, the axis of symmetry, and the maximum or minimum of the function and its graph.

3 EXAMPLE Modeling Quadratic Functions in Standard Form

The function $h(t) = -16t^2 + 64t$ gives the height h in feet of a golf ball t seconds after it is hit. The ball has a height of 48 feet after 1 second. Use the symmetry of the function's graph to determine the other time at which the ball will have a height of 48 feet.

A Write the function in vertex form.

$h(t) = \boxed{-16}\ (t^2 - 4t)$ Factor so that the coefficient of t^2 is 1.

$h(t) = -16\left(t^2 - 4t + \boxed{4}\right) - (-16)\ \boxed{4}$ Complete the square and keep the equation balanced.

$h(t) = -16\left(t - \boxed{2}\right)^2 - (-16)4$ Write the expression in parentheses as a binomial squared.

$h(t) = -16(t - 2)^2 + \boxed{64}$ Simplify.

B Use symmetry to sketch a graph of the function and solve the problem.

The vertex is $\underline{(2,\ 64)}$.

The point $\left(0,\ \boxed{0}\right)$ is on the graph.

This point is 2 units to the left of the vertex. Based on symmetry, there is a point 2 units to the right of the vertex with the same y-coordinate at $\left(\boxed{4}\ , 0\right)$.

The point $(1, 48)$ is on the graph. Based on symmetry, the point $\left(\boxed{3}\ , 48\right)$ is also on the graph.

So, the ball will have a height of 48 feet after 1 second and again after $\underline{3}$ seconds.

REFLECT

3a. How can you check your answer to the problem?

Evaluate the original function for $t = 3$ and check that the value of the function is 48.

© Houghton Mifflin Harcourt Publishing Company

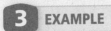

Questioning Strategies

- In this problem, which variable describes the horizontal distance that the golf ball travels? **There isn't a variable that describes horizontal distance. t describes the time, and $h(t)$ describes the vertical distance above the ground.**

- What is the axis of symmetry for this parabola? **$x = 2$**

- For how long is the ball in the air? How can you tell? **4 sec; the ball is on the ground when $h(t) = 0$. This occurs at $t = 0$ and at $t = 4$.**

EXTRA EXAMPLE

The function $h(t) = -16t^2 + 48t$ gives the height h in feet of a football t seconds after it is kicked off a tee. The ball has a height of 32 feet after 1 second. Write the function in vertex form and then graph the function. Use the symmetry of the function's graph to determine the other time at which the ball will have a height of 32 feet.
$h(t) = -16(t - 1.5)^2 + 36$

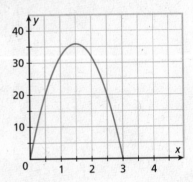

At 2 seconds, the ball will have a height of 32 feet.

CLOSE

Essential Question

How do you convert quadratic functions to vertex form $f(x) = a(x - h)^2 + k$?
You can convert quadratic functions from standard form $f(x) = ax^2 + bx + c$ to vertex form by completing the square on $ax^2 + bx$. You have to add and subtract the same constant to keep the equation balanced.

Summarize

Students should write a journal entry that summarizes what they know about the graphs of quadratic functions. They should write a quadratic function in vertex form, sketch its graph, and then write the function in standard form. To complete their summary, students should complete the square on the standard form to move back to the (original) vertex form of the function.

PRACTICE

Where skills are taught	Where skills are practiced
2 EXAMPLE	EXS. 1–4
3 EXAMPLE	EXS. 5, 6

3b. What is the maximum height that the ball reaches? How do you know?

The vertex form of the function indicates that the vertex is (2, 64). This means

that the ball reaches a maximum height of 64 feet 2 seconds after it is hit.

3c. If you know the coordinates of a point to the left of the vertex of the graph of a quadratic function, how can you use symmetry to find the coordinates of another point on the graph?

The second point will be the same distance to the right of the vertex as the

first point is to the left of the vertex. The second point will have the same

y-coordinate as the first point.

PRACTICE

Graph each function by first writing it in vertex form. Then give the maximum or minimum of the function and identify its zeros.

1. $f(x) = x^2 - 6x + 9$

$f(x) = (x - 3)^2$; min: 0; 3

2. $f(x) = x^2 - 2x - 3$

$f(x) = (x - 1)^2 - 4$; min: -4; -1 and 3

3. $f(x) = -7x^2 - 14x$

$f(x) = -7(x + 1)^2 + 7$; max: 7; -2 and 0

4. $f(x) = 3x^2 - 12x + 9$

$f(x) = 3(x - 2)^2 - 3$; min: -3; 1 and 3

---

5. A company is marketing a new toy. The function $s(p) = -50p^2 + 3000p$ models how the total sales s of the toy, in dollars, depend on the price p of the toy, in dollars.

a. Complete the square to write the function in vertex form and then graph the function.

$s(p) = -50(p - 30)^2 + 45,000$

b. What is the vertex of the graph of the function? What does the vertex represent in this situation?

(30, 45,000); the toy price ($30) that is

predicted to result in the greatest total

sales ($45,000)

c. The model predicts that total sales will be $40,000 when the toy price is $20. At what other price does the model predict that total sales will be $40,000? Use the symmetry of the graph to support your answer.

$40; The point (20, 40,000) is 10 units to the left of the vertex. Based on

the symmetry of the graph, there will also be a point 10 units to the right

of the vertex with a y-coordinate of 40,000. This point is (40, 40,000).

6. A circus performer throws a ball from a height of 32 feet. The model $h(t) = -16t^2 + 16t + 32$ gives the height of the ball in feet t seconds after it is thrown.

a. Complete the square to write the function in vertex form and then graph the function.

$h(t) = -16(t - 0.5)^2 + 36$

b. What is the maximum height that the ball reaches?

36 feet

c. What is a reasonable domain of the function? Explain.

$\{t \mid 0 \le t \le 2\}$; Only nonnegative values of

t and h make sense, so t cannot be less than 0.

h is negative for values of t greater than 2, so t

must be less than equal to 2.

d. What is the y-intercept of the function's graph? What does it represent in this situation? What do you notice about the y-intercept and the value of c when the function is written in standard form?

32; The height in feet from which the ball is thrown.

The y-intercept and the value of c are the same.

Writing Quadratic Functions in Intercept Form

Essential question: *How do you determine where the graph of a quadratic function crosses the x-axis?*

© Houghton Mifflin Harcourt Publishing Company

COMMON CORE Standards for Mathematical Content

CC.9-12.A.SSE.3 Choose and produce an equivalent form of an expression to reveal and explain properties of the quantity represented by the expression.*

CC.9-12.A.SSE.3a Factor a quadratic expression to reveal the zeros of the function it defines.*

CC.9-12.A.CED.2 ... graph equations on coordinate axes with labels and scales.*

CC.9-12.F.IF.2 Use function notation, evaluate functions for inputs in their domains and interpret statements that use function notation in terms of a context.

CC.9-12.F.IF.7 Graph functions expressed symbolically and show key features of the graph ...*

CC.9-12.F.IF.7a Graph ... quadratic functions and show intercepts, maxima, and minima.*

CC.9-12.F.IF.8 Write a function defined by an expression in different but equivalent forms to reveal and explain different properties of the function.

CC.9-12.F.IF.8a Use the process of factoring ... in a quadratic function to show zeros, extreme values, and symmetry of the graph, and interpret these in terms of a context.

Vocabulary
intercept form

Prerequisites
Factoring $ax^2 + bx + c$, Algebra 1

Math Background
Zeros can be found for many different types of functions, such as linear, quadratic, polynomial, logarithmic, exponential, and trigonometric. These functions are used to describe many different physical phenomena. Finding zeros of functions is a useful tool for determining information about the real-world situations modeled by these functions.

INTRODUCE

Have students state the general vertex form of a quadratic function. Ask them how they can find the coordinates of the vertex from this form. Ask them what other key characteristics they have found for quadratic functions (the zeros or *x*-intercepts). Explain that they will learn how to write a quadratic function in intercept form from which they can easily read the *x*-intercepts of the function's graph. Remind students that all three forms (standard, vertex, and intercept) of a given quadratic function are equivalent.

TEACH

1 EXPLORE

Questioning Strategies

- In part A, is there another method you can use to rewrite the expression? Explain. **Yes; you can use the FOIL method to multiply the binomials.**

- Describe a method you can use in parts A and B to check your work. **Substitute a value for *x* into both the original expression and the rewritten expression to ensure that the values of both expressions are the same.**

- In part B, if you were given the function $f(x) = x^2 - 3x - 4$ instead of the expression, explain how you would find the zeros of the function. **Set the function equal to zero and use the zero-product property.**

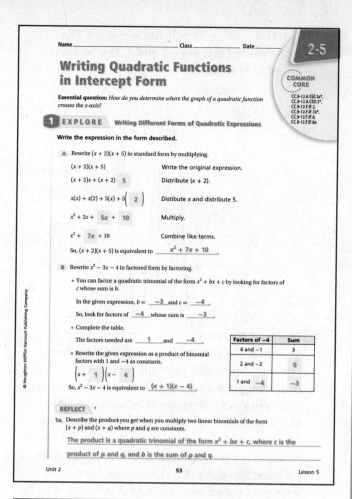

Writing Quadratic Functions in Intercept Form

2-5

COMMON CORE

CC.9-12.A.SSE.3a*,
CC.9-12.A.CED.2*,
CC.9-12.F.IF.2,
CC.9-12.F.IF.7a*,
CC.9-12.F.IF.8,
CC.9-12.F.IF.8a

Essential question: *How do you determine where the graph of a quadratic function crosses the x-axis?*

1 EXPLORE Writing Different Forms of Quadratic Expressions

Write the expression in the form described.

A Rewrite $(x + 2)(x + 5)$ in standard form by multiplying.

$(x + 2)(x + 5)$	Write the original expression.
$(x + 2)x + (x + 2)\ \boxed{5}$	Distribute $(x + 2)$.
$x(x) + x(2) + 5(x) + 5\boxed{2}$	Distibute x and distribute 5.
$x^2 + 2x + \boxed{5x} + \boxed{10}$	Multiply.
$x^2 + \boxed{7x} + 10$	Combine like terms.

So, $(x + 2)(x + 5)$ is equivalent to $\underline{x^2 + 7x + 10}$.

B Rewrite $x^2 - 3x - 4$ in factored form by factoring.

- You can factor a quadratic trinomial of the form $x^2 + bx + c$ by looking for factors of c whose sum is b.

In the given expression, $b = \underline{-3}$ and $c = \underline{-4}$.

So, look for factors of $\underline{-4}$ whose sum is $\underline{-3}$.

- Complete the table.

The factors needed are $\underline{1}$ and $\underline{-4}$.

Factors of −4	Sum
4 and −1	3
2 and −2	0
1 and −4	−3

- Rewrite the given expression as a product of binomial factors with 1 and −4 as constants.

$\left(x + \boxed{1}\right)\left(x - \boxed{4}\right)$

So, $x^2 - 3x - 4$ is equivalent to $\underline{(x + 1)(x - 4)}$.

REFLECT

1a. Describe the product you get when you multiply two linear binomials of the form $(x + p)$ and $(x + q)$ where p and q are constants.

The product is a quadratic trinomial of the form $x^2 + bx + c$, where c is the product of p and q, and b is the sum of p and q.

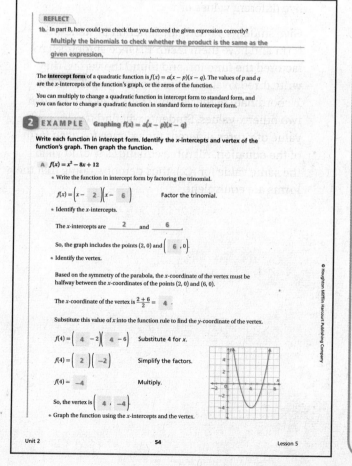

REFLECT

1b. In part B, how could you check that you factored the given expression correctly?

Multiply the binomials to check whether the product is the same as the given expression.

The **intercept form** of a quadratic function is $f(x) = a(x - p)(x - q)$. The values of p and q are the x-intercepts of the function's graph, or the zeros of the function.

You can multiply to change a quadratic function in intercept form to standard form, and you can factor to change a quadratic function in standard form to intercept form.

2 EXAMPLE Graphing $f(x) = a(x - p)(x - q)$

Write each function in intercept form. Identify the x-intercepts and vertex of the function's graph. Then graph the function.

A $f(x) = x^2 - 8x + 12$

- Write the function in intercept form by factoring the trinomial.

$f(x) = \left(x - \boxed{2}\right)\left(x - \boxed{6}\right)$ Factor the trinomial.

- Identify the x-intercepts.

The x-intercepts are $\underline{2}$ and $\underline{6}$.

So, the graph includes the points (2, 0) and $\left(\boxed{6}, 0\right)$.

- Identify the vertex.

Based on the symmetry of the parabola, the x-coordinate of the vertex must be halfway between the x-coordinates of the points (2, 0) and (6, 0).

The x-coordinate of the vertex is $\frac{2 + 6}{2} = \boxed{4}$.

Substitute this value of x into the function rule to find the y-coordinate of the vertex.

$f(4) = \left(\boxed{4} - 2\right)\left(\boxed{4} - 6\right)$ Substitute 4 for x.

$f(4) = \left(\boxed{2}\right)\left(\boxed{-2}\right)$ Simplify the factors.

$f(4) = \boxed{-4}$ Multiply.

So, the vertex is $\left(\boxed{4}, \boxed{-4}\right)$.

- Graph the function using the x-intercepts and the vertex.

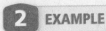

2 EXAMPLE

Questioning Strategies

- In part A, state the two conditions that must be satisfied by the factors of the constant term. **Their product must be 12, and their sum must be −8.**

- In part A, how do you know that both binomial factors are of the form $(x - \underline{\quad})$? **The constant term is positive, so its factors must both be negative or must both be positive. Because the coefficient of x is negative, the factors of the constant term must both be negative.**

- In part A, what is the value of a? **1** Which way should the parabola open? **up**

- In part B, why was $-\frac{1}{3}$ factored out instead of just $\frac{1}{3}$? **To make the factoring easier, you want the coefficient of x^2 to be positive.**

- In part B, does the parabola open up or down? How do you know? **Down; a is negative.**

EXTRA EXAMPLE

Write each function in intercept form. Identify the x-intercepts and vertex of the function's graph. Then graph the function.

A. $f(x) = x^2 - 6x + 5$ $f(x) = (x - 5)(x - 1)$; the x-intercepts are 5 and 1. The vertex is (3, −4).

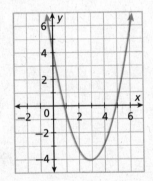

B. $f(x) = -5x^2 - 5x + 10$ $f(x) = -5(x + 2)(x - 1)$; the x-intercepts are −2 and 1. The vertex is (−0.5, 11.25).

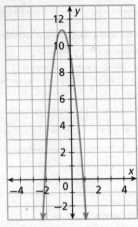

Teaching Strategy

To help students solidify the fact that the three forms of a quadratic function are equivalent, have them complete a 4-column table. The first column is for values of x; the second column, for values of $f(x)$ when the function is written in intercept form; the third column, for values of $f(x)$ when the function is written in standard form; and the last column, for values of $f(x)$ when the function is written in vertex form. Include at least five rows for five different values of x.

Give students a quadratic function in standard form and have them factor it. Once students have factored the function and found the vertex, they write three x-values—the two intercepts and the x-coordinate of the vertex. Then, they can choose two other x-values. Students will find $f(x)$ for each value of x three different times, once for each form of the equation. All three equations should yield the same value for $f(x)$, thus demonstrating that the forms are equivalent.

B $f(x) = -\frac{1}{3}x^2 + \frac{4}{3}x + \frac{5}{3}$

- Write the function in intercept form by factoring the trinomial.

$f(x) = -\frac{1}{3}\left(x^2 - \boxed{4}\ x - \boxed{5}\right)$ Factor out $-\frac{1}{3}$ so that the coefficient of x^2 is 1.

$f(x) = -\frac{1}{3}\left(x - \boxed{5}\right)\left(x + \boxed{1}\right)$ Factor the trinomial.

- Identify the x-intercepts.

The x-intercepts are $\underline{\ \ 5\ \ }$ and $\underline{\ \ -1\ \ }$.

So, the graph includes the points $\left(\boxed{5}, 0\right)$ and $\left(\boxed{-1}, 0\right)$.

- Identify the vertex.

The x-coordinate of the vertex must be halfway between the x-coordinates of the

points $(5, 0)$ and $\left(\boxed{-1}, 0\right)$.

The x-coordinate of the vertex is $\dfrac{5 + -1}{2} = \boxed{2}$.

Substitute this value of x into the function rule to find the y-coordinate of the vertex.

$f(2) = -\frac{1}{3}\left(\boxed{2} - 5\right)\left(\boxed{2} + 1\right)$ Substitute 2 for x.

$f(2) = -\frac{1}{3}\left(\boxed{-3}\right)\left(\boxed{3}\right)$ Simplify the factors.

$f(2) = \boxed{3}$ Multiply.

So, the vertex is $\left(\boxed{2}, \boxed{3}\right)$.

- Graph the function using the x-intercepts and the vertex.

REFLECT

2a. Describe another way that you could have found the vertex of the graph of the function in part A.

Sample answer: Write the function in vertex form. Then use the values of

h and k in the vertex form to write the coordinates of the vertex.

2b. In part B, how could you tell that the parabola opens downward by looking at the standard form of the quadratic function?

The value of a is negative, which means that the graph of the function is a

reflection of the graph of the parent function across the x-axis.

2c. A student claims that you can find the x-coordinate of the vertex of the graph of a quadratic function by averaging the values of p and q from the intercept form of the function. Is the student's claim correct? Explain.

Correct; The values of p and q are the x-intercepts of the function. Averaging p

and q gives an x-value that is halfway between them. Based on symmetry, the

x-coordinate of the vertex is halfway between the x-intercepts.

3 **EXAMPLE**   Writing a Quadratic Model in Intercept Form

The cross-sectional shape of the archway of a bridge is modeled by the function $f(x) = -0.5x^2 + 2x$, where $f(x)$ is the height in meters of a point on the arch and x is the distance in meters from the left end of the arch's base. How wide is the arch at its base? Will a wagon that is 2 meters wide and 1.75 meters tall fit under the arch?

A   Write the function in intercept form.

$f(x) = -0.5\left(x^2 - \boxed{4}\ x\right)$ Factor out -0.5 so that the coefficient of x^2 is 1.

$f(x) = -0.5(x)\left(x - \boxed{4}\right)$ Factor the binomial.

$f(x) = -0.5(x - 0)\left(x - \boxed{4}\right)$ Write the intercept form.

B   Identify the x-intercepts and the vertex.

The x-intercepts are $\underline{\ \ 0\ \ }$ and $\underline{\ \ 4\ \ }$.

The x-coordinate of the vertex is $\dfrac{0 + 4}{2} = \boxed{2}$.

Find the y-coordinate of the vertex.

$f(2) = -0.5\left(\boxed{2} - 0\right)\left(\boxed{2} - 4\right)$ Substitute 2 for x.

$f(2) = -0.5\left(\boxed{2}\right)\left(\boxed{-2}\right) = \boxed{2}$ Simplify.

The vertex is $\left(\boxed{2}, \boxed{2}\right)$.

C   Graph the function using the x-intercepts and the vertex.

D   Use the graph to solve the problem.

The width of the arch at its base is $\underline{\ \ 4\ \ }$ meters.
Sketch the wagon on your graph. Will the wagon fit under the arch? Explain.

No; when the wagon is centered on the arch,

the top corners are slightly higher than the arch.

Distance from left end (m)

Questioning Strategies

- What does the shape of the parabola represent in terms of the situation? **the actual shape of the archway**

- Which way do you expect the parabola to open? How do you know both mathematically and in terms of the situation? **Down; $a < 0$; also, the arch under a bridge must open down.**

EXTRA EXAMPLE

The shape of a tunnel is modeled by the function $f(x) = -0.2x^2 + 2x$ where $f(x)$ is the height from the ground in meters of a point on the tunnel and x is the distance in meters from the left edge of the tunnel. How wide is the tunnel at its base? Will 2 trucks that are each 4 meters tall and 2.6 meters wide be able to pass through the tunnel? **10 meters wide; no**

MATHEMATICAL PRACTICE **Highlighting the Standards**

3 EXAMPLE is an opportunity to address Mathematical Practice Standard 4 (Model with mathematics). Students must not only model the archway of the bridge described in the problem by drawing its graph but also determine whether a wagon will fit under the arch. This is done by modeling the wagon using a rectangle on the same grid as that of the model of the archway. Students must then look at the two models together and correctly determine that the wagon will not fit.

Essential Question

How do you determine where the graph of a quadratic function crosses the x-axis?

You can find the x-intercepts of the graph of a quadratic function in standard form by factoring the function to get its intercept form. If the function is not factorable, the x-intercepts can be found by using the quadratic formula to find the zeros of the function.

Summarize

Have students construct a graphic organizer showing the graph of a quadratic function and its equation in vertex form, intercept form, and standard form. The organizer should show how to "translate" among the forms. Students should choose an initial function in intercept form to be sure its graph has two real x-intercepts. A sample is shown.

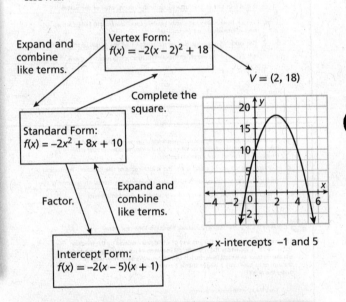

PRACTICE

Where skills are taught	Where skills are practiced
2 EXAMPLE	EXS. 1–4
3 EXAMPLE	EXS. 5, 6

REFLECT

3a. What do the *x*-intercepts represent in this situation?

The *x*-coordinates of the points where the arch touches the ground, where an

x-coordinate is the horizontal distance in meters from the left end of the arch.

3b. Explain how you used the graph to find the width of the arch at its base.

I found the distance between the points where the graph crosses the *x*-axis.

This distance is 4 units, so the arch is 4 meters wide.

3c. Explain how you modeled the shape of the wagon on the graph.

I drew a rectangle 2 units wide and 1.75 units high. I placed the bottom side of

the rectangle on the *x*-axis and centered the rectangle horizontally on the axis of

symmetry of the parabola.

3d. What are the *x*-coordinates of the left and right sides of the model of the wagon? Evaluate the function modeling the arch for these *x*-values. Do the results verify your conclusion about whether the wagon will fit under the arch? Explain.

1 and 3; $f(1) = f(3) = 1.5$; yes; The arch is 1.5 meters high at these *x*-values,

and the height of the wagon is 1.75 meters, so the wagon is too tall to fit.

PRACTICE

Write each function in intercept form. Identify the *x*-intercepts and vertex of the function's graph. Then graph the function.

1. $f(x) = x^2 + 6x + 5$

$f(x) = (x + 5)(x + 1)$;

−5 and −1; (−3, −4)

2. $f(x) = x^2 - 2x - 8$

$f(x) = (x + 2)(x - 4)$;

−2 and 4; (1, −9)

Write each function in intercept form. Identify the *x*-intercepts and vertex of the function's graph. Then graph the function.

3. $f(x) = 2x^2 - 8x + 6$

$f(x) = 2(x - 1)(x - 3)$; 1 and 3; (2, −2)

4. $f(x) = -3x^2 + 24x - 45$

$f(x) = -3(x - 3)(x - 5)$; 3 and 5; (4, 3)

5. In a football game, Tony attempts to kick a field goal at a distance of 40 yards from the goal post. The path of the kicked football is given by the equation $y = -0.02x^2 + 0.9x$ where *x* is the horizontal distance in yards and *y* is the vertical distance in yards.

a. Write the equation in intercept form.

$y = -0.02x(x - 45)$

b. Identify the *x*-intercepts and the vertex.

0, 45; (22.5, 10.125)

c. Graph the equation in the first quadrant.

d. The horizontal bar of the goal post is 10 feet above the ground. Does the ball go over the bar? Explain.

Yes, because the height of the ball at *x* = 40 yards

is *y* = 4 yards = 12 feet, so the ball clears the bar

by 2 feet.

6. Consider the function $f(x) = 2x^2 + 12x + 18$.

a. Write the function in intercept form. What is the relationship between *p* and *q*?

$f(x) = 2(x + 3)(x + 3)$; $p = q$

b. What is the relationship between the graph's *x*-intercepts and its vertex? Explain.

There is a single *x*-intercept that occurs at the vertex because the graph is

tangent to the *x*-axis at the vertex.

c. What is the vertex form of a quadratic function if $p = q$ in the intercept form of the function?

$f(x) = a(x - p)^2$

FOCUS ON MODELING
Modeling with Quadratic Functions

Essential question: *How can you model changes in revenue from season-ticket sales using a quadratic function?*

© Houghton Mifflin Harcourt Publishing Company

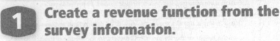

COMMON CORE Standards for Mathematical Content

The following standards are addressed in this lesson. (An asterisk indicates that a standard is also a Modeling standard.) For more detailed information, see each section of the lesson.

Number and Quantity: CC.9-12.N.Q.1*, CC.9-12.N.Q.2*

Algebra: CC.9-12.A.SSE.1*, CC.9-12.A.APR.1, CC.9-12.A.CED.1*, CC.9-12.A.CED.2*, CC.9-12.A.CED.3*, CC.9-12.A.REI.3, CC.9-12.A.REI.4

Functions: CC.9-12.F.IF.2, CC.9-12.F.IF.4*, CC.9-12.F.IF.5*, CC.9-12.F.IF.6, CC.9-12.F.IF.7*, CC.9-12.F.IF.7a*, CC.9-12.F.IF.8, CC.9-12.F.IF.8a, CC.9-12.F.BF.1* CC.9-12.F.BF.1a*

Prerequisites
- Quadratic functions in intercept form, Lesson 2-5
- Quadratic functions in vertex form, Lesson 2-4
- Real solutions of quadratic equations, Algebra 1

Math Background
In this lesson, students write a quadratic function that models revenue from season-ticket sales. When they study calculus, students will learn how to use differentiation to solve maximization problems like this one. In the meantime, this modeling lesson will show students that the tools and concepts they already have at their disposal can be used to solve the problem.

INTRODUCE

Ask students to discuss the repercussions that may occur when a business raises the price of an item. Help students understand that, on the one hand, revenue (which is the price of the item times the number of items sold) is likely to increase. On the other hand, these gains could be offset by fewer items being sold. Explain to students that they will use a quadratic function to model a business situation involving a price increase.

TEACH

1 Create a revenue function from the survey information.

Standards
CC.9-12.N.Q.1 Use units as a way to understand problems and to guide the solution of multi-step problems; ... *

CC.9-12.N.Q.2 Define appropriate quantities for the purpose of descriptive modeling.*

CC.9-12.A.SSE.1 Interpret expressions that represent a quantity in terms of its context.*

CC.9-12.A.CED.2 Create equations in two ... variables to represent relationships between quantities; ... *

CC.9-12.F.IF.2 Use function notation, evaluate functions for inputs in their domains, and interpret statements that use function notation in terms of a context.

CC.9-12.F.BF.1 Write a function that describes a relationship between two quantities.*

CC.9-12.F.BF.1a Determine an explicit expression ... from a context.*

Questioning Strategies
- What is the current revenue from season-ticket sales? How do you know? 200 • $50 = $10,000; this is the value that you obtain from $R(n)$ when $n = 0$.

- How can you use your revenue function to find the revenue after three $5 price increases? What is the price in this case? How many season-ticket holders are there? Evaluate $R(n)$ when $n = 3$; price is $50 + $5 • 3 = $65; number of season-ticket holders is 200 − 10 • 3 = 170.

Teaching Strategy
If students have difficulty writing an expression for the number of season-ticket holders after n price increases, suggest that they make a table showing values of n and the corresponding numbers of season-ticket holders. Then, encourage students to look for and describe any patterns in the table.

Name_____ Class_____ Date_____

2-6

FOCUS ON MODELING

Modeling with Quadratic Functions

COMMON CORE

CC-9-12.N.Q.1*,
CC-9-12.A.SSE.1*,
CC-9-12.A.CED.2*,
CC-9-12.A.CED.3*,
CC-9-12.F.IF.4*,
CC-9-12.F.IF.7a*

Essential question: *How can you model changes in revenue from season-ticket sales using a quadratic function?*

A community theater currently sells 200 season tickets at $50 each. In order to increase its season-ticket revenue, the theater surveys its season-ticket holders to see if they would be willing to pay more. The survey finds that for every $5 increase in the price of a season ticket, the theater would lose 10 season-ticket holders. What action, if any, should the theater take to increase revenue?

1 Create a revenue function from the survey information.

A Let *n* be the number of $5 price increases in the cost of a season ticket. Write an expression for the cost of a season ticket after *n* price increases.

$50 + 5n$

B Write an expression for the number of season-ticket holders after *n* price increases.

$200 - 10n$

C The revenue generated from season-ticket sales is given below in words. Use this verbal model and your expressions from steps 1A and 1B to write an algebraic rule for the revenue function $R(n)$.

Revenue from season tickets	=	Number of season-ticket holders	·	Price of a season ticket

$$R(n) = (200 - 10n)(50 + 5n)$$

D As a check on your function rule, find the value of $R(0)$. Tell what this number represents and whether it agrees with the problem statement.

$R(0) = 10,000$; this is the current revenue and agrees with the problem.

REFLECT

1a. What units are associated with the expressions that you wrote in steps 1A and 1B?

For $50 + 5n$, the units are dollars per ticket; for $200 - 10n$, the units are tickets.

1b. When you multiply the units for the expressions, what units do you get for the revenue? Are they the units you expect?

Dollars; yes, because (dollars per ticket) · (tickets) = dollars

© Houghton Mifflin Harcourt Publishing Company

Unit 2   59   Lesson 6

2 Determine the domain of the revenue function.

A Because *n* is the number of $5 price increases in the cost of a season ticket, you might think that the domain of the revenue function $R(n)$ is the set of whole numbers. However, given that increases in price result in losses of customers, what eventually happens to the number of season-ticket holders as *n* increases?

The number of season-ticket holders eventually becomes negative.

B Determine a constraint on the values of *n*. That is, write and solve an inequality that represents an upper bound on the values of *n*.

$200 - 10n \geq 0$; $n \leq 20$

C State a reasonable domain for the revenue function.

$\{0, 1, 2, \ldots, 20\}$

REFLECT

2. When the value of *n* reaches its upper bound, what will happen to the value of $R(n)$? Why?

$R(20) = 0$ because the number of season-ticket holders becomes 0.

3 Graph the revenue function.

A Complete the tables of values for the revenue function.

n	R(n)
0	10,000
1	10,450
2	10,800
3	11,050
4	11,200
5	11,250
6	11,200
7	11,050
8	10,800
9	10,450
10	10,000

n	R(n)
11	9,450
12	8,800
13	8,050
14	7,200
15	6,250
16	5,200
17	4,050
18	2,800
19	1,450
20	0

© Houghton Mifflin Harcourt Publishing Company

Unit 2   60   Lesson 6

2 Determine the domain of the revenue function.

Standards

CC.9-12.A.CED.3 Represent constraints by ... inequalities, ... and interpret solutions as viable or nonviable options in a modeling context.*

CC.9-12.A.REI.3 Solve linear ... inequalities in one variable ...

CC.9-12.F.IF.2 Use function notation, evaluate functions for inputs in their domains, and interpret statements that use function notation in terms of a context.

CC.9-12.F.IF.5 Relate the domain of a function to its graph and, where applicable, to the quantitative relationship it describes.*

Questioning Strategies

- What happens if you evaluate the revenue function for $n = 21$? Why does this happen? $R(21)$ is negative because the number of season-ticket holders becomes negative when $n = 21$.

- What is the domain of a function? The domain of a function is the values of the independent variable for which the function is defined.

- What is meant by a *reasonable domain*? A reasonable domain consists of the values of the independent variable that make sense in the context of the real-world situation.

Teaching Strategy

If students are unable to determine the domain of the revenue function based on its equation, encourage them to move on and make the tables and/or graph in step 3 of the problem. Once students have had this additional hands-on experience working with the function, they may find it easier to describe the domain.

3 Graph the revenue function.

Standards

CC.9-12.N.Q.1 ... choose and interpret the scale and the origin in graphs and data displays.*

CC.9-12.A.CED.2 Create equations in two or more variables to represent relationships between quantities; graph equations on coordinate axes with labels and scales.*

CC.9-12.F.IF.7a Graph ... quadratic functions and show intercepts, maxima, and minima.

Questioning Strategies

- In general, how do the values of $R(n)$ change in your tables? They increase and then decrease.

- What range of values should you show on the horizontal axis of your graph? on the vertical axis? $0 \leq n \leq 20$; $0 \leq R(n) \leq 12{,}000$

Avoid Common Errors

When students draw the graph of $R(n)$, they may draw a smooth curve through the points they plotted. Remind them that a reasonable domain of $R(n)$ consists of whole-number values of n from 0 to 20, inclusive. Therefore, the graph of the function is actually a set of discrete points rather than a smooth curve.

4 Analyze the revenue function.

Standards

CC.9-12.F.IF.4 For a function that models a relationship between two quantities, interpret key features of graphs and tables in terms of the quantities ...*

Questioning Strategies

- Which values of n result in an increase in revenue? Which values of n result in a decrease in revenue? How do you know? $0 \leq n \leq 5$; the plotted plots rise on the interval $0 \leq n \leq 5$; $5 \leq n \leq 20$; the plotted plots fall on the interval $5 \leq n \leq 20$

- How can you find the maximum value of $R(n)$ from your tables? How can you find the maximum value from your graph? Look for the greatest value in the $R(n)$ column; look for the highest point on the graph and read its y-coordinate.

continued

B. Graph the revenue function. Be sure to label the axes with the quantities they represent and indicate the axis scales by showing numbers for some grid lines.

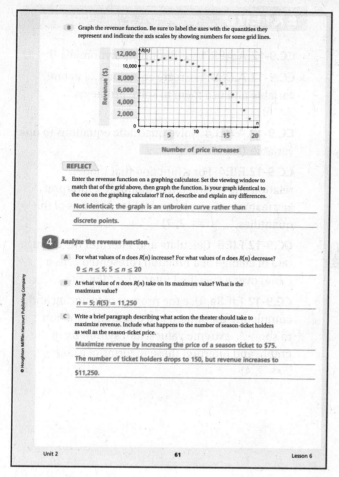

REFLECT

3. Enter the revenue function on a graphing calculator. Set the viewing window to match that of the grid above, then graph the function. Is your graph identical to the one on the graphing calculator? If not, describe and explain any differences.

Not identical; the graph is an unbroken curve rather than

discrete points.

4 Analyze the revenue function.

A. For what values of n does $R(n)$ increase? For what values of n does $R(n)$ decrease?

$0 \le n \le 5; 5 \le n \le 20$

B. At what value of n does $R(n)$ take on its maximum value? What is the maximum value?

$n = 5; R(5) = 11,250$

C. Write a brief paragraph describing what action the theater should take to maximize revenue. Include what happens to the number of season-ticket holders as well as the season-ticket price.

Maximize revenue by increasing the price of a season ticket to $75.

The number of ticket holders drops to 150, but revenue increases to

$11,250.

REFLECT

4. Identify the intercepts of the graph, and explain what they represent in the context of generating revenue from season-ticket sales.

Vertical intercept: 10,000, the current revenue;

horizontal intercept: 20, the greatest number of price increases

EXTEND

1. Show that the revenue function from step 1C is a quadratic function by multiplying the two factors and collecting like terms to obtain a function of the form $R(n) = an^2 + bn + c$ where a, b, and c are constants.

$R(n) = (200 - 10n)(50 + 5n) = 10,000 + 1,000n - 500n - 50n^2 =$

$-50n^2 + 500n + 10,000$

2. A quadratic function $f(x) = ax^2 + bx + c$ has a maximum value at $x = -\frac{b}{2a}$ if $a < 0$ or a minimum value at $x = -\frac{b}{2a}$ if $a > 0$. Confirm that this property is true for the rewritten revenue function from Exercise 1.

For $R(n) = -50n^2 + 500n + 10,000$, $a = -50$ and $b = 500$, so

$-\frac{b}{2a} = 5$, which agrees with the fact that the function has a

maximum at $n = 5$.

3. Complete the square on the rewritten revenue function from Exercise 1 to obtain a function of the form $R(n) = a(n - h)^2 + k$ where a, h, and k are constants. Using this vertex form, identify the vertex of the graph of $R(n)$ and check to see whether it agrees with your answers for step 4B.

$R(n) = -50n^2 + 500n + 10,000 = -50(n^2 - 10n) + 10,000 =$

$-50(n^2 - 10n + 25) + 10,000 + 50(25) = -50(n - 5)^2 + 11,250$,

so a maximum of 11,250 occurs at $n = 5$.

4. When graphing the revenue function in step 3B, you may have noticed that $R(0) = R(10)$, $R(1) = R(9)$, $R(2) = R(8)$, $R(3) = R(7)$, and $R(4) = R(6)$. Use the rewritten revenue function from Exercise 3 to explain those observations.

Each pair of n-values (0 and 10, 1 and 9, etc.) is the same

distance from 5, so $(n - 5)^2$, and therefore $R(n)$, has the same

value for each pair.

Teaching Strategy

You may wish to have students use their calculators to find the maximum. To do so, have students display the graph on the calculator. Then, have them press **2nd** **TRACE** and select **4:maximum**. The calculator will ask for a left bound, a right bound, and a guess. Students should use the arrow keys to move along the graph to enter these values. Once the guess has been entered, the calculator will give the coordinates of the vertex, whose y-coordinate is the function's maximum.

CLOSE

Essential Question

How can you model changes in revenue from season-ticket sales using a quadratic function? Write expressions for the cost of a ticket after n price increases and for the number of season-ticket holders after n price increases. Use these expressions to write a quadratic revenue function $R(n)$. Then, use a table or graph to find the maximum value of $R(n)$.

Summarize

Have students write a journal entry in which they provide a one-page summary of their findings for the manager of the community theater.

┄┄┄┄┄┄┄
MATHEMATICAL PRACTICE | **Highlighting the Standards**

If you have students summarize their findings as suggested in the preceding Summarize note, you can use the summaries to address Mathematical Practice Standard 3 (Construct viable arguments and critique the reasoning of others). Have pairs of students exchange their summaries and comment on the clarity and completeness of the argument made by their partner to the manager of the community theater.

EXTEND

CC.9-12.A.APR.1 ... multiply polynomials. (Ex. 1)

CC.9-12.A.CED.1 Create equations ... in one variable and use them to solve problems.* (Ex. 6)

CC.9-12.A.REI.4 Solve quadratic equations in one variable. (Ex. 6)

CC.9-12.F.IF.4 For a function that models a relationship between two quantities, interpret key features of graphs and tables in terms of the quantities, ... * (Exs. 2, 7)

CC.9-12.F.IF.6 Calculate and interpret the average rate of change of a function (presented ... as a table) over a specified interval ... * (Ex. 5)

CC.9-12.F.IF.8a Use the process of factoring and completing the square in a quadratic function to show ... extreme values, and symmetry of the graph, and interpret these in terms of a context. (Exs. 3, 4)

5. Using your tables of values from step 3A, calculate the rate of change in $R(n)$ for consecutive values of n. (That is, calculate the change in $R(n)$ from $n = 0$ to $n = 1$, from $n = 1$ to $n = 2$, and so on.) Describe what happens to the rates of change in $R(n)$, and relate them to your answers to the questions in step 4A.

n	$R(n)$	Change in $R(n)$		n	$R(n)$	Change in $R(n)$
0	10,000	—		11	9,450	−550
1	10,450	450		12	8,800	−650
2	10,800	350		13	8,050	−750
3	11,050	250		14	7,200	−850
4	11,200	150		15	6,250	−950
5	11,250	50		16	5,200	−1050
6	11,200	−50		17	4,050	−1150
7	11,050	−150		18	2,800	−1250
8	10,800	−250		19	1,450	−1350
9	10,450	−350		20	0	−1450
10	10,000	−450				

The rates are positive and then negative, which means

that $R(n)$ increases and then decreases.

6. Rather than maximize season-ticket revenue, suppose the theater wants to increase the current revenue by just 8%. Using the revenue function from step 1C, write and solve a quadratic equation, and interpret the solution(s).

$(200 − 10n)(50 + 5n) = 1.08(10,000)$; $−50n^2 + 500n + 10,000 =$

$10,800$; $n^2 − 10n + 16 = 0$; $(n − 2)(n − 8) = 0$; $n = 2$ or 8; set

ticket price at $60 or $90

7. Predict what would happen to revenue if the theater lost fewer than 10 season-ticket holders for every $5 increase in the price of a ticket. Then check your prediction by creating and analyzing a model for the situation.

Prediction: The maximum revenue would increase. For instance, if only

5 season-ticket holders are lost per $5 increase, the revenue function is

$R(n) = (200 − 5n)(50 + 5n)$ and the maximum revenue is $15,625.

© Houghton Mifflin Harcourt Publishing Company

© Houghton Mifflin Harcourt Publishing Company

COMMON CORE CORRELATION

Standard	Items
CC.9-12.N.Q.1*	13
CC.9-12.A.CED.2*	12
CC.9-12.A.CED.3*	13
CC.9-12.A.SSE.3a	4
CC.9-12.A.SSE.3b	7
CC.9-12.F.IF.2	2
CC.9-12.F.IF.4	13
CC.9-12.F.IF.5	13
CC.9-12.F.IF.7a*	8, 9, 10
CC.9-12.F.IF.8a	5
CC.9-12.F.IF.9	3
CC.9-12.F.BF.1	12
CC.9-12.F.BF.3	1, 6, 11

TEST PREP DOCTOR ⊕

Multiple Choice: Item 1
- Students who chose **A** or **B** did not include the reflection of the parent function.
- Students who chose **B** or **D** did not recognize the effect of $|a| < 1$, which is a vertical shrink.

Multiple Choice: Item 4
- Students who chose **G** or **J** did not factor the function correctly.
- Students who chose **F** did not set the factor $(x - 2)$ equal to 0 and solve for x.

Multiple Choice: Item 5
- Students who chose **B** or **D** found the intercepts, not the axis of symmetry.
- Students who chose **C** either did not correctly evaluate the midpoint between the intercepts or thought that the y-axis is always the axis of symmetry.

Multiple Choice: Item 6
- Students who chose **G** mistakenly thought the graph is reflected across the y-axis. It is symmetric about the y-axis but reflected across the x-axis.
- Students who chose **H** or **J** confused the effect of h or k on the graph of the parent function with the effect of a on the parent graph.

Multiple Choice: Item 8
- Students who chose **F** did not recognize the equivalence of this form of the function with the forms in **G** and **H**.
- Students who chose **G** did not recognize that the vertex is $(-1, 32)$.
- Students who chose **H** did not recognize the intercepts are -5 and 3.

Free Response: Item 9
- Students may not have completed the square correctly. If they did complete the square correctly, they could have made an error with the signs of h and k in identifying the coordinates of the vertex.

Free Response: Item 11
- Students who did not write the correct equation likely mixed up the values of h and k or misunderstood that h is subtracted while k is added in the general vertex form.

Free Response: Item 12
- Likely errors in writing the function include writing a function for the area of the entire quilt with the border, or failing to account for needing a border on all four sides of the quilt, which increases both the length and the width by $2x$.
- Students who did not interpret the meaning of $f(0.5)$ correctly may not understand the functional dependence of area on the width of the border.

Name _____ Class _____ Date _____

MULTIPLE CHOICE

1. The graph of which function is a reflection and vertical stretch of the parent quadratic function?

A. $f(x) = 3x^2$ **C.** $f(x) = -3x^2$

B. $f(x) = 0.3x^2$ **D.** $f(x) = -0.3x^2$

2. What is the value of $f(-2)$ for the quadratic function $f(x) = -2(x + 1)^2 - 5$?

F. -7 **H.** 3

G. -3 **J.** 7

3. Which of the following quadratic functions has a maximum greater than the quadratic function whose graph is shown below?

A. $f(x) = -(x + 2)^2 - 3$

B. $f(x) = -(x + 1)^2 + 1$

C. $f(x) = -2(x - 1)^2$

D. $f(x) = -3(x - 3)^2 + 2$

4. What are the zeros of $f(x) = x^2 - 2x$?

F. -2 and 0

G. -2 and 1

H. 0 and 2

J. 1 and 2

5. What is the axis of symmetry of the graph of $f(x) = (x + 1)(x + 5)$?

A. $x = -3$ **C.** $x = 0$

B. $x = -1$ **D.** $x = 5$

6. Which of the following describes the graph of $f(x) = -2x^2$ as a transformation of the graph of the parent quadratic function?

F. reflection across the x-axis and vertical stretch by a factor of 2

G. reflection across the y-axis and vertical shrink by a factor of 2

H. translation 2 units left

J. translation 2 units down

7. What is the minimum value of $f(x) = 5x^2 + 10x + 10$?

A. -5 **C.** 1

B. -1 **D.** 5

8. Which of the following functions does *not* have the graph shown below?

F. $f(x) = -2x^2 - 4x + 30$

G. $f(x) = -2(x + 1)^2 + 32$

H. $f(x) = -2(x + 5)(x - 3)$

J. $f(x) = -2(x - 5)(x + 3)$

© Houghton Mifflin Harcourt Publishing Company

FREE RESPONSE

9. Write the function $f(x) = 3x^2 - 6x + 5$ in vertex form. Identify the vertex of the function's graph. Then graph the function.

$f(x) = 3(x - 1)^2 + 2$

vertex: (1 , 2)

10. Write the quadratic function $f(x) = x^2 + 6x$ in intercept form. Identify the x-intercepts. Then graph the function.

$f(x) = (x + 0)(x + 6)$

x-intercepts: 0 and -6

11. The graph of a quadratic function is a translation of the graph of the parent quadratic function 2 units left and 5 units up.

a. Write the equation of the quadratic function.

$f(x) = (x + 2)^2 + 5$

b. Did you use standard form, vertex form, or intercept form to write the equation? Why?

vertex form because you know that

$a = 1$, $h = -2$, and $k = 5$ in

$f(x) = a(x - h)^2 + k$

12. Amanda is adding a border to a rectangular quilt with a length of 4 feet and a width of 3 feet. The border has a width of x feet. Write a quadratic function $f(x)$ in standard form for the area of the border in square feet. What is $f(0.5)$ and what does it represent?

$f(x) = 4x^2 + 14x$; $f(0.5) = 8$; the area

in square feet of the border when the

width of the border is 0.5 foot

13. The function $f(x) = -16x^2 + 40x$ models the height in feet of a football x seconds after it is kicked from the ground.

a. Graph the function.

b. What does the origin of the graph represent?

The height of the ball when it is

kicked; the ball has a height of 0 feet

after 0 seconds.

c. What is a reasonable domain of the function? Explain.

Domain: $\{x \mid 0 \le x \le 2.5\}$; The height

of the ball must be nonnegative; this

occurs only between 0 seconds and

2.5 seconds.

d. What is the maximum of the function, and what does it represent in this situation?

25; The greatest height that the ball

reaches is 25 feet.

© Houghton Mifflin Harcourt Publishing Company

Polynomial Functions

Unit Vocabulary

degree of a monomial	(3-4)
degree of a polynomial	(3-1)
end behavior	(3-1)
even function	(3-1)
monomial	(3-4)
odd function	(3-1)
polynomial	(3-4)
polynomial function	(3-4)
synthetic division	(3-8)
synthetic substitution	(3-8)

Polynomial Functions

Unit Focus

In this unit, you will learn various methods of graphing polynomial functions and you will learn to find zeros of such functions. You will apply your knowledge by modeling a real-world situation involving a volume function.

Unit at a Glance

COMMON CORE

Lesson		Standards for Mathematical Content
3-1	Investigating the Graph of $f(x) = x^n$	CC.9-12.F.IF.7*, CC.9-12.F.IF.7c*, CC.9-12.F.BF.3
3-2	Translating the Graph of $f(x) = x^n$	CC.9-12.F.IF.7*, CC.9-12.F.IF.7c*, CC.9-12.F.BF.3
3-3	Stretching, Shrinking, and Reflecting the Graph of $f(x) = x^n$	CC.9-12.F.IF.7*, CC.9-12.F.IF.7c*, CC.9-12.F.BF.3
3-4	Polynomial Functions	CC.9-12.F.IF.2, CC.9-12.F.IF.7*, CC.9-12.F.IF.7c*
3-5	Adding and Subtracting Polynomials	CC.9-12.A.APR.1, CC.9-12.F.BF.1*, CC.9-12.F.BF.1b*
3-6	Multiplying Polynomials	CC.9-12.A.APR.1, CC.9-12.A.APR.4
3-7	The Binomial Theorem	CC.9-12.A.APR.1, CC.9-12.A.APR.5(+)
3-8	Polynomial Division and the Remainder and Factor Theorems	CC.9-12.A.APR.1, CC.9-12.A.APR.2
3-9	Graphing Factorable Polynomial Functions	CC.9-12.A.SSE.2, CC.9-12.A.APR.3, CC.9-12.A.CED.2*, CC.9-12.F.IF.7*, CC.9-12.F.IF.7c*
3-10	Finding Zeros of Polynomial Functions	CC.9-12.N.CN.9(+), CC.9-12.A.SSE.2
3-11	Modeling with Polynomial Functions	CC.9-12.A.SSE.1*, CC.9-12.A.CED.1*, CC.9-12.A.CED.2*, CC.9-12.A.CED.3*, CC.9-12.F.IF.4*, CC.9-12.F.BF.1*
	Test Prep	

Unpacking the Common Core State Standards

Use the table to help you understand the Standards for Mathematical Content that are taught in this unit. Refer to the lessons listed after each standard for exploration and practice.

COMMON CORE Standards for Mathematical Content	What It Means For You
CC.9-12.N.CN.9(+) Know the Fundamental Theorem of Algebra; show that it is true for quadratic polynomials. Lesson 3-10	You will learn that a polynomial of degree n has n complex zeros, assuming repeated zeros are counted multiple times. You will use the quadratic formula to show why this is true for polynomials of degree 2.
CC.9-12.A.SSE.1 Interpret expressions that represent a quantity in terms of its context.* **CC.9-12.A.SSE.1a** Interpret parts of an expression, such as terms, factors, and coefficients.* **CC.9-12.A.SSE.1b** Interpret complicated expressions by viewing one or more of their parts as a single entity.* Lessons 3-5, 3-11	You will write expressions to represent length, width, and height in a volume function and interpret the meaning of these expressions in a third-degree polynomial.
CC.9-12.A.SSE.2 Use the structure of an expression to identify ways to rewrite it. Lessons 3-9, 3-10	Recognizing and rewriting polynomials as special products can help you find zeros of polynomial functions. For example, you will recognize $a^4 - b^4$ as a difference of two squares and rewrite the expression as $(a^2 - b^2)(a^2 + b^2)$.
CC.9-12.A.APR.1 Understand that polynomials form a system analogous to the integers, namely, they are closed under the operations of addition, subtraction, and multiplication; add, subtract, and multiply polynomials. Lessons 3-5, 3-6, 3-7, 3-8 (Also 3-11)	You will add, subtract, and multiply polynomials to solve problems and as a foundation for understanding related topics, such as the Binomial Theorem and polynomial division.
CC.9-12.A.APR.2 Know and apply the Remainder Theorem: For a polynomial $p(x)$ and a number a, the remainder on division by $x - a$ is $p(a)$, so $p(a) = 0$ if and only if $(x - a)$ is a factor of $p(x)$. Lesson 3-8	As you will see, there are many similarities between whole-number division and polynomial division. You will use the Remainder Theorem to solve problems involving polynomial division and to understand the Factor Theorem.
CC.9-12.A.APR.3 Identify zeros of polynomials when suitable factorizations are available, and use the zeros to construct a rough graph of the function defined by the polynomial. Lesson 3-9	You will learn to sketch the graph of a polynomial function by identifying zeros and understanding the behavior of the function near those zeros.
CC.9-12.A.APR.4 Prove polynomial identities and use them to describe numerical relationships. Lesson 3-6	You will prove identities for special products of polynomials and use the identities to rewrite polynomials in different forms.

Unpacking the Common Core State Standards

This page lists and explains the Standards for Mathematical Content that are addressed in this unit. For information about the Standards for Mathematical Practice, which are integrated throughout the text, see Teacher Edition pages x–xiii.

Notes

_____

_____

_____

_____

_____

_____

_____

_____

_____

_____

UNIT 3

Additional Standards in This Unit

CC.9-12.N.CN.8(+) Extend polynomial identities to the complex numbers. Lesson 3-10

CC.9-12.A.REI.11 Explain why the x-coordinates of the points where the graphs of the equations $y = f(x)$ and $y = g(x)$ intersect are the solutions of the equation $f(x) = g(x)$; find the solutions approximately, e.g., using technology to graph the functions, make tables of values, or find successive approximations. Include cases where $f(x)$ and/or $g(x)$ are linear, polynomial, rational, absolute value, exponential, and logarithmic functions.* Lesson 3-11

COMMON CORE Standards for Mathematical Content	What It Means For You
CC.9-12.A.APR.5(+) Know and apply the Binomial Theorem for the expansion of $(x + y)^n$ in powers of x and y for a positive integer n, where x and y are any numbers, with coefficients determined for example by Pascal's Triangle. Lesson 3-7	You will look for patterns to generate the numbers in Pascal's Triangle, and you will use Pascal's Triangle to determine coefficients for powers of binomials of the form $(x + y)^n$. You will see how binomial expansion can be used to solve problems, including finding zeros of polynomial functions.
CC.9-12.A.CED.1 Create equations and inequalities in one variable and use them to solve problems.* Lesson 3-11	You will write an equation in one variable to help you find the dimensions of a piece of cardboard that can be folded to form a box with a given volume.
CC.9-12.A.CED.2 Create equations in two or more variables to represent relationships between quantities; graph equations on coordinate axes with labels and scales.* Lessons 3-9, 3-11 (Also 3-2, 3-3, 3-4)	Polynomial equations can be used to represent relationships between quantities in real-world situations. You will create and graph polynomial functions to model these situations.
CC.9-12.A.CED.3 Represent constraints by equations or inequalities, and by systems of equations and/or inequalities, and interpret solutions as viable or nonviable options in a modeling context.* Lesson 3-11	Polynomial functions that model real-world situations often include constraints on the quantities involved. You will be able to use those constraints to determine the domain of the function.
CC.9-12.F.IF.2 Use function notation, evaluate functions for inputs in their domains, and interpret statements that use function notation in terms of a context. Lesson 3-4 (Also 3-2, 3-3, 3-9)	You will learn techniques for evaluating polynomial functions, including synthetic substitution. You will apply these techniques to make graphing polynomial functions easier.
CC.9-12.F.IF.4 For a function that models a relationship between two quantities, interpret key features of graphs and tables in terms of the quantities, and sketch graphs showing key features given a verbal description of the relationship.* Lesson 3-11	You will graph a volume function, identify the local maximum, and interpret its meaning in the context of the problem.
CC.9-12.F.IF.5 Relate the domain of a function to its graph and, where applicable, to the quantitative relationship it describes.* Lesson 3-11	You will determine the domain of a volume function based on the constraints imposed on the dimensions of the object.
CC.9-12.F.IF.7 Graph functions expressed symbolically and show key features of the graph, by hand in simple cases and using technology for more complicated cases.* **CC.9-12.F.IF.7c** Graph polynomial functions, identifying zeros when suitable factorizations are available, and showing end behavior.* Lessons 3-1, 3-2, 3-3, 3-4, 3-9, 3-11	You will sketch the graph of a polynomial function by identifying zeros and recognizing end behavior. You will also use a calculator to graph polynomial functions.

Notes

_____

_____

_____

_____

_____

_____

_____

_____

_____

COMMON CORE Standards for Mathematical Content	What It Means For You
CC.9-12.F.BF.1 Write a function that describes a relationship between two quantities.* **CC.9-12.F.BF.1a Determine an explicit expression, a recursive process, or steps for calculation from a context.*** **CC.9-12.F.BF.1b Combine standard function types using arithmetic operations.*** Lessons 3-5, 3-11	To solve a real-world problem, you will write a function that describes the relationship between the height of a box and the volume of the box. In doing so, you will express the width and length of the box in terms of the height.
CC.9-12.F.BF.3 Identify the effect on the graph of replacing $f(x)$ by $f(x) + k$, $kf(x)$, $f(kx)$, and $f(x + k)$ for specific values of k (both positive and negative); find the value of k given the graphs. Experiment with cases and illustrate an explanation of the effects on the graph using technology. Lessons 3-1, 3-2, 3-3	You will transform the graphs of parent functions like $f(x) = x^3$ and $f(x) = x^4$ by translating, reflecting, stretching, and shrinking the graphs. You will also learn what it means for a function to be an even function or an odd function and understand how these properties are displayed in the graph of a function.

Notes

_____

_____

_____

_____

_____

_____

_____

_____

_____

3-1

Investigating the Graph of $f(x) = x^n$

Essential question: *How does the value of n affect the behavior of the function* $f(x) = x^n$?

© Houghton Mifflin Harcourt Publishing Company

COMMON CORE Standards for Mathematical Content

CC.9-12.F.IF.7 Graph functions expressed symbolically and show key features of the graph, by hand in simple cases and using technology for more complicated cases.*

CC.9-12.F.IF.7c Graph polynomial functions, identifying zeros when suitable factorizations are available, and showing end behavior.*

CC.9-12.F.BF.3 Identify the effect on the graph of replacing $f(x)$ by ... $f(kx)$ ... for specific values of k ...

Vocabulary

end behavior
even function
odd function

Prerequisites

Graphing $f(x) = x^2$, Lesson 2-1

Math Background

Students are familiar with the graphs of $f(x) = x$ and $f(x) = x^2$ and their characteristics, such as symmetry and end behavior. In this lesson, students will extend their understanding to graphs of functions of the form $f(x) = x^n$ where n is a whole number as they investigate how the value of n affects the behavior of the graph.

INTRODUCE

Compare and contrast the graphs of the parent linear function, $f(x) = x$, and the parent quadratic function, $f(x) = x^2$. Note that both graphs pass through the origin, but the graph of $f(x) = x$ *crosses* the x-axis while the graph of $f(x) = x^2$ is *tangent* to the x-axis. Also note that both functions increase without bound as x increases without bound, so both graphs rise without bound in Quadrant I. But as x decreases without bound, $f(x) = x$ *decreases* without bound while $f(x) = x^2$ *increases* without bound. So, the graph of $f(x) = x$ falls without bound in Quadrant III while the graph of $f(x) = x^2$ rises without bound in Quadrant II.

TEACH

 1 EXPLORE

Materials
graphing calculator

Questioning Strategies
- If you graph $f(x) = x^8$, what will the function have in common with the functions $f(x) = x^2$, $f(x) = x^4$, and $f(x) = x^6$? **All of the functions have a zero at $x = 0$, a minimum value of 0, the y-axis as a line of symmetry for their graphs, and the same end behavior.**

- For the function $f(x) = x^{10}$, what happens to the values of $f(x)$ as x increases without bound, and how is this observed in its graph? **The values of $f(x)$ also increase without bound, and the graph rises without bound as you move along the positive y-axis.**

Technology
Students may benefit from using different viewing windows to observe how the graphs of $f(x) = x^n$ are related for different values of n. For example, have students set the viewing window to Xmin = 0, Xmax = 1, Ymin = 0, and Ymax = 1 and graph all three functions. Then, set the window to Xmin = −10, Xmax = 10, Ymin = 0, and Ymax = 100. Note that the order of the graphs of $f(x) = x^2$, $f(x) = x^4$, and $f(x) = x^6$, from top to bottom, is reversed for the intervals $0 < x < 1$ and $x > 1$ as well as for the intervals $−1 < x < 0$ and $x < −1$.

2 EXPLORE

Questioning Strategies
- Compare the symmetry of the graphs of $f(x) = x^{11}$ and $f(x) = x^{12}$. **The graph of $f(x) = x^{11}$ has 180° rotational symmetry about the origin. The graph of $f(x) = x^{12}$ has reflection symmetry in the y-axis.**

continued

Name_____ Class_____ Date_____

3-1

Investigating the Graph of $f(x) = x^n$

COMMON CORE

Essential question: *How does the value of n affect the behavior of the function $f(x) = x^n$?*

CC.9-12.F.IF.7*,
CC.9-12.F.IF.7c*,
CC.9-12.F.BF.3

1 EXPLORE Graphing $f(x) = x^n$ When n is Even

Follow these steps to investigate the graphs of $f(x) = x^2$, $f(x) = x^4$, and $f(x) = x^6$.

A Set the viewing window of your graphing calculator as shown.

B Enter the functions $f(x) = x^2$, $f(x) = x^4$, and $f(x) = x^6$ in the equation editor as shown.

C Graph the functions on the coordinate plane at right by sketching what you see on your calculator.

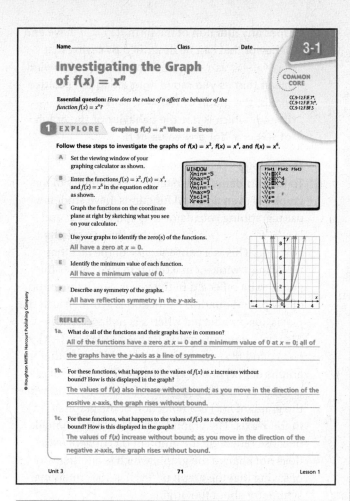

D Use your graphs to identify the zero(s) of the functions.

All have a zero at $x = 0$.

E Identify the minimum value of each function.

All have a minimum value of 0.

F Describe any symmetry of the graphs.

All have reflection symmetry in the y-axis.

REFLECT

1a. What do all of the functions and their graphs have in common?

All of the functions have a zero at $x = 0$ and a minimum value of 0 at $x = 0$; all of the graphs have the y-axis as a line of symmetry.

1b. For these functions, what happens to the values of $f(x)$ as x increases without bound? How is this displayed in the graph?

The values of $f(x)$ also increase without bound; as you move in the direction of the positive x-axis, the graph rises without bound.

1c. For these functions, what happens to the values of $f(x)$ as x decreases without bound? How is this displayed in the graph?

The values of $f(x)$ increase without bound; as you move in the direction of the negative x-axis, the graph rises without bound.

© Houghton Mifflin Harcourt Publishing Company

2 EXPLORE Graphing $f(x) = x^n$ When n is Odd

Follow these steps to investigate the graphs of $f(x) = x$, $f(x) = x^3$, and $f(x) = x^5$.

A Set the viewing window of your graphing calculator as shown.

B Enter the functions $f(x) = x$, $f(x) = x^3$, and $f(x) = x^5$ in the equation editor as shown.

C Graph the functions on the coordinate plane at right by sketching what you see on your calculator.

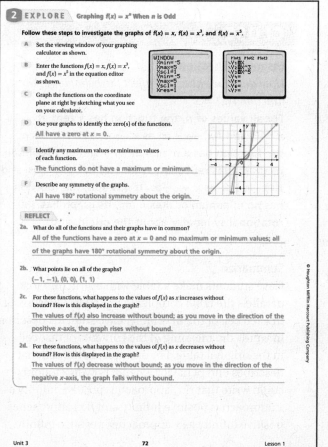

D Use your graphs to identify the zero(s) of the functions.

All have a zero at $x = 0$.

E Identify any maximum values or minimum values of each function.

The functions do not have a maximum or minimum.

F Describe any symmetry of the graphs.

All have 180° rotational symmetry about the origin.

REFLECT

2a. What do all of the functions and their graphs have in common?

All of the functions have a zero at $x = 0$ and no maximum or minimum values; all of the graphs have 180° rotational symmetry about the origin.

2b. What points lie on all of the graphs?

$(-1, -1)$, $(0, 0)$, $(1, 1)$

2c. For these functions, what happens to the values of $f(x)$ as x increases without bound? How is this displayed in the graph?

The values of $f(x)$ also increase without bound; as you move in the direction of the positive x-axis, the graph rises without bound.

2d. For these functions, what happens to the values of $f(x)$ as x decreases without bound? How is this displayed in the graph?

The values of $f(x)$ decrease without bound; as you move in the direction of the negative x-axis, the graph falls without bound.

© Houghton Mifflin Harcourt Publishing Company

© Houghton Mifflin Harcourt Publishing Company

• Compare what happens to the graphs of $f(x) = x^{11}$ and $f(x) = x^{12}$ as x decreases without bound.
  The graph of $f(x) = x^{11}$ falls without bound. The graph of $f(x) = x^{12}$ rises without bound.

Teaching Strategy

Have students graph all the following functions on the same axes: $f(x) = x, f(x) = x^2, f(x) = x^3,$ $f(x) = x^4, f(x) = x^5,$ and $f(x) = x^6$ Have students compare the graphs for $0 < x < 1, x > 1,$ $-1 < x < 0,$ and $x < -1$. Ask students how the graphs of $f(x) = x^n$ are related for different values of n. Have students predict how the graphs would change if they used the absolute value of each odd function: $f(x) = |x|, f(x) = |x^3|,$ and $f(x) = |x^5|$. Then, have them graph to confirm their conjectures.

╱┈┈ **MATHEMATICAL**   **Highlighting**
╱   **PRACTICE**   **the Standards**

2 EXPLORE   and its Reflect questions offer an opportunity to address Mathematical Practice Standard 7 (Look for and make use of structure). In this Explore and the previous Explore, students investigate the graph of $f(x) = x^n$ for different values of n. Students discover that the characteristics of the graphs, including minimum values, symmetry, and end behavior, are determined by whether the value of n is even or odd.

3 ENGAGE

Questioning Strategies

• Suppose $f(x) \to +\infty$ as $x \to -\infty$. What does this statement tell you about the graph of $f(x) = x^n$ and the direction in which you are moving on the x-axis? What can you say about the value of n?
  The statement says that as you move to the left along the negative x-axis so that x decreases without bound, the graph of $f(x) = x^n$ rises without bound. This is a characteristic of the graph of $f(x) = x^n$ when n is even.

• Does any function of the form $f(x) = x^n$ have end behavior that can be described by saying that $f(x) \to -\infty$ as $x \to +\infty$? Explain. No; this would mean that as you move right along the positive x-axis, the graph of $f(x) = x^n$ falls without bound, which is not the behavior of the graph of $f(x) = x^n$ for any value of n.

Technology

To help students understand the symmetry of the graphs of even and odd functions, have students use a graphing calculator to graph $f(x) = x^2$ and $g(x) = f(-x) = (-x)^2$ to see that the two graphs coincide. This is a consequence of the fact that replacing x with $-x$ in a function rule causes the graph to be reflected in the y-axis. Since the graph of the parent quadratic function is symmetric in the y-axis, it is unaffected when x is replaced with $-x$. Also have students graph $f(x) - x^3, g(x) = f(-x) = (-x)^3,$ and $h(x) = -f(x) = -x^3$ and observe that the graphs of $g(x)$ and $h(x)$ coincide. The graph of $g(x)$ is a reflection of the graph of $f(x)$ in the y-axis, while the graph of $h(x)$ is a reflection of the graph of $f(x)$ in the x-axis. The graphs of $g(x)$ and $h(x)$ coincide because reflecting the graph of $f(x)$ in *both* axes does not change the graph, which is another way of saying that the graph of $f(x)$ has $180°$ rotational symmetry about the origin.

CLOSE

Essential Question

How does the value of n affect the behavior of the function $f(x) = x^n$?
For all values of n, the function has a zero at $x = 0$, and $f(x) \to +\infty$ as $x \to +\infty$. If n is even, the function has a minimum at 0 and no maximum, its graph has reflection symmetry in the y-axis, and $f(x) \to +\infty$ as $x \to -\infty$. If n is odd, the function has no minimum or maximum, its graph has $180°$ rotational symmetry about the origin, and $f(x) \to -\infty$ as $x \to -\infty$.

Summarize

Have students make a table with a structure that parallels the table completed in Reflect Question 3f. In each cell of the new table, have students describe in words the meaning of the contents of that cell in the original table. For example, in the cell that describes end behavior when n is even, students could write that $f(x)$ approaches positive infinity as x approaches positive infinity and $f(x)$ approaches positive infinity as x approaches negative infinity.

3 ENGAGE Describing Characteristics of Functions

The **end behavior** of a function is a description of the values of the function as x increases without bound or decreases without bound.

For example, for $f(x) = x^3$, the values of $f(x)$ increase without bound as x increases without bound. You can say that $f(x)$ approaches positive infinity as x approaches positive infinity. This may be abbreviated as "$f(x) \to +\infty$ as $x \to +\infty$."

Also, the values of $f(x)$ decrease without bound as x decreases without bound. You can say that $f(x)$ approaches negative infinity as x approaches negative infinity. This may be abbreviated as "$f(x) \to -\infty$ as $x \to -\infty$."

A function is an **even function** if $f(-x) = f(x)$ for all values of x. This means that if the point (x, y) is on the graph, then the point $(-x, y)$ is also on the graph, so the graph is symmetric with respect to the y-axis.

A function is an **odd function** if $f(-x) = -f(x)$ for all values of x. This means that if the point (x, y) is on the graph, then the point $(-x, -y)$ is also on the graph, so the graph has 180° rotational symmetry about the origin.

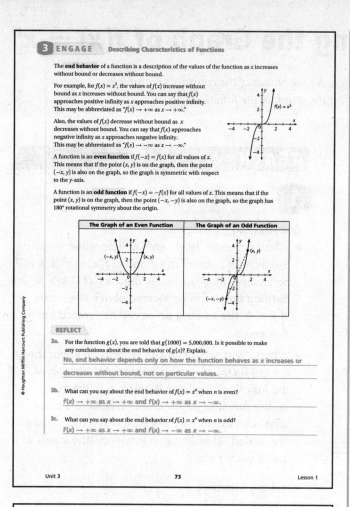

The Graph of an Even Function	The Graph of an Odd Function

REFLECT

3a. For the function $g(x)$, you are told that $g(1000) = 5{,}000{,}000$. Is it possible to make any conclusions about the end behavior of $g(x)$? Explain.

No, end behavior depends only on how the function behaves as x increases or decreases without bound, not on particular values.

3b. What can you say about the end behavior of $f(x) = x^n$ when n is even?

$f(x) \to +\infty$ as $x \to +\infty$ and $f(x) \to +\infty$ as $x \to -\infty$.

3c. What can you say about the end behavior of $f(x) = x^n$ when n is odd?

$f(x) \to +\infty$ as $x \to +\infty$ and $f(x) \to -\infty$ as $x \to -\infty$.

© Houghton Mifflin Harcourt Publishing Company

Unit 3   73   Lesson 1

3d. Explain why any function of the form $f(x) = x^n$ is an even function if n is even.

If n is even, then $(-x)^n = x^n$ for all values of x. So, $f(-x) = f(x)$ for all values of x and $f(x)$ is even.

3e. Explain why any function of the form $f(x) = x^n$ is an odd function if n is odd.

If n is odd, then $(-x)^n = -x^n$ for all values of x. So, $f(-x) = -f(x)$ for all values of x and $f(x)$ is odd.

3f. Complete the table.

Characteristics of $f(x) = x^n$		
	n is even	**n is odd**
Sketch of graph of $f(x) = x^n$		
End behavior	As $x \to +\infty$, $f(x) \to +\infty$. As $x \to -\infty$, $f(x) \to +\infty$.	As $x \to +\infty$, $f(x) \to +\infty$. As $x \to -\infty$, $f(x) \to -\infty$.
Zeros	$x = 0$	$x = 0$
Maximum or minimum values	Maximum: none Minimum: 0	Maximum: none Minimum: none
Symmetry	reflection symmetry in y-axis	180° rotational symmetry about origin
Even or odd function	even	odd

© Houghton Mifflin Harcourt Publishing Company

Unit 3   74   Lesson 1

3-2 Translating the Graph of $f(x) = x^n$

Essential question: *How do the values of the constants h and k in $f(x) = (x - h)^n + k$ affect the graph of the function?*

COMMON Standards for
CORE Mathematical Content

CC.9-12.F.IF.7 Graph functions expressed symbolically and show key features of the graph, by hand in simple cases ...*

CC.9-12.F.IF.7c Graph polynomial functions, identifying zeros when suitable factorizations are available, and showing end behavior.*

CC.9-12.F.BF.3 Identify the effect on the graph of replacing $f(x)$ by $f(x) + k$ ... and $f(x + k)$ for specific values of k (both positive and negative); find the value of k given the graphs. Experiment with cases and illustrate an explanation of the effects on the graph ...

Also: CC.9-12.F.IF.2, CC.9-12.F.IF.9, CC.9-12.A.CED.2*

Prerequisites

Translating the graph of $f(x) = x^2$, Lesson 2-1

Graphing $f(x) = x^n$, Lesson 3-1

Math Background

In Lesson 2-1, students became familiar with the graph of the parent quadratic function $f(x) = x^2$ and how values of the constants h and k affect the graph of $f(x) = (x - h)^2 + k$. In the previous lesson, students investigated graphs of functions of the form $f(x) = x^n$ and found that whether n is even or odd has a great effect on the graph of $f(x) = x^n$. In this lesson, students will extend that knowledge to translating the graph of $f(x) = x^n$ and understanding how values of the constants h and k affect the graph of $f(x) = (x - h)^n + k$.

INTRODUCE

Review the function $f(x) = x^2$ and how values of the constants h and k in $f(x) = (x - h)^2 + k$ affect the graph of the function. Also, review how the value of n affects the graph of $f(x) = x^n$.

TEACH

 EXAMPLE

Questioning Strategies

- When n is even, how can you determine whether the turning point of the graph of $f(x) = x^n + k$ will be located above or below the x-axis? **If $k > 0$, the turning point will be located above the x-axis. If $k < 0$, the turning point will be located below the x-axis.**

- When $k > 0$, what can you determine about the zero of $f(x) = x^3 + k$ by looking at the graph of the function? Explain. **When $k > 0$, the zero of the function $f(x) = x^3 + k$ will have a value that is less than zero because when the graph is translated $|k|$ units up, it intersects the x-axis at a point where $x < 0$.**

Teaching Strategy

Students should be reminded that when a graph of a function is translated, the location of the graph on the coordinate plane changes, but the graph otherwise stays the same. As a way to help students understand this, have them trace the graph of $f(x) = x^n$. Students can then either relocate the tracing on the same coordinate plane or use it on a different coordinate plane of the same size and scale.

EXTRA EXAMPLE

Graph $g(x) = x^4 - 5$. **It is the graph of the parent function $f(x) = x^4$ translated 5 units down.**

© Houghton Mifflin Harcourt Publishing Company

Name_____ Class_____ Date_____

Translating the Graph of
$f(x) = x^n$

Essential question: *How do the values of the constants h and k in*
$f(x) = (x - h)^n + k$ *affect the graph of the function?*

In this lesson and the next, you will explore transformations of the graph of
$f(x) = x^n$. In this lesson, the focus is on translations.

1 EXAMPLE Graphing $f(x) = x^n + k$

Graph each function.

A $g(x) = x^4 - 1$

Complete the table of values and use it to help you graph
the function. The graph of the parent function $f(x) = x^4$
is shown.

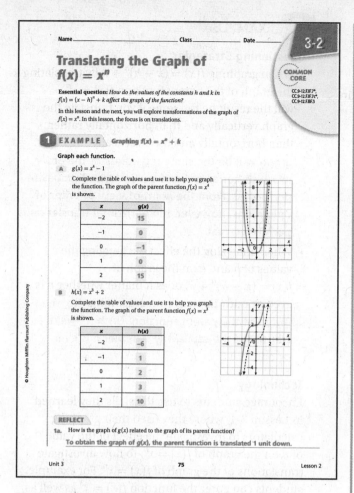

x	g(x)
−2	15
−1	0
0	−1
1	0
2	15

B $h(x) = x^3 + 2$

Complete the table of values and use it to help you graph
the function. The graph of the parent function $f(x) = x^3$
is shown.

x	h(x)
−2	−6
−1	1
0	2
1	3
2	10

REFLECT

1a. How is the graph of $g(x)$ related to the graph of its parent function?

To obtain the graph of $g(x)$, the parent function is translated 1 unit down.

1b. How is the graph of $h(x)$ related to the graph of its parent function?

To obtain the graph of $h(x)$, the parent function is translated 2 units up.

1c. In general, how do you think the graph of $f(x) = x^n + k$ is related to the graph of its
parent function?

To obtain the graph of $f(x)$, the parent function is translated $|k|$ units up if

$k > 0$ and $|k|$ units down if $k < 0$.

2 EXAMPLE Graphing $f(x) = (x - h)^n$

Graph each function.

A $g(x) = (x - 3)^4$

Complete the table of values and use it to help you graph
the function. The graph of the parent function $f(x) = x^4$
is shown.

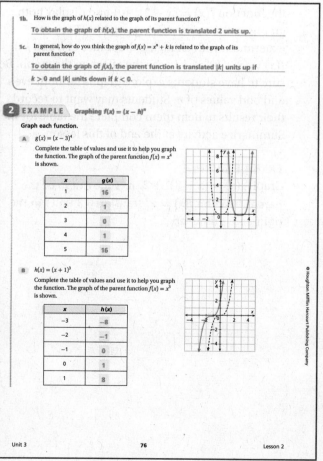

x	g(x)
1	16
2	1
3	0
4	1
5	16

B $h(x) = (x + 1)^3$

Complete the table of values and use it to help you graph
the function. The graph of the parent function $f(x) = x^3$
is shown.

x	h(x)
−3	−8
−2	−1
−1	0
0	1
1	8

Questioning Strategies

- If n is even, how does the value of h affect the minimum of the function $f(x) = (x - h)^n$? Explain. When n is even, the minimum of the function $f(x) = (x - h)^n$ is zero for any value of h; changing the value of h results only in a horizontal translation of the graph, so the minimum is not affected.

- How does the value of h affect the zero of the function $f(x) = (x - h)^n$? Explain. The zero is h, because the graph of $f(x) = (x - h)^n$ intersects the x-axis at $(h, 0)$.

Avoid Common Errors

When translating the graph of $f(x) = (x - h)^n$, students commonly interpret the sign of h incorrectly and translate the parent graph in the wrong direction. A major cause of this error is the presence of the subtraction sign in the expression $x - h$. Remind students that this subtraction sign is not the sign of h. In the expression $x - 2$, for instance, $h = 2$ (a positive number), so the translation is to the right. To identify the value of h in the expression $x + 2$, students should rewrite it as $x - (-2)$, which means that $h = -2$, so the translation is to the left.

EXTRA EXAMPLE

Graph $h(x) = (x + 2)^3$. It is the graph of the parent function $f(x) = x^3$ translated 2 units left.

Questioning Strategies

- When graphing $f(x) = (x - h)^n + k$ by translating the graph of the parent function $f(x) = x^n$, will the result be the same if you translate the graph vertically and then horizontally rather than horizontally and then vertically? Yes, the graph will be the same regardless of the order in which horizontal and vertical translations are performed. From the point of view of order of operations, however, the horizontal translation is performed first.

- When analyzing the effect of changing the values of h and k on the graph of $f(x) = (x - h)^n + k$, does it matter whether n is even or odd? Explain your reasoning. No, the graph of the parent function $f(x) = x^n$ will be translated the same way whether n is even or odd.

Technology

Encourage students to use the skills they learned in Lesson 3-1, where they used their graphing calculators to investigate the effect of the value of n on the graph of $f(x) = x^n$, to now investigate translations of the graph of $f(x) = x^n$. For example, students can enter the function $f(x) = x^3$ as well as the function $f(x) = (x - 2)^3 + 1$ and display both graphs in the same viewing window. They can experiment with changing the values of h and k in $f(x) = (x - h)^n + k$ to see the effect on the graph. Be sure to have students explore graphs for both even and odd values of n. Students may want to record their results to help them complete the table for the Summarize activity at the end of this lesson.

EXTRA EXAMPLE

Graph $g(x) = (x - 3)^4 + 2$. It is the graph of the parent function $f(x) = x^4$ translated 3 units to the right and 2 units up.

REFLECT

2a. How is the graph of $g(x)$ related to the graph of its parent function?

To obtain the graph of $g(x)$, the parent function is translated 3 units right.

2b. How is the graph of $h(x)$ related to the graph of its parent function?

To obtain the graph of $h(x)$, the parent function is translated 1 unit left.

2c. In general, how do you think the graph of $j(x) = (x - h)^n$ is related to the graph of its parent function?

To obtain the graph of $j(x)$, the parent function is translated $|h|$ units right if $h > 0$ and $|h|$ units left if $h < 0$.

---

3 EXAMPLE Graphing $f(x) = (x - h)^n + k$

Graph $g(x) = (x - 2)^3 + 1$.

A The graph of the parent function, $f(x) = x^3$, is shown. Determine how the graph of $g(x)$ is related to the graph of $f(x)$.

Since $g(x) = (x - 2)^3 + 1$, $h = \underline{2}$ and $k = \underline{1}$.

Complete the table to describe how the graph of the parent function must be translated to obtain the graph of $g(x)$.

Type of Translation	Number of Units	Direction
Horizontal	2	right
Vertical	1	up

B Use the translations you identified to help you draw the graph of $g(x)$.

REFLECT

3a. Compare the domain and range of $g(x) = (x - 2)^3 + 1$ to the domain and range of the parent function $f(x) = x^3$.

The domain and range of both functions are all real numbers.

3b. How is the graph of $h(x) = (x + 17)^8 - 6$ related to the graph of $f(x) = x^8$?

To obtain the graph of $h(x)$, the graph of $f(x)$ is translated 17 units left and 6 units down.

---

4 EXAMPLE Writing the Equation of a Function

The graph of $g(x)$ is the graph of $f(x) = x^4$ after a horizontal and vertical translation. Write the equation of $g(x)$.

A Complete the table to describe how the graph of the parent function must be translated to obtain the graph of $g(x)$.
(*Hint:* Consider how the "turning point" $(0, 0)$ on the graph of $f(x)$ must be translated to obtain the turning point on the graph of $g(x)$.)

Type of Translation	Number of Units	Direction
Horizontal	1	left
Vertical	6	down

B Determine the values of h and k in the equation $g(x) = (x - h)^4 + k$.

Based on the translations, $h = \underline{-1}$ and $k = \underline{-6}$.

So, $g(x) = \underline{(x + 1)^4 - 6}$.

REFLECT

4a. Compare the domain and range of $g(x)$ to the domain and range of the parent function $f(x) = x^4$.

The domain of both functions is all real numbers. The range of $f(x)$ is all real numbers greater than or equal to 0; the range of $g(x)$ is all real numbers greater than or equal to −6.

4b. Suppose the graph of $g(x)$ is translated 3 units right and 2 units up to give the graph of $h(x)$. Explain how you can write the equation of $h(x)$.

These translations move the turning point of the graph to $(2, -4)$, so the equation is $h(x) = (x - 2)^4 - 4$.

4c. In general, do translations change the end behavior of a function of the form $f(x) = x^n$? Give a specific example.

No, translations do not change end behavior. For example, the end behavior of $f(x) = x^4$ is $f(x) \to +\infty$ as $x \to +\infty$ and $f(x) \to +\infty$ as $x \to -\infty$. The function $g(x) = (x - 1)^4 - 6$ has the same end behavior.

Questioning Strategies

- What is the value of $g(x) = (x - h)^4 + k$ for $x = h$? How is the corresponding point on the graph of $g(x)$ related to the turning point on the graph of $f(x)$? $g(h) = k$; the corresponding point (h, k) on the graph of $g(x)$ is the translation of the turning point $(0, 0)$ on the graph of $f(x)$, so it is the turning point on the graph of $g(x)$.

- What is the equation of the axis of symmetry for the graph of $g(x)$? Which translation (horizontal or vertical) determines the location of the axis of symmetry? Why? $x = -1$; horizontal; vertical lines are affected by horizontal translations but not vertical translations.

MATHEMATICAL PRACTICE	Highlighting the Standards

4 EXAMPLE and its Reflect questions offer an opportunity to address Mathematical Practice Standard 2 (Reason abstractly and quantitatively). Students look at a graph of a function of the form $f(x) = x^n$ and determine the distance and direction that the graph has been translated horizontally and vertically. They then use this quantitative information algebraically as they determine the values of h and k and write an equation of the form $f(x) = (x - h)^n + k$ for the translated graph.

EXTRA EXAMPLE

The graph of $g(x)$ is the graph of $f(x) = x^5$ after a horizontal translation 3 units to the left and a vertical translation 2 units down. Write the equation of $g(x)$. $g(x) = (x + 3)^5 - 2$

CLOSE

Essential Question

How do the values of the constants h and k in $f(x) = (x - h)^n + k$ *affect the graph of the function?*
The graph of $f(x) = (x - h)^n + k$ is a translation of the graph of the parent function $f(x) = x^n$. The graph of the parent function is translated h units to the right if $h > 0$, $|h|$ units to the left if $h < 0$, k units up if $k > 0$, and $|k|$ units down if $k < 0$.

Summarize

Have students make a table showing the effect on the graph of the function $f(x) = (x - h)^n + k$ if $h > 0$, $h < 0$, $k > 0$, and $k < 0$. In the table, have students include a sketch of the graph, as well as information about function characteristics like zeros, minimum and maximum values, symmetry, and end behavior.

PRACTICE

Where skills are taught	Where skills are practiced
1 EXAMPLE	EXS. 1, 2
2 EXAMPLE	EXS. 3, 4
3 EXAMPLE	EXS. 5–7
4 EXAMPLE	EXS. 8–10

Exercise 11: Students investigate turning points of the graphs of $f(x) = (x - h)^n + k$ and how turning points are related to whether n is even or odd.

Exercise 12: Students identify an error when a graph is translated.

PRACTICE

Graph each function.

1. $f(x) = x^3 - 2$

2. $f(x) = x^6 + 1$

3. $f(x) = (x+2)^4$

4. $f(x) = (x-3)^5$

5. $f(x) = (x-1)^4 + 2$

6. $f(x) = (x+2)^3 - 2$

7. Without graphing, explain how the graph of $g(x) = (x-5)^7 - 1.3$ is related to the graph of $f(x) = x^7$.

To obtain the graph of $g(x)$, the graph of $f(x)$ is translated 5 units right and 1.3 units down.

Unit 3   79   Lesson 2

The graph of $g(x)$ is the graph of $f(x) = x^3$ after a horizontal and vertical translation. Write the equation of $g(x)$.

8.

$y = (x-3)^3 + 2$

9.

$y = (x+2)^3 - 3$

10. Suppose you translate the graph of $y = (x-2)^5 - 7$ left 4 units and up 3 units. What is the equation of the resulting graph?

$y = (x+2)^5 - 4$

11. A turning point on the graph of a function is a point where the graph changes from increasing to decreasing, or from decreasing to increasing. A turning point corresponds to a local maximum or local minimum.

a. Does the graph of $y = x^4$ have a turning point? If so, what is it?

Yes; (0, 0)

b. Does the graph of $y = (x+5)^4 + 4$ have a turning point? If so, what is it?

Yes; (−5, 4)

c. For even values of n, what is the turning point of $y = (x-h)^n + k$? Why is this true only when n is even?

(h, k); there is no turning point when n is odd.

12. **Error Analysis** A student was asked to graph the function $g(x) = (x+3)^4 - 2$. The student's work is shown at right. Identify the error and explain how the student should have graphed the function. Graph the function correctly.

The student translated the graph of $f(x) = x^4$ right 3 units and down 2 units, but the student should have translated the graph of $f(x)$ left 3 units and down 2 units.

Unit 3   80   Lesson 2

Unit 3   **80**   Lesson 2

Notes

Stretching, Shrinking, and Reflecting the Graph of $f(x) = x^n$

Essential question: *What are the effects of the constant a on the graph of* $f(x) = a(x - h)^n + k?$

COMMON **Standards for**
CORE **Mathematical Content**

CC.9-12.F.IF.7 Graph functions expressed symbolically and show key features of the graph, by hand in simple cases ...*

CC.9-12.F.IF.7c Graph polynomial functions, identifying zeros when suitable factorizations are available, and showing end behavior.*

CC.9-12.F.BF.3 Identify the effect on the graph of replacing $f(x)$ by $f(x) + k$, $k f(x)$, ... and $f(x + k)$ for specific values of k (both positive and negative); find the value of k given the graphs. Experiment with cases and illustrate an explanation of the effects on the graph ...

Also: CC.9-12.A.CED.2*, CC.9-12.F.IF.2, CC.9-12.F.IF.9

Prerequisites

Translating the graph of $f(x) = x^n$, Lesson 3-2

Math Background

Students have investigated the effects of n, h, and k on the graph of $f(x) = (x - h)^n + k$.

INTRODUCE

Review the effects of the constants n, h, and k on the graph of $f(x) = (x - h)^n + k$. In this lesson, students will explore additional transformations of the parent graph.

TEACH

1 EXAMPLE

Questioning Strategies

• How is the graph of $j(x) = \frac{1}{2} x^4$ related to the graphs of $f(x)$ and $g(x)$ in part A? **The graph of f(x) is shrunk vertically by a factor of 0.5 to obtain the graph of j(x). The graph of g(x) is stretched vertically by a factor of 2 to obtain the graph of j(x). All three functions have the same minimum and end behavior.**

• If (x, y) is a point on the graph of $g(x) = ax^n$ where n is even, is $(-x, -y)$ a point of the graph of $h(x) = -ax^n$? Explain. **Yes; the graph of the function h(x) = −axⁿ is a reflection across the x-axis of the graph of g(x) = axⁿ, so if (x, y) is on the graph of g(x), then (x, −y) is on the reflected graph. The point (−x, −y) is a reflection of the point (x, −y) across the y-axis. If n is even, then the graph has reflection symmetry in the y-axis, so the point (−x, −y) is on the graph of h(x).**

EXTRA EXAMPLE
Graph $g(x) = \frac{1}{2}x^2$ and $h(x) = -\frac{1}{2}x^2$. **The graph of g(x) is a vertical shrink of the graph of f(x) = x² that passes through (−2, 2), (0, 0), and (2, 2). The graph of h(x) is a reflection of the graph of g(x) across the x-axis.**

2 EXAMPLE

Questioning Strategies

• If n is even and $a < 0$, how is the turning point of the graph of $g(x) = a(x - h)^n + k$ related to the turning point of the graph of $f(x) = x^n$? What about the maximum or minimum value that occurs at the turning point? **The turning point of the graph of g(x) is (h, k) and k is a maximum. The turning point of the graph of f(x) is (0, 0) and 0 is a minimum.**

• If n is odd and $a < 0$, how is the end behavior of $g(x) = a(x - h)^n + k$ related to the end behavior of $f(x) = x^n$? **The end behaviors are opposites: As x → +∞, f(x) → +∞ and g(x) → −∞. As x → −∞, f(x) → −∞ and g(x) → +∞.**

continued

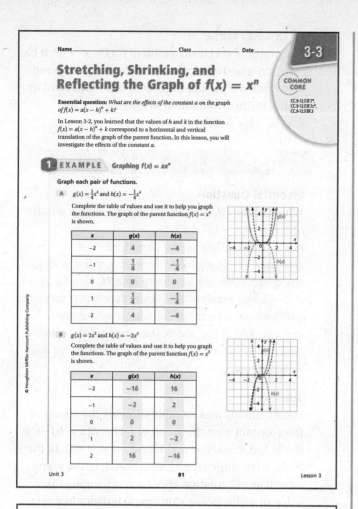

Name_____ Class_____ Date_____

3-3

Stretching, Shrinking, and Reflecting the Graph of $f(x) = x^n$

COMMON
CORE

CC.9-12.F.IF.7*,
CC.9-12.F.IF.7c*,
CC.9-12.F.BF.3

Essential question: *What are the effects of the constant a on the graph of* $f(x) = a(x − h)^n + k$?

In Lesson 3-2, you learned that the values of h and k in the function $f(x) = a(x − h)^n + k$ correspond to a horizontal and vertical translation of the graph of the parent function. In this lesson, you will investigate the effects of the constant a.

1 EXAMPLE Graphing $f(x) = ax^n$

Graph each pair of functions.

A $g(x) = \frac{1}{4}x^4$ and $h(x) = -\frac{1}{4}x^4$

Complete the table of values and use it to help you graph the functions. The graph of the parent function $f(x) = x^4$ is shown.

x	g(x)	h(x)
−2	4	−4
−1	$\frac{1}{4}$	$-\frac{1}{4}$
0	0	0
1	$\frac{1}{4}$	$-\frac{1}{4}$
2	4	−4

B $g(x) = 2x^3$ and $h(x) = -2x^3$

Complete the table of values and use it to help you graph the functions. The graph of the parent function $f(x) = x^3$ is shown.

x	g(x)	h(x)
−2	−16	16
−1	−2	2
0	0	0
1	2	−2
2	16	−16

Unit 3   81   Lesson 3

REFLECT

1a. How is the graph of $f(x) = ax^n$ related to the graph of the parent function $f(x) = x^n$ when $a > 1$? when $0 < a < 1$?

For $a > 1$, the graph of the parent function is stretched vertically.

For $0 < a < 1$, the graph is shrunk vertically.

1b. How is the graph of $f(x) = ax^n$ related to the graph of the parent function $f(x) = x^n$ when $a < −1$? when $−1 < a < 0$?

For $a < −1$, the graph of the parent function is stretched vertically and reflected

across the x-axis. For $−1 < a < 0$, the graph is shrunk vertically and reflected

across the x-axis.

1c. How is the end behavior of the graph of $f(x) = ax^n$ related to the end behavior of the graph of the parent function $f(x) = x^n$?

If $a > 0$, the end behavior of both graphs is the same.

If $a < 0$, the end behavior is the opposite.

2 EXAMPLE Graphing $f(x) = a(x − h)^n + k$

Graph $g(x) = 3(x − 2)^4 − 4$.

A The graph of the parent function $f(x) = x^4$ is shown. Determine how the graph of $g(x)$ is related to the graph of $f(x)$.

First perform any vertical stretches, shrinks, and reflections.

For $g(x)$, $a =$ __3__. The graph of $f(x)$ is stretched vertically and there is no reflection.

B For $g(x)$, $h =$ __2__ and $k =$ __−4__.

Complete the table to describe how the graph of the parent function must be translated to obtain the graph of $g(x)$.

Type of Translation	Number of Units	Direction
Horizontal	2	right
Vertical	4	down

C Use the transformations you identified to help you draw the graph of $g(x)$.

Unit 3   82   Lesson 3

EXTRA EXAMPLE
Graph $g(x) = 2(x - 1)^4 - 3$. The graph of $f(x) = x^4$ is stretched vertically by a factor of 2 and then translated 1 unit to the right and 3 units down.

MATHEMATICAL PRACTICE **Highlighting the Standards**

2 EXAMPLE and its Reflect questions offer an opportunity to address Mathematical Practice Standard 8 (Look for and express regularity in repeated reasoning). In this unit, students build upon patterns they have observed regarding the effects of parameters on the graph of the function $f(x) = a(x - h)^n + k$.

---

3 EXAMPLE

Questioning Strategies
- What is the image of the point $(0, 0)$? How can you tell? How does this relate to the values of h and k? $(-2, 3)$; the "symmetry point" of the graph of the parent function is translated to the symmetry point of $g(x)$. The x-coordinate of the image of $(0, 0)$ is h, and the y-coordinate is k.

- If n were even, how would you determine the values of h and k? The point $(0, 0)$ is the turning point of the graph of the parent function. The image of this point is the turning point of the translated graph and has coordinates (h, k).

- How can you use the images of $(0, 0)$ and $(1, 1)$ to find the value of a? Find the difference in the y-coordinates in the image points. The image of $(0, 0)$ is (h, k), and the image of $(1, 1)$ is $(h + 1, k + a)$.

Technology
Students can check the equations they write by graphing the functions on their graphing calculators. Use the TRACE or TABLE feature to identify coordinates of points in the resulting graph.

EXTRA EXAMPLE
The graph of $g(x)$ is the graph of $f(x) = x^3$ after it has been stretched vertically by a factor of 3, reflected across the x-axis, and translated left 4 units and up 1 unit. Write the equation of $g(x)$.
$g(x) = -3(x + 4)^3 + 1$

CLOSE

Essential Question
What are the effects of the constant a on the graph of $f(x) = a(x - h)^n + k$?
If $a > 1$, the graph of the parent function is stretched vertically by a factor of a. If $0 < a < 1$, the graph is shrunk vertically by a factor of a. If $a < -1$, the graph of the parent function is stretched vertically by a factor of $|a|$ and reflected across the x-axis. If $-1 < a < 0$, the graph of the parent function is shrunk vertically by a factor of $|a|$ and reflected across the x-axis.

Summarize
Have students make a table showing the effects of the constant a on the graph of $f(x) = a(x - h)^n + k$ if $a > 1$, $a < -1$, $0 < a < 1$, and $-1 < a < 0$. In the table, have students include a sketch of the graph, as well as information about how changing the value of a affects function characteristics like zeros, minimum and maximum values, symmetry, and end behavior.

PRACTICE

Where skills are taught	Where skills are practiced
1 EXAMPLE	EXS. 1, 2
2 EXAMPLE	EXS. 3, 4
3 EXAMPLE	EXS. 5, 6

Exercise 7: Students apply their knowledge of stretching, shrinking, and reflecting the graph of $f(x) = x^3$ to a problem involving the volumes of spheres and cubes.

REFLECT

2a. Describe how you think the graph of $g(x) = -0.5(x + 1)^5 - 1$ is related to the graph of the parent function $f(x) = x^5$. Check your prediction by graphing the functions on your calculator.

The graph of $f(x)$ is reflected in the x-axis, shrunk vertically by a factor of

0.5, and translated 1 unit left and 1 unit down.

---

3 EXAMPLE Writing the Equation of a Function

The graph of $g(x)$ is the graph of $f(x) = x^3$ after a series of transformations. Write the equation of $g(x)$.

A Complete the table to describe how the graph of the parent function must be translated to obtain the graph of $g(x)$. (*Hint*: Consider how the "symmetry point" $(0, 0)$ on the graph of $f(x)$ must be translated to obtain the symmetry point on the graph of $g(x)$.)

Type of Translation	Number of Units	Direction
Horizontal	2	left
Vertical	3	up

So, $h = $ _____-2_____ and $k = $ _____3_____.

B Determine the value of a in the equation $g(x) = a(x - h)^3 + k$.

The image of the point $(0, 0)$ is __(−2, 3)__. The image of the point $(1, 1)$ is

__(−1, 1)__. The vertical distance between $(0, 0)$ and $(1, 1)$ is 1 unit.

The vertical distance between the images of $(0, 0)$ and $(1, 1)$ is ___2___ units.

This means that $|a| = $ ___2___

The graph of the parent function is reflected across the x-axis, so a ___$<$___ 0.

So, the value of a is ___-2___

C Use the values of h, k, and a to write the equation: $g(x) = $ ___$-2(x + 2)^3 + 3$___

REFLECT

3a. The graph of $g(x)$ contains $(-3, 5)$. Check that your equation from part C is correct by showing that $(-3, 5)$ satisfies the equation.

$g(-3) = -2(-3 + 2)^3 + 3 = -2(-1)^3 + 3 = -2(-1) + 3 = 2 + 3 = 5$

3b. Suppose the graph of $g(x)$ is translated 4 units right and 5 units down to give the graph of $h(x)$. What is the equation of $h(x)$?

$h(x) = -2(x - 2)^3 - 2$

PRACTICE

Graph each function.

1. $f(x) = 2x^4$

2. $f(x) = -\frac{1}{2}x^3$

3. $f(x) = -(x - 3)^4 + 1$

4. $f(x) = 2(x + 1)^3 - 2$

The graph of $g(x)$ is the graph of $f(x) = x^4$ after a series of transformations. Write the equation of $g(x)$.

5.

$g(x) = -(x + 3)^4 + 4$

6.

$g(x) = \frac{1}{4}x^4 - 4$

7. $S(x) = \frac{4}{3}\pi\left(\frac{x}{2}\right)^3$ gives the volume of a sphere with diameter x, and $C(x) = x^3$ gives the volume of a cube with edge length x. Explain why the volume of a sphere with diameter x is less than the volume of a cube with edge length x.

$S(x) = \frac{4}{3}\pi\left(\frac{x}{2}\right)^3 = \frac{4}{3}\pi\left(\frac{x^3}{8}\right) = \frac{\pi}{6}x^3$ and $C(x) = x^3$, so $S(x) < C(x)$ because $\frac{\pi}{6} < 1$.

3-4 Polynomial Functions

Essential question: *What are polynomial functions and how do you graph them?*

COMMON Standards for
CORE Mathematical Content

CC.9-12.F.IF.2 Use function notation, evaluate functions for inputs in their domains, and interpret statements that use function notation in terms of a context.

CC.9-12.F.IF.7 Graph functions expressed symbolically and show key features of the graph, by hand in simple cases ...*

CC.9-12.F.IF.7c Graph polynomial functions, identifying zeros when suitable factorizations are available, and showing end behavior.*

Also: CC.9-12.A.CED.2, CC.9-12.F.IF.9

Vocabulary

monomial, polynomial, degree of a monomial, degree of a polynomial, polynomial function

Prerequisites

Understanding end behavior, Lesson 3-1

Math Background

In previous lessons, students investigated polynomials functions written in the form $f(x) = a(x - h)^n + k$. This form enables students to graph polynomial functions by transforming the graphs of parent functions. In this lesson, students will explore polynomial functions written in the form $f(x) = a_n x^n + a_{n-1} x^{n-1} + \cdots + a_1 x + a_0$, which is called standard form.

INTRODUCE

Explain to students that they have already been graphing polynomial functions that are written in the form $f(x) = a(x - h)^n + k$. They will now be graphing polynomial functions written in standard form, and this form requires different graphing techniques.

TEACH

1 ENGAGE

Questioning Strategies

- What is the degree of the polynomial $3x^2 + 2x^4$? Explain. **The degree is 4, which is the degree of $2x^4$, the term with the greatest degree. The degree of the polynomial is easier to determine if the polynomial is written in standard form: $2x^4 + 3x^2$.**

- The end behavior of a polynomial function $f(x)$ is $f(x) \to -\infty$ as $x \to +\infty$ and $f(x) \to +\infty$ as $x \to -\infty$. What can you tell about the degree of the polynomial and the coefficient a_n? **The degree is odd, and the coefficient a_n is negative.**

Differentiated Instruction

Understanding the concept of the degree of a polynomial is important in determining the end behavior of polynomial functions and, therefore, in graphing polynomial functions. English language learners may benefit from a rigorous review of finding degrees of polynomials, some in standard form and others with terms in varying orders of degree. Focus on polynomials that contain only single-variable monomials.

2 EXAMPLE

Questioning Strategies

- When a polynomial is in nested form, how is the number of pairs of parentheses related to the degree of the polynomial? **The number of pairs of parentheses is one less than the degree of the polynomial.**

- If a polynomial is in nested form, how can you write it in standard form? **Start with the leftmost expression in parentheses and multiply it by the x that was factored out. Repeat until all parentheses are removed.**

© Houghton Mifflin Harcourt Publishing Company

continued

Name_____ Class_____ Date_____

3-4

Polynomial Functions

Essential question: *What are polynomial functions and how do you graph them?*

COMMON CORE
CC.9-12.F.IF.2,
CC.9-12.F.IF.7*,
CC.9-12.F.IF.7c*

1 ENGAGE Understanding Polynomial Functions

A **monomial** is a number or a product of numbers and variables with whole-number exponents. For example, 6, $3x^5$, and $-2xy^2$ are all monomials. A **polynomial** is a monomial or a sum of monomials. For example, $-4x^9 + 5x^2 + 1$ is a polynomial.

The **degree of a monomial** is the sum of the exponents of the variables. The **degree of a polynomial** is the degree of the term with the greatest degree. For example, the polynomial $-4x^9 + 5x^2 + 1$ has degree 9.

A **polynomial function** can be written as $f(x) = a_n x^n + a_{n-1}x^{n-1} + \cdots + a_1x + a_0$ where the coefficients $a_n, \ldots, a_1, a_0$ are real numbers. This is known as *standard form*. Note that linear functions are polynomial functions of degree 1 and quadratic functions are polynomial functions of degree 2. The functions you have graphed in the form $f(x) = a(x-h)^n + k$ are also polynomial functions, as you will see in later lessons.

The end behavior of a polynomial function $f(x) = a_n x^n + a_{n-1}x^{n-1} + \cdots + a_1x + a_0$ is determined by the term with the greatest degree, $a_n x^n$.

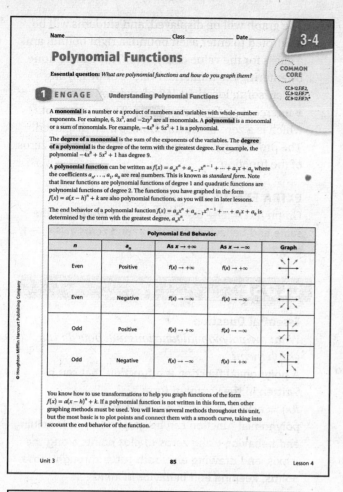

Polynomial End Behavior				
n	a_n	As $x \to +\infty$	As $x \to -\infty$	Graph
Even	Positive	$f(x) \to +\infty$	$f(x) \to +\infty$	
Even	Negative	$f(x) \to -\infty$	$f(x) \to -\infty$	
Odd	Positive	$f(x) \to +\infty$	$f(x) \to -\infty$	
Odd	Negative	$f(x) \to -\infty$	$f(x) \to +\infty$	

You know how to use transformations to help you graph functions of the form $f(x) = a(x-h)^n + k$. If a polynomial function is not written in this form, then other graphing methods must be used. You will learn several methods throughout this unit, but the most basic is to plot points and connect them with a smooth curve, taking into account the end behavior of the function.

Unit 3　　85　　Lesson 4

In general, the higher the degree of a polynomial, the more complex the graph. Here are some typical graphs for polynomials of degree n.

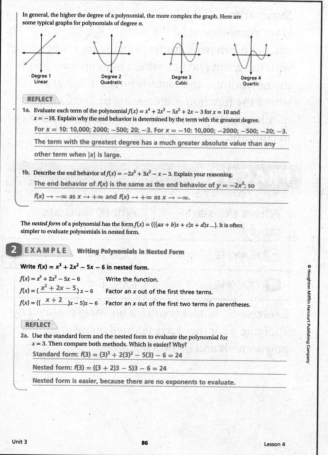

Degree 1
Linear

Degree 2
Quadratic

Degree 3
Cubic

Degree 4
Quartic

REFLECT

1a. Evaluate each term of the polynomial $f(x) = x^4 + 2x^3 - 5x^2 + 2x - 3$ for $x = 10$ and $x = -10$. Explain why the end behavior is determined by the term with the greatest degree.

For $x = 10$: 10,000; 2000; -500; 20; -3. For $x = -10$: 10,000; -2000; -500; -20; -3.

The term with the greatest degree has a much greater absolute value than any other term when $|x|$ is large.

1b. Describe the end behavior of $f(x) = -2x^3 + 3x^2 - x - 3$. Explain your reasoning.

The end behavior of $f(x)$ is the same as the end behavior of $y = -2x^3$; so

$f(x) \to -\infty$ as $x \to +\infty$ and $f(x) \to +\infty$ as $x \to -\infty$.

The *nested form* of a polynomial has the form $f(x) = (((ax + b)x + c)x + d)x \ldots)$. It is often simpler to evaluate polynomials in nested form.

2 EXAMPLE Writing Polynomials in Nested Form

Write $f(x) = x^3 + 2x^2 - 5x - 6$ in nested form.

$f(x) = x^3 + 2x^2 - 5x - 6$　　　Write the function.

$f(x) = (\,\underline{x^2 + 2x - 5}\,)x - 6$　　　Factor an x out of the first three terms.

$f(x) = ((\,\underline{x + 2}\,)x - 5)x - 6$　　　Factor an x out of the first two terms in parentheses.

REFLECT

2a. Use the standard form and the nested form to evaluate the polynomial for $x = 3$. Then compare both methods. Which is easier? Why?

Standard form: $f(3) = (3)^3 + 2(3)^2 - 5(3) - 6 = 24$

Nested form: $f(3) = ((3 + 2)3 - 5)3 - 6 = 24$

Nested form is easier, because there are no exponents to evaluate.

Unit 3　　86　　Lesson 4

Avoid Common Errors

When writing any expression that contains many parentheses, a common error is that the number of left parentheses and the number of right parentheses do not match. Remind students that parentheses come in pairs and encourage them to count the number of left parentheses and the number of right parentheses to make sure they are the same.

EXTRA EXAMPLE

Write $f(x) = x^3 + 3x^2 - 6x - 8$ in nested form.
$f(x) = ((x + 3)x - 6)x - 8$

3 EXAMPLE

Questioning Strategies

- What do you notice about the degree of $f(x)$ and the number of zeros $f(x)$ has? **The degree is 3 and there are 3 zeros.**

- When does a polynomial function of degree 8 have a minimum? a maximum? **If a_n is positive, the function has a minimum; if a_n is negative, the function has a maximum. The graph can also have local minimums and maximums.**

MATHEMATICAL PRACTICE — Highlighting the Standards

3 EXAMPLE and its Reflect questions offer an opportunity to address Mathematical Practice Standard 3 (Construct viable arguments and critique the reasoning of others). Based on the degree of a polynomial and the characteristics of its coefficients, students can give a viable description of the graph of the polynomial. Students can also use what they know about polynomials to critique a description of the graph given by another student.

Technology

Students can check their graphs by using their graphing calculators. Remind students that if the graph is not visible, they may have to change the settings for the viewing window. Once the graph is displayed, students can also check the zeros by pressing **2nd** **TRACE** (CALC) and choosing **2:zero.**

The graph will be displayed, and students will be prompted to enter a left bound, a right bound, and a guess for the value of the zero. This can be done by entering the numerical values or by moving the cursor to locations left of, right of, or near an x-intercept and pressing **ENTER**. The x-intercept, which is a zero of the function, is then displayed. The process can be repeated for finding other zeros of the function.

EXTRA EXAMPLE

Graph $f(x) = x^3 + 3x^2 - 6x - 8$. The graph has the same end behavior as $f(x) = x^3$ and zeros at $-4, -1,$ and 2.

CLOSE

Essential Question

What are polynomial functions and how do you graph them?

A polynomial function is a function that can be written in the standard form $f(x) = a_n x^n + a_{n-1} x^{n-1} + \cdots + a_1 x + a_0$. A polynomial function can be graphed by determining end behavior, using zeros to plot points along the x-axis, and drawing a smooth curve through those points, keeping end behavior in mind.

Summarize

Have students extend the table in 1 ENGAGE. For each end behavior, students can write a polynomial with the given end behavior. They can then graph the polynomial and identify its zeros, intervals where the function is increasing or decreasing, minimums or maximums, and local minimums or maximums.

PRACTICE

Where skills are taught	Where skills are practiced
2 EXAMPLE	EXS. 1–4
3 EXAMPLE	EXS. 1–4

Exercise 5: Students solve a business problem by applying what they have learned about graphing polynomials and identifying zeros.

3 EXAMPLE Graphing Polynomials

Graph $f(x) = x^3 + 2x^2 - 5x - 6$.

A. Determine the end behavior of the graph. The end behavior is determined by the leading term, x^3.

So, as $x \to +\infty$, $f(x) \to$ __+∞__, and as $x \to -\infty$, $f(x) \to$ __−∞__.

B. Complete the table of values. Use the nested form from the previous example to evaluate the polynomial.

x	−3	−2	−1	0	1	2	3
f(x)	0	4	0	−6	−8	0	24

C. Plot the points from the table on the graph, omitting any points whose y-values are much greater than or much less than the other y-values on the graph.

D. Draw a smooth curve through the plotted points, keeping in mind the end behavior of the graph.

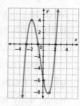

REFLECT

3a. What are the zeros of the function? How can you identify them from the graph?

−3, −1, and 2; the zeros occur where the graph intersects the x-axis.

3b. What are the approximate values of x for which the function is increasing? decreasing?

The function is increasing for approximately $x < -2$ and $x > 1$; the function is decreasing for approximately $-2 < x < 1$.

3c. A student wrote that $f(x)$ has a minimum value of approximately −8. Do you agree or disagree? Why?

Disagree; there is a *local* minimum of approximately −8, but the function has no minimum value.

3d. Without graphing, what do you think the graph of $g(x) = -x^3 - 2x^2 + 5x + 6$ looks like? Why?

The graph of $g(x)$ is a reflection of the graph of $f(x)$ in the x-axis because $g(x) = -f(x)$.

PRACTICE

Write each polynomial function in nested form. Then sketch the graph by plotting points and using end behavior.

1. $f(x) = x^4 - 4x^2$

$f(x) =$ __(((x)x − 4)x)x__

2. $f(x) = -x^3 + 4x^2 - x - 6$

$f(x) =$ __((−x + 4)x − 1)x − 6__

3. $f(x) = x^3 - x^2 - 4x + 4$

$f(x) =$ __((x − 1)x − 4)x + 4__

4. $f(x) = -x^4 + 4x^3 - 2x^2 - 4x + 3$

$f(x) =$ __(((−x + 4)x − 2)x − 4)x + 3__

5. From 2000 to 2010, the profit (in thousands of dollars) for a small business is modeled by $P(x) = -x^3 + 9x^2 - 6x - 16$, where x is the number of years since 2000.

a. Sketch a graph of the function at right.

b. What are the zeros of the function in the domain $0 \le x \le 10$?

2 and 8

c. What do the zeros represent?

The business broke even in 2002 and 2008.

3-5 Adding and Subtracting Polynomials

Essential question: *How do you add and subtract polynomials?*

COMMON **Standards for**
CORE **Mathematical Content**

CC.9-12.A.APR.1 Understand that polynomials form a system analogous to the integers, namely, they are closed under the operations of addition, subtraction, ...; add, subtract ... polynomials.

CC.9-12.F.BF.1 Write a function that describes a relationship between two quantities.*

CC.9-12.F.BF.1b Combine standard function types using arithmetic operations.*

Also: CC.9-12.A.SSE.1

Prerequisites
Closure of the set of integers, Lesson 1-1
Defining polynomials, Lesson 3-4

Math Background
Students are familiar with integer operations and understand that the integer system is closed under the operations of addition, subtraction, and multiplication. Students are also familiar with polynomials, have learned to identify the degree of a polynomial, and can write a polynomial in standard form.

INTRODUCE

Review integer operations, emphasizing that the integer system is closed under the operations of addition, subtraction, and multiplication.

TEACH

1 EXAMPLE

Questioning Strategies
- Are the commutative and associative properties of addition true for the addition of polynomials? Yes, the sum will be the same regardless of the order in which polynomials are added. If there are three or more polynomials being added, the sum will be the same regardless of how the polynomials are grouped.

- Compare the advantages and disadvantages of adding polynomials vertically and horizontally. If the polynomials have many terms, adding them vertically may prevent errors because you can line up like terms and leave gaps if terms of some degrees are missing. If the polynomials have only a few terms, adding them horizontally may be more convenient, and you may be able to add the coefficients using mental math without having to rewrite the polynomials.

- Is it possible to add three or more polynomials? If so, explain how. Yes, you can add three or more polynomials, either by writing the polynomials vertically, aligning like terms, and adding their coefficients or by writing the polynomials horizontally, grouping like terms, and adding their coefficients.

EXTRA EXAMPLE
Add $(4x^3 + 11x^2 + 8x + 5) + (7x^2 - 5x + 9)$.
$4x^3 + 18x^2 + 3x + 14$

2 EXAMPLE

Questioning Strategies
- Is it necessary to write polynomials in standard form before subtracting them? No, as long as you group like terms before subtracting and keep track of signs correctly, the results will be the same. However, it is good practice to write the difference as a polynomial in standard form.

- Is it necessary to use the method of rewriting the subtraction of polynomials as the addition of the opposite as in the given examples? No, although this may reduce the chance of error. If you can accurately subtract the coefficients of like terms rather than adding opposites, the results will be the same.

© Houghton Mifflin Harcourt Publishing Company

continued

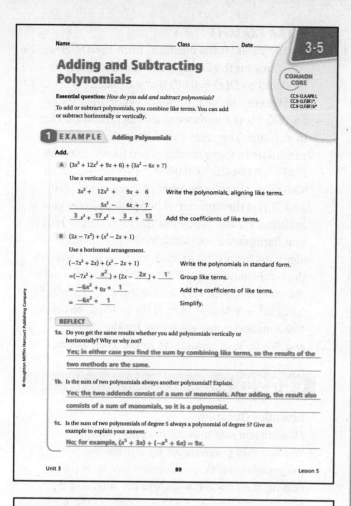

Name_____ Class_____ Date_____

3-5

Adding and Subtracting Polynomials

COMMON CORE
CC.9-12.A.APR.1,
CC.9-12.F.BF.1*,
CC.9-12.F.BF.1b*

Essential question: *How do you add and subtract polynomials?*

To add or subtract polynomials, you combine like terms. You can add or subtract horizontally or vertically.

1 EXAMPLE   Adding Polynomials

Add.

A $(3x^3 + 12x^2 + 9x + 6) + (5x^2 - 6x + 7)$

Use a vertical arrangement.

$3x^3 + 12x^2 + 9x + 6$ Write the polynomials, aligning like terms.
$\underline{ 5x^2 - 6x + 7}$
$\underline{3}\,x^3 + \underline{17}\,x^2 + \underline{3}\,x + \underline{13}$ Add the coefficients of like terms.

B $(2x - 7x^2) + (x^2 - 2x + 1)$

Use a horizontal arrangement.

$(-7x^2 + 2x) + (x^2 - 2x + 1)$ Write the polynomials in standard form.

$= (-7x^2 + \underline{x^2}) + (2x - \underline{2x}) + \underline{1}$ Group like terms.

$= \underline{-6x^2} + 0x + \underline{1}$ Add the coefficients of like terms.

$= \underline{-6x^2} + \underline{1}$ Simplify.

REFLECT

1a. Do you get the same results whether you add polynomials vertically or horizontally? Why or why not?

Yes; in either case you find the sum by combining like terms, so the results of the two methods are the same.

1b. Is the sum of two polynomials always another polynomial? Explain.

Yes; the two addends consist of a sum of monomials. After adding, the result also consists of a sum of monomials, so it is a polynomial.

1c. Is the sum of two polynomials of degree 5 always a polynomial of degree 5? Give an example to explain your answer.

No; for example, $(x^5 + 3x) + (-x^5 + 6x) = 9x$.

Unit 3   89   Lesson 5

To subtract polynomials, you add the opposite of the subtracted polynomial. The following example shows how to use this method with the vertical and horizontal formats.

2 EXAMPLE   Subtracting Polynomials

Subtract.

A $(2 + 9x^2) - (-6x^2 - 2x + 1)$

Use a vertical arrangement.

$9x^2 + 2$ Write the first polynomial in standard form.
$\underline{ 6x^2 + 2x - 1}$ Add the opposite of the second polynomial.
$\underline{15}\,x^2 + \underline{2}\,x + \underline{1}$ Add the coefficients of like terms.

B $(6x^3 + 3x^2 + 2x + 9) - (4x^3 + 8x^2 - 2x + 5)$

Use a horizontal arrangement.

$(6x^3 + 3x^2 + 2x + 9) - (4x^3 + 8x^2 - 2x + 5)$ Write the polynomials.

$= (6x^3 + 3x^2 + 2x + 9) + (-4x^3 - 8x^2 + 2x - 5)$ Add the opposite.

$= (6x^3 - \underline{4x^3}) + (3x^2 - \underline{8x^2}) + (\underline{2x} + 2x) + (\underline{9} - 5)$ Group like terms.

$= \underline{2}\,x^3 - \underline{5}\,x^2 + \underline{4}\,x + \underline{4}$ Add the coefficients of like terms.

REFLECT

2a. How is subtracting polynomials similar to subtracting integers?

You subtract integers by adding the opposite of the subtracted integer; you subtract polynomials by adding the opposite of the subtracted polynomial.

2b. In part A, you leave a gap in the polynomial $9x^2 + 2$ when you write the subtraction problem vertically. Why?

The polynomial does not have an x term, so you must leave a gap for like terms to align properly.

2c. Is the difference of two polynomials always another polynomial? Explain.

Yes; finding a difference of two polynomials is equivalent to finding the sum of the first polynomial and the opposite of the second polynomial, and the sum of two polynomials is always another polynomial.

Unit 3   90   Lesson 5

© Houghton Mifflin Harcourt Publishing Company

Avoid Common Errors

Regardless of the method students use to subtract polynomials, a common error is that instead of distributing the subtraction operation to all terms in the second polynomial, only the first term is subtracted while the others are added. Remind students to always be aware of this potential mistake. Also, encourage students to check their answers. Just as a numerical difference can be checked by addition, students can check a polynomial difference by addition.

EXTRA EXAMPLE

Subtract $(4 + 7x^2) - (-5x^2 - 3x + 2)$.
$12x^2 + 3x + 2$

3 EXAMPLE

Questioning Strategies

• Would adding or subtracting polynomials help you find the difference between the estimated number of female students in 2000 and 2005? Explain. **No; you would have to evaluate $F(x)$ for $x = 0$ and $x = 5$ and find the difference between the results.**

• How could you use the model to find the total enrollment in 2003? **Since x represents the number of years since 2000, evaluate $T(x)$ for $x = 3$.**

MATHEMATICAL PRACTICE **Highlighting the Standards**

3 EXAMPLE and its Reflect questions offer an opportunity to address Mathematical Practice Standard 4 (Model with mathematics). Many real-world situations in fields ranging from education and business to engineering and physics can be modeled by polynomial functions. In this example, students are given polynomials that model male and female high school enrollment in the United States. By adding and subtracting polynomials, students extend the model to determine the total high school enrollment and the difference between male and female enrollment.

EXTRA EXAMPLE

For the presidential elections from 1980 to 2008, the votes cast for the Democratic candidate can be modeled by $D(x) = 0.00230x^3 - 0.0625x^2 + 1.17x + 34.9$ where x is the number of years since 1980 and $D(x)$ is the number of Democratic votes cast in millions. The votes cast for the Republican candidate in these elections can be modeled by $R(x) = -0.00140x^4 + 0.0809x^3 - 1.41x^2 + 7.29x + 43.5$ where x is the number of years since 1980 and $R(x)$ is the number of Republican votes cast in millions. Write a model for the total Democratic and Republican votes cast in the presidential elections from 1980 to 2008, and use it to estimate the total Democratic and Republican votes cast in the 2000 election. $T(x) = -0.00140x^4 + 0.0832x^3 - 1.4725x^2 + 8.46x + 78.4$; $T(20) = 100.2$, so about 100.2 million votes were cast for the Democratic and Republican candidates in the 2000 election.

CLOSE

Essential Question

How do you add and subtract polynomials?
You can add polynomials by writing the polynomials vertically, aligning like terms, and adding their coefficients. You can also add the polynomials by writing them horizontally, grouping like terms, and adding their coefficients. To subtract polynomials, you can add the opposite of the polynomial being subtracted by using either the vertical or the horizontal addition method.

Summarize

Have students make a table describing the methods for adding and subtracting polynomials horizontally and vertically. For each method, students should provide an example.

PRACTICE

Where skills are taught	Where skills are practiced
1 EXAMPLE	EXS. 1–4
2 EXAMPLE	EXS. 5–10
3 EXAMPLE	EX. 11

Exercise 12: Students identify an error made by another student when subtracting polynomials.

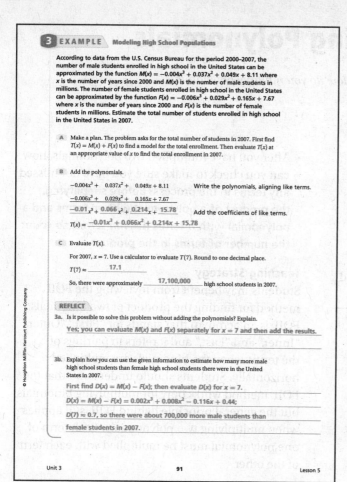

3 EXAMPLE Modeling High School Populations

According to data from the U.S. Census Bureau for the period 2000–2007, the number of male students enrolled in high school in the United States can be approximated by the function $M(x) = -0.004x^3 + 0.037x^2 + 0.049x + 8.11$ where x is the number of years since 2000 and $M(x)$ is the number of male students in millions. The number of female students enrolled in high school in the United States can be approximated by the function $F(x) = -0.006x^3 + 0.029x^2 + 0.165x + 7.67$ where x is the number of years since 2000 and $F(x)$ is the number of female students in millions. Estimate the total number of students enrolled in high school in the United States in 2007.

A Make a plan. The problem asks for the total number of students in 2007. First find $T(x) = M(x) + F(x)$ to find a model for the total enrollment. Then evaluate $T(x)$ at an appropriate value of x to find the total enrollment in 2007.

B Add the polynomials.

$-0.004x^3 + 0.037x^2 + 0.049x + 8.11$ Write the polynomials, aligning like terms.

$-0.006x^3 + 0.029x^2 + 0.165x + 7.67$

$\underline{-0.01}x^3 + \underline{0.066}x^2 + \underline{0.214}x + \underline{15.78}$ Add the coefficients of like terms.

$T(x) = \underline{-0.01x^3 + 0.066x^2 + 0.214x + 15.78}$

C Evaluate $T(x)$.

For 2007, $x = 7$. Use a calculator to evaluate $T(7)$. Round to one decimal place.

$T(7) \approx \underline{\hspace{1em} 17.1 \hspace{1em}}$

So, there were approximately $\underline{\hspace{1em} 17,100,000 \hspace{1em}}$ high school students in 2007.

REFLECT

3a. Is it possible to solve this problem without adding the polynomials? Explain.

Yes; you can evaluate $M(x)$ and $F(x)$ separately for $x = 7$ and then add the results.

3b. Explain how you can use the given information to estimate how many more male high school students than female high school students there were in the United States in 2007.

First find $D(x) = M(x) - F(x)$; then evaluate $D(x)$ for $x = 7$.

$D(x) = M(x) - F(x) = 0.002x^3 + 0.008x^2 - 0.116x + 0.44;$

$D(7) \approx 0.7$, so there were about 700,000 more male students than

female students in 2007.

© Houghton Mifflin Harcourt Publishing Company

PRACTICE

Add or subtract.

1. $(2x^4 - 6x^2 + 8) + (-x^4 + 2x^2 - 12)$

$x^4 - 4x^2 - 4$

2. $(7x^2 - 2x + 1) + (8x^3 + 2x^2 + 5x - 4)$

$8x^3 + 9x^2 + 3x - 3$

3. $(5x^2 - 6x^3 + 16) + (9x^3 + 3x + 7x^4)$

$7x^4 + 3x^3 + 5x^2 + 3x + 16$

4. $(-3x^3 - 7x^5 - 3) + (5x^2 + 3x^3 + 7x^5)$

$5x^2 - 3$

5. $(2x^4 - 6x^2 + 8) - (-x^4 + 2x^2 - 12)$

$3x^4 - 8x^2 + 20$

6. $(x^3 + 25) - (-x^2 - 18x - 8)$

$x^3 + x^2 + 18x + 33$

7. $(2x^2 + 3x + 1) - (7x^3 - 2x + 7x^3)$

$-7x^3 - 5x^2 + 5x + 1$

8. $(12x^2 + 3) - (15x^2 - 4x + 9x^4 + 7)$

$-9x^4 - 3x^2 + 4x - 4$

9. $(14x^4 - x^3 + 2x^2 + 5x + 15) - (10x^4 + 3x^3 - 5x^2 - 6x + 4)$

$4x^4 - 4x^3 + 7x^2 + 11x + 11$

10. $(-6x^3 + 10x + 26) + (5x^2 - 6x^5 + 7x) + (3 - 22x^4)$

$-6x^5 - 22x^4 - 6x^3 + 5x^2 + 17x + 29$

11. According to data from the U.S. Census Bureau, the total number of people in the United States labor force can be approximated by the function $T(x) = -0.011x^2 + 2x + 107$, where x is the number of years since 1980 and $T(x)$ is the number of workers in millions. The number of women in the United States labor force can be approximated by the function $W(x) = -0.012x^2 + 1.26x + 45.5$.

a. Write a polynomial function $M(x)$ that models the number of men in the labor force.

$M(x) = 0.001x^2 + 0.74x + 61.5$

b. Estimate the number of men in the labor force in 2008. Explain how you made your estimate.

Approximately 83,000,000; evaluate $M(x)$ for $x = 28$.

12. Error Analysis A student was asked to find the difference $(4x^5 - 3x^4 + 6x^2) - (7x^5 - 6x^4 + x^3)$. The student's work is shown at right. Identify the student's error and give the correct difference.

$\begin{array}{r} 4x^5 - 3x^4 + 6x^2 \\ -7x^5 - 6x^4 + x^3 \\ \hline -3x^5 - 9x^4 + x^3 + 6x^2 \end{array}$

The student did not distribute the negative sign in the

second polynomial. The correct difference is

$-3x^5 + 3x^4 - x^3 + 6x^2.$

© Houghton Mifflin Harcourt Publishing Company

© Houghton Mifflin Harcourt Publishing Company

Multiplying Polynomials

Essential question: *How do you multiply polynomials?*

COMMON
CORE
Standards for Mathematical Content

CC.9-12.A.APR.1 Understand that polynomials form a system analogous to the integers, namely, they are closed under the operations of … multiplication; … multiply polynomials.

CC.9-12.A.APR.4 Prove polynomial identities and use them to describe numerical relationships.

Prerequisites

Closure of the set of integers, Lesson 1-1

Adding polynomials, Lesson 3-5

Math Background

Students are familiar with integer operations and understand that the integers are closed under the operations of addition, subtraction, and multiplication. In the previous lesson, students learned to add and subtract polynomials, and discovered that like the integers, polynomials are closed under addition and subtraction.

INTRODUCE

Review polynomial addition and subtraction, emphasizing that like the integers, polynomials are closed under addition and subtraction. Ask students if they think that polynomials are also closed under multiplication, and have them explain their reasoning.

TEACH

1 EXAMPLE

Questioning Strategies

• Is the Commutative Property of Multiplication true for the multiplication of polynomials? Yes, the product will be the same regardless of the order in which polynomials are multiplied.

• After you have multiplied two polynomials, how can you check to make sure you have not missed any terms in the process? Before simplifying, the product of a polynomial with *m* terms and a polynomial with *n* terms has *mn* terms, so count the number of terms in the product .

Teaching Strategy

Students may benefit from reviewing the FOIL method for finding the product of two binomials. FOIL is an acronym that stands for "First," "Outer," "Inner," and "Last," and it refers to pairings of the terms when the binomials are multiplied horizontally. Students should understand that the FOIL method works only for multiplying binomials, but the general principle behind FOIL still applies when multiplying two polynomials: Each term of one polynomial must be multiplied with each term of the other.

EXTRA EXAMPLE

Find the product $(2x - 3)(3x^3 - x^2 + 6)$.
$6x^4 - 11x^3 + 3x^2 + 12x - 18$

2 EXAMPLE

Questioning Strategies

• In part A, how could the FOIL method help you? It would help you find the four terms in the product (before like terms are combined).

• In part B, what would the product be if the binomials being multiplied were $4x + 15$ and $4x - 15$? $16x^2 - 225$

continued

Name_____ Class_____ Date_____

3-6

Multiplying Polynomials

Essential question: *How do you multiply polynomials?*

To multiply two polynomials, you use the distributive property so that every term in the first factor is multiplied by every term in the second factor. You also use the product of powers property ($a^m \cdot a^n = a^{m+n}$) each time you multiply two terms.

COMMON CORE
CC.9-12.A.APR.1,
CC.9-12.A.APR.4

1 EXAMPLE Multiplying Polynomials

Find the product.

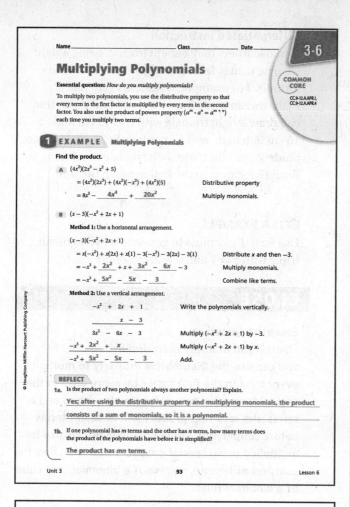

A $(4x^2)(2x^3 - x^2 + 5)$

$= (4x^2)(2x^3) + (4x^2)(-x^2) + (4x^2)(5)$ Distributive property

$= 8x^5 - \underline{4x^4} + \underline{20x^2}$ Multiply monomials.

B $(x - 3)(-x^2 + 2x + 1)$

Method 1: Use a horizontal arrangement.

$(x - 3)(-x^2 + 2x + 1)$

$= x(-x^2) + x(2x) + x(1) - 3(-x^2) - 3(2x) - 3(1)$ Distribute x and then -3.

$= -x^3 + \underline{2x^2} + x + \underline{3x^2} - \underline{6x} - 3$ Multiply monomials.

$= -x^3 + \underline{5x^2} - \underline{5x} - \underline{3}$ Combine like terms.

Method 2: Use a vertical arrangement.

$-x^2 + 2x + 1$ Write the polynomials vertically.

$\underline{\qquad x - 3}$

$3x^2 - 6x - 3$ Multiply $(-x^2 + 2x + 1)$ by -3.

$\underline{-x^3 + 2x^2 + x}$ Multiply $(-x^2 + 2x + 1)$ by x.

$-x^3 + 5x^2 - 5x - 3$ Add.

REFLECT

1a. Is the product of two polynomials always another polynomial? Explain.

Yes; after using the distributive property and multiplying monomials, the product

consists of a sum of monomials, so it is a polynomial.

1b. If one polynomial has m terms and the other has n terms, how many terms does the product of the polynomials have before it is simplified?

The product has mn terms.

There are several special products that occur so frequently that it is helpful to recognize their patterns and develop rules for the products. These rules are summarized in the table.

Special Product Rules	
Sum and Difference	$(a + b)(a - b) = a^2 - b^2$
Square of a Binomial	$(a + b)^2 = a^2 + 2ab + b^2$
	$(a - b)^2 = a^2 - 2ab + b^2$
Cube of a Binomial	$(a + b)^3 = a^3 + 3a^2b + 3ab^2 + b^3$
	$(a - b)^3 = a^3 - 3a^2b + 3ab^2 - b^3$

2 EXAMPLE Justifying and Applying a Special Product Rule

Justify the sum and difference rule. Then use it to find the product $(4x^2 + 15)(4x^2 - 15)$.

A Justify the rule.

$(a + b)(a - b) = a \cdot a + a(-b) + \underline{ba} + b(-b)$ Distribute a and then b.

$= a^2 - ab + \underline{ba} + \underline{-b^2}$ Multiply monomials.

$= \underline{a^2} - \underline{b^2}$ Combine like terms.

B Find the product $(4x^2 + 15)(4x^2 - 15)$.

$(4x^2 + 15)(4x^2 - 15) = (\underline{4x^2})^2 - (\underline{15})^2$ Sum and difference rule

$= \underline{16x^4 - 225}$ Simplify.

REFLECT

2a. **Error Analysis** A student was asked to find the square of $7x + 3$. The student quickly wrote $(7x + 3)^2 = 49x^2 + 9$. Identify the student's error and provide the correct answer.

The student forgot the middle term, $2ab$, in the rule for the square of a binomial.

The correct answer is $49x^2 + 42x + 9$.

2b. Show how to justify the rule for the cube of a binomial, $(a + b)^3$.

$(a + b)^3 = (a + b)(a + b)(a + b)$

$= (a + b)(a^2 + 2ab + b^2)$

$= a^3 + 2a^2b + ab^2 + ba^2 + 2ab^2 + b^3$

$= a^3 + 3a^2b + 3ab^2 + b^3$

**EXAMPLE** continued

Avoid Common Errors

When using the rules for special products, students often forget to apply exponents to the coefficients of terms in the binomial. Suggest that students first write the coefficient and variable within parentheses, with the exponent applied to both, and then simplify.

EXTRA EXAMPLE

Find the product $(2x^2 + 7)(2x^2 - 7)$. $4x^4 - 49$

3 EXAMPLE

Questioning Strategies

- When applying the special product rule for the square of a binomial to $(x^2 - y^2)^2$, which terms are substituted for a and b in the rule $(a - b)^2 = a^2 - 2ab + b^2$? **The term x^2 is substituted for a, and the term y^2 is substituted for b.**

- What is another way to find the product $(x^2 + y^2)^2$ if the special product rule for the square of a binomial is not applied? **Write the product as $(x^2 + y^2)(x^2 + y^2)$ and use the Distributive Property to multiply every term in the first factor by every term in the second factor, resulting in a total of four terms. Then, simplify the product by combining the two x^2y^2-terms.**

MATHEMATICAL PRACTICE | **Highlighting the Standards**

2 EXAMPLE, **3 EXAMPLE**, and their Reflect questions offer an opportunity to address Mathematical Practice Standard 3 (Construct viable arguments and critique the reasoning of others). Students use what they have learned about multiplying polynomials to justify the special product rule for the sum and difference. Then, students identify an error made by another student when applying the special product rule for the square of a binomial. Finally, students extend their understanding of multiplying polynomials and applying special product rules when they verify Euclid's formula.

Differentiated Instruction

Visual learners may benefit from drawing a right triangle with side lengths generated by Euclid's formula. For example, if students generate a Pythagorean triple by using $x = 4$ and $y = 2$, they can draw a right triangle with legs 12 cm and 16 cm in length, and a hypotenuse 20 cm in length. Students can then use their triangle to relate Euclid's formula to the Pythagorean theorem $a^2 + b^2 = c^2$.

EXTRA EXAMPLE

Use Euclid's formula to generate a Pythagorean triple with $x = 7$ and $y = 2$. **45, 28, 53**

CLOSE

Essential Question

How do you multiply polynomials?
You can use the Distributive Property to multiply every term in the first factor by every term in the second factor. For two polynomials with m and n terms, the resulting product will have mn terms before simplifying. Some polynomials can also be multiplied using special product rules, including the sum and difference, square of a binomial, and cube of a binomial rules.

Summarize

Have students make a table describing the methods for multiplying polynomials. Give examples for multiplying monomials, binomials, and trinomials, as well as for using special product rules.

PRACTICE

Where skills are taught	Where skills are practiced
1 EXAMPLE	EXS. 1–10
2 EXAMPLE	EX. 11
3 EXAMPLE	EX. 13

Exercise 12: Students apply the sum and difference rule to multiply integers by mental math.

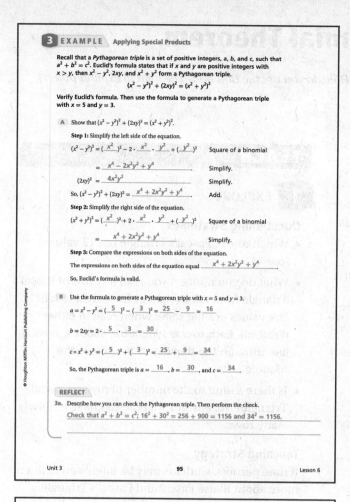

3 EXAMPLE Applying Special Products

Recall that a *Pythagorean triple* is a set of positive integers, a, b, and c, such that $a^2 + b^2 = c^2$. Euclid's formula states that if x and y are positive integers with $x > y$, then $x^2 - y^2$, $2xy$, and $x^2 + y^2$ form a Pythagorean triple.

$$(x^2 - y^2)^2 + (2xy)^2 = (x^2 + y^2)^2$$

Verify Euclid's formula. Then use the formula to generate a Pythagorean triple with $x = 5$ and $y = 3$.

A Show that $(x^2 - y^2)^2 + (2xy)^2 = (x^2 + y^2)^2$.

Step 1: Simplify the left side of the equation.

$(x^2 - y^2)^2 = (\underline{x^2})^2 - 2 \cdot \underline{x^2} \cdot \underline{y^2} + (\underline{y^2})^2$ Square of a binomial

$= \underline{x^4 - 2x^2y^2 + y^4}$ Simplify.

$(2xy)^2 = \underline{4x^2y^2}$ Simplify.

So, $(x^2 - y^2)^2 + (2xy)^2 = \underline{x^4 + 2x^2y^2 + y^4}$ Add.

Step 2: Simplify the right side of the equation.

$(x^2 + y^2)^2 = (\underline{x^2})^2 + 2 \cdot \underline{x^2} \cdot \underline{y^2} + (\underline{y^2})^2$ Square of a binomial

$= \underline{x^4 + 2x^2y^2 + y^4}$ Simplify.

Step 3: Compare the expressions on both sides of the equation.

The expressions on both sides of the equation equal $\underline{x^4 + 2x^2y^2 + y^4}$

So, Euclid's formula is valid.

B Use the formula to generate a Pythagorean triple with $x = 5$ and $y = 3$.

$a = x^2 - y^2 = (\underline{5})^2 - (\underline{3})^2 = \underline{25} - \underline{9} = \underline{16}$

$b = 2xy = 2 \cdot \underline{5} \cdot \underline{3} = \underline{30}$

$c = x^2 + y^2 = (\underline{5})^2 + (\underline{3})^2 = \underline{25} + \underline{9} = \underline{34}$

So, the Pythagorean triple is $a = \underline{16}$, $b = \underline{30}$, and $c = \underline{34}$.

REFLECT

3a. Describe how you can check the Pythagorean triple. Then perform the check.

Check that $a^2 + b^2 = c^2$; $16^2 + 30^2 = 256 + 900 = 1156$ and $34^2 = 1156$.

PRACTICE

Find each product.

1. $(2x^3)(2x^2 - 9x + 3)$

$4x^5 - 18x^4 + 6x^3$

2. $(x + 5)(3x^2 - x + 1)$

$3x^3 + 14x^2 - 4x + 5$

3. $(x - 4)(x - 6)$

$x^2 - 10x + 24$

4. $(3 + x^3)(-x + x^2 + 7)$

$x^5 - x^4 + 7x^3 + 3x^2 - 3x + 21$

5. $(4x^2 + 2x + 2)(2x^2 - x + 3)$

$8x^4 + 14x^2 + 4x + 6$

6. $(2x^4 - 5x^2)(6x + 4x^2)$

$8x^6 + 12x^5 - 20x^4 - 30x^3$

7. $(x + y)(2x - y)$

$2x^2 + xy - y^2$

8. $(x + 2y)(x^2 + xy + y^2)$

$x^3 + 3x^2y + 3xy^2 + 2y^3$

9. $(3x^2 - x + 2x^3 - 2)(2x + 3)$

$4x^4 + 12x^3 + 7x^2 - 7x - 6$

10. $(x^3)(x^2 - 3)(3x + 1)$

$3x^6 + x^5 - 9x^4 - 3x^3$

11. Justify the rule for the square of a binomial, $(a + b)^2 = a^2 + 2ab + b^2$. Then use it to expand $(2x^3 + 6y)^2$.

$(a + b)^2 = (a + b)(a + b) = a \cdot a + a \cdot b + b \cdot a + b \cdot b = a^2 + ab + ba + b^2 = a^2 + 2ab + b^2$;

$(2x^3 + 6y)^2 = (2x^3)^2 + 2(2x^3)(6y) + (6y)^2 = 4x^6 + 24x^3y + 36y^2$

12. The sum and difference rule is useful for mental-math calculations. Explain how you can use the rule and mental math to calculate $32 \cdot 28$. (*Hint:* $32 \cdot 28 = (30 + 2)(30 - 2)$.)

$32 \cdot 28 = (30 + 2)(30 - 2)$; by the sum and difference rule, this is equal to

$30^2 - 2^2$, which is easy to calculate by mental math: $30^2 - 2^2 = 900 - 4 = 896$.

13. You can generate a Pythagorean triple by choosing a positive integer m and letting $a = 2m$, $b = m^2 - 1$, and $c = m^2 + 1$. Show that this formula generates a Pythagorean triple. Then use the formula to generate a Pythagorean triple with $m = 5$.

$a^2 + b^2 = (2m)^2 + (m^2 - 1)^2 = 4m^2 + m^4 - 2m^2 + 1 = m^4 + 2m^2 + 1$;

$c^2 = (m^2 + 1)^2 = m^4 + 2m^2 + 1$; so $a^2 + b^2 = c^2$.

When $m = 5$, the Pythagorean triple is $a = 10$, $b = 24$, and $c = 26$.

The Binomial Theorem

Essential question: *How do you use the Binomial Theorem to expand powers of binomials?*

COMMON CORE

Standards for Mathematical Content

CC.9-12.A.APR.1 ... multiply polynomials.

CC.9-12.A.APR.5(+) Know and apply the Binomial Theorem for the expansion of $(x + y)^n$ in powers of x and y for a positive integer n, where x and y are any numbers, with coefficients determined for example by Pascal's Triangle.

Prerequisites

Multiplying polynomials, Lesson 3-6

Math Background

In Lesson 3-6, students learned to multiply polynomials. The techniques students learned include using the Distributive Property to multiply individual terms and then simplifying the result, as well as using rules for squares and cubes of binomials.

INTRODUCE

Revisit the techniques that students learned in Lesson 3-6 for multiplying polynomials. Remind students that the product of two polynomials, one with m terms and the other with n terms, will have mn terms before simplifying. Review the rules for squares and cubes of binomials. Ask students to think about how they would find a product like $(2x + 3y)^5$ using the techniques they learned in Lesson 3-6. For example, each factor has 2 terms, so the product would have $2^5 = 32$ terms before simplifying. Once students have realized how time-consuming that process would be, they will be ready to learn how using the Binomial Theorem can make expansion of powers of binomials a much easier task.

TEACH

1 EXPLORE

Questioning Strategies

- Which row of Pascal's Triangle has 12 values? row 11

- What do you notice if you read any row of Pascal's Triangle from left to right or from right to left? The values are the same when read in either direction. Each row is symmetric about a vertical line through the number at the top of the triangle.

- Is there a limit to the number of rows in Pascal's Triangle? No, Pascal's Triangle can have infinitely many rows.

Teaching Strategy

If time permits, students may be interested to learn more about Blaise Pascal and Pascal's Triangle. Born in 1623, Pascal was a child prodigy who was building calculating machines by the time he was a teenager. The computer programming language Pascal is named for him. Encourage students to look for other patterns in Pascal's Triangle, such as horizontal sums (the rows add to powers of 2) and patterns that form the Fibonacci sequence.

Differentiated Instruction

Kinesthetic learners may benefit from moving a physical object, such as coin or other marker, along the paths in Pascal's Triangle. For instance, you can give each of 16 students a unique pathway to follow using a four-letter sequence of Ls and Rs, such as RRLR. Those 16 students can then move their markers along the paths to determine at what node in row 4 of the triangle they land. By surveying the 16 students, you can find how many students landed at each of the five nodes in row 4, thereby generating the numbers in that row of Pascal's Triangle.

The Binomial Theorem

Name_____ Class_____ Date_____

Essential question: *How do you use the Binomial Theorem to expand powers of binomials?*

Pascal's Triangle is a famous number pattern named after the French mathematician Blaise Pascal (1623–1662). You can use Pascal's Triangle to help you expand a power of a binomial of the form $(a + b)^n$.

1 EXPLORE   Generating Pascal's Triangle

You can generate Pascal's Triangle by making a tree diagram as shown below. Starting at the top of the diagram, there are two paths from each node to the nodes beneath it, the left path (L) and the right path (R). You can describe a path from the top down to any node using lefts and rights.

There is only one possible path to each node in row 1. In row 2, there is only one possible path (LL) to the first node and only one possible path (RR) to the last node, but there are two possible paths (LR and RL) to the center node.

A Complete rows 3 and 4 of Pascal's Triangle. In each node, write the number of possible paths from the top down to that node.

B Look for patterns in the tree diagram.

What is the value in the first and last node in each row? ____1____

For the other nodes, what is the relationship of the value in the node to the two values above it?

Each value is the sum of the two values above it.

C Use the patterns to complete rows 5 and 6 of Pascal's Triangle.

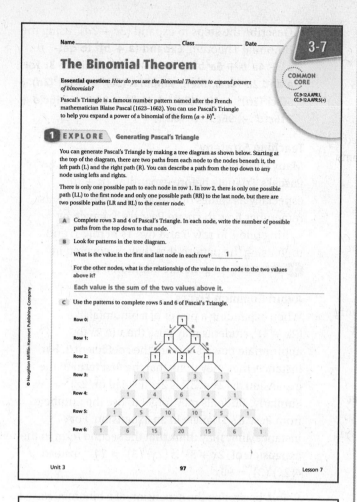

Row 0:   1
Row 1:   1   1
Row 2: 1   2   1
Row 3: 1   3   3   1
Row 4: 1   4   6   4   1
Row 5: 1   5   10   10   5   1
Row 6: 1   6   15   20   15   6   1

REFLECT

1a. What are all the paths to get to the second node in row 3? Write the paths in terms of L and R. How are the paths alike? How are they different?

LLR, LRL, RLL; every path has 2 Ls and 1 R, but they are in different orders.

1b. Which node in which row of Pascal's Triangle is located by the path LLRLR? What is the value at that node?

The third node in row 5; the value is 10.

The value in position r of row n of Pascal's Triangle is written as $_nC_r$, where the position numbers in each row start with 0. In the next Explore, you will see how the values in Pascal's Triangle are related to powers of a binomial.

Row 0 $\longrightarrow$ $_0C_0$
Row 1 $\longrightarrow$ $_1C_0$ $_1C_1$
Row 2 $\longrightarrow$ $_2C_0$ $_2C_1$ $_2C_2$
Row 3 $\longrightarrow$ $_3C_0$ $_3C_1$ $_3C_2$ $_3C_3$

2 EXPLORE   Expanding a Power of a Binomial

A Expand each power.

$(a + b)^0 = $ ____1____
$(a + b)^1 = $ ___$a + b$___
$(a + b)^2 = $ ___$a^2 + 2ab + b^2$___   Square of a binomial
$(a + b)^3 = $ ___$a^3 + 3a^2b + 3ab^2 + a^3$___   Multiply $(a + b)^2$ by $(a + b)$.
$(a + b)^4 = $ ___$a^4 + 4a^3b + 6a^2b^2 + 4ab^3 + b^4$___   Multiply $(a + b)^3$ by $(a + b)$.

B Identify patterns in the expanded power $(a + b)^n$.

What do you notice about the exponents of a?

The exponents start at n and decrease by 1 each term.

What do you notice about the exponents of b?

The exponents start at 0 and increase by 1 each term.

What is the sum of the exponents in each term? ___n___

What is the pattern in the coefficients of the terms?

The coefficients of the terms of the expanded power $(a + b)^n$ are the

values in the nth row of Pascal's Triangle.

Questioning Strategies

• In part A, what is another way of obtaining the expansion of $(a + b)^3$? Use the special product rule for the cube of a binomial.

• What position in Pascal's Triangle is represented as $_5C_2$? Explain. Position 2 of row 5; $_nC_r$ represents position r of row n.

• How is the number of paths to any given node in row n of Pascal's Triangle related to the corresponding term of the expanded form of $(a + b)^n$? The number of paths is the coefficient of the corresponding term.

Teaching Strategy

By the time students expand $(a + b)^4$ by multiplying $(a + b)(a + b)^3$ in step A, they will recognize that there is an advantage to learning an easier way to expand powers of binomials. Point out how the simple pattern of Pascal's Triangle gives the coefficients of terms in a binomial expansion that were previously so difficult to calculate. Explain to students that as they become mathematically fluent, they will learn many more ways that mathematics can make a seemingly complex task easy.

3 **EXAMPLE**

Questioning Strategies

• If a term in a binomial being raised to a power has a coefficient other than 1, what happens to that coefficient when the power is expanded using the Binomial Theorem? Give an example. The coefficient is raised to the same power as the variable for each term and then multiplied by the corresponding value from Pascal's triangle. For example, the expansion rule for $(2x + y)^3$ is $a^3 + 3a^2b + 3ab^2 + b^3$. Substituting $2x$ for a and y for b, the expansion becomes $((2x)^3 + 3(2x)^2y + 3(2x)y^2 + y^3) = 8x^3 + 12x^2y + 6xy^2 + y^3$.

• Describe the steps to expand $(3c + 2d)^4$ using the Binomial Theorem. Expand $(a + b)^4$ to get $a^4 + 4a^3b + 6a^2b^2 + 4ab^3 + b^4$. Substitute $3c$ for a and $2d$ for b; then, simplify: $(3c)^4 + 4(3c)^3(2d) + 6(3c)^2(2d)^2 + 4(3c)(2d)^3 + (2d)^4 = 81c^4 + 216c^3d + 216c^2d^2 + 96cd^3 + 16d^4$.

Teaching Strategy

Many students find it helpful to write out a copy of Pascal's Triangle before expanding $(a + b)^n$, especially as values of n increase. Help students remember how to create Pascal's Triangle by writing one 1 in row 0 and two 1s in row 1, and then using the pattern that they discovered in **1** **EXPLORE** to generate additional rows.

Avoid Common Errors

When expanding a power of a binomial like $(2x + 3)^4$, students may raise the x in $2x$ to appropriate powers but not the coefficient 2. For instance, they may think that the first term in the expansion of $(2x + 3)^4$ is $2x^4$ instead of $(2x)^4 = 16x^4$. Similarly, students may forget to use the numbers from Pascal's Triangle in an expansion. For instance, they may think that the second term in the expansion of $(2x + 3)^4$ is $(2x)^3(3)^1 = 24x^3$ instead of $4(2x)^3(3)^1 = 96x^3$.

Before beginning the expansion of a binomial raised to a power, some students may find it helpful to write out a "fill-in-the-blank" product, such as $(\_ + \_)^4 = (\_)^4 + 4(\_)^3(\_) + 6(\_)^2(\_)^2 + 4(\_)(\_)^3 + (\_)^4$. First, have them find the appropriate numbers from Pascal's Triangle. Then, they can fill in the exponents for the powers of the first term of the binomial in descending order: 4, 3, 2, 1, 0, and the exponents for the powers of the second term of the binomial in ascending order: 0, 1, 2, 3, 4. If the binomial has the form $(a - b)^n$, remind students to alternate the signs of the terms in the expansion, starting with a positive first term. They can then enter the values of a and b and simplify, being sure to apply each exponent to both the variable and its coefficient for variable terms.

continued

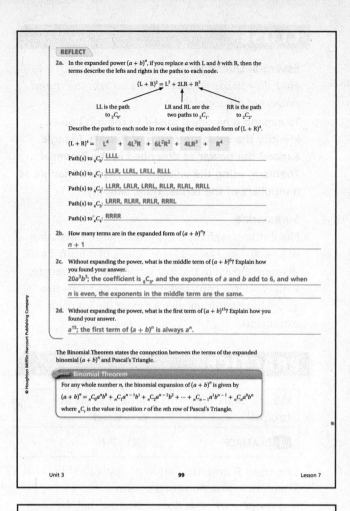

REFLECT

2a. In the expanded power $(a + b)^n$, if you replace a with L and b with R, then the terms describe the lefts and rights in the paths to each node.

$$(L + R)^2 = L^2 + 2LR + R^2$$

LL is the path to $_2C_0$.   LR and RL are the two paths to $_2C_1$.   RR is the path to $_2C_2$.

Describe the paths to each node in row 4 using the expanded form of $(L + R)^4$.

$$(L + R)^4 = \quad L^4 \quad + \quad 4L^3R \quad + \quad 6L^2R^2 \quad + \quad 4LR^3 \quad + \quad R^4$$

Path(s) to $_4C_0$: __LLLL__

Path(s) to $_4C_1$: __LLLR, LLRL, LRLL, RLLL__

Path(s) to $_4C_2$: __LLRR, LRLR, LRRL, RLLR, RLRL, RRLL__

Path(s) to $_4C_3$: __LRRR, RLRR, RRLR, RRRL__

Path(s) to $_4C_4$: __RRRR__

2b. How many terms are in the expanded form of $(a + b)^n$?

__$n + 1$__

2c. Without expanding the power, what is the middle term of $(a + b)^6$? Explain how you found your answer.

__$20a^3b^3$; the coefficient is $_6C_3$, and the exponents of a and b add to 6, and when__

__n is even, the exponents in the middle term are the same.__

2d. Without expanding the power, what is the first term of $(a + b)^{15}$? Explain how you found your answer.

__a^{15}; the first term of $(a + b)^n$ is always a^n.__

The Binomial Theorem states the connection between the terms of the expanded binomial $(a + b)^n$ and Pascal's Triangle.

> **Binomial Theorem**
>
> For any whole number n, the binomial expansion of $(a + b)^n$ is given by
>
> $$(a + b)^n = {}_nC_0 a^n b^0 + {}_nC_1 a^{n-1}b^1 + {}_nC_2 a^{n-2}b^2 + \cdots + {}_nC_{n-1}a^1 b^{n-1} + {}_nC_n a^0 b^n$$
>
> where $_nC_r$ is the value in position r of the nth row of Pascal's Triangle.

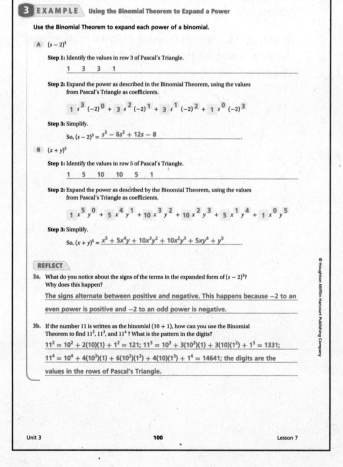

3 EXAMPLE Using the Binomial Theorem to Expand a Power

Use the Binomial Theorem to expand each power of a binomial.

A $(s - 2)^3$

Step 1: Identify the values in row 3 of Pascal's Triangle.

1   3   3   1

Step 2: Expand the power as described in the Binomial Theorem, using the values from Pascal's Triangle as coefficients.

$$1\, s^3 (-2)^0 + 3\, s^2 (-2)^1 + 3\, s^1 (-2)^2 + 1\, s^0 (-2)^3$$

Step 3: Simplify.

So, $(s - 2)^3 = \underline{s^3 - 6s^2 + 12s - 8}$.

B $(x + y)^5$

Step 1: Identify the values in row 5 of Pascal's Triangle.

1   5   10   10   5   1

Step 2: Expand the power as described by the Binomial Theorem, using the values from Pascal's Triangle as coefficients.

$$1\, x^5 y^0 + 5\, x^4 y^1 + 10\, x^3 y^2 + 10\, x^2 y^3 + 5\, x^1 y^4 + 1\, x^0 y^5$$

Step 3: Simplify.

So, $(x + y)^5 = \underline{x^5 + 5x^4y + 10x^3y^2 + 10x^2y^3 + 5xy^4 + y^5}$.

REFLECT

3a. What do you notice about the signs of the terms in the expanded form of $(s - 2)^3$? Why does this happen?

__The signs alternate between positive and negative. This happens because −2 to an__

__even power is positive and −2 to an odd power is negative.__

3b. If the number 11 is written as the binomial $(10 + 1)$, how can you use the Binomial Theorem to find 11^2, 11^3, and 11^4? What is the pattern in the digits?

__$11^2 = 10^2 + 2(10)(1) + 1^2 = 121$; $11^3 = 10^3 + 3(10^2)(1) + 3(10)(1^2) + 1^3 = 1331$;__

__$11^4 = 10^4 + 4(10^3)(1) + 6(10^2)(1^2) + 4(10)(1^3) + 1^4 = 14641$; the digits are the__

__values in the rows of Pascal's Triangle.__

Technology

Students can use their graphing calculators to check their use of the Binomial Theorem to expand the power of a binomial. They can enter the power of the binomial and the expanded form as two separate functions and compare their graphs.

MATHEMATICAL PRACTICE	Highlighting the Standards

3 EXAMPLE and its Reflect questions offer an opportunity to address Mathematical Practice Standard 2 (Reason abstractly and quantitatively). At the beginning of this lesson, students reasoned quantitatively as they identified the pattern of Pascal's Triangle and performed simple arithmetic calculations to fill in additional rows. Then, they related the values in Pascal's Triangle to the variable n representing the nth row of the triangle and reasoned abstractly to make connections between n and the exponents and coefficients of the expanded power $(a + b)^n$. The process culminates in this example as they extend the abstraction to expand the power of any binomial as described by the Binomial Theorem, using the values from Pascal's Triangle as multipliers of the terms in the expansion.

EXTRA EXAMPLE

Use the Binomial Theorem to expand $(t - 4)^3$.

$t^3 - 12t^2 + 48t - 64$

CLOSE

Essential Question

How do you use the Binomial Theorem to expand powers of binomials?

To expand a binomial raised to the nth power, identify the values in row n of Pascal's Triangle. Expand the power as described in the Binomial Theorem, using the values from Pascal's Triangle as multipliers of the terms. Then, simplify.

Summarize

Have students make a list showing the expansion of $(a + b)^n$ and $(a - b)^n$ for values of n from 2 to 6. Arrange the list in the format of Pascal's Triangle, with each row centered below the previous row. Then, have students give an example for each expansion.

PRACTICE

Where skills are taught	Where skills are practiced
3 EXAMPLE	EXS. 1–8

Exercises 9 and 10: Students apply the Binomial Theorem to functions of the form $f(x) = a(x - h)^n + k$, demonstrating that they are polynomial functions.

Exercise 11: Students use a calculator to expand the power of a binomial using the Binomial Theorem.

PRACTICE

Use the Binomial Theorem to expand each power of a binomial.

1. $(x - 1)^4$

$x^4 - 4x^3 + 6x^2 - 4x + 1$

2. $(2m + 5)^3$

$8m^3 + 60m^2 + 150m + 125$

3. $(c + 2d)^3$

$c^3 + 6c^2d + 12cd^2 + 8d^3$

4. $(2x - 2)^4$

$16x^4 - 64x^3 + 96x^2 - 64x + 16$

5. $(8 - m)^3$

$512 - 192m + 24m^2 - m^3$

6. $(3s + 2t)^4$

$81s^4 + 216s^3t + 216s^2t^2 + 96st^3 + 16t^4$

7. $(3 + t)^5$

$243 + 405t + 270t^2 + 90t^3 + 15t^4 + t^5$

8. $(p - 2q)^6$

$p^6 - 12p^5q + 60p^4q^2 - 160p^3q^3 + 240p^2q^4 - 192pq^5 + 64q^6$

9. Previously, you graphed functions of the form $f(x) = a(x - h)^n + k$.

   a. What is the expanded form of $a(x - h)^3 + k$?

      $ax^3 - 3ax^2h + 3axh^2 - ah^3 + k$

   b. Is this function a polynomial? Why or why not?

      Yes; the function consists of a sum of monomials.

   c. What is the constant term in the expanded form of $a(x - h)^3 + k$? What does this represent in the graph of the function?

      $-ah^3 + k$; it is the y-intercept of the graph.

10. What is the leading term of the expanded form of $f(x) = a(x - h)^n + k$? What is the constant term? Explain how you know.

   ax^n; $a(-h)^n + k$; when $(x - h)^n$ is expanded using the Binomial Theorem, the first term is x^n and the last term is $(-h)^n$. Each term of the expanded form is multiplied by a, and k is added to the constant term.

11. You can use a graphing calculator to evaluate $_nC_r$. First enter the value of n, then press [MATH], select **PRB**, then select **3:nCr**. Now enter the value of r, and then press [ENTER]. Use a calculator to help you expand $(x + 1)^9$.

   $x^9 + 9x^8 + 36x^7 + 84x^6 + 126x^5 + 126x^4 + 84x^3 + 36x^2 + 9x + 1$

Polynomial Division and the Remainder and Factor Theorems

Essential question: *What is the relationship between polynomial division and the Remainder and Factor Theorems?*

COMMON CORE Standards for Mathematical Content

CC.9-12.A.APR.1 Understand that polynomials form a system analogous to the integers, namely, they are closed under the operations of addition, subtraction, and multiplication ...

CC.9-12.A.APR.2 Know and apply the Remainder Theorem: For a polynomial $p(x)$ and a number a, the remainder on division by $x - a$ is $p(a)$, so $p(a) = 0$ if and only if $(x - a)$ is a factor of $p(x)$.

Vocabulary

synthetic division, synthetic substitution

Prerequisites

Closure of the set of integers, Lesson 1-1

Multiplying polynomials, Lesson 3-6

Math Background

In Lessons 3-5 and 3-6, students learned to add, subtract, and multiply polynomials. Students also explored the property of closure and concluded that the set of polynomials is closed under addition, subtraction, and multiplication in a way that is analogous to the set of integers. In this lesson, they will explore division of polynomials, discovering that the set of polynomials, like the set of integers, is *not* closed under the operation of division.

INTRODUCE

Point out the parallels between addition, subtraction, and multiplication of integers and the same operations for the set of polynomials. Ask: Is the set of integers closed under division? No. Do you think the set of polynomials is closed under division? No. Review numerical long division and explain that polynomial long division is similar.

TEACH

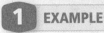

Questioning Strategies

• When using long division to find $4517 \div 58$, you may think that the first digit of the quotient is 9, because $45 \div 5 = 9$. However, $9 \times 58 = 522$, which is greater than 451, so 9 is too large for the first digit. Do similar situations arise when using long division to divide polynomials? No, because at each step of the division process, you are dividing monomials to obtain the next term in the quotient. As long as the degree of the monomial from the dividend is greater than or equal to the monomial from the divisor, the quotient of the monomials is another monomial.

• Why is the quotient of the polynomials in the Example *not* a polynomial? A polynomial does not have variables in the denominators in any of its terms.

• How could you check that division of polynomials using long division has been performed correctly? Multiply the quotient by the divisor and then add the remainder. The resulting polynomial should be equal to the polynomial that is the dividend.

Teaching Strategies

Students who normally divide with a calculator may benefit from a review of numerical long division. As a review, work a numerical long division and a polynomial long division side-by-side, showing the steps of each simultaneously. Remind students to take special care with the signs when subtracting polynomials to avoid careless mistakes. Encourage students to write neatly and keep terms aligned.

EXTRA EXAMPLE

Divide $3x^3 + x^2 - 4x$ by $x - 1$ using long division.
$3x^2 + 4x$

Name_____ Class_____ Date_____

3-8

Polynomial Division and the Remainder and Factor Theorems

COMMON CORE

CC.9-12.A.APR.1, CC.9-12.A.APR.2

Essential question: *What is the relationship between polynomial division and the Remainder and Factor Theorems?*

You can use long division to divide a polynomial by another polynomial of a lower degree. The process is similar to dividing numbers.

1 EXAMPLE Using Long Division to Divide Polynomials

Divide $2x^3 + 4x^2 + 5$ by $x - 3$ using long division.

A Write the quotient in long division format. Remember to include terms with a coefficient of 0.

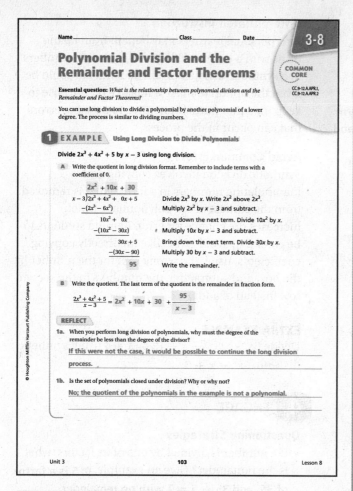

$$\begin{array}{r} 2x^2 + 10x + 30 \\ x-3\overline{)2x^3 + 4x^2 + 0x + 5} \\ -(2x^3 - 6x^2) \\ \hline 10x^2 + 0x \\ -(10x^2 - 30x) \\ \hline 30x + 5 \\ -(30x - 90) \\ \hline 95 \end{array}$$

Divide $2x^3$ by x. Write $2x^2$ above $2x^3$.

Multiply $2x^2$ by $x - 3$ and subtract.

Bring down the next term. Divide $10x^2$ by x.

Multiply $10x$ by $x - 3$ and subtract.

Bring down the next term. Divide $30x$ by x.

Multiply 30 by $x - 3$ and subtract.

Write the remainder.

B Write the quotient. The last term of the quotient is the remainder in fraction form.

$$\frac{2x^3 + 4x^2 + 5}{x - 3} = 2x^2 + 10x + 30 + \frac{95}{x - 3}$$

REFLECT

1a. When you perform long division of polynomials, why must the degree of the remainder be less than the degree of the divisor?

If this were not the case, it would be possible to continue the long division process.

1b. Is the set of polynomials closed under division? Why or why not?

No; the quotient of the polynomials in the example is not a polynomial.

Unit 3   103   Lesson 8

---

2 ENGAGE Understanding the Remainder Theorem

When you divide $2x^3 + 4x^2 + 5$ by $x - 3$, you get a remainder of 95. If you evaluate the polynomial $2x^3 + 4x^2 + 5$ for $x = 3$, you get $2(3)^3 + 4(3)^2 + 5 = 2(27) + 4(9) + 5 = 95$. This is an illustration of the Remainder Theorem.

> **Remainder Theorem**
>
> If a polynomial $p(x)$ is divided by $x - a$, then the remainder r is $p(a)$.

You can use the Remainder Theorem to evaluate polynomials. To find $p(a)$, you divide the polynomial $p(x)$ by $x - a$ and find the remainder.

A shorthand method for dividing a polynomial by $x - a$ is called **synthetic division**. The process is similar to long division, but you work only with the coefficients. Here are the steps for using synthetic division to find the quotient $(2x^3 + 4x^2 + 5) \div (x - 3)$. In this case, $p(x) = 2x^3 + 4x^2 + 5$ and $a = 3$.

Step 1: Write the coefficients of $p(x)$ in the top row.

Step 2: Write the value of a to the left.

Step 3: Bring down the first coefficient.

Step 4: Multiply by a and place the result below the next coefficient, then add. Continue to the last column.

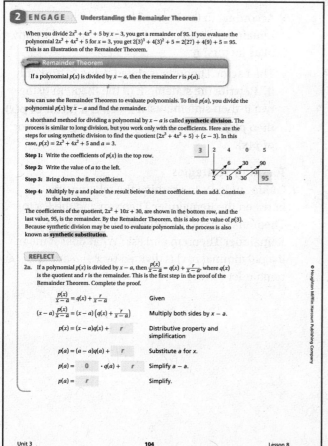

$$\begin{array}{c|cccc} 3 & 2 & 4 & 0 & 5 \\ & & 6 & 30 & 90 \\ & & \times3 & \times3 & \times3 \\ \hline & 2 & 10 & 30 & \boxed{95} \end{array}$$

The coefficients of the quotient, $2x^2 + 10x + 30$, are shown in the bottom row, and the last value, 95, is the remainder. By the Remainder Theorem, this is also the value of $p(3)$. Because synthetic division may be used to evaluate polynomials, the process is also known as **synthetic substitution**.

REFLECT

2a. If a polynomial $p(x)$ is divided by $x - a$, then $\frac{p(x)}{x-a} = q(x) + \frac{r}{x-a}$, where $q(x)$ is the quotient and r is the remainder. This is the first step in the proof of the Remainder Theorem. Complete the proof.

$$\frac{p(x)}{x-a} = q(x) + \frac{r}{x-a}$$ Given

$$(x-a)\frac{p(x)}{x-a} = (x-a)\left(q(x) + \frac{r}{x-a}\right)$$ Multiply both sides by $x - a$.

$$p(x) = (x-a)q(x) + \boxed{r}$$ Distributive property and simplification

$$p(a) = (a-a)q(a) + \boxed{r}$$ Substitute a for x.

$$p(a) = \boxed{0} \cdot q(a) + \boxed{r}$$ Simplify $a - a$.

$$p(a) = \boxed{r}$$ Simplify.

Unit 3   104   Lesson 8

© Houghton Mifflin Harcourt Publishing Company

2 ENGAGE

Questioning Strategies

- If a polynomial $p(x)$ is divided by $x - a$ and $p(a) \neq 0$, is the quotient a polynomial? Explain. **No; if $p(a) \neq 0$, then the quotient contains a term with the remainder $p(a) = r$ in the numerator and $x - a$ in the denominator.**

- In the synthetic division shown, if you replaced the 3 in the box at the upper left with a 4, what division problem would be represented by the synthetic division? **$(2x^3 + 4x^2 + 5) \div (x - 4)$**

- If you replaced the 3 in the box at the upper left in the synthetic division with a -3, what division problem would be represented by the synthetic division? **$(2x^3 + 4x^2 + 5) \div (x + 3)$**

Avoid Common Errors

Students may think that the entire bottom row of numbers in a synthetic division represents the quotient. For instance, in the problem shown, students may think that the quotient is $2x^3 + 10x^2 + 30x + 95$. Point out to students that if they were to multiply this "quotient" by the divisor, $x - 3$, they would get a polynomial of degree 4, which is obviously not the degree of the dividend. Students should understand that using a divisor of degree 1 results in a quotient whose degree is 1 less than the degree of the dividend. So, the quotient has 1 less term than the dividend does. In the bottom row of a synthetic division, then, all the numbers *except for the last one* are coefficients of the quotient, and the last number (which can be "boxed off" from the others) is the remainder.

3 EXAMPLE

Questioning Strategies

- A student filled in the bottom row of the synthetic division as 3, 29, -146, and -710. What error did the student make? **The student subtracted the second line of numbers from the top line of numbers instead of adding.**

- What number would you place in the box at the upper left to find $(3x^3 + 14x^2 - x + 20) \div (x - 7)$ using synthetic division? **7**

- What numbers would be placed along the top row to find $(2x^3 - 13x^2 + x - 25) \div (x + 5)$ using synthetic division? **2, -13, 1, and -25**

Differentiated Instruction

Interpersonal learners may benefit from taking turns with a partner filling in the missing numbers in a synthetic division problem. Students could be given the option to make a mistake on purpose to keep the other partner attentive to possible errors that can occur in the process.

Avoid Common Errors

Synthetic division involves copying and manipulating numbers in a format that is removed from the context of the polynomials, which increases the chance for error. Remind students to be careful to avoid errors like incorrectly copying coefficients, using the wrong sign for the number in the box, and subtracting the numbers in the second row instead of adding.

EXTRA EXAMPLE

Divide $6x^3 + 23x^2 - x + 12$ by $x + 4$ using synthetic division. **$6x^2 - x + 3$**

4 ENGAGE

Questioning Strategies

- If a number is divided by one of its factors, what is the remainder? Give an example. **0; 5 is a factor of 35, and $35 \div 5 = 7$ with no remainder.**

- According to the Factor Theorem, what is the remainder when a polynomial is divided by any of its factors? **0**

- The Factor Theorem is stated using "if and only if." Rewrite the statement of the theorem using two if-then statements. **If $x - a$ is a factor of $p(x)$, then $p(a) = 0$. If $p(a) = 0$, then $x - a$ is a factor of $p(x)$.**

Teaching Strategies

Guide students to examine the relationship between the Remainder Theorem and the Factor Theorem. Revisit the Engage section for the Remainder Theorem and ask: What does it mean if a polynomial $p(x)$ is divided by $x - a$ and the remainder r is 0?

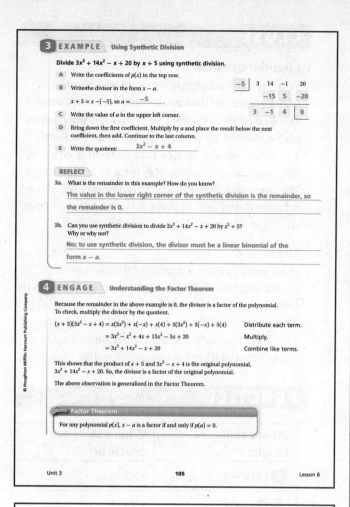

3 EXAMPLE Using Synthetic Division

Divide $3x^3 + 14x^2 - x + 20$ by $x + 5$ using synthetic division.

A Write the coefficients of $p(x)$ in the top row.

B Write the divisor in the form $x - a$.

$x + 5 = x - (-5)$, so $a = \underline{-5}$.

C Write the value of a in the upper left corner.

$$
\begin{array}{r|rrrr}
-5 & 3 & 14 & -1 & 20 \\
   &   & -15 & 5 & -20 \\
\hline
   & 3 & -1 & 4 & 0
\end{array}
$$

D Bring down the first coefficient. Multiply by a and place the result below the next coefficient, then add. Continue to the last column.

E Write the quotient: $\underline{3x^2 - x + 4}$

REFLECT

3a. What is the remainder in this example? How do you know?

The value in the lower right corner of the synthetic division is the remainder, so the remainder is 0.

3b. Can you use synthetic division to divide $3x^3 + 14x^2 - x + 20$ by $x^2 + 5$? Why or why not?

No; to use synthetic division, the divisor must be a linear binomial of the form $x - a$.

4 ENGAGE Understanding the Factor Theorem

Because the remainder in the above example is 0, the divisor is a factor of the polynomial. To check, multiply the divisor by the quotient.

$(x + 5)(3x^2 - x + 4) = x(3x^2) + x(-x) + x(4) + 5(3x^2) + 5(-x) + 5(4)$ Distribute each term.

$= 3x^3 - x^2 + 4x + 15x^2 - 5x + 20$ Multiply.

$= 3x^3 + 14x^2 - x + 20$ Combine like terms.

This shows that the product of $x + 5$ and $3x^2 - x + 4$ is the original polynomial, $3x^3 + 14x^2 - x + 20$. So, the divisor is a factor of the original polynomial.

The above observation is generalized in the Factor Theorem.

> **Factor Theorem**
>
> For any polynomial $p(x)$, $x - a$ is a factor if and only if $p(a) = 0$.

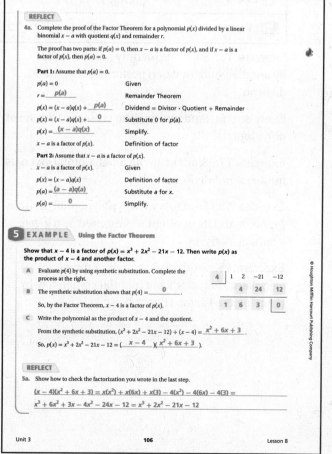

REFLECT

4a. Complete the proof of the Factor Theorem for a polynomial $p(x)$ divided by a linear binomial $x - a$ with quotient $q(x)$ and remainder r.

The proof has two parts: if $p(a) = 0$, then $x - a$ is a factor of $p(x)$, and if $x - a$ is a factor of $p(x)$, then $p(a) = 0$.

Part 1: Assume that $p(a) = 0$.

$p(a) = 0$	Given
$r = \underline{p(a)}$	Remainder Theorem
$p(x) = (x - a)q(x) + \underline{p(a)}$	Dividend = Divisor · Quotient + Remainder
$p(x) = (x - a)q(x) + \underline{0}$	Substitute 0 for $p(a)$.
$p(x) = \underline{(x - a)q(x)}$	Simplify.
$x - a$ is a factor of $p(x)$.	Definition of factor

Part 2: Assume that $x - a$ is a factor of $p(x)$.

$x - a$ is a factor of $p(x)$.	Given
$p(x) = (x - a)q(x)$	Definition of factor
$p(a) = \underline{(a - a)q(a)}$	Substitute a for x.
$p(a) = \underline{0}$	Simplify.

5 EXAMPLE Using the Factor Theorem

Show that $x - 4$ is a factor of $p(x) = x^3 + 2x^2 - 21x - 12$. Then write $p(x)$ as the product of $x - 4$ and another factor.

A Evaluate $p(4)$ by using synthetic substitution. Complete the process at the right.

$$
\begin{array}{r|rrrr}
4 & 1 & 2 & -21 & -12 \\
  &   & 4 & 24 & 12 \\
\hline
  & 1 & 6 & 3 & 0
\end{array}
$$

B The synthetic substitution shows that $p(4) = \underline{0}$.

So, by the Factor Theorem, $x - 4$ is a factor of $p(x)$.

C Write the polynomial as the product of $x - 4$ and the quotient.

From the synthetic substitution, $(x^3 + 2x^2 - 21x - 12) \div (x - 4) = \underline{x^2 + 6x + 3}$.

So, $p(x) = x^3 + 2x^2 - 21x - 12 = (\underline{x - 4})(\underline{x^2 + 6x + 3})$.

REFLECT

5a. Show how to check the factorization you wrote in the last step.

$(x - 4)(x^2 + 6x + 3) = x(x^2) + x(6x) + x(3) - 4(x^2) - 4(6x) - 4(3) =$

$x^3 + 6x^2 + 3x - 4x^2 - 24x - 12 = x^3 + 2x^2 - 21x - 12$

© Houghton Mifflin Harcourt Publishing Company

Notes

MATHEMATICAL PRACTICE
Highlighting the Standards

4 ENGAGE and its Reflect question offer an opportunity to address Mathematical Practice Standard 3 (Construct viable arguments and critique the reasoning of others). Students complete a proof of the Factor Theorem for a polynomial $p(x)$ divided by a linear binomial $x - a$ with quotient $q(x)$ and remainder r. Since the Factor Theorem is stated using the phrase "if and only if," students complete the proof for two parts. Students show that (1) if $p(a) = 0$, then $x - a$ is a factor of $p(x)$, and (2) if $x - a$ is a factor of $p(x)$, then $p(a) = 0$.

5 EXAMPLE

Questioning Strategies

- Could you show that $x^2 + 6x + 3$ is a factor of $p(x) = x^2 + 2x^2 - 21x - 12$ by using synthetic division to divide $p(x)$ by $x^2 + 6x + 3$? No, synthetic division can be used only when the divisor is a linear binomial of the form $x - a$.

- What does the Factor Theorem tell you if you use synthetic division to evaluate $p(-4)$? Since the remainder is not zero, $x + 4$ is not a factor of $p(x)$.

Technology

Students can use their graphing calculators and the Remainder Theorem to check their answer when performing synthetic division. Enter $Y_1 = p(x)$, and use the TABLE feature to find $p(a)$, which should match the remainder.

EXTRA EXAMPLE

Write $p(x) = x^3 + 2x^2 - 13x - 6$ as the product of $x - 3$ and another factor. $(x - 3)(x^2 + 5x + 2)$

Essential Question

What is the relationship between polynomial division and the Remainder and Factor Theorems?
The Remainder Theorem says that if a polynomial $p(x)$ is divided by a linear binomial of the form $x - a$, the remainder r of that division is equal to the result of evaluating $p(x)$ for $x = a$. The Factor Theorem says that for any polynomial $p(x)$, $x - a$ is a factor if and only if there is no remainder r (that is, $p(a) = 0$) when $p(x)$ is divided by $x - a$.

Summarize

Have students make a table with one row describing how polynomial division is related to the Remainder Theorem and another row describing how polynomial division is related to the Factor Theorem. For each theorem, provide at least two examples that illustrate the relationship.

PRACTICE

Where skills are taught	Where skills are practiced
1 EXAMPLE	EXS. 1–6
3 EXAMPLE	EXS. 7–12
5 EXAMPLE	EXS. 13–14

Exercise 15: Students identify an error made by another student when performing synthetic division.

Exercise 16: Students analyze closure of the set of polynomials.

Exercise 17: Students write a polynomial given its quotient and divisor.

Exercise 18: Students write a polynomial division problem and its quotient represented by a given synthetic division.

Exercise 19: Students use their graphing calculators to factor a polynomial completely by applying the Factor Theorem.

PRACTICE

Divide using long division.

1. $(5x^3 - 8x^2 - x - 4) \div (x - 2)$

$5x^2 + 2x + 3 + \dfrac{2}{x-2}$

2. $(6x^3 + 16x^2 + 3x - 2) \div (x + 1)$

$6x^2 + 10x - 7 + \dfrac{5}{x+1}$

3. $(x^3 + 7x^2 + 5x + 35) \div (x + 7)$

$x^2 + 5$

4. $(7x^3 + 9x^2 + 13) \div (x - 3)$

$7x^2 + 30x + 90 + \dfrac{283}{x-3}$

5. $(4x^2 - 6x + 6) \div (2x + 1)$

$2x - 4 + \dfrac{10}{2x+1}$

6. $(15x^3 + 16x^2 + x - 1) \div (3x + 2)$

$5x^2 + 2x - 1$

Divide using synthetic division.

7. $(4x^3 + 5x^2 + 2x + 16) \div (x + 2)$

$4x^2 - 3x + 8$

8. $(2x^3 - 22x^2 + 3x - 33) \div (x - 11)$

$2x^2 + 3$

9. $(4x^4 + 2x^2 - 3x - 9) \div (x + 1)$

$4x^3 - 4x^2 + 6x - 9$

10. $(6x^3 - 5x^2 - 3x + 2) \div \left(x - \dfrac{1}{2}\right)$

$6x^2 - 2x - 4$

11. $(3x^3 - x + 7) \div (x + 3)$

$3x^2 - 9x + 26 - \dfrac{71}{x+3}$

12. $(6x^3 - 4x^2 + 2x + 17) \div (x - 4)$

$6x^2 + 20x + 82 + \dfrac{345}{x-4}$

13. Show that $x + 2$ is a factor of $p(x) = x^4 + 2x^3 + 4x^2 + x - 14$. Then write $p(x)$ as the product of $x + 2$ and another factor.

Using synthetic substitution, $p(-2) = 0$, so by the Factor Theorem, $x + 2$ is a

factor of $p(x)$; $p(x) = (x + 2)(x^3 + 4x - 7)$.

14. a. Show that $x + 6$ is a factor of $p(x) = x^3 + 6x^2 - 16x - 96$. Then write $p(x)$ as the product of $x + 6$ and another factor.

Using synthetic substitution, $p(-6) = 0$, so by the Factor Theorem, $x + 6$ is a

factor of $p(x)$; $p(x) = (x + 6)(x^2 - 16)$.

b. Factor $p(x) = x^3 + 6x^2 - 16x - 96$ completely. That is, write $p(x)$ as a product of linear factors. Describe the strategy you used.

$x^2 - 16$ is a difference of squares, so $x^2 - 16 = (x + 4)(x - 4)$ and

$p(x) = (x + 6)(x + 4)(x - 4)$.

---

15. Error Analysis A student was asked to find the quotient $(4x^3 + x^2 + 2x + 1) \div (x + 2)$. The student's work is shown at right. Identify the student's error and provide the correct quotient.

The student should have used −2 in the upper

left corner of the synthetic division. The

correct quotient is $4x^2 - 7x + 16 - \dfrac{31}{x+2}$.

2	4	1	2	1
		8	18	40
	4	9	20	41

So, $(4x^3 + x^2 + 2x + 1) \div (x + 2) =$

$4x^2 + 9x + 20 + \dfrac{41}{x+2}$.

16. The set of polynomials is analogous to a set of numbers you have studied. To determine this set of numbers, consider the following questions about closure.

a. Under which operations is the set of polynomials closed?

addition, subtraction, and multiplication

b. Which set of the numbers discussed in Lesson 1-1 is closed under the same set of operations?

integers

17. When the polynomial $p(x)$ is divided by $x - 1$, the quotient is $-2x^2 + 3x + 5 + \dfrac{12}{x-1}$. What is $p(x)$? How did you find $p(x)$?

$p(x) = -2x^3 + 5x^2 + 2x + 7$; multiply the quotient by $x - 1$.

18. Determine the values of a, b, and c in the synthetic division shown at right. Then tell what polynomial division problem and quotient are represented by the synthetic division.

$a = 1$, $b = -5$, $c = 4$; $(x^3 - 2x^2 + 4x + 1) \div (x + 3)$

$= x^2 - 5x + 19 - \dfrac{56}{x+3}$.

−3	a	−2	c	1
		−3	15	−57
	1	b	19	−56

19. Use the Table feature of your graphing calculator to complete the table of values for $p(x) = x^4 - 2x^3 - 9x^2 + 2x + 8$. Use your results to factor $p(x)$ completely. Justify your answer.

$p(x) = (x + 2)(x + 1)(x - 1)(x - 4)$; the

zeros of $p(x)$ are $-2, -1, 1$, and 4, so by

the Factor Theorem, $x + 2$, $x + 1$,

$x - 1$, and $x - 4$ are factors of $p(x)$.

x	p(x)	x	p(x)
−4	240	1	0
−3	56	2	−24
−2	0	3	−40
−1	0	4	0
0	8	5	168

Graphing Factorable Polynomial Functions

Essential question: *How do you graph factorable polynomial functions?*

© Houghton Mifflin Harcourt Publishing Company

COMMON CORE Standards for Mathematical Content

CC.9-12.A.SSE.2 Use the structure of an expression to identify ways to rewrite it.

CC.9-12.A.APR.3 Identify zeros of polynomials when suitable factorizations are available, and use the zeros to construct a rough graph of the function defined by the polynomial.

CC.9-12.A.CED.2 Create equations in two ... variables to represent relationships between quantities; graph equations on coordinate axes with labels and scales.*

CC.9-12.F.IF.7 Graph functions expressed symbolically and show key features of the graph, by hand in simple cases and using technology for more complicated cases.*

CC.9-12.F.IF.7c Graph polynomial functions, identifying zeros when suitable factorizations are available, and showing end behavior.*

Also: CC.9-12.F.IF.2, CC.9-12.F.IF.9

Prerequisite
Determining end behavior, Lesson 3-4
Dividing polynomials, Lesson 3-8

Math Background
In previous lessons, students have examined the graphs of polynomial functions in the form $f(x) = a(x - h)^n + k$ and in standard form. Now that they know how to find the factors of a polynomial using the Remainder Theorem and Factor Theorem, they will graph factorable polynomial functions in factored form.

INTRODUCE

This lesson brings together many of the topics covered in the previous lessons of this unit. Start by drawing the graph of a general polynomial function on the board, and discuss the important features of the function, such as end behavior, zeros, maxima and minima. Ask students how they would determine the degree of the polynomial and what they could determine about the leading coefficient and the factors of the polynomial, based on the end behavior and zeros and using the Factor Theorem. Tell students they will learn to put all of these pieces together in order to graph polynomials that can be factored.

TEACH

1 EXPLORE

Questioning Strategies
- If you write all four polynomial functions in standard form, what do you notice about the degree of each polynomial? **Each polynomial has a degree of 4.**

- Looking at the table, how are the zeros of the functions related to the degrees of the functions? **Each polynomial has a degree of 4 and the total number of times zeros occur for each function is 4.**

Teaching Strategy
To review previous lessons, as well as reinforce new concepts learned in this example, draw the graph for part B on the board. Have students take turns identifying the parts of the graph that show what the function's end behavior is, where the function increases or decreases, where minimum or maximum values occur, and where zeros occur. Also have students keep count of the zeros, with separate totals for zeros at which the graph crosses the x-axis and zeros at which the graph is tangent to the x-axis.

continued

Name_____ Class_____ Date_____

3-9

Graphing Factorable Polynomial Functions

COMMON CORE

CC.9-12.A.SSE.2,
CC.9-12.A.APR.3,
CC.9-12.A.CED.2*,
CC.9-12.F.IF.7*,
CC.9-12.F.IF.7c*

Essential question: *How do you graph factorable polynomial functions?*

In this lesson you will sketch a variety of polynomial functions. When you make a sketch you do not need to put values on the *y*-axis. The emphasis is on showing the overall shape of the graph and its *x*-intercepts.

1 EXPLORE Investigating the Behavior of Graphs Near Zeros

Use a graphing calculator to graph each function. Sketch the graphs on the axes provided below. Then complete the table.

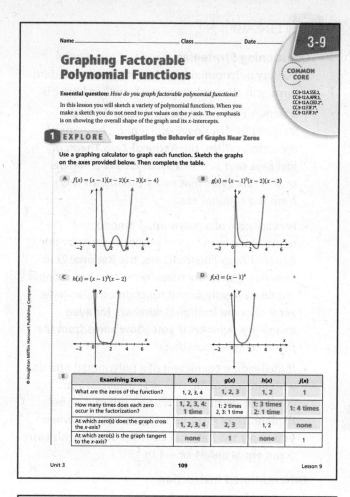

A $f(x) = (x-1)(x-2)(x-3)(x-4)$

B $g(x) = (x-1)^2(x-2)(x-3)$

C $h(x) = (x-1)^3(x-2)$

D $j(x) = (x-1)^4$

E

Examining Zeros	f(x)	g(x)	h(x)	j(x)
What are the zeros of the function?	1, 2, 3, 4	1, 2, 3	1, 2	1
How many times does each zero occur in the factorization?	1, 2, 3, 4: 1 time	1: 2 times 2, 3: 1 time	1: 3 times 2: 1 time	1: 4 times
At which zero(s) does the graph cross the *x*-axis?	1, 2, 3, 4	2, 3	1, 2	none
At which zero(s) is the graph tangent to the *x*-axis?	none	1	none	1

Unit 3   109   Lesson 9

REFLECT

1a. Based on your results, make a generalization about the number of times a zero occurs in the factorization of a function and whether the graph of the function crosses or is tangent to the *x*-axis at that zero.

The graph crosses the *x*-axis at the zero if the zero occurs an odd number of times.

The graph is tangent to the *x*-axis at the zero if the zero occurs an even number

of times.

The factored form of a polynomial is useful for graphing because the zeros can easily be determined. The degree of a polynomial in factored form is the sum of the degrees of the factors.

2 EXAMPLE Sketching the Graph of a Factored Polynomial Function

Sketch the graph of $f(x) = (x+2)^2(x+1)(x-2)(x-3)$.

A Determine the end behavior.

The degree of the polynomial is the sum of the degrees of the factors.

So, the degree of $f(x)$ is ___5___.

If you multiply the factors to write $f(x)$ standard form, $a_nx^n + a_{n-1}x^{n-1} + \cdots + a_1x + a_0$, the leading coefficient a_n is ___1___.

Because the degree is odd and the leading coefficient is positive,

$f(x) \to$ ___$+\infty$___ as $x \to +\infty$ and $f(x) \to$ ___$-\infty$___ as $x \to -\infty$.

B Describe the behavior at the zeros.

The zeros of the function are ___$-2, -1, 2,$ and 3___.

Identify how many times each zero occurs in the factorization.
-2 occurs 2 times; -1, 2, and 3 each occur 1 time.

Determine the zero(s) at which the graph crosses the *x*-axis.
-1, 2, and 3

Determine the zero(s) at which the graph is tangent to the *x*-axis.
-2

C Sketch the graph at right. Use the end behavior to determine where to start and end. You may find it helpful to plot a few points between the zeros to help get the general shape of the graph.

Unit 3   110   Lesson 9

Technology

Have students zoom in very closely around each zero and compare the shape of the graph with the graph of a function of the form $f(x) = x^n$. Students should notice that when they zoom in around a zero that occurs once in the factorization, the graph will look like the graph of $f(x) = x$ (a line). If the zero occurs twice, the graph will look like the graph of $f(x) = x^2$ (a parabola). If the zero occurs three times, the graph will look like the graph of $f(x) = x^3$. And if the zero occurs four times, the graph will look like the graph of $f(x) = x^4$.

2 EXAMPLE

Questioning Strategies

• What is $f(0)$? What does this tell you about the graph? **12; it is the graph's y-intercept.**

• How do you know that the graph is tangent to the x-axis at $x = -2$? **The zero -2 occurs twice in the factorization, and the graph of a polynomial function is tangent to the x-axis at the zero if the zero occurs an even number of times.**

Avoid Common Errors

To determine end behavior, students can multiply all factors, but they may make errors in the complex calculation. Point out to students that the end behavior is determined by the term with the greatest degree. If a function is written in factored form, then the highest-degree term is the product of all the first terms of the factors, as long as any repeated factors are considered individually. So, if $f(x) = (3x + 1)^2(x - 1) = (3x + 1)(3x + 1)(x - 1)$, then the leading term is $(3x)(3x)(x) = 9x^3$, and the polynomial has the same end behavior as $f(x) = x^3$.

The y-intercept can also be found by multiplying the constant terms in the factors, $(1)(1)(-1) = -1$.

EXTRA EXAMPLE

Sketch the graph of $f(x) = (x - 2)^2(x + 1)(x + 2)(x + 3)$. **The graph shows that $f(x) \longrightarrow -\infty$ as $x \longrightarrow -\infty$ and $f(x) \longrightarrow +\infty$ as $x \longrightarrow +\infty$, and has x-intercepts -3, -2, -1, and 2, crossing the x-axis at each negative x-intercept and tangent to the x-axis at the positive x-intercept.**

3 ENGAGE

Questioning Strategies

• For any polynomial function written in standard form, will all numbers of the form $\frac{c}{b}$, where c is a factor of the constant term a_0 and b is a factor of the leading coefficient a_n, be zeros of the function? **No, the Rational Zero Theorem just says that every rational zero is a number of this form, not that every number of this form is a rational zero.**

• Is every zero of a polynomial function represented in the set of numbers given by the Rational Zero Theorem? **No, the Rational Zero Theorem gives only those zeros that are rational numbers. A polynomial function can also have zeros that are irrational numbers (or even imaginary numbers if you allow zeros from the set of complex numbers).**

• If the leading coefficient of a polynomial function with integer coefficients is 1, what can you conclude about the function's rational zeros? Explain. **They must be integers because when you apply the Rational Zero Theorem in this case, b can equal only 1 or -1 in $\frac{c}{b}$.**

Differentiated Instruction

Analytical learners may benefit from answering the Reflect question and then testing their algebraic reasoning by working through the zeros given for the functions $f(x)$ and $g(x)$ in the Engage. Point out that in the algebraic conclusion of the Reflect question, the function $q(x)$ represents the quotient when $p(x)$ is divided by $x - \frac{c}{b}$.

REFLECT

2a. Can you determine how many times a zero occurs in the factorization of a polynomial function just by looking at the graph of the function? Explain.

No; you can tell only whether a zero occurs an even or odd number of times in the factorization.

3 ENGAGE   The Rational Zero Theorem

If you multiply the factors of the function $f(x) = (x - 1)(x - 2)(x - 3)(x - 4)$, you can write $f(x)$ in standard form as follows.

$$f(x) = x^4 - 10x^3 + 35x^2 - 50x + 24$$

So, $f(x)$ is a polynomial with integer coefficients that begins with the term x^4 and ends with the term 24. The zeros of $f(x)$ are 1, 2, 3, and 4. Notice that each zero is a factor of the constant term, 24.

Now consider the function $g(x) = (2x - 1)(3x - 2)(4x - 3)(5x - 4)$. If you multiply the factors, you can write $g(x)$ in standard form as follows.

$$g(x) = 120x^4 - 326x^3 + 329x^2 - 146x + 24$$

So, $g(x)$ is a polynomial with integer coefficients that begins with the term $120x^4$ and ends with the term 24. The zeros of $g(x)$ are $\frac{1}{2}$, $\frac{2}{3}$, $\frac{3}{4}$, and $\frac{4}{5}$. In this case, the numerator of each zero is a factor of the constant term, 24, and the denominator of each zero is a factor of the leading coefficient, 120.

These examples illustrate the Rational Zero Theorem.

> **Rational Zero Theorem**
>
> If $p(x) = a_n x^n + a_{n-1} x^{n-1} + \cdots + a_2 x^2 + a_1 x + a_0$ has integer coefficients, then every rational zero of $p(x)$ is a number of the following form:
>
> $$\frac{c}{b} = \frac{\text{factor of constant term } a_0}{\text{factor of leading coefficient } a_n}$$

REFLECT

3a. If $\frac{c}{b}$ is a rational zero of a polynomial function $p(x)$, explain why $bx - c$ must be a factor of the polynomial.

Since $p\left(\frac{c}{b}\right) = 0$, $x - \frac{c}{b}$ is a factor of $p(x)$ by the Factor Theorem.

So, $p(x) = \left(x - \frac{c}{b}\right)q(x)$ and $p(x) = \frac{b}{b}\left(x - \frac{c}{b}\right)q(x) = \frac{1}{b}(bx - c)q(x)$, which shows that $bx - c$ is a factor of $p(x)$.

---

4 EXAMPLE   Using the Rational Zero Theorem

Sketch the graph of $f(x) = x^3 - x^2 - 8x + 12$.

A Use the Rational Zero Theorem to identify the possible rational zeros of $f(x)$.

The constant term is 12.

Integer factors of the constant term are ± 1, ± 2, ± 3, ± 4, ± 6, and ± 12.

The leading coefficient is __1__

Integer factors of the leading coefficient are __± 1__

By the Rational Zero Theorem, the possible rational zeros of $f(x)$ are all rational numbers of the form $\frac{c}{b}$ where c is a factor of the constant term and b is a factor of the leading coefficient.

List all the possible rational zeros.

Possible rational zeros: __± 1, ± 2, ± 3, ± 4, ± 6, ± 12__

B Test the possible rational zeros until you find one that is an actual zero.

Use synthetic substitution to test 1 and 2.

1	1	-1	-8	12
		1	0	-8
	1	0	-8	4

2	1	-1	-8	12
		2	2	-12
	1	1	-6	0

So, __2__ is a zero, and therefore __$x - 2$__ is a factor of $f(x)$.

C Factor $f(x) = x^3 - x^2 - 8x + 12$ completely.

Use the results of the synthetic substitution to write $f(x)$ as the product of a linear factor and a quadratic factor.

$f(x) = (\underline{x - 2})(\underline{x^2 + x - 6})$

Factor the quadratic factor to write $f(x)$ as a product of linear factors.

$f(x) = (\underline{x - 2})(\underline{x - 2})(\underline{x + 3})$

Use the factorization to identify the other zeros of $f(x)$.

2 and -3

How many times does each zero occur in the factorization?

2 occurs two times; -3 occurs one time.

D Determine the end behavior.

$f(x) \to \underline{+\infty}$ as $x \to +\infty$ and $f(x) \to \underline{-\infty}$ as $x \to -\infty$.

E Sketch the graph of the function on the coordinate plane at right.

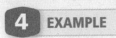

4 EXAMPLE

Questioning Strategies

- Since the Rational Zero Theorem can generate many possible rational zeros, what rule of thumb could you follow to determine which possible zero(s) to test first? **You can first test possible zeros that are integers because the function will be easier to evaluate for those numbers.**

- Describe the steps to find the other zeros of $f(x) = x^3 - x^2 - 8x + 12$ if the possible rational zero -3 is tested first. **The results of the synthetic substitution can be used to write the product $(x + 3)(x^2 - 4x + 4)$, which can then be factored as $(x + 3)(x - 2)(x - 2)$. The result is the same: the zeros are -3 and 2, with 2 occurring twice.**

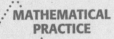

MATHEMATICAL PRACTICE

Highlighting the Standards

4 EXAMPLE and its Reflect questions offer an opportunity to address Mathematical Practice Standard 8 (Look for and express regularity in repeated reasoning). Students use the Rational Zero Theorem to identify a list of possible rational zeros for a polynomial function of degree three and then test possible zeros until one actual zero is found. Students identify one linear factor and then use the results of the synthetic substitution to rewrite the polynomial as the product of a linear factor and a quadratic factor. They then factor the quadratic factor, identify the zeros and end behavior, and graph the function. For functions of greater degree, the process can be repeated by testing for other actual zeros from the list of possible rational zeros generated by the Rational Zero Theorem. Another approach is to use the Rational Zero Theorem to identify one actual zero and its related linear factor, rewrite the polynomial as a product of that linear factor and another polynomial factor, and repeat the process for the other polynomial factor. (The second approach greatly reduces the number of possible rational zeros at each stage.)

EXTRA EXAMPLE

For the polynomial $p(x) = 2x^3 - 7x^2 + 2x + 3$, use the Rational Zero Theorem to identify the possible rational zeros; then, factor the polynomial completely, and sketch the function's graph. Possible zeros: $\pm 1, \pm 3, \pm\frac{1}{2}, \pm\frac{3}{2}$; $p(x) = (x - 1)(x - 3)(2x + 1)$; the graph shows that $f(x) \rightarrow -\infty$ as $x \rightarrow -\infty$ and $f(x) \rightarrow +\infty$ as $x \rightarrow +\infty$, and has x-intercepts $1, 3,$ and $-\frac{1}{2}$, crossing the x-axis at each x-intercept.

CLOSE

Essential Question

How do you graph factorable polynomial functions?
Factor the polynomial. You can use the Rational Zero Theorem to help identify possible rational zeros and factors. Once the polynomial is factored, identify the zeros. Plot the zeros on the coordinate plane, identify end behavior, and sketch the graph.

Summarize

Have students make a flow chart illustrating the process of graphing a factorable polynomial function. Choose one polynomial function from Practice Exercises 5–8 and describe how each step would be applied.

PRACTICE

Where skills are taught	Where skills are practiced
2 EXAMPLE	EXS. 1–4
4 EXAMPLE	EXS. 5–7

Exercise 8: Given the zeros of a polynomial function, students write the function.

REFLECT

4a. How did you determine where the graph crosses the *x*-axis and where it is tangent to the *x*-axis?

The graph crosses at any zero that occurs an odd number of times in the
factorization (i.e., at $x = -3$) and is tangent at any zero that occurs an even
number of times (i.e., at $x = 2$).

4b. How did factoring the polynomial help you graph the function?

By setting each factor equal to zero and solving, you can identify all the zeros of
the function, which are the *x*-intercepts of the function's graph.

4c. How did using the Rational Zero Theorem to find one zero help you find
the other zeros?

Using synthetic substitution to find one zero gives the coefficients of the
quadratic factor, which can easily be factored into two linear factors.

PRACTICE

Sketch the graph of each factored polynomial function.

1. $f(x) = (x - 3)(x + 2)^2$

2. $g(x) = (x + 1)^6$

3. $h(x) = (x + 3)(x + 1)^2(x - 1)$

4. $j(x) = (x + 2)^3(x - 3)^2$

Use the Rational Zero Theorem to identify the possible zeros of each function.
Then factor the polynomial completely. Finally, identify the actual zeros and
sketch the graph of the function.

5. $f(x) = x^3 - 2x^2 - x + 2$

Possible zeros:
$\pm 1, \pm 2$

Factored form of function:
$f(x) = (x + 1)(x - 1)(x - 2)$

Actual zeros:
$-1, 1, 2$

6. $g(x) = x^3 - 2x^2 - 11x + 12$

Possible zeros:
$\pm 1, \pm 2, \pm 3, \pm 4, \pm 6, \pm 12$

Factored form of function:
$g(x) = (x + 3)(x - 1)(x - 4)$

Actual zeros:
$-3, 1, 4$

7. $h(x) = 2x^4 - 5x^3 - 11x^2 + 20x + 12$

Possible zeros:
$\pm\frac{1}{2}, \pm 1, \pm\frac{3}{2}, \pm 2, \pm 3, \pm 4, \pm 6, \pm 8, \pm 12$

Factored form of function:
$h(x) = (x + 2)(2x + 1)(x - 2)(x - 3)$

Actual zeros:
$-2, -\frac{1}{2}, 2, 3$

8. The polynomial function $p(x)$ has degree 3, and its zeros are −3, 4, and 6. What
do you think is the equation of $p(x)$? Do you think there could be more than one
possibility? Explain.

$p(x) = (x + 3)(x - 4)(x - 6)$; any constant multiple of $p(x)$ will also have degree 3
and the same zeros, so the equation could be any function of the form
$p(x) = a(x + 3)(x - 4)(x - 6)$ where $a \neq 0$.

Finding Zeros of Polynomial Functions

Essential question: *How can you find zeros of polynomial functions?*

COMMON Standards for
CORE Mathematical Content

CC.9-12.N.CN.9(+) Know the Fundamental Theorem of Algebra; show that it is true for quadratic polynomials.

CC.9-12.A.SSE.2 Use the structure of an expression to identify ways to rewrite it.

Also: CC.9-12.N.CN.8(+)

Prerequisites
Recognizing special products, Lesson 3-6
Expanding powers of binomials, Lesson 3-7
Finding rational zeros, Lesson 3-9

Math Background
In Lesson 3-9, students used the Rational Zero Theorem to identify possible rational zeros for polynomial functions written in standard form and then used synthetic substitution to test for actual zeros. An alternative method of finding zeros is to factor a polynomial and then set each factor equal to 0. Factoring a polynomial is the reverse of multiplying its factors, so the skills that students learned in Lessons 3-6 and 3-7, such as finding special products and expanding powers of binomials using the Binomial Theorem, are useful in this lesson.

INTRODUCE

Review the special product rules and the Binomial Theorem. Explain that rules for special products and the Binomial Theorem can be applied in reverse to factor polynomials. Write some polynomials on the board and ask students to identify them as sum-and-difference, square of a binomial, cube of a binomial, or other expanded power of a binomial. Then, have them work backward to try to figure out what factors were multiplied to get each special product.

TEACH

1 EXAMPLE

Questioning Strategies

- Will the coefficients in the expansion of $f(x) = (2x + 5)^3$ exactly match the numbers 1, 3, 3, and 1 in row 3 of Pascal's Triangle? Explain. **No; the numbers from Pascal's Triangle get multiplied by powers of 2 and 5: the expansion of $f(x) = (2x + 5)^3$ is $f(x) = 8x^3 + 60x^2 + 150x + 125$.**

- Can you use the Binomial Theorem to find the zeros of $f(x) = 8x^3 + 60x^2 + 150x + 125$? If so, explain how. **Yes; examining the relationship between the numbers 1, 3, 3, and 1 from row 3 of Pascal's triangle and the coefficients 8, 60, 150, and 125 shows that $8 = 2^3$, $60 = 3 \cdot 2^2 \cdot 5$, $150 = 3 \cdot 2 \cdot 5^2$, and $125 = 5^3$. So, $f(x) = (2x + 5)^3$ and the only zero of $f(x)$ is $-\frac{5}{2}$, which occurs 3 times.**

Teaching Strategy
To gain facility in recognizing polynomials that are special products, students might benefit from some sort of game or matching exercise between a set of polynomials in standard form and another equivalent set in factored form.

Avoid Common Errors
When finding the zeros of $f(x) = (x + 1)^3$, students may say the zero is 1 because they are accustomed to thinking that a is a zero when $x - a$ is a factor without realizing that $x + 1$ needs to be in the form of a difference: $x - (-1)$. Remind students to check whether $f(x) = 0$: in this case, $f(-1) = 0$ but $f(1) = 8$.

continued

Name_____ Class_____ Date_____

Finding Zeros of Polynomial Functions

COMMON CORE
CC.9-12.N.CN.9(+),
CC.9-12.A.SSE.2

Essential question: *How can you find zeros of polynomial functions?*

So far, you have found only rational zeros of polynomial functions. In this lesson you will review the various techniques for finding rational zeros and employ those techniques on polynomial functions whose zeros may not all be rational numbers.

1 EXAMPLE Using the Binomial Theorem to Find Zeros

Find the zeros of $f(x) = x^3 + 3x^2 + 3x + 1$ and write the function in factored form.

A Write the coefficients of the terms of the polynomial.

1, 3, 3, 1

How are these coefficients related to Pascal's Triangle?

They are the values from row 3 of Pascal's Triangle.

Identify the corresponding binomial expansion.

$(a + b)^3 = a^3 + 3a^2b + 3ab^2 + b^3$

B Use the binomial expansion to rewrite the function in the form $(a + b)^n$.

$f(x) = \left(x + 1 \right)^3$

C Identify the zero(s) of the function.

The only zero of $f(x)$ is -1.

How many times does each zero occur? Explain.

The only zero, -1, occurs 3 times because the factor $x + 1$ occurs 3 times.

So, the zero of $f(x)$ is -1.

The factored form of $f(x)$ is $f(x) = (x + 1)^3$.

REFLECT

1a. Can you always use the Binomial Theorem in this way to find the zeros of a polynomial function? Explain.

No, but the Binomial Theorem is useful if the coefficients of the terms of

the polynomial correspond to a row of Pascal's Triangle.

1b. Without actually graphing, describe the graph of $f(x)$.

The graph has the same shape as the graph of $y = x^3$ but is translated 1 unit left.

Unit 3   115   Lesson 10

2 EXAMPLE Using the Rational Zero Theorem to Find Zeros

Find the zeros of $g(x) = x^3 - x^2 - 2x + 2$ and write the function in factored form.

A Use the Rational Zero Theorem to identify possible rational zeros.

Integer factors of the constant term are $\pm1, \pm2$.

Integer factors of the leading coefficient are ±1.

By the Rational Zero Theorem, the possible rational zeros of $g(x)$ are all rational numbers of the form $\frac{c}{b}$ where c is a factor of the constant term and b is a factor of the leading coefficient.

Possible rational zeros are $\pm1, \pm2$.

B Use synthetic substitution to test each possible rational zero to identify any actual rational zeros.

The function $g(x)$ has one rational zero, which is 1.

So, $x - 1$ is a factor of $g(x)$.

C Use synthetic division to identify the other factors of the polynomial.

Divide $g(x)$ by $x - 1$. Complete the synthetic division at right.

$$\begin{array}{r|rrrr} 1 & 1 & -1 & -2 & 2 \\ & & 1 & 0 & -2 \\ \hline & 1 & 0 & -2 & 0 \end{array}$$

The quotient is $1 x^2 + 0 x - 2$.

Write $g(x)$ as a product of two factors.

$g(x) = (x - 1)(x^2 - 2)$

The zeros of the quadratic factor are $\pm\sqrt{2}$.

Write the quadratic factor as a product of two linear factors.

$(x - \sqrt{2})(x + \sqrt{2})$

D Identify the zeros of the function.

The zeros of $g(x)$ are $1, \sqrt{2}, -\sqrt{2}$.

E Write the function in factored form.

The factored form is $g(x) = (x - 1)(x - \sqrt{2})(x + \sqrt{2})$.

REFLECT

2a. When you used the Rational Zero Theorem, did your list of possible zeros include all of the actual zeros of $g(x)$? Why or why not?

No; only the rational zero, 1, is in the list. The other zeros, $\pm\sqrt{2}$, are irrational,

so they are not included.

2b. How can you check that you wrote the factored form of $g(x)$ correctly?

Multiply the factors; the product should be the original function $g(x)$.

Unit 3   116   Lesson 10

EXTRA EXAMPLE
Find the zeros of
$g(x) = x^6 + 6x^5 + 15x^4 + 20x^3 + 15x^2 + 6x + 1$ and write the function in factored form. -1, which occurs six times; $g(x) = (x + 1)^6$

2 EXAMPLE

Questioning Strategies

• Explain how the Rational Zero Theorem can help you find zeros that are not rational. The Rational Zero Theorem can be used to identify rational zeros and the corresponding factors. Then, other methods, such as the quadratic formula, may be used to find other zeros that are irrational or imaginary.

• Can you use the Rational Zero Theorem to help you write a polynomial function in factored form if the function has no rational zeros? No, the Rational Zero Theorem can only be used to find rational zeros.

Teaching Strategy
To reinforce how to find both rational and irrational zeros, have students create their own polynomial functions that have both rational and irrational zeros. To do this, have students write one factor of the form $x - a$, where a is rational, and another factor of the form $x^2 + b$ where $b > 0$. Have them multiply these factors to obtain a polynomial in standard form. Students can exchange their polynomial functions and use the Rational Zero Theorem to find all the zeros.

EXTRA EXAMPLE
Find the zeros of $g(x) = x^3 - x^2 - 7x + 7$ and write the function in factored form. $1, \sqrt{7}, -\sqrt{7}$; $g(x) = (x - 1)(x - \sqrt{7})(x + \sqrt{7})$

3 EXAMPLE

Questioning Strategies

• Could you use a special product to find the zeros of $h(x) = 25x^4 + 20x^2 + 4$? If so, explain how. Yes; the function can be rewritten as the square of a binomial: $h(x) = (5x^2 + 2)^2$. Then find the zeros of $5x^2 + 2$.

• If you do not recognize the form of a function as a special product, is it still possible to find the zeros of the function? Yes, you can still use other factoring techniques and the Rational Zero Theorem to write the function in factored form.

Avoid Common Errors
When using special products to factor polynomial functions, remind students to write the exponents correctly. For example, since the difference of two squares is given by $a^2 - b^2 = (a + b)(a - b)$, students may factor $x^4 - 16$ as $(x + 4)(x - 4)$ rather than as $(x^2 + 4)(x^2 - 4)$.

⋰ MATHEMATICAL   **Highlighting**
⋱ PRACTICE   **the Standards**

3 EXAMPLE and its Reflect questions offer an opportunity to address Mathematical Practice Standard 7 (Look for and make use of structure). In previous lessons, students learned to multiply polynomials in a more efficient way by using rules for special products. Specific patterns were identified in the structure of some polynomial products: the difference of two squares, the square of a binomial, and the cube of a binomial. In this example, students recognize that the structure of the polynomial $x^4 - 16$ is the difference of two squares.

EXTRA EXAMPLE
Find the zeros of $h(x) = x^4 - 256$ and write the function in factored form. $-4i, 4i, -4, 4$; $h(x) = (x + 4i)(x - 4i)(x + 4)(x - 4)$

3 EXAMPLE Using Special Products to Find Zeros

Find the zeros of $h(x) = x^4 - 16$ and write the function in factored form.

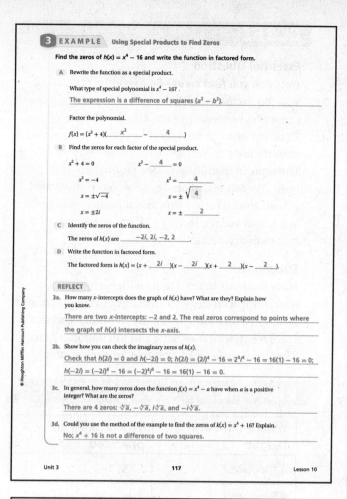

A. Rewrite the function as a special product.

What type of special polynomial is $x^4 - 16$?

The expression is a difference of squares ($a^2 - b^2$).

Factor the polynomial.

$f(x) = (x^2 + 4)(\underline{\quad x^2 \quad} - \underline{\quad 4 \quad})$

B. Find the zeros for each factor of the special product.

$x^2 + 4 = 0$ $x^2 - \underline{4} = 0$

$x^2 = -4$ $x^2 = \underline{4}$

$x = \pm\sqrt{-4}$ $x = \pm\sqrt{\underline{4}}$

$x = \pm 2i$ $x = \pm \underline{2}$

C. Identify the zeros of the function.

The zeros of $h(x)$ are $\underline{\quad -2i,\ 2i,\ -2,\ 2 \quad}$.

D. Write the function in factored form.

The factored form is $h(x) = (x + \underline{2i})(x - \underline{2i})(x + \underline{2})(x - \underline{2})$.

REFLECT

3a. How many x-intercepts does the graph of $h(x)$ have? What are they? Explain how you know.

There are two x-intercepts: −2 and 2. The real zeros correspond to points where the graph of $h(x)$ intersects the x-axis.

3b. Show how you can check the imaginary zeros of $h(x)$.

Check that $h(2i) = 0$ and $h(-2i) = 0$; $h(2i) = (2i)^4 - 16 = 2^4 i^4 - 16 = 16(1) - 16 = 0$; $h(-2i) = (-2i)^4 - 16 = (-2)^4 i^4 - 16 = 16(1) - 16 = 0$.

3c. In general, how many zeros does the function $j(x) = x^4 - a$ have when a is a positive integer? What are the zeros?

There are 4 zeros: $\sqrt[4]{a}$, $-\sqrt[4]{a}$, $i\sqrt[4]{a}$, and $-i\sqrt[4]{a}$.

3d. Could you use the method of the example to find the zeros of $k(x) = x^4 + 16$? Explain.

No; $x^4 + 16$ is not a difference of two squares.

© Houghton Mifflin Harcourt Publishing Company

4 ENGAGE Understanding the Fundamental Theorem of Algebra

The table summarizes the functions from the three examples. Notice that the number of zeros equals the degree of the polynomial, as long as repeated zeros are counted multiple times. Irrational and imaginary zeros must also be taken into account.

Function	Degree	Zeros	Number of Zeros
$f(x) = x^3 + 3x^2 + 3x + 1$	3	−1 (occurs 3 times)	3
$g(x) = x^3 - x^2 - 2x + 2$	3	$1, \sqrt{2}, -\sqrt{2}$	3
$h(x) = x^4 - 16$	4	$-2i, 2i, -2, 2$	4

The table can help you understand the Fundamental Theorem of Algebra.

> **Fundamental Theorem of Algebra**
>
> If $f(x)$ is a polynomial of degree n, then $f(x)$ has at least one zero in the set of complex numbers.
>
> **Corollary:** If $f(x)$ is a polynomial of degree n, then $f(x)$ has exactly n zeros, provided that repeated zeros are counted multiple times.

REFLECT

4a. How does the quadratic formula prove the Fundamental Theorem of Algebra for the case $n = 2$?

The formula gives two real zeros if $b^2 - 4ac > 0$, one real zero if $b^2 - 4ac = 0$, and two complex zeros if $b^2 - 4ac < 0$. In every case, there is at least one zero in the set of complex numbers.

4b. If you apply the Fundamental Theorem of Algebra to any polynomial function $f(x)$, you can conclude that $f(x)$ has one complex zero z_1. So, by the Factor Theorem, $x - z_1$ is a factor of $f(x)$. This means $f(x) = (x - z_1)q_1(x)$ where $q_1(x)$ is a polynomial whose degree is one less than the degree of $f(x)$. Explain how you can use this idea and repeatedly apply the Fundamental Theorem of Algebra to prove the corollary of the theorem.

The quotient $q_1(x)$ is a polynomial function, so by the Fundamental Theorem of Algebra, $q_1(x)$ has one complex zero z_2. So, $f(x) = (x - z_1)(x - z_2)q_2(x)$ where $q_2(x)$ is a polynomial whose degree is two less than the degree of $f(x)$. You can continue this process until $q_n(x)$ is a factor of degree 1 and n complex zeros of $f(x)$ have been identified.

4c. Can you conclude that $f(x) = x^5 - 4x^2 + \frac{1}{x}$ has 5 zeros? Why or why not?

No; the Fundamental Theorem of Algebra applies only to polynomials.

© Houghton Mifflin Harcourt Publishing Company

Questioning Strategies

- Suppose that a polynomial function has two zeros, $\frac{1}{2}$ and $-\frac{1}{2}$. Do these zeros satisfy the requirement of the Fundamental Theorem of Algebra which states that a polynomial $f(x)$ of degree n has at least one zero in the set of complex numbers? Yes, $\frac{1}{2}$ and $-\frac{1}{2}$ are real numbers. Complex numbers are numbers of the form $a + bi$, where a and b are real numbers, and real numbers are complex numbers for which the value of b is 0. So, all real numbers are complex numbers, and $\frac{1}{2}$ and $-\frac{1}{2}$ satisfy the requirement.

- A polynomial function of degree 4 has only the zeros -2, 3, and 4. How can this be true given the requirement of the Corollary of the Fundamental Theorem of Algebra which states that a polynomial of degree n has exactly n zeros? One of the zeros must occur twice. The corollary requires that repeated zeros be counted multiple times.

Technology

Encourage students to use their graphing calculators to check their factorizations of polynomials. Have students enter the polynomial functions into their graphing calculators and display the graphs so they can see the points where the graph crosses or is tangent to the x-axis. (Remind students that they may have to adjust window settings.)

By examining graphs, students should see that if a polynomial function of degree n has n different real zeros, then its graph crosses the x-axis at n different points, and that if the graph crosses or is tangent to the x-axis at fewer than n points, then some zeros are repeated.

Essential Question

How can you find zeros of polynomial functions? You can factor the polynomial to find zeros. For some polynomials, you can use the Binomial Theorem or rules for special products to help you identify factors. You can also use the Rational Zero Theorem to identify possible rational zeros and then you can test them to see whether they are actual zeros. If one factor has degree 2, you can use the quadratic formula to find irrational or imaginary zeros.

Summarize

Have students make a table with each row describing a strategy for finding zeros of polynomial functions, including using the Binomial Theorem, rules for special products, and the Rational Zero Theorem. Include an example for each strategy.

PRACTICE

Where skills are taught	Where skills are practiced
1 EXAMPLE	EXS. 1–3
2 EXAMPLE	EXS. 4, 5
3 EXAMPLE	EXS. 6–8

Exercise 9: Given the zeros of a polynomial function, students write the function.

Exercise 10: Students use the corollary of the Fundamental Theorem of Algebra to determine the number of zeros for a function $p(x)$ that is the product of two polynomials whose degrees are given.

PRACTICE

Find the zeros of the function and write the function in factored form.

1. $f(x) = x^4 + 4x^3 + 6x^2 + 4x + 1$

The zeros of $f(x)$ are

  -1 (occurs 4 times) .

The factored form is

  $f(x) = \underline{\quad (x+1)^4 \quad}$.

2. $g(x) = x^3 - 3x^2 + 3x - 1$

The zeros of $g(x)$ are

  1 (occurs 3 times) .

The factored form is

  $g(x) = \underline{\quad (x-1)^3 \quad}$.

3. $f(x) = x^5 + 5x^4 + 10x^3 + 10x^2 + 5x + 1$

The zeros of $f(x)$ are

  -1 (occurs 5 times) .

The factored form is

  $f(x) = \underline{\quad (x+1)^5 \quad}$.

4. $g(x) = x^3 - x^2 - 3x + 3$

The zeros of $g(x)$ are

  $1, \sqrt{3}, -\sqrt{3}$.

The factored form is

  $g(x) = \underline{\quad (x-1)(x+\sqrt{3})(x-\sqrt{3}) \quad}$.

5. $f(x) = x^3 + 2x^2 - 5x - 10$

The zeros of $f(x)$ are

  $-2, \sqrt{5}, -\sqrt{5}$.

The factored form is

  $f(x) = \underline{\quad (x+2)(x+\sqrt{5})(x-\sqrt{5}) \quad}$.

6. $g(x) = x^4 - 81$

The zeros of $g(x)$ are

  $-3i, 3i, -3, 3$.

The factored form is

  $g(x) = \underline{\quad (x+3i)(x-3i)(x+3)(x-3) \quad}$.

7. $f(x) = x^4 - 8x^2 + 16$

The zeros of $f(x)$ are

  $2, -2$ (each occurs 2 times) .

The factored form is

  $f(x) = \underline{\quad (x+2)^2(x-2)^2 \quad}$.

8. $g(x) = 16x^4 - 1$

The zeros of $g(x)$ are

  $\frac{1}{2}i, -\frac{1}{2}i, \frac{1}{2}, -\frac{1}{2}$.

The factored form is

  $g(x) = \underline{\quad (2x+i)(2x-i)(2x+1)(2x-1) \quad}$.

9. A polynomial function has exactly four zeros: $2, -2, \sqrt{3},$ and $-\sqrt{3}$. Use standard form to write the simplest function with these zeros. Describe your method.

  $f(x) = x^4 - 7x^2 + 12$; use the zeros to write the factors, then multiply the factors:

  $f(x) = (x-2)(x+2)(x-\sqrt{3})(x+\sqrt{3}) = (x^2-4)(x^2-3) = x^4 - 7x^2 + 12.$

10. Suppose $p(x)$ is the product of a polynomial of degree 5 and a cubic polynomial. How many zeros does $p(x)$ have? Explain.

  8; $p(x)$ has degree $5 + 3 = 8$, so it has 8 zeros by the Fundamental Theorem of

  Algebra.

FOCUS ON MODELING
Modeling with Polynomial Functions

Essential question: *How can you use polynomial functions to model and solve real-world problems?*

© Houghton Mifflin Harcourt Publishing Company

COMMON CORE   Standards for Mathematical Content

The following standards are addressed in this lesson. (An asterisk indicates that a standard is also a Modeling standard.) For more detailed information, see each section of the lesson.

Algebra: CC.9-12.A.SSE.1*, CC.9-12.A.SSE.1a*, CC.9-12.A.APR.1, CC.9-12.A.CED.1*, CC.9-12.A.CED.2*, CC.9-12.A.CED.3*, CC.9-12.A.REI.11

Functions: CC.9-12.F.IF.4*, CC.9-12.F.IF.5*, CC.9-12.F.IF.7*, CC.9-12.F.IF.7c*, CC.9-12.F.BF.1*, CC.9-12.F.BF.1a*

Prerequisites

- Graphing polynomial functions, Lessons 3-1, 3-2, and 3-3

- Adding, subtracting, and multiplying polynomial expressions, Lessons 3-5 and 3-6

- Solving polynomial equations, Lessons 3-9 and 3-10

Math Background

Students write a polynomial function for the volume of a box. They use the Rational Zero Theorem to find the dimensions of the box and analyze the graph of the function to find the maximum volume of the box.

INTRODUCE

Point out that volume models can be used for a wide range of real-world situations, from engineering and manufacturing to everyday applications like mailing a package.

TEACH

1 Write a volume function.

Standards
CC.9-12.A.SSE.1 Interpret expressions that represent a quantity in terms of its context.*

CC.9-12.A.SSE.1a Interpret parts of an expression, such as ... factors ...*

CC.9-12.A.CED.2 Create equations in two ... variables to represent relationships between quantities ...*

CC.9-12.A.F.BF.1 Write a function that describes a relationship between two quantities.*

CC.9-12.F.BF.1a Determine an explicit expression ... from a context.*

Questioning Strategies

- How is the expression for the height of the box related to expressions for the length and the width of the box? The expression for the height is x, which is the amount cut from each end of the 10-inch length, represented as $10 - 2x$, and from each end of the 8-inch width, represented as $8 - 2x$.

- What would the rule for $V(x)$ be if the piece of cardboard were a square with side length 8 inches? $V(x) = x(8 - 2x)^2$

2 Determine the domain of the volume function.

Standards
CC.9-12.A.CED.3 Represent constraints by ... inequalities ...*

CC.9-12.F.IF.5 Relate the domain of a function ... to the quantitative relationship it describes.*

Questioning Strategies

- Why do the constraints on x for the length and width not simply require that x be nonnegative? The constraints on x describe those values of x that make the expressions for the length and width result in nonnegative values.

- How can you generalize from this situation to finding the domain for any volume function? Since length, height, and width will always be nonnegative, the domain of a volume function will always require that the independent variable takes on only values that make each dimension nonnegative.

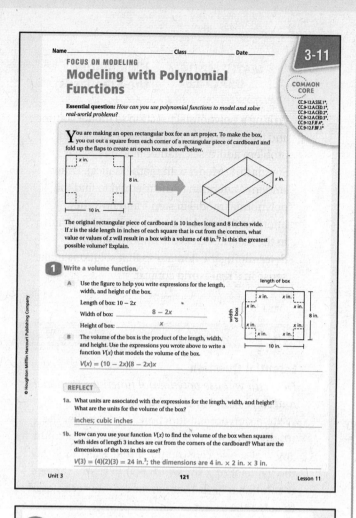

Name_____ Class_____ Date_____

FOCUS ON MODELING

Modeling with Polynomial Functions

Essential question: *How can you use polynomial functions to model and solve real-world problems?*

COMMON CORE

CC-12.A.SSE.1*
CC.9-12.A.CED.1*
CC.9-12.A.CED.2*
CC.9-12.A.CED.3*
CC.9-12.F.IF.4*
CC.9-12.F.BF.1*

You are making an open rectangular box for an art project. To make the box, you cut out a square from each corner of a rectangular piece of cardboard and fold up the flaps to create an open box as shown below.

The original rectangular piece of cardboard is 10 inches long and 8 inches wide. If x is the side length in inches of each square that is cut from the corners, what value or values of x will result in a box with a volume of 48 in.^{3}? Is this the greatest possible volume? Explain.

1 **Write a volume function.**

A Use the figure to help you write expressions for the length, width, and height of the box.

Length of box: $10 - 2x$

Width of box: $\underline{8 - 2x}$

Height of box: $\underline{x}$

B The volume of the box is the product of the length, width, and height. Use the expressions you wrote above to write a function $V(x)$ that models the volume of the box.

$V(x) = (10 - 2x)(8 - 2x)x$

REFLECT

1a. What units are associated with the expressions for the length, width, and height? What are the units for the volume of the box?

inches; cubic inches

1b. How can you use your function $V(x)$ to find the volume of the box when squares with sides of length 3 inches are cut from the corners of the cardboard? What are the dimensions of the box in this case?

$V(3) = (4)(2)(3) = 24$ in.^{3}; the dimensions are 4 in. × 2 in. × 3 in.

© Houghton Mifflin Harcourt Publishing Company

---

2 **Determine the domain of the volume function.**

A To find the domain of the volume function, use the fact that each dimension of the box must be positive.

Find the constraint on the values of x for the length of the box.

$10 - 2x > 0$ Write an inequality stating that the length of the box must be positive.

$\underline{x < 5}$ Solve the inequality.

Find the constraint on the values of x for the width of the box.

$\underline{8 - 2x} > 0$ Write an inequality stating that the width of the box must be positive.

$\underline{x < 4}$ Solve the inequality.

Find the constraint on the values of x for the height of the box.

$\underline{x > 0}$ Write an inequality stating that the height of the box must be positive.

B For a value of x to be in the domain of $V(x)$, it must simultaneously satisfy all three of the inequalities you wrote.

So, the domain of $V(x)$ is all x such that $\underline{0} < x < \underline{4}$.

REFLECT

2a. What would happen to the volume if x took on either of the endpoint values in the domain inequality? Explain why this makes sense in the context of the problem.

In either case, the volume would be 0. When $x = 0$, no cuts are made and the box would have a height of 0. When $x = 4$, the box would have a width of 0.

2b. Explain why the domain of $V(x)$ is not $0 < x < 5$.

Although values of x between 4 and 5 satisfy the constraint for the length of the box, they do not satisfy the constraint for the width, so they must be excluded.

3 **Write and solve an equation.**

A Multiply the factors in $V(x)$ to write $V(x)$ as a polynomial in standard form.

$V(x) = 4x^3 - 36x^2 + 80x$

B To find the value of x that results in a box with a volume of 48 in.^{3}, set the polynomial $V(x)$ equal to 48. Write the resulting equation.

$4x^3 - 36x^2 + 80x = 48$

C Write your equation in the form $p(x) = 0$. To make calculations easier, divide both sides of your equation by the greatest common factor of the coefficients of $p(x)$.

$x^3 - 9x^2 + 20x - 12 = 0$

© Houghton Mifflin Harcourt Publishing Company

3 **Write and solve an equation.**

Standards

CC.9-12.A.APR.1 ... multiply polynomials.

CC.9-12.A.CED.1 Create equations ... in one variable and use them to solve problems.*

Questioning Strategies

- How does writing the polynomial in standard form help you solve the equation? You can then use the Rational Zero Theorem to identify possible rational zeros.

- According to the Fundamental Theorem of Algebra, how many zeros will any volume function have? Explain. 3; a volume function is always of degree 3.

4 **Graph the volume function and determine the local maximum.**

Standards

CC.9-12.F.IF.4 For a function that models a relationship between two quantities, interpret key features of graphs ... in terms of the quantities ...*

CC.9-12.F.IF.7 Graph functions expressed symbolically and show key features of the graph, ... using technology for more complicated cases.*

CC.9-12.F.IF.7c Graph polynomial functions ...*

Questioning Strategies

- How can you use your graphing calculator to find the values of x that result in a volume of 48 in.^{3}? Enter and graph a second function as $Y_2 = 48$ and then use the Intersect feature to find the x-values where the two graphs intersect.

- For any volume less than the maximum, how many different boxes are possible? Explain. 2, because there are two x-values for any $V(x)$-value less than the maximum, and each x-value results in a unique box.

CLOSE

Essential Question

How can you use polynomial functions to model and solve real-world problems?
Write a polynomial function $f(x)$ to model the situation. Restrict the domain of $f(x)$ to account for any real-world constraints. If you want to know the value(s) of x for which $f(x) = c$, you can use the Rational Zero Theorem and other techniques to solve the equation once you write it in the form $f(x) - c = 0$. If you want to know the maximum value of $f(x)$ on its domain, you can graph the function.

Summarize

Have students write a one-page summary of how to use a polynomial model to write a volume function and solve volume problems.

EXTEND

CC.9-12.A.CED.2 Create equations in two ... variables to represent relationships between quantities ...* (Ex. 1)

CC.9-12.A.CED.3 Represent constraints by ... inequalities ...* (Ex. 2)

CC.9-12.A.REI.11 Explain why the x-coordinates of the points where the graphs of the equations $y = f(x)$ and $y = g(x)$ intersect are the solutions of the equation $f(x) = g(x)$ ... Include cases where $f(x)$ and/or $g(x)$ are ... polynomial ... functions.* (Ex. 3)

CC.9-12.F.IF.4 For a function that models a relationship between two quantities, interpret key features of graphs ... in terms of the quantities ...* (Exs. 4, 5)

D   Solve the equation. First determine the possible rational zeros of $p(x)$.

$\pm 1, \pm 2, \pm 3, \pm 4, \pm 6, \pm 12$

Use synthetic substitution to find a zero of $p(x)$. Then factor $p(x)$ completely to find the remaining zeros.

The zeros of $p(x)$ are 1, 2, and 6

E   Interpret the results. Which of the zeros are in the domain of $V(x)$?

1 and 2

For each of these zeros, what are the corresponding dimensions of the box?

When $x = 1$, the box is 8 in. $\times$ 6 in. $\times$ 1 in.

When $x = 2$, the box is 6 in. $\times$ 4 in. $\times$ 2 in.

REFLECT

3a. Check that the values of x that you found above result in a box with a volume of 48 in.^{3}

When $x = 1$, the volume is $8 \times 6 \times 1 = 48$ in.^{3}

When $x = 2$, the volume is $6 \times 4 \times 2 = 48$ in.^{3}

3b. Given that it's possible to create a box with a volume of 48 in.^{3}, do you think it's possible to create a box with a volume of 24 in.^{3}? Explain.

Yes; if $V(x)$ takes on a value of 0 when $x = 0$ and $V(x)$ takes on a value of 48

when $x = 1$, then $V(x)$ must take on all values between 0 and 48 for $0 < x < 1$.

4   Graph the volume function and determine the local maximum.

A   Use a graphing calculator to graph the volume function $V(x)$.

Step 1: Enter $V(x)$ in the equation editor.

Step 2: Use the domain of $V(x)$ and the fact that the volume can be at least 48 in.^{3} to help you choose an appropriate viewing window.

Step 3: Graph the function. Sketch the graph on the coordinate plane at right.

B   Find the maximum value of the function within the domain.

Step 1: Press `2nd` `TRACE`, then select **4:maximum.**

Step 2: Use the arrow keys to move along the graph to select a left bound, a right bound, and a guess. Press `ENTER` after each of these.

At what point does the maximum value occur? Round the coordinates to the nearest tenth.

(1.5, 52.5)

REFLECT

4a. Interpret the result. What do the coordinates of the point where the maximum value occurs represent in the context of the problem?

The box has a maximum volume of about 52.5 in.^{3} when the squares cut from

each corner have side lengths of about 1.5 in.

4b. How does your graph of $V(x)$ support the domain you found earlier?

The graph shows that the volume is positive for values of x between 0 and 4.

4c. You know that $V(x)$ has a maximum value on the domain $0 < x < 4$, but does $V(x)$ have a maximum value when the domain is not restricted (that is, when x can be any real number)? Explain.

No; the graph of $V(x)$ eventually rises without bound as x increases without

bound, so $V(x)$ has no greatest value when x can be any real number.

EXTEND

1. Suppose you have a second piece of cardboard that is 16 inches long and 6 inches wide. What is the volume function for this box when squares of side length x are cut from the corners of the cardboard?

$V(x) = (16 - 2x)(6 - 2x)x$

2. What is the domain of this volume function?

$0 < x < 3$

3. Graph this volume function in the same viewing window as the volume function for the box made from the 10-by-8 piece of cardboard. Then use the calculator's Intersect feature to find the coordinates of the point or points where the graphs intersect.

The graphs intersect at (2, 48).

4. What do the coordinates of the points of intersection represent in the context of the problem?

When $x = 2$ in., both boxes have a volume of 48 in.^{3}

5. Suppose you can make a box from only one of the pieces of cardboard and you want to make a box with the greatest possible volume. Which piece of cardboard should you use? How is your answer supported by the graphs of the volume functions?

The graphs show that the box with the greatest possible volume made from

the 16-by-6 piece of cardboard has a greater volume (approximately 59.3 in.^{3})

than the box with the greatest possible volume made from the 10-by-8 piece

of cardboard.

COMMON CORE CORRELATION

Standard	Items
CC.9-12.N.CN.9(+)	1
CC.9-12.A.SSE.2	2
CC.9-12.A.APR.1	4, 10
CC.9-12.A.APR.2	6, 11
CC.9-12.A.APR.3	7, 8
CC.9-12.A.APR.5(+)	5
CC.9-12.A.CED.1*	14
CC.9-12.A.CED.2*	12
CC.9-12.A.CED.3*	13
CC.9-12.F.IF.2	11
CC.9-12.F.IF.4*	3
CC.9-12.F.IF.7c*	3
CC.9-12.F.BF.1*	12, 15
CC.9-12.F.BF.3	9

TEST PREP DOCTOR ⊕

Multiple Choice: Item 3

- Students who chose **A** did not take into account the negative sign in the leading term $-x^5$.

- Students who chose **B** or **C** identified the end behavior for a polynomial of even degree.

Multiple Choice: Item 5

- Students who chose **B** used a 4 instead of a 1 for the constant term.

- Students who chose **C** used a 4 instead of a 1 as the leading coefficient.

- Students who chose **D** used a 4 instead of a 1 for both the leading coefficient and the constant term.

Multiple Choice: Item 7

- Students who chose **A** factored $f(x) = x^2 - 9$.

- Students who chose **C** incorrectly identified $f(x) = x^2 + 9$ as the square of a binomial.

- Students who chose **D** used the wrong sign in one of the factors.

Free Response: Item 9

- Students who incorrectly graphed and described the end behavior of $g(x)$ may not understand the effect of the value of n on the graph of $g(x) = a(x - h)^n + k$.

- Students who incorrectly graphed and described the stretching of the graph of $f(x)$ may not understand the effect of the value of a on the graph of $g(x) = a(x - h)^n + k$.

- Students who incorrectly graphed and described the reflection of the graph of $f(x)$ may not understand the effect of the sign of a on the graph of $g(x) = a(x - h)^n + k$.

- Students who incorrectly graphed and described the horizontal and/or vertical translations of the graph of $f(x)$ may not understand the effects of the values of h and k on the graph of $g(x) = a(x - h)^n + k$.

Free Response: Item 11

- Students who performed the synthetic substitution correctly and determined that -6 is a zero of $f(x)$ do not understand how to interpret the results of synthetic substitution. They may not understand that -6 would be a zero only if $f(-6)$, the last number in the bottom row, were zero.

- Students who determined that -6 is a zero of $f(x)$ may have mistakenly tested to see whether 6 is a zero of $f(x)$. Evaluating $f(x)$ for $x = 6$ results in 0.

- Students who performed the synthetic substitution incorrectly may not have understood the process of synthetic substitution, such as subtracting numbers in the second row from numbers in the top row instead of adding.

Notes

Name _____ Class _____ Date _____

MULTIPLE CHOICE

1. Which theorem states that if $f(x)$ is a polynomial of degree n, then $f(x)$ has at least one zero in the set of complex numbers?

   A. Rational Zero Theorem

   B. Factor Theorem

   C. Remainder Theorem

   D. Fundamental Theorem of Algebra ✓

2. Which is a factored form of $x^4 - 16$?

   F. $(x^2 - 2)(x^2 + 2)$

   G. $(x^2 + 4)(x^2 - 2)(x^2 + 2)$

   H. $(x^2 + 4)(x - 2)(x + 2)$ ✓

   J. $(x^2 + 4)(x - 4)(x + 4)$

3. Christopher is drawing the graph of $f(x) = -x^5 + 2x^4 + x^3 + 3x^2 - 8x + 1$. How should he show the end behavior of the function?

   A. $f(x) \to +\infty$ as $x \to +\infty$ and $f(x) \to -\infty$ as $x \to -\infty$

   B. $f(x) \to -\infty$ as $x \to +\infty$ and $f(x) \to -\infty$ as $x \to -\infty$

   C. $f(x) \to +\infty$ as $x \to +\infty$ and $f(x) \to +\infty$ as $x \to -\infty$

   D. $f(x) \to -\infty$ as $x \to +\infty$ and $f(x) \to +\infty$ as $x \to -\infty$ ✓

4. Under which operation(s) is the set of polynomials closed?

   F. addition only

   G. addition and multiplication only

   H. addition, subtraction, and multiplication only ✓

   J. addition, subtraction, multiplication, and division

5. Which expression is the expansion of $(x + 1)^4$?

   A. $x^4 + 4x^3 + 6x^2 + 4x + 1$ ✓

   B. $x^4 + 4x^3 + 6x^2 + 4x + 4$

   C. $4x^4 + 4x^3 + 6x^2 + 4x + 1$

   D. $4x^4 + 4x^3 + 6x^2 + 4x + 4$

6. If $x - a$ is a factor of a polynomial $p(x)$, which statement *must* be true?

   F. $x + a$ is a factor of $p(x)$.

   G. $p(a) = 1$

   H. If $p(x)$ is divided by $x - a$, the remainder is 0. ✓

   J. If $p(x)$ is divided by $x - a$, the remainder is a.

7. Which factorization can you use to find the zeros of $f(x) = x^2 + 9$?

   A. $(x + 3)(x - 3)$ C. $(x + 3)(x + 3)$

   B. $(x + 3i)(x - 3i)$ ✓   D. $(x + 3i)(x + 3i)$

8. Which could be the rule for the function $f(x)$ whose graph is below?

   F. $f(x) = 2x^3 - 2x^2 - 16x + 24$

   G. $f(x) = 2x^3 + 2x^2 - 16x - 24$ ✓

   H. $f(x) = 2x^3 + 16x^2 + 42x + 36$

   J. $f(x) = 2x^3 - 16x^2 + 42x - 36$

FREE RESPONSE

9. Graph $g(x) = -2(x - 1)^3 - 4$. Describe the transformations of the graph of the parent function $f(x) = x^3$ that produce this graph.

   The graph of $f(x)$ is stretched vertically by a factor of 2, reflected across the x-axis, and translated 1 unit right and 4 units down.

10. Given the functions $p(x) = 3x^3 - 4x^2 + 7$ and $q(x) = 4x + 10 + 4x^2$, find $p(x) + q(x)$ and $p(x) - q(x)$.

   $p(x) + q(x) = 3x^3 + 4x + 17$;

   $p(x) - q(x) = 3x^3 - 8x^2 - 4x - 3$

11. Is -6 a zero of $f(x) = x^3 - 5x^2 - 8x + 12$? Show how you can use synthetic substitution to determine the answer.

   No; use synthetic substitution to evaluate $f(x)$ for $x = -6$:

-6	1	-5	-8	12
		-6	66	-348
	1	-11	58	-336

   The remainder is not 0, so -6 is not a zero.

For Items 12–15, use the figure and the information below.

You make a box by cutting out a square from each corner of a rectangular sheet of cardboard and folding up the flaps as shown below.

12. Write a function $V(x)$ to represent the volume of the box. Explain how you wrote $V(x)$.

   $V(x) = 4x^3 - 30x^2 + 56x$; multiply expressions that represent length $(8 - 2x)$, width $(7 - 2x)$, and height (x).

13. What is the domain of $V(x)$? Justify your answer.

   $0 < x < 3.5$; each dimension must be positive, so find the intersection of $8 - 2x > 0$, $7 - 2x > 0$, and $x > 0$.

14. Write and solve an equation to find the two values of x that result in a box with a volume of 15 in.³ Use your calculator to help you solve the equation.

   $4x^3 - 30x^2 + 56x - 15 = 0$;

   $x \approx 0.32$ in. and $x = 2.5$ in.

15. What maximum volume can a box made from a 7-by-8 sheet of cardboard have? What size square must you cut from each corner?

   About 30.9 in.³; a square with a side length of about 1.24 in.

UNIT 4

Rational Functions

Unit Vocabulary

extraneous
  solutions   (4-6)

rational function (4-3)

UNIT 4

Rational Functions

Unit Focus

In this unit, you will learn about *rational functions*, which can be written as the ratio of two polynomial functions. You will learn to graph simple rational functions, perform basic operations on rational functions, and solve rational equations. You will also model real-world situations using rational functions.

Unit at a Glance

COMMON CORE

Lesson		Standards for Mathematical Content
4-1	Graphing $f(x) = \frac{a}{x}$	CC.9-12.A.CED.2*, CC.9-12.F.IF.2, CC.9-12.F.IF.4*, CC.9-12.F.IF.7d(+)*, CC.9-12.F.BF.1*, CC.9-12.F.BF.3
4-2	Translating the Graph of $f(x) = \frac{a}{x}$	CC.9-12.A.CED.2*, CC.9-12.F.IF.2, CC.9-12.F.IF.4*, CC.9-12.F.IF.7d(+)*, CC.9-12.F.BF.1*, CC.9-12.F.BF.3
4-3	Graphing Simple Rational Functions	CC.9-12.A.APR.6, CC.9-12.A.CED.2*, CC.9-12.F.IF.2, CC.9-12.F.IF.4*, CC.9-12.F.IF.7d(+)*, CC.9-12.F.BF.1*
4-4	Adding and Subtracting Rational Expressions	CC.9-12.A.SSE.1*, CC.9-12.A.SSE.1b*, CC.9-12.A.APR.7(+), CC.9-12.F.BF.1*, CC.9-12.F.BF.1b*
4-5	Multiplying and Dividing Rational Expressions	CC.9-12.A.SSE.1*, CC.9-12.A.SSE.1b*, CC.9-12.A.APR.7(+), CC.9-12.F.BF.1*, CC.9-12.F.BF.1b*
4-6	Solving Rational Equations	CC.9-12.A.CED.1*, CC.9-12.A.REI.2, CC.9-12.A.REI.11*
4-7	Modeling with Rational Functions	CC.9-12.A.CED.2*, CC.9-12.F.IF.2, CC.9-12.F.IF.4*, CC.9-12.F.IF.7d(+)*, CC.9-12.F.IF.9, CC.9-12.F.BF.1*
	Test Prep	

Unpacking the Common Core State Standards

Use the table to help you understand the Standards for Mathematical Content that are taught in this unit. Refer to the lessons listed after each standard for exploration and practice.

COMMON CORE Standards for Mathematical Content	What It Means For You
CC.9-12.A.SSE.1 Interpret expressions that represent a quantity in terms of its context.* **CC.9-12.A.SSE.1b** Interpret complicated expressions by viewing one or more of their parts as a single entity.* Lessons 4-4, 4-5 (Also 4-6, 4-7)	By combining simple rational models through basic operations like addition and division, you can create more complicated rational models.
CC.9-12.A.APR.6 Rewrite simple rational expressions in different forms; write $a(x)/b(x)$ in the form $q(x) + r(x)/b(x)$, where $a(x)$, $b(x)$, $q(x)$, and $r(x)$ are polynomials with the degree of $r(x)$ less than the degree of $b(x)$, using inspection, long division, or, for the more complicated examples, a computer algebra system. Lesson 4-3 (Also 4-7)	You will learn how using polynomial long division allows you to write rational functions in a form that is more convenient for graphing.
CC.9-12.A.APR.7(+) Understand that rational expressions form a system analogous to the rational numbers, closed under addition, subtraction, multiplication, and division by a nonzero rational expression; add, subtract, multiply, and divide rational expressions. Lessons 4-4, 4-5 (Also 4-7)	You will see that performing operations on rational expressions is just like performing operations on rational numbers.
CC.9-12.A.CED.1 Create equations and inequalities in one variable and use them to solve problems.* Lesson 4-6	You will learn to write and solve rational equations, including those that arise from rational models.
CC.9-12.A.CED.2 Create equations in two or more variables to represent relationships between quantities; graph equations on coordinate axes with labels and scales.* Lessons 4-1, 4-2, 4-3, 4-7	You will learn to model real-world situations with rational functions, representing them both as equations and as graphs.
CC.9-12.A.REI.2 Solve simple rational and radical equations in one variable, and give examples showing how extraneous solutions may arise. Lesson 4-6 (Also 4-7)	When you solve a rational equation, you may obtain a value that appears to be a solution, but one of the rational expressions within the equation becomes undefined when you attempt to check the apparent solution. You will learn how to identify such an *extraneous solution*.

Unpacking the Common Core State Standards

This page lists and explains the Standards for Mathematical Content that are addressed in this unit. For information about the Standards for Mathematical Practice, which are integrated throughout the text, see Teacher Edition pages x–xiii.

Notes

COMMON CORE Standards for Mathematical Content	What It Means For You
CC.9-12.A.REI.11 Explain why the *x*-coordinates of the points where the graphs of the equations $y = f(x)$ and $y = g(x)$ intersect are the solutions of the equation $f(x) = g(x)$; find the solutions approximately, e.g., using technology to graph the functions, make tables of values, or find successive approximations. Include cases where $f(x)$ and/or $g(x)$ are linear, polynomial, rational, absolute value, exponential, and logarithmic functions.* Lesson 4-6 (Also 4-7)	One way to solve a rational equation is to treat each side of the equation as a function. Then you can graph the functions to see where the graphs intersect.
CC.9-12.F.IF.2 Use function notation, evaluate functions for inputs in their domains, and interpret statements that use function notation in terms of a context. Lessons 4-1, 4-2, 4-3, 4-7	You will write rational functions using function notation. Function notation is especially helpful when modeling, because it underscores the dependency of one real-world quantity on another.
CC.9-12.F.IF.4 For a function that models a relationship between two quantities, interpret key features of graphs and tables in terms of the quantities, and sketch graphs showing key features given a verbal description of the relationship.* Lessons 4-1, 4-2, 4-3, 4-7	You will examine the properties of rational models in order to draw conclusions about their problem situations.
CC.9-12.F.IF.7 Graph functions expressed symbolically and show key features of the graph, by hand in simple cases and using technology for more complicated cases.* **CC.9-12.F.IF.7d(+)** Graph rational functions, identifying zeros and asymptotes when suitable factorizations are available, and showing end behavior.* Lessons 4-1, 4-2, 4-3, 4-7	Because a rational function $f(x)$ involves division, you will examine what happens to the value of $f(x)$ as the value of x approaches an x-value for which $f(x)$ is undefined. You will also examine the function's *end behavior*, which refers to what happens to the value of $f(x)$ as x increases or decreases without bound. Knowing how the function behaves helps you graph the function.
CC.9-12.F.IF.9 Compare properties of two functions each represented in a different way (algebraically, graphically, numerically in tables, or by verbal descriptions). Lesson 4-7 (Also 4.2)	When modeling with a rational function, you will investigate what happens to the model when some aspect of the problem situation changes. You will then analyze the revised model to see what new information the revised model gives you.

© Houghton Mifflin Harcourt Publishing Company

UNIT 4

Notes

_____

_____

_____

_____

_____

_____

_____

_____

_____

© Houghton Mifflin Harcourt Publishing Company

COMMON CORE Standards for Mathematical Content	What It Means For You
CC.9-12.F.BF.1 Write a function that describes a relationship between two quantities.* **CC.9-12.F.BF.1a** Determine an explicit expression, a recursive process, or steps for calculation from a context.* **CC.9-12.F.BF.1b** Combine standard function types using arithmetic operations.* Lessons 4-1, 4-2, 4-3, 4-4, 4-5, 4-7	You will learn how to use rational functions to model real-world quantities, and then how to combine those functions using basic operations to model other quantities.
CC.9-12.F.BF.3 Identify the effect on the graph of replacing $f(x)$ by $f(x) + k$, $k\,f(x)$, $f(kx)$, and $f(x + k)$ for specific values of k (both positive and negative); find the value of k given the graphs. Experiment with cases and illustrate an explanation of the effects on the graph using technology. Lessons 4-1, 4-2 (Also 4-7)	You will learn how to use transformations to obtain the graphs of some rational functions by starting with the graph of the simplest rational function, $f(x) = \frac{1}{x}$.

Additional Standards in this Unit

CC.9-12.A.SSE.1a Interpret parts of an expression, such as terms, factors, and coefficients.* Lesson 4-7

CC.9-12.F.IF.5 Relate the domain of a function to its graph and, where applicable, to the quantitative relationship it describes.* Lessons 4-1, 4-2, 4-3

CC.9-12.F.IF.6 Calculate and interpret the average rate of change of a function (presented symbolically or as a table) over a specified interval. Estimate the rate of change from a graph.* Lessons 4-1, 4-7

Notes

Graphing $f(x) = \dfrac{a}{x}$

Essential question: *What is the effect of changing the value of a on the graph of* $f(x) = \dfrac{a}{x}$?

COMMON **Standards for**
CORE **Mathematical Content**

CC.9-12.A.CED.2 Create equations in two or more variables to represent relationships between quantities; graph equations on coordinate axes with labels and scales.*

CC.9-12.F.IF.2 Use function notation, evaluate functions for inputs in their domains ...

CC.9-12.F.IF.4 For a function that models a relationship between two quantities, interpret key features of graphs and tables in terms of the quantities, and sketch graphs showing key features given a verbal description of the relationship.*

CC.9-12.F.IF.7 Graph functions expressed symbolically and show key features of the graph ...*

CC.9-12.F.IF.7d(+) Graph rational functions, identifying zeros and asymptotes when suitable factorizations are available, and showing end behavior.*

CC.9-12.F.BF.1 Write a function that describes a relationship between two quantities.*

CC.9-12.F.BF.1a Determine an explicit expression ... from a context.*

CC.9-12.F.BF.3 Identify the effect on the graph of replacing $f(x)$ by ... $k\,f(x)$ ... for specific values of k (both positive and negative) ...

Also: CC.9-12.F.IF.5*, CC.9-12.F.IF.6*

Prerequisites
Transformations of parent functions, Algebra 1

Math Background
Students have previously explored the parent functions $f(x) = x^2$ and $f(x) = x^n$. Students investigated the relationship between variations of the parent functions and the corresponding transformations of their graphs.

For rational functions of the form $f(x) = \dfrac{a}{x}$, the parent function is $f(x) = \dfrac{1}{x}$. In this lesson, students will learn about transformations that are a result of changing the value of a. Students should recognize that because division by zero is undefined, x cannot have a value of zero for $f(x) = \dfrac{a}{x}$.

INTRODUCE

Revisit the concept of parent functions by referencing the function $f(x) = x^n$ and its relationship to the function $f(x) = ax^n$. Review how changing the value of a can result in vertically stretching the graph of the parent function $(a > 1)$, vertically shrinking the graph of the parent function $(0 < a < 1)$, or reflecting the graph of the parent function across the x-axis $(a < 0)$. Explain that a similar relationship exists between the parent function $f(x) = \dfrac{1}{x}$ and rational functions of the form $f(x) = \dfrac{a}{x}$. Remind students that because division by zero is undefined, $x \neq 0$ for $f(x) = \dfrac{a}{x}$.

TEACH

1 ENGAGE

Questioning Strategies

- Is it possible to substitute zero for x in the function $f(x) = \dfrac{1}{x}$? Explain. No; division by zero is undefined.

- The domain of $f(x) = \dfrac{1}{x}$ is $\{x \mid x \neq 0\}$. How is this reflected in the function's graph? The graph approaches the line $x = 0$ but never actually reaches it.

continued

Name_____ Class_____ Date_____

4-1

Graphing $f(x) = \dfrac{a}{x}$

Essential question: *What is the effect of changing the value of a on the graph of $f(x) = \frac{a}{x}$?*

COMMON CORE

CC.9-12.A.CED.2*,
CC.9-12.F.IF.2,
CC.9-12.F.IF.4*,
CC.9-12.F.IF.7d(+)*,
CC.9-12.F.BF.1*,
CC.9-12.F.BF.3

1 ENGAGE Understanding the Parent Function $f(x) = \frac{1}{x}$

The function $f(x) = \frac{1}{x}$ is the parent function of all functions of the form $g(x) = \frac{a}{x}$. The graph of $f(x) = \frac{1}{x}$ consists of two separate curves, one in Quadrant III and one in Quadrant I, called *branches*. As you can see from the tables and graph below, the ends of the branches approach the axes, which are called the graph's *asymptotes*.

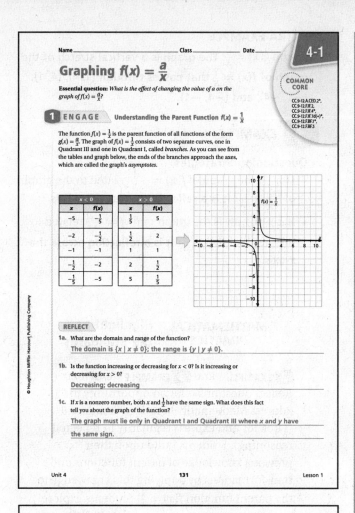

$x < 0$	
x	$f(x)$
-5	$-\frac{1}{5}$
-2	$-\frac{1}{2}$
-1	-1
$-\frac{1}{2}$	-2
$-\frac{1}{5}$	-5

$x > 0$	
x	$f(x)$
$\frac{1}{5}$	5
$\frac{1}{2}$	2
1	1
2	$\frac{1}{2}$
5	$\frac{1}{5}$

REFLECT

1a. What are the domain and range of the function?

The domain is $\{x \mid x \neq 0\}$; the range is $\{y \mid y \neq 0\}$.

1b. Is the function increasing or decreasing for $x < 0$? Is it increasing or decreasing for $x > 0$?

Decreasing; decreasing

1c. If x is a nonzero number, both x and $\frac{1}{x}$ have the same sign. What does this fact tell you about the graph of the function?

The graph must lie only in Quadrant I and Quadrant III where x and y have

the same sign.

Unit 4   131   Lesson 1

1d. If a is a nonzero number, then both $\left(a, \frac{1}{a}\right)$ and $\left(\frac{1}{a}, a\right)$ are points on the graph of the function. What does this fact tell you about the symmetry of the graph?

The graph is symmetric about the line $y = x$.

1e. The function's *end behavior* is determined by what happens to the value of $f(x)$ as the value of x increases or decreases without bound. The notation $x \to +\infty$, which is read "x approaches positive infinity," means that x is increasing without bound, while the notation $x \to -\infty$, which is read "x approaches negative infinity," means that x is decreasing without bound. Complete each table and then describe the function's end behavior.

x increases without bound.	
x	$f(x) = \frac{1}{x}$
100	0.01
1000	0.001
10,000	0.0001
100,000	0.00001

x decreases without bound.	
x	$f(x) = \frac{1}{x}$
-100	-0.01
-1000	-0.001
$-10,000$	-0.0001
$-100,000$	-0.00001

As $x \to +\infty$, $f(x) \to$ 0   As $x \to -\infty$, $f(x) \to$ 0

1f. The break in the function's graph at $x = 0$ is called an *infinite discontinuity*. To see why this is so, complete each table and then describe the function's behavior. The notation $x \to 0^+$ means that x approaches 0 from the right, while the notation $x \to 0^-$ means that x approaches 0 from the left.

x approaches 0 from the right.	
x	$f(x) = \frac{1}{x}$
0.01	100
0.001	1000
0.0001	10,000
0.00001	100,000

x approaches 0 from the left.	
x	$f(x) = \frac{1}{x}$
-0.01	-100
-0.001	-1000
-0.0001	$-10,000$
-0.00001	$-100,000$

As $x \to 0^+$, $f(x) \to$ $+\infty$ As $x \to 0^-$, $f(x) \to$ $-\infty$

Unit 4   132   Lesson 1

Teaching Strategies

As students look at the table of values for $f(x) = \frac{1}{x}$, have them locate each corresponding point on the graph in the order that the points are listed in the table. Encourage students to observe how the points get closer and closer to the x- and y-axes as x decreases without bound, as x approaches 0, and as x increases without bound. Ask: Will the graph ever actually touch or cross the line $x = 0$? Will the graph ever actually touch or cross the line $y = 0$?

2 EXAMPLE

Questioning Strategies

- If the graph of a function $g(x) = \frac{a}{x}$ passes through $(1, 3)$, $(3, 1)$, $(-1, -3)$, and $(-3, -1)$, what is the value of a? **3**

- If the graph of $g(x) = \frac{a}{x}$ passes through $(0.1, 6)$, $(0.2, 3)$, $(-0.1, -6)$, and $(-0.2, -3)$, what is the value of a? **0.6**

- If $a > 1$, is the graph of $g(x) = \frac{a}{x}$ closer to or farther from the x- and y-axes than the graph of the parent function? **farther from the axes**

- If $0 < a < 1$, is the graph of $g(x) = \frac{a}{x}$ closer to or farther from the x- and y-axes than the graph of the parent function? **closer to the axes**

Differentiated Instruction

Visual learners may benefit from finding the value of $g(x) = \frac{2}{x}$ as x increases from -4 to 4:

$$-\frac{2}{4}, -\frac{2}{2}, -\frac{2}{1}, -\frac{2}{0.5}, \frac{2}{0.5}, \frac{2}{1}, \frac{2}{2}, \frac{2}{4}$$

As they simplify each fraction in the sequence, have them follow the path of the corresponding points on the graph of $g(x) = \frac{2}{x}$, paying close attention to what happens as x increases from -0.5 to 0.5.

Repeat the process for $g(x) = \frac{0.4}{x}$ as the values of x increase from -2 to 2:

$$-\frac{0.4}{2}, -\frac{0.4}{1}, -\frac{0.4}{0.4}, -\frac{0.4}{0.2}, -\frac{0.4}{0.1}, \frac{0.4}{0.1}, \frac{0.4}{0.2}, \frac{0.4}{1}, \frac{0.4}{2}$$

Have them pay close attention to what happens as x increases from -0.1 to 0.1.

3 EXAMPLE

Questioning Strategies

- How is the graph of $f(x) = -\frac{1}{x}$ related to the graph of $f(x) = \frac{1}{x}$? **It is a reflection across the x-axis.**

- If $a > 0$, how is the graph of $f(x) = -\frac{a}{x}$ related to the graph of $f(x) = \frac{a}{x}$? **It is a reflection across the x-axis.**

MATHEMATICAL PRACTICE	Highlighting the Standards

2 EXAMPLE and **3 EXAMPLE** and their Reflect questions offer an opportunity to address Mathematical Practice Standard 8 (Look for and express regularity in repeated reasoning). Students build upon their previous knowledge of parent functions and transformations by applying this knowledge to the parent function $f(x) = \frac{1}{x}$. Students explore how changing the value of a in the function $f(x) = \frac{a}{x}$ transforms the graph of the function by shrinking, stretching, and/or reflecting.

2 EXAMPLE Graphing $g(x) = \frac{a}{x}$ when $a > 0$

Graph each function. (The parent function is shown in gray.)

A $g(x) = \frac{2}{x}$

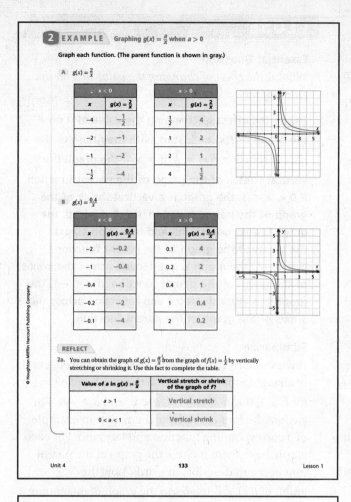

x < 0	
x	$g(x) = \frac{2}{x}$
−4	$-\frac{1}{2}$
−2	−1
−1	−2
$-\frac{1}{2}$	−4

x > 0	
x	$g(x) = \frac{2}{x}$
$\frac{1}{2}$	4
1	2
2	1
4	$\frac{1}{2}$

B $g(x) = \frac{0.4}{x}$

x < 0	
x	$g(x) = \frac{0.4}{x}$
−2	−0.2
−1	−0.4
−0.4	−1
−0.2	−2
−0.1	−4

x > 0	
x	$g(x) = \frac{0.4}{x}$
0.1	4
0.2	2
0.4	1
1	0.4
2	0.2

REFLECT

2a. You can obtain the graph of $g(x) = \frac{a}{x}$ from the graph of $f(x) = \frac{1}{x}$ by vertically stretching or shrinking it. Use this fact to complete the table.

Value of a in $g(x) = \frac{a}{x}$	Vertical stretch or shrink of the graph of f?
a > 1	Vertical stretch
0 < a < 1	Vertical shrink

Unit 4   133   Lesson 1

3 EXAMPLE Graphing $g(x) = \frac{a}{x}$ when $a < 0$

Graph each function. (The parent function is shown in gray.)

A $g(x) = -\frac{2}{x}$

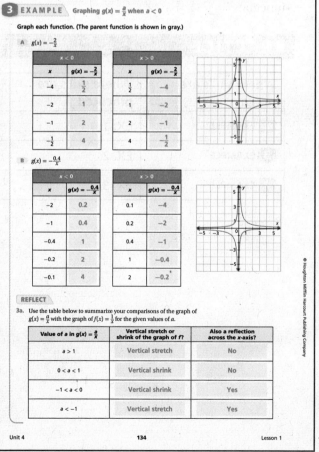

x < 0	
x	$g(x) = -\frac{2}{x}$
−4	$\frac{1}{2}$
−2	1
−1	2
$-\frac{1}{2}$	4

x > 0	
x	$g(x) = -\frac{2}{x}$
$\frac{1}{2}$	−4
1	−2
2	−1
4	$-\frac{1}{2}$

B $g(x) = -\frac{0.4}{x}$

x < 0	
x	$g(x) = -\frac{0.4}{x}$
−2	0.2
−1	0.4
−0.4	1
−0.2	2
−0.1	4

x > 0	
x	$g(x) = -\frac{0.4}{x}$
0.1	−4
0.2	−2
0.4	−1
1	−0.4
2	−0.2

REFLECT

3a. Use the table below to summarize your comparisons of the graph of $g(x) = \frac{a}{x}$ with the graph of $f(x) = \frac{1}{x}$ for the given values of a.

Value of a in $g(x) = \frac{a}{x}$	Vertical stretch or shrink of the graph of f?	Also a reflection across the x-axis?
a > 1	Vertical stretch	No
0 < a < 1	Vertical shrink	No
−1 < a < 0	Vertical shrink	Yes
a < −1	Vertical stretch	Yes

Unit 4   134   Lesson 1

Questioning Strategies

- What is the domain of the function $t(r) = \frac{30}{r}$ from a purely mathematical perspective? **The domain is $\{r \mid r \neq 0\}$.**

- Does the domain of the function accurately reflect the possible values of r in the context of this problem? Explain. **No; in addition to the rate not being equal to zero, the rate cannot have a negative value. Also, assuming Mrs. Jacobs obeys speed limits, her rate would always be the posted speed limit or less.**

Avoid Common Errors

When graphing a function that represents a real-world inverse variation situation, students may graph both branches of the function even though the context of the problem requires that only positive values be used. Ask: What if the graph also consisted of the branch in Quadrant III? Have students identify several points on that branch of the graph and analyze whether those points represent solutions that make sense in the context of the situation. Finally, encourage students to read every real-world problem carefully, identifying practical restrictions on values for any variables and solutions.

EXTRA EXAMPLE

Each day, Jim rides his bike 7 miles to work. His commuting time depends on his average speed, which varies from day to day. If r is his average speed and t is time, write and graph an equation that gives his commuting time as a function of his average speed. $t(r) = \frac{7}{r}$; **The graph is a vertical stretch of the graph of $f(x) = \frac{1}{x}$ that passes through (1, 7) and (7, 1), consisting only of the branch in Quadrant I (horizontal axis labeled r and vertical axis labeled $t(r)$).**

CLOSE

Essential Question

What is the effect of changing the value of a on the graph of $f(x) = \frac{a}{x}$?

To see the effect of changing the value of a on the graph of $f(x) = \frac{a}{x}$, start with the graph of the parent function $f(x) = \frac{1}{x}$. If $a > 1$, the graph is a vertical stretch of the graph of the parent function. If $0 < a < 1$, the graph is a vertical shrink of the graph of the parent function. If $-1 < a < 0$, the graph is a vertical shrink and reflection across the x-axis of the graph of the parent function. If $a = -1$, the graph is a reflection across the x-axis of the graph of the parent function. If $a < -1$, the graph is a vertical stretch and reflection across the x-axis of the graph of the parent function.

Summarize

Have students make a table that shows the effects of changing the value of a on the graph of $f(x) = \frac{a}{x}$ for $a > 1$, $0 < a < 1$, $-1 < a < 0$, and $a < -1$. For each of the four cases, have them give an example of a corresponding function and its graph. For each graph, have them include the graph of the parent function and describe, in words, how the graph of $f(x) = \frac{a}{x}$ relates to the graph of the parent function.

PRACTICE

Where skills are taught	Where skills are practiced
2 EXAMPLE	EX. 1
3 EXAMPLE	EX. 2
4 EXAMPLE	EX. 3

Inverse Variation When the relationship between two real-world quantities x and y has the form $y = \frac{a}{x}$ for some nonzero constant a, the relationship is called *inverse variation* and y is said to *vary inversely* as x.

4 EXAMPLE Writing and Graphing an Equation for Inverse Variation

Mrs. Jacobs drives 30 miles to her job in the city. Her commuting time depends on her average speed, which varies from day to day as a result of weather and traffic conditions. Write and graph an equation that gives her commuting time as a function of her average speed.

A Use the formula $d = rt$ where d is distance, r is rate (average speed), and t is time to write t as a function of r given that $d = 30$.

$rt =$ [30] The product of rate and time gives distance.

$t = \dfrac{30}{r}$ Solve for t.

B Use the table to help you graph the function $t(r)$.

r	$t(r)$
10	3
15	2
30	1
60	0.5

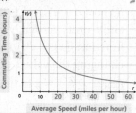

REFLECT

4a. Why does the graph consist only of the branch in Quadrant I?

Rate and time have only positive values in this problem.

4b. Do equal changes in average speed result in equal changes in commuting time? Give an example to support your answer.

No; going from 10 mi/h to 20 mi/h decreases the commuting time by 1.5 h, but going from 20 mi/h to 30 mi/h decreases the commuting time by only 0.5 h.

PRACTICE

For each function, plot the points at which $x = \pm 1$, then draw the complete graph.

1. $f(x) = \dfrac{0.3}{x}$

2. $f(x) = -\dfrac{4}{x}$

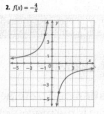

3. Shaun is paid $20 each week to mow a lawn. The time he spends mowing varies from week to week based on factors such as how much the grass has grown and how wet the grass is. His effective hourly pay rate is therefore a function of the time he spends mowing.

a. Use the formula $p = rt$ where p is total pay, r is hourly pay rate, and t is time to write r as a function of t given that $p = 20$. Describe the relationship between r and t.

$r = \dfrac{20}{t}$; r varies inversely as t.

b. Use the table below to help you graph the function $r(t)$.

t	$r(t)$
0.5	40
1	20
2	10
2.5	8

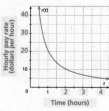

Translating the Graph of $f(x) = \dfrac{a}{x}$

Essential question: *How does changing the values of h and k affect the graph of* $f(x) = \dfrac{a}{x - h} + k$*?*

COMMON Standards for
CORE Mathematical Content

CC.9-12.A.CED.2 Create equations in two or more variables to represent relationships between quantities; graph equations on coordinate axes with labels and scales.*

CC.9-12.F.IF.2 Use function notation, evaluate functions for inputs in their domains ...

CC.9-12.F.IF.4 For a function that models a relationship between two quantities, interpret key features of graphs and tables in terms of the quantities, and sketch graphs showing key features given a verbal description of the relationship.*

CC.9-12.F.IF.7 Graph functions expressed symbolically and show key features of the graph ...*

CC.9-12.F.IF.7d(+) Graph rational functions, identifying zeros and asymptotes when suitable factorizations are available, and showing end behavior.*

CC.9-12.F.BF.1 Write a function that describes a relationship between two quantities.*

CC.9-12.F.BF.1a Determine an explicit expression ... from a context.*

CC.9-12.F.BF.3 Identify the effect on the graph of replacing $f(x)$ by ... $f(x) + k$ ... and $f(x + k)$ for specific values of k (both positive and negative) ...

Also: CC.9-12.F.IF.5*, CC.9-12.F.IF.9*

Prerequisites
Graphing $f(x) = \dfrac{a}{x}$, Lesson 4-1

Math Background
In the previous lesson, students graphed rational functions of the form $f(x) = \dfrac{a}{x}$ by transforming the graph of the parent function $f(x) = \dfrac{1}{x}$.

Students will now extend that knowledge by investigating how the values of h and k are related to the graph of $f(x) = \dfrac{a}{x - h} + k$. Students should recall that the graph of the polynomial function $f(x) = (x - h)^n + k$ is translated h units horizontally and k units vertically from the graph of the parent function $f(x) = x^n$. In this lesson, they will see that changing the values of h and k affect the graph of $f(x) = \dfrac{a}{x - h} + k$ in the same way.

INTRODUCE

Review the process of graphing the rational function $f(x) = \dfrac{a}{x}$. Remind students of the parallels between the graphs of rational functions and polynomials functions and how they are affected by changing the value of a.

Ask students to recall what they know about the graph of the polynomial function $f(x) = (x - h)^n + k$ and the effects of changing the values of h and k. Ask them to predict the effects of changing the values of h and k on the graph of the rational function $f(x) = \dfrac{a}{x - h} + k$.

TEACH

1 EXAMPLE

Questioning Strategies
- How is the process of graphing a rational function of the form $f(x) = \dfrac{1}{x - h} + k$ related to the process of graphing a polynomial function of the form $f(x) = (x - h)^n + k$? **In both cases, you start with the graph of the parent function and translate the graph h units horizontally and k units vertically.**

continued

Name_____ Class_____ Date_____

4-2

COMMON CORE

CC.9-12.A.CED.2*,
CC.9-12.F.IF.2,
CC.9-12.F.IF.4*,
CC.9-12.F.IF.7d(+)*,
CC.9-12.F.BF.1*,
CC.9-12.F.BF.3

Translating the Graph of $f(x) = \frac{a}{x}$

Essential question: *How does changing the values of h and k affect the graph of $f(x) = \frac{a}{x-h} + k$?*

In Lesson 4-1, you saw that the graphs of functions of the form $g(x) = \frac{a}{x}$ are vertical stretches or shrinks, coupled with a reflection in the x-axis when $a < 0$, of the graph of the parent function $f(x) = \frac{1}{x}$. In this lesson, you will learn how the graphs of functions of the form $s(x) = \frac{a}{x-h} + k$ are related to the graph of the parent function.

1 EXAMPLE Graphing $s(x) = \frac{a}{x-h} + k$ when a = 1

Graph the function $s(x) = \frac{1}{x-3} + 2$.

A Determine the graph's horizontal asymptote. You know from examining the end behavior of the parent function that its graph has the x-axis as a horizontal asymptote. Now consider the end behavior of the given function.

x increases without bound.		x decreases without bound.	
x	$s(x) = \frac{1}{x-3} + 2$	**x**	$s(x) = \frac{1}{x-3} + 2$
103	2.01	−97	1.99
1003	2.001	−997	1.999
10,003	2.0001	−9997	1.9999
100,003	2.00001	−99,997	1.99999

As $x \to +\infty$, $s(x) \to$ __2__.   As $x \to -\infty$, $s(x) \to$ __2__.

So, the graph's horizontal asymptote is the line __$y = 2$__.

B Determine the graph's vertical asymptote. You know that the parent function is undefined when $x = 0$. You also know from examining the behavior of the parent function near $x = 0$ that the graph has the y-axis as a vertical asymptote.

For what value of x is the given function undefined? __$x = 3$__

Complete the tables below to show that the graph's vertical asymptote is the line $x = 3$.

x approaches 3 from the right.		x approaches 3 from the left.	
x	$s(x) = \frac{1}{x-3} + 2$	**x**	$s(x) = \frac{1}{x-3} + 2$
3.01	102	2.99	−98
3.001	1002	2.999	−998
3.0001	10,002	2.9999	−9998
3.00001	100,002	2.99999	−99,998

As $x \to 3^+$, $s(x) \to$ __$+\infty$__.   As $x \to 3^-$, $s(x) \to$ __$-\infty$__.

C Identify the coordinates of two reference points. You know that one branch of the graph of the parent function $f(x) = \frac{1}{x}$ includes the point (1, 1) while the other branch includes the point (−1, −1). These points are 1 unit to the right and 1 unit to the left of the vertical asymptote. What are the corresponding points on the graph of $s(x) = \frac{1}{x-3} + 2$?

__(4, 3) and (2, 1)__

D Draw the graph by first drawing the horizontal and vertical asymptotes as dashed lines and then plotting the reference points. Each branch of the graph should pass through one of the reference points and approach the asymptotes. (The graph of the parent function is shown in gray.)

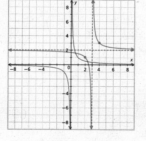

REFLECT

1a. Describe how to graph $s(x) = \frac{1}{x-3} + 2$ as a transformation of the graph of $f(x) = \frac{1}{x}$.

__Translate the graph of f right 3 units and up 2 units.__

1b. What are the domain and range of the function $s(x) = \frac{1}{x-3} + 2$?

__$D = \{x \mid x \neq 3\}$; $R = \{y \mid y \neq 2\}$__

- Why is the function $h(x) = \frac{1}{x-3} + 2$ undefined for the value $x = 3$? because $x - 3$ equals 0, and division by zero is undefined

Teaching Strategies

Encourage students to use mental math when completing the tables in parts A and B. For instance, when determining the value of $h(x)$ for $x = 103$, students should follow the order of operations and perform these calculations mentally: The difference of 103 and 3 is 100. The reciprocal of 100 is 0.01. The sum of 0.01 and 2 is 2.01, which is the value of $h(x)$.

When graphing the function in part D, students may need to plot other points besides the reference points. For instance, they can plot $(-1, 1.75)$, $(2.5, 0)$, $(3.5, 4)$, and $(5, 2.5)$. But they should recognize that each branch of the graph will follow the asymptotes as you move away from the reference points.

EXTRA EXAMPLE

Graph the function $h(x) = \frac{1}{x-4} + 1$. The graph is a translation of the graph of $f(x) = \frac{1}{x}$ with horizontal asymptote at $y = 1$, vertical asymptote at $x = 4$, and reference points at $(3, 0)$ and $(5, 2)$.

2 EXAMPLE

Questioning Strategies

- What horizontal and vertical translations are performed on the graph of $g(x) = \frac{3}{x}$ to obtain the graph of $h(x) = \frac{3}{x+2} + 1$? Given that the asymptotes of the graph of $g(x)$ are $x = 0$ and $y = 0$, what asymptotes do you get for the graph of $h(x)$ when you perform the translations on the asymptotes for the graph of $g(x)$? Translate 2 units left and 1 unit up; $x = -2$ and $y = 1$

- After graphing $h(x) = \frac{3}{x+2} + 1$ by plotting horizontal and vertical asymptotes of $y = 1$ and $x = -2$ and reference points $(-1, 4)$ and $(-3, -2)$, how could you check that you have graphed the function correctly? Since the graph also appears to include the points $(-5, 0)$ and $(1, 2)$, substitute these values into the function.

Differentiated Instruction

After the horizontal and vertical asymptotes of the graph have been identified, visual learners may benefit from drawing horizontal and vertical arrows to find the reference points.

They already know that the graph of $g(x) = \frac{3}{x}$ includes the reference points $(1, 3)$ and $(-1, -3)$, and that the horizontal and vertical asymptotes of the graph of $h(x) = \frac{3}{x+2} + 1$ intersect at $(-2, 1)$. By starting at the intersection and drawing a pair of arrows 1 unit right and 3 units up to get to the translation of $(1, 3)$, and a second pair 1 unit left and 3 units down to get to the translation of $(-1, -3)$, they will identify the reference points of $(-1, 4)$ and $(-3, -2)$.

EXTRA EXAMPLE

Graph the function $h(x) = \frac{2}{x+1} + 3$. The graph is a translation of the graph of $f(x) = \frac{2}{x}$ with horizontal asymptote at $y = 3$, vertical asymptote at $x = -1$, and reference points at $(0, 5)$ and $(-2, 1)$.

3 EXAMPLE

Questioning Strategies

- If you started with the parent function $f(x) = \frac{1}{x}$, was the graph of the function $C(s)$ translated horizontally, vertically, or both? Explain.

  Vertically; although $C(s) = \frac{100}{s} + 10$ is a function of the form $f(x) = \frac{a}{x-h} + k$, the value of h is zero, meaning there is no horizontal translation.

- How would the function $C(s)$ and its graph change if the $100 cost of the tour guide were evenly shared by s students and 3 teachers who chaperoned the tour? The function would change to $C(s) = \frac{100}{s+3} + 10$, and the graph would be translated 3 units to the left.

continued

You have seen how to graph $h(x) = \frac{a}{x-h} + k$ when $a = 1$. The method is the same when $a \neq 1$, except that you translate the graph of $g(x) = \frac{a}{x}$ rather than the graph of $f(x) = \frac{1}{x}$.

2 EXAMPLE Graphing $h(x) = \frac{a}{x-h} + k$ when $a \neq 1$

Graph the function $g(x) = \frac{3}{x+2} + 1$.

A Identify the graph's horizontal asymptote. $y = 1$

B Identify the graph's vertical asymptote. $x = -2$

C Identify the coordinates of two reference points. You know that one branch of the graph of $g(x) = \frac{3}{x}$ includes the point $(1, 3)$ while the other branch includes the point $(-1, -3)$. These points are 1 unit to the right and 1 unit to the left of the vertical asymptote. What are the coordinates of the corresponding points on the graph of $h(x) = \frac{3}{x+2} + 1$?
$(-1, 4)$ and $(-3, -2)$

D Draw the graph by first drawing the horizontal and vertical asymptotes as dashed lines and then plotting the reference points. Each branch of the graph should pass through one of the reference points and approach the asymptotes. (The graph of $g(x) = \frac{3}{x}$ is shown in gray.)

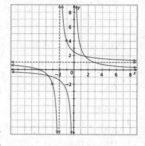

REFLECT

2a. Describe how to graph $h(x) = \frac{3}{x+2} + 1$ as a transformation of the graph of $f(x) = \frac{1}{x}$.

Vertically stretch the graph of f by

a factor of 3, then translate the

stretched graph 2 units left and

1 unit up.

Unit 4   139   Lesson 2

2b. Complete the table to summarize the characteristics of the graphs of the functions listed there.

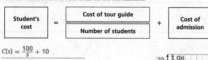

	$f(x) = \frac{1}{x}$	$g(x) = \frac{a}{x}$	$s(x) = \frac{a}{x-h} + k$
Horizontal Asymptote	$y = 0$	$y = 0$	$y = k$
Vertical Asymptote	$x = 0$	$x = 0$	$x = h$
Reference Points	$(1, 1), (-1, -1)$	$(1, a), (-1, -a)$	$(1 + h, a + k),$ $(-1 + h, -a + k)$

3 EXAMPLE Modeling with $s(x) = \frac{a}{x-h} + k$

A student art club has arranged a tour of an art museum. Students who go on the tour will pay $10 each for admission. They will also evenly share the $100 cost to hire a tour guide for the group. A student's cost C is therefore a function of the number s of students who go on the tour. Write a rule for the function $C(s)$ and then graph the function.

A Use the verbal model to write a rule for the cost function.

$$\text{Student's cost} = \frac{\text{Cost of tour guide}}{\text{Number of students}} + \text{Cost of admission}$$

$C(s) = \frac{100}{s} + 10$

B Write the equations of the asymptotes and complete the table of values. Then use the information to graph the function.

Vertical asymptote: $s = 0$

Horizontal asymptote: $C(s) = 10$

s	10	20	50	100
$C(s)$	20	15	12	11

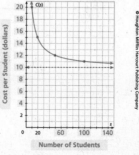

Unit 4   140   Lesson 2

Teaching Strategies

In elementary grades, students are introduced to the concept that division can be used to model real-world situations that involve sharing. Have students recall this concept as they write the rule for the cost function. Point out that since the cost of the tour guide is shared, the $100 cost is divided by *s*, the number of students. On the other hand, the $10 admission cost is not shared and is not divided.

MATHEMATICAL PRACTICE | **Highlighting the Standards**

3 EXAMPLE and its Reflect questions offer an opportunity to address Mathematical Practice Standard 2 (Reason abstractly and quantitatively). Students develop an algebraic model for determining the cost per student for a tour when part of that cost is constant and part depends on the number of students who go on the tour. Students analyze their model to draw conclusions, and then apply those conclusions back to the real world. They see that only the branch in Quadrant I, representing positive values, makes sense in the context of the problem. They also see that the graph in the real-world context consists of discrete points representing individual students. Finally, they interpret how the horizontal asymptote represents the lower limit of the cost per student as the number of students increases.

EXTRA EXAMPLE

A student drama club is planning a trip to see a play at the local theater. Each student will pay $15 for a ticket, and the group will evenly share the $120 cost of bus transportation. A student's cost *C* is therefore a function of the number *s* of students who go to see the play. Write a rule for the function $C(s)$ and then graph the function. $C(s) = \frac{120}{s} + 15$; the graph has horizontal asymptote $s = 0$ and vertical asymptote $C(s) = 15$, and passes through (10, 27), (20, 21), (30, 19), and (40, 18).

Avoid Common Errors

When modeling a real-world situation with a rational function of the form $h(x) = \frac{a}{x - h} + k$, remind students that the context of the problem may require that only positive values be used.

CLOSE

Essential Question

How does changing the values of h and k affect the graph of $f(x) = \frac{a}{x - h} + k$?

Changing the values of *h* and *k* will result in a translation of the graph of $f(x) = \frac{a}{x - h} + k$. The graph of $f(x) = \frac{a}{x - h} + k$ is the graph of $f(x) = \frac{a}{x}$ translated *h* units horizontally and *k* units vertically. The horizontal asymptote will be $y = k$, the vertical asymptote will be $x = h$, and the reference points will be $(1 + h, a + k)$ and $(-1 + h, -a + k)$.

Summarize

Have students make a table that shows the effects of changing the values of *h* and *k* on the graph of $f(x) = \frac{a}{x - h} + k$ for $a = 1$ and $a \neq 1$. For each of the two cases, have them give an example of a corresponding function and its graph. For each graph, have them include the graph of the parent function and describe, in words, how the graph of $f(x) = \frac{a}{x - h} + k$ relates to the graph of the parent function.

PRACTICE

Where skills are taught	Where skills are practiced
1 EXAMPLE	EX. 5
2 EXAMPLE	EXS. 1–4, 6–8
3 EXAMPLE	EX. 9

REFLECT

3a. Although you graphed the function as an unbroken curve, the graph really consists
of a series of distinct points. Explain why.

The values of the independent variable are nonzero whole numbers because

students are being counted, so the graph should consist only of points with

nonzero whole-number *s*-coordinates.

3b. Is the function increasing or decreasing? What does this tell you about the cost per
student as the number of students going on the tour increases?

Decreasing; as the number of students increases, the cost per student decreases.

3c. Interpret the graph's horizontal asymptote in the context of the problem.

As the number of students increases, the cost per student approaches $10

(but never reaches that amount).

PRACTICE

Identify the asymptotes of the graph of each function.

1. $f(x) = \frac{5}{x-4}$

$x = 4, y = 0$

2. $f(x) = \frac{0.2}{x} - 1$

$x = 0, y = -1$

3. $f(x) = \frac{-4}{x+1} + 3$

$x = -1, y = 3$

4. $f(x) = \frac{11}{x-9} + 9$

$x = 9, y = 9$

Graph each function.

5. $f(x) = \frac{1}{x-2} + 4$

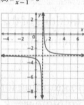

6. $f(x) = -\frac{1}{x+1} - 2$

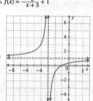

7. $f(x) = \frac{0.5}{x-1} - 3$

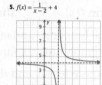

8. $f(x) = -\frac{2}{x+3} + 1$

9. A sports club is organizing a trip to an out-of-town football game. Members who
go on the trip will pay $40 each for a ticket to the game. They will also evenly
share the $320 cost of a bus for transportation to and from the game. A member's
cost C is therefore a function of the number m of members who go on the trip.

a. Write a rule for the function $C(m)$.

$C(m) = \frac{320}{m} + 40$

b. Identify the asymptotes of the
function's graph.

Horizontal: $C(m) = 40$;

vertical: $m = 0$

c. Graph the function.

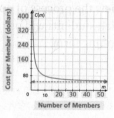

d. Suppose the club decides to hold
a lottery where the winner gets to go
to the game for free. The winner's ticket
cost is added to the cost of the bus,
with the total cost evenly shared by
everyone but the winner. Write a rule
for the new function $C(m)$ where m
includes the winner.

$C(m) = \frac{360}{m-1} + 40$

e. Identify the asymptotes of the new
function's graph.

Horizontal: $C(m) = 40$;

vertical: $m = 1$

f. Graph the new function.

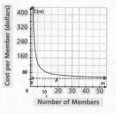

Graphing Simple Rational Functions

Essential question: *How can you graph a function of the form* $f(x) = \frac{bx + c}{dx + e}$*?*

Standards for Mathematical Content

CC.9-12.A.APR.6 Rewrite simple rational expressions in different forms; write $a(x)/b(x)$ in the form $q(x) + r(x)/b(x)$, where $a(x)$, $b(x)$, $q(x)$, and $r(x)$ are polynomials with the degree of $r(x)$ less than the degree of $b(x)$, using inspection, long division, ...

CC.9-12.A.CED.2 Create equations in two or more variables to represent relationships between quantities; graph equations on coordinate axes with labels and scales.*

CC.9-12.F.IF.2 Use function notation, evaluate functions for inputs in their domains, and interpret statements that use function notation in terms of a context.

CC.9-12.F.IF.4 For a function that models a relationship between two quantities, interpret key features of graphs and tables in terms of the quantities, and sketch graphs showing key features given a verbal description of the relationship.*

CC.9-12.F.IF.7 Graph functions expressed symbolically and show key features of the graph, by hand in simple cases and using technology for more complicated cases.*

CC.9-12.F.IF.7d(+) Graph rational functions, identifying zeros and asymptotes when suitable factorizations are available, and showing end behavior.*

CC.9-12.F.BF.1 Write a function that describes a relationship between two quantities.*

CC.9-12.F.BF.1a Determine an explicit expression ... from a context.*

Also: CC.9-12.F.IF.5*

Vocabulary
rational function

Prerequisites
Graphing and translating $f(x) = \frac{a}{x}$, Lessons 4-1, 4-2

Polynomial long division, Lesson 3-8

Math Background
In Lessons 4-1 and 4-2, students learned to graph rational functions in the graphing form $f(x) = \frac{a}{x - h} + k$. Now, they will graph rational functions in the general form $f(x) = \frac{p(x)}{q(x)}$, where $p(x)$ and $q(x)$ are polynomial functions and $q(x) \neq 0$. In this lesson, students will graph rational functions of the form $f(x) = \frac{bx + c}{dx + e}$, where $bx + c$ and $dx + e$ are both linear functions. Although such functions can be graphed by rewriting in the graphing form, students will also learn how to graph these functions without rewriting them first.

INTRODUCE

Students will begin graphing functions of the form $f(x) = \frac{bx + c}{dx + e}$ by first rewriting them in the graphing form $f(x) = \frac{a}{x - h} + k$.

Review the process for using the graphing form to determine the horizontal asymptote $y = k$, the vertical asymptote $x = h$, and reference points $(1 + h, a + k)$ and $(-1 + h, -a + k)$. Also review the process of polynomial long division, which students will use to rewrite functions in graphing form.

Name_____ Class_____ Date_____

Graphing Simple Rational Functions

COMMON CORE

CC-9-12.A.APR.6,
CC-9-12.A.CED.2*,
CC-9-12.F.IF.2,
CC-9-12.F.IF.4*,
CC-9-12.F.IF.7d(+)*,
CC-9-12.F.BF.1*

Essential question: *How can you graph a function of the form* $f(x) = \frac{bx + c}{dx + e}$?

A **rational function** has the form $f(x) = \frac{p(x)}{q(x)}$ where $p(x)$ and $q(x)$ are polynomial functions and $q(x) \neq 0$. The functions that you learned to graph in Lessons 4-1 and 4-2 are rational functions because they can be written as the ratio of two polynomials. For instance, you can write

$$f(x) = \frac{2}{x+1} + 3 \text{ as } f(x) = \frac{2}{x+1} + 3 = \frac{2}{x+1} + \frac{3(x+1)}{x+1} = \frac{3x+5}{x+1}.$$

Notice that the numerator and denominator of this function are both linear. Because the process of writing $f(x) = \frac{a}{x-h} + k$ as $f(x) = \frac{bx+c}{dx+e}$ is reversible, you have a means of graphing rational functions with linear numerators and denominators by putting them in the *graphing form* $f(x) = \frac{a}{x-h} + k$.

1 EXAMPLE Graphing $f(x) = \frac{bx+c}{dx+e}$ when $d = 1$

Graph the function $f(x) = \frac{3x+2}{x-1}$.

A Use long division to write the function in graphing form.

$$\begin{array}{r} 3 \\ x-1 \overline{)3x+2} \end{array}$$ Divide $3x$ by x and write down the quotient, 3.

$$\begin{array}{r} 3 \\ x-1 \overline{)3x+2} \\ \underline{3x-3} \\ 5 \end{array}$$ Multiply the divisor, $x - 1$, by the quotient and subtract the result from the dividend, $3x + 2$, to get the remainder, 5.

So, the division of $3x + 2$ by $x - 1$ results in a quotient of 3 with a remainder of 5. Use the relationship below to rewrite the function's rule.

$$\frac{dividend}{divisor} = quotient + \frac{remainder}{divisor}$$

$$\frac{3x+2}{x-1} = 3 + \frac{5}{x-1}$$

Write the function in graphing form: $f(x) = \frac{5}{x-1} + 3$

B Use the graphing form to complete the information below about the graph. Then graph the function.

- Horizontal asymptote: $y = 3$
- Vertical asymptote: $x = 1$
- Reference point that is 1 unit to the right of the vertical asymptote: $(2, 8)$
- Reference point that is 1 unit to the left of the vertical asymptote: $(0, -2)$

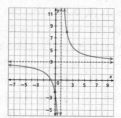

REFLECT

1a. Describe how you can find the vertical asymptote of the graph of $f(x) = \frac{3x+2}{x-1}$ without writing the function in graphing form first.

The vertical asymptote occurs at the value of x for which the function is undefined, which is when the denominator equals 0.

1b. If you divide the numerator and denominator of $f(x) = \frac{3x+2}{x-1}$ by x, you get $f(x) = \frac{3 + \frac{2}{x}}{1 - \frac{1}{x}}$. Use this form of the function to complete the table.

	What the value of the numerator approaches	What the value of the denominator approaches	What the value of the function approaches
As x increases without bound	3	1	$\frac{3}{1} = 3$
As x decreases without bound	3	1	$\frac{3}{1} = 3$

1c. What does the table above tell you about the graph of the function?

The line $y = 3$ is a horizontal asymptote for the graph.

© Houghton Mifflin Harcourt Publishing Company

TEACH

1 EXAMPLE

Questioning Strategies

- How can you use what you know about translating the graph of $f(x) = \frac{a}{x}$ to graph $f(x) = \frac{3x+2}{x-1}$? Rewrite the function in graphing form as $f(x) = \frac{5}{x-1} + 3$; translate the graph of $f(x) = \frac{5}{x}$ right 1 unit and up 3 units.

- When $f(x) = \frac{3x+2}{x-1}$ is written in graphing form, what are the values of a, h, and k? 5, 1, 3

Differentiated Instruction

Interpersonal learners may benefit from working in pairs, with one student graphing $f(x) = \frac{3x+2}{x-1}$ by rewriting the function in graphing form and the other graphing the function by making a table of values and plotting points. Students should compare the strategies by identifying at least one advantage and one disadvantage for each method. Then have them swap methods to complete the Extra Example.

EXTRA EXAMPLE

Graph the function $f(x) = \frac{2x-5}{x-4}$. The horizontal asymptote is $y = 2$. The vertical asymptote is $x = 4$. The reference points are (5, 5) and (3, −1).

2 EXAMPLE

Questioning Strategies

- How are the domain and the range of $f(x) = \frac{3x+4}{4x-5}$ related to the graph of the function? The domain is $\{x \mid x \neq 1.25\}$ and the vertical asymptote is $x = 1.25$, so the value excluded from the domain is where the vertical asymptote occurs. The range is $\{y \mid y \neq 0.75\}$, and the horizontal asymptote is $y = 0.75$, so the value excluded from the range is also where the horizontal asymptote occurs.

- How can you use the graphing form of $f(x) = \frac{3x+4}{4x-5}$ to determine reference points on each side of the vertical asymptote? The graphing form $f(x) = \frac{1.9375}{x-1.25} + 0.75$ represents a translation of the graph of $f(x) = \frac{1.9375}{x}$, which includes reference points (1, 1.9375) and (−1, −1.9375). The graphing form tells you that the graph is translated 1.25 units to the right and 0.75 units up, so the translated reference points are (2.25, 2.6875) and (0.25, −1.1875).

EXTRA EXAMPLE

Graph the function $f(x) = \frac{2x+4}{5x-3}$. The horizontal asymptote is $y = 0.4$, the vertical asymptote is $x = 0.6$, and the reference points are $(0, -\frac{4}{3})$ and (1, 3).

3 EXAMPLE

Questioning Strategies

- What would be the rule for $C(a)$ if the initial amount of acid were 3 mL instead of 5 mL? Explain. $C(a) = \frac{a+3}{a+18}$; the concentration of acid in the acid-and-water mix would be $\frac{3}{3+15} = \frac{3}{18} \approx$ 16.7%, and when the additional amount a of acid is added, $C(a) = \frac{3+a}{(3+a)+15} = \frac{a+3}{a+18}$.

- How could you graph $C(a) = \frac{a+5}{a+20}$ without using a graphing calculator? You know that the graph begins at (0, 0.25). You can also determine that the graph has $C(a) = 1$ as its horizontal asymptote (which is the function's end behavior as a increases without bound). Make a table of values for several positive values of a, such as $a = 10, 20,$ and 30. Plot the points and draw a smooth curve that approaches the line $C(a) = 1$ for greater values of a.

© Houghton Mifflin Harcourt Publishing Company

continued

The Reflect questions on the previous page suggest another way to find the asymptotes of the graph of $f(x) = \frac{bx + c}{dx + e}$.

- To find the vertical asymptote, set the denominator equal to 0 and solve for x. (You are finding the value of x for which the function is undefined. This value is sometimes called an *excluded value* because it cannot be included in the function's domain.)
- To find the horizontal asymptote, divide the numerator and the denominator of the function's rule by x, and then determine what value the function approaches as x increases or decreases without bound.

2 EXAMPLE Graphing $f(x) = \frac{bx + c}{dx + e}$ when $d \neq 1$

Graph the function $f(x) = \frac{3x + 4}{4x - 5}$.

A Find the vertical asymptote. Set $4x - 5$ equal to 0 and solve for x to get

$x = \underline{1.25}$

B Find the horizontal asymptote. Rewrite the function rule as $f(x) = \frac{3 + \frac{4}{x}}{4 - \frac{5}{x}}$.

As x increases or decreases without bound, the y-value that the value

of $f(x)$ approaches is $y = \underline{0.75}$

C Draw the graph after determining a reference point on each side of the vertical asymptote.

- A reference point to the right of the vertical asymptote: *Sample answer:* About (2, 3.3)

- A reference point to the left of the vertical asymptote: *Sample answer:* (0, −0.8)

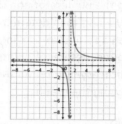

REFLECT

2a. State the domain and range of the function.

$D = \{x \mid x \neq 1.25\}; R = \{y \mid y \neq 0.75\}$

2b. Follow the steps below to write $f(x) = \frac{3x + 4}{4x - 5}$ in graphing form.

Step 1: Divide the numerator and denominator by the coefficient of x in the denominator.

$f(x) = \dfrac{0.75\ x + 1}{x - 1.25}$

Step 2: Divide the numerator in Step 1 by the denominator in Step 1 using long division.

$x - 1.25 \overline{)\,0.75\ x + 1\,}$

$0.75\ x - 0.9375$

1.9375

Step 3: Write the function in graphing form.

$f(x) = \dfrac{1.9375}{x - 1.25} + 0.75$

How does the graphing form help you check the graph that you drew?

It confirms that the vertical asymptote is $x = 1.25$ and the horizontal asymptote is $y = 0.75$.

3 EXAMPLE Modeling with Rational Functions

A chemist mixes 5 mL of an acid with 15 mL of water. The concentration of acid in the acid-and-water mix is $\frac{5}{5 + 15} = \frac{5}{20} = 25\%$. If the chemist adds more acid to the mix, then the concentration C becomes a function of the additional amount a of acid added to the mix. Write a rule for the function $C(a)$ and then graph the function using a graphing calculator.

A Use the verbal model below to write the rule for $C(a)$.

$$\frac{\text{Concentration of acid in mix}}{} = \frac{\text{Initial amount of acid} + \text{Additional acid}}{\text{Total amount of acid} + \text{Amount of water}}$$

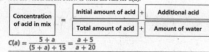

$C(a) = \dfrac{5 + a}{(5 + a) + 15} = \dfrac{a + 5}{a + 20}$

B Determine a good viewing window by answering the following questions.

- What is a reasonable domain for the function? That is, what values can the variable a have in this situation?
The amount of acid added must be nonnegative, so $a \geq 0$.

© Houghton Mifflin Harcourt Publishing Company

Essential Question

How can you graph a function of the form

$f(x) = \dfrac{bx + c}{dx + e}$?

One method is to write the function in graphing

form $h(x) = \dfrac{a}{x - h} + k$, and then use that form

to determine the horizontal asymptote $y = k$, the
vertical asymptote $x = h$, and the reference points
$(1 + h, a + k)$ and $(-1 + h, -a + k)$. Another
method is to leave the function in the form

$f(x) = \dfrac{bx + c}{dx + e}$ and determine the vertical asymptote

by setting the denominator equal to 0 and solving
for x. The horizontal asymptote can be determined
by dividing the numerator and denominator of the
function by x and then determining what value
the function approaches as x increases or decreases
without bound. Reference points on either side
of the vertical asymptote can then be determined
before drawing the graph.

MATHEMATICAL PRACTICE · **Highlighting the Standards**

3 EXAMPLE and its Reflect questions offer
an opportunity to address Mathematical
Practice Standard 5 (Use appropriate tools
strategically). Students write a rational
function to model a real-world situation and
then use a graphing calculator to graph the
function. Although the vertical asymptote of
the graph intersects the x-axis at a negative
value of x, the reasonable domain for the
function consists of only nonnegative values.
Students manipulate the model by setting the
viewing window of the graphing calculator
to show only the portion of the graph that is
relevant to the real-world situation.

Summarize

Have students make a table that shows the steps for

graphing a function of the form $f(x) = \dfrac{bx + c}{dx + e}$ by

two methods: (1) writing the function in graphing
form before graphing and (2) graphing the function
without writing the function in graphing form first.

Teachnology

After students have graphed $C(a) = \dfrac{a + 5}{a + 20}$ using

a graphing calculator, they can use the TRACE
function to explore the relationship between
the additional amount a of acid added and the
concentration of acid in the acid-and-water mix.
After TRACE is pressed, the left and right arrow keys
move the cursor along the graph. As the cursor
moves, its x- and y-coordinates are updated at
the bottom of the viewing window. The x-value
represents the amount a of acid added to the mix.
The corresponding y-value represents, as a decimal,
the percent of acid in the acid-and-water mix.

EXTRA EXAMPLE

An artist mixes 2 mL of red paint with 18 mL
of white paint. The concentration of red in the

red-and-white mix is $\dfrac{2}{2 + 18} = \dfrac{2}{20} = 10\%$.

If the painter adds more red to the mix, then the
concentration of red C becomes a function of the
additional amount r of red added to the mix. Write
a rule for the function $C(r)$ and then graph the

function using a graphing calculator. $C(r) = \dfrac{r + 2}{r + 20}$;

graph the function on a graphing calculator with
viewing window set to $x \geq 0$ and $0 \leq y \leq 1$.

PRACTICE

Where skills are taught	Where skills are practiced
1 EXAMPLE	EXS. 1, 2
2 EXAMPLE	EX. 3
3 EXAMPLE	EX. 4

- What concentration of acid does pure water have? What concentration of acid does pure acid have? So, what are the possible values of $C(a)$?

  Pure water is 0% acid; pure acid is 100% acid; $0\% \le C(a) \le 100\%$ or $0 \le C(a) \le 1$

- On a graphing calculator, you will let x represent a and y represent $C(a)$. Specify a viewing window by stating the least and greatest x-values and the least and greatest y-values that you will use.

  Answers for the greatest x-value will vary. *Sample answer:* $0 \le x \le 20$; $0 \le y \le 1$

C Press [WINDOW] and set the viewing window. (Choose appropriate scales for the two axes.) Then press [Y=] and enter the rule for the function. Finally, press [GRAPH] to see the graph. It should look like the one shown.

REFLECT

3a. Analyze the function's rule to determine the vertical asymptote of the function's graph. Why is the asymptote irrelevant in this situation?

Vertical asymptote: $x = -20$; only nonnegative values of x are being considered.

3b. Analyze the function's rule to determine the horizontal asymptote of the function's graph. What is the relevance of the asymptote in this situation?

Horizontal asymptote: $y = 1$; when the chemist adds lots of acid to the mix, the

concentration of acid in the mix approaches that of pure acid (concentration = 1).

PRACTICE

Write each function in graphing form and then graph the function.

1. $f(x) = \frac{3x - 14}{x - 5}$ $f(x) = \frac{1}{x - 5} + 3$

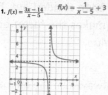

2. $f(x) = \frac{-4x + 5}{x + 2}$ $f(x) = \frac{3}{x + 2} - 4$

Unit 4   147   Lesson 3

---

3. Graph $f(x) = \frac{2x + 1}{5x - 2}$ after finding the asymptotes and plotting a reference point on each side of the vertical asymptote.

- Vertical asymptote: $x = 0.4$
- Horizontal asymptote: $y = 0.4$
- A reference point to the right of the vertical asymptote: Sample answer: (1, 1)
- A reference point to the left of the vertical asymptote: Sample answer: (0, −0.5)

4. A baseball team has won 18 games and lost 12. Its current percent of wins is $\frac{18}{18 + 12} = \frac{18}{30} = 0.6$, or 60%. Suppose the team experiences a winning streak where every game played is a win. Then its percent P of wins becomes a function of the number w of wins in the streak.

a. Use the verbal model below to write a rule for $P(w)$.

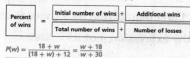

$$P(w) = \frac{18 + w}{(18 + w) + 12} = \frac{w + 18}{w + 30}$$

b. Before graphing the function on a graphing calculator, decide what a good viewing window would be. Explain your reasoning.

Answers will vary, but students should recognize that x (representing w) should

be nonnegative and that y (representing $P(w)$) should be between 0 and 1.

c. Again, before graphing the function on a graphing calculator, state what the graph's y-intercept is and whether the graph is increasing or decreasing. Explain your reasoning.

The y-intercept is 0.6 because that is the initial percent of wins; the graph is

increasing because winning more games increases the percent of wins.

d. Graph the function on a graphing calculator. Describe the end behavior in terms of the context of the problem.

The graph approaches the horizontal asymptote $y = 1$, which represents a

perfect winning percentage.

Unit 4   148   Lesson 3

© Houghton Mifflin Harcourt Publishing Company

Adding and Subtracting Rational Expressions

Essential question: *How do you find sums and differences of rational expressions?*

© Houghton Mifflin Harcourt Publishing Company

COMMON CORE Standards for Mathematical Content

CC.9-12.A.SSE.1 Interpret expressions that represent a quantity in terms of its context.*

CC.9-12.A.SSE.1b Interpret complicated expressions by viewing one or more of their parts as a single entity.*

CC.9-12.A.APR.7(+) ... add, subtract ... rational expressions.

CC.9-12.F.BF.1 Write a function that describes a relationship between two quantities.*

CC.9-12.F.BF.1b Combine standard function types using arithmetic operations.*

Also: CC.9-12.N.Q.1*

Prerequisites

Multiplying polynomials, Lesson 3-6

Factoring polynomials, Lesson 3-8

Math Background

Students are familiar with the process of multiplying polynomials as well as the reverse process of factoring polynomials. In this lesson, they will use these skills to add and subtract rational expressions.

INTRODUCE

Point out to students that the process of adding and subtracting rational expressions follows the same general steps as the process of adding and subtracting rational numbers: First, write the fractions with a common denominator, if necessary. Then, add or subtract the numerators and write the result over the common denominator. Finally, simplify the answer, if possible. Students may find it helpful to add and subtract a couple of rational numbers before attempting to add and subtract rational expressions.

TEACH

1 EXAMPLE

Questioning Strategies

- When working with equivalent expressions, how can you determine excluded values of the simplified form of the expression? **Look at the denominator after the expression in the denominator has been factored, but before any common factors have been divided out. For each factor, any value that makes the factor equal to zero is an excluded value.**

Avoid Common Errors

Encourage students to always use the factored but unsimplified form of a rational expression to identify any excluded values.

EXTRA EXAMPLE

Simplify: $\dfrac{3x-6}{x^2-5x+6}$. Identify any excluded values. $\dfrac{3}{x-3}; x \neq 3; x \neq 2$

2 EXAMPLE

Questioning Strategies

- Does the value of the second expression of the sum change when it is multiplied by $\dfrac{x-1}{x-1}$? **No, $\dfrac{x-1}{x-1} = 1$ and multiplying by 1 changes only the form of the expression, not its value.**

- Why is $x = 0$ used to check the work instead of $x = 1$ or some other value of x? **When $x = 0$, the x^2- and x-terms evaluate to 0, which simplifies the calculations.**

EXTRA EXAMPLE

Find the sum: $\dfrac{x+3}{x^2-2x-8} + \dfrac{3}{x+2} \cdot$ $\dfrac{4x-9}{(x+2)(x-4)}$

Name_____ Class_____ Date_____

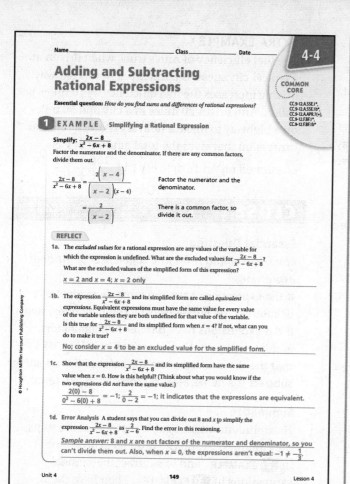

Adding and Subtracting Rational Expressions

4-4

COMMON CORE

CC.9-12.A.SSE.1*,
CC.9-12.A.SSE.1b*,
CC.9-12.A.APR.7(+),
CC.9-12.F.BF.1*,
CC.9-12.F.BF.1b*

Essential question: *How do you find sums and differences of rational expressions?*

1 EXAMPLE Simplifying a Rational Expression

Simplify: $\dfrac{2x-8}{x^2-6x+8}$

Factor the numerator and the denominator. If there are any common factors, divide them out.

$\dfrac{2x-8}{x^2-6x+8}=\dfrac{2\left(\boxed{x}-4\right)}{\left(\boxed{x}-2\right)(x-4)}$ Factor the numerator and the denominator.

$=\dfrac{2}{\left(\boxed{x}-2\right)}$ There is a common factor, so divide it out.

REFLECT

1a. The *excluded values* for a rational expression are any values of the variable for which the expression is undefined. What are the excluded values for $\dfrac{2x-8}{x^2-6x+8}$? What are the excluded values of the simplified form of this expression?

$x = 2$ and $x = 4$; $x = 2$ only

1b. The expression $\dfrac{2x-8}{x^2-6x+8}$ and its simplified form are called *equivalent expressions*. Equivalent expressions must have the same value for every value of the variable unless they are both undefined for that value of the variable. Is this true for $\dfrac{2x-8}{x^2-6x+8}$ and its simplified form when $x = 4$? If not, what can you do to make it true?

No; consider $x = 4$ to be an excluded value for the simplified form.

1c. Show that the expression $\dfrac{2x-8}{x^2-6x+8}$ and its simplified form have the same value when $x = 0$. How is this helpful? (Think about what you would know if the two expressions did *not* have the same value.)

$\dfrac{2(0)-8}{0^2-6(0)+8}=-1$; $\dfrac{2}{0-2}=-1$; it indicates that the expressions are equivalent.

1d. **Error Analysis** A student says that you can divide out 8 and x to simplify the expression $\dfrac{2x-8}{x^2-6x+8}$ as $\dfrac{2}{x-6}$. Find the error in this reasoning.

Sample answer: 8 and x are not factors of the numerator and denominator, so you can't divide them out. Also, when $x = 0$, the expressions aren't equal: $-1 \neq -\dfrac{1}{3}$.

Unit 4   149   Lesson 4

© Houghton Mifflin Harcourt Publishing Company

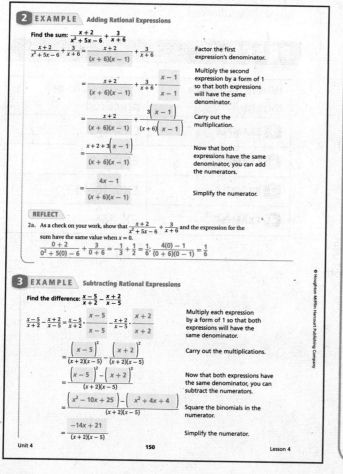

2 EXAMPLE Adding Rational Expressions

Find the sum: $\dfrac{x+2}{x^2+5x-6}+\dfrac{3}{x+6}$

$\dfrac{x+2}{x^2+5x-6}+\dfrac{3}{x+6}=\dfrac{x+2}{(x+6)(x-1)}+\dfrac{3}{x+6}$ Factor the first expression's denominator.

$=\dfrac{x+2}{(x+6)(x-1)}+\dfrac{3}{x+6}\cdot\dfrac{x-1}{x-1}$ Multiply the second expression by a form of 1 so that both expressions will have the same denominator.

$=\dfrac{x+2}{(x+6)(x-1)}+\dfrac{3\left(x-1\right)}{(x+6)\left(x-1\right)}$ Carry out the multiplication.

$=\dfrac{x+2+3\left(x-1\right)}{(x+6)(x-1)}$ Now that both expressions have the same denominator, you can add the numerators.

$=\dfrac{4x-1}{(x+6)(x-1)}$ Simplify the numerator.

REFLECT

2a. As a check on your work, show that $\dfrac{x+2}{x^2+5x-6}+\dfrac{3}{x+6}$ and the expression for the sum have the same value when $x = 0$.

$\dfrac{0+2}{0^2+5(0)-6}+\dfrac{3}{0+6}=-\dfrac{1}{3}+\dfrac{1}{2}=\dfrac{1}{6}$; $\dfrac{4(0)-1}{(0+6)(0-1)}=\dfrac{1}{6}$

3 EXAMPLE Subtracting Rational Expressions

Find the difference: $\dfrac{x-5}{x+2}-\dfrac{x+2}{x-5}$

$\dfrac{x-5}{x+2}-\dfrac{x+2}{x-5}=\dfrac{x-5}{x+2}\cdot\dfrac{x-5}{x-5}-\dfrac{x+2}{x-5}\cdot\dfrac{x+2}{x+2}$ Multiply each expression by a form of 1 so that both expressions will have the same denominator.

$=\dfrac{\left(x-5\right)^2}{(x+2)(x-5)}-\dfrac{\left(x+2\right)^2}{(x+2)(x-5)}$ Carry out the multiplications.

$=\dfrac{\left(x-5\right)^2-\left(x+2\right)^2}{(x+2)(x-5)}$ Now that both expressions have the same denominator, you can subtract the numerators.

$=\dfrac{\left(x^2-10x+25\right)-\left(x^2+4x+4\right)}{(x+2)(x-5)}$ Square the binomials in the numerator.

$=\dfrac{-14x+21}{(x+2)(x-5)}$ Simplify the numerator.

Unit 4   150   Lesson 4

© Houghton Mifflin Harcourt Publishing Company

Unit 4

Lesson 4

3 EXAMPLE

Questioning Strategies

• After rational expressions have been subtracted, why is it important to check whether the numerator of the expression for the difference is factorable? **If the numerator is factorable, it may be possible that the expression for the difference can be simplified further.**

Avoid Common Errors

When students subtract a numerator that has more than one term, they may subtract only the first term and then add the remaining terms. Remind students that each term in the numerator must be subtracted. Some students may benefit from adding the opposite rather than subtracting.

| MATHEMATICAL PRACTICE | Highlighting the Standards |

2 EXAMPLE and **3 EXAMPLE** and their Reflect questions offer an opportunity to address Mathematical Practice Standard 8 (Look for and express regularity in repeated reasoning). Students observe that rational expressions can be both added and subtracted by multiplying one or both expressions by a form of 1 so that the denominators are the same.

EXTRA EXAMPLE

Find the difference: $\dfrac{x-4}{x+3} - \dfrac{x+3}{x-4}$. $\dfrac{-14x+7}{(x+3)(x-4)}$

4 EXAMPLE

Questioning Strategies

• What form of 1 is $\dfrac{25}{E}$ multiplied by so that both expressions have the same denominator? $\dfrac{E-5}{E-5}$

• What form of 1 is $\dfrac{10}{E-5}$ multiplied by so that both expressions have the same denominator? $\dfrac{E}{E}$

EXTRA EXAMPLE

The fuel efficiency of Ann's truck when driven at a typical city speed is E miles per hour. Highway driving increases the fuel efficiency by 10 miles per gallon. Ann drives 20 miles in a city and 50 miles on a highway to make a delivery. Write a rational expression that gives the total amount of gas consumed on Ann's delivery trip. $\dfrac{70E+200}{E(E+10)}$

CLOSE

Essential Question

How do you find sums and differences of rational expressions?
If the expressions have the same denominator, add or subtract the numerators by combining like terms. If the expressions have different denominators, multiply one or both expressions by a form of 1 so that the denominators are the same and then add or subtract the numerators by combining like terms.

Summarize

Have students make a table that shows the steps they followed to add the rational expressions in **2 EXAMPLE** and to subtract the rational expressions in **3 EXAMPLE**. Then have them identify the similarities and differences between the steps they followed.

PRACTICE

Where skills are taught	Where skills are practiced
1 EXAMPLE	EXS. 1–3
2 EXAMPLE	EXS. 4–9
3 EXAMPLE	EXS. 10–15
4 EXAMPLE	EX. 16

REFLECT

3a. As a check on your work, show that $\frac{x-5}{x+2} - \frac{x+2}{x-5}$ and the expression for the difference have the same value when $x = 0$.

$$\frac{0-5}{0+2} - \frac{0+2}{0-5} = -\frac{5}{2} - \left(-\frac{2}{5}\right) = -\frac{25}{10} + \frac{4}{10} = -\frac{21}{10}; \frac{-14(0)+21}{(0+2)(0-5)} = -\frac{21}{10}$$

3b. In the expression for the difference, is the numerator factorable? If so, can the expression be simplified? Explain.

The numerator can be factored as $-7(2x - 3)$; the expression cannot be simplified

because there are no common factors in the numerator and denominator.

4 EXAMPLE Modeling with a Sum of Rational Expressions

The fuel efficiency of Mr. Garcia's car when driven at a typical highway speed is E miles per gallon. City driving reduces the fuel efficiency by 5 miles per gallon. Mr. Garcia drives 25 miles on a highway and 10 miles in a city to get to work. Write a rational expression that gives the total amount of gas consumed on Mr. Garcia's trip to work.

A Divide the distance traveled by the fuel efficiency to find an expression for the amount of gas consumed on each portion of the trip.

Gas consumed on highway $= \dfrac{25}{E}$ Gas consumed in city $= \dfrac{10}{E-5}$

B Use the verbal model to write an expression involving addition for the total gas consumed.

Total gas consumed	=	Gas consumed on highway	+	Gas consumed in city

Total gas consumed $= \dfrac{25}{E} + \dfrac{10}{E-5}$

C Carry out the addition to get a combined expression for the total gas consumed.

Total gas consumed $= \dfrac{25(E-5) + 10E}{E(E-5)} = \dfrac{35E - 125}{E(E-5)}$

REFLECT

4a. Use unit analysis to show why dividing distance traveled by fuel efficiency gives the amount of gas consumed.

$$\text{miles} \div \frac{\text{miles}}{\text{gallons}} = \text{miles} \cdot \frac{\text{gallons}}{\text{miles}} = \text{gallons}$$

PRACTICE

Simplify each expression.

1. $\dfrac{2x-4}{3x-6}$

$\dfrac{2}{3}$

2. $\dfrac{4x+8}{8x+4}$

$\dfrac{x+2}{2x+1}$

3. $\dfrac{2x-10}{x^2-3x-10}$

$\dfrac{2}{x+2}$

Find each sum or difference.

4. $\dfrac{2}{x+1} + \dfrac{3}{x}$

$\dfrac{5x+3}{x(x+1)}$

5. $\dfrac{x-5}{x+3} + \dfrac{x+4}{x-2}$

$\dfrac{2x^2+22}{(x+3)(x-2)}$

6. $\dfrac{3x}{2x+6} + \dfrac{x}{x^2+7x+12}$

$\dfrac{3x^2-14x}{2(x+4)(x+3)}$

7. $\dfrac{3}{x^2-25} + \dfrac{9x}{x+5}$

$\dfrac{9x^2-45x+3}{(x+5)(x-5)}$

8. $\dfrac{x+4}{x+7} + \dfrac{x-1}{x-2}$

$\dfrac{2x^2+8x-15}{(x+7)(x-2)}$

9. $\dfrac{1}{x^2+2x+1} + \dfrac{1}{x^2-1}$

$\dfrac{2x}{(x+1)^2(x-1)}$

10. $\dfrac{x}{x+9} - \dfrac{4}{x}$

$\dfrac{x^2-4x-36}{x(x+9)}$

11. $\dfrac{4}{2x+3} - \dfrac{5x}{x-6}$

$\dfrac{10x^2+11x+24}{(2x+3)(x+6)}$

12. $\dfrac{7}{x^2-4x+4} - \dfrac{3x}{x-2}$

$\dfrac{-3x^2+6x+7}{(x-2)^2}$

13. $\dfrac{x+2}{x-1} - \dfrac{x+8}{3x^2+3x-6}$

$\dfrac{3x^2+11x+4}{3(x+2)(x-1)}$

14. $\dfrac{x+2}{x+1} - \dfrac{x+1}{x+2}$

$\dfrac{2x+3}{(x+1)(x+2)}$

15. $\dfrac{x}{x^2-2x+1} - \dfrac{x}{x^2-1}$

$\dfrac{2x}{(x-1)^2(x+1)}$

16. Anita exercises by running and walking. When she runs, she burns c Calories per minute for a total of 500 Calories. When she walks, she burns $(c-8)$ Calories per minute for a total of 100 Calories.

a. Write an expression for the time that she spends running and another expression for the time that she spends walking.

Running time $= \dfrac{500}{c}$; walking time $= \dfrac{100}{c-8}$

b. Use unit analysis to show that your expressions are a unit of time.

$$\text{Calories} \div \frac{\text{Calories}}{\text{minutes}} = \text{Calories} \cdot \frac{\text{minutes}}{\text{Calories}} = \text{minutes}$$

c. Write two equivalent expressions for her total time.

Total time $= \dfrac{500}{c} + \dfrac{100}{c-8} = \dfrac{600c-4000}{c(c-8)}$

Multiplying and Dividing Rational Expressions

Essential question: *How do you find products and quotients of rational expressions?*

COMMON Standards for
CORE Mathematical Content

CC.9-12.A.SSE.1 Interpret expressions that represent a quantity in terms of its context.*

CC.9-12.A.SSE.1b Interpret complicated expressions by viewing one or more of their parts as a single entity.*

CC.9-12.A.APR.7(+) Understand that rational expressions form a system analogous to the rational numbers, closed under addition, subtraction, multiplication, and division by a nonzero rational expression; ... multiply, and divide rational expressions.

CC.9-12.F.BF.1 Write a function that describes a relationship between two quantities.*

CC.9-12.F.BF.1b Combine standard function types using arithmetic operations.

Also: CC.9-12.N.Q.1*

Prerequisites

Multiplying polynomials, Lesson 3-6

Factoring polynomials, Lesson 3-8

Excluded values, Lesson 4-4

Math Background

Students are familiar with factoring polynomials, as well as with multiplying polynomials. In the previous lesson, they learned to simplify rational expressions. In this lesson, they will use these skills to multiply and divide rational expressions.

INTRODUCE

Point out to students that the process of multiplying and dividing rational expressions follows the same general steps as the process of multiplying and dividing rational numbers: First, if division is involved, rewrite to multiply by the reciprocal of the divisor instead. Then, write the product of the numerators over the product of the denominators. Finally, simplify the answer, if possible. Point out that for rational expressions, unlike rational numbers, the factoring that is needed to simplify the answer should be done *before* multiplying to avoid having difficult-to-factor polynomials in the

numerator and denominator at the end. Students may find it helpful to multiply and divide a couple of rational numbers before attempting to multiply and divide rational expressions.

TEACH

1 EXAMPLE

Questioning Strategies

- Would the product be the same if you multiplied the numerators and denominators and then factored each numerator and denominator? **Yes, the expressions would be equivalent.**

- What is the purpose of factoring each numerator and denominator before multiplying the numerators and denominators? **To have the product in factored form so that common factors in the numerator and denominator can be divided out.**

EXTRA EXAMPLE

Find the product: $\dfrac{4x}{x^2 + x - 6} \cdot \dfrac{2x - 4}{x^2 + x} \cdot \dfrac{8}{(x + 1)(x + 3)}$

2 EXAMPLE

Questioning Strategies

- How is the process for dividing rational expressions related to the process for multiplying rational expressions? **Dividing by an expression is equivalent to multiplying by its reciprocal. Once division is converted to multiplication, you can carry out the steps for multiplying rational expressions.**

- Why is $x = 0$ an excluded value? **The denominator $x^2 - 4x$ equals 0 when $x = 0$.**

Avoid Common Errors

When identifying excluded values for quotients of rational expressions, students may consider values that cause the denominators to be zero, but they may not consider values that cause the divisor itself to be 0. For example, the divisor $\dfrac{x^2 - 36}{x^2 - 4x}$ will have a value of 0 when $x = 6$ or $x = -6$, so these values must also be excluded values.

continued

© Houghton Mifflin Harcourt Publishing Company

Name_____ Class_____ Date_____

4-5

COMMON
CORE

Multiplying and Dividing Rational Expressions

Essential question: *How do you find products and quotients of rational expressions?*

CC.9-12.A.SSE.1*,
CC.9-12.A.SSE.1b*,
CC.9-12.A.APR.7(+),
CC.9-12.F.BF.1*,
CC.9-12.F.BF.1b*

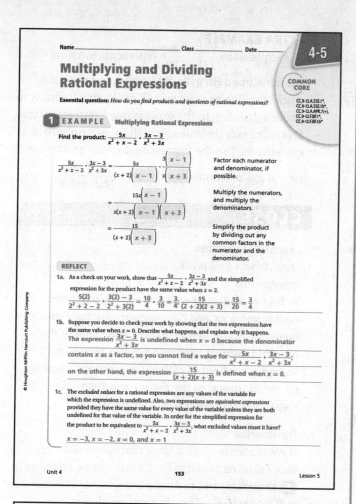

1 EXAMPLE Multiplying Rational Expressions

Find the product: $\dfrac{5x}{x^2 + x - 2} \cdot \dfrac{3x - 3}{x^2 + 3x}$

$$\dfrac{5x}{x^2+x-2} \cdot \dfrac{3x-3}{x^2+3x} = \dfrac{5x}{(x+2)(x-1)} \cdot \dfrac{3(x-1)}{x(x+3)}$$
Factor each numerator and denominator, if possible.

$$= \dfrac{15x(x-1)}{x(x+2)(x-1)(x+3)}$$
Multiply the numerators, and multiply the denominators.

$$= \dfrac{15}{(x+2)(x+3)}$$
Simplify the product by dividing out any common factors in the numerator and the denominator.

REFLECT

1a. As a check on your work, show that $\dfrac{5x}{x^2+x-2} \cdot \dfrac{3x-3}{x^2+3x}$ and the simplified expression for the product have the same value when $x = 2$.

$$\dfrac{5(2)}{2^2+2-2} \cdot \dfrac{3(2)-3}{2^2+3(2)} = \dfrac{10}{4} \cdot \dfrac{3}{10} = \dfrac{3}{4}; \quad \dfrac{15}{(2+2)(2+3)} = \dfrac{15}{20} = \dfrac{3}{4}$$

1b. Suppose you decide to check your work by showing that the two expressions have the same value when $x = 0$. Describe what happens, and explain why it happens.

The expression $\dfrac{3x-3}{x^2+3x}$ is undefined when $x = 0$ because the denominator

contains x as a factor, so you cannot find a value for $\dfrac{5x}{x^2+x-2} \cdot \dfrac{3x-3}{x^2+3x}$;

on the other hand, the expression $\dfrac{15}{(x+2)(x+3)}$ is defined when $x = 0$.

1c. The *excluded values* for a rational expression are any values of the variable for which the expression is undefined. Also, two expressions are *equivalent expressions* provided they have the same value for every value of the variable unless they are both undefined for that value of the variable. In order for the simplified expression for the product to be equivalent to $\dfrac{5x}{x^2+x-2} \cdot \dfrac{3x-3}{x^2+3x}$, what excluded values must it have?

$x = -3, x = -2, x = 0,$ and $x = 1$

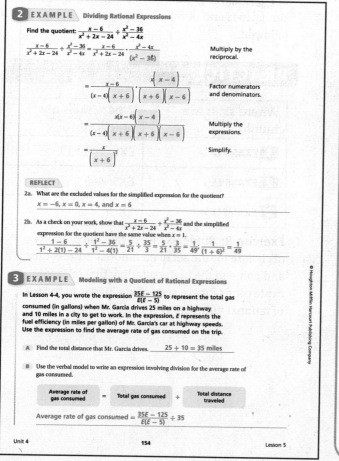

2 EXAMPLE Dividing Rational Expressions

Find the quotient: $\dfrac{x-6}{x^2+2x-24} \div \dfrac{x^2-36}{x^2-4x}$

$$\dfrac{x-6}{x^2+2x-24} \div \dfrac{x^2-36}{x^2-4x} = \dfrac{x-6}{x^2+2x-24} \cdot \dfrac{x^2-4x}{(x^2-36)}$$
Multiply by the reciprocal.

$$= \dfrac{x-6}{(x-4)(x+6)} \cdot \dfrac{x(x-4)}{(x+6)(x-6)}$$
Factor numerators and denominators.

$$= \dfrac{x(x-6)(x-4)}{(x-4)(x+6)(x+6)(x-6)}$$
Multiply the expressions.

$$= \dfrac{x}{(x+6)^2}$$
Simplify.

REFLECT

2a. What are the excluded values for the simplified expression for the quotient?

$x = -6, x = 0, x = 4,$ and $x = 6$

2b. As a check on your work, show that $\dfrac{x-6}{x^2+2x-24} \div \dfrac{x^2-36}{x^2-4x}$ and the simplified expression for the quotient have the same value when $x = 1$.

$$\dfrac{1-6}{1^2+2(1)-24} \div \dfrac{1^2-36}{1^2-4(1)} = \dfrac{5}{21} \div \dfrac{35}{3} = \dfrac{5}{21} \cdot \dfrac{3}{35} = \dfrac{1}{49}; \quad \dfrac{1}{(1+6)^2} = \dfrac{1}{49}$$

3 EXAMPLE Modeling with a Quotient of Rational Expressions

In Lesson 4-4, you wrote the expression $\dfrac{35E - 125}{E(E-5)}$ to represent the total gas consumed (in gallons) when Mr. Garcia drives 25 miles on a highway and 10 miles in a city to get to work. In the expression, E represents the fuel efficiency (in miles per gallon) of Mr. Garcia's car at highway speeds. Use the expression to find the average rate of gas consumed on the trip.

A Find the total distance that Mr. Garcia drives. ____ $25 + 10 = 35$ miles

B Use the verbal model to write an expression involving division for the average rate of gas consumed.

Average rate of gas consumed	=	Total gas consumed	÷	Total distance traveled

Average rate of gas consumed $= \dfrac{35E - 125}{E(E-5)} \div 35$

EXTRA EXAMPLE

Find the quotient: $\dfrac{x-5}{x^2+3x-10} \div \dfrac{x^2-25}{x^2-2x} \cdot \dfrac{x}{(x+5)^2}$

3 EXAMPLE

Questioning Strategies

- What are the steps to carry out the division in part C? $\dfrac{35E-125}{E(E-5)}$ is multiplied by $\dfrac{1}{35}$, the reciprocal of 35, to get $\dfrac{35E-125}{35E(E-5)}$. Then, the numerator is factored as $5(7E-25)$. Finally, the common factor of 5 is divided out, resulting in the simplified expression $\dfrac{7E-25}{7E(E-5)}$.

- Suppose the fuel efficiency of Mr. Garcia's car at highway speeds is $E = 30$ miles per gallon. Evaluate the expression $\dfrac{35E-125}{E(E-5)}$ to get the total gas consumed on his trip to work. Then divide this total by the 35 miles he drives to get the average rate of gas consumed. How does this result help you check the expression that you wrote in part C? Show that it checks. **About 1.23 gallons; about 0.035 gallon per mile; evaluate the expression in part C to see if you get the same average rate of gas consumed;** $\dfrac{7(30)-25}{7(30)(30-5)} \approx 0.035$

```
. . . . . . . .            Highlighting
.  MATHEMATICAL            the Standards
.     PRACTICE
. . . . . . . .
```

3 EXAMPLE and its Reflect questions offer an opportunity to address Mathematical Practice Standard 4 (Model with mathematics). Over the course of two lessons, students use rational expressions to model the relationship between fuel economy and rate of gas consumption. Students see how operations on rational expressions can be applied to real-world situations.

EXTRA EXAMPLE

The expression $\dfrac{70E+200}{E(E+10)}$ represents the total gas consumed (in gallons) when Ann drives her truck 20 miles in a city and 50 miles on a highway to make a delivery. In the expression, E represents the fuel efficiency (in miles per gallon) of Ann's truck at city speeds. Use the expression to find the average rate of gas consumed on the trip. $\dfrac{7E+20}{7E(E+10)}$

CLOSE

Essential Question

How do you find products and quotients of rational expressions?

To find a product of rational expressions, factor each numerator and denominator, multiply the numerators and denominators, and simplify the resulting rational expression that is the product.

To find a quotient of rational expressions, multiply by the reciprocal of the divisor and then follow the steps for multiplying rational expressions.

Summarize

Have students make a table that shows the steps they followed to multiply the rational expressions in 1 EXAMPLE and to divide the rational expressions in 2 EXAMPLE. Then have them identify the similarities and differences between the steps they followed.

PRACTICE

Where skills are taught	Where skills are practiced
1 EXAMPLE	EXS. 1–3
2 EXAMPLE	EXS. 4–6
3 EXAMPLE	EX. 7

Exercise 8: Students investigate the property of closure for the set of all rational expressions, and come to the understanding that rational expressions form a system analogous to the set of rational numbers.

c Carry out the division to get a combined expression for the average rate of gas consumed.

$$\text{Average rate of gas consumed} = \frac{35E - 125}{35E(E-5)} = \frac{7E - 25}{7E(E-5)}$$

REFLECT

3a. What unit of measurement applies to the expression for the average rate of gas consumed? Explain.

Gallons per mile; total gas consumed is measured in gallons, and total distance traveled is measured in miles, so the quotient of gas consumed to distance traveled is measured in gallons per mile.

3b. Mr. Garcia's car has a highway fuel efficiency of E miles per gallon and a city fuel efficiency of $(E - 5)$ miles per gallon. Unit analysis and an understanding of averaging would suggest that the average rate of gas consumed is given by $\left(\frac{1}{E} + \frac{1}{E-5}\right) \div 2$. Carry out the operations in this expression to get a combined expression for the average rate of gas consumed.

$$\left(\frac{1}{E} + \frac{1}{E-5}\right) \div 2 = \frac{2E - 5}{E(E-5)} \div 2 = \frac{2E - 5}{2E(E-5)}$$

3c. Suppose Mr. Garcia drives 10 miles on a highway and 10 miles in a city to get to work. Find a combined expression for the total gas consumed (see Lesson 4-4 for help) and then divide it by the total distance traveled to get a combined expression for the average rate of gas consumed. Compare this result with the one in the previous Reflect question.

Total gas consumed $= \frac{10}{E} + \frac{10}{E-5} = \frac{10(E-5) + 10E}{E(E-5)} = \frac{20E - 50}{E(E-5)}$; total distance

traveled $= 20$; average rate of gas used $= \frac{20E - 50}{E(E-5)} \div 20 = \frac{20E - 50}{20E(E-5)} = \frac{2E - 5}{2E(E-5)}$;

the expressions are identical.

3d. Show that $\left(\frac{d_1}{E} + \frac{d_2}{E-5}\right) \div (d_1 + d_2) = \frac{2E - 5}{2E(E-5)}$ when $d_1 = d_2$ but not when $d_1 \neq d_2$.

If $d_1 = d_2$, then $\left(\frac{d_1}{E} + \frac{d_2}{E-5}\right) \div (d_1 + d_2) = \left(\frac{d_1}{E} + \frac{d_1}{E-5}\right) \div (d_1 + d_1) = $

$d_1\left(\frac{1}{E} + \frac{1}{E-5}\right) \div 2d_1 = d_1\left(\frac{2E-5}{E(E-5)}\right) \div 2d_1 = \frac{d_1(2E-5)}{2d_1(E(E-5))} = \frac{2E-5}{2E(E-5)}$, but d_1

cannot be substituted for d_2 when $d_1 \neq d_2$, so $\left(\frac{d_1}{E} + \frac{d_2}{E-5}\right) \div (d_1 + d_2)$

can only be rewritten as $\frac{(d_1 + d_2)E - 5d_1}{(d_1 + d_2)E(E-5)}$.

PRACTICE

Find each product or quotient. State all excluded values.

1. $\frac{4x}{x-3} \cdot \frac{3x-9}{x^2}$

$\frac{12}{x}$; 0, 3

2. $\frac{3x+15}{x-2} \cdot \frac{7x-14}{x^2+5x}$

$\frac{21}{x}$; −5, 0, 2

3. $\frac{x+1}{x^2+7x-8} \cdot \frac{x-1}{5x+5}$

$\frac{1}{5(x+8)}$; −8, ±1

4. $\frac{5}{x^2-2x} \div \frac{3x}{x-2}$

$\frac{5}{3x^2}$; 0, 2

5. $\frac{7x-21}{x^2+7x} \div \frac{x-3}{x^2-5x}$

$\frac{7(x-5)}{x+7}$; −7, 0, 3, 5

6. $\frac{x^2+5x-6}{4x} \div \frac{x+6}{x^2-x}$

$\frac{(x-1)^2}{4}$; −6, 0, 1

7. On his trip to work, Mr. Garcia drives at a speed of s miles per hour on the highway and $(s - 30)$ miles per hour in the city. Recall that the distances he drives are 25 miles on the highway and 10 miles in the city.

a. Write an expression for the time that he spends driving on the highway and the time that he spends driving in the city.

Highway time $= \frac{25}{s}$; city time $= \frac{10}{s-30}$

b. Write his total time as a sum and then carry out the addition.

Total time $= \frac{25}{s} + \frac{10}{s-30} = \frac{35s - 750}{s(s-30)}$

c. Find his average speed on the trip by dividing the total distance that he travels by the total time. Write the average speed as a quotient and then carry out the division.

Average speed $= 35 \div \frac{35s - 750}{s(s-30)} = \frac{35s(s-30)}{35s - 750} = \frac{7s(s-30)}{7s - 150}$

8. a. In the second row of the table, write the result after performing the operation given in the first row of the table.

$\frac{x}{x+2} + \frac{1}{x^2-4}$	$\frac{x}{x+2} - \frac{1}{x^2-4}$	$\frac{x}{x+2} \cdot \frac{1}{x^2-4}$	$\frac{x}{x+2} \div \frac{1}{x^2-4}$
$\frac{(x-1)^2}{(x+2)(x-2)}$	$\frac{x^2-2x-1}{(x+2)(x-2)}$	$\frac{x}{(x+2)^2(x-2)}$	$x(x-2)$

b. Do the results support or refute the claim that the set of all rational expressions is closed under all four basic operations? Explain.

Support; all results are rational expressions including the last, which can be written as $\frac{x^2 - 2x}{1}$.

c. Based on closure, what subset of real numbers is the set of rational expressions most like?

The set of rational numbers

Solving Rational Equations

Essential question: *What methods are there for solving rational equations?*

© Houghton Mifflin Harcourt Publishing Company

⊙ COMMON **Standards for**
  CORE **Mathematical Content**

CC.9-12.A.CED.1 Create equations ... in one variable and use them to solve problems.*

CC.9-12.A.REI.2 Solve simple rational ... equations in one variable, and give examples showing how extraneous solutions may arise.

CC.9-12.A.REI.11 Explain why the x-coordinates of the points where the graphs of the equations $y = f(x)$ and $y = g(x)$ intersect are the solutions of the equation $f(x) = g(x)$; find the solutions approximately, e.g., using technology to graph the functions ... Include cases where $f(x)$ and/or $g(x)$ are linear, ... rational ... functions.*

Also: CC.9-12.A.SSE.1*, CC.9-12.A.SSE.1b*

Vocabulary
Extraneous solutions

Prerequisites
Multiplying rational expressions, Lesson 4-5
Finding zeros of polynomial functions, Lesson 3-10

Math Background
Students are familiar with methods for multiplying rational expressions and solving polynomial equations. In this lesson, students will combine these skills to solve rational equations.

INTRODUCE

Review techniques for factoring polynomials. Also, review the process for identifying excluded values in rational expressions.

TEACH

1 EXAMPLE

Questioning Strategies
• If the two sides of the equation are graphed as $y = \dfrac{2}{x-1}$ and $y = \dfrac{6}{x^2 - x}$, will the two graphs intersect, and if so, where? Yes, the graphs will intersect at (3, 1), or when $x = 3$.

• How does finding the LCM of the denominators of the rational expressions and multiplying each side of the equation by the LCM turn the rational equation into a polynomial equation? After the multiplication of both sides by the LCM has been carried out, common factors in the numerators and denominators can be divided out. The resulting denominators on each side are 1, and since the numerators are both polynomials, the equation becomes a polynomial equation.

Differentiated Instruction
After seeing the relationship between solving rational equations and solving polynomial equations, analytical learners may recall that when solving polynomial equations, the first step is often to rewrite the equation so that one side of the equation is set equal to 0. Analytical learners may benefit from rewriting this rational equation as $\dfrac{2}{x-1} - \dfrac{6}{x^2 - 1} = 0$. They can then use what they know about subtracting rational expressions to solve the equation, and draw additional conclusions about the parallels between solving rational and polynomial equations.

EXTRA EXAMPLE
Solve $\dfrac{4}{x-3} = \dfrac{8}{x^2 - 3x}$. $x = 2$

2 EXAMPLE

Questioning Strategies
• Why is the first step of the solution to factor the denominator of the rational expression on the right side of the equation? Factoring the denominator makes it easier to determine the LCM.

continued

Name_____ Class_____ Date_____

Solving Rational Equations

Essential question: *What methods are there for solving rational equations?*

As you might expect, a rational equation consists of rational expressions and polynomials (which are themselves rational expressions if you write them over 1). You can solve a rational equation algebraically by finding the least common multiple (LCM) of the denominators of the rational expressions and multiplying each side of the equation by it. Doing so turns the equation into a polynomial equation.

COMMON
CORE

CC.9-12.A.CED.1*,
CC.9-12.A.REI.2,
CC.9-12.A.REI.11*

1 EXAMPLE Solving a Rational Equation Algebraically

Solve $\frac{2}{x-1} = \frac{6}{x^2-x}$.

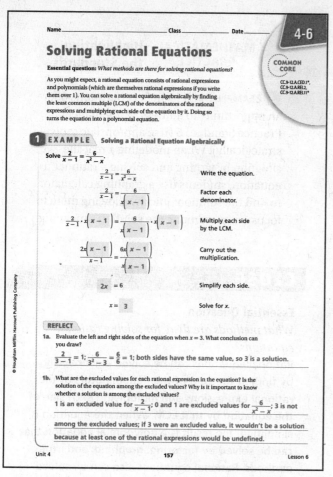

$\frac{2}{x-1} = \frac{6}{x^2-x}$ Write the equation.

$\frac{2}{x-1} = \frac{6}{x(x-1)}$ Factor each denominator.

$\frac{2}{x-1} \cdot x(x-1) = \frac{6}{x(x-1)} \cdot x(x-1)$ Multiply each side by the LCM.

$\frac{2x(x-1)}{x-1} = \frac{6x(x-1)}{x(x-1)}$ Carry out the multiplication.

$2x = 6$ Simplify each side.

$x = 3$ Solve for x.

REFLECT

1a. Evaluate the left and right sides of the equation when $x = 3$. What conclusion can you draw?

$\frac{2}{3-1} = 1$; $\frac{6}{3^2-3} = \frac{6}{6} = 1$; both sides have the same value, so 3 is a solution.

1b. What are the excluded values for each rational expression in the equation? Is the solution of the equation among the excluded values? Why is it important to know whether a solution is among the excluded values?

1 is an excluded value for $\frac{2}{x-1}$; 0 and 1 are excluded values for $\frac{6}{x^2-x}$; 3 is not

among the excluded values; if 3 were an excluded value, it wouldn't be a solution

because at least one of the rational expressions would be undefined.

Unit 4   157   Lesson 6

When solving rational equations algebraically, you must always check any apparent solutions to see if they are excluded values. If they are, then they are called **extraneous solutions** and must be rejected.

2 EXAMPLE Solving Rational Equations Having Extraneous Solutions

Solve $\frac{x}{x-2} + \frac{1}{x-4} = \frac{2}{x^2-6x+8}$.

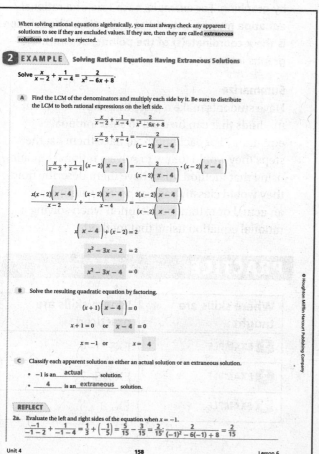

A Find the LCM of the denominators and multiply each side by it. Be sure to distribute the LCM to both rational expressions on the left side.

$\frac{x}{x-2} + \frac{1}{x-4} = \frac{2}{x^2-6x+8}$

$\frac{x}{x-2} + \frac{1}{x-4} = \frac{2}{(x-2)(x-4)}$

$\left[\frac{x}{x-2} + \frac{1}{x-4}\right](x-2)(x-4) = \frac{2}{(x-2)(x-4)} \cdot (x-2)(x-4)$

$\frac{x(x-2)(x-4)}{x-2} + \frac{(x-2)(x-4)}{x-4} = \frac{2(x-2)(x-4)}{(x-2)(x-4)}$

$x(x-4) + (x-2) = 2$

$x^2 - 3x - 2 = 2$

$x^2 - 3x - 4 = 0$

B Solve the resulting quadratic equation by factoring.

$(x+1)(x-4) = 0$

$x+1 = 0$ or $x-4 = 0$

$x = -1$ or $x = 4$

C Classify each apparent solution as either an actual solution or an extraneous solution.

• −1 is an ___actual___ solution.

• ___4___ is an ___extraneous___ solution.

REFLECT

2a. Evaluate the left and right sides of the equation when $x = -1$.

$\frac{-1}{-1-2} + \frac{1}{-1-4} = \frac{1}{3} + \left(-\frac{1}{5}\right) = \frac{5}{15} - \frac{3}{15} = \frac{2}{15}$; $\frac{2}{(-1)^2 - 6(-1) + 8} = \frac{2}{15}$

Unit 4   158   Lesson 6

• After multiplying both sides of the equation by the LCM, why is the equation rewritten as $x^2 - 3x - 4 = 0$ before being solved by factoring? **Simplifying the left side reveals that it is a quadratic expression. In order to solve the resulting quadratic equation by factoring and applying the Zero Product Property, one side of the equation must be 0.**

Avoid Common Errors
To make sure that students reject all extraneous solutions, have them evaluate the equation for each actual solution to double check that there are no excluded values that they may have overlooked.

EXTRA EXAMPLE
Solve $\frac{x}{x-3} + \frac{1}{x-5} = \frac{2}{x^2 - 8x + 15}$. $x = -1$
($x = 5$ is an extraneous solution.)

3 EXAMPLE

Questioning Strategies
• What steps would you follow to algebraically solve the equation that models the canoe trip? **Multiply each side of $\frac{6}{4+s} + \frac{6}{4-s} = 4$ by the LCM $(4 + s)(4 - s)$ and simplify to get $4s^2 - 16 = 0$. The solutions of the equation are $x = 2$ and $x = -2$, but only the positive value is reasonable in the context of the problem.**

• How would the equation that models the canoe trip change if the total trip time were 5 hours instead of 4 hours? **The right side of the equation would change from 4 to 5: $\frac{6}{4+s} + \frac{6}{4-s} = 5$.**

EXTRA EXAMPLE
Suppose you paddle a kayak at a steady speed of 5 miles per hour. You go 8 miles downstream and then 8 miles upstream to get back to where you started. The trip takes 5 hours. What is the speed of the current? **3 miles per hour**

3 EXAMPLE and its Reflect questions offer an opportunity to address Mathematical Practice Standard 5 (Use appropriate tools strategically). When modeling a real-life situation by writing and solving a rational equation, students use a graphing calculator to find the solution quickly, allowing them to focus on interpreting the solution's meaning.

CLOSE

Essential Question
What methods are there for solving rational equations?
Rational equations can be solved algebraically by finding the LCM of the denominators of the rational expressions and multiplying each side of the equation by that LCM. When the equation is simplified, the result is a polynomial equation that can be solved by factoring, graphing, and other methods. Rational equations also can be solved by graphing. For example, each side of a rational equation may be entered as a function. The solution is the x-coordinate(s) of the point(s) at which the graphs intersect.

Summarize
Have students make a table that shows different methods that can be used to solve rational equations. For each method, have them list the steps they would follow to solve a rational equation using that method. Also, have them describe how they would classify each apparent solution as an actual or extraneous solution when solving a rational equation using that method.

PRACTICE

Where skills are taught	Where skills are practiced
1 EXAMPLE	EXS. 1–4
2 EXAMPLE	EXS. 5–7
3 EXAMPLE	EX. 8

3 EXAMPLE Modeling with Rational Equations

If you're in a canoe on a river and not paddling, you will travel in the same direction and at the same speed as the river's current. When you paddle *with* the current (downstream), the canoe's speed is the *sum* of your paddling speed and the current's speed. When you paddle *against* the current (upstream), the canoe's speed is the *difference* of your paddling speed and the current's speed.

Suppose you paddle a canoe at a steady speed of 4 miles per hour. You go 6 miles downstream and then 6 miles upstream to get back to where you started. The trip takes 4 hours. What is the speed of the current?

A   Write expressions for the canoe's downstream and upstream speeds. Let s be the speed of the current.

Downstream speed = $4 + s$ Upstream speed = $4 - s$

B   Divide the distance traveled in each direction by the canoe's speed in that direction to find the time for that part of the trip.

Downstream time = $\dfrac{6}{4 + s}$ Upstream time = $\dfrac{6}{4 - s}$

C   Use the verbal model to write an equation that models the canoe trip.

Downstream time	+	Upstream time	=	Total trip time

$$\dfrac{6}{4 + s} + \dfrac{6}{4 - s} = 4$$

D   Solve the equation. Although can you solve the equation using algebra, you can also solve it using a graphing calculator. Treat the left side of the equation as a rational function $f(x)$. (You will need to substitute x for s when you enter the function on the graphing calculator.) Treat the right side of the equation as the constant function $g(x) = 4$.

• What viewing window should you use for graphing? Why?

Answers will vary. *Sample answer:* $0 \le x \le 4$ and $0 \le y \le 5$ because both the current's speed x and the trip time y are nonnegative, the current's speed will not exceed your paddling speed, and the trip time is 4 hours.

• Enter the functions and graph them. At what point do the graphs intersect? Interpret the coordinates of this point in the context of the problem.

(2, 4); the current's speed is 2 miles per hour, which results in a trip time of 4 hours.

REFLECT

3a. The graph of $f(x)$ has a vertical asymptote at $x = 4$. Based on the context of the problem, why *should* there be a vertical asymptote at $x = 4$?

As the current's speed approaches 4 miles per hour (which is your paddling speed), the canoe's speed will approach 0, which means that your upstream time will grow without bound.

3b. Solve the equation in part C algebraically. How many solutions does the equation have? Do all the solutions make sense in the context of the problem? Why or why not?

$s = \pm 2$; there are two solutions, but the negative one doesn't make sense because the current's speed must be positive.

PRACTICE

Solve each equation.

1. $\dfrac{3}{x + 1} = \dfrac{1}{x^2 - 1}$

$\dfrac{4}{3}$

2. $\dfrac{2}{x} = x - 1$

$-1, 2$

3. $\dfrac{3}{2x} - \dfrac{5}{3x} = 2$

$-\dfrac{1}{12}$

4. $\dfrac{x}{4} + 3 = \dfrac{x + 4}{x - 2}$

$-10, 4$

5. $\dfrac{x}{x - 1} - \dfrac{3}{x} = \dfrac{1}{x^2 - x}$

2

6. $\dfrac{4}{x^2 - 4} - \dfrac{1}{x + 2} = \dfrac{x - 1}{x - 2}$

-4

7. Explain why the equation $\dfrac{x + 1}{x - 3} = \dfrac{4}{x - 3}$ has no solution.

The only apparent solution, $x = 3$, is extraneous.

8. You paddle a canoe at a steady speed on a river where the current's speed is 1 kilometer per hour. You go 7.7 kilometers downstream and then 7.7 kilometers upstream to get back to where you started. The trip takes 3.6 hours.

a. Write a rational equation that models the problem. State what the variable in your equation represents.

$\dfrac{7.7}{s + 1} + \dfrac{7.7}{s - 1} = 3.6$ where s is your paddling speed

b. Solve the equation and state the solution in terms of the context of the problem.

$s = 4.5$; your paddling speed is 4.5 kilometers per hour

FOCUS ON MODELING
Modeling with Rational Functions

Essential question: *How can you model profit-per-item using a rational function?*

© Houghton Mifflin Harcourt Publishing Company

COMMON CORE Standards for Mathematical Content

The following standards are addressed in this lesson. (An asterisk indicates that a standard is also a Modeling standard.) For more detailed information, see each section of the lesson.

Algebra: CC.9-12.A.CED.2*, CC.9-12.A.SSE.1*, CC.9-12.A.SSE.1a*, CC.9-12.A.SSE.1b*, CC.9-12.A.APR.6, CC.9-12.A.APR.7(+), CC.9-12.A.CED.1*, CC.9-12.A.REI.2, CC.9-12.A.REI.11*

Functions: CC.9-12.F.IF.2, CC.9-12.F.IF.4*, CC.9-12.F.IF.6*, CC.9-12.F.IF.7*, CC.9-12.F.IF.7(d)+*, CC.9-12.F.IF.9, CC.9-12.F.BF.1*, CC.9-12.F.BF.1a*, CC.9-12.F.BF.3

Prerequisites
• Graphing rational functions, Lesson 4-3

Math Background
In this lesson, students develop a profit-per-item model for a fundraising project. Finding the *per-item* cost, sales income, and profit means that students must divide each quantity by the number of items. Therefore, students model the situation using rational functions. Students use their knowledge of asymptotes and reference points to graph the profit-per-item function and analyze the graph by looking at key features like end behavior and intercepts.

INTRODUCE

By modeling their fundraising projects with mathematics, students can avoid the pitfall of expending energy and money on an activity that does not generate profit. In this lesson, they will learn to model both total and per-item profits for a project that involves making and selling T-shirts.

TEACH

1 Create a profit-per-item model from the given information.

Standards
CC.9-12.A.CED.2 Create equations in two or more variables to represent relationships between quantities ...*

CC.9-12.F.IF.2 ... interpret statements that use function notation in terms of a context.

CC.9-12.F.BF.1 Write a function that describes a relationship between two quantities.*

Questioning Strategies
• How are $C(t)$ and $S(t)$ different from $C_{PI}(t)$ and $S_{PI}(t)$? $C(t)$ and $S(t)$ represent total costs and total sales income; $C_{PI}(t)$ and $S_{PI}(t)$ represent cost *per item* and sales income *per item*.

• How are $C_{PI}(t)$ and $S_{PI}(t)$ obtained? $C_{PI}(t)$, the cost to make one T-shirt, is obtained by dividing total costs $C(t)$ for making all the T-shirts by t, the number of T-shirts made. $S_{PI}(t)$, the income from selling one T-shirt, is obtained by dividing total sales income $S(t)$ from selling all the T-shirts by t, the number of T-shirts sold.

2 Graph $P_{PI}(t)$.

Standards
CC.9-12.A.CED.2 ... graph equations on coordinate axes with labels and scales.*

CC.9-12.F.IF.4 For a function that models a relationship between two quantities, interpret key features of graphs and tables in terms of the quantities, and sketch graphs showing key features given a verbal description of the relationship.*

continued

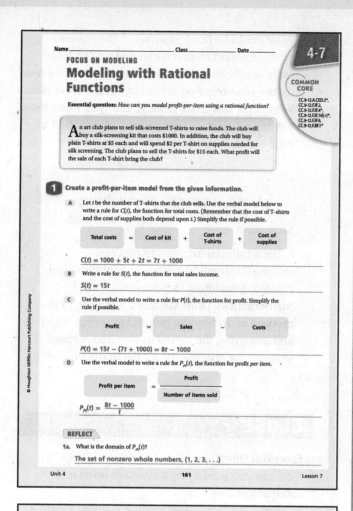

FOCUS ON MODELING

Modeling with Rational Functions

4-7

COMMON CORE

CC-9-12.A.CED.2*,
CC-9-12.F.IF.2,
CC-9-12.F.IF.4*,
CC-9-12.F.IF.7d(+)*,
CC-9-12.F.IF.9,
CC-9-12.F.BF.1*

Essential question: *How can you model profit-per-item using a rational function?*

An art club plans to sell silk-screened T-shirts to raise funds. The club will buy a silk-screening kit that costs $1000. In addition, the club will buy plain T-shirts at $5 each and will spend $2 per T-shirt on supplies needed for silk screening. The club plans to sell the T-shirts for $15 each. What profit will the sale of each T-shirt bring the club?

1 Create a profit-per-item model from the given information.

A Let *t* be the number of T-shirts that the club sells. Use the verbal model below to write a rule for $C(t)$, the function for total costs. (Remember that the cost of T-shirts and the cost of supplies both depend upon *t*.) Simplify the rule if possible.

| Total costs | = | Cost of kit | + | Cost of T-shirts | + | Cost of supplies |

$C(t) = 1000 + 5t + 2t = 7t + 1000$

B Write a rule for $S(t)$, the function for total sales income.

$S(t) = 15t$

C Use the verbal model to write a rule for $P(t)$, the function for profit. Simplify the rule if possible.

| Profit | = | Sales | − | Costs |

$P(t) = 15t − (7t + 1000) = 8t − 1000$

D Use the verbal model to write a rule for $P_{pi}(t)$, the function for profit *per item*.

| Profit per item | = | Profit / Number of items sold |

$P_{pi}(t) = \dfrac{8t − 1000}{t}$

REFLECT

1a. What is the domain of $P_{pi}(t)$?

The set of nonzero whole numbers, {1, 2, 3, . . .}

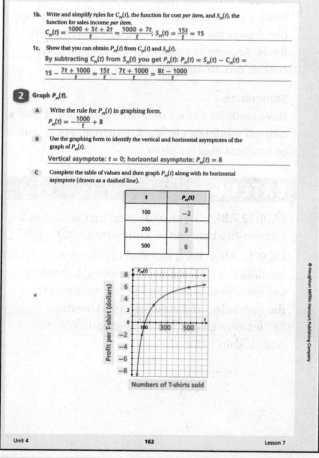

1b. Write and simplify rules for $C_{pi}(t)$, the function for cost *per item*, and $S_{pi}(t)$, the function for sales income *per item*.

$C_{pi}(t) = \dfrac{1000 + 5t + 2t}{t} = \dfrac{1000 + 7t}{t}$; $S_{pi}(t) = \dfrac{15t}{t} = 15$

1c. Show that you can obtain $P_{pi}(t)$ from $C_{pi}(t)$ and $S_{pi}(t)$.

By subtracting $C_{pi}(t)$ from $S_{pi}(t)$ you get $P_{pi}(t)$: $P_{pi}(t) = S_{pi}(t) − C_{pi}(t) =$

$15 − \dfrac{7t + 1000}{t} = \dfrac{15t}{t} − \dfrac{7t + 1000}{t} = \dfrac{8t − 1000}{t}$

2 Graph $P_{pi}(t)$.

A Write the rule for $P_{pi}(t)$ in graphing form.

$P_{pi}(t) = −\dfrac{1000}{t} + 8$

B Use the graphing form to identify the vertical and horizontal asymptotes of the graph of $P_{pi}(t)$.

Vertical asymptote: $t = 0$; horizontal asymptote: $P_{pi}(t) = 8$

C Complete the table of values and then graph $P_{pi}(t)$ along with its horizontal asymptote (drawn as a dashed line).

t	$P_{pi}(t)$
100	−2
200	3
500	6

Profit per T-shirt (dollars)

Numbers of T-shirts sold

2 continued

CC.9-12.F.IF.7 Graph functions expressed symbolically and show key features of the graph ...*

CC.9-12.F.IF.7d(+) Graph rational functions, identifying zeros and asymptotes when suitable factorizations are available, and showing end behavior.*

Questioning Strategies

- What are the advantages of writing the rule for $P_{Pl}(t)$ in graphing form? **Graphing form makes it easier to identify the vertical and horizontal asymptotes, and to perform the translation of the parent graph.**

- Although you graphed the function as an unbroken curve, the graph really consists of a series of distinct points. Explain why. **The independent variable is the number of T-shirts made and sold, which is a nonzero whole number. So, the graph should consist of only points with nonzero whole-number t-coordinates.**

3 **Analyze the graph of $P_{Pl}(t)$.**

Standards

CC.9-12.F.IF.2 ... interpret statements that use function notation in terms of a context.

CC.9-12.F.IF.4 For a function that models a relationship between two quantities, interpret key features of graphs ... in terms of the quantities ...*

CC.9-12.F.IF.9 Compare properties of two functions each represented in a different way (algebraically, graphically ... or by verbal descriptions).*

Questioning Strategies

- Is it possible for the club to make a profit greater than $8 per T-shirt? Explain. **No; the horizontal asymptote is $P_{Pl}(t) = 8$, which means that the profit per T-shirt will never go above $8.**

- What could be done to increase the possible profit-per-item so that it can exceed $8? **Total costs would have to be reduced by spending less on the silk-screening kit or supplies, buying plain T-shirts for less than $5 each, charging more than $15 for a T-shirt, or using some combination of all three strategies.**

> ┌─────────────────────────────────────┐
> **MATHEMATICAL PRACTICE** **Highlighting the Standards**
>
> Using a rational function to model a real-world situation addresses Mathematical Practice Standard 4 (Model with mathematics). Draw students' attention to the method of finding the rational model in step 1 and analyzing the model in step 3 to prepare students for altering the model in the Extend.
> └─────────────────────────────────────┘

CLOSE

Essential Question

How can you model profit-per-item using a rational function?
To model profit-per-item using a rational function, write a profit-per-item function by dividing profit (total sales minus total costs) by the number of items. Analyze the model graphically to draw conclusions about the situation.

Summarize

Have students write a one-page summary of how a rational model can be used to help an organization or business analyze profit.

EXTEND

CC.9-12.F.BF.1 Write a function that describes a relationship between two quantities.* **(Ex. 1)**

CC.9-12.F.IF.4 For a function that models a relationship between two quantities, interpret key features of graphs and tables in terms of the quantities, and sketch graphs showing key features given a verbal description of the relationship.* **(Ex. 1)**

REFLECT

2a. When completing the table of values, you should have found that $P_{PI}(100)$ is negative. Explain why the profit per item *should* be negative in this case.

When 100 T-shirts are sold, the total sales income is $1500, but the

total costs are $1700. The profit in this case is −$200, so the profit

per item is −$2.

2b. Describe the transformations you would have to perform on the graph of the parent function $f(t) = \frac{1}{t}$ to produce the graph of $P_{PI}(t)$.

Vertical stretch by a factor of 1000; reflection in the t-axis; vertical

translation by 8 units

3 Analyze the graph of $P_{PI}(t)$.

A Are the values of $P_{PI}(t)$ increasing or decreasing, and what does that mean for the club?

Increasing; the more T-shirts the club sells, the greater the profit

per item that the club makes

B What t-intercept does the graph of $P_{PI}(t)$ have, and what does that mean for the club?

125; this is the number of T-shirts that the club must sell in order for

sales income to equal total costs so that the club is breaking even.

C For what t-values is the value of $P_{PI}(t)$ negative? For what t-values is the value of $P_{PI}(t)$ positive? What does that mean for the club?

$0 < t < 125$; $t > 125$; the club must sell more than 125 T-shirts if it

wants to raise funds rather than lose money.

D What end behavior does $P_{PI}(t)$ have, and what does that mean for the club?

The values of $P_{PI}(t)$ approach 8; the club's profit per item will

approach $8 as the number of T-shirts sold increases without bound.

© Houghton Mifflin Harcourt Publishing Company

REFLECT

3a. Suppose the club hopes to make a profit per item of $5. Use the graph to estimate the number of T-shirts that must be sold. Then write and solve an equation to find the exact number. Does the exact number make sense in this situation? Explain.

About 340; $-\frac{1000}{t} + 8 = 5$; $t = 333\frac{1}{3}$; the exact number does not make

sense because it is not a whole number.

3b. Does the profit per item increase faster when the number of T-shirts sold increases from 150 to 250 or from 250 to 350? Explain.

From 150 to 250; the graph is more vertical between $t = 150$ and $t = 250$

than it is between $t = 250$ and $t = 350$, so the rate of change in the profit

per item is greater.

EXTEND

1. Concerned about how many T-shirts must be sold before the profit per item becomes positive, the club's treasurer proposes three options, described below. For each option, give the new rule for $P_{PI}(t)$, describe how the function's graph changes, and find the graph's new t-intercept.

a. Buy a "gently used" silk-screening kit for $800.

$P_{PI}(t) = -\frac{800}{t} + 8$; compared with the graph of the original function,

the vertical stretch is less; 100

b. Increase the price of a silk-screened T-shirt to $18.

$P_{PI}(t) = -\frac{1000}{t} + 11$; the new graph is a translation of the original

graph up 3 units; about 91

c. Buy plain T-shirts in bulk to reduce their cost to $4 each.

$P_{PI}(t) = -\frac{1000}{t} + 9$; the new graph is a translation of the original

graph up 1 unit; about 111

d. Which of the three options has the greatest impact on the t-intercept?

Increasing the price of a silk-screened T-shirt to $18

© Houghton Mifflin Harcourt Publishing Company

Standard	Items
CC.9-12.A.APR.6	5
CC.9-12.A.APR.7(+)	7, 8, 11, 12
CC.9-12.A.CED.1*	12
CC.9-12.A.CED.2*	3, 10
CC.9-12.A.REI.2	4
CC.9-12.A.REI.11*	12
CC.9-12.F.IF.4*	10
CC.9-12.F.IF.7d(+)*	1, 6, 12
CC.9-12.F.BF.1*	3, 10, 12
CC.9-12.F.BF.3	2, 9, 12

TEST PREP DOCTOR ⊕

Multiple Choice: Item 1
- Students who chose **C** identified what the graph of $f(x) = \frac{a}{x}$ would be if a were changed to $-a$.
- Students who chose **A** or **D** did not understand what the graph of a rational function of the form $f(x) = \frac{a}{x}$ looks like.

Multiple Choice: Item 2
- Students who chose **G** used the wrong sign when determining the effect of changing h on the graph of $f(x) = \frac{a}{x - h} + k$.
- Students who chose **H** or **J** mixed up the parameters h and k when determining the effect of changing the parameter h on the graph of $f(x) = \frac{a}{x - h} + k$.

Multiple Choice: Item 3
- Students who chose **A** placed the variable x in the numerator rather than in the denominator.
- Students who chose **B** both incorrectly placed x in the numerator and mixed up the cost that was shared (the dinner) and the cost that was not shared (the dessert).
- Students who chose **D** mixed up the shared cost and the cost that was not shared.

Multiple Choice: Item 4
- Students who chose **F** included an extraneous solution instead of rejecting it. Because $x = -2$ is an excluded value for the second expression in the sum, it is an extraneous solution of the equation.
- Students who chose **G** solved the equation as if the right side of the equation did not have a negative sign in front of the expression and included an extraneous solution.
- Students who chose **J** solved the equation as if the right side of the equation did not have a negative sign in front of the expression.

Free Response: Item 9
- Students who incorrectly described the transformation of the graph may have mixed up the parameters a, h, and k when analyzing the effects of those parameters on the graph of $f(x) = \frac{a}{x - h} + k$.
- They may have used the wrong sign for the parameters.
- They may not have understood that changing a results in vertical stretching or shrinking, that making a negative results in a reflection, that changing h results in a horizontal translation, or that changing k results in a vertical translation.

Free Response: Item 11
- Students who found an incorrect sum may have incorrectly factored the denominator of the second expression, incorrectly determined the LCM for the denominators, or multiplied the first expression incorrectly when multiplying by a form of 1 so that both expressions would have the same denominator.
- Students who found an incorrect difference may have added instead of subtracted, or made any of the errors listed above.
- Students who found an incorrect product may have factored or simplified incorrectly or did not simplify at all.
- Students who found an incorrect quotient may not have multiplied by the reciprocal of the divisor.

Name _____ Class _____ Date _____

MULTIPLE CHOICE

1. In which quadrants does the graph of $f(x) = \frac{2}{x}$ lie?

A. I and II C. II and IV

B. I and III D. III and IV

2. How can you obtain the graph of $g(x) = \frac{1}{x-2}$ from the graph of $f(x) = \frac{1}{x}$?

F. Translate the graph of f right 2 units.

G. Translate the graph of f left 2 units.

H. Translate the graph of f up 2 units.

J. Translate the graph of f down 2 units.

3. A group of x friends splits the cost of a family-style dinner for $50. In addition to the cost of the dinner, each person orders a $5 dessert. Which function gives the amount $A(x)$ that each person pays?

A. $A(x) = \frac{x}{50} + 5$ **C.** $A(x) = \frac{50}{x} + 5$

B. $A(x) = \frac{x}{5} + 50$ D. $A(x) = \frac{5}{x} + 50$

4. What are the solutions of the equation $\frac{x}{x-1} + \frac{1}{x+2} = -\frac{3}{x^2+x-2}$?

F. $-1, -2$ **H.** -1

G. $-4, 1$ J. -4

5. Which function is the graphing form of $f(x) = \frac{4x+3}{x-1}$?

A. $f(x) = \frac{4}{x-1} + 7$

B. $f(x) = \frac{4}{x-1} - 1$

C. $f(x) = \frac{-1}{x-1} + 4$

D. $f(x) = \frac{7}{x-1} + 4$

6. The graph of which function is shown?

F. $f(x) = \frac{1}{x+1} + 1$

G. $f(x) = \frac{1}{x+1} - 1$

H. $f(x) = \frac{1}{x-1} + 1$

J. $f(x) = \frac{1}{x-1} - 1$

7. Find the sum: $\frac{x+4}{x^2-4} + \frac{15}{x-2}$

A. $\frac{16x+34}{(x+2)(x-2)}$

B. $\frac{-14x+13}{(x+2)(x-2)}$

C. $\frac{16x+34}{(x+2)^2}$

D. $\frac{16x+34}{(x-2)^2}$

8. Find the quotient: $\frac{x^2-4x-21}{5x+15} \div \frac{x^2+3x-70}{x^2-100}$

F. $\frac{(x-7)^2}{5(x-10)}$

G. $\frac{x-10}{5}$

H. $\frac{x^2-14x-49}{5x-50}$

J. $\frac{5}{x-10}$

FREE RESPONSE

9. Describe how to graph $g(x) = \frac{-2}{x-4} + 3$ as a transformation of the graph of $f(x) = \frac{1}{x}$.

Vertically stretch the graph of f(x) by

a factor of 2. Then reflect it over the

x-axis. Finally, translate it 4 units to

the right and 3 units up.

10. Kelsey is making bracelets to sell at a craft fair. She spends $50 on a jewelry-making kit and $.50 on beads for each bracelet. She plans to sell the bracelets for $3 each.

a. Write and simplify a rule for the profit-per-bracelet function $P(b)$ if she sells b bracelets.

$P(b) = \frac{3b - (50 + 0.5b)}{b} = -\frac{50}{b} + 2.5$

b. As the number of bracelets sold increases, what happens to the profit per bracelet?

The profit per bracelet

approaches $2.50.

11. Use the expressions $\frac{x}{x+1}$ and $\frac{1}{x^2+x}$ to complete the following.

a. Find the sum of the expressions.

$\frac{x}{x+1} + \frac{1}{x(x+1)} = \frac{x^2+1}{x(x+1)}$

b. Find the difference of the expressions (first expression minus second expression).

$\frac{x}{x+1} - \frac{1}{x(x+1)} = \frac{x^2-1}{x(x+1)} = \frac{x-1}{x}$

c. Find the product of the expressions.

$\frac{x}{x+1} \cdot \frac{1}{x(x+1)} = \frac{1}{(x+1)^2}$

d. Find the quotient of the expressions (first expression divided by second expression).

$\frac{x}{x+1} \div \frac{1}{x(x+1)} =$

$\frac{x}{x+1} \cdot \frac{x(x+1)}{1} = x^2$

12. While canoeing on a river, your paddling speed is twice the river's current. You travel 3 miles downstream and then 3 miles upstream to get back to where you started.

a. Write a rule for $T(s)$, the function that gives your total trip time (in hours) as a function of the current's speed s (in miles per hour). The rule should involve a sum of two rational expressions. Carry out the addition to simplify the rule as much as possible.

$T(s) = \frac{3}{2s+s} + \frac{3}{2s-s} = \frac{1}{s} + \frac{3}{s} = \frac{4}{s}$

b. Use the coordinate plane below to graph $T(s)$. Include axis labels and scales.

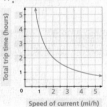

Speed of current (mi/h)

c. How is the graph of $T(s)$ related to the graph of the parent function $f(s) = \frac{1}{s}$?

Vertical stretch by a factor of 4

d. Use the graph to estimate the current's speed when the total trip time is 2.5 hours.

About 1.6 miles per hour

e. Write and solve an equation to find the current's speed exactly when the total trip time is 2.5 hours.

$\frac{4}{s} = 2.5$; $s = 1.6$ miles per hour

UNIT 5

Radical Functions

Unit Vocabulary

cube root
function (5-3)

extraneous
solution (5-7)

inverse functions (5-1)

one-to-one
function (5-2)

square root
function (5-2)

Radical Functions

Unit Focus

In this unit, you will learn about square root and cube root functions, as well as some of their applications. Square root and cube root functions are examples of *radical functions* because their rules are radical expressions, such as $\sqrt{x}$. Square root and cube root functions are defined in relation to quadratic and cubic functions; specifically, they are the *inverses* of these functions. In preparation for learning about radical functions, you will learn about inverses of functions in general.

Unit at a Glance

COMMON CORE

Lesson		Standards for Mathematical Content
5-1	Inverses of Functions	CC.9-12.A.CED.2*, CC.9-12.F.IF.2, CC.9-12.F.IF.7*, CC.9-12.F.IF.7a*, CC.9-12.F.BF.4, CC.9-12.F.BF.4a
5-2	Inverses of Quadratic Functions	CC.9-12.A.CED.2*, CC.9-12.F.IF.2, CC.9-12.F.IF.7a*, CC.9-12.F.IF.7b*, CC.9-12.F.BF.4, CC.9-12.F.BF.4d(+)
5-3	Inverses of Cubic Functions	CC.9-12.A.CED.2*, CC.9-12.F.IF.2, CC.9-12.F.IF.7b*, CC.9-12.F.IF.7c*, CC.9-12.F.BF.4, CC.9-12.F.BF.4a
5-4	Graphing Square Root and Cube Root Functions	CC.9-12.F.IF.7*, CC.9-12.F.IF.7b*, CC.9-12.F.BF.3
5-5	Modeling with Square Root Functions	CC.9-12.A.CED.2*, CC.9-12.F.IF.4*, CC.9-12.F.IF.7b*, CC.9-12.F.BF.1*, CC.9-12.F.BF.4d(+), CC.9-12.S.ID.6a*
5-6	Modeling with Cube Root Functions	CC.9-12.A.CED.2*, CC.9-12.F.IF.4*, CC.9-12.F.IF.7b*, CC.9-12.F.BF.1*, CC.9-12.F.BF.4a, CC.9-12.S.ID.6a*
5-7	Solving Radical Equations	CC.9-12.A.REI.2, CC.9-12.A.REI.11*
	Test Prep	

Unpacking the Common Core State Standards

Use the table to help you understand the Standards for Mathematical Content that are taught in this unit. Refer to the lessons listed after each standard for exploration and practice.

COMMON CORE Standards for Mathematical Content	What It Means For You
CC.9-12.A.CED.2 Create equations in two or more variables to represent relationships between quantities; graph equations on coordinate axes with labels and scales.* Lessons 5-1, 5-2, 5-3; 5-5, 5-6	In this unit, you will write equations containing radical expressions to represent relationships between real-world quantities. Graphing these equations can provide useful information. You will learn to use appropriate viewing windows, scales, and labels so the information can be understood.
CC.9-12.A.REI.2 Solve simple rational and radical equations in one variable, and give examples showing how extraneous solutions may arise. Lesson 5-7	When you solve radical equations, you may find values that appear to be solutions, but that do not satisfy the original equations. You will learn how to identify these *extraneous* solutions.
CC.9-12.A.REI.11 Explain why the *x*-coordinates of the points where the graphs of the equations $y = f(x)$ and $y = g(x)$ intersect are the solutions of the equation $f(x) = g(x)$; find the solutions approximately, e.g., using technology to graph the functions, make tables of values, or find successive approximations. Include cases where $f(x)$ and/or $g(x)$ are linear, polynomial, rational, absolute value, exponential, and logarithmic functions.* Lesson 5-7	To solve a complicated equation, you can represent each side of the equation as a separate function. You can then graph the functions and find the points where they intersect. The *x*-coordinates of these points are the solutions of the original equation.
CC.9-12.F.IF.2 Use function notation, evaluate functions for inputs in their domains, and interpret statements that use function notation in terms of a context. Lessons 5-1, 5-2, 5-3; 5-5, 5-6	You will use functions to describe relationships and solve real-world problems. To do so, you will need to understand and apply function notation.
CC.9-12.F.IF.4 For a function that models a relationship between two quantities, interpret key features of graphs and tables in terms of the quantities, and sketch graphs showing key features given a verbal description of the relationship.* Lessons 5-5, 5-6	Graphing a function that models a real-world situation can help you understand the relationship between two quantities. Analyzing and interpreting a graph can reveal information that would be difficult to determine solely from the symbolic form of a function.

Unpacking the Common Core State Standards

This page lists and explains the Standards for Mathematical Content that are addressed in this unit. For information about the Standards for Mathematical Practice, which are integrated throughout the text, see Teacher Edition pages x–xiii.

Notes

Additional Standards in This Unit

CC.9-12.A.SSE.3 Choose and produce an equivalent form of an expression to reveal and explain properties of the quantity represented by the expression. Lesson 5-5

CC.9-12.A.SSE.3b Complete the square in a quadratic expression to reveal the maximum or minimum value of the function it defines. Lesson 5-5

CC.9-12.N.Q.1 Use units as a way to understand problems and to guide the solution of multi-step problems; choose and interpret units consistently in formulas; choose and interpret the scale and the origin in graphs and data displays.* Lesson 5-6

CC.9-12.A.CED.1 Create equations and inequalities in one variable and use them to solve problems.* Lesson 5-7

CC.9-12.A.CED.4 Rearrange formulas to highlight a quantity of interest, using the same reasoning as in solving equations.* Lessons 5-1, 5-2

CC.9-12.F.IF.7d(+) Graph rational functions, identifying zeros and asymptotes when suitable factorizations are available, and showing end behavior. Lesson 5-1

COMMON CORE Standards for Mathematical Content	What It Means For You
CC.9-12.F.IF.7 Graph functions expressed symbolically and show key features of the graph, by hand in simple cases and using technology for more complicated cases.* **CC.9-12.F.IF.7a** Graph linear and quadratic functions and show intercepts, maxima, and minima.* **CC.9-12.F.IF.7b** Graph square root, cube root, and piecewise-defined functions, including step functions and absolute value functions.* **CC.9-12.F.IF.7c** Graph polynomial functions, identifying zeros when suitable factorizations are available, and showing end behavior.* Lessons 5-1, 5-2, 5-3, 5-4, 5-5, 5-6	In this unit, you will graph inverse functions, including the inverses of linear functions. You will also learn to graph square root and cube root functions by reflecting the graphs of quadratic and cubic functions across the line $y = x$.
CC.9-12.F.BF.1 Write a function that describes a relationship between two quantities.* **CC.9-12.F.BF.1a** Determine an explicit expression, a recursive process, or steps for calculation from a context.* Lessons 5-5, 5-6	You will learn to write radical functions to model real-world situations. You can then use these functions to solve practical problems.
CC.9-12.F.BF.3 Identify the effect on the graph of replacing $f(x)$ by $f(x) + k$, $k\,f(x)$, $f(kx)$, and $f(x + k)$ for specific values of k (both positive and negative); find the value of k given the graphs. Experiment with cases and illustrate an explanation of the effects on the graph using technology. Lesson 5-4 (Also 5-2, 5-3)	Groups of functions with common properties are often transformations of a *parent function*, which is the simplest function of the same type. You will graph square root and cube root functions as transformations of their parent functions.
CC.9-12.F.BF.4 Find inverse functions. **CC.9-12.F.BF.4a** Solve an equation of the form $f(x) = c$ for a simple function f that has an inverse and write an expression for the inverse. **CC.9-12.F.BF.4d(+)** Produce an invertible function from a non-invertible function by restricting the domain. Lessons 5-1, 5-2, 5-3, 5-5, 5-6	Finding inverse functions is a useful skill for solving some real-life problems. For example, if a formula expresses quantity A in terms of quantity B, you can find the inverse to express quantity B in terms of quantity A. You will also learn that square root and cube root functions can be defined as inverses of quadratic and cubic functions, respectively.
CC.9-12.S.ID.6 Represent data on two quantitative variables on a scatter plot, and describe how the variables are related.* **CC.9-12.S.ID.6a** Fit a function to the data; use functions fitted to data to solve problems in the context of the data.* Lessons 5-5, 5-6	You will fit square root functions and cube root functions to real-world data.

Unit 5   169   Radical Functions

UNIT 5

Notes

Notes

_____

_____

_____

_____

_____

_____

_____

_____

_____

_____

_____

_____

_____

_____

_____

_____

_____

_____

_____

_____

_____

_____

_____

_____

_____

_____

CC.9-12.F.IF.8 Write a function defined by an expression in different but equivalent forms to reveal and explain different properties of the function. Lesson 5-5

CC.9-12.F.IF.8a Use the process of factoring and completing the square in a quadratic function to show zeros, extreme values, and symmetry of the graph, and interpret these in terms of a context. Lesson 5-5

CC.9-12.F.IF.9 Compare properties of two functions each represented in a different way (algebraically, graphically, numerically in tables, or by verbal descriptions). Lessons 5-4, 5-6

UNIT 5

Inverses of Functions

Essential question: *How do you find the inverse of a function, and how is the original function related to its inverse?*

COMMON CORE **Standards for Mathematical Content**

CC.9-12.A.CED.2 Create equations in two ... variables to represent relationships between quantities; graph equations on coordinate axes with labels and scales.*

CC.9-12.F.IF.2 Use function notation, evaluate functions for inputs in their domains, and interpret statements that use function notation in terms of a context.

CC.9-12.F.IF.7 Graph functions expressed symbolically and show key features of the graph ...*

CC.9-12.F.IF.7a Graph linear ... functions ...*

CC.9-12.F.BF.4 Find inverse functions.

CC.9-12.F.BF.4a Solve an equation of the form $f(x) = c$ for a simple function f that has an inverse and write an expression for the inverse.

Also: CC.9-12.A.CED.4*, CC.9-12.F.IF.7d(+)

Vocabulary

inverse functions

Prerequisites

Functions, Algebra 1

Graphing linear functions, Algebra 1

Graphing rational functions, Lesson 4-1

Math Background

A relation is a mapping of the elements of one set of numbers to the elements of another set, which produces a set of ordered pairs. A relation is a function if, for every input, there is exactly one output. The graph of a relation is a function if it passes the *vertical line test*, that is, if every possible vertical line drawn through the graph intersects it in at most one point.

A function takes an input, applies a rule, and gives an output. The inverse of that function will use that output as its input and apply a rule to give the input of the original function as its output.

INTRODUCE

Tell students you have a secret number. If you multiply by 2, add 3, and divide by 7, in that order, the number becomes 5. Have students find your secret number and explain how they found it. The number is 16. Perform inverse operations on 5 in the reverse order.

TEACH

1 ENGAGE

Questioning Strategies

- What are some points on the graph of $f(x) = 2$? Sample answers: (—3, 2), (0, 2), (4, 2)

- Is $f(x) = 2$ a function? Is its inverse a function? Explain. Yes, each input has only one output. No, the input of 2 has infinitely many outputs.

- What must be true about a function if its inverse is not a function? The function must pair at least two inputs with the same output.

Avoid Common Errors

Students often read $f^{-1}(x)$ as raising a function to the −1 power. Stress that −1 is not an exponent even though it is written as a superscript.

2 EXPLORE

Questioning Strategies

- In part A, how do you know that the multiplication is performed before the subtraction? By the order of operations, multiplication is performed before subtraction.

- In part A, what would be the rule if the subtraction were performed first? $f(x) = 3(x - 2)$

- What is the inverse function of $f(x) = 3(x - 2)$? $f^{-1}(x) = \frac{x}{3} + 2$

Name_____ Class_____ Date_____

5-1
COMMON CORE
CC-9-12.A.CED.2*,
CC-9-12.F.IF.2,
CC-9-12.F.IF.7*,
CC-9-12.F.IF.7a*,
CC-9-12.F.BF.4,
CC-9-12.F.BF.4a

Inverses of Functions

Essential question: *How do you find the inverse of a function, and how is the original function related to its inverse?*

1 ENGAGE   Understanding the Inverse of a Function

The mapping diagram on the left shows a function. If you reverse the arrows in the mapping diagram as shown on the right, the original outputs become the inputs, and the original inputs become the outputs.

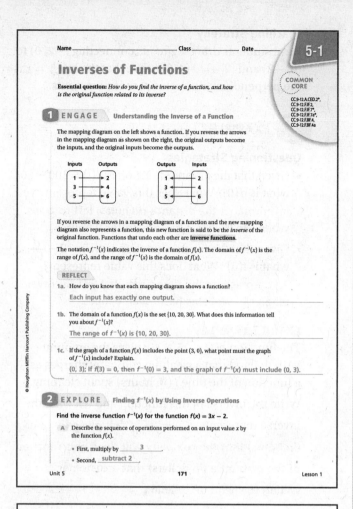

If you reverse the arrows in a mapping diagram of a function and the new mapping diagram also represents a function, this new function is said to be the *inverse* of the original function. Functions that undo each other are **inverse functions**.

The notation $f^{-1}(x)$ indicates the inverse of a function $f(x)$. The domain of $f^{-1}(x)$ is the range of $f(x)$, and the range of $f^{-1}(x)$ is the domain of $f(x)$.

REFLECT

1a. How do you know that each mapping diagram shows a function?

Each input has exactly one output.

1b. The domain of a function $f(x)$ is the set {10, 20, 30}. What does this information tell you about $f^{-1}(x)$?

The range of $f^{-1}(x)$ is {10, 20, 30}.

1c. If the graph of a function $f(x)$ includes the point (3, 0), what point must the graph of $f^{-1}(x)$ include? Explain.

(0, 3); If $f(3) = 0$, then $f^{-1}(0) = 3$, and the graph of $f^{-1}(x)$ must include (0, 3).

2 EXPLORE   Finding $f^{-1}(x)$ by Using Inverse Operations

Find the inverse function $f^{-1}(x)$ for the function $f(x) = 3x - 2$.

A   Describe the sequence of operations performed on an input value x by the function $f(x)$.

• First, multiply by ___3___.

• Second, _subtract 2_.

B   Describe the inverse of each operation listed in step A, but in reverse order.

• First, add ___2___.

• Second, _divide_ by 3.

C   Write a function rule for $f^{-1}(x)$ that matches the steps you described in step B.

$x + $ 2   First, add 2 to the variable.

$\dfrac{x+2}{3}$ Second, _divide_ the sum by 3.

$f^{-1}(x) = \dfrac{x+2}{3}$ Write the rule for the inverse function.

D   Complete the tables to verify that you found the rule for the inverse function correctly. Use the outputs from the first table as the inputs for the second table.

| Function $f(x) = 3x - 2$ | | Inverse Function | |
Input x	Output $f(x)$	Input x	Output $f^{-1}(x)$
0	−2	−2	0
2	4	4	2
4	10	10	4
6	16	16	6

REFLECT

2a. Explain how the tables show that you found the inverse of the function correctly.

The inputs in one table are the same as the outputs in the other table, and vice versa.

2b. Why do you reverse the order of the steps when writing the inverse operations in part B?

To undo the operations in the original function, you need to work backward. Start by undoing the last operation in the original function. Then undo the first operation.

2c. Could the rule for $f^{-1}(x)$ be written as $\frac{x}{3} + 2$? Explain why or why not.

No; to undo the operations in the original function, first add 2 and then divide by 3. This expression shows dividing by 3 first and then adding 2.

Questioning Strategies

- What are the two operations in $f(x)$ in the order they are performed?
  multiplication and subtraction

- What are the two operations in $f^{-1}(x)$ in the order they are performed?
  addition and division

- What is $f(0)$? -2

- What is $f^{-1}(-2)$? 0

EXTRA EXAMPLE
Find the inverse function $f^{-1}(x)$ for the function $f(x) = \frac{x-4}{3}$. $f^{-1}(x) = 3x + 4$

Teaching Strategy
Show students that they can reverse the steps in finding the inverse function. They could first switch x and y and then solve for y.

Teaching Strategy
Encourage students to always test an inverse function using the fact that if $f(a) = b$, then $f^{-1}(b) = a$.

4 **EXAMPLE**

Questioning Strategies

- How do you know from their function rules that both $f(x)$ and $f^{-1}(x)$ are linear?
  Each has the form $y = mx + b$.

- What is the y-intercept of the graph of $f(x)$? -2

- What is the x-intercept of the graph of $f^{-1}(x)$? -2

- Why does the y-intercept of the graph of $f(x)$ equal the x-intercept of the graph of $f^{-1}(x)$?
  When you switch the coordinates of $(0, -2)$, you get $(-2, 0)$.

EXTRA EXAMPLE
Graph the function $f(x) = \frac{1}{2}x + 5$ and its inverse.
The graph of $f(x)$ passes through $(0, 5)$ and $(2, 6)$.
The graph of $f^{-1}(x) = 2(x - 5) = 2x - 10$ passes through $(5, 0)$ and $(6, 2)$.

Differentiated Instruction
Visual learners will benefit from folding their papers over the line $y = x$. They will easily be able to see that $f(x)$ and $f^{-1}(x)$ are reflections of each other over that line.

Teaching Strategy
Have students draw segments connecting $(-2, 0)$ to $(0, -2)$ and $(2, 4)$ to $(4, 2)$ to see that the line $y = x$ is the perpendicular bisector of those segments.

5 **EXAMPLE**

Questioning Strategies

- Given that the distance function is $d(t) = 100 - 50t$, what is $d(0)$? What does this value represent? 100;
  it represents the distance (in miles) left to travel when Mr. Williams has driven for 0 hours.

- Given that the inverse function is $t(d) = 2 - \frac{d}{50}$, what is $t(0)$? What does this value represent?
  2; it represents the time (in hours) left to travel when Mr. Williams has driven 0 miles.

EXTRA EXAMPLE
The function $a(t) = 25 + 40t$ gives the amount a (in dollars) that a cleaning company charges as a function of the time t (in hours) spent cleaning. Write the inverse of this function and tell what the inverse represents. $t(a) = \frac{a - 25}{40}$; it gives the time t (in hours) that the company will clean as a function of the amount a (in dollars) that a customer is willing to spend on cleaning.

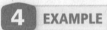

MATHEMATICAL PRACTICE | Highlighting the Standards

5 EXAMPLE includes opportunities to address Mathematical Practice Standard 4 (Model with mathematics). After finding an inverse function, students must be able to interpret it in the context of the situation. Discuss how the units are switched in the domain and range because the input and the output of the function are reversed. Draw a simple mapping diagram for the situation. Label the left side *hours* and the right side *miles*. Include a few values in each set, such as 0 in the *hours* set and 100 in the *miles* set. Ask students to draw arrows in the proper direction for the function $d(t)$. Then, on a copy of the mapping diagram, have them draw arrows in the proper direction for the function $t(d)$.

3 EXAMPLE Finding $f^{-1}(x)$ by Solving an Equation

Find the inverse function $f^{-1}(x)$ for the function $f(x) = 3x - 2$.

A   Substitute y for $f(x)$, and then solve for x.

$y = 3x - 2$	Replace $f(x)$ with y.
$y + \boxed{2} = 3x$	Add 2 to both sides.
$\dfrac{y + 2}{3} = x$	Divide both sides by $\underline{\quad 3 \quad}$

B   Write the rule for $f^{-1}(x)$.

$\dfrac{x + 2}{3} = y$ Switch x and y in the equation from part A.

$\dfrac{x + 2}{3} = f^{-1}(x)$ Replace y with $f^{-1}(x)$.

So, the inverse function is $f^{-1}(x) = \underline{\dfrac{x+2}{3}}$.

REFLECT

3a. How are the steps of solving the equation in part A similar to what you did when writing inverse operations in reverse order in the Explore?

Both activities involve adding 2 first and then dividing by 3.

3b. Why does it make sense to switch the variables when writing the inverse function?

The inputs and outputs are switched in the inverse function compared

with the original function.

4 EXAMPLE Graphing a Function and Its Inverse

Graph the function $f(x) = 3x - 2$ and its inverse.

A   Graph the function $f(x) = 3x - 2$.

The function is linear.

slope = $\boxed{3}$; y-intercept = $\boxed{-2}$

B   Graph the inverse function $f^{-1}(x)$.

From the previous Example, you know that $f^{-1}(x) = \dfrac{x+2}{3}$.

The function is linear.

$f^{-1}(x) = \boxed{\dfrac{1}{3}} \, x + \boxed{\dfrac{2}{3}}$ Write in slope-intercept form.

slope = $\boxed{\dfrac{1}{3}}$; y-intercept = $\boxed{\dfrac{2}{3}}$

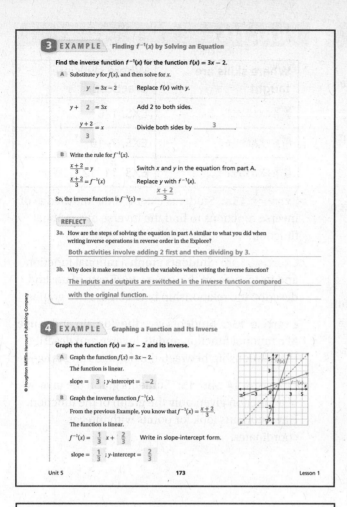

REFLECT

4a. Describe the relationship between coordinates of the points on the graph of a function and those on the graph of its inverse.

The x- and y-coordinates are switched.

4b. Graph the line $y = x$ on the same coordinate plane as the graphs of $f(x)$ and f^{-1} (x). Use the graph of $y = x$ to describe the graph of $f^{-1}(x)$ as a transformation of the graph of $f(x)$.

The graph of $f^{-1}(x)$ is a reflection of the graph of $f(x)$ across the line $y = x$.

Real-World Functions The variables in functions that model real-world situations typically refer to the real-world quantities that they represent. For instance, the function that gives the amount a (in dollars) that you spend when you buy g gallons of gas for $4 per gallon at a gas station is $a = 4g$. You can write $a(g) = 4g$ to emphasize the dependency of a on g.

You can find the inverse of a function that models a real-world situation by solving for the independent variable in terms of the dependent variable. You do not, however, switch the variables at the end of the process as you would switch x and y when finding the inverse of a purely mathematical function. The reason for not switching is that the variables have real-world meanings that cannot be interchanged.

In the case of the real-world function $a = 4g$, the inverse function is $g = \dfrac{a}{4}$, which gives the amount of gas (in gallons) that you can buy for a given amount of money (in dollars). To emphasize the dependency of g on a, you can write $g(a) = \dfrac{a}{4}$.

5 EXAMPLE Finding the Inverse of a Real-World Function

Mr. Williams is driving on a highway at an average speed of 50 miles per hour. His destination is 100 miles away. The equation $d = 100 - 50t$ gives the distance d (in miles) that he has left to travel as a function of the time t (in hours) that he has been driving. Write and interpret the inverse of this function.

A   Solve the equation for t.

$d = 100 - 50t$	Write the equation.
$d - \boxed{100} = -50t$	Subtract 100 from both sides.
$\dfrac{d - \boxed{100}}{-50} = t$	Divide both sides by -50.
$\boxed{2} - \dfrac{d}{50} = t$	Simplify the left side.

B   Interpret the inverse function.

The inverse function gives the $\underline{\text{time } t \text{ (in hours)}}$ that Mr. Williams has left to travel as a function of the $\underline{\text{distance } d \text{ (in miles)}}$ that he has driven.

Essential Question

How do you find the inverse of a function, and how is the original function related to its inverse?

To find the inverse of a function, replace $f(x)$ with y, solve for x, and then switch x and y. The output of a function is the input of the inverse function. The output of the inverse function is the input of the function. Because the coordinates of the ordered pairs are reversed, the graphs of the function and the inverse function are reflections across the line $y = x$.

Summarize

Have students write a journal entry that explains how they can draw the graph of an inverse function if they are given only the graph of the original function.

Where skills are taught	Where skills are practiced
3 EXAMPLE	EXS. 1–6
4 EXAMPLE	EXS. 7–10
5 EXAMPLE	EXS. 11, 12

Exercise 13a: Students extend their knowledge of inverse functions to find the inverse of a rational function.

Exercise 13b: Students graph a rational function and its inverse on the same coordinate plane and describe the relationship between the two graphs.

Exercise 13c: Students give the domain and range of a rational function and its inverse and describe the relationship between the domains and ranges.

Exercises 14 and 15: Students graph the inverse of a function given only the graph of the function. Have students look for points with integer coordinates.

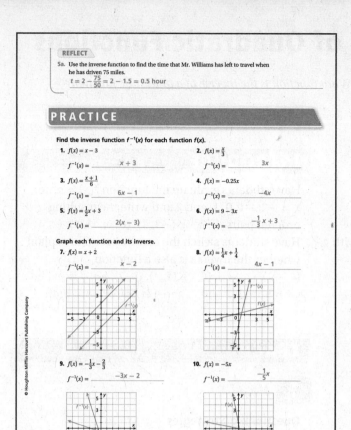

REFLECT

5a. Use the inverse function to find the time that Mr. Williams has left to travel when he has driven 75 miles.

$t = 2 - \frac{75}{50} = 2 - 1.5 = 0.5$ hour

PRACTICE

Find the inverse function $f^{-1}(x)$ for each function $f(x)$.

1. $f(x) = x - 3$

   $f^{-1}(x) = $ _____ $x + 3$

2. $f(x) = \frac{x}{3}$

   $f^{-1}(x) = $ _____ $3x$

3. $f(x) = \frac{x + 1}{6}$

   $f^{-1}(x) = $ _____ $6x - 1$

4. $f(x) = -0.25x$

   $f^{-1}(x) = $ _____ $-4x$

5. $f(x) = \frac{1}{2}x + 3$

   $f^{-1}(x) = $ _____ $2(x - 3)$

6. $f(x) = 9 - 3x$

   $f^{-1}(x) = $ _____ $-\frac{1}{3}x + 3$

Graph each function and its inverse.

7. $f(x) = x + 2$

   $f^{-1}(x) = $ _____ $x - 2$

8. $f(x) = \frac{1}{4}x + \frac{1}{4}$

   $f^{-1}(x) = $ _____ $4x - 1$

9. $f(x) = -\frac{1}{3}x - \frac{2}{3}$

   $f^{-1}(x) = $ _____ $-3x - 2$

10. $f(x) = -5x$

    $f^{-1}(x) = $ _____ $-\frac{1}{5}x$

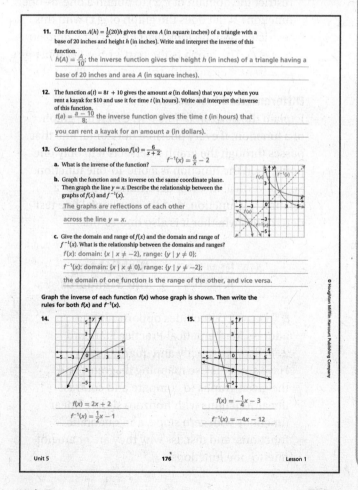

11. The function $A(h) = \frac{1}{2}(20)h$ gives the area A (in square inches) of a triangle with a base of 20 inches and height h (in inches). Write and interpret the inverse of this function.

    $h(A) = \frac{A}{10}$; the inverse function gives the height h (in inches) of a triangle having a base of 20 inches and area A (in square inches).

12. The function $a(t) = 8t + 10$ gives the amount a (in dollars) that you pay when you rent a kayak for $10 and use it for time t (in hours). Write and interpret the inverse of this function.

    $t(a) = \frac{a - 10}{8}$; the inverse function gives the time t (in hours) that you can rent a kayak for an amount a (in dollars).

13. Consider the rational function $f(x) = \frac{6}{x + 2}$.

    a. What is the inverse of the function? $f^{-1}(x) = \frac{6}{x} - 2$

    b. Graph the function and its inverse on the same coordinate plane. Then graph the line $y = x$. Describe the relationship between the graphs of $f(x)$ and $f^{-1}(x)$.

       The graphs are reflections of each other across the line $y = x$.

    c. Give the domain and range of $f(x)$ and the domain and range of $f^{-1}(x)$. What is the relationship between the domains and ranges?

       $f(x)$: domain: $\{x \mid x \neq -2\}$, range: $\{y \mid y \neq 0\}$;

       $f^{-1}(x)$: domain: $\{x \mid x \neq 0\}$, range: $\{y \mid y \neq -2\}$;

       the domain of one function is the range of the other, and vice versa.

Graph the inverse of each function $f(x)$ whose graph is shown. Then write the rules for both $f(x)$ and $f^{-1}(x)$.

14.

    $f(x) = 2x + 2$

    $f^{-1}(x) = \frac{1}{2}x - 1$

15.

    $f(x) = -\frac{1}{4}x - 3$

    $f^{-1}(x) = -4x - 12$

Inverses of Quadratic Functions

Essential question: *What function is the inverse of a quadratic function?*

COMMON CORE Standards for Mathematical Content

CC.9-12.A.CED.2 Create equations in two ... variables to represent relationships between quantities; graph equations on coordinate axes with labels and scales.*

CC.9-12.F.IF.2 Use function notation, evaluate functions for inputs in their domains, and interpret statements that use function notation in terms of a context.

CC.9-12.F.IF.7 Graph functions expressed symbolically and show key features of the graph ...*

CC.9-12.F.IF.7a Graph ... quadratic functions ...*

CC.9-12.F.IF.7b Graph square root ... functions ...*

CC.9-12.F.BF.4 Find inverse functions.

CC.9-12.F.BF.4d(+) Produce an invertible function from a non-invertible function by restricting the domain.

Also: CC.9-12.A.CED.4*, CC.9-12.F.BF.3

Vocabulary
one-to-one function
square root function

Prerequisites
Inverses of functions, Lesson 5-1
Quadratic functions, Lessons 2-1 and 2-2

Math Background
The domain of a quadratic function needs to be restricted in order for the inverse of the function to also be a function. If the domain of a quadratic function is not restricted, then reflecting its graph across the line $y = x$ yields a graph that fails the vertical line test.

INTRODUCE

Have students evaluate the function $f(x) = x^2$ for $x = -2, -1, 0, 1,$ and 2 and write the resulting ordered pairs. (−2, 4), (−1, 1), (0, 0), (1, 1), (2, 4) Have students switch the coordinates and explain whether the inverse is also a function.
(4, −2), (1, −1), (0, 0), (1, 1), (4, 2); no; 4 is paired with both −2 and 2, and 1 is paired with both −1 and 1.

TEACH

1 ENGAGE

Questioning Strategies
- Give an example of a linear function that is not one-to-one. Sample answer: $f(x) = 2$
- In Reflect Question 1d, what is another way to restrict the domain of $g(x)$ to obtain a one-to-one function? What does the graph of $g(x)$ with this restricted domain look like? Restrict the domain to $x \le 0$. The graph is the part of the parabola in Quadrant II along with the vertex (0, 0).

Differentiated Instruction
Explain the *horizontal line test*: Given the graph of a function, if every possible horizontal line that passes through the graph intersects it in only one point, then the function is a one-to-one function. So, the vertical line test determines whether a relation is a function, and the horizontal line test determines whether it is also one-to-one.

MATHEMATICAL PRACTICE | **Highlighting the Standards**

1 ENGAGE includes opportunities to address Mathematical Practice Standard 2 (Reason abstractly and quantitatively). Have students use mapping diagrams and the given graphs to compare and contrast linear functions with nonzero slopes, linear functions with zero slope, and quadratic functions, and discuss why they are or are not one-to-one functions.

Name_____ Class_____ Date_____

5-2

Inverses of Quadratic Functions

COMMON CORE

CC 9-12.A.CED.2*,
CC 9-12.F.IF.2,
CC 9-12.F.IF.7a*,
CC 9-12.F.IF.7b*,
CC 9-12.F.BF.4,
CC 9-12.F.BF.4a

Essential question: *What function is the inverse of a quadratic function?*

1 ENGAGE   Understanding One-to-One Functions

A function is **one-to-one** if each output of the function is paired with exactly one input. Only one-to-one functions have inverses that are also functions.

Recall that the graph of $f^{-1}(x)$ is the reflection of the graph of $f(x)$ across the line $y = x$.

Linear functions with nonzero slopes are always one-to-one, so their inverses are always functions.

Quadratic functions with unrestricted domains are not one-to-one. The reflection of the parabola labeled $g(x)$ across the line $y = x$ is not a function.

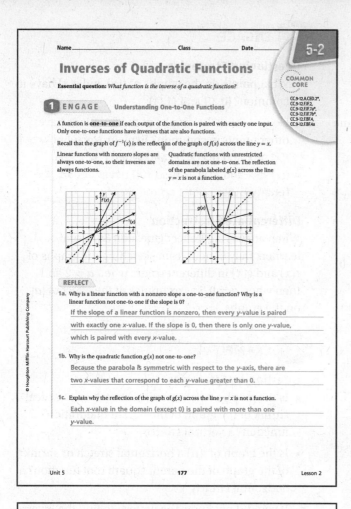

REFLECT

1a. Why is a linear function with a nonzero slope a one-to-one function? Why is a linear function not one-to-one if the slope is 0?

If the slope of a linear function is nonzero, then every *y*-value is paired
with exactly one *x*-value. If the slope is 0, then there is only one *y*-value,
which is paired with every *x*-value.

1b. Why is the quadratic function $g(x)$ not one-to-one?

Because the parabola is symmetric with respect to the *y*-axis, there are
two *x*-values that correspond to each *y*-value greater than 0.

1c. Explain why the reflection of the graph of $g(x)$ across the line $y = x$ is not a function.

Each *x*-value in the domain (except 0) is paired with more than one
y-value.

1d. Consider the quadratic function $g(x) = x^2$. How could you restrict its domain so that the resulting function is one-to-one? Explain. Graph the function for the restricted domain.

Sample answer: Restrict the domain to
$x \geq 0$. For this domain, every *y*-value will
correspond to exactly one *x*-value.

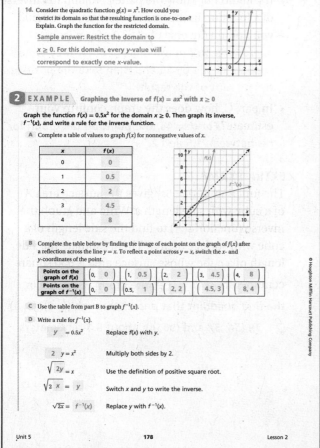

2 EXAMPLE   Graphing the Inverse of $f(x) = ax^2$ with $x \geq 0$

Graph the function $f(x) = 0.5x^2$ for the domain $x \geq 0$. Then graph its inverse, $f^{-1}(x)$, and write a rule for the inverse function.

A Complete a table of values to graph $f(x)$ for nonnegative values of *x*.

x	f(x)
0	0
1	0.5
2	2
3	4.5
4	8

B Complete the table below by finding the image of each point on the graph of $f(x)$ after a reflection across the line $y = x$. To reflect a point across $y = x$, switch the *x*- and *y*-coordinates of the point.

Points on the graph of $f(x)$	(0, 0)	(1, 0.5)	(2, 2)	(3, 4.5)	(4, 8)
Points on the graph of $f^{-1}(x)$	(0, 0)	(0.5, 1)	(2, 2)	(4.5, 3)	(8, 4)

C Use the table from part B to graph $f^{-1}(x)$.

D Write a rule for $f^{-1}(x)$.

$y = 0.5x^2$ Replace $f(x)$ with *y*.

$2 \; y = x^2$ Multiply both sides by 2.

$\sqrt{2y} = x$ Use the definition of positive square root.

$\sqrt{2\,x} = y$ Switch *x* and *y* to write the inverse.

$\sqrt{2x} = f^{-1}(x)$ Replace *y* with $f^{-1}(x)$.

Questioning Strategies

- Why is the domain restricted to nonnegative numbers? so that the inverse is a function

- In part C, how can you visually check whether the graph of $f^{-1}(x)$ is correct?
  The graph should be a reflection of the graph of $f(x)$ across the line $y = x$.

- In part D, why multiply both sides by 2 to isolate x^2?
  The multiplicative inverse of 0.5 is 2.

EXTRA EXAMPLE

Graph the function $f(x) = 3x^2$ for the domain $x \geq 0$. Then graph its inverse, $f^{-1}(x)$, and write a rule for the inverse function. The graph of $f(x)$ is a curve in the first quadrant passing through (0, 0), (1, 3), and (2, 12). The graph of $f^{-1}(x)$ is a curve in the first quadrant passing through (0, 0), (3, 1), and (12, 2). $f^{-1}(x) = \sqrt{\frac{x}{3}}$

Teaching Strategy

Have students state the sequence of operations performed on x in both the function and its inverse. For $f(x)$, square x and take half of the result. For $f^{-1}(x)$, multiply x by 2 and take the positive square root of the result.

Avoid Common Errors

Students sometimes fail to draw the radical sign far enough to the right to cover the expression they wish to cover. For example, they may write $f(x) = \sqrt{3}x$ instead of $f(x) = \sqrt{3x}$.

Questioning Strategies

- What points do the graphs of $f(x)$ and $g(x)$ have in common? (0, 0) and (1, 1)

- Do you think the graphs of the functions have other points in common? Explain. No; when $x > 1$, $f(x) > x$ and $g(x) < x$, and when $0 < x < 1$, $f(x) < x$ and $g(x) > x$, so $f(x)$ never equals $g(x)$ for any other points on the graphs.

Differentiated Instruction

When answering Reflect Question 3a, visual learners may benefit from sketching the graphs of $f(x)$ and $g(x)$ in different colors when $a = 2$ and then when $a = 0.5$ as examples of the effect of $|a|$ on the graphs.

Questioning Strategies

- Is the graph of $d(t)$ a vertical stretch or a vertical shrink of the graph of the parent quadratic function? a vertical stretch

- Is the graph of $t(d)$ a horizontal stretch or shrink of the graph of the parent square root function? a horizontal stretch

- If you did not know the pattern to find the inverse of a function in the form $f(x) = ax^2$, how could you find the inverse of $d(t)$? Perform inverse operations on t in the reverse order they were applied: divide by 16 and then take the positive square root of the result.

- In part C, how does the graph confirm your estimate? For $d = 48$, the point on the graph for t is between 1.5 and 2.

EXTRA EXAMPLE

The function $A(s) = 6s^2$ gives the surface area A of a cube with side length s. Write and graph the inverse function $s(A)$ to find the side length of a cube with surface area A. Then, estimate the side length of a cube whose surface area is 500 square centimeters. $s(A) = \sqrt{\frac{A}{6}}$; the graph is a curve in the first quadrant that passes through (0, 0), (6, 1), (24, 2), (54, 3), and (96, 4); about 9.1 centimeters

REFLECT

2a. When solving the equation $2y = x^2$ for x in part D, you use the definition of a positive square root. Why can you ignore negative square roots?

Because the domain of $f(x)$ is restricted to $x \geq 0$, x cannot be negative.

2b. How else could you restrict the domain of $f(x)$ in order to get an inverse that is a function? What is the inverse function given that restriction?

The domain could be restricted to any interval where the function is one-to-one; for example, $x \leq 0$, where the inverse would be $f^{-1}(x) = -\sqrt{2x}$.

3 ENGAGE   Understanding Square Root Functions

A quadratic function of the form $f(x) = ax^2$ for $x \geq 0$ is a one-to-one function, so its inverse is also a function. In general, the inverse of $f(x) = ax^2$ for $x \geq 0$ is the *square root function* $g(x) = \sqrt{\frac{x}{a}}$.

A **square root function** is a function whose rule involves $\sqrt{x}$. The parent square root function is $g(x) = \sqrt{x}$. The graph shows that $g(x) = \sqrt{x}$ is the inverse of $f(x) = x^2$ for $x \geq 0$.

A square root function is defined only for values of x that make the expression under the radical sign nonnegative.

REFLECT

3a. What are the domain and range of the parent square root function $g(x) = \sqrt{x}$? Explain.

The expression under the radical sign must be nonnegative, so the domain of the function is $x \geq 0$. The square root of a real number is never negative, so the range of the function is $y \geq 0$.

3b. When $a > 1$, the graph of $f(x) = ax^2$ for $x \geq 0$ is a vertical stretch by a factor of a of the graph of the parent quadratic function for $x \geq 0$. When $a > 1$, is the graph of $g(x) = \sqrt{\frac{x}{a}}$ a horizontal stretch or a horizontal shrink by a factor of a of the graph of the parent square root function? Explain.

When reflected across the line $y = x$, a vertical stretch of the graph of the parent quadratic function for $x \geq 0$ results in a graph that is a horizontal stretch of the parent square root function. So, the graph of $g(x)$ is a horizontal stretch by a factor of a of the parent square root function.

4 EXAMPLE   Modeling the Inverse of a Quadratic Function

The function $d(t) = 16t^2$ gives the distance d in feet that a dropped object falls in t seconds. Write and graph the inverse function $t(d)$ to find the time t in seconds it takes for an object to fall a distance of d feet. Then estimate how long it will take a penny dropped into a well to fall 48 feet.

A Write the inverse function.

The original function is a ___quadratic___ function with a domain restricted to $t \geq$ ___0___.

The function fits the pattern $f(x) = ax^2$ for $x \geq 0$, so its inverse will have the form $g(x) = \sqrt{\frac{x}{a}}$.

Original Function	Inverse Function
$d(t) = 16t^2$ for $t \geq 0$	$t(d) = \sqrt{\dfrac{d}{16}}$ for $d \geq 0$

B Complete the table of values and use it to graph the function $t(d)$.

d	0	4	16	36	64	100
t	0	0.5	1	1.5	2	2.5

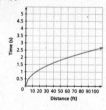

C Use the function $t(d)$ to estimate how long it will take a penny to fall 48 feet.

$t(d) = \sqrt{\dfrac{d}{16}}$ Write the function.

$t(48) = \sqrt{\dfrac{48}{16}}$ Substitute 48 for d.

$t(48) = \sqrt{3}$ Simplify.

$t(48) \approx 1.7$ Use a calculator to estimate.

So, it will take about ___1.7___ seconds for a penny to fall 48 feet.

© Houghton Mifflin Harcourt Publishing Company

Essential Question

What function is the inverse of a quadratic function?
A square root function is the inverse of a quadratic function whose domain is restricted. The inverse of $f(x) = ax^2$ for $x \geq 0$ is $f^{-1}(x) = \sqrt{\frac{x}{a}}$.

Summarize

Have students do the following: Draw the graph of the parent quadratic function and discuss why the function is not one-to-one. Erase the "left side" of the parabola and discuss why the function is now one-to-one. Draw the line $y = x$ and use it to draw the graph of the inverse function. Discuss why it is a function.

Where skills are taught	Where skills are practiced
2 EXAMPLE	EXS. 1–4
3 EXAMPLE	EXS. 5, 6

Exercises 7 and 8: These exercises are extensions of Reflect Question 3b, which showed that the graph of $g(x) = \sqrt{\frac{x}{a}}$ is a horizontal stretch of the parent square root function by a factor of a when $a > 1$ (and, through similar reasoning, a horizontal shrink by a factor of a when $0 < a < 1$). When completing Exercises 7 and 8, some students may compare the graph of $g(x)$ with the given graph of the parent square root function and see vertical stretches and shrinks instead of horizontal stretches and shrinks. If so, this would be an opportunity to show students that the constant a can be pulled out of the radicand. For instance, in Exercise 7, you can rewrite $g(x)$ as $g(x) = \sqrt{\frac{x}{3}} = \sqrt{\frac{1}{3}} \cdot \sqrt{x} \approx 0.58\sqrt{x}$. This shows that the graph of $g(x)$ can be characterized as either a horizontal stretch by a factor of 3 or a vertical shrink by a factor of 0.58. In Exercise 8, you can write $g(x)$ as either $g(x) = \sqrt{\frac{x}{0.25}}$ or $g(x) = 2\sqrt{x}$. The former tells you that the graph of $g(x)$ is a horizontal shrink of the parent square root function by a factor of 0.25, while the latter tells you that the graph of $g(x)$ is a vertical stretch by a factor of 2.

© Houghton Mifflin Harcourt Publishing Company

REFLECT

4a. Explain why the domain is restricted to $t \geq 0$ for the original function $d(t) = 16t^2$.

The domain is restricted because t represents time in seconds, which can only be

nonnegative.

4b. Describe another way that you could estimate the time it would take a penny
to fall 48 feet.

Sample answer: Set $d(t)$ equal to 48 in the original function $d(t) = 16t^2$.

Then solve for t.

PRACTICE

Graph the function $f(x)$ for the domain $x \geq 0$. Then graph its inverse, $f^{-1}(x)$, and
write a rule for the inverse function.

1. $f(x) = 2x^2$

$f^{-1}(x) = \sqrt{\dfrac{x}{2}}$

2. $f(x) = -x^2$

$f^{-1}(x) = \sqrt{-x}$

3. $f(x) = \frac{1}{3}x^2$

$f^{-1}(x) = \sqrt{3x}$

4. $f(x) = -\frac{1}{2}x^2$

$f^{-1}(x) = \sqrt{-2x}$

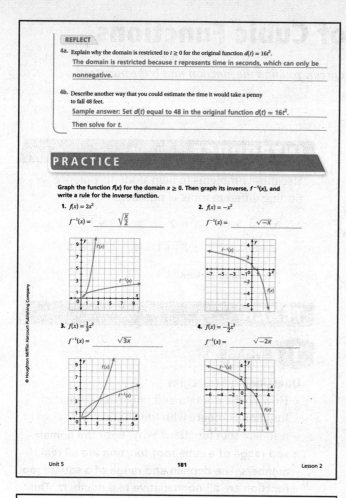

5. A company manufactures square tabletops that are covered by 16 square tiles.
If s is the side length of each tile in inches, then the area A of a tabletop in square
feet is given by $A(s) = \frac{1}{9}s^2$.

a. Write and graph the inverse function $s(A)$ to find the side
length of the tiles in inches for a tabletop with an area of
A square feet.

$s(A) = \sqrt{9A}$

b. What is the side length of the tiles that make up a tabletop
with an area of 4 square feet?

6 inches

6. The function $A(r) = \pi r^2$ gives the area A in square meters of
a circle with a radius of r meters.

a. Write and graph the inverse function $r(A)$ to find the radius
in meters of a circle with an area of A square meters.

$r(A) = \sqrt{\dfrac{A}{\pi}}$

b. Estimate the radius of a circular swimming pool that has
a surface area of 120 square meters.

6.2 meters

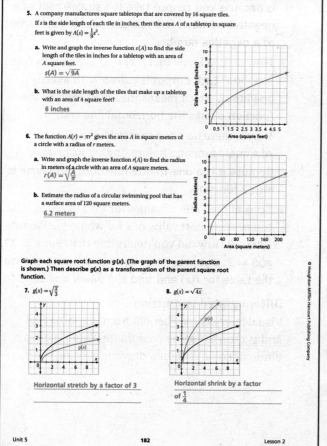

Graph each square root function $g(x)$. (The graph of the parent function
is shown.) Then describe $g(x)$ as a transformation of the parent square root
function.

7. $g(x) = \sqrt{\dfrac{x}{3}}$

Horizontal stretch by a factor of 3

8. $g(x) = \sqrt{4x}$

Horizontal shrink by a factor
of $\frac{1}{4}$

Inverses of Cubic Functions

Essential question: *How can you find the function that is the inverse of a cubic function?*

© Houghton Mifflin Harcourt Publishing Company

COMMON Standards for
CORE Mathematical Content

CC.9-12.A.CED.2 Create equations in two ... variables to represent relationships between quantities; graph equations on coordinate axes with labels and scales. *

CC.9-12.F.IF.2 Use function notation, evaluate functions for inputs in their domains, and interpret statements that use function notation in terms of a context.

CC.9-12.F.IF.7 Graph functions expressed symbolically and show key features of the graph ...*

CC.9-12.F.IF.7b Graph ... cube root ... functions ...*

CC.9-12.F.IF.7c Graph polynomial functions ...*

CC.9-12.F.BF.4 Find inverse functions.

CC.9-12.F.BF.4a Solve an equation of the form $f(x) = c$ for a simple function f that has an inverse and write an expression for the inverse.

Also: CC.9-12.F.BF.3

Vocabulary
cube root function

Prerequisites
Finding cube roots, Grade 8
Graphing polynomial functions, Lesson 3-1
Inverses of functions, Lesson 5-1
Inverses of quadratic functions, Lesson 5-2

Math Background
If $a^3 = b$, then a is the cube root of b. Every real number has a single cube root. This is in contrast to square roots, where positive real numbers have two square roots, 0 has one square root (itself), and negative real numbers have no (real) square roots.

This lesson is similar in nature to the previous lesson on inverses of quadratic functions. As you move through the lesson, point out the concepts that are repeated between the previous lesson on quadratics and this lesson. Students who experienced success in that lesson should be successful here also.

INTRODUCE

Use these problems to help students practice finding different roots of numbers.

$\sqrt[3]{125}$ 5 $\sqrt[3]{8}$ 2 $\sqrt[4]{16}$ 2

$\sqrt[3]{-8}$ −2 $\sqrt[3]{-64}$ −4 $\sqrt[5]{0}$ 0

$\sqrt{-4}$ does not exist

TEACH

1 ENGAGE

Questioning Strategies

- How do the domain and range of a cube root function compare with the domain and range of a square root function? Why? **Both the domain and range of a cube root function are all real numbers. The domain and range of a square root function are all nonnegative real numbers. This is because you cannot take the square root of a negative number, but you can take the cube root of a negative number.**

- How do you know that $f(x) = x^3$ is a one-to-one function? **Each output is paired with exactly one input, which means that the graph of the function passes the horizontal line test.**

- Why is there no need to restrict the domain of a cubic function before finding its inverse? **Because it is a one-to-one function, its inverse is also a function.**

- Look at the table of values for $g(x)$. What is the next greatest value of x for which $g(x)$ is an integer? How did you determine that? **For $x = 27$, $g(x) = 3$. One way to determine this is to extend the table for $f(x)$ and find $f(x)$ when $x = 3$.**

Differentiated Instruction

Visual learners may benefit from graphing $f(x)$ and $g(x)$ on the same coordinate plane, each in a different color, and then drawing the line $y = x$.

Name_____ Class_____ Date_____

Inverses of Cubic Functions

COMMON
CORE

CC-12.A.CED.2*,
CC-9-12.F.IF.2,
CC-9-12.F.IF.7b*,
CC-9-12.F.IF.7c*,
CC-9-12.F.BF.4,
CC-9-12.F.BF.4a

Essential question: *How can you find the function that is the inverse of a cubic function?*

1 ENGAGE   Understanding the Cube Root Function

A table of values for the parent cubic function, $f(x) = x^3$, is shown below, along with its graph.

x	f(x)
−2	−8
−1	−1
0	0
1	1
2	8

Because $f(x) = x^3$ is a one-to-one function, its inverse is also a function. The inverse of $f(x) = x^3$ is the *cube root function* $g(x) = \sqrt[3]{x}$.

A **cube root function** is a function whose rule involves $\sqrt[3]{x}$. The parent cube root function is $g(x) = \sqrt[3]{x}$.

A table of values for $g(x) = \sqrt[3]{x}$ is shown below, along with its graph.

x	g(x)
−8	−2
−1	−1
0	0
1	1
8	2

REFLECT

1a. Explain how the values in the tables for $f(x) = x^3$ and $g(x) = \sqrt[3]{x}$ show that the graphs of these functions are reflections of each other across the line $y = x$.

The x- and y-coordinates in the table for $f(x)$ are switched in the table for $g(x)$.

1b. Is $g(x) = \sqrt[3]{x}$ also a one-to-one function? Explain.

Yes; each y-value is paired with exactly one x-value.

1c. What are the domain and range of $f(x) = x^3$? What are the domain and range of $g(x) = \sqrt[3]{x}$?

The domains of both functions are all real numbers.

The ranges of both functions are also all real numbers.

2 EXAMPLE   Graphing the Inverse of $f(x) = ax^3$

Graph the function $f(x) = 0.5x^3$. Then graph its inverse, $f^{-1}(x)$, and write a rule for the inverse function.

A Complete the table of values to graph the function $f(x) = 0.5x^3$.

x	f(x)
−2	−4
−1	−0.5
0	0
1	0.5
2	4

B Complete the table below by finding the image of each point on the graph of $f(x)$ after a reflection across the line $y = x$.

Points on the graph of f(x)	−2, −4	−1, −0.5	0, 0	1, 0.5	2, 4
Points on the graph of $f^{-1}(x)$	−4, −2	−0.5, −1	(0, 0)	(0.5, 1)	(4, 2)

C Use the table from part B to graph $f^{-1}(x)$.

D Write a rule for $f^{-1}(x)$.

$y = 0.5x^3$ Replace $f(x)$ with y.

$2\ y = x^3$ Solve for x. Multiply both sides by 2.

$\sqrt[3]{2y} = x$ Use the definition of cube root.

$\sqrt[3]{2\ x} = y$ Switch x and y to write the inverse.

$\sqrt[3]{2x} = f^{-1}(x)$ Replace y with $f^{-1}(x)$.

Questioning Strategies

- When finding the inverse of $f(x) = x^2$ for $x \geq 0$, you use the definition of a positive square root. In part D, why don't you use the definition of a positive cube root? **Positive real numbers have two square roots (one positive and one negative), but you want only the positive square root due to the restriction $x \geq 0$. Real numbers have a single cube root, so you're simply finding** *the* **cube root.**

- In part D, how can you write the radicand $2x$ in the form $\frac{x}{a}$? What is a? **Multiplying x by 2 is the same as dividing x by $\frac{1}{2}$, so $g(x) = \sqrt[3]{2x} = \sqrt[3]{\frac{x}{0.5}}$; $a = 0.5$**

EXTRA EXAMPLE

Graph the function $f(x) = -\frac{1}{2}x^3$. Then graph its inverse, $f^{-1}(x)$, and write a rule for the inverse function. **The graph of $f(x)$ is a curve passing through $(-2, 4)$, $(-1, 0.5)$, $(0, 0)$, $(1, -0.5)$, and $(2, -4)$. The graph of $f^{-1}(x)$ is a curve passing through $(4, -2)$, $(0.5, -1)$, $(0, 0)$, $(-0.5, 1)$, and $(-4, 2)$. $f^{-1}(x) = \sqrt[3]{-2x}$**

Teaching Strategy

Have students state the sequence of operations performed on x in both the function and its inverse. **For $f(x)$, cube x and take half of the result. For $f^{-1}(x)$, multiply x by 2 and take the cube root of the result.**

Technology

To cube a number on a graphing calculator, enter the base followed by the caret key [∧] and the exponent, 3. To take a cube root, press [MATH], choose 4: $\sqrt[3]{}$ (, and type the radicand. Another way to take a cube root is to enter the base followed by [∧] (1/3), making sure to enclose the fractional exponent in parentheses.

Highlighting the Standards

2 EXAMPLE includes opportunities to address Mathematical Practice Standard 8 (Look for and express regularity in repeated reasoning). In Reflect Question 2a, students find that the inverse of the general cubic function $f(x) = ax^3$ is $f^{-1}(x) = \sqrt[3]{\frac{x}{a}}$. Have students compare these two general functions to the general quadratic and square root functions they found previously: $f(x) = ax^2$ for $x \geq 0$ and $f^{-1}(x) = \sqrt{\frac{x}{a}}$. Ask students what they think the inverses of $f(x) = ax^4$ and $f(x) = ax^5$ would be.

Questioning Strategies

- How does the graph of $l(w)$ compare to the graph of the parent cube root function? **It's a horizontal shrink.**

- How can you use the original function $w(l)$ to answer the question? **Substitute 7 for $w(l)$ and solve for l by multiplying each side by 3500 and then applying the definition of cube root.**

EXTRA EXAMPLE

The function $t(w) = \frac{w^3}{9}$ gives the number of full truckloads t of cement needed to form a bridge pillar of width w yards. Write and graph the inverse function $w(t)$ to find the approximate width of a pillar requiring t truckloads of cement. Then estimate the width of a bridge pillar requiring 40 truckloads of cement. **$w(t) = \sqrt[3]{9t}$; The graph is a curve in the first quadrant passing approximately through $(0, 0)$, $(1, 2)$, $(3, 3)$, $(8, 4)$, and $(14, 5)$; about 7 yards**

REFLECT

2a. What is the inverse of the function $f(x) = ax^3$?

$f^{-1}(x) = \sqrt[3]{\frac{x}{a}}$

2b. When $0 < a < 1$, the graph of $f(x) = ax^3$ is a vertical shrink by a factor of a of the graph of the parent cubic function. When $0 < a < 1$, is the graph of $f^{-1}(x) = \sqrt[3]{\frac{x}{a}}$ a horizontal stretch or a horizontal shrink by a factor of a of the graph of the parent cube root function? Explain.

When reflected across the line $y = x$, a vertical shrink of the

graph of the parent cubic function results in a graph that is a

horizontal shrink of the graph of the parent cube root function.

So, the graph of $f^{-1}(x)$ is a horizontal shrink by a factor of a of

the graph of the parent cube root function.

2c. Complete the chart below by describing the graph of each function as a transformation of the graph of its parent function.

Value of a	$f(x) = ax^3$	$g(x) = \sqrt[3]{\frac{x}{a}}$
$a > 1$	vertical stretch by a factor of a	horizontal stretch by a factor of a
$0 < a < 1$	vertical shrink by a factor of a	horizontal shrink by a factor of a

3 EXAMPLE Modeling the Inverse of a Cubic Function

A pike is a type of freshwater fish. The function $w(l) = \frac{l^3}{3500}$ gives the approximate weight w in pounds of a pike with length l inches. Write and graph the inverse function $l(w)$ to find the approximate length l in inches of a pike weighing w pounds. Then estimate how long a 7-pound pike would be.

A Write the inverse function.

The original function is a __cubic__ function.

It can be written in the form $f(x) = ax^3$ where $a = \frac{1}{3500}$.

Its inverse will have the form $g(x) = \sqrt[3]{\frac{x}{a}}$.

Original Function	Inverse Function
$w(l) = \frac{1}{3500}\,l^3$	$l(w) = \sqrt[3]{3500w}$

B Complete the table of values and use it to graph the function $l(w)$. Round the values of l to the nearest whole number.

w	0	1	2	3	4	5
l	0	15	19	22	24	26

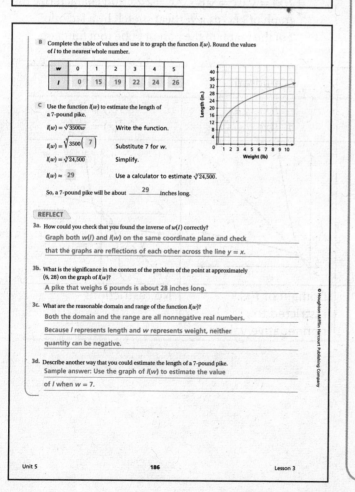

C Use the function $l(w)$ to estimate the length of a 7-pound pike.

$l(w) = \sqrt[3]{3500w}$ Write the function.

$l(w) = \sqrt[3]{3500\left(\boxed{7}\right)}$ Substitute 7 for w.

$l(w) = \sqrt[3]{24,500}$ Simplify.

$l(w) \approx 29$ Use a calculator to estimate $\sqrt[3]{24,500}$.

So, a 7-pound pike will be about ___29___ inches long.

REFLECT

3a. How could you check that you found the inverse of $w(l)$ correctly?

Graph both $w(l)$ and $l(w)$ on the same coordinate plane and check

that the graphs are reflections of each other across the line $y = x$.

3b. What is the significance in the context of the problem of the point at approximately (6, 28) on the graph of $l(w)$?

A pike that weighs 6 pounds is about 28 inches long.

3c. What are the reasonable domain and range of the function $l(w)$?

Both the domain and the range are all nonnegative real numbers.

Because l represents length and w represents weight, neither

quantity can be negative.

3d. Describe another way that you could estimate the length of a 7-pound pike.

Sample answer: Use the graph of $l(w)$ to estimate the value

of l when $w = 7$.

© Houghton Mifflin Harcourt Publishing Company

Essential Question

How can you find the function that is the inverse of a cubic function?

Algebraically, substitute y for $f(x)$, solve for x, and then switch x and y. The inverse of $f(x) = ax^3$ is the function $f^{-1}(x) = \sqrt[3]{\frac{x}{a}}$. Graphically, graph the cubic function and reflect the graph across the line $y = x$, which switches the coordinates in each ordered pair for $f(x)$ and thereby results in ordered pairs for $f^{-1}(x)$.

Summarize

Create a graphic organizer that compares and contrasts inverse linear, quadratic, and cubic functions. One possibility is shown below.

Where skills are taught	Where skills are practiced
2 EXAMPLE	EXS. 1–4
3 EXAMPLE	EXS. 5, 6

Exercise 7: Students analyze a cubic function that is not a one-to-one function. Point out how this function is not in the form $f(x) = ax^3$, as are those studied in the lesson.

Exercises 8 and 9: Students describe the graphs of cube root functions that involve multiplying the function by a or multiplying x by a as horizontal or vertical stretches or shrinks of the graph of the parent cube root function. While students should be familiar with the transformation in Exercise 8, they may have trouble with the transformation in Exercise 9. This exercise is an extension of Reflect Questions 2a–2c. Students will need to rewrite $g(x)$ as $g(x) = \sqrt[3]{8x} = \sqrt[3]{\frac{x}{0.125}}$ in order to see that its graph is a horizontal stretch by a fator of 0.125 of the graph of the parent cube root function. Alternatively, students can rewrite $g(x)$ as $g(x) = \sqrt[3]{8x} = \sqrt[3]{8} \cdot \sqrt[3]{x} = 2\sqrt[3]{x}$ and characterize the graph of $g(x)$ as a vertical stretch by a factor of 2 of the graph of the parent cube root function.

	Linear	**Quadratic**	**Cubic**
Equations	$f(x) = ax$ $f^{-1}(x) = \frac{x}{a}$	$f(x) = ax^2$ $f^{-1}(x) = \sqrt{\frac{x}{a}}$	$f(x) = ax^3$ $f^{-1}(x) = \sqrt[3]{\frac{x}{a}}$
Graphs			
Restrictions	$f(x)$ must have nonzero slope.	Domain of $f(x)$ restricted to nonnegative values	No restrictions

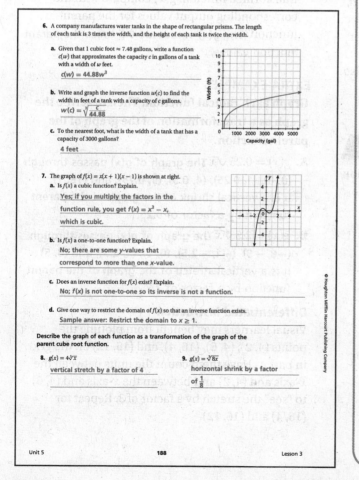

PRACTICE

Graph the function $f(x)$. Then graph its inverse, $f^{-1}(x)$, and write a rule for the inverse function.

1. $f(x) = 2x^3$

$f^{-1}(x) =$ _____ $\sqrt[3]{\dfrac{x}{2}}$ _____

2. $f(x) = -x^3$

$f^{-1}(x) =$ _____ $\sqrt[3]{-x}$ _____

3. $f(x) = \frac{1}{4}x^3$

$f^{-1}(x) =$ _____ $\sqrt[3]{4x}$ _____

4. $f(x) = -\frac{1}{3}x^3$

$f^{-1}(x) =$ _____ $\sqrt[3]{-3x}$ _____

5. The function $V(r) = \frac{4}{3}\pi r^3$ gives the volume V in cubic inches of a sphere with a radius of r inches.

a. Write and graph the inverse function $r(V)$ to find the radius in inches of a sphere with a volume of V cubic inches.

$r(V) = \sqrt[3]{\dfrac{3}{4\pi}V}$

b. To the nearest inch, what is the radius of a basketball with a volume of 455 cubic inches?

5 inches

Unit 5   187   Lesson 3

6. A company manufactures water tanks in the shape of rectangular prisms. The length of each tank is 3 times the width, and the height of each tank is twice the width.

a. Given that 1 cubic foot ≈ 7.48 gallons, write a function $c(w)$ that approximates the capacity c in gallons of a tank with a width of w feet.

$c(w) = 44.88w^3$

b. Write and graph the inverse function $w(c)$ to find the width in feet of a tank with a capacity of c gallons.

$w(c) = \sqrt[3]{\dfrac{c}{44.88}}$

c. To the nearest foot, what is the width of a tank that has a capacity of 3000 gallons?

4 feet

7. The graph of $f(x) = x(x+1)(x-1)$ is shown at right.

a. Is $f(x)$ a cubic function? Explain.

Yes; if you multiply the factors in the function rule, you get $f(x) = x^3 - x$, which is cubic.

b. Is $f(x)$ a one-to-one function? Explain.

No; there are some y-values that correspond to more than one x-value.

c. Does an inverse function for $f(x)$ exist? Explain.

No; $f(x)$ is not one-to-one so its inverse is not a function.

d. Give one way to restrict the domain of $f(x)$ so that an inverse function exists.

Sample answer: Restrict the domain to $x \geq 1$.

Describe the graph of each function as a transformation of the graph of the parent cube root function.

8. $g(x) = 4\sqrt[3]{x}$

vertical stretch by a factor of 4

9. $g(x) = \sqrt[3]{8x}$

horizontal shrink by a factor of $\frac{1}{8}$

Unit 5   188   Lesson 3

© Houghton Mifflin Harcourt Publishing Company

Graphing Square Root and Cube Root Functions

Essential question: *How can you graph transformations of the parent square root and cube root functions?*

© Houghton Mifflin Harcourt Publishing Company

COMMON CORE Standards for Mathematical Content

CC.9-12.F.IF.7 Graph functions expressed symbolically and show key features of the graph ...*

CC.9-12.F.IF.7b Graph square root, cube root ... functions ...*

CC.9-12.F.BF.3 Identify the effect on the graph of replacing $f(x)$ by $f(x) + k$, $kf(x)$, ... and $f(x + k)$ for specific values of k (both positive and negative); find the value of k given the graphs. ...

Also: CC.9–12.F.IF.9

Prerequisites

Inverses of quadratic functions, Lesson 5-2

Inverses of cubic functions, Lesson 5-3

Math Background

Students will explore how changing the values of a, h, and k in a square root or cube root function affect its graph. They will find that changing a parameter affects the graph in the same way it did for other functions they have encountered. Students will also write an equation given the graph of one of these transformed radical functions.

INTRODUCE

Remind students that the parent quadratic function is $f(x) = x^2$ and that the vertex form of a quadratic function is $f(x) = a(x - h)^2 + k$. Next, write the equation of the parent square root function, $f(x) = \sqrt{x}$. Ask students how to write $af(x)$, $f(x) + k$ and $f(x - h)$. $f(x) = a\sqrt{x}$, $f(x) = \sqrt{x} + k$, $f(x) = \sqrt{x - h}$

Show students that the general form for a square root function is $f(x) = a\sqrt{x - h} + k$, and in the parent function, $a = 1$, $h = 0$, and $k = 0$. Finally, ask the students how to write the general form for a cube root function. $f(x) = a\sqrt[3]{x - h} + k$

TEACH

1 EXAMPLE

Questioning Strategies

- For the x-values shown in the table in part A, what are the output values of the parent function? From the top down, they are 0, 1, 2, 3, and 4.

- In part A, how do the output values for the transformed function $g(x)$ compare with the corresponding output values for the parent function? The $g(x)$-values are 3 times the parent function values.

- For the x-values shown in the table in part B, what are the output values of the parent function? From the top down, they are −2, −1, 0, 1, and 2.

- In part B, how do the output values for the transformed function $g(x)$ compare with the corresponding output values for the parent function? The $g(x)$-values are 0.5 times the parent function values.

EXTRA EXAMPLES

Graph each radical function. Then describe the graph as a transformation of the graph of the parent function.

A. $g(x) = 0.25\sqrt{x}$ The graph of $g(x)$ passes through (0, 0), (1, 0.25), (4, 0.5), (9, 0.75), and (16, 1). It is a vertical shrink of the graph of the parent function by a factor of 0.25.

B. $g(x) = 2.5\sqrt[3]{x}$ The graph of $g(x)$ passes through (−8, −5), (−1, −2.5), (0, 0), (1, 2.5), and (8, 5). It is a vertical stretch of the graph of the parent function by a factor of 2.5.

Differentiated Instruction

Visual learners may benefit from plotting the points (4, 2), (4, 6), (16, 4), and (16, 12) on the grid in part A. Have them count the units between the x-axis and (4, 2) and between the x-axis and (4, 6) to "see" the stretch by a factor of 3. Repeat for (16, 4) and (16, 12).

Name _____ Class _____ Date _____

Graphing Square Root and Cube Root Functions

COMMON
CORE

CC.9-12.F.IF.7*,
CC.9-12.F.IF.7b*,
CC.9-12.F.BF.3

Essential question: *How can you graph transformations of the parent square root and cube root functions?*

You can transform the parent square root and parent cube root functions by changing the values of *a*, *h*, and *k* in the general forms of the equations shown below.

$$f(x) = a\sqrt{x - h} + k \qquad\qquad f(x) = a\sqrt[3]{x - h} + k$$

1 EXAMPLE Changing the Value of *a*

Graph each radical function. Then describe the graph as a transformation of the graph of the parent function. (The graph of the parent function is shown.)

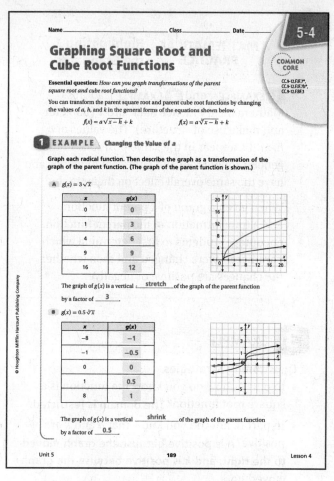

A $g(x) = 3\sqrt{x}$

x	g(x)
0	0
1	3
4	6
9	9
16	12

The graph of g(x) is a vertical ___stretch___ of the graph of the parent function

by a factor of ___3___ .

B $g(x) = 0.5\sqrt[3]{x}$

x	g(x)
−8	−1
−1	−0.5
0	0
1	0.5
8	1

The graph of g(x) is a vertical ___shrink___ of the graph of the parent function

by a factor of ___0.5___ .

Unit 5   189   Lesson 4

REFLECT

1a. In part A, why does it make sense to use x-values of 0, 1, 4, 9, and 16 when finding points on the graph of g(x)?

The rule for g(x) involves finding the square root of x, so using x-values that are

perfect squares will make the calculations easier.

1b. Explain how you know in part B that the graph of g(x) is a vertical shrink of the graph of the parent function.

For a given x-value, the value of g(x) is half the value of the parent function.

1c. Generalize from your observations to complete the sentences below.

For $g(x) = a\sqrt{x}$ or $g(x) = a\sqrt[3]{x}$:

• when |a| > 1, the graph of g(x) is a vertical ___stretch___ of the graph of the parent function.

• when 0 < |a| < 1, the graph of g(x) is a vertical ___shrink___ of the graph of the parent function.

2 EXAMPLE Changing the Values of *h* and *k*

Graph each radical function. Then describe the graph as a transformation of the graph of the parent function, and give its domain and range. (The graph of the parent function is shown.)

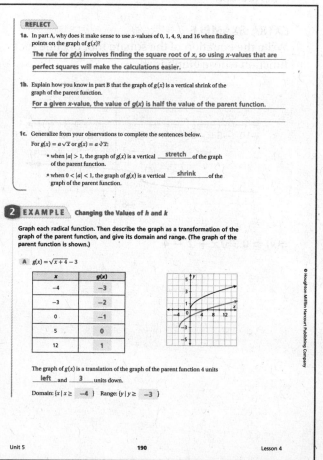

A $g(x) = \sqrt{x + 4} - 3$

x	g(x)
−4	−3
−3	−2
0	−1
5	0
12	1

The graph of g(x) is a translation of the graph of the parent function 4 units

___left___ and ___3___ units down.

Domain: {x | x ≥ ___−4___ }   Range: {y | y ≥ ___−3___ }

Unit 5   190   Lesson 4

© Houghton Mifflin Harcourt Publishing Company

Questioning Strategies

- In part A, how can you determine the x-intercept just by analyzing the function rule? The x-intercept is the value of x when $g(x) = 0$. If $g(x) = 0$, then $\sqrt{x + 4}$ equals 3. This means the radicand must equal 9, so x must be 5.

- Does the graph of the square root function have a vertical or horizontal asymptote? Explain. No; the graph does not *approach* a value, but it does have a *starting point*.

- In the function $g(x) = 5 + \sqrt{x + 1}$, is 5 the value of a or of k? Explain. It is the value of k. It is being added to the radical. The function can be rewritten as $g(x) = \sqrt{x + 1} + 5$.

EXTRA EXAMPLE

Graph each radical function. Then describe the graph as a transformation of the graph of the parent function and give its domain and range.

A. $g(x) = \sqrt{x - 3} - 5$ The graph of $g(x)$ starts at $(3, -5)$ and passes through $(4, -4)$, $(7, -3)$, $(12, -2)$, and $(19, -1)$. It is a translation 3 units right and 5 units down; domain: $\{x \mid x \geq 3\}$; range: $\{y \mid y \geq -5\}$

B. $g(x) = \sqrt[3]{x + 6} + 2$ The graph of $g(x)$ passes through $(-14, 0)$, $(-7, 1)$, $(-6, 2)$, $(-5, 3)$, and $(2, 4)$. It is a translation 6 units left and 2 units up; domain: all real numbers; range: all real numbers

Teaching Strategy

In part A, have students add a column for $\sqrt{x + 4}$ between x and $g(x)$. Have them plot the ordered pairs that result from this intermediate step to see that the graph is first shifted 4 units left. Similarly, they can add a middle column for the results of $\sqrt[3]{x - 2}$ in part B to see that the graph is first shifted 2 units right.

---

3 EXAMPLE

Questioning Strategies

- In part A, how do you know the function is a square root function? The domain is restricted.

- In part B, how do you know that h and k are positive? h is positive because the graph moved to the right, and k is positive because the graph moved up.

EXTRA EXAMPLE

Write the equation of the square root or cube root function whose graph is shown.

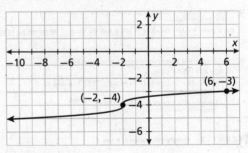

$g(x) = 0.5 \sqrt[3]{x + 2} - 4$

8 $g(x) = \sqrt[3]{x-2} + 4$

x	g(x)
−6	2
1	3
2	4
3	5
10	6

The graph of $g(x)$ is a translation of the graph of the parent function 2 units __right__ and __4__ units up.

Domain: __all real numbers__   Range: __all real numbers__

REFLECT

2a. How can you determine the domain of $g(x) = \sqrt{x+4} - 3$ by looking at its function rule?

The expression under the radical sign must be nonnegative, which means that x cannot be less than −4. So, the domain is $\{x \mid x \geq -4\}$.

2b. In part B, what are the values of h and k in $g(x) = \sqrt[3]{x-2} + 4$? What effect do h and k have on the function's graph?

$h = 2$; $k = 4$; h determines how the graph is translated horizontally, and k determines how the graph is translated vertically.

2c. Generalize from your observations to complete the sentences below.

For $g(x) = \sqrt{x-h} + k$ and $g(x) = \sqrt[3]{x-h} + k$:

• the graph of $g(x)$ is a translation of the parent function $|h|$ units __left__ if $h < 0$ and h units __right__ if $h > 0$.

• the graph of $g(x)$ is a translation of the parent function $|k|$ units __down__ if $k < 0$ and k units __up__ if $k > 0$.

---

3 **EXAMPLE**   Writing the Equation of a Radical Function

Write the equation of the square root or cube root function whose graph is shown.

A Identify the function type. The shape of the graph indicates a __square root__ function.

B Identify the values of h and k.

The endpoint (0, 0) from the parent square root function was translated to (1, 3).

$h = $ __1__ $k = $ __3__

The equation has the form $g(x) = a\sqrt{x - \boxed{1}} + \boxed{3}$.

C Use the point (5, 7) to identify a.

$g(x) = a\sqrt{x-1} + 3$	Function form
$7 = a\sqrt{\boxed{5} - 1} + 3$	Substitute 7 for $g(x)$ and 5 for x.
$7 = a\left(\boxed{2}\right) + 3$	Simplify the radical.
$\boxed{4} = a(2)$	Subtract 3 from both sides.
$2 = a$	Divide both sides by 2.

So, the equation of the function is $g(x) = $ __$2\sqrt{x-1} + 3$__

REFLECT

3a. Does the given graph represent a vertical stretch or a vertical shrink of the graph of the parent function? Does this agree with the value of a that you found? Explain.

Vertical stretch; yes, because $|2| > 1$.

3b. How can you identify the point to which (0, 0) from the graph of the parent function was translated in the graph of a square root function? in the graph of a cube root function?

For a square root function, the point (0, 0) is translated to the endpoint of the graph. For a cube root function, the point (0, 0) is translated to the point at which the curvature of the graph changes.

Essential Question

How can you graph transformations of the parent square root and cube root functions?

The general form a square root function is $f(x) = a\sqrt{x - h} + k$. The general form of a cube root function is $f(x) = a\sqrt[3]{x - h} + k$.

For both functions, use a to stretch the graph vertically if $|a|$ is greater than 1 and to shrink the graph vertically if $|a|$ is between 0 and 1. If a is negative, the graph is also reflected across the x-axis.

Use h to translate the graph to the right if h is positive and to the left if h is negative.

Use k to translate the graph up if k is positive and down if k is negative.

Summarize

Have students write a journal entry explaining how to find the equation of a transformed square root function given the starting point and another point on the graph.

Where skills are taught	Where skills are practiced
1 EXAMPLE	EXS. 1–4
2 EXAMPLE	EXS. 1–4
3 EXAMPLE	EXS. 5–8

Exercise 9: Students summarize the domains and ranges of the general square root and cube root functions for $a > 0$ and $a < 0$.

Exercise 10: Students compare the minimums of two square root functions. They need to realize that in square root functions with $a > 0$, the minimum occurs at the graph's starting point.

PRACTICE

Graph each radical function. Then describe the graph as a transformation of the graph of the parent function, and give its domain and range. (The graph of the parent function is shown.)

1. $f(x) = 0.5\sqrt{x+2}$

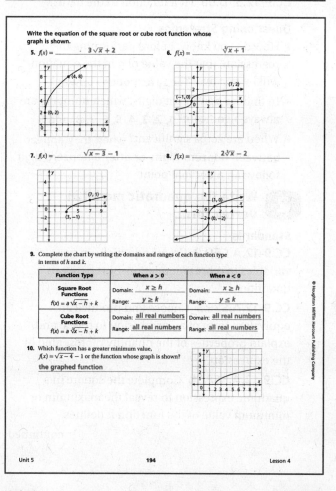

vertical shrink by a factor of $\frac{1}{2}$;

translation 2 units left

Domain: $\{x \mid x \geq -2\}$

Range: $\{y \mid y \geq 0\}$

2. $f(x) = 2\sqrt[3]{x} - 4$

vertical stretch by a factor of 2;

translation 4 units down

Domain: all real numbers

Range: all real numbers

3. $f(x) = -\sqrt{x} + 5$

reflection across the x-axis;

translation 5 units up

Domain: $\{x \mid x \geq 0\}$

Range: $\{y \mid y \leq 5\}$

4. $f(x) = -\sqrt[3]{x-1}$

reflection across the x-axis;

translation 1 unit right

Domain: all real numbers

Range: all real numbers

Unit 5   193   Lesson 4

Write the equation of the square root or cube root function whose graph is shown.

5. $f(x) = \underline{3\sqrt{x} + 2}$

(4, 8)

(0, 2)

6. $f(x) = \underline{\sqrt[3]{x+1}}$

(7, 2)

(-1, 0)

7. $f(x) = \underline{\sqrt{x-3} - 1}$

(7, 1)

(3, -1)

8. $f(x) = \underline{2\sqrt[3]{x} - 2}$

(1, 0)

(0, -2)

9. Complete the chart by writing the domains and ranges of each function type in terms of h and k.

Function Type	When $a > 0$	When $a < 0$
Square Root Functions $f(x) = a\sqrt{x-h} + k$	Domain: $x \geq h$ Range: $y \geq k$	Domain: $x \geq h$ Range: $y \leq k$
Cube Root Functions $f(x) = a\sqrt[3]{x-h} + k$	Domain: all real numbers Range: all real numbers	Domain: all real numbers Range: all real numbers

10. Which function has a greater minimum value, $f(x) = \sqrt{x-4} - 1$ or the function whose graph is shown?

the graphed function

Unit 5   194   Lesson 4

FOCUS ON MODELING
Modeling with Square Root Functions

Essential question: How can you model age as a function of body mass index given a data set?

© Houghton Mifflin Harcourt Publishing Company

COMMON CORE Standards for Mathematical Content

The following standards are addressed in this lesson. (An asterisk indicates that a standard is also a Modeling standard.) For more detailed information, see each section of the lesson.

Algebra: CC.9-12.A.CED.2*, CC.9-12.A.SSE.3, CC.9-12.A.SSE.3b

Functions: CC.9-12.F.IF.2, CC.9-12.F.IF.4*, CC.9-12.F.IF.7*, CC.9-12.F.IF.7b*, CC.9-12.F.IF.8, CC.9-12.F.IF.8a, CC.9-12.F.BF.1*, CC.9-12.F.BF.1a*, CC.9-12.F.BF.4, CC.9-12.F.BF.4d(+)

Statistics and Probability: CC.9-12.S.ID.6*, CC.9-12.S.ID.6a*

Prerequisites

- Writing a quadratic function in vertex form, Lesson 2-4
- Finding a regression equation, Algebra 1
- Inverses of quadratic functions, Lesson 5-2
- Writing a rule for a square root function given a graph, Lesson 5-4

Math Background

In this lesson, students obtain a quadratic function by using their calculators to perform quadratic regression on a set of data. The calculator gives the equation in standard form. Students use previously learned skills to rewrite the equation in vertex form. They then find the inverse of the quadratic model.

INTRODUCE

Children's physical characteristics, such as size and weight, tend to follow predictable trends as children grow. Given a child's age, you can predict his or her height within a few inches, although there are always exceptions. Another fairly predictable characteristic is a child's body mass index, or BMI, which is a measure used to determine healthy body mass based on height.

TEACH

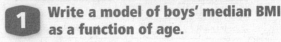

1 Write a model of boys' median BMI as a function of age.

Standards

CC.9-12.A.CED.2 Create equations in two ... variables to represent relationships between quantities ...*

CC.9-12.F.IF.2 Use function notation ...

CC.9-12.F.BF.1 Write a function that describes a relationship between two quantities.*

CC.9-12.F.BF.1a Determine an explicit expression ... from a context.*

CC.9-12.S.ID.6 Represent data on two quantitative variables on a scatter plot, and describe how the variables are related.*

CC.9-12.S.ID.6a Fit a function to the data ...*

Questioning Strategies

- How do you know, before performing the regression, that the value of a in the equation will be positive? **The graph opens upward.**
- In finding significant digits, which numbers are always significant? **1, 2, 3, 4, 5, 6, 7, 8, and 9**
- When are zeros significant? **when they appear between nonzero digits or after a nonzero digit following a decimal point**

2 Write the quadratic model in vertex form.

Standards

CC.9-12.A.CED.2 Create equations in two ... variables to represent relationships between quantities ...*

CC.9-12.A.SSE.3 Choose and produce an equivalent form of an expression to reveal and explain properties of the quantity represented by the expression.

CC.9-12.A.SSE.3b Complete the square in a quadratic expression to reveal the maximum or minimum value of the function it defines.

continued

Name_____ Class_____ Date_____

5-5

FOCUS ON MODELING

Modeling with Square Root Functions

COMMON CORE

CC-9-12.A.CED.2*,
CC-9-12.F.IF.4*,
CC-9-12.F.IF.7b*,
CC-9-12.F.BF.1*,
CC-9-12.F.BF.4d(+),
CC-9-12.S.ID.6a*

Essential question: *How can you model age as a function of body mass index given a data set?*

Body mass index (BMI) is a measure used to determine healthy body mass based on a person's height. BMI is calculated by dividing a person's mass in kilograms by the square of his or her height in meters. The median BMI measures for a group of boys ages 2 to 10 years are given in the chart below.

Age of Boys	2	3	4	5	6	7	8	9	10
Median BMI	16.6	16.0	15.6	15.4	15.4	15.5	15.8	16.2	16.6

How can you use the data to develop a model for predicting the age of a boy with a given BMI?

1 Write a model of boys' median BMI as a function of age.

A   Create a scatter plot for the data in the table, treating age as the independent variable x and median BMI as the dependent variable y.

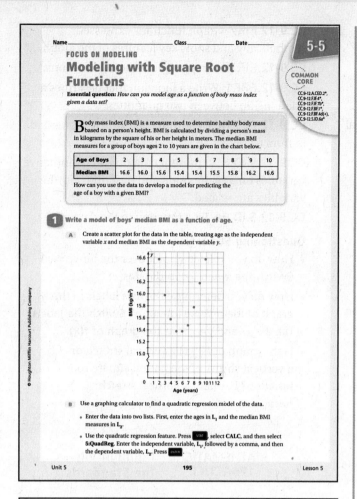

B   Use a graphing calculator to find a quadratic regression model of the data.

- Enter the data into two lists. First, enter the ages in L_1 and the median BMI measures in L_2.

- Use the quadratic regression feature. Press [STAT], select **CALC**, and then select **5:QuadReg**. Enter the independent variable, L_1, followed by a comma, and then the dependent variable, L_2. Press [ENTER].

© Houghton Mifflin Harcourt Publishing Company

- The values for a, b, and c correspond to the values in the standard form of a quadratic function, $f(x) = ax^2 + bx + c$. Record each value to three significant digits to complete the quadratic model below.

$f(x) = \underline{0.0763}\,x^2 - \underline{0.897}\,x + \underline{18.0}$

REFLECT

1a. Explain why it is appropriate to use a quadratic model for this data set, rather than another type of model, such as linear or cubic.

The data points appear to lie on a curve that approximates a parabola.

1b. Use a calculator to make a scatter plot of the data and then graph $f(x)$ on the same screen. Is the model a good fit for the data? Explain.

Yes; the curve appears to pass through or near almost all of the

data points.

2 Write the quadratic model in vertex form.

Complete the square to write the function in vertex form, $f(x) = a(x - h)^2 + k$.

$f(x) = 0.0763x^2 - 0.897x + 18.0$ Write the equation in standard form.

$f(x) = \underline{0.0763}\,(x^2 - 11.76x) + 18.0$ Factor the variable terms so that the coefficient of x^2 is 1.

$f(x) = 0.0763\left(x^2 - 11.76x + \boxed{}\right) + 18.0 - \boxed{}$ Set up for completing the square.

$f(x) = 0.0763\left(x^2 - 11.76x + \underline{34.5744}\right) + 18.0 - 0.0763 \cdot \underline{34.5744}$ Complete the square: $\left(\frac{11.76}{2}\right)^2 = \underline{34.5744}$

$f(x) = 0.0763\left(x - \underline{5.88}\right)^2 + 15.4$ Write the expression in parentheses as a binomial squared. Simplify the product being subtracted, rounding to 3 significant digits.

REFLECT

2a. Based on the vertex form of the equation, what is the approximate vertex of the graph of $f(x)$? Explain how you determined your answer.

(5.88, 15.4); for an equation in vertex form, the coordinates of the vertex

are (h, k). For $f(x)$, $h = 5.88$ and $k = 15.4$.

© Houghton Mifflin Harcourt Publishing Company

© Houghton Mifflin Harcourt Publishing Company

CC.9-12.F.IF.2 Use function notation ... and interpret statements that use function notation in terms of a context.

CC.9-12.F.IF.8 Write a function defined by an expression in different but equivalent forms to reveal and explain different properties of the function.

CC.9-12.F.IF.8a Use the process of ... completing the square in a quadratic function to show ... extreme values ...

CC.9-12.F.BF.1 Write a function that describes a relationship between two quantities.*

CC.9-12.F.BF.1a Determine an explicit expression ... from a context.*

CC.9-12.F.BF.4 Find inverse functions.

CC.9-12.F.BF.4d(+) Produce an invertible function from a non-invertible function by restricting the domain.

Questioning Strategies

- How do you determine the constant term in the trinomial when completing the square? Divide the coefficient of the *x*-term by 2 and square the result.

- Why is the product of 0.0763 and 34.5744, instead of 34.5744, subtracted from the equation? Because the trinomial is multiplied by 0.0763, the amount added to the trinomial to complete the square, 34.5744, is multiplied by 0.0763, so the product of 0.0763 and 34.5744 must be subtracted to maintain balance.

- How do you factor the perfect square trinomial into a squared binomial? The square root of 34.5744 is 5.88 (to three significant digits), and the *x*-term is negative, so the trinomial factors as $(x - 5.88)^2$.

3 **Graph and write the inverse of the quadratic model.**

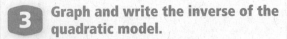

Standards

CC.9-12.A.CED.2 Create equations in two ... variables to represent relationships between quantities; graph equations on coordinate axes with labels and scales.*

CC.9-12.F.IF.2 Use function notation, evaluate functions for inputs in their domains, and interpret statements that use function notation in terms of a context.

CC.9-12.F.IF.4 For a function that models a relationship between two quantities, interpret key features of graphs and tables in terms of the quantities, and sketch graphs showing key features ...*

CC.9-12.F.IF.7 Graph functions expressed symbolically and show key features of the graph ...*

CC.9-12.F.IF.7b Graph square root ... functions.*

CC.9-12.F.BF.1 Write a function that describes a relationship between two quantities.*

CC.9-12.F.BF.1a Determine an explicit expression ... from a context.*

CC.9-12.S.ID.6 Represent data on two quantitative variables on a scatter plot, and describe how the variables are related.*

CC.9-12.S.ID.6a Fit a function to the data ...*

Questioning Strategies

- How do you reflect a point over the line $y = x$? Switch the *x* and *y* coordinates.

- How do you determine the axis labels in the graph of the inverse function? Switch the labels for the *x*- and *y*-axes in the graph of *f*(*x*).

- Is the graph of $f^{-1}(x)$ a vertical stretch or a vertical shrink of the parent square root function? Explain. a vertical stretch; because $a > 1$

MATHEMATICAL PRACTICE **Highlighting the Standards**

The steps in this lesson address Mathematical Practice Standard 6 (Attend to precision). All of the steps require students to round to 3 significant digits. You may need to review how to determine significant digits. In decimal numbers, zeros to the right of the decimal point, but to the left of the first nonzero digit, are not significant, because they are placeholders. For example, in 0.005060, the two zeros between the decimal point and the 5 are not significant. The other two zeros are significant.

Discuss the balance between using enough digits to give a certain degree of accuracy and using few enough digits to keep the handling of the equations manageable.

In step 3, students round coordinates to the nearest tenth. This rounding should occur only in the final step. Rounding in intermediate steps compromises accuracy by compounding round-off errors.

2b. Do the coordinates you found for the vertex agree with the information in the scatter plot? Explain.

Yes, the data in the scatter plot can be modeled by a parabola with a vertex close to (5.88, 15.4).

2c. Interpret the meaning of the vertex in the context of the problem.

The vertex gives the age (about 5.88 years) at which boys' median BMI is least (about 15.4).

2d. Give the domain of $f(x)$ based on the data set.

$\{x \mid 2 \leq x \leq 10\}$

3 Graph and write the inverse of the quadratic model.

A Because $f(x)$ is quadratic, it is not one-to-one and its inverse is not a function. Restrict the domain of $f(x)$ to values of x for which $f(x)$ is increasing so that its inverse will be a function. What is the restricted domain of $f(x)$?

$\{x \mid 5.88 \leq x \leq 10\}$

B Enter the coordinates of the vertex in the first row of the table below. Complete the table of values and use it to graph $f(x)$ with the restricted domain. Round the values of $f(x)$ to the nearest tenth.

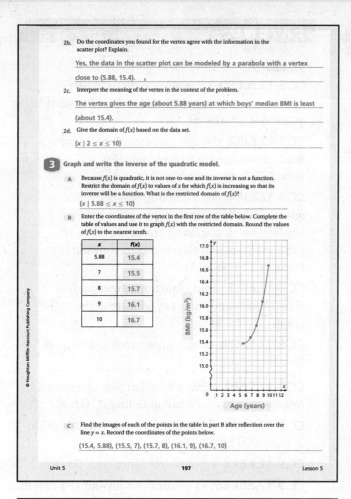

x	f(x)
5.88	15.4
7	15.5
8	15.7
9	16.1
10	16.7

C Find the images of each of the points in the table in part B after reflection over the line $y = x$. Record the coordinates of the points below.

(15.4, 5.88), (15.5, 7), (15.7, 8), (16.1, 9), (16.7, 10)

D Plot the points from part C and draw a smooth curve through them to graph the inverse function, $f^{-1}(x)$.

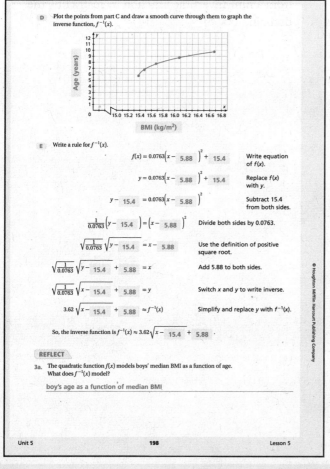

E Write a rule for $f^{-1}(x)$.

$f(x) = 0.0763\left(x - \boxed{5.88}\right)^2 + \boxed{15.4}$ Write equation of $f(x)$.

$y = 0.0763\left(x - \boxed{5.88}\right)^2 + \boxed{15.4}$ Replace $f(x)$ with y.

$y - \boxed{15.4} = 0.0763\left(x - \boxed{5.88}\right)^2$ Subtract 15.4 from both sides.

$\frac{1}{0.0763}\left(y - \boxed{15.4}\right) = \left(x - \boxed{5.88}\right)^2$ Divide both sides by 0.0763.

$\sqrt{\frac{1}{0.0763}}\sqrt{y - \boxed{15.4}} = x - \boxed{5.88}$ Use the definition of positive square root.

$\sqrt{\frac{1}{0.0763}}\sqrt{y - \boxed{15.4}} + \boxed{5.88} = x$ Add 5.88 to both sides.

$\sqrt{\frac{1}{0.0763}}\sqrt{x - \boxed{15.4}} + \boxed{5.88} = y$ Switch x and y to write inverse.

$3.62\sqrt{x - \boxed{15.4}} + \boxed{5.88} \approx f^{-1}(x)$ Simplify and replace y with $f^{-1}(x)$.

So, the inverse function is $f^{-1}(x) \approx 3.62\sqrt{x - \boxed{15.4}} + \boxed{5.88}$.

REFLECT

3a. The quadratic function $f(x)$ models boys' median BMI as a function of age. What does $f^{-1}(x)$ model?

boy's age as a function of median BMI

Notes

Essential Question

How can you model age as a function of body mass index given a data set?

The graph of BMI as a function of age appears to be parabolic, so use a quadratic regression equation with *x* representing age and *y* representing BMIs. Restrict the domain so that the function is a one-to-one function and then find its inverse, which is a square root function that accepts BMIs as inputs and gives ages as outputs.

Summarize

In their journals, have students explain why they must be able to identify the vertex of the graph of a quadratic function to determine the inverse function.

Standards

CC.9-12.A.CED.2 Create equations in two variables ... to represent relationships between quantities ...* (Ex. 5)

CC.9-12.F.IF.2 Use function notation, evaluate functions for inputs in their domains ... (Exs. 1, 2, 3, 5)

CC.9-12.F.IF.4 For a function that models a relationship between two quantities, interpret key features of graphs and tables in terms of the quantities, and sketch graphs showing key features ...* (Exs. 4, 5)

CC.9-12.F.IF.7 Graph functions expressed symbolically and show key features of the graph ...* (Ex. 5)

CC.9-12.F.IF.7b Graph square root ... functions.* (Ex. 5)

CC.9-12.F.BF.1 Write a function that describes a relationship between two quantities.* (Ex. 5)

CC.9-12.F.BF.1a Determine an explicit expression ... from a context.* (Ex. 5)

CC.9-12.F.BF.4 Find inverse functions. (Ex. 5)

CC.9-12.F.BF.4d(+) Produce an invertible function from a non-invertible function by restricting the domain. (Ex. 5)

3b. Why does it make sense to make the least x-value in the domain of $f(x)$ be 5.88 when finding the inverse function?

5.88 is the x-coordinate of the vertex of the graph of the quadratic model.

The function is one-to-one to the left or right of the vertex.

3c. What are the domain and range of $f(x)$? of $f^{-1}(x)$?

Domain of $f(x)$: $\{x \mid 5.88 \leq x \leq 10\}$; range of $f(x)$: $\{y \mid 15.4 \leq y \leq 16.7\}$;

domain of $f^{-1}(x)$: $\{x \mid 15.4 \leq x \leq 16.7\}$; range of $f^{-1}(x)$: $\{y \mid 5.88 \leq y \leq 10\}$

3d. Use a graphing calculator to graph $f(x)$, $f^{-1}(x)$, and the line $y = x$ in the same window. How can you use these graphs to check that you found the inverse function correctly?

If the inverse was found correctly, then the two graphs should appear

to be reflections across the line $y = x$.

EXTEND

Use the inverse function $f^{-1}(x)$ to make predictions for Exercises 1 and 2. (In Exercise 2, allow the domain to include x-values greater than 10.)

1. A boy over the age of 6 has a BMI of 15.9. How old do you expect him to be, to the nearest tenth of a year?

8.4 years old

2. A boy over the age of 6 has a BMI of 20.4. How old do you expect him to be, to the nearest tenth of a year?

14.0 years old

3. Which of your predictions, the one in Exercise 1 or the one in Exercise 2, do you think is more reliable? Explain your reasoning.

The prediction in Exercise 1 is more reliable. The original data set had a maximum

age of 10 years. Because the age in Exercise 2 is outside the age range of the

original data set, it is less likely to be reliable.

4. Over what interval, if any, does the inverse function $f^{-1}(x)$ increase? Over what interval, if any, does it decrease? Does this make sense given what you know about $f(x)$?

The function increases throughout its domain. There is no interval for which it

decreases. Because $f(x)$ increases throughout its restricted domain, it makes sense

that its inverse will also increase throughout its domain.

---

5. The model you found for $f^{-1}(x)$ applies to boys aged 5.88 years or older. Consider how you could change your model so that it applies to boys aged 5.88 years or younger.

a. How else could you restrict the domain of $f(x) = 0.0763(x - 5.88)^2 + 15.4$ to find an inverse that is a function?

Restrict the domain to $2 \leq x \leq 5.88$.

b. Complete the table of values and use it to graph $f(x)$ with the restricted domain. Round the values of $f(x)$ to the nearest hundredth.

x	$f(x)$
2	16.55
3	16.03
4	15.67
5.88	15.4

c. What is the range of $f(x)$ with the restricted domain?

$15.4 \leq y \leq 16.55$

d. Graph the inverse of $f(x)$ with the restricted domain. Give the domain and range of the inverse.

Domain:

$15.4 \leq x \leq 16.55$

Range:

$2 \leq y \leq 5.88$

e. The equation of $f^{-1}(x)$ when the domain of $f(x)$ is restricted to $\{x \mid 5.88 \leq x \leq 10\}$ is $f^{-1}(x) = 3.62\sqrt{x - 15.4} + 5.88$. What is the equation of $f^{-1}(x)$ when the domain of $f(x)$ is restricted to $\{x \mid 2 \leq x \leq 5.88\}$? Explain.

$f^{-1}(x) = -3.62\sqrt{x - 15.4} + 5.88$; writing the rule proceeds exactly as in part

E of step 3, except that you use a negative square root instead of a positive

square root.

FOCUS ON MODELING
Modeling with Cube Root Functions

Essential question: *How can you model the radius of a stainless steel ball bearing as a function of its mass?*

COMMON CORE Standards for Mathematical Content

The following standards are addressed in this lesson. (An asterisk indicates that a standard is also a Modeling standard.) For more detailed information, see each section of the lesson.

Number & Quantity: CC.9-12.N.Q.1*

Algebra: CC.9-12.A.CED.2*

Functions: CC.9-12.F.IF.2, CC.9-12.F.IF.4*, CC.9-12.F.IF.7*, CC.9-12.F.IF.7b*, CC.9-12.F.IF.9, CC.9-12.F.BF.1*, CC.9-2.F.BF.1a*, CC.9-12.F.BF.4, CC.9-12.F.BF.4a

Statistics and Probability: CC.9-12.S.ID.6*, CC.9-12.S.ID.6a*

Prerequisites

- Graphing $f(x) = ax^3$, Lesson 3-3
- Inverses of functions, Lesson 5-1
- Graphing cube root functions, Lesson 5-4

Math Background

The general structure of this lesson follows that of the previous lesson on modeling with square root functions.

Although cube root functions have unrestricted domains and ranges, the domain and range are restricted in this lesson because neither mass nor radius can be negative.

INTRODUCE

Imagine five people in a small room. Now imagine ten people in a house. Even though there are fewer people in the room, the people in the room would be more crowded because the amount of floor space in a room is much less than that of a whole house. You can use the word *density* to compare the two scenarios. Those in the room are more *densely* packed than those in the house.

TEACH

  Find the density of stainless steel.

Standards

CC.9-12.N.Q.1 Use units as a way to understand problems ...*

CC.9-12.F.BF.1a Determine an explicit expression ... from a context.*

Questioning Strategies

- How do you find the volume of a cube given its edge length? Cube the side length: $V = s^3$.
- How can you write a formula for density d using m for mass and V for volume? $d = \frac{m}{V}$
- How could you find the edge length in centimeters of a stainless steel cube if you knew its mass in grams? Divide the mass by the density, 8 g/cm³, and then take the cube root of the result.

2 **Write a model for the mass of a stainless steel sphere as a function of its radius.**

Standards

CC.9-12.N.Q.1 Use units as a way to understand problems ...*

CC.9-12.A.CED.2 Create equations in two or more variables to represent relationships between quantities ...*

CC.9-12.F.IF.2 Use function notation ... and interpret statements that use function notation in terms of a context.

CC.9-12.F.BF.1 Write a function that describes a relationship between two quantities.*

CC.9-12.F.BF.1a Determine an explicit expression ... from a context.*

continued

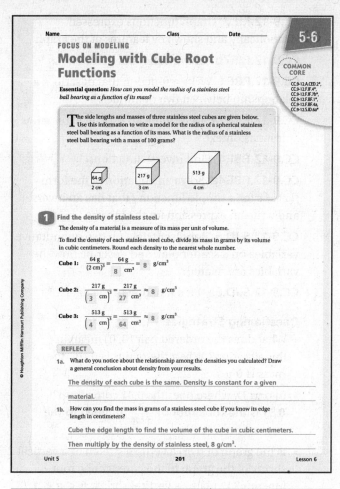

Name _____ **Class** _____ **Date** _____

FOCUS ON MODELING

Modeling with Cube Root Functions

5-6

COMMON CORE

CC.9-12.A.CED.2*,
CC.9-12.F.IF.4*,
CC.9-12.F.IF.7b*,
CC.9-12.F.IF.1*,
CC.9-12.F.BF.4a,
CC.9-12.S.ID.6a*

Essential question: *How can you model the radius of a stainless steel ball bearing as a function of its mass?*

The side lengths and masses of three stainless steel cubes are given below. Use this information to write a model for the radius of a spherical stainless steel ball bearing as a function of its mass. What is the radius of a stainless steel ball bearing with a mass of 100 grams?

64 g — 2 cm

217 g — 3 cm

513 g — 4 cm

1 Find the density of stainless steel.

The density of a material is a measure of its mass per unit of volume.

To find the density of each stainless steel cube, divide its mass in grams by its volume in cubic centimeters. Round each density to the nearest whole number.

Cube 1: $\dfrac{64 \text{ g}}{(2 \text{ cm})^3} = \dfrac{64 \text{ g}}{8 \text{ cm}^3} = 8 \text{ g/cm}^3$

Cube 2: $\dfrac{217 \text{ g}}{(3 \text{ cm})^3} = \dfrac{217 \text{ g}}{27 \text{ cm}^3} \approx 8 \text{ g/cm}^3$

Cube 3: $\dfrac{513 \text{ g}}{(4 \text{ cm})^3} = \dfrac{513 \text{ g}}{64 \text{ cm}^3} \approx 8 \text{ g/cm}^3$

REFLECT

1a. What do you notice about the relationship among the densities you calculated? Draw a general conclusion about density from your results.

The density of each cube is the same. Density is constant for a given

material.

1b. How can you find the mass in grams of a stainless steel cube if you know its edge length in centimeters?

Cube the edge length to find the volume of the cube in cubic centimeters.

Then multiply by the density of stainless steel, 8 g/cm³.

Unit 5   201   Lesson 6

© Houghton Mifflin Harcourt Publishing Company

---

2 Write a model for the mass of a stainless steel sphere as a function of its radius.

A Explain how you can use an object's volume in cubic centimeters and its density in grams per cubic centimeter to find its mass.

When you multiply the volume by the density, units of cubic centimeters

cancel. The product is the object's mass in grams.

B Write the formula for the volume of a sphere.

$V = \dfrac{4}{3}\pi r^3$

C Write a function $m(r)$ for the mass in grams of a stainless steel ball bearing with a radius of r centimeters.

$m(r) = \dfrac{32}{3}\pi r^3$

REFLECT

2a. How could you find the mass of a stainless steel ball bearing with a radius of 2 centimeters? Find the mass to the nearest gram.

Evaluate the function $m(r)$ for $r = 2$; 268 grams.

2b. What are the reasonable domain and range of $m(r)$?

Domain: $\{r \mid r \geq 0\}$; range: $\{m \mid m \geq 0\}$

3 Graph and write the inverse function $r(m)$.

A Complete the table of values and use it to graph $m(r)$ for $r \geq 0$. Round the function values to the nearest whole number.

r	$m(r)$
0	0
0.5	4
1	34
1.5	113
2	268
2.5	524
3	905

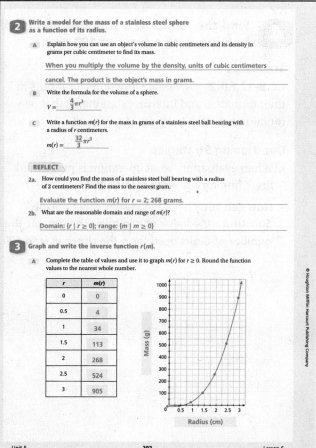

Unit 5   202   Lesson 6

© Houghton Mifflin Harcourt Publishing Company

2 continued

Questioning Strategies
- What is the result of solving the equation $d = \frac{m}{V}$ for m? $m = dV$
- Explain why the constant in the function $m(r)$ is $\frac{32}{3}\pi$. **To find mass, you multiply volume by density. The density is 8 g/cm³, so the constant becomes $8 \cdot \frac{4}{3}\pi$, or $\frac{32}{3}\pi$.**

Teaching Strategy
Show the multiplication of the density of 8 g/cm³ by the volume of a sphere with units clearly placed in the numerator or denominator so that it is obvious to students why cm³ divides out.

$$m = d \cdot V$$
$$= \frac{8\,\text{g}}{\text{cm}^3} \cdot \frac{4}{3}\pi r^3\ \text{cm}^3$$
$$= \frac{8\,\text{g}}{\text{cm}^3} \cdot \frac{4\pi r^3}{3}\ \text{cm}^3$$
$$= \frac{32\pi r^3\ \text{g}}{3}$$
$$= \frac{32\pi r^3}{3}\ \text{g}$$

3 ### Graph and write the inverse function $r(m)$.

Standards
CC.9-12.A.CED.2 Create equations in two ... variables to represent relationships between quantities; graph equations on coordinate axes with labels and scales.*

CC.9-12.F.IF.2 Use function notation, evaluate functions for inputs in their domains, and interpret statements that use function notation in terms of a context.

CC.9-12.F.IF.4 For a function that models a relationship between two quantities, interpret key features of graphs and tables in terms of the quantities, and sketch graphs showing key features ...*

CC.9-12.F.IF.7 Graph functions expressed symbolically and show key features of the graph ...*

CC.9-12.F.IF.7b Graph cube root ... functions.*

CC.9-12.F.BF.1 Write a function that describes a relationship between two quantities.*

CC.9-12.F.BF.1a Determine an explicit expression ... from a context.*

CC.9-12.F.BF.4 Find inverse functions.

CC.9-12.F.BF.4a Solve an equation of the form $f(x) = c$ for a simple function f that has an inverse and write an expression for the inverse.

CC.9-12.S.ID.6 Represent data on two quantitative variables on a scatter plot, and describe how the variables are related.*

CC.9-12.S.ID.6a Fit a function to the data ...*

Questioning Strategies
- What does the ordered pair (0, 0) mean in this situation? **When the radius is 0 cm, the mass is 0 g.**
- In part D, where does the 0.31 come from? **0.31 is the cube root of $\frac{3}{32\pi}$ rounded to the nearest hundredth.**
- Is the graph of $r(m)$ a vertical stretch or a vertical shrink of the graph of the parent cube root function? Explain. **a vertical shrink; $0 < a < 1$**

4 ### Find the radius of a stainless steel ball bearing with a mass of 100 grams.

Standards
CC.9-12.F.IF.2 ... evaluate functions for inputs in their domains, and interpret statements that use function notation in terms of a context.

Questioning Strategies
- When evaluating, what operation is performed first? **finding the cube root of 100**
- How can you check the answer algebraically? **Substitute the value of r in $m(r)$. The greater the number of digits used for r, the closer m is to 100.**

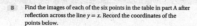

B Find the images of each of the six points in the table in part A after reflection across the line $y = x$. Record the coordinates of the points below.

(0, 0), (4, 0.5), (34, 1), (113, 1.5), (268, 2), (524, 2.5), (905, 3)

C Plot the points from part B and draw a smooth curve through them to graph the inverse function, $r(m)$.

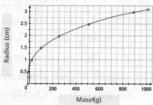

D Write the equation for the inverse function, $r(m)$.

$m(r) = \frac{32}{3}\pi r^3$	Write the equation for $m(r)$.
$m = \frac{32}{3}\pi r^3$	Replace $m(r)$ with m.
$\frac{3}{32\pi}m = r^3$	Solve for r. Divide both sides by $\frac{32}{3}\pi$.
$\sqrt[3]{\frac{3}{32\pi}m} = r$	Use the definition of cube root.
$\sqrt[3]{\frac{3}{32\pi}m} = r(m)$	Replace r with $r(m)$.
$0.31\sqrt[3]{m} = r(m)$	Write $r(m)$ in the form $r(m) = a\sqrt[3]{m}$. Round a to the nearest hundredth.

REFLECT

3a. Show that the equation for the inverse function in part D checks by using one of the coordinate pairs (other than (0, 0)) that you listed in part B. Why is the coordinate pair (0, 0) a poor choice to use as a check?

Sample answer: Using (4, 0.5), $r(4) = 0.31\sqrt[3]{4} \approx 0.31(1.6) \approx 0.5$, so the equation

checks; using (0, 0) is a poor choice because the product of $\sqrt[3]{0}$, which is 0, and

any number is 0, which doesn't show whether 0.31 is the correct coefficient.

3b. What type of function is $m(r)$? What type of function is its inverse $r(m)$?

$m(r)$ is a cubic function. $r(m)$ is a cube root function.

3c. The function $m(r)$ models the mass in grams of a stainless steel ball bearing as a function of its radius in centimeters. What does $r(m)$ model?

the radius in centimeters of a stainless steel ball bearing as a function

of its mass in grams

3d. Why does it make sense to restrict the domain of $m(r)$ to $r \geq 0$? Must the domain of $m(r)$ be restricted for the inverse function $r(m)$ to exist?

The domain is restricted because r represents a radius, which is nonnegative.

No; because $m(r)$ is a cubic function, an inverse function exists even for an

unrestricted domain.

3e. What are the domain and range of $r(m)$?

Domain: $\{m \mid m \geq 0\}$; range: $\{r \mid r \geq 0\}$

4 Find the radius of a stainless steel ball bearing with a mass of 100 grams.

$r(m) = 0.31\sqrt[3]{m}$	Write the model that gives radius in centimeters as a function of mass in grams.
$r(100) = 0.31\sqrt[3]{100}$	Substitute 100 for m.
$r(100) = 1.4$	Simplify. Round to the nearest tenth.

So, a stainless steel ball bearing with a mass of 100 grams has a radius
of about __1.4__ centimeters.

REFLECT

4a. How could you check that you found the radius correctly?

Sample answer: Check that the point (100, 1.4) lies on the graph

of $r(m)$.

4b. Could the function $r(m)$ be used to determine the radius of a ceramic ball bearing with a mass of 100 grams? Explain.

No, because ceramic likely has a different density than stainless steel does.

Highlighting the Standards

The examples in this lesson address Mathematical Practice Standard 2 (Reason abstractly and quantitatively). Density is a rate (a ratio of two measures with different units), and it is important for students to understand the meaning of the units for the individual quantities, as well as how to simplify and reinterpret the units in the ratio.

In step 1, be sure students understand that when mass is divided by volume, the units remain. In step 2, the units of volume divide out when density and volume are multiplied. Like common factors, common units divide out when one is in the numerator and the other is in the denominator.

CLOSE

Essential Question

How can you model the radius of a stainless steel ball bearing as a function of its mass?

Once you determine the density of stainless steel, multiply it by the formula for the volume of a sphere (the shape of a ball bearing). The resulting cubic function gives the mass of a stainless steel ball bearing in terms of its radius. Find the inverse of this function to determine a cube root function that gives the radius of the ball bearing in terms of its mass.

Summarize

In their journals, have students use examples to explain why the product of density and volume results in mass.

EXTEND

Standards

CC.9-12.A.CED.2 Create equations in two ... variables to represent relationships between quantities; graph equations on coordinate axes with labels and scales.* (Exs. 4, 5, 6)

CC.9-12.F.IF.2 Use function notation, evaluate functions for inputs in their domains, and interpret statements that use function notation in terms of a context. (Exs. 1, 2, 3, 5, 6, 7)

CC.9-12.F.IF.4 For a function that models a relationship between two quantities, interpret key features of graphs and tables in terms of the quantities, and sketch graphs showing key features ...* (Exs. 4, 6)

CC.9-12.F.IF.9 Compare properties of two functions ... (Ex. 7)

CC.9-12.F.BF.1 Write a function that describes a relationship between two quantities.* (Exs. 4, 5, 6)

CC.9-12.F.BF.1a Determine an explicit expression ... from a context.* (Exs. 4, 5, 6)

CC.9-12.F.BF.9 Find inverse functions. (Exs. 6, 7)

CC.9-12.F.BF.4a Solve an equation of the form $f(x) = c$ for a simple function f that has an inverse and write an expression for the inverse. (Exs. 6, 7)

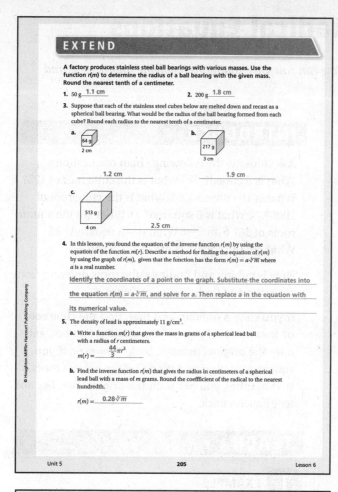

EXTEND

A factory produces stainless steel ball bearings with various masses. Use the function $r(m)$ to determine the radius of a ball bearing with the given mass. Round the nearest tenth of a centimeter.

1. 50 g ___1.1 cm___
2. 200 g ___1.8 cm___

3. Suppose that each of the stainless steel cubes below are melted down and recast as a spherical ball bearing. What would be the radius of the ball bearing formed from each cube? Round each radius to the nearest tenth of a centimeter.

a. [64 g, 2 cm cube]   ___1.2 cm___

b. [217 g, 3 cm cube]   ___1.9 cm___

c. [513 g, 4 cm cube]   ___2.5 cm___

4. In this lesson, you found the equation of the inverse function $r(m)$ by using the equation of the function $m(r)$. Describe a method for finding the equation of $r(m)$ by using the graph of $r(m)$, given that the function has the form $r(m) = a\sqrt[3]{m}$ where a is a real number.

Identify the coordinates of a point on the graph. Substitute the coordinates into

the equation $r(m) = a\sqrt[3]{m}$, and solve for a. Then replace a in the equation with

its numerical value.

5. The density of lead is approximately 11 g/cm³.

a. Write a function $m(r)$ that gives the mass in grams of a spherical lead ball with a radius of r centimeters.

$m(r) = $ ___$\frac{44}{3}\pi r^3$___

b. Find the inverse function $r(m)$ that gives the radius in centimeters of a spherical lead ball with a mass of m grams. Round the coeffficient of the radical to the nearest hundredth.

$r(m) = $ ___$0.28\sqrt[3]{m}$___

---

6. The function whose graph is shown models the radius r in centimeters of a spherical zinc ball as a function of the ball's mass m in grams.

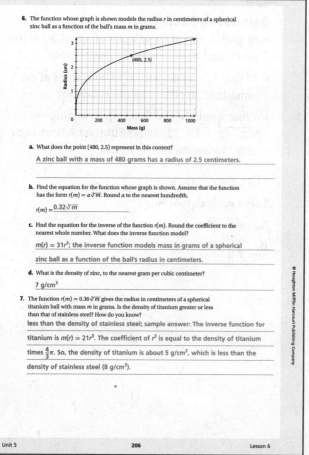

a. What does the point (480, 2.5) represent in this context?

A zinc ball with a mass of 480 grams has a radius of 2.5 centimeters.

b. Find the equation for the function whose graph is shown. Assume that the function has the form $r(m) = a\sqrt[3]{m}$. Round a to the nearest hundredth.

$r(m) = $ ___$0.32\sqrt[3]{m}$___

c. Find the equation for the inverse of the function $r(m)$. Round the coefficient to the nearest whole number. What does the inverse function model?

$m(r) = 31r^3$; the inverse function models mass in grams of a spherical

zinc ball as a function of the ball's radius in centimeters.

d. What is the density of zinc, to the nearest gram per cubic centimeter?

7 g/cm³

7. The function $r(m) = 0.36\sqrt[3]{m}$ gives the radius in centimeters of a spherical titanium ball with mass m in grams. Is the density of titanium greater or less than that of stainless steel? How do you know?

less than the density of stainless steel; sample answer: The inverse function for

titanium is $m(r) = 21r^3$. The coefficient of r^3 is equal to the density of titanium

times $\frac{4}{3}\pi$. So, the density of titanium is about 5 g/cm³, which is less than the

density of stainless steel (8 g/cm³).

Solving Radical Equations

Essential question: *How can you solve equations involving square roots and cube roots?*

COMMON CORE **Standards for Mathematical Content**

CC.9-12.A.REI.2 Solve simple ... radical equations in one variable, and give examples showing how extraneous solutions may arise.

CC.9-12.A.REI.11 Explain why the *x*-coordinates of the points where the graphs of the equations $y = f(x)$ and $y = g(x)$ intersect are the solutions of the equation $f(x) = g(x)$; find the solutions approximately, e.g. using technology to graph the functions, make tables of values, or find successive approximations.*

Also: CC.9-12.A.CED.1*

Vocabulary

extraneous solution

Prerequisites

Graphing square root and cube root functions, Lesson 5-4

Math Background

Students will use inverse operations to solve radical equations, which are equations in which the variable is in the radicand. The inverse of taking a root is raising to a power. For example, the cube root of 27 is 3, and 3 cubed is 27.

Squaring both sides of an equation may produce a solution that the original equation does not have. For example, the solution of $x = 4$ is 4. If both sides of $x = 4$ are squared, the result is $x^2 = 16$. This equation has two solutions: 4 and −4. Because of this, students must check that any solutions that result from squaring both sides of an equation are not extraneous (not a solution to the original equation).

While students solve only square and cube root equations in this lesson, extraneous solutions could appear when solving radical equations with *n*th roots when *n* is even.

INTRODUCE

Ask students the following chain of questions. What is 5 cubed? 125 What is the cube root of 125? 5 What is 10 cubed? 1000 What is the cube root of 1000? 10 What is 6 squared? 36 What are the square roots of 36? 6 and −6 What is −5 squared? 25 What are the square roots of 25? 5 and −5

How is cubing and finding cube roots different from squaring and finding square roots?

If you cube a number and then find the cube root of that number, you get the original number, and only the original number, back. However, if you square a number and then find the square roots of that number, you get both the original number and its opposite back.

TEACH

1 EXAMPLE

Questioning Strategies

• In part A, why do you square both sides of the equation? to eliminate the square root

• In part B, why do you cube both sides of the equation? to eliminate the cube root

• What would be the first step in solving $\sqrt{x - 2} + 7 = 12$? Why? Subtract 7 from both sides to isolate the radical.

EXTRA EXAMPLE

Solve each equation.

A. $\sqrt{x - 5} = 4$ $x = 21$

B. $\sqrt[3]{\dfrac{x}{5}} = 2$ $x = 40$

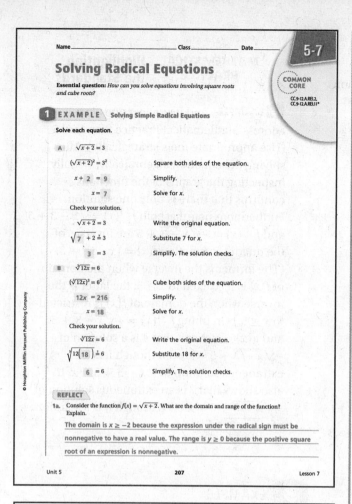

5-7

Solving Radical Equations

Essential question: *How can you solve equations involving square roots and cube roots?*

COMMON CORE

CC.9-12.A.REL2,
CC.9-12.A.REL11*

1 EXAMPLE — Solving Simple Radical Equations

Solve each equation.

A $\sqrt{x+2} = 3$

$(\sqrt{x+2})^2 = 3^2$ — Square both sides of the equation.

$x + 2 = 9$ — Simplify.

$x = 7$ — Solve for x.

Check your solution.

$\sqrt{x+2} = 3$ — Write the original equation.

$\sqrt{7 + 2} \stackrel{?}{=} 3$ — Substitute 7 for x.

$3 = 3$ — Simplify. The solution checks.

B $\sqrt[3]{12x} = 6$

$(\sqrt[3]{12x})^3 = 6^3$ — Cube both sides of the equation.

$12x = 216$ — Simplify.

$x = 18$ — Solve for x.

Check your solution.

$\sqrt[3]{12x} = 6$ — Write the original equation.

$\sqrt[3]{12(18)} \stackrel{?}{=} 6$ — Substitute 18 for x.

$6 = 6$ — Simplify. The solution checks.

REFLECT

1a. Consider the function $f(x) = \sqrt{x+2}$. What are the domain and range of the function? Explain.

The domain is $x \geq -2$ because the expression under the radical sign must be

nonnegative to have a real value. The range is $y \geq 0$ because the positive square

root of an expression is nonnegative.

© Houghton Mifflin Harcourt Publishing Company

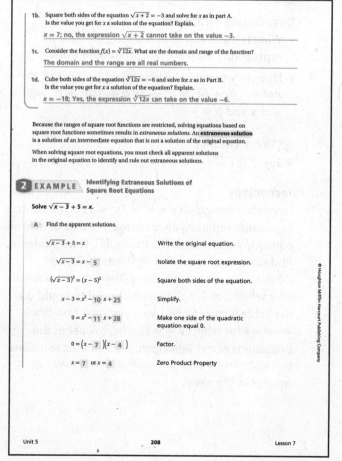

1b. Square both sides of the equation $\sqrt{x+2} = -3$ and solve for x as in part A. Is the value you get for x a solution of the equation? Explain.

$x = 7$; no, the expression $\sqrt{x+2}$ cannot take on the value -3.

1c. Consider the function $f(x) = \sqrt[3]{12x}$. What are the domain and range of the function?

The domain and the range are all real numbers.

1d. Cube both sides of the equation $\sqrt[3]{12x} = -6$ and solve for x as in Part B. Is the value you get for x a solution of the equation? Explain.

$x = -18$; Yes, the expression $\sqrt[3]{12x}$ can take on the value -6.

Because the ranges of square root functions are restricted, solving equations based on square root functions sometimes results in *extraneous solutions*. An **extraneous solution** is a solution of an intermediate equation that is not a solution of the original equation.

When solving square root equations, you must check all apparent solutions in the original equation to identify and rule out extraneous solutions.

2 EXAMPLE — Identifying Extraneous Solutions of Square Root Equations

Solve $\sqrt{x-3} + 5 = x$.

A Find the apparent solutions.

$\sqrt{x-3} + 5 = x$ — Write the original equation.

$\sqrt{x-3} = x - 5$ — Isolate the square root expression.

$(\sqrt{x-3})^2 = (x-5)^2$ — Square both sides of the equation.

$x - 3 = x^2 - 10x + 25$ — Simplify.

$0 = x^2 - 11x + 28$ — Make one side of the quadratic equation equal 0.

$0 = (x-7)(x-4)$ — Factor.

$x = 7$ or $x = 4$ — Zero Product Property

© Houghton Mifflin Harcourt Publishing Company

© Houghton Mifflin Harcourt Publishing Company

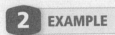

2 EXAMPLE

Questioning Strategies

- Why do you not square both sides of the equation as the first step? **Squaring both sides as the first step does not eliminate the radical from the equation.**

- After squaring and obtaining a quadratic equation, how would you solve the equation if you could not factor it? **Use the quadratic formula.**

EXTRA EXAMPLE

Solve $x - 5 = \sqrt{3x - 5}$. **The solution is $x = 10$. ($x = 3$ is an extraneous solution.)**

Teaching Strategy

After students find that 7 is a solution and 4 is an extraneous solution, have them substitute 4 for x in each equation in the solution while working backward to see in which step the 4 quit being a solution.

$x = 7$ or $x = 4$
True: $4 = 4$ (Only one part of an *or* statement needs to be satisfied.)

$0 = (x - 7)(x - 4)$
True: $x = 4$ makes the right side equal to $-3(0)$, or 0.

$0 = x^2 - 11x + 28$
True: $4^2 - 11(4) + 28 = 0$

$x - 3 = x^2 - 10x + 25$
True: $4 - 3 = 1$ and $4^2 - 10(4) + 25 = 1$.

$(\sqrt{x - 3})^2 = (x - 5)^2$
True: $(\sqrt{4 - 3})^2 = 1$ and $(4 - 5)^2 = 1$.

$\sqrt{x - 3} = x - 5$
False: $\sqrt{4 - 3} = 1$, but $4 - 5 = -1$.

Students should discover that the extraneous solution was introduced when both sides were squared.

---

3 EXAMPLE

Questioning Strategies

- What is the first step in isolating the radical expression? **subtracting 3 from both sides**

- How do you cube the binomial $(x - 2)$? **Use the pattern $(a + b)^3 = a^3 + 3a^2b + 3ab^2 + b^3$ with $a = x$ and $b = -2$.**

EXTRA EXAMPLE

Solve $\sqrt[3]{13x - 1} - 4 = x - 5$. **$x = -2$, 0, and 5**

Technology

Have students graph $y = x^3 - 7x^2 + 12x$ (the cubic expression obtained after setting one side of the equation equal to 0 in the Example). Have students find the x-intercepts. **0, 3, and 4** Ask why the x-intercepts are the solutions. **They are the values of x when $y = 0$.** Ask students how they could use the Table feature to find the solutions. **Find the x-values for which $y = 0$.** Finally, ask about the limitations of the Table feature for finding solutions this way. **The x-values for which $y = 0$ may not appear in the table.**

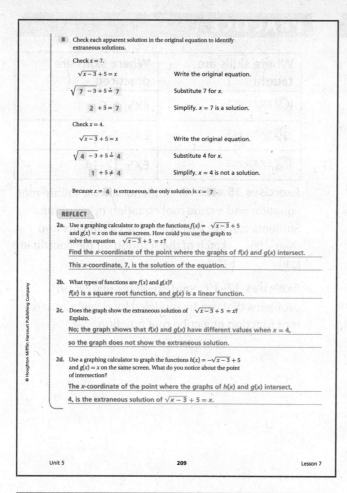

B Check each apparent solution in the original equation to identify extraneous solutions.

Check $x = 7$.

$\sqrt{x-3} + 5 = x$	Write the original equation.
$\sqrt{7-3} + 5 \stackrel{?}{=} 7$	Substitute 7 for x.
$2 + 5 = 7$	Simplify. $x = 7$ is a solution.

Check $x = 4$.

$\sqrt{x-3} + 5 = x$	Write the original equation.
$\sqrt{4-3} + 5 \stackrel{?}{=} 4$	Substitute 4 for x.
$1 + 5 \neq 4$	Simplify. $x = 4$ is not a solution.

Because $x = \boxed{4}$ is extraneous, the only solution is $x = \boxed{7}$.

REFLECT

2a. Use a graphing calculator to graph the functions $f(x) = \sqrt{x-3} + 5$ and $g(x) = x$ on the same screen. How could you use the graph to solve the equation $\sqrt{x-3} + 5 = x$?

Find the x-coordinate of the point where the graphs of $f(x)$ and $g(x)$ intersect.

This x-coordinate, 7, is the solution of the equation.

2b. What types of functions are $f(x)$ and $g(x)$?

$f(x)$ is a square root function, and $g(x)$ is a linear function.

2c. Does the graph show the extraneous solution of $\sqrt{x-3} + 5 = x$? Explain.

No; the graph shows that $f(x)$ and $g(x)$ have different values when $x = 4$,

so the graph does not show the extraneous solution.

2d. Use a graphing calculator to graph the functions $h(x) = -\sqrt{x-3} + 5$ and $g(x) = x$ on the same screen. What do you notice about the point of intersection?

The x-coordinate of the point where the graphs of $h(x)$ and $g(x)$ intersect,

4, is the extraneous solution of $\sqrt{x-3} + 5 = x$.

---

3 EXAMPLE Solving Cube Root Equations

Solve $2\sqrt[3]{x^2 - 8} + 3 = 2x - 1$.

$2\sqrt[3]{x^2 - 8} + 3 = 2x - 1$	Write the equation.
$2\sqrt[3]{x^2 - 8} = 2x - \boxed{4}$	Isolate the cube root expression.
$\sqrt[3]{x^2 - 8} = x - \boxed{2}$	Divide both sides by 2.
$\left(\sqrt[3]{x^2 - 8}\right)^3 = (x - 2)^3$	Cube both sides of the equation.
$x^2 - 8 = x^3 - \boxed{6}\,x^2 + 12\,x - \boxed{8}$	Expand $(x - 2)^3$.
$0 = x^3 - \boxed{7}\,x^2 + 12\,x$	Make one side of the equation equal 0.
$0 = x\left(x - \boxed{4}\right)\left(x - \boxed{3}\right)$	Factor.
$x = \boxed{0}, x = \boxed{4}, \text{ or } x = \boxed{3}$	Zero Product Property

Check your solutions.

$2\sqrt[3]{x^2 - 8} + 3 = 2x - 1$	$2\sqrt[3]{x^2 - 8} + 3 = 2x - 1$	$2\sqrt[3]{x^2 - 8} + 3 = 2x - 1$
$2\sqrt[3]{0^2 - 8} + 3 \stackrel{?}{=} 2\left(0\right) - 1$	$2\sqrt[3]{4^2 - 8} + 3 \stackrel{?}{=} 2\left(4\right) - 1$	$2\sqrt[3]{3^2 - 8} + 3 \stackrel{?}{=} 2\left(3\right) - 1$
$2\left(-2\right) + 3 \stackrel{?}{=} -1$	$2\left(2\right) + 3 \stackrel{?}{=} 7$	$2\left(1\right) + 3 \stackrel{?}{=} 5$
$-1 = -1$	$7 = 7$	$5 = 5$

REFLECT

3a. Explain how you could use a graph to check your solutions.

Graph $f(x) = 2\sqrt[3]{x^2 - 8} + 3$ and $g(x) = 2x - 1$ on the same coordinate

plane. Find the x-coordinates of the points where the graph of $f(x)$

intersects the graph of $g(x)$. These x-coordinates are the solutions of

$2\sqrt[3]{x^2 - 8} + 3 = 2x - 1$.

3b. Cube root equations that have no restrictions on the variable do not yield extraneous solutions when solved. Why is it still important to check your solutions?

Checking solutions is still important, because it may identify an

algebraic or arithmetic error in the solving process.

Essential Question

How can you solve equations involving square roots and cube roots? Isolate the radical expression. If it is a square root, square both sides of the equation. If it is a cube root, cube both sides of the equation. Continue to solve by isolating the variable.

For square root equations, check for extraneous solutions by substituting the solution(s) back into the original equation.

Summarize

Have students write an entry in their journals that compares and contrasts solving square root equations and cube root equations, using examples as appropriate. The entry should include a discussion of extraneous solutions in the case of square root equations.

Where skills are taught	Where skills are practiced
1 EXAMPLE	EXS. 1–6
2 EXAMPLE	EXS. 7–11
3 EXAMPLE	EXS. 12–14

Exercises 15 and 16: Students solve a square root equation and a cube root equation by graphing. Students can use their graphing calculators and then draw a sketch of the solution on the coordinate grid.

Exercises 17–19: Students solve real-world problems that can be modeled by either a square root function or a cube root function.

PRACTICE

Solve each equation.

1. $\sqrt{x+5} = 5$

$x = 20$

2. $\sqrt[3]{4x} = -2$

$x = -2$

3. $\sqrt{3x} = 9$

$x = 27$

4. $\sqrt{x+1} = 6$

$x = 215$

5. $\sqrt{4x-7} = 5$

$x = 8$

6. $\sqrt[3]{x-4} + 3 = -1$

$x = -60$

7. $\sqrt{-3x-5} = x+3$

$x = -2$

8. $\sqrt{12+2x} = x+2$

$x = 2$

9. $\sqrt{-6x-14} = x+1$

no real solutions

10. $\sqrt{2x-7} = x-5$

$x = 8$

11. $\sqrt{9x+90} = x+6$

$x = 6$

12. $\sqrt[3]{1-x^2} = x+1$

$x = 0, x = -1, x = -3$

13. $\sqrt[3]{9x^2+22x+8} = x+2$

$x = 0, x = -2, x = 5$

14. $\sqrt[3]{x^2-x-1} = x-1$

$x = 0, x = 2$

Solve each equation by graphing.

15. $2\sqrt{x+1} = 3x+2$

$x = 0$

16. $2\sqrt[3]{x+1} + 3 = -2x+1$

$x = -1$

---

17. The function $s(l) = 1.34\sqrt{l}$ models the maximum speed s in knots for a sailboat with length l in feet at the waterline.

a. Use the model to find the length of a sailboat with a maximum speed of 12 knots. Round to the nearest foot.

80 feet

b. Explain how you can check your solution using a graphing calculator. Then use the method you described to check your result.

Graph the functions $f(x) = 12$ and $g(x) = 1.34\sqrt{x}$. Find the x-coordinate of the

point where the graphs intersect.

18. The function $a(h) = 20\sqrt[3]{h-8.3} + 40$ models the age a in years of a sassafras tree that is h meters high.

a. Use the model to find the height of the sassafras tree when it was 50 years old. Round to the nearest tenth of a meter.

8.4 meters

b. Explain how you can check your solution using a graphing calculator. Then use the method you described to check your result.

Graph the functions $f(x) = 50$ and $g(x) = 20\sqrt[3]{x-8.3} + 40$. Find the

x-coordinate at the point of intersection of the two graphs.

19. When a car skids to a stop on a dry asphalt road, the equation $s = \sqrt{21d}$ models the relationship between the car's speed s in miles per hour at the beginning of the skid and the distance d in feet that the car skids.

a. Use the model to find the distance that a car will skid to a stop if it is traveling at 40 miles per hour at the beginning of the skid. Round to the nearest foot.

76 feet

b. Use the model to find the distance that a car will skid to a stop if it is traveling at 20 miles per hour at the beginning of the skid. Round to the nearest foot. Compare this result with the result from part (a), where the speed was twice as great.

19 feet; a speed that is twice as great results in a skid that is 4 times as long.

c. A car skids to a stop and leaves skid marks that are 65 feet long. The speed limit on the road is 35 miles per hour. Was the car speeding when it went into the skid? Explain.

Yes; possible explanation: If the car were traveling at 35 mi/h, its skid marks

would have been about 58 ft long. Since the skid marks were longer than this,

the car must have been speeding.

CORRELATION

Standard	Items
CC.9-12.A.CED.2*	12
CC.9-12.A.REI.2	5, 9
CC.9-12.A.REI.11*	8
CC.9-12.F.IF.2	1
CC.9-12.F.IF.4*	12
CC.9-12.F.IF.7b*	4, 11
CC.9-12.F.BF.1*	7
CC.9-12.F.BF.3	6, 11
CC.9-12.F.BF.4	3
CC.9-12.F.BF.4a	2
CC.9-12.F.BF.4d(+)	7, 10

TEST PREP DOCTOR ✚

Multiple Choice: Item 2
- Students who chose **F** performed the inverse of the operations performed on x, but not in the reverse order.
- Students who chose **G** interpreted the superscript -1 as an exponent and took the reciprocal of the function rule.
- Students who chose **J** found the correct inverse but then took its reciprocal.

Multiple Choice: Item 4
- Students who chose **F** confused the general shapes of the graphs of a square root function and cube root function.
- Students who chose **H** read the coordinates in $(8, 2)$ in the reverse order.
- Students who chose **J** took the reciprocal instead of the inverse of the parent cubic function.

Multiple Choice: Item 5
- Students who chose **A** or **C** may have incorrectly factored $x^2 - 7x - 18$, the polynomial that arises after squaring both sides of the equation and getting one side equal to 0.
- Students who chose **B** chose the extraneous solution.

Multiple Choice: Item 7
- Students who chose **A** found a by dividing 1 by 4.9, but they forgot to take the square root of the result.
- Students who chose **C** found a by taking the square root of 4.9.
- Students who chose **D** used the value of a from the original function.

Free Response: Item 9
- Students who answered incorrectly may have written $x^3 + 8$ for the cube of $x + 2$.
- Students who did not get 0 as an answer may have forgotten to set x equal to 0 when they used the Zero Product Property.
- In their explanation regarding extraneous solutions, it is also correct for students to say that they know that none are extraneous because cubing both sides of an equation does not lead to extraneous solutions.

Free Response: Item 10
- Students who answered $\dfrac{1}{x^2 + 3}$ confused the inverse and the reciprocal.

Free Response: Item 11
- Students whose graphs start at $(-1, 2)$ used -1 for h and translated the parent graph left.

© Houghton Mifflin Harcourt Publishing Company

UNIT 5 TEST PREP

Name _____ Class _____ Date _____

MULTIPLE CHOICE

1. What is $f(-3)$, given that $f(x) = -\sqrt[3]{x-5} + 6$?

  A. -8 C. 4

  B. 0 D. 8

2. What is the inverse of $f(x) = 2x + 9$?

  F. $f^{-1}(x) = \frac{x}{2} - 9$

  G. $f^{-1}(x) = \frac{1}{2x+9}$

  H. $f^{-1}(x) = \frac{x-9}{2}$

  J. $f^{-1}(x) = \frac{2}{x-9}$

3. What is the inverse of the quadratic function whose graph is shown?

  A. $f^{-1}(x) = -\frac{1}{2}\sqrt{x}$

  B. $f^{-1}(x) = \frac{1}{2}\sqrt{x}$

  C. $f^{-1}(x) = -2\sqrt{x}$

  D. $f^{-1}(x) = 2\sqrt{x}$

4. Which function is graphed below?

  F. $f(x) = \sqrt{x}$ H. $f(x) = x^3$

  G. $f(x) = \sqrt[3]{x}$ J. $f(x) = \frac{1}{x^3}$

5. What is the solution of the equation $\sqrt{x+27} = x - 3$?

  A. $x = -9$ C. $x = 2$

  B. $x = -2$ D. $x = 9$

6. Which best describes the graph of $g(x) = 4\sqrt[3]{x}$ as a transformation of the graph of $f(x) = \sqrt[3]{x}$?

  F. vertical stretch by a factor of 4

  G. vertical shrink by a factor of $\frac{1}{4}$

  H. translation 4 units up

  J. translation 4 units to the right

7. The function $d(t) = 4.9t^2$ models the distance in meters an object falls after t seconds where $t \geq 0$. Which function $t(d)$ best models the time in seconds that it will take an object to fall d meters?

  A. $t(d) = 0.20\sqrt{d}$

  B. $t(d) = 0.45\sqrt{d}$

  C. $t(d) = 2.2\sqrt{d}$

  D. $t(d) = 4.9\sqrt{d}$

FREE RESPONSE

8. A student solves $\sqrt{-2x-12} = x + 6$ and gets the apparent solutions $x = -6$ or $x = -8$. Explain how the student could use a graph to determine whether either of the apparent solutions is extraneous.

Sample answer: Graph the functions

$f(x) = \sqrt{-2x - 12}$ and $g(x) = x + 6$,

and determine whether the graphs

intersect when $x = -6$. If they do

not, then $x = -6$ is an extraneous

solution. Repeat for $x = -8$.

9. Solve the equation $\sqrt[3]{8 - x^2} = x + 2$. Show your work.

$\left(\sqrt[3]{8 - x^2}\right)^3 = (x + 2)^3$

$8 - x^2 = x^3 + 6x^2 + 12x + 8$

$0 = x^3 + 7x^2 + 12x$

$0 = x(x + 3)(x + 4)$

$x = \dfrac{0}{}$ or $x = \dfrac{-3}{}$ or $x = \dfrac{-4}{}$

Are any of the solutions extraneous? Explain.

No; sample answer: When you

substitute each apparent solution

into the original equation, the

equation is true.

10. Find the inverse function of $f(x) = x^2 + 3$ by using algebra. Include any necessary restrictions on the domain of $f(x)$.

Restrict the domain of $f(x)$ to $x \geq 0$.

$f(x) = x^2 + 3 \rightarrow y = x^2 + 3$

$y - 3 = x^2$

$\sqrt{y - 3} = x$

Switch x and y to write the inverse:

$\sqrt{x - 3} = y$. So, $f^{-1}(x) = \sqrt{x - 3}$.

11. Graph $g(x) = \sqrt{x-1} + 2$ on the coordinate plane below. Then describe the graph of $g(x)$ as a transformation of the graph of the parent function $f(x) = \sqrt{x}$.

The graph of $g(x)$ is a translation of

the graph of $f(x)$ right 1 unit and up

2 units.

12. The function $d(h) = \sqrt{1.50h}$ approximates the distance in miles to the horizon for an observer whose eye level is h feet above the ground.

  a. Sketch a graph of the function on the grid below.

  b. Identify the coordinates of a point on the graph other than $(0, 0)$, and explain what the coordinates mean in the context of the situation.

Sample answer: (6, 3); for a person

whose eye level is 6 feet above the

ground, the horizon is 3 miles away.

Exponential Functions

Unit Vocabulary

e	(6-5)
exponential decay function	(6-1)
exponential function	(6-1)
exponential growth function	(6-1)

UNIT 6

Exponential Functions

Unit Focus

This unit is about exponential functions, which are functions in which the variable appears in the exponent. You will learn the characteristics of the basic growth and decay functions and then use your graphing calculator to explore transformations of these functions. Along the way, you will learn about the irrational number e and see applications of exponential functions, including compound interest and population growth. Finally, you will learn to solve exponential equations both algebraically and graphically.

Unit at a Glance

COMMON CORE

Lesson		Standards for Mathematical Content
6-1	Graphing Basic Exponential Functions	CC.9-12.F.IF.2, CC.9-12.F.IF.7*, CC.9-12.F.IF.7e*, CC.9-12.F.LE.3*
6-2	Graphing $f(x) = ab^{x-h} + k$ when $b > 1$	CC.9-12.F.IF.2, CC.9-12.F.IF.4*, CC.9-12.F.IF.7*, CC.9-12.F.IF.7e*, CC.9-12.F.BF.3, CC.9-12.F.LE.2*
6-3	Graphing $f(x) = ab^{x-h} + k$ when $0 < b < 1$	CC.9-12.F.IF.2, CC.9-12.F.IF.4*, CC.9-12.F.IF.7*, CC.9-12.F.IF.7e*, CC.9-12.F.BF.3, CC.9-12.F.LE.2*
6-4	Changing the Base of an Exponential Function	CC.9-12.A.SSE.3c, CC.9-12.A.CED.2*, CC.9-12.F.IF.2, CC.9-12.F.IF.7e*, CC.9-12.F.IF.8b, CC.9-12.F.BF.3
6-5	The Base e	CC.9-12.A.CED.2*, CC.9-12.F.IF.2, CC.9-12.F.IF.7e*, CC.9-12.F.BF.3, CC.9-12.F.LE.2*, CC.9-12.F.LE.5*
6-6	Modeling with Exponential Functions	CC.9-12.A.SSE.3c, CC.9-12.F.IF.8b, CC.9-12.F.BF.1*, CC.9-12.F.LE.3*, CC.9-12.S.ID.6a*, CC.9-12.S.ID.6b*
6-7	Solving Exponential Equations	CC.9-12.A.CED.1*, CC.9-12.A.REI.11*, CC.9-12.F.IF.7*, CC.9-12.F.IF.7e*
	Test Prep	

Unpacking the Common Core State Standards

This page lists and explains the Standards for Mathematical Content that are addressed in this unit. For information about the Standards for Mathematical Practice, which are integrated throughout the text, see Teacher Edition pages x–xiii.

Unpacking the Common Core State Standards

Use the table to help you understand the Standards for Mathematical Content that are taught in this unit. Refer to the lessons listed after each standard for exploration and practice.

COMMON CORE Standards for Mathematical Content	What It Means For You
CC.9-12.A.SSE.3 Choose and produce an equivalent form of an expression to reveal and explain properties of the quantity represented by the expression.* **CC.9-12.A.SSE.3c** Use the properties of exponents to transform expressions for exponential functions.* Lessons 6-4, 6-6 (Also 6-5)	You will learn how using the properties of exponents allows you to write equivalent forms of function rules. These different forms may explain why certain graphs behave as they do. In the context of a population growth model, different forms can reveal growth rates for the same data over different time periods.
CC.9-12.A.CED.1 Create equations and inequalities in one variable and use them to solve problems.* Lesson 6-7	In an exponential equation, the variable appears in an exponent. You will solve exponential equations algebraically and graphically. This includes writing equations by setting two function rules equal to each other.
CC.9-12.A.CED.2 Create equations in two or more variables to represent relationships between quantities; graph equations on coordinate axes with labels and scales.* Lessons 6-2, 6-3, 6-4, 6-5, 6-6	There are many applications of exponential functions in the real world. You will write and graph such functions, sometimes by hand and sometimes on a graphing calculator.
CC.9-12.A.REI.11 Explain why the x-coordinates of the points where the graphs of the equations $y = f(x)$ and $y = g(x)$ intersect are the solutions of the equation $f(x) = g(x)$; find the solutions approximately, e.g., using technology to graph the functions, make tables of values, or find successive approximations. Include cases where $f(x)$ and/or $g(x)$ are linear, polynomial, rational, absolute value, **exponential**, and logarithmic functions.* Lesson 6-7	When two functions $f(x)$ and $g(x)$ have the same value for a given x-value, their graphs pass through the same point. This fact allows you to solve the equation $f(x) = g(x)$ graphically. You will solve some exponential equations using this graphical method and explain, in the context of real-world problems, the meanings of the x- and y-coordinates.
CC.9-12.F.IF.2 Use function notation, evaluate functions for inputs in their domains, and interpret statements that use function notation in terms of a context. Lessons 6-1, 6-2, 6-3, 6-4, 6-5	When you graph multiple functions, the functions will be named $f(x)$, $g(x)$, and so on, to make it easy to distinguish their graphs on the same coordinate plane. You will evaluate functions in order to graph them and to solve real-world problems.
CC.9-12.F.IF.4 For a function that models a relationship between two quantities, interpret key features of graphs and tables in terms of the quantities, and sketch graphs showing key features given a verbal description of the relationship.* Lessons 6-2, 6-3, 6-6 (Also 6-5)	When exploring the graphs of exponential functions, you will focus on the y-intercept, the domain, the range, the asymptote, and the end behavior. You will also create and analyze tables when making some of these graphs and describe and explain any patterns.

Notes

_____

_____

_____

_____

_____

_____

_____

_____

_____

_____

_____

COMMON CORE	Standards for Mathematical Content	What It Means For You
CC.9-12.F.IF.7 Graph functions expressed symbolically and show key features of the graph, by hand in simple cases and using technology for more complicated cases.* **CC.9-12.F.IF.7e** Graph exponential and logarithmic functions, showing intercepts and end behavior, and trigonometric functions, showing period, midline, and amplitude.* Lessons 6-1, 6-2, 6-3, 6-4, 6-5, 6-6, 6-7		At the start of the unit, you will graph exponential functions by hand to get a sense of how the functions increase and decrease as x increases and decreases. Later, especially when transforming the graphs, you will use a graphing calculator.
CC.9-12.F.IF.8 Write a function defined by an expression in different but equivalent forms to reveal and explain different properties of the function. **CC.9-12.F.IF.8b** Use properties of exponents to interpret expressions for exponential functions. Lessons 6-4, 6-6 (Also 6-5)		You will use the properties of exponents to write equivalent forms of function rules. These different forms may explain why certain graphs behave as they do. In the context of a population growth model, different forms can reveal growth rates for the same data over different time periods.
CC.9-12.F.BF.1 Write a function that describes a relationship between two quantities.* **CC.9-12.F.BF.1a** Determine an explicit expression, a recursive process, or steps for calculation from a context.* Lesson 6-2, 6-3, 6-4, 6-6		You will write exponential functions that model real-world data.
CC.9-12.F.BF.3 Identify the effect on the graph of replacing $f(x)$ by $f(x) + k$, $k\,f(x)$, $f(kx)$, and $f(x + k)$ for specific values of k (both positive and negative); find the value of k given the graphs. Experiment with cases and illustrate an explanation of the effects on the graph using technology. Lessons 6-2, 6-3, 6-4, 6-5		After learning the characteristics of basic exponential growth and decay functions, you will explore, describe, and apply transformations of exponential functions. These transformations include translations, reflections, stretches, and shrinks.
CC.9-12.F.LE.2 Construct linear and exponential functions, including arithmetic and geometric sequences, given a graph, a description of a relationship, or two input-output pairs (include reading these from a table).* Lessons 6-2, 6-3, 6-4, 6-5		You will use what you learn about the structure of an exponential function to write its equation from its graph by comparing the graph to the graph of the parent function. You will also learn to identify parameters from a verbal description of an exponential function in order to write an equation for the function.
CC.9-12.F.LE.3 Observe using graphs and tables that a quantity increasing exponentially eventually exceeds a quantity increasing linearly, quadratically, or (more generally) as a polynomial function. Lessons 6-1, 6-6		You will see that exponential growth outstrips any type of polynomial growth.

UNIT 6

Notes

_____

_____

_____

_____

_____

_____

_____

_____

_____

_____

COMMON CORE Standards for Mathematical Content	What It Means For You
CC.9-12.F.LE.5 Interpret the parameters in a linear or exponential function in terms of a context.* Lessons 6-4, 6-5 (Also 6-2, 6-3)	You will interpret growth rates for exponential functions that model interest earned over time in order to compare savings options.
CC.9-12.S.ID.6 Represent data on two quantitative variables on a scatter plot, and describe how the variables are related.* CC.9-12.S.ID.6a Fit a function to the data; use functions fitted to data to solve problems in the context of the data.* CC.9-12.S.ID.6b Informally assess the fit of a function by plotting and analyzing residuals.* Lesson 6-6	You will use your calculator to perform exponential regression in order to fit an exponential function to real-world population data. After graphing both the data and the equation, you will find the residuals and determine if the model is a good fit. You will also compare the function obtained from exponential regression to a function obtained from quadratic regression.

Additional Standards in this Unit

CC.9-12.F.IF.9 Compare properties of two functions each represented in a different way (algebraically, graphically, numerically in tables, or by verbal descriptions). Lessons 6-2, 6-3

Notes

_____

_____

_____

_____

_____

_____

_____

_____

Graphing Basic Exponential Functions

Essential question: What are the characteristics of an exponential function?

© Houghton Mifflin Harcourt Publishing Company

COMMON CORE Standards for Mathematical Content

CC.9-12.F.IF.2 Use function notation, evaluate functions for inputs in their domains, ...

CC.9-12.F.IF.7 Graph functions expressed symbolically and show key features of the graph, by hand in simple cases ...*

CC.9-12.F.IF.7e Graph exponential ... functions, showing intercepts and end behavior, ...*

CC.9-12.F.LE.3 Observe using graphs and tables that a quantity increasing exponentially eventually exceeds a quantity increasing linearly, quadratically, or (more generally) as a polynomial function.*

Vocabulary

exponential function

exponential growth function

exponential decay function

Prerequisites

Evaluating integer exponents, Grade 8

Properties of exponents, Grade 8

Math Background

An exponential function is not just a function with an exponent but a function whose independent variable is the exponent. Therefore, $f(x) = 2^x$ is an exponential function, but $g(x) = x^2$ is not. Students should enter this lesson comfortable with evaluating powers with zero and negative exponents.

Students will graph most of the exponential functions in this lesson by hand. They will see that the graphs of exponential growth functions approach the negative x-axis as x decreases without bound while the graphs of exponential decay functions approach the positive x-axis as x increases without bound, so the x-axis is an asymptote for the graph of any function of the form $f(x) = b^x$ where $b > 0$ and $b \neq 1$. In subsequent lessons, students will transform the graphs of exponential functions and discover how the transformations affect the asymptote, y-intercept, and rate of increase or decrease.

INTRODUCE

To help remind students of some of the laws of exponents, have them evaluate each of the following expressions.

$$4^0 \quad 1 \quad \left(\frac{1}{8}\right)^{-3} \quad 512 \quad 10^{-2} \quad \frac{1}{100}$$

TEACH

1 EXAMPLE

Questioning Strategies

- Does the graph have a horizontal asymptote? If so, what is it? Yes; the x-axis

- How do you know that there is no vertical asymptote? The function is defined for all real values of x.

EXTRA EXAMPLE

Graph $f(x) = 4^x$. The curve passes through $\left(-2, \frac{1}{16}\right)$, $\left(-1, \frac{1}{4}\right)$, (0, 1), (1, 4), and (2, 16).

Teaching Strategy

Have students find $f(x)$ for $x = 4, 5, 6, 7$, and 8 to see that the *amount* of increase between output values will increase dramatically as x continues to increase.

2 EXAMPLE

Questioning Strategies

- Compared with the graph in the previous example, the x-axis is still a horizontal asymptote, but what is different in this case? The graph approaches the positive x-axis in this case, but the graph approached the negative x-axis in the previous example.

- How are the function rules in 1 EXAMPLE and 2 EXAMPLE related? How are their outputs related? The bases in the function rules are reciprocals, and the corresponding outputs are reciprocals.

continued

Name_____ Class_____ Date_____

6-1

Graphing Basic Exponential Functions

COMMON CORE

CC.9-12.F.IF.2,
CC.9-12.F.IF.7*,
CC.9-12.F.IF.7e*,
CC.9-12.F.LE.3*

Essential question: *What are the characteristics of an exponential function?*

In an **exponential function**, the variable is an exponent. The parent function is $f(x) = b^x$, where b is any real number greater than 0, except 1.

1 EXAMPLE Graphing $f(x) = b^x$ for $b > 1$

Graph $f(x) = 2^x$.

A Complete the table of values below.

B Plot the points on the graph and connect the points with a smooth curve.

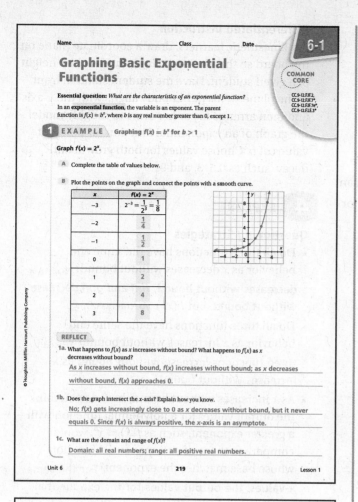

x	$f(x) = 2^x$
−3	$2^{-3} = \frac{1}{2^3} = \frac{1}{8}$
−2	$\frac{1}{4}$
−1	$\frac{1}{2}$
0	1
1	2
2	4
3	8

REFLECT

1a. What happens to $f(x)$ as x increases without bound? What happens to $f(x)$ as x decreases without bound?

As x increases without bound, $f(x)$ increases without bound; as x decreases without bound, $f(x)$ approaches 0.

1b. Does the graph intersect the x-axis? Explain how you know.

No; $f(x)$ gets increasingly close to 0 as x decreases without bound, but it never equals 0. Since $f(x)$ is always positive, the x-axis is an asymptote.

1c. What are the domain and range of $f(x)$?

Domain: all real numbers; range: all positive real numbers.

Unit 6   219   Lesson 1

© Houghton Mifflin Harcourt Publishing Company

2 EXAMPLE Graphing $f(x) = b^x$ for $0 < b < 1$

Graph $f(x) = \left(\frac{1}{2}\right)^x$.

A Complete the table of values below.

B Plot the points on the graph and connect the points with a smooth curve.

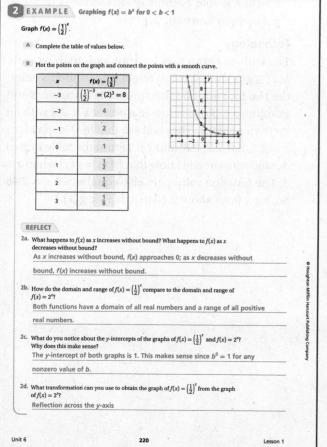

x	$f(x) = \left(\frac{1}{2}\right)^x$
−3	$\left(\frac{1}{2}\right)^{-3} = (2)^3 = 8$
−2	4
−1	2
0	1
1	$\frac{1}{2}$
2	$\frac{1}{4}$
3	$\frac{1}{8}$

REFLECT

2a. What happens to $f(x)$ as x increases without bound? What happens to $f(x)$ as x decreases without bound?

As x increases without bound, $f(x)$ approaches 0; as x decreases without bound, $f(x)$ increases without bound.

2b. How do the domain and range of $f(x) = \left(\frac{1}{2}\right)^x$ compare to the domain and range of $f(x) = 2^x$?

Both functions have a domain of all real numbers and a range of all positive real numbers.

2c. What do you notice about the y-intercepts of the graphs of $f(x) = \left(\frac{1}{2}\right)^x$ and $f(x) = 2^x$? Why does this make sense?

The y-intercept of both graphs is 1. This makes sense since $b^0 = 1$ for any nonzero value of b.

2d. What transformation can you use to obtain the graph of $f(x) = \left(\frac{1}{2}\right)^x$ from the graph of $f(x) = 2^x$?

Reflection across the y-axis

Unit 6   220   Lesson 1

© Houghton Mifflin Harcourt Publishing Company

EXTRA EXAMPLE
Graph $f(x) = \left(\frac{1}{4}\right)^x$. The curve passes through $(-2, 16)$, $(-1, 4)$, $(0, 1)$, $\left(1, \frac{1}{4}\right)$, and $\left(2, \frac{1}{16}\right)$.

Differentiated Instruction
Have students copy the graph of $f(x) = \left(\frac{1}{2}\right)^x$ on the same grid used for the graph of $f(x) = 2^x$ so they can confirm that the y-axis acts as a line of reflection for transforming one graph to the other.

<table>
<tr><td>

MATHEMATICAL PRACTICE   **Highlighting the Standards**

1 EXAMPLE and **2 EXAMPLE** include opportunities to address Mathematical Practice Standard 8 (Look for and express regularity in repeated reasoning). Show students how they can continue the patterns in the output columns. As x increases in **2 EXAMPLE**, the numbers in the denominators of the unit fractions double. So, without even evaluating the function, you can determine that $f(x)$ equals $\frac{1}{16}$, $\frac{1}{32}$, and $\frac{1}{64}$ when x equals 4, 5, and 6, respectively.

</td></tr>
</table>

3 ENGAGE

Questioning Strategies
- How can you determine whether an exponential function models growth or decay just by looking at its graph? Exponential growth functions increase from left to right, and exponential decay functions decrease from left to right.

- Can you automatically conclude that an exponential function models decay if the base of the power is a fraction or decimal? Explain. No, some fractions and decimals have a value greater than one, such as 2.5 and $\frac{7}{2}$, and these bases produce exponential growth functions.

- For any acceptable value of b in an exponential function $f(x) = b^x$, what is the value of $f(x)$ if $x = -1$? $\frac{1}{b}$

Differentiated Instruction
For kinesthetic learners, draw a coordinate plane on the board so that the origin is about shoulder height of a given student. Have the student stand in front of the plane so his or her body aligns with the y-axis and then arrange his or her arms to roughly model the graph of an exponential function for different values of b. Choose values for both growth and decay, such as 0.5, 3, and 8.

4 EXPLORE

Questioning Strategies
- Do all three functions have the same end behavior as x decreases without bound? No, as x decreases without bound, $f(x)$ and $g(x)$ decrease without bound, but $h(x)$ approaches 0.

- Do all three functions have the same end behavior as x increases without bound? Yes, all three functions increase without bound as x increases without bound.

- As x increases without bound, how do you think the output values for a polynomial function with a greater exponent, such as $f(x) = x^5$, would compare to those of an exponential function whose base matches the exponent? For the same x-values, the output values for the exponential function would eventually exceed those of the polynomial function.

Technology
The table in part A may lead students to think that $h(x) \geq g(x)$ for all x. You might have students enter the two functions on their graphing calculators and examine a table of values starting at $x = 2.4$ with an increment of 0.1. They will see that $h(x) < g(x)$ for $x = 2.5, 2.6, 2.7, 2.8,$ and 2.9. (From the table in part A, students already know that $h(x) = g(x)$ when $x = 3$. The function values are also equal when $x \approx 2.48$. So, for x from about 2.48 to 3, $h(x) < g(x)$.)

3 ENGAGE | Recognizing Types of Exponential Functions

A function of the form $f(x) = b^x$ is an **exponential growth function** if $b > 1$ and an **exponential decay function** if $0 < b < 1$.

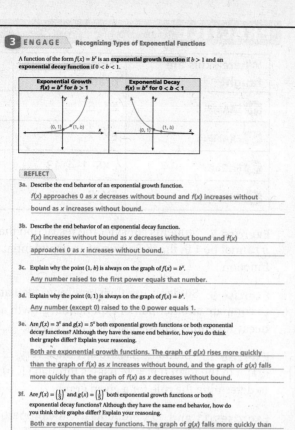

| Exponential Growth $f(x) = b^x$ for $b > 1$ | Exponential Decay $f(x) = b^x$ for $0 < b < 1$ |

REFLECT

3a. Describe the end behavior of an exponential growth function.

$f(x)$ approaches 0 as x decreases without bound and $f(x)$ increases without bound as x increases without bound.

3b. Describe the end behavior of an exponential decay function.

$f(x)$ increases without bound as x decreases without bound and $f(x)$ approaches 0 as x increases without bound.

3c. Explain why the point $(1, b)$ is always on the graph of $f(x) = b^x$.

Any number raised to the first power equals that number.

3d. Explain why the point $(0, 1)$ is always on the graph of $f(x) = b^x$.

Any number (except 0) raised to the 0 power equals 1.

3e. Are $f(x) = 3^x$ and $g(x) = 5^x$ both exponential growth functions or both exponential decay functions? Although they have the same end behavior, how you do think their graphs differ? Explain your reasoning.

Both are exponential growth functions. The graph of $g(x)$ rises more quickly than the graph of $f(x)$ as x increases without bound, and the graph of $g(x)$ falls more quickly than the graph of $f(x)$ as x decreases without bound.

3f. Are $f(x) = \left(\frac{1}{3}\right)^x$ and $g(x) = \left(\frac{1}{5}\right)^x$ both exponential growth functions or both exponential decay functions? Although they have the same end behavior, how do you think their graphs differ? Explain your reasoning.

Both are exponential decay functions. The graph of $g(x)$ falls more quickly than the graph of $f(x)$ as x increases without bound, and the graph of $g(x)$ rises more quickly than the graph of $f(x)$ as x decreases without bound.

4 EXPLORE | Comparing Linear, Quadratic, and Exponential Functions

Compare each of the functions $f(x) = x + 3$ and $g(x) = x^3$ to the exponential function $h(x) = 3^x$ for $x \geq 0$.

A Complete the table of values for the three functions.

x	$f(x) = x + 3$	$g(x) = x^3$	$h(x) = 3^x$
0	3	0	1
1	4	1	3
2	5	8	9
3	6	27	27
4	7	64	81
5	8	125	243

B The graph of $h(x) = 3^x$ is shown on the coordinate grid below. Graph $f(x) = x + 3$ on the same grid.

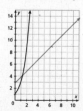

C The graph of $h(x) = 3^x$ is shown on the coordinate grid below. Graph $g(x) = x^3$ on the same grid.

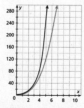

REFLECT

4a. How do the values of $h(x)$ compare to those of $f(x)$ and $g(x)$ as x increases without bound?

For the same x-value, the value of $h(x)$ may start out less than the values of $f(x)$ and $g(x)$, but the value of $h(x)$ eventually becomes greater than the values of $f(x)$ and $g(x)$ as x increases without bound.

Essential Question

What are the characteristics of an exponential function?

The graph is a curve that rises from left to right at an increasing rate when the base is greater than 1. The curve falls from left to right when the base is between 0 and 1. The domain is all real numbers, but the range is restricted to positive numbers because a power with a positive base cannot yield a negative number. This gives the graph a horizontal asymptote at the *x*-axis.

Summarize

Have students make a graphic organizer to compare and contrast exponential growth functions and exponential decay functions. One possibility is shown below.

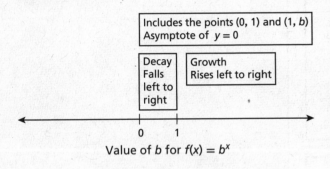

Value of *b* for $f(x) = b^x$

Where skills are taught	Where skills are practiced
1 EXAMPLE	EX. 6
2 EXAMPLE	EX. 7
3 ENGAGE	EXS. 1–4, 13
4 EXPLORE	EX. 8

Exercise 5: Students consider the restriction that *b* cannot be 1 in the definition of an exponential function.

Exercise 9: Students use their graphing calculators to compare another pair of exponential growth and decay functions whose bases are reciprocals.

Exercise 10: Students use the fact that every graph in the form $f(x) = b^x$ passes through $(1, b)$ to determine the rule for a given graph.

Exercises 11 and 12: Students use the properties of exponents to explain, generally, how *y* will change under certain circumstances.

Exercise 14: Students compare linear growth with exponential growth.

© Houghton Mifflin Harcourt Publishing Company

PRACTICE

Tell whether the function describes an exponential growth function or an exponential decay function. Explain how you know without graphing.

1. $f(x) = 0.9^x$

Exponential decay; $b = 0.9$ and 0.9 is between 0 and 1.

2. $g(x) = 4.5^x$

Exponential growth; $b = 4.5$ and 4.5 is greater than 1.

3. $h(x) = \left(\frac{5}{2}\right)^x$

Exponential growth; $b = 2.5$ and 2.5 is greater than 1.

4. $k(x) = \left(\frac{3}{4}\right)^x$

Exponential decay; $b = 0.75$ and 0.75 is between 0 and 1.

5. In an exponential function, $f(x) = b^x$, b is not allowed to be 1. Explain why this restriction exists.

If $b = 1$, the function is not exponential; in this case, it is the constant function $f(x) = 1$ because 1 raised to any power equals 1.

6. Complete the table for $f(x) = 4^x$. Then sketch the graph of the function.

x	f(x)
−1	0.25
0	1
1	4
2	16
3	64

7. Complete the table for $f(x) = \left(\frac{1}{3}\right)^x$. Then sketch the graph of the function.

x	f(x)
−3	27
−2	9
−1	3
0	1
1	$\frac{1}{3}$

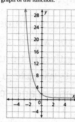

8. Compare the graph of $f(x) = 2^x$ to the graph of $g(x) = x^2$.

The graph of $g(x)$ has a line of symmetry, while the graph of $f(x)$ does not. As x increases without bound, the graph of $f(x)$ rises more quickly than the graph of $g(x)$. As x decreases without bound, the graph of $f(x)$ approaches 0 while the graph of $g(x)$ increases without bound.

9. Enter the functions $f(x) = 10^x$ and $g(x) = \left(\frac{1}{10}\right)^x$ into your graphing calculator.

a. Look at a table of values for the two functions. For a given x-value, how do the corresponding function values compare?

They are reciprocals of each other.

b. Look at graphs of the two functions. How are the two graphs related to each other?

The graphs are reflections of each other across the y-axis.

10. The graph of an exponential function $f(x) = b^x$ is shown.

a. Which of the labeled points, (0, 1) or (1, 5), allows you to determine the value of b? Why doesn't the other point help?

(1, 5); (0, 1) doesn't help because the graphs of all functions of the form $f(x) = b^x$ pass through (0, 1)

b. What is the value of b? Explain how you know.

$b = 5$ because $f(1) = b^1 = b = 5$

11. Given an exponential function $y = b^x$, when you double the value of x, how does the value of y change? Explain.

The value of y is squared because $b^{2x} = (b^x)^2 = y^2$.

12. Given an exponential function $y = b^x$, when you add 2 to the value of x, how does the value of y change? Explain.

The value of y is multiplied by b^2 because $b^{x+2} = b^x \cdot b^2 = b^2 \cdot y$.

13. **Error Analysis** A student says that the function $f(x) = \left(\frac{1}{0.5}\right)^x$ is an exponential decay function. Explain the student's error.

$f(x) = b^x$ is an exponential decay function when $0 < b < 1$, but in this case $b = 2$.

14. One method of cutting a long piece of string into smaller pieces is to make individual cuts, so that 1 cut results in 2 pieces, 2 cuts result in 3 pieces, and so on. Another method of cutting the string is to fold it onto itself and cut the folded end, then fold the pieces onto themselves and cut their folded ends at the same time, and continue to fold and cut, so that 1 cut results in 2 pieces, 2 cuts result in 4 pieces, and so on. For each method, write a function that gives the number p of pieces in terms of the number c of cuts. Which function grows faster? Why?

Method 1: $p = c + 1$; method 2: $p = 2^c$; $p = 2^c$ because exponential growth beats linear growth

Notes

Graphing $f(x) = ab^{x-h} + k$ when $b > 1$

Essential question: *How does changing the values of a, h, and k affect the graph of an exponential growth function?*

COMMON CORE Standards for Mathematical Content

CC.9-12.A.CED.2 Create equations in two or more variables to represent relationships between quantities; graph equations on coordinate axes with labels and scales.*

CC.9-12.F.IF.2 Use function notation, evaluate functions for inputs in their domains ...

CC.9-12.F.IF.4 For a function that models a relationship between two quantities, interpret key features of graphs ... in terms of the quantities, and sketch graphs showing key features given a verbal description of the relationship.*

CC.9-12.F.IF.7 Graph functions expressed symbolically and show key features of the graph, by hand in simple cases and using technology for more complicated cases.*

CC.9-12.F.IF.7e Graph exponential ... functions, showing intercepts and end behavior, ...*

CC.9–12.F.BF.1 Write a function that describes a relationship between two quantities.*

CC.9–12.F.BF.1a Determine an explicit expression ... from a context.*

CC.9-12.F.BF.3 Identify the effect on the graph of replacing $f(x)$ by $f(x) + k$, $kf(x)$, ..., and $f(x + k)$ for specific values of k (both positive and negative); find the value of k given the graphs. Experiment with cases and illustrate an explanation of the effects on the graph using technology.

CC.9-12.F.LE.2 Construct ... exponential functions, ... given a graph, a description of a relationship, ...*

Also: CC.9-12.F.IF.9, CC.9-12.F.LE.5*

Prerequisites
Graphing basic exponential functions, Lesson 6–1

Math Background
The process of transforming the graphs of parent exponential functions is the same as it is for other functions. You can add a number to or subtract a number from the independent variable for a horizontal translation and add a number to or subtract a number from the function for a vertical translation. You can multiply the function by a positive number to vertically stretch or shrink the graph.

In this lesson, students will work only with functions where $b > 1$. In the next lesson, they will work with functions where $0 < b < 1$. In both cases, students will use graphing calculators to conduct explorations and solve problems.

INTRODUCE

Review the general characteristics of an exponential function in the form $f(x) = b^x$, where $b > 0$ and $b \neq 1$, by asking students the following questions:

- What is the domain? all real numbers
- What is the range? all positive real numbers
- What is the graph's shape if $b > 1$? a curve that rises in greater and greater amounts as x increases

TEACH

 EXPLORE

Materials
graphing calculator

Questioning Strategies
- In parts B and C, how do you indicate on the calculator that you are subtracting 4 from x rather than 2^x or adding 6 to x rather than 2^x? by enclosing the entire expression for the exponent in parentheses
- Which parameter, h or k, changes the function's range? Why? changing k; because it causes a vertical shift in the graph, and the range is determined by the y-coordinates of points on the graph

Name_____ Class_____ Date_____

6-2

COMMON CORE

CC9-12.F.IF.2,
CC9-12.F.IF.4*,
CC9-12.F.IF.7*,
CC9-12.F.IF.7e*,
CC9-12.F.BF.3,
CC9-12.F.LE.2*

Graphing $f(x) = ab^{x-h} + k$ when $b > 1$

Essential question: *How does changing the values of a, h, and k affect the graph of an exponential growth function?*

A general exponential growth function has the form $f(x) = ab^{x-h} + k$ where $b > 0$ and a, h, and k are real numbers with $a > 0$. Every value of b represents a different family of functions that can be transformed by changing the values of a, h, and k.

1 EXPLORE Changing h and k

Use your graphing calculator to help you with this activity.

A Graph $f(x) = 2^x$. Confirm that it matches the graph shown at right.

B Graph $g(x) = 2^{x-4}$. Sketch and label $g(x)$ at right.

C Graph $h(x) = 2^{x+6}$. Sketch and label $h(x)$ at right.

D Compare the three graphs. How is the graph of $g(x)$ related to the graph of $f(x)$? How is the graph of $h(x)$ related to the graph of $f(x)$?

The graph of $g(x)$ is a horizontal translation of the

graph of $f(x)$ right 4 units; the graph of $h(x)$ is a

horizontal translation of the graph of $f(x)$ left 6 units.

E Delete all equations from the equation editor. Then graph $f(x) = 3^x$. Confirm that it matches the graph shown at right.

F Graph $g(x) = 3^x + 3$. Sketch and label $g(x)$ at right.

G Graph $h(x) = 3^x - 5$. Sketch and label $h(x)$ at right.

H Compare the three graphs. How is the graph of $g(x)$ related to the graph of $f(x)$? How is the graph of $h(x)$ related to the graph of $f(x)$?

The graph of $g(x)$ is a vertical translation of the

graph of $f(x)$ up 3 units; the graph of $h(x)$ is a

vertical translation of the graph of $f(x)$ down 5 units.

© Houghton Mifflin Harcourt Publishing Company

Unit 6   225   Lesson 2

REFLECT

1a. How do you think the value of h affects the graph of $g(x) = b^{x-h}$?

The graph of $g(x) = b^{x-h}$ is a translation of the graph of $f(x) = b^x$ by $|h|$ units to

the right when $h > 0$ and $|h|$ units to the left when $h < 0$.

1b. How do you think the value of k affects the graph of $g(x) = b^x + k$?

The graph of $g(x) = b^x + k$ is a translation of the graph of $f(x) = b^x$ by $|k|$ units up

when $k > 0$ and $|k|$ units down when $k < 0$.

2 EXPLORE Changing a

Use your graphing calculator to help you with this activity.

A Graph $f(x) = 4^x$. Confirm that it matches the graph shown.

B Graph $g(x) = 3(4)^x$. Sketch and label $g(x)$ at right.

C Graph $h(x) = \frac{1}{2}(4)^x$. Sketch and label $h(x)$ at right.

D Compare the three graphs. How is the graph of $g(x)$ related to the graph of $f(x)$? How is the graph of $h(x)$ related to the graph of $f(x)$?

The graph of $g(x)$ is a vertical stretch of the graph of $f(x)$ by a factor of 3; the

graph of $h(x)$ is a vertical shrink of the graph of $f(x)$ by a factor of $\frac{1}{2}$.

REFLECT

2a. For $a > 0$, how do you think the value of a affects the graph of $g(x) = ab^x$?

The graph of $g(x) = ab^x$ is a vertical stretch of the graph of $f(x) = b^x$ by a factor of

a when $a > 1$, and a vertical shrink of the graph of $f(x) = b^x$ by a factor of a when

$0 < a < 1$.

2b. Without graphing, explain how the graph of $g(x) = 4(2)^{x+1} - 7$ compares to the graph of $f(x) = 2^x$.

The graph of $g(x)$ is the graph of $f(x)$ stretched vertically by a factor of 4 and

translated 1 unit left and 7 units down.

The following table summarizes how the values of the parameters a, h, and k affect the graph of an exponential growth function.

	$f(x) = ab^{x-h} + k$
Parameter	**Effect**
h	If $h > 0$, the graph of the parent function is translated $|h|$ units to the right. If $h < 0$, the graph of the parent function is translated $|h|$ units to the left.
k	If $k > 0$, the graph of the parent function is translated $|k|$ units up. If $k < 0$, the graph of the parent function is translated $|k|$ units down.
a	If $a > 1$, the graph of the parent function is stretched vertically by a factor of a. If $0 < a < 1$, the graph of the parent function is shrunk vertically by a factor of a.

© Houghton Mifflin Harcourt Publishing Company

Unit 6   226   Lesson 2

© Houghton Mifflin Harcourt Publishing Company

Materials
graphing calculator

Questioning Strategies
- Explain how you can enter the rule for $g(x)$ in the calculator and not use parentheses. If you enter a multiplication symbol between 3 and 4, the power of x will apply only to the base because of the order of operations.
- Why does it make sense for the graph to stretch when $a > 1$ and for the graph to shrink when $0 < a < 1$? Multiplying by a factor greater than 1 increases the outputs compared with the parent function, and multiplying by a factor between 0 and 1 decreases the outputs compared with the parent function.
- Why does the y-intercept of $f(x) = ab^x + k$ equal a when $k = 0$? The y-intercept occurs when $x = 0$, and $ab^0 + 0 = a(1) = a$.

Differentiated Instruction
For Reflect Question 2b, have students graph $y = 2^x$, $y = 2^{x+1}$, $y = 4(2)^{x+1}$, and $y = 4(2)^{x+1} - 7$, in that order, on a graphing calculator. Have them keep track of the changes by drawing sketches of each graph on the same coordinate grid.

Technology
A calculator will read numbers separated by parentheses as implied multiplication, so students can enter $3(4)^x$ for $g(x)$ as is (that is, without a multiplication symbol).

MATHEMATICAL PRACTICE **Highlighting the Standards**

1 EXAMPLE and **2** EXAMPLE implement Mathematical Practice Standard 5 (Use appropriate tools strategically). Because students are now proficient in graphing these functions, the graphing calculator lets them focus on how the graphs are changing and gives them more time to reason and analyze.

Questioning Strategies
- How does finding k help you determine a? Finding k tells you how to translate the graph before comparing the y-intercept to that for the parent function in order to find a.
- How do you use the y-coordinate of the point where $x = 1$ to determine b? The graph of the parent function passes through $(1, b)$. To find b, reverse any vertical translation then any vertical stretch or shrink.

EXTRA EXAMPLE
Write an equation of the exponential growth function whose graph is shown. $f(x) = 3(2)^x + 1$

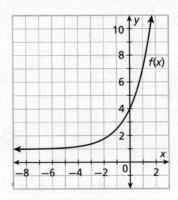

Questioning Strategies
- Why is the graph limited to Quadrant I? Time before 0 years does not make sense, and the balance will never be negative.
- When should you round calculations? Round during the last step only. Finding the value of 1.02^6 and rounding to two decimal places before multiplying by 5000 results in $5650.

Avoid Common Errors
Students may multiply the initial amount by the growth factor and then raise that product to the exponent. Remind students to apply the order of operations. The exponent applies only to the growth factor.

EXTRA EXAMPLE
Petra invested $6500 in an account that earns interest at a rate of 3.2% compounded annually. Write and graph a function that gives the balance in the account after t years. Then, find the balance after 10 years. $A(t) = 6500(1.032)^t$; the graph has a y-intercept of 6500 and passes through $(1, 6708)$. The balance after 10 years is $8906.57.

Using the properties of exponents, you can rewrite the expression $ab^{x-h} + k$ as follows:

$$ab^{x-h} + k = ab^x \cdot b^{-h} + k = (ab^{-h})b^x + k$$

where ab^{-h} is a constant because a, b, and h are constants. This means that the parameter h in the function $f(x) = ab^{x-h} + k$ can be eliminated by combining it with the parameter a. Therefore, when you are asked to find the equation of an exponential growth function, you can assume that it has the form $f(x) = ab^x + k$.

3 EXAMPLE Writing an Equation from a Graph

Write an equation of the exponential growth function $g(x)$ whose graph is shown.

A Let $g(x) = ab^x + k$. First find the value of k.

Since the graph has the line $y = 1$ as a horizontal asymptote, there is a vertical translation of the parent function.

So, $k = \underline{\quad 1 \quad}$.

B Find the value of a.

The y-intercept of the graph of $g(x)$ is $\underline{\quad 3 \quad}$.

If the graph of $g(x)$ is translated so that the x-axis is the asymptote, then the y-intercept of the graph will be $\underline{\quad 2 \quad}$.

The y-intercept of the parent exponential growth function $f(x) = b^x$ is $\underline{\quad 1 \quad}$.

This means the graph of the parent function is stretched vertically by a factor of $\underline{\quad 2 \quad}$.

So, $a = \underline{\quad 2 \quad}$.

C Find the value of b.

The graph of $g(x)$ passes through $(1, 7)$.

If the graph is translated as in part A, then it passes through $(1, \underline{\ 6\ })$.

Shrinking produces the graph of the parent function passing through $(1, \underline{\ 3\ })$.

The graph of the parent function passes through $(1, b)$, so $b = \underline{\quad 3 \quad}$.

D Write the equation.

Using the values of the parameters from above, $g(x) = \underline{\quad 2(3)^x + 1 \quad}$.

REFLECT

3a. How did you use the fact that $g(x)$ passes through $(1, 7)$ to find a point through which the parent function passes?

The graph of the parent function is stretched vertically by a factor of 2 then translated up 1 unit, so the parent function must pass through $(1, (7 - 1) \div 2)$, or $(1, 3)$.

3b. How can you check that you wrote a correct equation?

Graph the equation to check that it matches the given graph.

Exponential growth occurs when a quantity increases by the same fixed percent over equal periods of time. You can model such growth using the following formula.

The Exponential Growth Formula

The function $A(t) = a(1 + r)^t$ gives the amount $A(t)$ of a quantity after t time periods when the quantity is growing exponentially and the initial amount of the quantity is a. The constant r, which is the fixed percent by which the quantity increases each time period, is called the *growth rate* and is written in decimal form. The expression $1 + r$ is called the *growth factor*.

4 EXAMPLE Writing an Exponential Growth Function

Janelle invests \$5000 in an account that earns interest at a rate of 2% compounded annually. Write and graph a function that gives the balance in the account after t years. Then find the balance after 6 years.

A Write an exponential growth function.

The initial amount a is $\underline{\quad 5000 \quad}$.

The growth rate r is $\underline{\ 0.02\ }$ and the growth factor is $1 + r$, or $\underline{\ 1.02\ }$.

The balance A after t years is given by $A(t) = a(1 + r)^t$.

So, $A(t) = \underline{\ 5000(1.02)^t\ }$.

B Graph the function. Sketch the graph on the coordinate plane at right.

C Find the balance after 6 years.

$A(6) = \boxed{5000}\left(\boxed{1.02}\right)^6$ Substitute 6 for t.

≈ 5630.81 Use a calculator. Round to the nearest hundredth.

So, the balance after 6 years is $\underline{\ \$5630.81\ }$.

REFLECT

4a. What is the y-intercept of the graph? What does it represent?

5000; this represents the initial amount.

4b. Suppose Janelle decides to invest the money in an account that earns interest at a rate of 4% compounded annually. How would the graph for that exponential growth function compare to the one you graphed above?

It would have the same y-intercept, but the graph would rise more quickly as t increases without bound.

© Houghton Mifflin Harcourt Publishing Company

Essential Question

How does changing the values of a, h, and k affect the graph of an exponential growth function?
Changing *a* stretches the graph of the parent function vertically if $a > 1$ and shrinks the graph vertically if $0 < a < 1$. Changing *h* translates the graph right if *h* is positive and left if *h* is negative. Changing *k* translates the graph up if *k* is positive and down if *k* is negative.

Summarize

Write each equation below on the board. Have students state the equation for the parent function and then describe how the graph of the parent function is transformed to become the graph of the given function.

- $y = 0.75(4)^{x-7} - 3$ The parent function is $y = 4^x$. The parent graph is translated 7 units right, vertically shrunk by a factor of 0.75, and translated 3 units down.

- $y = 3(1.5)^{x+6}$ The parent function is $y = 1.5^x$. The parent graph is translated 6 units left and vertically stretched by a factor of 3.

Where skills are taught	Where skills are practiced
3 EXAMPLE	EXS. 10–12
4 EXAMPLE	EXS. 13, 14

Exercises 1–4: Students write function rules when given the parent function and a description of a transformation or set of transformations. They also graph the functions.

Exercises 5–8: Students write function rules when given the parent function and a description of a transformation or set of transformations. They also give the range of each function.

Exercise 9: Students explain and correct the error in a student's reasoning about the equation of a graphed function.

Exercise 15: Students are given the exponential growth function for a situation that involves interest compounded annually. They rewrite the function's rule for a change in the situation and tell how the graph would change.

Exercise 16: Students extend what they learned in 4 EXAMPLE to write and analyze a function representing a real-world situation that began in the past and continues into the future.

PRACTICE

The graph of $f(x) = 2.5^x$ is shown. Write the function rules for $g(x)$ and $h(x)$ based on the descriptions given. Then sketch and label the graphs of $g(x)$ and $h(x)$ on the same coordinate plane.

1. The graph of $g(x)$ is the translation of the graph of $f(x)$ to the left 3 units.

   $g(x) = 2.5^{x+3}$

2. The graph of $h(x)$ is the translation of the graph of $f(x)$ up 2 units.

   $h(x) = 2.5^x + 2$

The graph of $f(x) = 3^x$ is shown. Write the function rules for $g(x)$ and $h(x)$ based on the descriptions given. Then sketch and label the graphs of $g(x)$ and $h(x)$ on the same coordinate plane.

3. The graph of $g(x)$ is the translation of the graph of $f(x)$ to the right 2 units and down 1 unit.

   $g(x) = 3^{x-2} - 1$

4. The graph of $h(x)$ is a vertical stretch of the graph of $f(x)$ by a factor of 2.5.

   $h(x) = 2.5(3)^x$

Given $f(x) = 2^x$, write the function rules for $g(x)$, $h(x)$, $j(x)$, and $k(x)$ based on the descriptions given. Then give the range of each function.

5. The graph of $g(x)$ is a vertical shrink of the graph of $f(x)$ by a factor of $\frac{1}{3}$ and a vertical translation 6 units up.

   $g(x) = \frac{1}{3}(2)^x + 6$; the range is all real numbers greater than 6.

6. The graph of $h(x)$ is a vertical stretch of the graph of $f(x)$ by a factor of 5 and a horizontal translation 4 units left.

   $h(x) = 5(2)^{x+4}$; the range is all real numbers greater than 0.

7. The graph of $j(x)$ is a vertical stretch of the graph of $f(x)$ by a factor of 1.2, a horizontal translation 2 units right, and a vertical translation 4 units down.

   $j(x) = 1.2(2)^{x-2} - 4$; the range is all real numbers greater than −4.

8. The graph of $k(x)$ is a vertical shrink of the graph of $f(x)$ by a factor of 0.1, a horizontal translation 1 unit left, and a vertical translation 3 units up.

   $k(x) = 0.1(2)^{x+1} + 3$; the range is all real numbers greater than 3

9. **Error Analysis** A student is told that the graph shown at right is a vertical translation of $f(x) = 1.5^x$ and determines that the equation of the function must be $f(x) = 1.5^x - 3$ because the y-intercept is −3. Explain and correct the error in the student's reasoning.

   The y-intercept of the parent function is (0, 1), not

   (0, 0), so the graph was translated 4 units down.

   The equation is $f(x) = 1.5^x - 4$.

Write an equation of the exponential function $g(x)$ whose graph is shown.

10.

   $g(x) = 2^x + 2$

11.

   $g(x) = 2(2)^x$

12.

   $g(x) = 3^x - 4$

13. Skyler invests $480 in an account that earns interest at a rate of 3.5% compounded annually. Write a function that gives the balance in the account after t years. Then find the balance after 10 years.

   $A(t) = 480(1.035)^t$; $677.09

14. You invest money in an account for which the interest is compounded annually. The account balance after t years is given by $A(t) = 850(1.024)^t$. What is the initial amount of your investment? What is the interest rate? What is the account balance after 5 years?

   $850; 2.4%; $957.01

15. The function $A(t) = 2100(1.04)^t$ gives the amount in Howard's account after t years if he sticks with his savings plan. Write the function that would give the amount if Howard keeps the same rate but instead invests one-third of the original amount. Tell how this change affects the graph of the function.

   The new function is $A(t) = \frac{1}{3} \cdot 2100(1.04)^t = 700(1.04)^t$; the graph is a

   vertical shrink of the original graph by a factor of $\frac{1}{3}$.

16. Five years ago, Tonya invested $400 in an account that earns interest at a rate of 3% compounded annually. Write a function $A(t)$ that gives the balance in the account t years from *now*. That is, the function value $A(-5)$ should give the initial amount in the account. Find $A(0)$ and describe what it represents.

   $A(t) = 400(1.03)^{t+5}$; $A(0) \approx $463.71 is the current balance of the account

Graphing $f(x) = ab^{x-h} + k$ when $0 < b < 1$

Essential question: *How does changing the values of a, h, and k affect the graph of an exponential decay function?*

COMMON CORE **Standards for Mathematical Content**

CC.9-12.A.CED.2 Create equations in two or more variables to represent relationships between quantities; graph equations on coordinate axes with labels and scales.*

CC.9-12.F.IF.2 Use function notation, evaluate functions for inputs in their domains ...

CC.9-12.F.IF.4 For a function that models a relationship between two quantities, interpret key features of graphs ... in terms of the quantities, and sketch graphs showing key features given a verbal description of the relationship.*

CC.9-12.F.IF.7 Graph functions expressed symbolically and show key features of the graph, ...*

CC.9-12.F.IF.7e Graph exponential ... functions, showing intercepts and end behavior, ...*

CC.9–12.F.BF.1 Write a function that describes a relationship between two quantities.*

CC.9–12.F.BF.1a Determine an explicit expression ... from a context.*

CC.9-12.F.BF.3 Identify the effect on the graph of replacing $f(x)$ by $f(x) + k$, $kf(x)$, ..., and $f(x + k)$ for specific values of k (both positive and negative); find the value of k given the graphs...

CC.9-12.F.LE.2 Construct ... exponential functions, ... given a graph, a description of a relationship, ...*

Also: CC.9-12.F.IF.9, CC.9-12.F.LE.5*

Prerequisites
Graphing basic exponential functions, Lesson 6–1
Transforming exponential growth functions, Lesson 6–2

Math Background
Transforming an exponential decay function is just like transforming an exponential growth function. Students will extend what they learned in the previous lesson to graph transformed exponential decay functions, write equations from graphs, and use the exponential decay formula.

INTRODUCE

Discuss how the value of a new car drops drastically the moment it is driven off the lot. Its value continues to fall, but the amount of decrease reduces over time, never reaching $0, as the car is never completely worthless. This is an example of exponential decay.

Ask students to suggest other examples of exponential decay. Some suggestions might be the value of electronics over time, the amount of a radioactive element in a sample, or the rebound height of a tennis ball after each bounce.

TEACH

1 EXAMPLE

Questioning Strategies
- Why do you know that the graphs of the parent functions will fall from left to right? **The graph of $f(x) = b^x$ falls from left to right when b is between 0 and 1. Both $\frac{1}{2}$ and $\frac{1}{3}$ are between 0 and 1.**
- What are the values of h and k in the parent functions? **Both h and k are 0 in the parent functions.**

EXTRA EXAMPLE

Graph the exponential decay function.

A. $g(x) = \left(\frac{1}{4}\right)^{x-4}$ **The graph of $g(x)$ is a translation 4 units to the right of the graph of $f(x) = \left(\frac{1}{4}\right)^x$.**

B. $g(x) = (0.2)^{x+1} - 3.5$ **The graph of $g(x)$ is a translation 1 unit to the left and 3.5 units down of the graph of $f(x) = (0.2)^x$.**

Differentiated Instruction
Draw the graph of a parent exponential decay function on a grid on a clear transparency sheet. On another clear transparency sheet, trace over the graph only. Move the second sheet over the first sheet to show translations. Visual learners may wish to make and use their own pair of transparency sheets to practice with.

Name_____ Class_____ Date_____

6-3

Graphing $f(x) = ab^{x-h} + k$ when $0 < b < 1$

COMMON CORE

CC.9-12.F.IF.2,
CC.9-12.F.IF.4*,
CC.9-12.F.IF.7*,
CC.9-12.F.IF.7e*,
CC.9-12.F.BF.3,
CC.9-12.F.LE.2*

Essential question: *How does changing the values of a, h, and k affect the graph of an exponential decay function?*

A general exponential decay function has the form $f(x) = ab^{x-h} + k$ where $0 < b < 1$ and a, h, and k are real numbers with $a > 0$. The effect of changing the parameters a, h, and k in an exponential decay function is the same as the effect of changing these parameters in an exponential growth function.

1 EXAMPLE Graphing $f(x) = b^{x-h} + k$

Graph each exponential decay function.

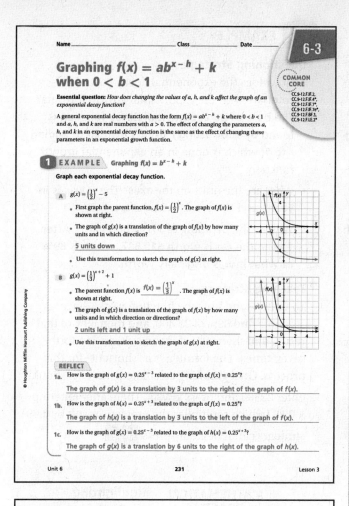

A $g(x) = \left(\frac{1}{2}\right)^x - 5$

- First graph the parent function, $f(x) = \left(\frac{1}{2}\right)^x$. The graph of $f(x)$ is shown at right.

- The graph of $g(x)$ is a translation of the graph of $f(x)$ by how many units and in which direction?

  5 units down

- Use this transformation to sketch the graph of $g(x)$ at right.

B $g(x) = \left(\frac{1}{3}\right)^{x+2} + 1$

- The parent function $f(x)$ is $\underline{f(x) = \left(\frac{1}{3}\right)^x}$. The graph of $f(x)$ is shown at right.

- The graph of $g(x)$ is a translation of the graph of $f(x)$ by how many units and in which direction or directions?

  2 units left and 1 unit up

- Use this transformation to sketch the graph of $g(x)$ at right.

REFLECT

1a. How is the graph of $g(x) = 0.25^{x-3}$ related to the graph of $f(x) = 0.25^x$?

The graph of $g(x)$ is a translation by 3 units to the right of the graph of $f(x)$.

1b. How is the graph of $h(x) = 0.25^{x+3}$ related to the graph of $f(x) = 0.25^x$?

The graph of $h(x)$ is a translation by 3 units to the left of the graph of $f(x)$.

1c. How is the graph of $g(x) = 0.25^{x-3}$ related to the graph of $h(x) = 0.25^{x+3}$?

The graph of $g(x)$ is a translation by 6 units to the right of the graph of $h(x)$.

Unit 6   231   Lesson 3

---

2 EXAMPLE Graphing $f(x) = ab^x$

Graph each exponential decay function.

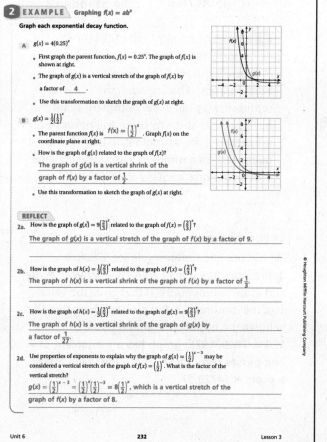

A $g(x) = 4(0.25)^x$

- First graph the parent function, $f(x) = 0.25^x$. The graph of $f(x)$ is shown at right.

- The graph of $g(x)$ is a vertical stretch of the graph of $f(x)$ by

  a factor of ___4___.

- Use this transformation to sketch the graph of $g(x)$ at right.

B $g(x) = \frac{1}{2}\left(\frac{1}{2}\right)^x$

- The parent function $f(x)$ is $\underline{f(x) = \left(\frac{1}{2}\right)^x}$. Graph $f(x)$ on the coordinate plane at right.

- How is the graph of $g(x)$ related to the graph of $f(x)$?

  The graph of $g(x)$ is a vertical shrink of the graph of $f(x)$ by a factor of $\frac{1}{2}$.

- Use this transformation to sketch the graph of $g(x)$ at right.

REFLECT

2a. How is the graph of $g(x) = 9\left(\frac{2}{3}\right)^x$ related to the graph of $f(x) = \left(\frac{2}{3}\right)^x$?

The graph of $g(x)$ is a vertical stretch of the graph of $f(x)$ by a factor of 9.

2b. How is the graph of $h(x) = \frac{1}{3}\left(\frac{2}{3}\right)^x$ related to the graph of $f(x) = \left(\frac{2}{3}\right)^x$?

The graph of $h(x)$ is a vertical shrink of the graph of $f(x)$ by a factor of $\frac{1}{3}$.

2c. How is the graph of $h(x) = \frac{1}{3}\left(\frac{2}{3}\right)^x$ related to the graph of $g(x) = 9\left(\frac{2}{3}\right)^x$?

The graph of $h(x)$ is a vertical shrink of the graph of $g(x)$ by a factor of $\frac{1}{27}$.

2d. Use properties of exponents to explain why the graph of $g(x) = \left(\frac{1}{2}\right)^{x-3}$ may be considered a vertical stretch of the graph of $f(x) = \left(\frac{1}{2}\right)^x$. What is the factor of the vertical stretch?

$g(x) = \left(\frac{1}{2}\right)^{x-3} = \left(\frac{1}{2}\right)^x\left(\frac{1}{2}\right)^{-3} = 8\left(\frac{1}{2}\right)^x$, which is a vertical stretch of the graph of $f(x)$ by a factor of 8.

Unit 6   232   Lesson 3

Questioning Strategies

- How do you use the graph of $f(x)$ to draw the graph of $g(x)$? **Find points on $f(x)$ that intersect the grid at integer coordinates. Then, multiply the y-coordinates by a to plot the corresponding points on $g(x)$.**

- What is the value of a in the parent functions? **The value of a is 1 in the parent functions.**

- In Reflect Question 2c, how can you use properties of exponents to explain how the graphs are related? **Write $\frac{1}{3}$ as 3^{-1} and 9 as 3^2. Then, 3^{-1} divided by 3^2 equals 3^{-1-2}, or 3^{-3}, or $\frac{1}{27}$.**

EXTRA EXAMPLE

Graph the exponential decay function.

A. $g(x) = 2\left(\frac{1}{3}\right)^x$ **The graph of $g(x)$ is a vertical stretch of the graph of $f(x) = \left(\frac{1}{3}\right)^x$ by a f actor of 2.**

B. $g(x) = 0.5(0.25)^x$ **The graph of $g(x)$ is a vertical shrink of the graph of $f(x) = (0.25)^x$ by a factor of 0.5.**

3 EXAMPLE

Questioning Strategies

- How do you know immediately that k will be negative? **because the asymptote is below the x-axis ($y = 0$)**

- Describe another way to find the value of b using the point $(-1, 5)$. **When you reverse the vertical translation you get $(-1, 6)$ and when you reverse the stretch by 2, you get $(-1, 3)$. The graph of every function in the form $f(x) = b^x$ $(0 < b < 1)$ includes the point $\left(-1, \frac{1}{b}\right)$, so $b = \frac{1}{3}$.**

EXTRA EXAMPLE

Write an equation of the exponential decay function whose graph is shown. $f(x) = 3\left(\frac{1}{2}\right)^x - 4$

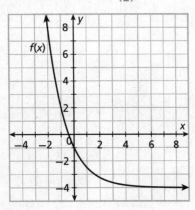

4 EXAMPLE

Questioning Strategies

- How does the exponential decay formula compare with the exponential growth formula? **The base of an exponential decay function is found by subtracting r from 1 instead of adding r to 1, which is done in an exponential growth function.**

- What are the units on the axes? **The x-axis is in years, and the y-axis is in dollars.**

- What is the meaning of $V(t)$ when $t = 1$? **After 1 year, the car is worth \$19,847, which is 89% of what it was originally worth.**

Teaching Strategy

To understand how the function works, have students find 89% of 22,300, and then 89% of that result, and then 89% of that result, and so forth, seven times. The formula is a "shortcut" for this process. On a graphing calculator, students should enter 22300 and press ENTER. Then, after entering $\times 0.89$ (which multiplies the previous result by 0.89), students can repeatedly press ENTER.

> MATHEMATICAL PRACTICE | Highlighting the Standards
>
> **4** EXAMPLE and its Reflect questions offer an opportunity to implement Mathematical Practice Standard 4 (Model with mathematics). Discuss what the y-intercept represents (initial value because 0 years have passed) and why there will never be an x-intercept (you cannot reach 0 by continually taking 89% of a number). Also, discuss why only a first-quadrant graph is needed.

EXTRA EXAMPLE

Harold bought a motorcycle for \$7800. It depreciates at a rate of about 8% per year. Write and graph a function $V(t)$ that gives the value V of the motorcycle after t years. Then, find the value of the motorcycle after 6 years.
$V(t) = 7800(0.92)^t$; graph has a y-intercept of 7800 and passes through $(1, 7176)$; the value after 6 years is \$4729.57.

As you saw in Lesson 6-2, the parameter h in the equation of an exponential decay function can be eliminated by using properties of exponents to combine it with the multiplicative constant a. When you are asked to find the equation of an exponential decay function, you can assume that the equation has the form $f(x) = ab^x + k$.

3 EXAMPLE — Writing an Equation from a Graph

Write an equation of the exponential decay function $g(x)$ whose graph is shown.

A Let $g(x) = ab^x + k$. First find the value of k.

Since the graph has the line $y = -1$ as a horizontal asymptote, there is a vertical translation of the parent function 1 unit down.

So, $k = \underline{-1}$.

B Find the value of a. The equation of $g(x)$ has the form $y = ab^x - 1$.

The graph passes through $(0, 1)$. Substitute these values in the equation.

$y = ab^x - 1$ Write the equation of $g(x)$.

$\boxed{1} = ab^{\boxed{0}} - 1$ Substitute 0 for x and 1 for y.

$\boxed{1} = \boxed{a} - 1$ Simplify.

$a = \boxed{2}$ Solve for a.

C Find the value of b.

Using the values of k and a from above, the equation of $g(x)$ has the form $y = 2b^x - 1$.

The graph passes through $(-1, 5)$. Substitute these values in the equation.

$y = 2b^x - 1$ Write the equation of $g(x)$.

$\boxed{5} = 2b^{\boxed{-1}} - 1$ Substitute -1 for x and 5 for y.

$\boxed{5} = \dfrac{\boxed{2}}{b} - 1$ Simplify.

$\boxed{6} = \dfrac{2}{b}$ Add 1 to both sides.

$b = \boxed{\dfrac{1}{3}}$ Solve for b.

D Write the equation.

Using the values of the parameters from above, $g(x) = \boxed{2\left(\dfrac{1}{3}\right)^x - 1}$.

REFLECT

3a. What is the parent function of $g(x)$? How is the graph of $g(x)$ related to the graph of its parent function?

The parent function is $f(x) = \left(\dfrac{1}{3}\right)^x$. The graph of $f(x)$ is stretched vertically

by a factor 2 and translated down 1 unit to give the graph of $g(x)$.

3b. How can you check that you wrote a correct equation for $g(x)$?

Graph the equation to check that it matches the given graph.

Exponential decay occurs when a quantity decreases by the same fixed percent over equal periods of time. You can model such decay using the following formula.

> **The Exponential Decay Formula**
>
> The function $A(t) = a(1 - r)^t$ gives the amount $A(t)$ of a quantity after t time periods when the quantity is decaying exponentially and the initial amount of the quantity is a. The constant r, which is the fixed percent by which the quantity decreases each time period, is called the *decay rate* and is written in decimal form. The expression $1 - r$ is called the *decay factor*.

4 EXAMPLE — Writing an Exponential Decay Function

A car sells for $22,300 and is known to depreciate at a rate of approximately 11% per year. Write and graph a function $V(t)$ that gives the value V of the car after t years. Then find the value of the car after 7 years.

A Write an exponential decay function.

The initial amount a is $\underline{22,300}$.

The decay rate r is $\underline{0.11}$ and the decay factor is $1 - r$, or $\underline{0.89}$.

The value V after t years is given by $V(t) = a(1 - r)^t$.

So, $V(t) = \underline{22,300(0.89)^t}$.

B Graph the function. Sketch the graph on the coordinate plane at right.

C Find the value after 7 years.

$V(7) = \boxed{22,300}\left(\boxed{0.89}\right)^{\boxed{7}}$ Substitute 7 for t.

$\approx \boxed{9863.59}$ Use a calculator. Round to the nearest hundredth.

So, the value of the car after 7 years is $\underline{\$9863.59}$.

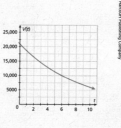

© Houghton Mifflin Harcourt Publishing Company

Essential Question

How does changing the values of a, h, and k affect the graph of an exponential decay function?
Changing *a* stretches or shrinks the graph.
Changing *h* translates the graph right or left.
Changing *k* translates the graph up or down.

Summarize

In their journals, have students write the rule for, and sketch the graph of, any parent exponential decay function. Then, have them write and show how the rule and graph change first when $h = 2$, then when $a = 2$, and finally when $k = 2$, such that each change is added to the previous change.

Where skills are taught	Where skills are practiced
1 EXAMPLE	EXS. 1, 2
2 EXAMPLE	EXS. 3, 4
3 EXAMPLE	EXS. 9–11
4 EXAMPLE	EXS. 12, 13

Exercise 5: Students study the rule of a transformed function and use what they know about changing certain parameters to determine the *y*-intercept and equation of the asymptote without graphing the equation.

Exercises 6–8: Students write function rules when given the parent function and a description of a transformation or set of transformations.

Exercise 14: Students work with a binary search model, which has the form of an exponential decay function. To answer part (b), students can graph the equation, continually take one-half (or 50%) of 8564, or use a guess-and-check approach after making a reasonable first guess. Discuss why the value of *a* must be a whole number.

4a. How can you use your graph to find the approximate number of years it takes for the car to have a value of $12,500?

Find the value of t corresponding to the point where the graph crosses the

line $V = 12,500$; this value of t is approximately 5 years.

4b. A different car sells for $22,300 but depreciates at a rate of 9% per year. How would the graph for that exponential decay function compare to the one you graphed in the example?

It would have the same y-intercept, but the graph would fall more slowly

as t increases without bound.

PRACTICE

Graph each exponential decay function.

1. $f(x) = \left(\frac{1}{4}\right)^x + 1$

2. $f(x) = 0.5^{x-2} - 1$

3. $f(x) = 3\left(\frac{1}{3}\right)^x$

4. $f(x) = 2(0.5)^{x+1}$

5. Without graphing, give the y-intercept and the horizontal asymptote of the graph of $f(x) = 7(0.2)^x - 4$.

The y-intercept is 3; the horizontal asymptote is $y = -4$.

Write the equation of $g(x)$ given that $g(x)$ is a transformation of the graph of $f(x) = 0.6^x$ as described.

6. A translation 2 units right and 1 unit up $g(x) = 0.6^{x-2} + 1$

7. A vertical stretch by a factor of 3.5 $g(x) = 3.5(0.6)^x$

8. A vertical shrink by a factor of 0.1 and a translation 5 units left $g(x) = 0.1(0.6)^{x+5}$

Write an equation of the exponential function $g(x)$ whose graph is shown.

9.

$g(x) = \left(\frac{1}{3}\right)^x + 2$

10.

$g(x) = 2\left(\frac{1}{2}\right)^x$

11.

$g(x) = \left(\frac{1}{4}\right)^x - 4$

12. A computer costs $1240 when it is new and is known to depreciate at a rate of approximately 22% per year. Write a function $V(t)$ that gives the value V of the computer after t years. Then find the value of the computer after 3 years.

$V(t) = 1240(0.78)^t$; $588.44

13. The value V of a laser printer after t years is given by $V(t) = 371(0.82)^t$. What is the cost of the printer when it is new? At what annual rate does the value of the printer depreciate?

$371; 18% per year

14. If you are asked to guess an integer between 0 and 100, and you are given the clues *higher* or *lower* after each guess, it is best to start by guessing 50. Then you should choose the middle number in the correct remaining half of the integers. This process is known as a binary search. The number of items I left to be searched after a attempts to locate the correct item in an ordered list that initially has I_0 items is given by $I = I_0\left(\frac{1}{2}\right)^a$.

a. Write a function that gives the number of items left to be searched after a attempts in a binary search of an ordered list with 8564 items.

$I(a) = 8564\left(\frac{1}{2}\right)^a$

b. How many attempts are needed so that the number of items remaining is less than 50? (*Hint:* Use your graphing calculator.)   8

Changing the Base of an Exponential Function

Essential question: *How does the value of c in $f(x) = b^{cx}$ affect the graph of f(x)?*

© Houghton Mifflin Harcourt Publishing Company

COMMON CORE Standards for Mathematical Content

CC.9-12.A.SSE.3 Choose and produce an equivalent form of an expression to reveal and explain properties of the quantity represented by the expression.

CC.9-12.A.SSE.3c Use the properties of exponents to transform expressions for exponential functions.

CC.9-12.A.CED.2 Create equations in two or more variables to represent relationships between quantities; graph equations on coordinate axes with labels and scales.*

CC.9-12.F.IF.2 Use function notation, evaluate functions for inputs in their domains, and interpret statements that use function notation in terms of a context.

CC.9-12.F.IF.7 Graph functions expressed symbolically and show key features of the graph... .*

CC.9-12.F.IF.7e Graph exponential ... functions, showing intercepts and end behavior, ...*

CC.9-12.F.IF.8 Write a function defined by an expression in different but equivalent forms to reveal and explain different properties of the function.

CC.9-12.F.IF.8b Use properties of exponents to interpret expressions for exponential functions.

CC.9-12.F.BF.1 Write a function that describes a relationship between two quantities.*

CC.9-12.F.BF.1a Determine an explicit expression ... from a context.*

CC.9-12.F.BF.3 Identify the effect on the graph of replacing $f(x)$ by ... $f(kx)$ ... for specific values of k (both positive and negative); find the value of k given the graphs. Experiment with cases and illustrate an explanation of the effects on the graph using technology.

CC.9-12.F.LE.2 Construct ... exponential functions, ... given ... a description of a relationship, ...*

CC.9-12.F.LE.5 Interpret the parameters in a ... exponential function in terms of a context.*

Prerequisites

Graphing basic exponential functions, Lesson 6–1

Transforming exponential growth and decay functions, Lessons 6–2 and 6–3

Math Background

The graphs of exponential functions can be horizontally stretched and shrunk by multiplying the independent variable by a nonzero constant. Students will draw graphs by hand to better understand why values of the constant that are greater than 1 shrink the graphs toward the *y*-axis, while values between 0 and 1 stretch them away from the *y*-axis.

Students will work with properties of exponents to see different but equivalent ways of writing the same function rule.

INTRODUCE

Use these examples to review properties of exponents.

$$(2^3)^2 = 2^{3(2)} = 2^6$$

$$5^{-2} = \frac{1}{5^2} = \frac{1}{25}$$

$$(3.5^6)^{\frac{1}{6}x} = 3.5^{6 \cdot \frac{1}{6}x} = 3.5^x$$

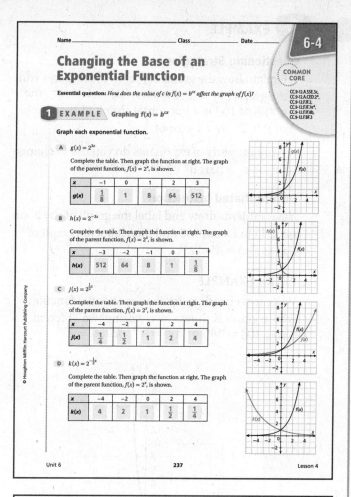

Name_____ Class_____ Date_____

6-4

Changing the Base of an Exponential Function

COMMON CORE

CC-9-12.A.SSE.3c,
CC-9-12.A.CED.2*,
CC-9-12.F.IF.2,
CC-9-12.F.IF.7e*,
CC-9-12.F.IF.8b,
CC-9-12.F.BF.3

Essential question: *How does the value of c in f(x) = b^{cx} affect the graph of f(x)?*

1 EXAMPLE Graphing $f(x) = b^{cx}$

Graph each exponential function.

A $g(x) = 2^{3x}$

Complete the table. Then graph the function at right. The graph of the parent function, $f(x) = 2^x$, is shown.

x	−1	0	1	2	3
g(x)	$\frac{1}{8}$	1	8	64	512

B $h(x) = 2^{-3x}$

Complete the table. Then graph the function at right. The graph of the parent function, $f(x) = 2^x$, is shown.

x	−3	−2	−1	0	1
h(x)	512	64	8	1	$\frac{1}{8}$

C $j(x) = 2^{\frac{1}{2}x}$

Complete the table. Then graph the function at right. The graph of the parent function, $f(x) = 2^x$, is shown.

x	−4	−2	0	2	4
j(x)	$\frac{1}{4}$	$\frac{1}{2}$	1	2	4

D $k(x) = 2^{-\frac{1}{2}x}$

Complete the table. Then graph the function at right. The graph of the parent function, $f(x) = 2^x$, is shown.

x	−4	−2	0	2	4
k(x)	4	2	1	$\frac{1}{2}$	$\frac{1}{4}$

Unit 6 237 Lesson 4

© Houghton Mifflin Harcourt Publishing Company

REFLECT

1a. Look at your graphs to make a conjecture: When c > 0, how is the graph of $g(x) = b^{cx}$ related to the graph of the parent function $f(x) = b^x$?

The graph of g(x) is a horizontal stretch or shrink of the graph of f(x) by a

factor of $\frac{1}{c}$.

1b. When c < 0, how is the graph of $g(x) = b^{cx}$ related to the graph of the parent function $f(x) = b^x$?

The graph of g(x) is a horizontal stretch or shrink of the graph of f(x) by a

factor of $\frac{1}{|c|}$ followed by a reflection in the y-axis.

2 EXPLORE Comparing Graphs

Use your graphing calculator for this activity.

A For each row of the first table, enter one function as Y_1 and enter the other function as Y_2. Graph both functions in the same viewing window and note your results. Do this for all three pairs of functions in the table.

What do you notice about the graphs for each pair?

The graphs are the same.

Y_1	Y_2
$f(x) = 2^{3x}$	$g(x) = 8^x$
$f(x) = 3^{2x}$	$g(x) = 9^x$
$f(x) = \left(\frac{1}{2}\right)^{2x}$	$g(x) = \left(\frac{1}{4}\right)^x$

B Repeat the process for the functions in the second table. What do you notice about the graphs for each pair?

The graphs are reflections of each other across

the y-axis.

Y_1	Y_2
$f(x) = 3^x$	$g(x) = \left(\frac{1}{3}\right)^x$
$f(x) = \left(\frac{1}{5}\right)^x$	$g(x) = 5^x$
$f(x) = \left(\frac{3}{2}\right)^x$	$g(x) = \left(\frac{2}{3}\right)^x$

REFLECT

2a. How can you use properties of exponents to explain your observation in step A?

By the power of a power property, $b^{cx} = (b^c)^x$, so $f(x) = b^{cx}$ has the same

graph as $g(x) = (b^c)^x$.

2b. How can you use properties of exponents to explain your observation in step B? (*Hint:* Use the fact that $\frac{1}{b} = b^{-1}$.)

By the power of a power property, $\left(\frac{1}{b}\right)^x = (b^{-1})^x = b^{-x}$, so $f(x) = b^x$ and

$g(x) = \left(\frac{1}{b}\right)^x = b^{-x}$ are reflections of each other across the y-axis.

2c. For what value of b are the graphs of $f(x) = b^x$ and $g(x) = 3^{-2x}$ the same? Explain.

$\frac{1}{9}$ because $3^{-2x} = (3^{-2})^x = \left(\frac{1}{9}\right)^x$

Unit 6 238 Lesson 4

© Houghton Mifflin Harcourt Publishing Company

1 EXAMPLE

Questioning Strategies

- Why does the graph shrink horizontally when $|c| > 1$ and stretch horizontally when $0 < |c| < 1$? If $|c| > 1$, the absolute value of the exponent increases, so inputs closer to 0 produce the same outputs as the parent function. If $0 < |c| < 1$, the absolute value of the exponent decreases, so inputs farther from 0 produce the same outputs as the parent function.

- In part A, how can you show that the graph shrinks by a factor of $\frac{1}{3}$ horizontally? For $y = 8$, $x = 3$ for $f(x)$ and $x = 1$ for $g(x)$.

- In part C, how can you show the graph is stretched by a factor of 2 horizontally? For $y = 4$, $x = 2$ for $f(x)$ and $x = 4$ for $j(x)$.

EXTRA EXAMPLE

Graph the exponential function.

A. $g(x) = 2^{2x}$ It is the graph of $f(x) = 2^x$ shrunk horizontally by a factor of $\frac{1}{2}$.

B. $h(x) = 2^{-2x}$ It is the graph of $f(x) = 2^x$ shrunk horizontally by a factor of $\frac{1}{2}$ and then reflected across the y-axis.

C. $j(x) = 2^{\frac{1}{4}x}$ It is the graph of $f(x) = 2^x$ stretched horizontally by a factor of 4.

D. $k(x) = 2^{-\frac{1}{4}x}$ It is the graph of $f(x) = 2^x$ stretched horizontally by a factor of 4 and then reflected across the y-axis.

2 EXPLORE

Materials

graphing calculator

Questioning Strategies

- In part A, how should you enter the function rule 2^{3x} on your calculator? Why? Enter the rule as $2^{(3x)}$ to indicate that the product of 3 and x is the exponent. Otherwise you graph the line $y = 8x$.

- In part B, how can you confirm on your calculator that the graph pairs are reflections across the y-axis? Examine a table of values to see that $f(x) = g(-x)$ for any x.

Technology

When graphing the functions in part A, have students use a thicker curve for the graph of $g(x)$ to see that its graph coincides with the graph of $f(x)$.

Questioning Strategies

- Explain how the graph of $f(x) = 4^x$ compares with the graph of $y = 2^x$. Because $f(x) = 4^x = 2^{2x}$, the graph of $f(x)$ is a horizontal shrink of the graph of $y = 2^x$ by a factor of $\frac{1}{2}$.

- What property of exponents do you use to change the base in part B? power of a power

Differentiated Instruction

Have students draw and label the graph of $y = 2^x$ on the grid in Example 3 and then label the graph of $f(x)$ as $f(x) = 4^x = 2^{2x}$.

EXTRA EXAMPLE

Write two equations for the exponential function whose graph is shown by choosing two different bases. $f(x) = 16^x$, or $f(x) = 4^{2x}$, or $f(x) = 2^{4x}$

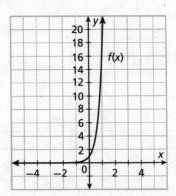

You have seen that $f(x) = b^{cx}$ has the same graph as $g(x) = (b^c)^x$ because $b^{cx} = (b^c)^x$. You can use this idea to change the base of an exponential function.

3 EXAMPLE Changing Bases

Write two equations for the exponential function whose graph is shown by choosing two different bases.

A Write an equation for $f(x)$.

The horizontal asymptote is the x-axis, so there is no vertical translation of the parent function. The function rule may be written in the form $f(x) = ab^x$.

The graph passes through (0, 1), so $a = \underline{\quad 1 \quad}$.

The graph passes through (1, 4), so $b = \underline{\quad 4 \quad}$.

So, an equation for the function is $\underline{\quad f(x) = 4^x \quad}$.

B Change the base.

$f(x) = \underline{\quad 4^x \quad}$ Write the equation from step A.

$\quad = \underline{\quad (2^2)^x \quad}$ Write the base of the function as a power.

$\quad = \underline{\quad 2^{2x} \quad}$ Use the fact that $(b^c)^x = b^{cx}$.

So, another equation for the function is $\underline{\quad f(x) = 2^{2x} \quad}$.

REFLECT

3a. Show how to write the exponential function with a base of $\frac{1}{4}$.

$\underline{f(x) = 4^x = (4^{-1})^{-x} = \left(\frac{1}{4}\right)^{-x}}$

When an initial amount P (called the *principal*) is invested in an account that earns interest compounded annually at a rate r (a fixed percent), the amount $A(t)$ in the account after t years is given by the function $A(t) = P(1 + r)^t$. If the interest is compounded n times per year at an annual rate r, called the *nominal rate*, then the interest earned each compounding period is $\frac{r}{n}$, and the amount in the account is

$$A(t) = P\left(1 + \frac{r}{n}\right)^{nt}.$$

You can think of this as an exponential growth function $f(t) = ab^t$ where $a = P$ and $b = \left(1 + \frac{r}{n}\right)^n$. If you subtract 1 from the base, you get the growth rate R, which is also called the *effective rate*: $R = \left(1 + \frac{r}{n}\right)^n - 1$.

The effective rate is the rate of interest earned in 1 year as a result of compounding interest n times during the year at a rate $\frac{r}{n}$. So, another way you can write the function $A(t) = P\left(1 + \frac{r}{n}\right)^{nt}$ is $A(t) = P(1 + R)^t$. The effective rate is useful for comparing accounts that have different nominal rates and different compounding periods.

4 EXAMPLE Comparing Interest Rates

Arturo plans to deposit $850 in one of the accounts shown in the table. He chooses the account with the greater effective rate. How much money will he have in his account after 5 years?

	Account X	Account Y
Nominal interest rate	2.5%	2.48%
Compounding period	Quarterly	Monthly

A Compare the accounts' effective rates.

For Account X, interest is compounded quarterly, so $n = \underline{\quad 4 \quad}$.

The nominal interest rate is 2.5%, so $r = \underline{\quad 0.025 \quad}$.

$R_X = \left(1 + \frac{r}{n}\right)^n - 1$ Use the formula for the effective rate.

$\quad = \left(1 + \dfrac{0.025}{4}\right)^4 - 1$ Substitute the values of r and n from above.

$\quad \approx \underline{\quad 0.02524 \quad}$ Use a calculator. Round to 5 decimal places.

For Account Y, interest is compounded monthly, so $n = \underline{\quad 12 \quad}$.

The nominal interest rate is 2.48%, so $r = \underline{\quad 0.0248 \quad}$.

$R_Y = \left(1 + \frac{r}{n}\right)^n - 1$ Use the formula for the effective rate.

$\quad = \left(1 + \dfrac{0.0248}{12}\right)^{12} - 1$ Substitute the values of r and n from above.

$\quad \approx \underline{\quad 0.02508 \quad}$ Use a calculator. Round to 5 decimal places.

So, Account $\underline{\quad X \quad}$ has a greater effective rate.

B Find the amount in Arturo's account after 5 years.

$A(t) = P\left(1 + \frac{r}{n}\right)^{nt}$ Use the formula for interest compounded n times per year.

$A(5) = 850\left(1 + \dfrac{0.025}{4}\right)^{4 \cdot 5}$ Substitute 850 for P and 5 for t. Use the values of r and n for the account with the greater effective rate.

$\quad \approx \underline{\quad 962.80 \quad}$ Use a calculator. Round to the nearest hundredth.

So, Arturo will have $\underline{\quad \$962.80 \quad}$ in his account after 5 years.

REFLECT

4a. How can you use the effective rate to find the amount in Arturo's account?

$\underline{\text{Use the formula } A(t) = P(1 + R)^t \text{ with the value of } R \text{ calculated}}$

$\underline{\text{above } (R \approx 0.02524) \text{ and } t = 5.}$

© Houghton Mifflin Harcourt Publishing Company

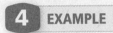

Questioning Strategies

- Which account has a bigger difference between its stated interest rate and its effective rate? Account Y, because $2.508 - 2.48 = 0.28$, and for Account X, $2.524 - 2.5 = 0.24$.

- How would you find R if the compounding period were weekly? daily? Use $n = 52$ and $n = 365$, respectively.

MATHEMATICAL PRACTICE **Highlighting the Standards**

4 EXAMPLE and its Reflect questions offer an opportunity to implement Mathematical Practice Standard 6 (Attend to precision). Have students use their calculators to find the amount in Arturo's account after 5 years in Reflect Question 4a with R_X rounded to 2, 3, 4, and 5 decimal places and compare their answers. Then, have students find and compare the amounts again leaving all the digits in their calculators for the value of R_X.

EXTRA EXAMPLE

Maxwell plans to deposit $1300 in one of the accounts shown below.

Account X: interest rate 1.735% compounded semi-annually

Account Y: interest rate 1.73% compounded monthly

He chooses the account with the greater effective rate. How much money will he have in his account after 11 years? $1572.28

CLOSE

Essential Question

How does the value of c in $f(x) = b^{cx}$ affect the graph of $f(x)$?
The value of c causes the graph to shrink horizontally ($|c| > 1$) or stretch horizontally ($0 < |c| < 1$) by a factor of $\frac{1}{|c|}$. If c is negative, it also causes a reflection in the y-axis.

Summarize

Write $f(x) = 64^x$ on the board. Have students give equivalent forms of the function with bases of 2, 4, and 8 and explain how the graph of each compares with the graph of its corresponding parent function $y = 2^x$, $y = 4^x$, or $y = 8^x$. $f(x) = 2^{6x}$ (horizontal shrink by a factor of $\frac{1}{6}$); $f(x) = 4^{3x}$ (horizontal shrink by a factor of $\frac{1}{3}$); $f(x) = 8^{2x}$ (horizontal shrink by a factor of $\frac{1}{2}$)

PRACTICE

Where skills are taught	Where skills are practiced
1 EXAMPLE	EXS. 1–4
3 EXAMPLE	EXS. 9–11
4 EXAMPLE	EX. 12

Exercises 5, 6: Students write function rules when given the parent function and a description of a horizontal stretch or shrink.

Exercises 7, 8: Students write function rules when given the parent function and a description of a set of transformations that combine horizontal stretches or shrinks with other types of transformations.

Exercises 13, 14: Students determine whether the value of c has an impact on the range and end behavior of a function.

Exercise 15: Students rewrite an exponential function involving an annual interest rate into one involving a monthly interest rate using two different methods.

PRACTICE

Graph each exponential function.

1. $f(x) = 3^{2x}$

2. $f(x) = 3^{-2x}$

3. $f(x) = 4^{\frac{1}{2}x}$

4. $f(x) = 4^{-\frac{1}{2}x}$

The graph of $f(x) = 3^x$ is shown. Write the function rules for $g(x)$ and $h(x)$ based on the descriptions given. Then sketch the graphs of $g(x)$ and $h(x)$ on the same coordinate plane.

5. The graph of $g(x)$ is a horizontal stretch of the graph of $f(x)$ by a factor of 4.

$g(x) = 3^{\frac{1}{4}x}$

6. The graph of $h(x)$ is a horizontal shrink of the graph of $f(x)$ by a factor of $\frac{1}{4}$.

$h(x) = 3^{4x}$

Write the equation for each transformation of the graph of $f(x) = \left(\frac{1}{2}\right)^x$.

7. The graph of $g(x)$ is a horizontal shrink of the graph of $f(x)$ by a factor of $\frac{1}{2}$ and a translation up by 4 units. $g(x) = \left(\frac{1}{2}\right)^{2x} + 4$

8. The graph of $h(x)$ is a horizontal stretch of the graph of $f(x)$ by a factor of 1.2, a vertical stretch by a factor of 3, and a translation 8 units down. $h(x) = 3\left(\frac{1}{2}\right)^{\frac{5}{6}x} - 8$

Write two equations for the exponential function whose graph is shown by choosing two different bases.

9.

$f(x) = 8^x$

$f(x) = 2^{3x}$

10.

$f(x) = 9^x$

$f(x) = 3^{2x}$

11.

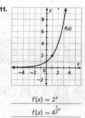

$f(x) = 2^x$

$f(x) = 4^{\frac{1}{2}x}$

12. Leah plans to deposit $625 in one of the accounts shown in the table. She chooses the account with the greater effective rate. In which account will she invest? How much money will she have in her account after 4 years?

Account A; $683.41

	Account A	Account B
Nominal interest rate	2.24%	2.23%
Compounding period	Quarterly	Daily

13. Provided $c \neq 0$, can changing the value of c in $f(x) = b^{cx}$ affect the range of the function? Explain.

No; a change in c results in a horizontal stretch or shrink of the graph of $f(x)$ and, if c changes from positive to negative (or vice versa), a reflection in the y-axis, but the range remains the set of all positive real numbers.

14. Provided $c \neq 0$, can changing the value of c in $f(x) = b^{cx}$ affect the end behavior of the function? Explain.

Yes; a change in c from positive to negative (or vice versa) results in a reflection in the y-axis, which changes the end behavior.

15. Tyrell makes an investment that earns an annual interest rate of 8%. He wants to know the approximate equivalent monthly interest rate.

a. One way to find the equivalent monthly interest rate is to recognize that in this situation the effective rate R is 8% and the number n of compounding periods is 12. Use the formula $R = \left(1 + \frac{r}{n}\right)^n - 1$ to solve for $\frac{r}{n}$.

$0.08 = \left(1 + \frac{r}{12}\right)^{12} - 1; 1.08 = \left(1 + \frac{r}{12}\right)^{12}; 1.08^{\frac{1}{12}} = 1 + \frac{r}{12}, \frac{r}{12} = 1.08^{\frac{1}{12}} - 1 \approx 0.0064$, so $\frac{r}{12} \approx 0.64\%$

b. Another way to find the equivalent monthly interest rate is to rewrite the function $A(t) = (1.08)^t$ so that the exponent is $12t$. What must you do to the base to compensate for making the exponent $12t$? Carry out the rewriting of $A(t) = (1.08)^t$ to find the equivalent monthly interest rate.

Raise the base to the power of $\frac{1}{12}$; $A(t) = P(1.08)^t = P(1.08^{\frac{1}{12}})^{12t} \approx P(1.0064)^{12t}$, so the equivalent monthly interest rate is about 0.64%.

The Base *e*

Essential question: *How does the graph of $f(x) = e^x$ compare to graphs of exponential functions with other bases?*

COMMON **Standards for**
CORE **Mathematical Content**

CC.9-12.A.CED.2 Create equations in two or more variables to represent relationships between quantities; graph equations on coordinate axes with labels and scales.*

CC.9-12.F.IF.2 Use function notation, evaluate functions for inputs in their domains, ...

CC.9-12.F.IF.7 Graph functions expressed symbolically and show key features of the graph, by hand in simple cases ...*

CC.9-12.F.IF.7e Graph exponential ... functions, showing intercepts and end behavior, ...*

CC.9-12.F.BF.3 Identify the effect on the graph of replacing $f(x)$ by $f(x) + k$, $kf(x)$, $f(kx)$, and $f(x + k)$ for specific values of k (both positive and negative) ...

CC.9-12.F.LE.2 Construct ... exponential functions, ... given ... a description of a relationship, ...*

CC.9-12.F.LE.5 Interpret the parameters in a ... exponential function in terms of a context.*

Also: CC.9-12.A.SSE.3, CC.9-12.A.SSE.3c, CC.9-12.F.IF.4*, CC.9-12.F.IF.8, CC.9-12.F.IF.8b

Vocabulary

e

Prerequisites

Graphing basic exponential functions, Lesson 6–1
Transforming exponential growth functions, Lessons 6-2 and 6-4

Math Background

Like π, e is an irrational number, so its decimal form never repeats and never terminates. Its value is approximately 2.718. The function $f(x) = e^x$ is special in mathematics because it is the only exponential function $f(x) = b^x$ whose derivative is equal to itself. For that reason, e is sometimes called the *natural base*.

INTRODUCE

Have students find the values of $\frac{1}{x}$ for $x = 1, 10, 100,$ and 1000. Then, have them find the values of $1 + \frac{1}{x}$ for the same values. Ask them to describe what happens as x becomes greater.

TEACH

1 **EXPLORE**

Materials

graphing calculator

Questioning Strategies

- How do you enter the expression in part A into a graphing calculator? Enter (1 + 1/X)^X.

- Will the value of $1 + \frac{1}{x}$ ever reach 1 as x increases without bound? Why or why not? No; $\frac{1}{x}$ is always positive, so you are always adding a positive value to 1 no matter how great x becomes.

Name_____ Class_____ Date_____

The Base *e*

Essential question: *How does the graph of* $f(x) = e^x$ *compare to graphs of exponential functions with other bases?*

COMMON CORE
CC9-12.A.CED.2*,
CC9-12.F.IF.2,
CC9-12.F.IF.7e*,
CC9-12.F.IF.8b,
CC9-12.F.BF.3,
CC9-12.F.LE.2*,
CC9-12.F.LE.5*

1 EXPLORE Investigating $\left(1 + \frac{1}{x}\right)^x$

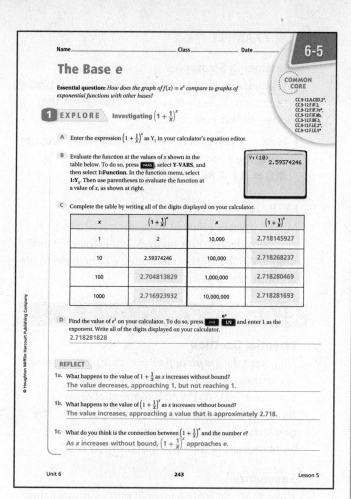

A Enter the expression $\left(1 + \frac{1}{x}\right)^x$ as Y_1 in your calculator's equation editor.

B Evaluate the function at the values of *x* shown in the table below. To do so, press [VARS], select **Y-VARS**, and then select **1:Function**. In the function menu, select **1:Y₁**. Then use parentheses to evaluate the function at a value of *x*, as shown at right.

Y₁(10)
          2.59374246

C Complete the table by writing all of the digits displayed on your calculator.

x	$\left(1 + \frac{1}{x}\right)^x$	*x*	$\left(1 + \frac{1}{x}\right)^x$
1	2	10,000	2.718145927
10	2.59374246	100,000	2.718268237
100	2.704813829	1,000,000	2.718280469
1000	2.716923932	10,000,000	2.718281693

D Find the value of e^1 on your calculator. To do so, press [2nd] [LN] e^x and enter 1 as the exponent. Write all of the digits displayed on your calculator.
2.718281828

REFLECT

1a. What happens to the value of $1 + \frac{1}{x}$ as *x* increases without bound?
The value decreases, approaching 1, but not reaching 1.

1b. What happens to the value of $\left(1 + \frac{1}{x}\right)^x$ as *x* increases without bound?
The value increases, approaching a value that is approximately 2.718.

1c. What do you think is the connection between $\left(1 + \frac{1}{x}\right)^x$ and the number *e*?
As *x* increases without bound, $\left(1 + \frac{1}{x}\right)^x$ approaches *e*.

Unit 6   243   Lesson 5

---

2 ENGAGE Introducing the Base *e*

The number *e* is defined as the value that the expression $\left(1 + \frac{1}{x}\right)^x$ approaches as *x* increases without bound. As you saw in the Explore, the decimal form of *e* is approximately 2.718281828. Despite the appearance of a pattern in the decimal digits, *e* is an irrational number whose actual decimal value neither repeats nor terminates. Like any other positive real number, *e* can be used as the base of an exponential function.

The graph of $f(x) = e^x$ is shown.

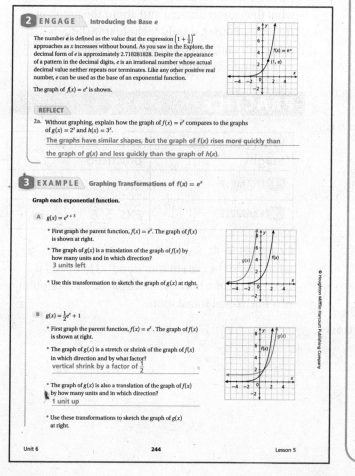

REFLECT

2a. Without graphing, explain how the graph of $f(x) = e^x$ compares to the graphs of $g(x) = 2^x$ and $h(x) = 3^x$.
The graphs have similar shapes, but the graph of $f(x)$ rises more quickly than the graph of $g(x)$ and less quickly than the graph of $h(x)$.

3 EXAMPLE Graphing Transformations of $f(x) = e^x$

Graph each exponential function.

A $g(x) = e^{x+3}$

* First graph the parent function, $f(x) = e^x$. The graph of $f(x)$ is shown at right.
* The graph of $g(x)$ is a translation of the graph of $f(x)$ by how many units and in which direction?
  3 units left
* Use this transformation to sketch the graph of $g(x)$ at right.

B $g(x) = \frac{1}{2}e^x + 1$

* First graph the parent function, $f(x) = e^x$. The graph of $f(x)$ is shown at right.
* The graph of $g(x)$ is a stretch or shrink of the graph of $f(x)$ in which direction and by what factor?
  vertical shrink by a factor of $\frac{1}{2}$
* The graph of $g(x)$ is also a translation of the graph of $f(x)$ by how many units and in which direction?
  1 unit up
* Use these transformations to sketch the graph of $g(x)$ at right.

Unit 6   244   Lesson 5

Questioning Strategies

- What is $f(0)$? What does this tell you about the graph of $f(x) = e^x$? **1; the graph passes through the point (0, 1).**

- Does the graph of $f(x) = e^x$ ever intersect the x-axis? Why or why not? **Not; there is no value of x for which $e^x = 0$. As x decreases without bound, e^x approaches but never reaches 0.**

> **MATHEMATICAL PRACTICE**   **Highlighting the Standards**
>
> Reflect Question 2a offers an opportunity to implement Mathematical Practice Standard 7 (Look for and make use of structure). Students must recognize that graphs of exponential growth functions rise faster as the base increases and that $2 < e < 3$.

Avoid Common Errors

Students are used to letters representing variables and may get confused when working with e. Remind them that, like π, e is a constant representing an irrational number.

Questioning Strategies

- In part A, how do you know that the graph of $g(x)$ will be a translation of the graph of $f(x)$ to the left? **The expression $x + 3$ equals $x - (-3)$, so h is negative.**

- In part B, how do you know that the shrink is vertical and not horizontal? **$f(x)$, and not x, is being multiplied by the constant.**

EXTRA EXAMPLE

Graph the exponential function.

A. $g(x) = e^x - 4$ **It is the graph of $f(x) = e^x$ translated 4 units down.**

B. $g(x) = e^{-\frac{1}{2}x}$ **It is the graph of $f(x) = e^x$ stretched horizontally by a factor of 2 and reflected across the y-axis.**

Questioning Strategies

- When using the formula $A = Pe^{rt}$, does r represent the rate or the effective rate? **r represents the rate—in this case, 0.025.**

- How can you find the amount in Keiko's account using the effective rate? **Substitute it for R in $A(t) = P(1 + R)^t$.**

EXTRA EXAMPLE

Miguel invests $4800 at 1.9% annual interest compounded continuously. What is the effective rate? **1.918%** How much money will he have in his account after 3 years? **$5081.55**

CLOSE

Essential Question

How does the graph of $f(x) = e^x$ compare to graphs of exponential functions with other bases? **Because $e > 1$, $f(x)$ is an exponential growth function, so its graph rises from left to right. The graph rises more quickly than the graph of $f(x) = 2^x$ and less quickly than the graph of $f(x) = 3^x$.**

Summarize

Have students write a journal entry summarizing what they know about e and about the graph of $f(x) = e^x$. Entries should include translations of the graph and how e is used to find interest compounded continuously.

PRACTICE

Where skills are taught	Where skills are practiced
3 EXAMPLE	EXS. 1, 2
4 EXAMPLE	EXS. 5, 6

Exercises 3–4: Students write a function rule when given the parent function $f(x) = e^x$ and a description of a horizontal shrink or a description of a horizontal translation.

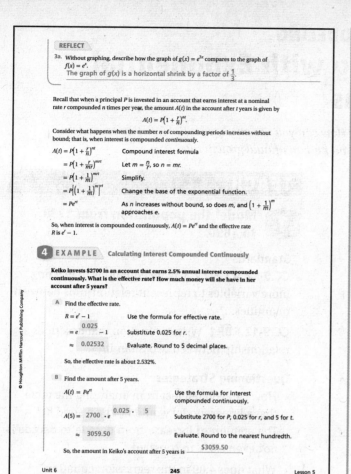

REFLECT

3a. Without graphing, describe how the graph of $g(x) = e^{3x}$ compares to the graph of $f(x) = e^x$.

The graph of $g(x)$ is a horizontal shrink by a factor of $\frac{1}{3}$.

Recall that when a principal P is invested in an account that earns interest at a nominal rate r compounded n times per year, the amount $A(t)$ in the account after t years is given by

$$A(t) = P\left(1 + \frac{r}{n}\right)^{nt}.$$

Consider what happens when the number n of compounding periods increases without bound; that is, when interest is compounded *continuously*.

$A(t) = P\left(1 + \frac{r}{n}\right)^{nt}$ Compound interest formula

$\quad = P\left(1 + \frac{r}{mr}\right)^{mrt}$ Let $m = \frac{n}{r}$, so $n = mr$.

$\quad = P\left(1 + \frac{1}{m}\right)^{mrt}$ Simplify.

$\quad = P\left[\left(1 + \frac{1}{m}\right)^{m}\right]^{rt}$ Change the base of the exponential function.

$\quad = Pe^{rt}$ As n increases without bound, so does m, and $\left(1 + \frac{1}{m}\right)^{m}$ approaches e.

So, when interest is compounded continuously, $A(t) = Pe^{rt}$ and the effective rate R is $e^r - 1$.

4 EXAMPLE   Calculating Interest Compounded Continuously

Keiko invests $2700 in an account that earns 2.5% annual interest compounded continuously. What is the effective rate? How much money will she have in her account after 5 years?

A Find the effective rate.

$R = e^r - 1$ Use the formula for effective rate.

$\quad = e^{\boxed{0.025}} - 1$ Substitute 0.025 for r.

$\quad \approx \boxed{0.02532}$ Evaluate. Round to 5 decimal places.

So, the effective rate is about 2.532%.

B Find the amount after 5 years.

$A(t) = Pe^{rt}$ Use the formula for interest compounded continuously.

$A(5) = \boxed{2700} \cdot e^{\boxed{0.025} \cdot \boxed{5}}$ Substitute 2700 for P, 0.025 for r, and 5 for t.

$\quad \approx \boxed{3059.50}$ Evaluate. Round to the nearest hundredth.

So, the amount in Keiko's account after 5 years is $\boxed{\$3059.50}$.

Unit 6   245   Lesson 5

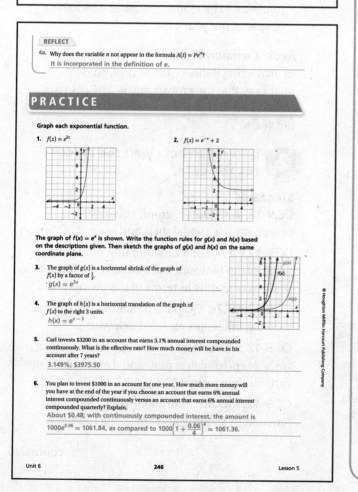

REFLECT

4a. Why does the variable n not appear in the formula $A(t) = Pe^{rt}$?

It is incorporated in the definition of e.

PRACTICE

Graph each exponential function.

1. $f(x) = e^{2x}$

2. $f(x) = e^{-x} + 2$

The graph of $f(x) = e^x$ is shown. Write the function rules for $g(x)$ and $h(x)$ based on the descriptions given. Then sketch the graphs of $g(x)$ and $h(x)$ on the same coordinate plane.

3. The graph of $g(x)$ is a horizontal shrink of the graph of $f(x)$ by a factor of $\frac{1}{3}$.

$g(x) = e^{3x}$

4. The graph of $h(x)$ is a horizontal translation of the graph of $f(x)$ to the right 3 units.

$h(x) = e^{x-3}$

5. Carl invests $3200 in an account that earns 3.1% annual interest compounded continuously. What is the effective rate? How much money will he have in his account after 7 years?

3.149%; $3975.50

6. You plan to invest $1000 in an account for one year. How much more money will you have at the end of the year if you choose an account that earns 6% annual interest compounded continuously versus an account that earns 6% annual interest compounded quarterly? Explain.

About $0.48; with continuously compounded interest, the amount is

$1000e^{0.06} \approx 1061.84$, as compared to $1000\left(1 + \frac{0.06}{4}\right)^{4} \approx 1061.36$.

Unit 6   246   Lesson 5

© Houghton Mifflin Harcourt Publishing Company

FOCUS ON MODELING
Modeling with Exponential Functions

Essential question: *How can you use an exponential function to model population growth and find an annual growth rate?*

COMMON CORE **Standards for Mathematical Content**

The following standards are addressed in this lesson. (An asterisk indicates that a standard is also a Modeling standard.) For more detailed information, see each section of the lesson.

Algebra: CC.9-12.A.SSE.3, CC.9-12.A.SSE.3c, CC.9-12.A.CED.2*

Functions: CC.9-12.F.IF.4*, CC.9-12.F.IF.7*, CC.9-12.F.IF.7e*, CC.9-12.F.IF.8, CC.9-12.F.IF.8b, CC.9-12.F.BF.1*, CC.9-12.F.BF.1a*, CC.9-12.F.LE.3*

Statistics and Probability: CC.9-12.S.ID.6*, CC.9-12.S.ID.6a*, CC.9-12.S.ID.6b*

Prerequisites

- Graphing an exponential function, Lesson 6-1
- Interpreting an exponential growth function, Lesson 6-2
- Finding a regression equation, Algebra 1
- Finding and interpreting residuals, Algebra 1

Math Background

In this lesson, students enter population data into their graphing calculators to determine an exponential regression equation. They use the graph of the exponential equation and residuals to determine whether the model is a good fit for the data and use properties of exponents to write an equivalent equation to gain new information about the situation. They see that while the model is a good fit for the given time period, it is a poor fit for times beyond it. In the extension, they compare the exponential model to a quadratic model.

INTRODUCE

Population can grow very quickly. As an example, have students use the census table and find the differences from one decade to the next. Students should see that each difference increases over the difference before it.

TEACH

 Model the population from 1790 to 1890.

Standards

CC.9-12.A.CED.2 Create equations in two or more variables to represent relationships between quantities...*

CC.9-12.F.BF.1 Write a function that describes a relationship between two quantities.*

Questioning Strategies

- How can you tell just from analyzing the table that a linear model would not be a good fit? The amount of increase from decade to decade is not even close to constant.

- What does 4.09 in the regression equation represent? The model estimates 4.09 million people in the year 1790.

Avoid Common Errors

In answering Reflect Question 1a, students might say that the growth rate is 33% per year. Remind them that the *x*-values represent decades, not years.

2 **Determine how well the model fits the data.**

Standards

CC.9-12. A.CED.2 ... graph equations on coordinate axes with labels and scales.*

CC.9-12.F.IF.4 For a function that models a relationship between two quantities, interpret key features of graphs in terms of the quantities, ...*

CC.9-12.F.IF.7e Graph exponential...functions, showing intercepts and end behavior ...*

CC.9-12.S.ID.6 Represent data on two quantitative variables on a scatter plot, and describe how the variables are related.*

CC.9-12.S.ID.6b Informally assess the fit of a function by plotting and analyzing residuals.*

continued

Name_____ Class_____ Date_____

FOCUS ON MODELING
Modeling with Exponential Functions

COMMON CORE
CC.9-12.A.SSE.3c,
CC.9-12.F.IF.8b,
CC.9-12.F.BF.1*,
CC.9-12.F.LE.3*,
CC.9-12.S.ID.6a*,
CC.9-12.S.ID.6b*

Essential question: *How can you use an exponential function to model population growth and find an annual growth rate?*

The United States government performs a census every 10 years. The census data from 1790 to 1890 are given in the table below. How can you use the data to predict the population in 1845 and 1990?

1 Model the population from 1790 to 1890.

A Complete the table. Round the population (in millions) to the nearest tenth.

Census Year	Decades Since First Census	Population	Population (in millions)
1790	0	3,929,214	3.9
1800	1	5,308,483	5.3
1810	2	7,239,881	7.2
1820	3	9,638,453	9.6
1830	4	12,866,020	12.9
1840	5	17,069,453	17.1
1850	6	23,191,876	23.2
1860	7	31,443,321	31.4
1870	8	39,818,449	39.8
1880	9	50,189,209	50.2
1890	10	62,979,766	63.0

B Use your graphing calculator to determine the exponential regression equation for the data as follows.
- Let the *x*-values be the number of decades since 1790. Enter these values in list L_1.
- Let the *y*-values be the population in millions. Enter these values in list L_2.
- Find the exponential regression equation by pressing [STAT], selecting the **CALC** menu, and then selecting **0:ExpReg**.

Write the exponential regression equation below, rounding the values of *a* and *b* to two decimal places.

$$y = 4.09(1.33)^x$$

REFLECT

1a. Write the regression equation in the form of an exponential growth function, $y = a(1 + r)^t$. What does *r* represent?

$y = 4.09(1 + 0.33)^t$; *r* represents the population's growth rate of 33%

per decade.

2 Determine how well the model fits the data.

A Plot the 11 data points (*decades since first census, population in millions*) on the coordinate plane below.

B Graph the exponential regression equation on the same coordinate plane.

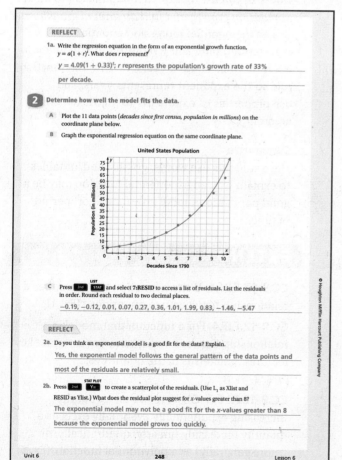

United States Population

C Press [2nd] [STAT] and select **7:RESID** to access a list of residuals. List the residuals in order. Round each residual to two decimal places.

−0.19, −0.12, 0.01, 0.07, 0.27, 0.36, 1.01, 1.99, 0.83, −1.46, −5.47

REFLECT

2a. Do you think an exponential model is a good fit for the data? Explain.

Yes, the exponential model follows the general pattern of the data points and
most of the residuals are relatively small.

2b. Press [2nd] [Y=] to create a scatterplot of the residuals. (Use L_1 as Xlist and RESID as Ylist.) What does the residual plot suggest for *x*-values greater than 8?

The exponential model may not be a good fit for the *x*-values greater than 8
because the exponential model grows too quickly.

Notes

2 continued

Questioning Strategies

- What does the absolute value of a residual reveal? the distance between a data value and the corresponding output value from the model

- What does the sign of a residual reveal? whether the data value is greater or less than the corresponding output value from the model

- For which decade (0–10) is the residual positive and its absolute value the greatest? For which decade is the residual negative and its absolute value the greatest? 7; 10

3 Write the exponential model in other forms.

Standards

CC.9-12.A.SSE.3 … produce an equivalent form of an expression to reveal and explain properties of the quantity represented by the expression.

CC.9-12.A.SSE.3c Use the properties of exponents to transform expressions for exponential functions.

CC.9-12.F.IF.8 Write a function defined by an expression in different but equivalent forms to reveal and explain different properties of the function.

CC.9-12.F.IF.8b Use properties of exponents to interpret expressions for exponential functions.

Questioning Strategies

- Why does raising 1.33 to the one-tenth power give the growth factor per year? When rewriting the function with an exponent of 10x representing years, you have to rewrite the base as 1.33 to the one-tenth power to produce an equivalent expression, and this base represents the annual growth factor. (In general, if the growth factor for n years is g, then the annual growth factor is the nth root of g.)

- Will using the equation in Reflect Question 3b for $x = 5$ give the same result as using the original equation for $x = 5$? Not exactly; 1.03 was rounded in part B.

4 Use the model to make predictions.

Standards

CC.9-12.S.ID.6a … use functions fitted to data to solve problems in the context of the data.*

Questioning Strategies

- How can you check the reasonableness of the prediction for 1845? See whether it is between the populations given for 1840 and 1850 in the table.

- How do you find the value of x when the year is 1990? Find 1990 − 1790 and divide by 10.

MATHEMATICAL PRACTICE   **Highlighting the Standards**

Answering the questions about the predictions addresses Mathematical Practice Standard 3 (Construct viable arguments and critique the reasoning of others). Let students discuss among themselves why the model was good for 1845 but very poor for 1990. Encourage students to look for a pattern in the residuals and think about the form of an exponential growth function.

CLOSE

Essential Question

How can you use an exponential function to model population growth and find an annual growth rate?
Use an exponential regression equation with x representing time and y representing population. If x is not measured in years, rewrite the function rule so the exponent represents years, and use properties of exponents to adjust the base accordingly.

Summarize

Have students use words, graphs, and/or tables to explain why an exponential function may be a good population model only for a short period of time.

EXTEND

CC.9-12.F.BF.1 Write a function that describes a relationship between two quantities.* (Ex. 1)

CC.9-12.F.IF.4 For a function that models a relationship between two quantities, interpret key features … in terms of the quantities, …* (Exs. 2, 3, 4)

CC.9-12.F.LE.3 Observe … that a quantity increasing exponentially eventually exceeds a quantity increasing linearly, quadratically, or (more generally) as a polynomial function. (Ex. 5)

© Houghton Mifflin Harcourt Publishing Company

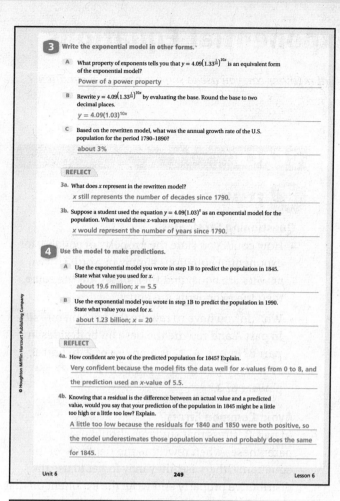

3 Write the exponential model in other forms.

A What property of exponents tells you that $y = 4.09(1.33^{\frac{1}{10}})^{10x}$ is an equivalent form of the exponential model?

Power of a power property

B Rewrite $y = 4.09(1.33^{\frac{1}{10}})^{10x}$ by evaluating the base. Round the base to two decimal places.

$y = 4.09(1.03)^{10x}$

C Based on the rewritten model, what was the annual growth rate of the U.S. population for the period 1790–1890?

about 3%

REFLECT

3a. What does x represent in the rewritten model?

x still represents the number of decades since 1790.

3b. Suppose a student used the equation $y = 4.09(1.03)^x$ as an exponential model for the population. What would these x-values represent?

x would represent the number of years since 1790.

4 Use the model to make predictions.

A Use the exponential model you wrote in step 1B to predict the population in 1845. State what value you used for x.

about 19.6 million; $x = 5.5$

B Use the exponential model you wrote in step 1B to predict the population in 1990. State what value you used for x.

about 1.23 billion; $x = 20$

REFLECT

4a. How confident are you of the predicted population for 1845? Explain.

Very confident because the model fits the data well for x-values from 0 to 8, and the prediction used an x-value of 5.5.

4b. Knowing that a residual is the difference between an actual value and a predicted value, would you say that your prediction of the population in 1845 might be a little too high or a little too low? Explain.

A little too low because the residuals for 1840 and 1850 were both positive, so the model underestimates those population values and probably does the same for 1845.

4c. The census for 1990 showed that the U.S. population was 248,718,302. Compare this to your prediction. What does this tell you about the growth rate of the population for the period 1890–1990 relative to the growth rate for the period 1790–1890?

The actual population in 1990 was about one-fifth of the population that the model predicted. For the period 1890–1990, the population must have grown at a rate less than 33% per decade (or 3% per year).

4d. Explain the difference between the predicted population and the actual population for 1990.

The prediction is based on an exponential model that grows very quickly. The residuals indicate that the actual population would not keep up with the model, and $x = 20$ is far beyond the data used to develop the model.

EXTEND

1. Use the data in the population table (still stored in your calculator as L_1 and L_2) to determine the quadratic regression equation. Round the values of a, b, and c to three decimal places.

$y = 0.638x^2 - 0.684x + 5.046$

2. List the residuals for the quadratic regression in order. Round each residual to two decimal places.

−1.15, 0.30, 0.97, 0.86, 0.38, −0.48, −0.72, −0.13, −0.62, −0.39, 0.97

3. Is the quadratic regression equation a better fit for the data than the exponential model? Explain.

Yes, the quadratic model has fewer large residuals than the exponential model.

4. Use the quadratic model to predict the population in 1990. Compare this prediction to the one you obtained from the exponential model.

246.57 million; this is much closer to the actual population than the prediction that was obtained from the exponential model.

5. On your calculator, graph the data and both regression equations in the same window. Discuss how the graphs compare.
(*Hint:* To make the graphs, perform the regressions again with the arguments shown at right. This stores the regression equations as Y_1 and Y_2.)

ExpReg L1,L2,Y1

QuadReg L1,L2,Y2

Both graphs start out about the same and model the data well, but then the graph of the exponential model rises more steeply than the graph of the quadratic model.

Notes

Solving Exponential Equations

Essential question: *What methods can you use to solve exponential equations?*

© Houghton Mifflin Harcourt Publishing Company

COMMON CORE Standards for Mathematical Content

CC.9-12.A.CED.1 Create equations ... in one variable and use them to solve problems. Include equations arising from ... exponential functions. *

CC.9-12.A.REI.11 Explain why the *x*-coordinates of the points where the graphs of the equations $y = f(x)$ and $y = g(x)$ intersect are the solutions of the equation $f(x) = g(x)$; find the solutions approximately, e.g., using technology to graph the functions, make tables of values, ...Include ... exponential... functions. *

CC.9-12.F.IF.7 Graph functions expressed symbolically ... using technology for more complicated cases.*

CC.9-12.F.IF.7e Graph exponential ... functions ... *

Prerequisites

Exponential growth and decay functions, Lessons 6-2 and 6-3

Properties of exponents, Grade 8

Math Background

Students will learn how to solve exponential equations algebraically and with a table or graph using their graphing calculators. The equations they solve algebraically are all in a form that can be solved by first rewriting the equation so that each side is a power with the same base and then setting the exponents equal to each other. This results in an equation that is not exponential (usually linear, sometimes quadratic) and that can usually be solved quite easily.

In the next unit, students will use logarithms to solve exponential equations for which it is not possible to write each side as a power with the same base.

INTRODUCE

Write $2^{2x} = 16$ on the board and ask what the value of $2x$ is and why. 4; because $2^4 = 16$ Ask for the value of *x*. 2 Ask students which of these could be solved the same way and why: $2^{2x} = 64$ or $2^{2x} = 50$. $2^{2x} = 64$ because 64 is a power of 2 and 50 is not

TEACH

1 EXAMPLE

Questioning Strategies

- How could you state the property of equality for exponential equations simply in words? If two powers are equal and their bases are the same, then the exponents are equal.

- Why do you have to rewrite the base on one side in part A and rewrite the base on both sides in part B? In part A, 32 is a power of 2. In part B, 27 is not a power of 9, but both 9 and 27 are powers of 3.

Avoid Common Errors

In part B, stress that students should use parentheses when rewriting the right side of the equation. Otherwise, they may forget to use the distributive property and write the exponent on that side as $3x + 1$.

EXTRA EXAMPLE

Solve the exponential equation.

A. $4^{x+5} = 64$ $x = -2$ **B.** $125^{x-4} = 25^x$ $x = 12$

2 EXAMPLE

Questioning Strategies

- Why is it not possible to solve this equation as you solved the equation in Example 1? You cannot write $(1.33)^x$ and the quotient of 45 and 4.1 as powers with a common base.

- Why are increments of 0.1 used in setting up the table? Each tenth represents one year, so the table displays in years, rather than decades, since 1790.

- In the table, the *y*-value of 45 is between $x = 8.4$ and $x = 8.5$. Why choose 8.4? The population reached 45 million *before* 1875 ($x = 8.5$), so it occurred *during* the year 1874 ($x = 8.4$).

continued

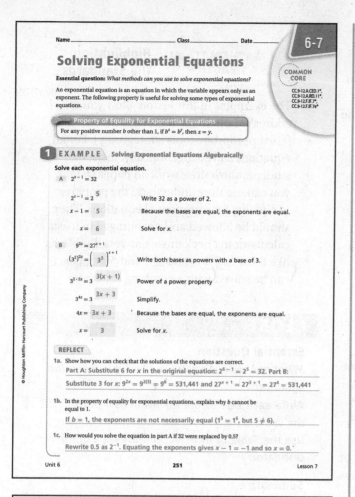

Name _____ Class _____ Date _____

6-7

Solving Exponential Equations

COMMON CORE
CC.9-12.A.CED.1*,
CC.9-12.A.REL1*,
CC.9-12.F.IF.7*,
CC.9-12.F.IF.7e*

Essential question: *What methods can you use to solve exponential equations?*

An exponential equation is an equation in which the variable appears only as an exponent. The following property is useful for solving some types of exponential equations.

Property of Equality for Exponential Equations

For any positive number b other than 1, if $b^x = b^y$, then $x = y$.

1 EXAMPLE Solving Exponential Equations Algebraically

Solve each exponential equation.

A $2^{x-1} = 32$

$2^{x-1} = 2^{\boxed{5}}$ Write 32 as a power of 2.

$x - 1 = \boxed{5}$ Because the bases are equal, the exponents are equal.

$x = \boxed{6}$ Solve for x.

B $9^{2x} = 27^{x+1}$

$(3^2)^{2x} = \left(\boxed{3^3}\right)^{x+1}$ Write both bases as powers with a base of 3.

$3^{2 \cdot 2x} = 3^{\boxed{3(x+1)}}$ Power of a power property

$3^{4x} = 3^{\boxed{3x+3}}$ Simplify.

$4x = \boxed{3x+3}$ Because the bases are equal, the exponents are equal.

$x = \boxed{3}$ Solve for x.

REFLECT

1a. Show how you can check that the solutions of the equations are correct.

Part A: Substitute 6 for x in the original equation: $2^{6-1} = 2^5 = 32$. Part B:

Substitute 3 for x: $9^{2x} = 9^{2(3)} = 9^6 = 531,441$ and $27^{x+1} = 27^{3+1} = 27^4 = 531,441$

1b. In the property of equality for exponential equations, explain why b cannot be equal to 1.

If $b = 1$, the exponents are not necessarily equal ($1^5 = 1^6$, but $5 \neq 6$).

1c. How would you solve the equation in part A if 32 were replaced by 0.5?

Rewrite 0.5 as 2^{-1}. Equating the exponents gives $x - 1 = -1$ and so $x = 0$.

Unit 6   251   Lesson 7

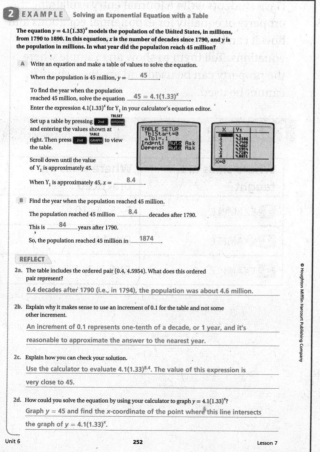

2 EXAMPLE Solving an Exponential Equation with a Table

The equation $y = 4.1(1.33)^x$ models the population of the United States, in millions, from 1790 to 1890. In this equation, x is the number of decades since 1790, and y is the population in millions. In what year did the population reach 45 million?

A Write an equation and make a table of values to solve the equation.

When the population is 45 million, $y = \boxed{45}$

To find the year when the population reached 45 million, solve the equation $45 = 4.1(1.33)^x$

Enter the expression $4.1(1.33)^x$ for Y_1 in your calculator's equation editor.

Set up a table by pressing [2nd] [WINDOW] and entering the values shown at right. Then press [2nd] [GRAPH] to view the table.

Scroll down until the value of Y_1 is approximately 45.

When Y_1 is approximately 45, $x = \boxed{8.4}$

B Find the year when the population reached 45 million.

The population reached 45 million $\boxed{8.4}$ decades after 1790.

This is $\boxed{84}$ years after 1790.

So, the population reached 45 million in $\boxed{1874}$

REFLECT

2a. The table includes the ordered pair (0.4, 4.5954). What does this ordered pair represent?

0.4 decades after 1790 (i.e., in 1794), the population was about 4.6 million.

2b. Explain why it makes sense to use an increment of 0.1 for the table and not some other increment.

An increment of 0.1 represents one-tenth of a decade, or 1 year, and it's

reasonable to approximate the answer to the nearest year.

2c. Explain how you can check your solution.

Use the calculator to evaluate $4.1(1.33)^{8.4}$. The value of this expression is

very close to 45.

2d. How could you solve the equation by using your calculator to graph $y = 4.1(1.33)^x$?

Graph $y = 45$ and find the x-coordinate of the point where this line intersects

the graph of $y = 4.1(1.33)^x$.

Unit 6   252   Lesson 7

EXTRA EXAMPLE

The equation $y = 1.3(1.04)^x$ models the population of a city, in millions, from 1950 to 2010, where x is the number of years after 1950. In what year did the population reach 5 million? **1984**

Teaching Strategy

Instead of scrolling down a long list, students can first use increments of 1 for x to see that the number of decades is between 8 and 9. Then, they can go back to TBLSET and start the x-values at 8 and increase them by tenths to fine-tune the table by year.

3 **EXAMPLE**

Questioning Strategies

- Why is graphing and finding the point of intersection a better method than using the table as in Example 2? It would be difficult to increment the x-values so that the two y-values would be equal. After graphing, the intersect feature will give a more accurate value for the intersection.

- Why should you round the y-value of the point of intersection to the hundredths place? The y-value represents dollars, with the hundredths place representing cents.

EXTRA EXAMPLE

Sylvester invested $700 at 2.5% annual interest compounded continuously. Judy invested $650 at 3.8% annual interest compounded continuously. When will they have the same amount in their accounts? What will the amount be when this occurs? after approximately 5.7 years; $807.22

Teaching Strategy

There are different ways to answer Reflect Question 3b. Students could substitute 10 for x in each equation manually. They can use the table to see each y-value when $x = 10$. Or they can graph the functions press `2nd` `TRACE` CALC, select **1: value,** type 10, press enter, and then use the up and down arrows to toggle between Y_1 and Y_2.

MATHEMATICAL PRACTICE   **Highlighting the Standards**

The examples in this lesson allow you to address Mathematical Practice Standard 5 (Use appropriate tools strategically). For all equations solved algebraically, insist that students show their work on paper so that you can see they understand the property of equality for exponential equations. They should be allowed and encouraged to use a calculator to check those answers. Problems like those in **2** EXAMPLE and **3** EXAMPLE can be solved with a graphing calculator.

CLOSE

Essential Question

What methods can you use to solve exponential equations?

Write each side of the equation as a power with the same base and set the exponents equal.
Use the Table or Intersect feature on a graphing calculator.

Summarize

Have students write a journal entry explaining the property of equality for exponential equations and how it can be used to solve certain exponential equations. Tell them to show an example where the property can be used and another where it cannot be used.

PRACTICE

Where skills are taught	Where skills are practiced
1 EXAMPLE	EXS. 1–10
2 EXAMPLE	EX. 11
3 EXAMPLE	EXS. 12, 13

3 EXAMPLE Solving an Exponential Equation by Graphing

Camilla invested $300 at 4% interest compounded continuously. Diego invested $275 at 6% interest compounded continuously. When will they have the same amount in their accounts? What will the amount be when this occurs?

A   Write equations to represent the amount in each account.

When interest is compounded continuously, $A(t) = Pe^{rt}$.

Camilla: $A(t) = \boxed{300} \cdot e^{0.04 \cdot t}$ Substitute 300 for P and 0.04 for r.

Diego: $A(t) = \boxed{275} \cdot e^{0.06 \cdot t}$ Substitute 275 for P and 0.06 for r.

B   Graph the equations.

Enter the equation for Camilla's account as Y_1 in your calculator's equation editor. Enter the equation for Diego's account as Y_2.

Graph both equations in the same viewing window. A good viewing in this situation is $0 \leq x \leq 10$ with a tick mark every 1 unit and $0 \leq y \leq 500$ with a tick mark every 50 units.

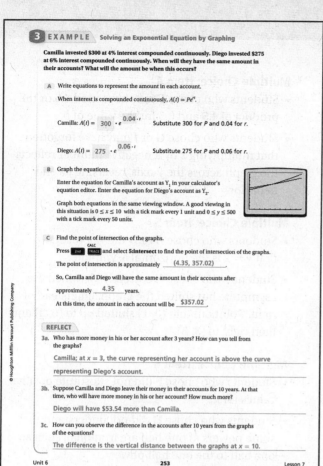

C   Find the point of intersection of the graphs.

Press [2nd] [TRACE]^CALC and select 5:Intersect to find the point of intersection of the graphs.

The point of intersection is approximately   (4.35, 357.02) .

So, Camilla and Diego will have the same amount in their accounts after approximately   4.35   years.

At this time, the amount in each account will be $357.02 .

REFLECT

3a. Who has more money in his or her account after 3 years? How can you tell from the graphs?

Camilla; at $x = 3$, the curve representing her account is above the curve representing Diego's account.

3b. Suppose Camilla and Diego leave their money in their accounts for 10 years. At that time, who will have more money in his or her account? How much more?

Diego will have $53.54 more than Camilla.

3c. How can you observe the difference in the accounts after 10 years from the graphs of the equations?

The difference is the vertical distance between the graphs at $x = 10$.

PRACTICE

Solve each exponential equation algebraically.

1. $16^{3x} = 64^{x+2}$

   $x = 2$

2. $\left(\frac{2}{5}\right)^{x+7} = \left(\frac{4}{25}\right)^{10}$

   $x = 13$

3. $27^x = \frac{1}{9}$

   $x = -\frac{2}{3}$

4. $6^{5x-1} = 36$

   $x = \frac{3}{5}$

5. $0.01^{x+1} = 1000^{x-9}$

   $x = 5$

6. $625 = \left(\frac{1}{25}\right)^{x+3}$

   $x = -5$

7. $6^{x^2} = 36^8$

   $x = \pm 4$

8. $0.75^{5x-2} = \left(\frac{27}{64}\right)^{x-6}$

   $x = -8$

9. $\left(\frac{1}{3}\right)^{x+2} = 81^{x-1}$

   $x = \frac{2}{5}$

10. Show that you can solve $\frac{1}{4} = 16^{x+5}$ by writing both sides of the equation with a base of 2 or with a base of 4.

    $2^{-2} = (2^4)^{x+5} \rightarrow 2^{-2} = 2^{4x+20} \rightarrow -2 = 4x + 20 \rightarrow -22 = 4x \rightarrow -5.5 = x$

    $4^{-1} = (4^2)^{x+5} \rightarrow 4^{-1} = 4^{2x+10} \rightarrow -1 = 2x + 10 \rightarrow -11 = 2x \rightarrow -5.5 = x$

11. The equation $y = 87.3(1.07)^x$ models the population of a city, in thousands, from 1980 to 2010. In this equation, x is the number of years since 1980, and y is the population in thousands.

    a. In what year did the population reach 150,000?   1988

    b. In what year did the population reach 250,000?   1995

12. In the lower stratosphere (between 36,152 feet and 82,345 feet), the equation $p = 473.1e^{1.73 - 0.000048h}$ represents the atmospheric pressure p in pounds per square foot at altitude h feet.

    a. At what altitude does the pressure equal 150 lb/ft²?   59,972 ft

    b. At what altitude does the pressure equal 300 lb/ft²?   45,532 ft

13. Rima and Trevor both bought a car in 2010. Rima's car cost $17,832 and Trevor's car cost $22,575. Rima's car is depreciating at a rate of 11% per year and Trevor's car is depreciating at a rate of 13.5% per year.

    a. Write each car's value as a function of time t (in years since 2010).

    Rima: $V(t) = 17,832(0.89)^t$; Trevor: $V(t) = 22,575(0.865)^t$

    b. During what year will the cars have an equal value? At that time, what will the value of the cars be?

    In 2018, both cars will be worth about $6796.

© Houghton Mifflin Harcourt Publishing Company

COMMON CORE CORRELATION

Standard	Items
CC.9-12.A.SSE.3c	9b
CC.9-12.A.CED.1*	7
CC.9-12.A.CED.2*	3, 9a
CC.9-12.A.REI.11*	7, 10
CC.9-12.F.IF.2	6, 11
CC.9-12.F.IF.4*	4, 11
CC.9-12.F.IF.7e*	1
CC.9-12.F.IF.8b	9c
CC.9-12.F.IF.9	2
CC.9-12.F.BF.1*	3
CC.9-12.F.BF.3	5
CC.9-12.F.LE.3	8
CC.9-12.S.ID.6a*	9a, 9e
CC.9-12.S.ID.6b*	9d

TEST PREP DOCTOR ✚

Multiple Choice: Item 1
- Students who chose **A**, **C**, or **D** did not understand how the values of a, h, and k affect the graph of $f(x) = ab^{x-h} + k$.

Multiple Choice: Item 3
- Students who chose **A** used the formula for exponential growth instead of exponential decay.
- Students who chose **C** did not understand that the decay factor is $1 - 0.14$, not 0.14.
- Students who chose **D** did not understand how to relate the decay factor to the initial population.

Multiple Choice: Item 4
- Students who chose **F** may have used 4.5 or the product of 4.5 and 0.5 for the value of b.
- Students who chose **G** or **J** may have forgotten that multiplying x by a negative number reflects the graph across the y-axis, reversing its end behavior.

Multiple Choice: Item 5
- Students who chose **A** or **D** did not recognize that $y = 2$ is the horizontal asymptote.
- Students who chose **C** correctly identified the asymptote but shifted the graph left instead of right. Point out that $(0, 1)$ shifted up to $(0, 3)$ and then right to $(3, 3)$.

Multiple Choice: Item 6
- Students who chose **F** did not substitute positive values for x.
- Students who chose **H** did not understand that some powers of one half are irrational, such as one half to the one half power.
- Students who chose **J** did not notice that $f(x)$ equals 2 when x equals 0.

Multiple Choice: Item 8
- Students who chose **G**, **H**, or **J** did not substitute enough values of x to observe that the value of the exponential function eventually exceeds the values of the other functions.

Free Response: Item 9a
- Students who wrote $y = 2.62(1.02)^x$ used x-values of 0, 10, 20, 30, 40, 50, and 60 instead of the number of decades: 0, 1, 2, 3, 4, 5, and 6.

Free Response: Item 9b
- Students who answered 118% forgot to subtract 1 from the growth factor.
- Students who answered 1.18% did not understand what the growth factor means.

Free Response: Item 10
- Students who answered 0.05 did not enclose the exponent in each function in parentheses on their graphing calculators. They ended up graphing $y = 5^x + 2$ and $y = 64x$.

UNIT 6 TEST PREP

Name _____ Class _____ Date _____

MULTIPLE CHOICE

1. Alicia graphed an exponential function that has a y-intercept of 3. Which of the following functions could she have graphed?

   A. $g(x) = 5^{x-3}$ C. $g(x) = 5^x + 3$

   B. $g(x) = 3(5)^x$ D. $g(x) = 5^{3x}$

2. You graph the function $f(x) = 300(1.015)^x$, which gives the total amount in your account after x years of interest that is compounded annually. The function $g(x)$ gives the amount in your account if you make the same initial investment, but at a rate of interest of 2.3% compounded annually. How would the graph of $g(x)$ compare to the graph of $f(x)$?

   F. It would have the same y-intercept, but rise more quickly over time.

   G. It would have the same y-intercept, but rise less quickly over time.

   H. It would have a greater y-intercept and rise more quickly over time.

   J. It would have a greater y-intercept and rise less quickly over time.

3. An initial population of 900 frogs decreases at a rate of 14% per year. Which function gives the population after x years?

   A. $f(x) = 900(1.14)^x$

   B. $f(x) = 900(0.86)^x$

   C. $f(x) = 900(0.14)^x$

   D. $f(x) = 900 - 0.86^x$

4. The graph of $f(x)$ decreases as x decreases and increases as x increases. Which of these could be the function described?

   F. $f(x) = 4.5(0.5)^x$ H. $h(x) = 4.5^{0.5x}$

   G. $g(x) = 4.5^{-2x}$ J. $j(x) = 4.5^{-0.5x}$

5. The graph below is a horizontal and vertical translation of the graph of $f(x) = \left(\frac{3}{4}\right)^x$.

   What is the equation of the graph?

   A. $y = \left(\frac{3}{4}\right)^{x-2} + 3$ C. $y = \left(\frac{3}{4}\right)^{x+3} + 2$

   B. $y = \left(\frac{3}{4}\right)^{x-3} + 2$ D. $y = \left(\frac{3}{4}\right)^{x+2} + 3$

6. Tyrell evaluates the function $f(x) = \left(\frac{1}{2}\right)^x + 1$ for a real number x. What must be true about the value of $f(x)$?

   F. The value of $f(x)$ is greater than 2.

   G. The value of $f(x)$ is greater than 1.

   H. The value of $f(x)$ is a rational number.

   J. The value of $f(x)$ is not equal to 2.

7. Ron invests $1200 at 4.5% compounded continuously and Dina invests $1500 at 3% compounded continuously. When will they have the same amount in their accounts?

   A. about 7 years   C. about 14 years

   B. about 8 years   D. about 15 years

8. As x increases without bound, the graph of which function rises at the fastest rate?

   F. $f(x) = 3^x$

   G. $g(x) = 3x^2$

   H. $h(x) = 5x + 30$

   J. $j(x) = x^4 + 1$

FREE RESPONSE

9. The table shows the total world population from 1950 to 2010 according to data from the U.S. Census Bureau.

Year	Population (in billions)
1950	2.6
1960	3.0
1970	3.7
1980	4.5
1990	5.3
2000	6.1
2010	6.9

a. Find the exponential regression equation, using the number of decades since 1950 as x-values. Round the values of a and b to two decimal places.

   $y = 2.62(1.18)^x$

b. What is the population's growth rate? Tell how you know.

   18% per decade because 1.18 is the growth factor $1 + r$, so $r = 0.18$.

c. Show how to transform the equation to find the annual growth rate.

   $y = 2.62\left(1.18^{\frac{1}{10}}\right)^{10x} \rightarrow$

   $y = 2.62(1.017)^{10x}$; the annual growth rate is about 1.7%.

d. Do you think the exponential model is a good fit for the data? Use residuals to explain.

   Yes; the residuals are all relatively close to 0. (They are approximately: $-0.02, -0.10, 0.03, 0.16, 0.17, 0.03, -0.29$.)

e. Would you use the model to predict the world population in the year 3000? Explain.

   No; exponential functions grow very quickly and a prediction that far beyond the given data would likely be much too high.

10. Explain how you can solve the exponential equation $5^{x+2} = 4^{3x}$ using your graphing calculator. Then give the approximate solution to two decimal places.

   Graph $y = 5^{x+2}$ and $y = 4^{3x}$ in the same viewing window. Use the calculator's Intersect tool to find the x-coordinate of the point of intersection of the graphs. The approximate solution is $x = 1.26$.

11. A cup of hot water is left to cool to room temperature. The water's temperature T (in degrees Fahrenheit) at time t (in minutes) is given by the function

    $T(t) = 60(0.95)^t + 65$.

a. What is $T(0)$? Give its meaning in terms of the situation.

   125; initially, the water's temperature is 125°F.

b. What asymptote does the graph of the function have? Give its meaning in terms of the situation.

   $T = 65$; the asymptote represents a room temperature of 65°F.

Logarithmic Functions

Unit Vocabulary

logarithm   (7-1)

logarithmic
  function   (7-1)

Logarithmic Functions

Unit Focus

This unit is about logarithmic functions. A logarithmic function is the inverse of an exponential function. In an exponential function, the exponent is the input, so in a logarithmic function, the exponent is the output. You will learn how to graph logarithmic functions by hand and by using a graphing calculator. You will explore and verify properties of logarithms and use those properties to solve logarithmic equations. You will also revisit exponential equations and learn a new way to solve them. Throughout this unit, you will see applications of logarithms, which include the decibel scale, compound interest, and half-lives of radioactive substances.

Unit at a Glance   COMMON CORE

Lesson		Standards for Mathematical Content
7-1	Logarithmic Functions as Inverses of Exponential Functions	CC.9-12.F.IF.2, CC.9-12.F.IF.7*, CC.9-12.F.IF.7e*, CC.9-12.F.BF.5(+)
7-2	Transforming the Graph of $f(x) = \log_b x$	CC.9-12.F.IF.7*, CC.9-12.F.IF.7e*, CC.9-12.F.BF.3
7-3	Properties of Logarithms	CC.9-12.F.BF.5(+)
7-4	Solving Exponential and Logarithmic Equations	CC.9-12.A.CED.1*, CC.9-12.A.REI.11*, CC.9-12.F.LE.4*
7-5	Modeling with Logarithmic Functions	CC.9-12.A.CED.2*, CC.9-12.A.CED.4*, CC.9-12.F.IF.2, CC.9-12.F.IF.4*, CC.9-12.F.BF.1*, CC.9-12.F.BF.1a*
	Test Prep	

Unpacking the Common Core State Standards

Use the table to help you understand the Standards for Mathematical Content that are taught in this unit. Refer to the lessons listed after each standard for exploration and practice.

COMMON CORE Standards for Mathematical Content	What It Means For You
CC.9-12.A.CED.1 Create equations and inequalities in one variable and use them to solve problems.* Lesson 7-4	You solved some exponential equations in Unit 6 by making the bases the same on both sides of the equation and setting the exponents equal. In this unit, you will learn how to solve exponential equations by using logarithms. This will allow you to solve exponential equations when you cannot make the bases the same.
CC.9-12.A.CED.2 Create equations in two or more variables to represent relationships between quantities; graph equations on coordinate axes with labels and scales.* Lesson 7-5	You will create both exponential and logarithmic equations to solve problems involving the decay of a radioactive substance given its half-life.
CC.9-12.A.CED.4 Rearrange formulas to highlight a quantity of interest, using the same reasoning as in solving equations.* Lesson 7-5	After writing an exponential equation to express the percent of a radioactive substance remaining as a function of time, you will rearrange the equation to highlight time.
CC.9-12.A.REI.11 Explain why the x-coordinates of the points where the graphs of the equations $y = f(x)$ and $y = g(x)$ intersect are the solutions of the equation $f(x) = g(x)$; find the solutions approximately, e.g., using technology to graph the functions, make tables of values, or find successive approximations. Include cases where $f(x)$ and/or $g(x)$ are linear, polynomial, rational, absolute value, exponential, and logarithmic functions.* Lesson 7-4	A point of intersection of two graphs is a solution of the system of the graphs' equations. You will use this graphical method to verify solutions obtained algebraically, and in some cases, as the only means to determine a solution.
CC.9-12.F.IF.2 Use function notation, evaluate functions for inputs in their domains, and interpret statements that use function notation in terms of a context. Lessons 7-1, 7-5	In this unit, you will evaluate logarithmic functions. This includes evaluating models of radioactive decay for different input values and interpreting the results.

Unpacking the Common Core State Standards

This page lists and explains the Standards for Mathematical Content that are addressed in this unit. For information about the Standards for Mathematical Practice, which are integrated throughout the text, see Teacher Edition pages x–xiii.

UNIT 7

Notes

COMMON CORE Standards for Mathematical Content	What It Means For You
CC.9-12.F.IF.4 For a function that models a relationship between two quantities, interpret **key features** of graphs and tables in terms of the quantities, and sketch graphs showing key features given a verbal description of the relationship.* Lesson 7-5	After writing a logarithmic function modeling the half-life of a radioactive substance, you will enter it into your graphing calculator and use the table feature to help answer questions about the model.
CC.9-12.F.IF.7 **Graph functions** expressed symbolically and show key features of the graph, by hand in simple cases and using technology for more complicated cases.* **CC.9-12.F.IF.7e** Graph exponential and logarithmic functions, showing intercepts and end behavior, and trigonometric functions, showing period, midline, and amplitude.* Lessons 7-1, 7-2	You will first graph a logarithmic function by reflecting the graph of an exponential function in the line $y = x$. You will then graph some logarithmic functions by making a table of values and plotting points. After learning properties of logarithms, you will also be able to graph logarithmic functions on a graphing calculator.
CC.9-12.F.BF.1 Write a function that describes a relationship between two quantities.* **CC.9-12.F.BF.1a** Determine an explicit expression, a recursive process, or steps for calculation from a context.* Lesson 7-5	You will use the general formula for exponential decay to write a model for the half-life of a radioactive substance.
CC.9-12.F.BF.3 Identify the effect on the graph of replacing $f(x)$ by $f(x) + k$, $k\,f(x)$, $f(kx)$, and $f(x + k)$ for specific values of k (both positive and negative); find the value of k given the graphs. Experiment with cases and illustrate an explanation of the effects on the graph using technology. Lesson 7-2	You will graph logarithmic functions of the form $f(x) = a \log_c (x - h) + k$ by changing the values of h, k, and a to create translations, stretches, and shrinks of the graph of the parent logarithmic function.
CC.9-12.F.BF.5(+) Understand the inverse relationship between exponents and logarithms and use this relationship to solve problems involving logarithms and exponents. Lessons 7-1, 7-3	You will use the inverse relationship between exponents and logarithms to investigate the characteristics of the graph of a logarithmic function. The relationship will also play an important role in understanding and verifying the properties of logarithms.
CC.9-12.F.LE.4 For exponential models, express as a logarithm the solution to $ab^{ct} = d$ where a, c, and d are numbers and the base is 2, 10, or e; evaluate the logarithm using technology.* Lesson 7-4	Just as you can raise each side of an equation to the same power, you can take a logarithm of both sides of an exponential equation. You can express the solution as a logarithmic expression, which is the exact value, or approximate it using a calculator.

Notes

_____

_____

_____

_____

_____

_____

_____

_____

_____

_____

_____

_____

_____

_____

_____

_____

_____

_____

_____

_____

_____

_____

_____

_____

_____

_____

_____

_____

_____

_____

_____

_____

_____

_____

_____

UNIT 7

Logarithmic Functions as Inverses of Exponential Functions

Essential question: *What are the characteristics of logarithmic functions?*

COMMON CORE **Standards for Mathematical Content**

CC.9-12.F.IF.2 Use function notation, evaluate functions for inputs in their domains, and interpret statements that use function notation in terms of a context.

CC.9-12.F.IF.7 Graph functions expressed symbolically and show key features of the graph ...*

CC.9-12.F.IF.7e Graph ... logarithmic functions, showing intercepts and end behavior, ...*

CC.9-12.F.BF.5(+) Understand the inverse relationship between exponents and logarithms and use this relationship to solve problems involving logarithms and exponents.

Vocabulary

logarithm

logarithmic function

Prerequisites

Basic exponential functions, Lesson 6-1

Inverses of functions, Lesson 5-1

The number e, Lesson 6-5

Math Background

The inverse of an exponential function is a logarithmic function. In the exponential function $f(x) = 5^x$, you input 2 and get 25 as the output. In the corresponding logarithmic function, written $f(x) = \log_5 x$, you input 25 and get 2 as the output because $5^2 = 25$. That is, the logarithm is the exponent that the base must be raised to in order to obtain a given number.

The base of a logarithm can be any positive number other than 1, but two bases are used so frequently that they have special names. The common logarithm has a base of 10, and the natural logarithm has a base of e.

INTRODUCE

Write these equations with empty boxes on the board. Have students determine the missing values.

$2^{\boxed{}} = 16$ **4** $7^{\boxed{}} = 49$ **2** $10^{\boxed{}} = 100{,}000$ **5**

$10^{\boxed{}} = 0.001$ **−3** $2^{\boxed{}} = \frac{1}{2}$ **−1** $e^{\boxed{}} = 1$ **0**

TEACH

1 EXPLORE

Questioning Strategies

- How do you know that $f(x) = 2^x$ is a one-to-one function? **Each *y*-value has only one *x*-value and the function's graph passes the horizontal line test.**

- How do you determine the ordered pairs for the graph of the inverse function? **Exchange the *x*- and *y*-coordinates.**

- How do you know that the graph of the inverse function has no horizontal asymptotes? **The graph of the exponential function has no vertical asymptotes.**

Differentiated Instruction

Have kinesthetic learners fold their paper over the line $y = x$ to check their graph of $f^{-1}(x)$.

2 ENGAGE

Questioning Strategies

- In the expression $\log_b y = x$, what does b represent? *b* **is the base in a power.**

- In the expression $\log_b y = x$, what does x represent? *x* **is the exponent in the power.**

- In the expression $\log_b y = x$, what does y represent? *y* **is the value of b^x.**

Teaching Strategy

When discussing Reflect Question 2c, input each *x*-coordinate from the table for $f^{-1}(x)$ in **1 EXPLORE** into $f^{-1}(x) = \log_2 x$. Show that if each input is written as a power (2^{-2}, 2^{-1}, 2^0, 2^1, and 2^2), then the outputs are the exponents in those powers.

© Houghton Mifflin Harcourt Publishing Company

7-1

Logarithmic Functions as Inverses of Exponential Functions

COMMON CORE
CC.9-12.F.IF.2,
CC.9-12.F.IF.7*,
CC.9-12.F.IF.7e*,
CC.9-12.F.BF.5(+)

Name_____ Class_____ Date_____

Essential question: *What are the characteristics of logarithmic functions?*

Recall that if $f(x)$ is a one-to-one function, then the graphs of $f(x)$ and its inverse, $f^{-1}(x)$, are reflections of each other about the line $y = x$. The domain of $f(x)$ is the range of $f^{-1}(x)$, and the range of $f(x)$ is the domain of $f^{-1}(x)$.

1 EXPLORE Graphing the Inverse of an Exponential Function

The graph of $f(x) = 2^x$ is shown. Graph $f^{-1}(x)$ by following these steps.

A   Complete the table by writing the image of each point on the graph of $f(x)$ after a reflection across the line $y = x$.

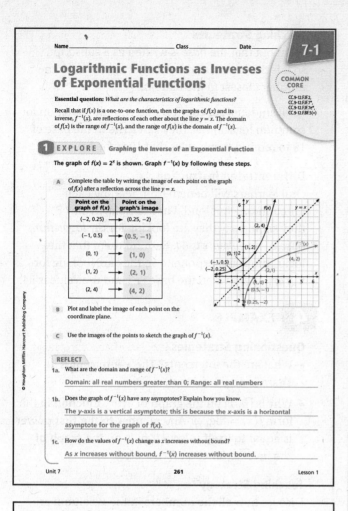

Point on the graph of $f(x)$	Point on the graph's image
$(-2, 0.25)$ →	$(0.25, -2)$
$(-1, 0.5)$ →	$(0.5, -1)$
$(0, 1)$ →	$(1, 0)$
$(1, 2)$ →	$(2, 1)$
$(2, 4)$ →	$(4, 2)$

B   Plot and label the image of each point on the coordinate plane.

C   Use the images of the points to sketch the graph of $f^{-1}(x)$.

REFLECT

1a.   What are the domain and range of $f^{-1}(x)$?

Domain: all real numbers greater than 0; Range: all real numbers

1b.   Does the graph of $f^{-1}(x)$ have any asymptotes? Explain how you know.

The y-axis is a vertical asymptote; this is because the x-axis is a horizontal

asymptote for the graph of $f(x)$.

1c.   How do the values of $f^{-1}(x)$ change as x increases without bound?

As x increases without bound, $f^{-1}(x)$ increases without bound.

Unit 7   261   Lesson 1

---

2 ENGAGE Defining Logarithmic Functions

A *logarithm* is the exponent to which a base must be raised in order to obtain a given value. For example, $2^3 = 8$, so the logarithm base 2 of 8 is 3, and you write $\log_2 8 = 3$.

Definition of Logarithm

For positive numbers y and b ($b \neq 1$), the **logarithm** of y with base b is written $\log_b y$ and is defined as follows:

$$\log_b y = x \text{ if and only if } b^x = y.$$

This definition means that every statement about exponents can be converted into an equivalent statement about logarithms, and vice versa. Note that you read $\log_b x$ as "the logarithm base b of x" or "log base b of x."

A **logarithmic function** with base b is the inverse of the exponential function with base b. For instance, the inverse of $f(x) = 2^x$ is $f^{-1}(x) = \log_2 x$, the graph of which you sketched in the Explore.

The table describes two special logarithms.

Special Logarithms		
Name	**Base**	**Notation**
Common logarithm	10	Write log x instead of $\log_{10} x$.
Natural logarithm	e	Write ln x instead of $\log_e x$.

REFLECT

2a.   Explain, in terms of a logarithmic function, how to write $7^2 = 49$ as an equivalent statement involving a logarithm.

The base of the logarithmic function is 7; it accepts 49 as input and gives 2

as output, so $\log_7 49 = 2$.

2b.   Explain, in terms of an exponential function, how to write log $1000 = 3$ as an equivalent statement involving an exponent.

The base of the exponential function is 10; it accepts 3 as input and gives

1000 as output, so $10^3 = 1000$.

2c.   The input of $f(x) = 2^x$ is an exponent and the output is a power of 2. Describe the input and output of $f^{-1}(x) = \log_2 x$. Give a specific example.

The input is a power of 2 and the output is the corresponding exponent.

For example, when the input value is 32 (which is 2^5), the output value is 5.

2d.   Find $\ln \frac{1}{e}$ by letting $\ln \frac{1}{e} = x$ and writing this statement in an equivalent form that involves an exponent. Explain your reasoning from that point on.

If $\ln \frac{1}{e} = x$, then $e^x = \frac{1}{e}$; since $\frac{1}{e} = e^{-1}$, $x = -1$.

Unit 7   262   Lesson 1

3 EXAMPLE

Questioning Strategies

- Can you input a negative number for x in $f(x) = \log_2 x$? **No, there is no power of 2 that will result in a negative number.**

- What is the base in Reflect Question 3c? How do you know? **The base is 10. When the base is not shown, it is understood to be 10.**

EXTRA EXAMPLE

Find each value of $f(x) = \log_3 x$.

A. $f(9)$ **2**

B. $f\left(\frac{1}{81}\right)$ **-4**

C. $f(3)$ **1**

D. $f(27)$ **3**

E. $f\left(\frac{1}{243}\right)$ **-5**

MATHEMATICAL PRACTICE — Highlighting the Standards

The Reflect questions for **3 EXAMPLE** address Mathematical Practice Standard 2 (Reason abstractly and quantitatively). Having students answer more questions like 3b and 3c will help them better understand logarithms.

For example, have students find the two integers that $f(40)$ lies between for $f(x) = \log_4 x$ and then explain why it lies between them. ($f(40)$ lies between 2 and 3 because $4^2 = 16$ and $4^3 = 64$.)

Also, have students estimate more outputs that are not whole numbers. For example, have them estimate $f(8,000)$ for $f(x) = \log x$ and explain their reasoning. ($f(8,000)$ is about 3.9 because 8,000 is between 1,000, or 10^3, and 10,000, or 10^4, but closer to 10^4.)

Teaching Strategies

Point out that the *base* is written as a subscript, so it is the lowest number in the equation, or the number closest to the *bottom*.

Until students get comfortable with the notation for common logarithms, they can write in the base of 10 to remind themselves that 10 is the base.

Differentiated Instruction

Oral learners will benefit from reading each function rule out loud. For example, in part B, they should say they are looking for *the logarithm, base 2, of x when x is 64*. Remind them that the logarithm is the exponent, so they are looking for the exponent when the base is 2 and the value is 64.

4 EXAMPLE

Questioning Strategies

- What are the intercepts? **The x-intercept is 1. There is no y-intercept.**

- Why is $(b, 1)$ on the graph of every function in the form $f(x) = \log_b x$? **Any number to the first power is equal to itself. Also, $(1, b)$ is on the graph of the inverse function $f(x) = b^x$.**

Teaching Strategy

Discuss how all the numbers in the x-column are powers of $\frac{1}{2}$. The domain is all real numbers, but these are the easiest to evaluate.

EXTRA EXAMPLE

Graph $f(x) = \log_5 x$. **The graph is a smooth curve that passes through $(0.2, -1)$, $(1, 0)$, $(5, 1)$, and $(25, 2)$.**

3 EXAMPLE Evaluating Logarithmic Functions

Find each value of $f(x) = \log_2 x$.

A $f(16)$

Write the function's input as a power of 2. The function's output is the exponent.

$16 = 2^4$, so $f(16) = \underline{\quad 4 \quad}$.

B $f(64)$

$64 = 2^6$, so $f(64) = \underline{\quad 6 \quad}$.

C $f\left(\frac{1}{32}\right)$

$\frac{1}{32} = 2^{-5}$, so $f\left(\frac{1}{32}\right) = \underline{\quad -5 \quad}$.

D $f\left(\frac{1}{8}\right)$

$\frac{1}{8} = 2^{-3}$, so $f\left(\frac{1}{8}\right) = \underline{\quad -3 \quad}$.

E $f(1)$

$1 = 2^0$, so $f(1) = \underline{\quad 0 \quad}$.

REFLECT

3a. Is it possible to evaluate $f(0)$? Why or why not?

No; it is not possible to write 0 as a power of 2.

3b. For $f(x) = \log_2 x$, between which two integers does $f(40)$ lie? Explain.

$f(40)$ must be between 5 and 6, since 40 is between 32 and 64; that is, 40 is between 2^5 and 2^6, so $\log_2 40$ is between 5 and 6.

3c. Estimate $g(95)$ for $g(x) = \log x$, without using a calculator. Explain.

$g(95)$ is very close to 2, because 95 is between 10^1 and 10^2, but much closer to 10^2.

3d. Without using a calculator, explain how you know that $\ln 20 > \log 20$.

$\ln 20$ has a base of e and $\log 20$ has a base of 10. Because $e < 10$, the power of e that equals 20 must be greater than the power of 10 that equals 20.

---

4 EXAMPLE Graphing a Logarithmic Function

Graph $f(x) = \log_{\frac{1}{2}} x$.

A Complete the table of values.

x	$f(x)$
$\frac{1}{4}$	2
$\frac{1}{2}$	1
1	0
2	-1
4	-2
8	-3

B Plot the points. Connect them with a smooth curve.

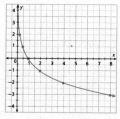

REFLECT

4a. How is the graph of $f(x) = \log_{\frac{1}{2}} x$ related to the graph of $f(x) = \log_2 x$ from the Explore? Why does this make sense?

The graph of $f(x) = \log_{\frac{1}{2}} x$ is a reflection in the x-axis of the graph of $f(x) = \log_2 x$. Because $\frac{1}{2} = 2^{-1}$, $\left(\frac{1}{2}\right)^m = 2^{-m}$ for any value of m; if you let $x = \left(\frac{1}{2}\right)^m = 2^{-m}$, then $\log_{\frac{1}{2}} x = m$ and $\log_2 x = -m$, so the two logarithmic functions have opposite values for any given value of x.

4b. What point do the graphs of $f(x) = \log_{\frac{1}{2}} x$ and $f(x) = \log_2 x$ have in common? Why?

$(1, 0)$ appears on both graphs because $\left(\frac{1}{2}\right)^0 = 1$ and $2^0 = 1$.

4c. Describe the end behavior of $f(x) = \log_{\frac{1}{2}} x$.

As x approaches 0, $f(x)$ increases without bound. As x increases without bound, $f(x)$ decreases without bound.

4d. How is the graph of $f(x) = \log_{\frac{1}{2}} x$ related to the graph of $f(x) = \left(\frac{1}{2}\right)^x$?

The graph of $f(x) = \log_{\frac{1}{2}} x$ is a reflection of the graph of $f(x) = \left(\frac{1}{2}\right)^x$ in the line $y = x$.

Essential Question

What are the characteristics of logarithmic functions?

A logarithmic function is an inverse of an exponential function, so the output is the exponent needed to raise the base to obtain a specific value. The graph is a reflection of its corresponding exponential function across the line $y = x$.

Summarize

Have students make a graphic organizer to compare and contrast exponential and logarithmic functions. One possibility is shown below.

Exponential		Logarithmic
$f(x) = b^x$	Function	$f(x) = \log_b x$
all real numbers	Domain	all real numbers > 0
all real numbers > 0	Range	all real numbers
$y = 0$	Asymptote	$x = 0$
	Graph if $b > 1$	

Where skills are taught	Where skills are practiced
1 EXPLORE	EX. 1
3 EXAMPLE	EXS. 2–13
4 EXAMPLE	EXS. 17, 18, 20

Exercises 14 and 15: Students estimate the value of a common logarithm and a natural logarithm by determining the powers of 10 or e that are just below and just above the given input value.

Exercise 16: Students use the definition of a logarithm to determine that the log, base b, of b, must be 1.

Exercise 19: Given a graph of a logarithmic function, students determine its function rule.

Exercise 21: Given two points on the graph of $f(x) = \log_b x$, students determine the value of b.

Exercise 22: Given a real-world scenario for the exponential function $f(x) = 2^x$, students describe the input and output of the inverse logarithmic function in terms of the scenario, evaluate the function for a given input, and then determine an area function and its inverse for a section of paper folded x times.

PRACTICE

1. The graph of $f(x) = 3^x$ is shown.

a. Use the labeled points to help you draw the graph of $f^{-1}(x)$. Label the corresponding points on $f^{-1}(x)$.

b. Write the inverse function, $f^{-1}(x)$, using logarithmic notation.

$f^{-1}(x) = \log_3 x$

c. State the domain and range of $f^{-1}(x)$.

D: positive real numbers; R: all real numbers

Find each value of $f(x) = \log_4 x$.

2. $f(16)$

2

3. $f\left(\frac{1}{64}\right)$

−3

4. $f(4)$

1

Find each value of $f(x) = \log x$.

5. $f(10{,}000)$

4

6. $f(0.1)$

−1

7. $f\left(\frac{1}{100}\right)$

−2

Find each value of $f(x) = \log_{\frac{1}{4}} x$.

8. $f(16)$

−2

9. $f(1)$

0

10. $f\left(\frac{1}{64}\right)$

3

Evaluate each expression.

11. $\log_8 64$

2

12. $\log_2 1024$

10

13. $\log 1{,}000{,}000$

6

14. For $f(x) = \log x$, between what two integers does $f(6)$ lie? Explain.

$f(6)$ must be between 0 and 1, since 6 is between 1 and 10; that is, 6 is between 10^0 and 10^1, so log 6 is between 0 and 1.

15. Explain how you can estimate the value of ln 10 without using a calculator.

e is a bit less than 3, so 10 is between e^2 and e^3. This means that ln 10 is between 2 and 3. It is closer to 2 because 10 is closer to e^2.

16. What is the value of $\log_b b$ for $b > 0$ and $b \neq 1$? Explain.

$\log_b b = 1$ because $b^1 = b$.

Graph each logarithmic function.

17. $f(x) = \log_4 x$

18. $f(x) = \log_{\frac{1}{3}} x$

19. The graph of what logarithmic function is shown? Explain your reasoning.

$f(x) = \log_{\frac{1}{10}} x$; the graph passes through $(10, -1)$,

so $\log_b 10 = -1$ and $b = 10^{-1} = \frac{1}{10}$.

20. Name some values you would choose for x if you were plotting points to sketch the graph of $f(x) = \log x$ without using a calculator. Explain.

Sample answer: $\frac{1}{10}$, 1, and 10; these are powers of 10 with integer exponents $(10^{-1}, 10^0, \text{ and } 10^1)$ giving the points $\left(\frac{1}{10}, -1\right)$, $(1, 0)$, and $(10, 1)$.

21. The graph of $f(x) = \log_b x$ passes through the points $(1, 0)$ and $(36, 2)$. What is the value of b? Explain.

6; $\log_b 36 = 2$, so $b^2 = 36$ and $b = 6$.

22. When you fold a sheet of paper in half x times, the function $f(x) = 2^x$ gives the number of sections that are created by the folds.

a. Describe the input and output of the function $f^{-1}(x) = \log_2 x$ in the problem context.

The input is the number of sections and the output is the number of folds needed to make that many sections.

b. Use $f^{-1}(x)$ to find the number of folds needed to create 64 sections.

$f^{-1}(64) = \log_2 64 = 6$, so 6 folds are needed.

c. Assume that a sheet of paper has an area of 1. Write an exponential function $g(x)$ that gives the area of a section of the paper after being folded in half x times.

$g(x) = \left(\frac{1}{2}\right)^x$

d. Write the rule for $g^{-1}(x)$ and describe the function's input and output.

$g^{-1}(x) = \log_{\frac{1}{2}} x$; the input is the area of a section and the output is the number of folds needed to make a section having that area.

Transforming the Graph of $f(x) = \log_b x$

Essential question: *How does changing the values of a, h, and k affect the graph of $f(x) = a \log_b (x - h) + k$?*

CC.9-12.F.IF.7 Graph functions expressed symbolically and show key features of the graph ...*

CC.9-12.F.IF.7e Graph ... logarithmic functions, showing intercepts and end behavior, ...*

CC.9-12.F.BF.3 Identify the effect on the graph of replacing $f(x)$ by $f(x) + k$, $k f(x)$, ... and $f(x + k)$ for specific values of k (both positive and negative); find the value of k given the graphs ...

Prerequisites

Transforming exponential functions, Lessons 6-2 and 6-3

Graphing logarithmic functions, Lesson 7–1

Math Background

Students will explore transformations of the graphs of logarithmic functions. As with previous types of functions, they will see how changing the values of a, h, and k in $f(x) = a \log_b (x - h) + k$ translate, shrink, or stretch the graph of the parent function $f(x) = a \log_b x$.

INTRODUCE

Review with students how changing the values of a, h, and k affected the graphs of the parent functions of quadratic, polynomial, rational, and exponential functions. Then, have students evaluate the functions below and compare their answers with what they would get if they evaluated the parent functions at the same values.

$g(8)$ for $g(x) = 3 \log_2 x$ 9
$g(4)$ for $g(x) = \log_2 x + 4$ 6
$g(1)$ for $g(x) = \log_2 \left(x - \frac{1}{2}\right) - 1$

TEACH

1 EXAMPLE

Questioning Strategies

- What is the difference between $\log_2 (x - 3)$ and $\log_2 x - 3$? In the first, 3 is subtracted from x, and then the log is taken. In the second, the log of x is taken, and then 3 is subtracted.

- What are the equations of the asymptotes for the graphs of $f(x)$, $g(x)$, and $h(x)$? $x = 0$ for $f(x)$ and $x = 3$ for $g(x)$ and $h(x)$.

- Which parameter, h or k, changes the domain of the function? Why? h; because it causes the graph to shift horizontally

- If you were finding values of $g(x)$ or $h(x)$ for an x-value less than 3.5 and an x-value greater than 11, which x-values would you use and why? *Sample answer*: 3.25 and 19; because after 3 is subtracted from each, the value is an integer power of 2 (2^{-2} and 2^4).

EXTRA EXAMPLE

The graph of $f(x) = \log_{\frac{1}{2}} x$ is shown. Graph $g(x) = \log_{\frac{1}{2}}(x + 4)$ and $h(x) = \log_{\frac{1}{2}}(x + 4) - 1$.

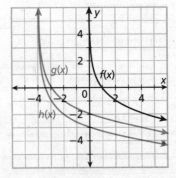

The graph of $g(x)$ is the graph of $f(x)$ shifted 4 units left, and the graph of $h(x)$ is the graph of $g(x)$ shifted 1 unit down.

Name_____ Class_____ Date_____

Transforming the Graph of $f(x) = \log_b x$

COMMON CORE

CC.9-12.F.IF.7*,
CC.9-12.F.IF.7e*,
CC.9-12.F.BF.3

Essential question: *How does changing the values of a, h, and k affect the graph of* $f(x) = a\log_b (x - h) + k$?

A general logarithmic function has the form $f(x) = a\log_b (x - h) + k$ where $b > 0$ ($b \neq 1$) and a, h, and k are real numbers. The effect of changing the parameters a, h, and k in a logarithmic function is similar to the effect of changing these parameters in other types of functions.

1 EXAMPLE Changing the Values of h and k

The graph of $f(x) = \log_2 x$ is shown. Graph $g(x) = \log_2 (x - 3)$ and $h(x) = \log_2 (x - 3) + 2$.

A Complete the table of values.

x	g(x)	h(x)
3.5	−1	1
4	0	2
5	1	3
7	2	4
11	3	5

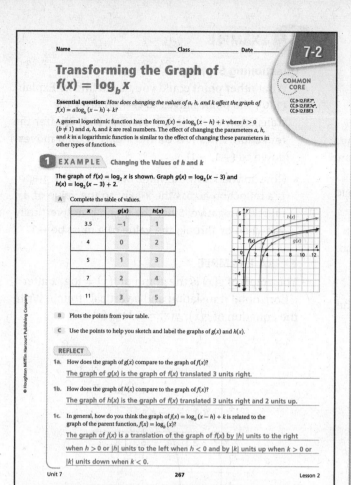

B Plots the points from your table.

C Use the points to help you sketch and label the graphs of $g(x)$ and $h(x)$.

REFLECT

1a. How does the graph of $g(x)$ compare to the graph of $f(x)$?

The graph of $g(x)$ is the graph of $f(x)$ translated 3 units right.

1b. How does the graph of $h(x)$ compare to the graph of $f(x)$?

The graph of $h(x)$ is the graph of $f(x)$ translated 3 units right and 2 units up.

1c. In general, how do you think the graph of $j(x) = \log_b (x - h) + k$ is related to the graph of the parent function, $f(x) = \log_b (x)$?

The graph of $j(x)$ is a translation of the graph of $f(x)$ by $|h|$ units to the right when $h > 0$ or $|h|$ units to the left when $h < 0$ and by $|k|$ units up when $k > 0$ or $|k|$ units down when $k < 0$.

Unit 7   267   Lesson 2

---

2 EXAMPLE Changing the Value of a

The graph of $f(x) = \log_{\frac{1}{2}} x$ is shown. Graph $g(x) = 2\log_{\frac{1}{2}} x$ and $h(x) = -\frac{1}{2}\log_{\frac{1}{2}} x$.

A Complete the table of values.

x	g(x)	h(x)
1	0	0
2	−2	$\frac{1}{2}$
4	−4	1
8	−6	$\frac{3}{2}$

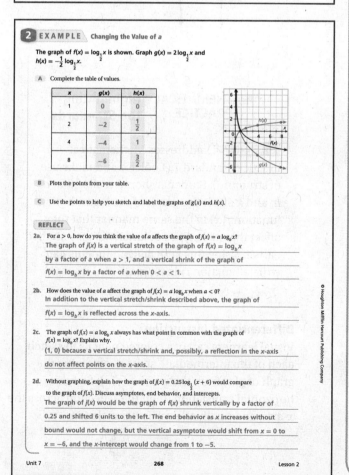

B Plots the points from your table.

C Use the points to help you sketch and label the graphs of $g(x)$ and $h(x)$.

REFLECT

2a. For $a > 0$, how do you think the value of a affects the graph of $j(x) = a\log_b x$?

The graph of $j(x)$ is a vertical stretch of the graph of $f(x) = \log_b x$ by a factor of a when $a > 1$, and a vertical shrink of the graph of $f(x) = \log_b x$ by a factor of a when $0 < a < 1$.

2b. How does the value of a affect the graph of $j(x) = a\log_b x$ when $a < 0$?

In addition to the vertical stretch/shrink described above, the graph of $f(x) = \log_b x$ is reflected across the x-axis.

2c. The graph of $j(x) = a\log_b x$ always has what point in common with the graph of $f(x) = \log_b x$? Explain why.

(1, 0) because a vertical stretch/shrink and, possibly, a reflection in the x-axis do not affect points on the x-axis.

2d. Without graphing, explain how the graph of $j(x) = 0.25\log_{\frac{1}{2}} (x + 6)$ would compare to the graph of $f(x)$. Discuss asymptotes, end behavior, and intercepts.

The graph of $j(x)$ would be the graph of $f(x)$ shrunk vertically by a factor of 0.25 and shifted 6 units to the left. The end behavior as x increases without bound would not change, but the vertical asymptote would shift from $x = 0$ to $x = -6$, and the x-intercept would change from 1 to −5.

Unit 7   268   Lesson 2

© Houghton Mifflin Harcourt Publishing Company

Questioning Strategies

- How did the value of *a* affect the graphs of *exponential* functions? How does this compare with its effect on the graphs of logarithmic functions? **For exponential functions, it stretched the graph vertically by a factor of *a* for $a > 1$ and shrunk the graph vertically by a factor of *a* for $0 < a < 1$. The effect is the same for logarithmic functions.**

- Why does a negative value of *a* reflect the graph across the *x*-axis? **The *y*-values are opposites, so points above the *x*-axis are moved below the *x*-axis and vice versa.**

- What are the equations of the asymptotes for the graphs of $f(x)$, $g(x)$, and $h(x)$? **$x = 0$ for each.**

EXTRA EXAMPLE

The graph of $f(x) = \log_2 x$ is shown. Graph $g(x) = -3 \log_2 x$ and $h(x) = \frac{1}{4} \log_2 x$.

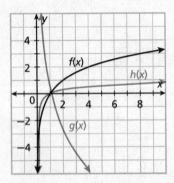

Relative to the graph of $f(x)$, the graph of $g(x)$ is vertically stretched by a factor of 3 and reflected across the *x*-axis, and the graph of $h(x)$ is shrunk vertically by a factor of $\frac{1}{4}$.

Teaching Strategy

Have students graph $j(x) = \frac{1}{2} \log_{\frac{1}{2}} x$ on the grid along with $g(x)$ and $h(x)$ so they can see that the graph of $j(x)$ is a reflection of the graph of $h(x)$ across the *x*-axis.

Questioning Strategies

- What other point could you use to find *k*? Explain. **(1, 0); the point moves to (−1, 0) after the translation to the left. It stays at (−1, 0) after the reflection, since it is on the *x*-axis. It then moves down to (−1, −1).**

- How do you know the value of *a* is −1? **The graph is a reflection across the *x*-axis, so the value of *a* must be negative. Since the graph is not vertically stretched or shrunk, the value of *a* must be −1.**

EXTRA EXAMPLE

The graph of $g(x)$ is the graph of $f(x) = \log_3 x$ after a horizontal translation and a vertical stretch. Write the equation of $g(x)$. **$g(x) = 2 \log_3 (x - 3)$**

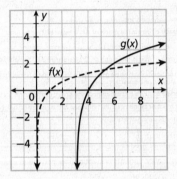

MATHEMATICAL PRACTICE · **Highlighting the Standards**

3 EXAMPLE addresses Mathematical Practice Standard 7 (Look for and make use of structure). Students should realize that *a*, *h*, and *k* affect the graph of the logarithmic function $f(x)$ in the same manner that they affect the other types of functions they studied earlier. Using this knowledge, students can write a function rule for $g(x)$.

Differentiated Instruction

Visual learners can use colored pencils to sketch each of the intermediate steps in obtaining the graph of $g(x)$ from the graph of $f(x)$: first the horizontal translation, then the reflection across the *x*-axis, and finally the vertical translation.

3 **EXAMPLE**   Writing an Equation from a Graph

The graph of $g(x)$ is the graph of $f(x) = \log_{\frac{1}{4}} x$ after a horizontal translation, a reflection in the x-axis, and a vertical translation. Write the equation of $g(x)$.

A   Let $g(x) = a \log_{\frac{1}{4}} (x - h) + k$. Find the value of h.

The vertical asymptote of $g(x)$ is the line $\underline{x = -2}$.

The vertical asymptote of the parent function $f(x)$ is $x = 0$. This means

$f(x)$ is translated $\underline{\quad 2 \quad}$ units to the left and so $h = \underline{\quad -2 \quad}$.

B   Find the sign of a.

Since the graph of the parent function $f(x)$ is reflected across the

x-axis, the sign of a is $\underline{\text{negative}}$. Since the transformation did not involve a stretch.

C   Find the value of k.

Consider the point $(4, -1)$ on the graph of $f(x)$ and the sequence of transformations that maps it to the corresponding point on the graph of $g(x)$.

The horizontal translation maps $(4, -1)$ to $(2, -1)$. Then the reflection across the x-axis maps $(2, -1)$ to $(2, 1)$. Finally, the vertical translation maps $(2, 1)$ to $(2, 0)$.

The final transformation is a translation of $\underline{\quad 1 \quad}$ unit(s) down, so $k = \underline{\quad -1 \quad}$.

D   Write the equation.

Using the values of the parameters from above, $g(x) = \underline{-\log_{\frac{1}{4}} (x + 2) - 1}$.

REFLECT

3a.   How can you use the x-intercept of the graph of $g(x)$ to check that you wrote a correct equation?

The x-intercept is 2. Check that the ordered pair (2, 0) satisfies the equation.

$-\log_{\frac{1}{4}} (2 + 2) - 1 = -\log_{\frac{1}{4}} 4 - 1 = -(-1) - 1 = 1 - 1 = 0$

3b.   Given the graph of a function $f(x) = ab^{x-h} + k$, which parameter (a, h, or k) is determined by the location of the graph's asymptote? Given the graph of a function $g(x) = a \log_b (x - h) + k$, which parameter (a, h, or k) is determined by the location of the graph's asymptote? Explain each of your answers.

k, because the parent function's graph has a horizontal asymptote that is affected

only by a vertical translation, which k controls;

h, because the parent function's graph has a vertical asymptote that is affected

only by a horizontal translation, which h controls.

Unit 7   269   Lesson 2

PRACTICE

The graph of $f(x) = \log_3 x$ is shown. Write the function rules for $g(x)$ and $h(x)$ based on the descriptions given. Then sketch and label the graphs of $g(x)$ and $h(x)$ on the same coordinate plane.

1.   The graph of $g(x)$ is the translation of the graph of $f(x)$ to the right 4 units and up 3 units.

$g(x) = \log_3 (x - 4) + 3$

2.   The graph of $h(x)$ is the reflection of the graph of $f(x)$ over the x-axis followed by a translation down 2 units

$h(x) = -\log_3 x - 2$

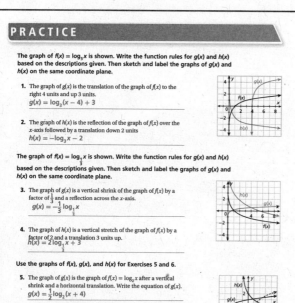

The graph of $f(x) = \log_{\frac{1}{3}} x$ is shown. Write the function rules for $g(x)$ and $h(x)$ based on the descriptions given. Then sketch and label the graphs of $g(x)$ and $h(x)$ on the same coordinate plane.

3.   The graph of $g(x)$ is a vertical shrink of the graph of $f(x)$ by a factor of $\frac{1}{3}$ and a reflection across the x-axis.

$g(x) = -\frac{1}{3} \log_{\frac{1}{3}} x$

4.   The graph of $h(x)$ is a vertical stretch of the graph of $f(x)$ by a factor of 2 and a translation 3 units up.

$h(x) = 2 \log_{\frac{1}{3}} x + 3$

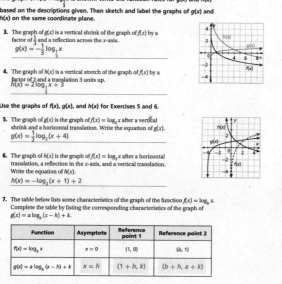

Use the graphs of $f(x)$, $g(x)$, and $h(x)$ for Exercises 5 and 6.

5.   The graph of $g(x)$ is the graph of $f(x) = \log_2 x$ after a vertical shrink and a horizontal translation. Write the equation of $g(x)$.

$g(x) = \frac{1}{2} \log_2 (x + 4)$

6.   The graph of $h(x)$ is the graph of $f(x) = \log_2 x$ after a horizontal translation, a reflection in the x-axis, and a vertical translation. Write the equation of $h(x)$.

$h(x) = -\log_2 (x + 1) + 2$

7.   The table below lists some characteristics of the graph of the function $f(x) = \log_b x$. Complete the table by listing the corresponding characteristics of the graph of $g(x) = a \log_b (x - h) + k$.

Function	Asymptote	Reference point 1	Reference point 2
$f(x) = \log_b x$	$x = 0$	$(1, 0)$	$(b, 1)$
$g(x) = a \log_b (x - h) + k$	$x = h$	$(1 + h, k)$	$(b + h, a + k)$

Unit 7   270   Lesson 2

Essential Question

How does changing the values of a, h, and k affect the graph of $f(x) = a \log_b (x - h) + k$?
The graph is stretched vertically for $|a| > 1$ and shrunk vertically for $0 < |a| < 1$. If a is negative, the graph is reflected across the *x*-axis as well. If *h* is positive, the graph is translated right, and if *h* is negative, it is translated left. If *k* is positive, the graph is translated up, and if *k* is negative, it is translated down.

Summarize

Have students create a table describing the effects of changing *a*, *h*, and *k* on the six types of functions they have studied so far. Students should list quadratic, polynomial, rational, radical, exponential, and logarithmic in that order. Students can revisit this table in Unit 8 when they graph trigonometric functions.

Where skills are taught	Where skills are practiced
1 EXAMPLE	EX. 1
2 EXAMPLE	EXS. 2–4
3 EXAMPLE	EXS. 5, 6

Exercise 7: Students complete a table showing how changing the values of *a*, *h*, and *k* in $g(x) = a \log_b (x - h) + k$ affect the asymptote and the points $(1, 0)$ and $(b, 1)$ for the graph of the parent function $f(x) = \log_b x$.

Exercise 8: Students explore horizontal stretches and shrinks. They see how a horizontal stretch or shrink by a factor of $\frac{1}{c}$ has the same effect as a vertical translation by the logarithm of *c*.

8. In this exercise, you will make a conjecture about horizontal stretches and shrinks of the graphs of logarithmic functions.

a. Let $f(x) = \log_2 8x$ and $g(x) = \log_2 x + 3$. Complete the table. Then graph $f(x)$ and $g(x)$ on the coordinate plane at right.

x	f(x)	g(x)
1	3	3
2	4	4
4	5	5
8	6	6

b. Describe the graphs of $f(x)$ and $g(x)$ as transformations of the parent base 2 logarithmic function.

The graph of $f(x)$ is a horizontal shrink by a factor of $\frac{1}{8}$;

The graph of $g(x)$ is a translation up 3 units.

c. Let $h(x) = \log_2 \frac{1}{2}x$ and $j(x) = \log_2 x - 1$. Complete the table. Then graph $h(x)$ and $j(x)$ on the coordinate plane at right.

x	h(x)	j(x)
1	−1	−1
2	0	0
4	1	1
8	2	2

d. Describe the graphs of $h(x)$ and $j(x)$ as transformations of the parent base 2 logarithmic function.

The graph of $h(x)$ is a horizontal stretch by a factor of 2;

The graph of $j(x)$ is a translation down 1 unit.

e. The rules for the functions $f(x)$ and $h(x)$ have the form $\log_2 cx$ while the rules for the functions $g(x)$ and $j(x)$ have the form $\log_2 x + k$. Write the values of k in $g(x)$ and $j(x)$ as logarithms with base 2.

$3 = \log_2 8$ and $-1 = \log_2 \frac{1}{2}$

f. Summarize the relationship between a horizontal stretch or horizontal shrink of the graph of a logarithmic function and a translation of the graph.

A horizontal stretch or shrink by a factor of $\frac{1}{c}$ is equivalent to a

vertical translation by k where $k = \log_b c$.

Properties of Logarithms

Essential question: *How do you prove properties of logarithms?*

© Houghton Mifflin Harcourt Publishing Company

Standards for Mathematical Content

CC.9-12.F.BF.5(+) Understand the inverse relationship between exponents and logarithms and use this relationship to solve problems involving logarithms and exponents.

Prerequisites

Properties of exponents, Algebra 1

Logarithmic functions as inverses of exponential functions, Lesson 7–1

Math Background

Because of the inverse relationship between logarithms and exponents, the properties of logarithms are similar to the properties of exponents. For example, to find a product of powers, such as $x^5(x^2)$, keep the base and add the exponents: x^{5+2}. To find the log of a product, such as $\log_b 5(2)$, add the log of each factor: $\log_b 5 + \log_b 2$.

INTRODUCE

Have students simplify these expressions to review properties of exponents. Students should state the names of the properties used. Then ask students to propose a similar property for logarithms.

$x^4 x^3$ x^7; **Product of Powers Property**

$\dfrac{x^6}{x^2}$ x^4; **Quotient of Powers Property**

$(x^5)^3$ x^{15}; **Power of a Power Property**

TEACH

1 EXPLORE

Materials
graphing calculator

Questioning Strategies

- What is the base for logarithms written $\log x$? for logarithms written $\ln x$? **The base for $\log x$ is 10. The base for $\ln x$ is e.**

- How do you enter e on a graphing calculator?

Press [2nd] [÷] .

2 ENGAGE

Questioning Strategies

- Which property of exponents is similar to the Product Property of Logarithms? Why? **Product of Powers Property; both use addition to rewrite an expression involving multiplication.**

- Which property of exponents is similar to the Quotient Property of Logarithms? Why? **Quotient of Powers Property; both use subtraction to rewrite an expression involving division.**

- How is the Power Property of Logarithms similar to the Power of a Power Property? **In $(x^m)^n$, there are n factors of x^m. Because $n \log_b m$ represents multiplication, you can think of it as n factors of $\log_b m$.**

Teaching Strategy

Give students examples of each property of logarithms using integers. Have students append these examples to the table given in 2 ENGAGE. Examples could include the following:

$$\log_3 9(27) = \log_3 9 + \log_3 27 = 2 + 3 = 5$$

$$\log_3 \frac{27}{9} = \log_3 27 - \log_3 9 = 3 - 2 = 1$$

$$\log_3 27^4 = 4(\log_3 27) = 4(3) = 12$$

Avoid Common Errors

Students sometimes employ the Product Property of Logarithms when there is no product. Show them that a logarithm is not distributive.

$$\log_2 (8 + 32) \neq \log_2 8 + \log_2 32$$

Students also may be tempted to write a difference of logarithms as a quotient, an improper use of the Quotient Property of Logarithms. Demonstrate the following:

$$\log_2 32 - \log_2 8 \neq \frac{\log_2 32}{\log_2 8}.$$

© Houghton Mifflin Harcourt Publishing Company

Name_____ Class_____ Date_____

7-3

Properties of Logarithms

Essential question: How do you prove properties of logarithms?

COMMON CORE
CC.9-12.F.BF.5(+)

1 EXPLORE   Comparing Logarithmic Expressions

Use a calculator to evaluate each of the following expressions. When necessary, round your answers to three decimal places.

A $\log e$ __0.434__

B $\log 10e$ __1.434__

C $\log \frac{e}{10}$ __−0.566__

D $\log e^{10}$ __4.343__

E $(\log e)(\ln 10)$ __1__

REFLECT

1a. How do $\log 10e$, $\log \frac{e}{10}$, and $\log e^{10}$ compare to $\log e$?

$\log 10e$ is 1 more than $\log e$; $\log \frac{e}{10}$ is 1 less than $\log e$; $\log e^{10}$ is 10 times

$\log e$.

1b. How do you know that $\log e$ and $\ln 10$ are reciprocals? Given that the expressions are reciprocals, show another way to represent each expression.

Since the product of $\log e$ and $\ln 10$ is 1, the expressions are reciprocals;

$\log e = \frac{1}{\ln 10}$ and $\ln 10 = \frac{1}{\log e}$.

2 ENGAGE   Properties of Logarithms

Recall that a logarithm is the exponent to which a base must be raised in order to obtain a given number. From this definition you can see that $\log_b b^m = m$. It follows that $\log_b b^0 = 0$, so $\log_b 1 = 0$. Also, $\log_b b^1 = 1$, so $\log_b b = 1$. These facts, and some additional properties of logarithms, are summarized below.

Properties of Logarithms

For any positive numbers a, m, n, b ($b \neq 1$), and c ($c \neq 1$), the following properties hold.

Definition-Based Properties	$\log_b b^m = m$ $\log_b 1 = 0$ $\log_b b = 1$
Product Property of Logarithms	$\log_b mn = \log_b m + \log_b n$
Quotient Property of Logarithms	$\log_b \frac{m}{n} = \log_b m - \log_b n$
Power Property of Logarithms	$\log_b m^n = n \log_b m$
Change of Base Property of Logarithms	$\log_c a = \frac{\log_b a}{\log_b c}$

REFLECT

2a. Use the definition of a logarithm to explain why $\log 10 = 1$ and $\ln e = 1$.

By the definition of a logarithm, $\log 10 = \log_{10} 10^1 = 1$ and $\ln e = \log_e e^1 = 1$.

2b. Use the Product Property of Logarithms to explain why $\log 10e$ is 1 more than $\log e$.

By the Product Property of Logarithms, $\log 10e = \log 10 + \log e = 1 + \log e$.

2c. Use the Quotient Property of Logarithms to explain why $\log \frac{e}{10}$ is 1 less than $\log e$.

By the Quotient Property of Logarithms, $\log \frac{e}{10} = \log e - \log 10 = \log e - 1$.

2d. Use the Power Property of Logarithms to explain why $\log e^{10}$ is 10 times $\log e$.

By the Power Property of Logarithms, $\log e^{10} = 10 \log e$.

2e. Use the Change of Base Property to change the base of $\ln 10$ from e to 10. What does the result tell you about $\ln 10$?

$\ln 10 = \frac{\log 10}{\log e} = \frac{1}{\log e}$; $\ln 10$ is the reciprocal of $\log e$.

2f. What is the relationship between $\log e$ and $\log \frac{1}{e}$? Explain your reasoning.

They are opposites; by the Quotient Property of Logarithms, $\log \frac{1}{e} = $

$\log 1 - \log e = 0 - \log e = -\log e$.

3 EXAMPLE   Proving the Product Property of Logarithms

Prove the Product Property of Logarithms.

A Given positive numbers m, n, and b ($b \neq 1$), show that $\log_b mn = \log_b m + \log_b n$.

To prove this property, convert statements about logarithms to statements about exponents. Then use properties of exponents.

Let $\log_b m = p$ and let $\log_b n = q$.

By the definition of a logarithm, $m = b^p$ and __$n = b^q$__.

B $\log_b mn = \log_b \left(\boxed{b^p b^q} \right)$ Substitution

$= \log_b b^{\boxed{p+q}}$ Product of Powers Property of Exponents

$= \boxed{p+q}$ Definition of a logarithm

$= \log_b m + \log_b n$ Substitution

So, $\log_b mn = \log_b m + \log_b n$.

Questioning Strategies

Can you extend the Product Property of Logarithms to three factors? If so, give an example. Yes; *Sample answer:* $\log_2 64 = \log_2 (2)(4)(8) = \log_2 2 + \log_2 4 + \log_2 8 = 1 + 2 + 3 = 6$ and $2^6 = 64$.

EXTRA EXAMPLE

Prove that you can extend the Product Property of Logarithms to three factors, or that $\log_b kmn = \log_b k + \log_b m + \log_b n$. Let $\log_b k = p$, $\log_b m = q$, and $\log_b n = r$. By the definition of a logarithm, $k = b^p$, $m = b^q$, and $n = b^r$. By substitution, $\log_b kmn = \log_b (b^p b^q b^r)$. By the Product of Powers Property of Exponents, $\log_b (b^p b^q b^r) = \log_b b^{p+q+r}$. By the definition of a logarithm, $\log_b b^{p+q+r} = p + q + r$, which equals $\log_b k + \log_b m + \log_b n$ by substitution.

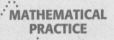

MATHEMATICAL PRACTICE **Highlighting the Standards**

3 EXAMPLE and many of the practice exercises address Mathematical Practice Standard 3 (Construct viable arguments and critique the reasoning of others). Students write formal proofs for the properties, verify the properties by showing they work in certain cases, and confirm properties by graphing equivalent equations on a graphing calculator.

Essential Question

How do you prove properties of logarithms?
You can prove properties of logarithms by converting the statements about logarithms to statements about exponents, using the properties of exponents, and then rewriting the exponential expressions as logarithmic expressions.

Summarize

Have students make a graphic organizer that compares the properties of logarithms with the corresponding properties of exponents.

Where skills are taught	Where skills are practiced
2 ENGAGE	EXS. 4–9
3 EXAMPLE	EXS. 1–3

Exercise 10: Students explore how the Change of Base Property can be used to enter logarithms of any base on a graphing calculator. Then, they use their results to evaluate $\log_2 5$.

Exercises 11 and 12: Students use their graphing calculators to confirm the Quotient and Power Properties of Logarithms. They graph functions with equivalent function rules and see that the graphs coincide.

Exercise 13: Students identify, explain, and correct an error commonly made when using the Power Property of Logarithms.

Exercise 14: Students use properties of logarithms to rewrite a formula involving the intensity of sound. Then, they use the rewritten formula to answer a question about the intensity of a sound with a given sound level.

REFLECT

3a. Suppose $m = n$ in $\log_b mn$. What result do you get when you apply the Product Property of Logarithms? This result is a particular case of what other property of logarithms? Explain.

When $m = n$, $\log_b mn = \log_b (m \cdot m) = \log_b m + \log_b m = 2 \log_b m$; this result is a

particular case of the Power Property of Logarithms when $n = 2$: $\log_b m^2 = 2 \log_b m$

PRACTICE

1. Prove the Quotient Property of Logarithms. Justify each step of your proof.

Let $\log_b m = p$ and $\log_b n = q$. Then $m = b^p$ and $n = b^q$. (Def. of a logarithm)

$$\log_b \frac{m}{n} = \log_b \frac{b^p}{b^q} \qquad \text{(Substitution)}$$
$$= \log_b b^{p-q} \qquad \text{(Quotient of Powers Property of Exponents)}$$
$$= p - q \qquad \text{(Definition of a logarithm)}$$
$$= \log_b m - \log_b n \qquad \text{(Substitution)}$$

2. Prove the Power Property of Logarithms. Justify each step of your proof.

Let $\log_b m = p$. Then $m = b^p$. (Definition of a logarithm)

$$\log_b m^n = \log_b (b^p)^n \qquad \text{(Substitution)}$$
$$= \log_b b^{pn} \qquad \text{(Power of a Power Property of Exponents)}$$
$$= pn \qquad \text{(Definition of a logarithm)}$$
$$= (\log_b m)(n) \qquad \text{(Substitution)}$$
$$= n \log_b m \qquad \text{(Commutative Property)}$$

3. When n is a positive integer, show how you can prove the Power Property of Logarithms using the Product Property of Logarithms. (*Hint:* When n is a positive integer, $m^n = m \cdot m \cdot m \cdot \cdots \cdot m$ where m appears as a factor n times.)

When n is a positive integer, $\log_b m^n = \log_b (m \cdot m \cdot m \cdot \cdots \cdot m) = \log_b m +$

$\log_b m + \log_b m + \cdots + \log_b m = n \log_b m.$

Simplify each expression.

4. $\log_3 3^4$

4

5. $\log_7 7^5$

5

6. $\log_6 36^9$

18

7. $\log_{\frac{1}{10}} 10^3$

−3

8. $\log_2 14 - \log_2 7$

1

9. $\log 25 + \log 4$

2

---

10. Your calculator has keys for evaluating only common logarithms and natural logarithms. Explain why you don't need a generic logarithm key where you must specify the base. Then describe how you can evaluate $\log_2 5$ using either one of your calculator's logarithm keys. Finally, find the value of $\log_2 5$ to 3 decimal places using each key to demonstrate that you get the same result.

You can use the Change of Base Property to convert any base to base 10 or

base e; enter log 5 divided by log 2 or ln 5 divided by ln 2; the result is 2.322

in both cases.

11. On a graphing calculator, graph $y = \log \frac{10}{x}$ and $y = 1 - \log x$ in the same viewing window. What do you notice? Which property of logarithms explains what you see? Why?

The graphs coincide. The Quotient Property of Logarithms explains this because

$\log \frac{10}{x} = \log 10 - \log x = 1 - \log x.$

12. On a graphing calculator, graph $y = \log 10^x$ and $y = x \log 10$ in the same viewing window.

a. What do you notice? Which property of logarithms explains what you see? Why?

The graphs coincide. The Power Property of Logarithms explains this because

$\log 10^x = x \log 10.$

b. What linear function are both functions equivalent to? Explain.

$y = x$; $y = \log 10^x = x$ by definition of a logarithm, and $y = x \log 10 = x \cdot 1 = x$

by a definition-based property of logarithms ($\log_b b = 1$).

13. **Error Analysis** A student simplified $(\log_3 81)^2$ as shown at right. Explain and correct the student's error.

The property applies to expressions of the form

$\log_b m^n$, not to expressions of the form $(\log_b m)^n$.

The correct answer is $(\log_3 81)^2 = (4)^2 = 16.$

$(\log_3 81)^2$	
$= 2 \log_3 81$	Power Property of Logs
$= 2 \log_3 3^4$	Write 81 as a power of 3.
$= 2 \cdot 4$	Definition of logarithm
$= 8$	Multiply.

14. The formula $L = 10 \log \frac{I}{I_0}$ gives the sound level L (in decibels) for a sound with intensity I (in watts per square meter). I_0 is the threshold of human hearing, 10^{-12} watts/m^2.

a. Rewrite the formula by using the Quotient Property of Logarithms, substituting 10^{-12} for I_0 and simplifying.

$L = 10(\log I - \log I_0) = 10(\log I - \log 10^{-12}) = 10(\log I + 12)$

b. Show how to use the formula from part (a) to find the intensity of a sound if its sound level L is 120 decibels.

Solve $120 = 10(\log I + 12)$. Dividing both sides by 10 gives $12 = \log I + 12$,

so $0 = \log I$ and $I = 1$. The intensity is 1 watt/m^2.

7-4

Solving Exponential and Logarithmic Equations

Essential question: *What is the general process for solving exponential and logarithmic equations?*

COMMON Standards for
CORE Mathematical Content

CC.9-12.A.CED.1 Create equations ... in one variable and use them to solve problems. Include equations arising from ... exponential functions.*

CC.9-12.A.REI.11 Explain why the x-coordinates of the points where the graphs of the equations $y = f(x)$ and $y = g(x)$ intersect are the solutions of the equation $f(x) = g(x)$; find the solutions approximately, e.g., using technology to graph the functions, ... include ... exponential, and logarithmic functions.*

CC.9-12.F.LE.4 For exponential models, express as a logarithm the solution to $ab^{ct} = d$ where a, c, and d are numbers and the base is 2, 10, or e; evaluate the logarithm using technology.*

Prerequisites

Interest compounded continuously, Lesson 6-5

Solving exponential equations, Lesson 6-7

Properties of logarithms, Lesson 7-3

Math Background

For students to solve exponential equations in Unit 6, the equation had to be in the form where both sides could be written as powers with the same base. Now that students know logarithms, they can solve exponential equations where this is not the case.

Students will solve these exponential equations by taking the logarithm of both sides. Students should notice the similarities between the Property of Equality for Logarithmic Equations and the Property of Equality for Exponential Equations.

Students will also solve some logarithmic equations graphically. They will use the Change of Base Property from the previous lesson to graph logarithmic equations with bases other than 10 or e.

INTRODUCE

Ask students how they can solve $2^{x+3} = 64$ algebraically. Write 64 as 2^6 and solve $x + 3 = 6$.

Ask why they cannot use the same method to solve $2^{x+3} = 50$. You cannot write 50 as an integer power of 2.

TEACH

1 EXAMPLE

Questioning Strategies

• What is the purpose of dividing both sides of the equation by log 2? The purpose is to isolate the variable expression $x - 3$ on one side of the equation.

• How do you get the value of x in the last step? Evaluate log 85 and log 2. Divide the value of log 85 by the value of log 2. Add that quotient to 3.

Avoid Common Errors

When finding the approximate value of x, be sure to close the parentheses for log 85 before dividing by log 2. Students should enter $\log(85) / \log(2) + 3$ into their graphing calculators.

Teaching Strategy

An alternate approach to 1 EXAMPLE is to write the equation as a logarithmic equation, isolate the variable, and use the Change of Base Property.

$2^{x-3} = 85$ is equivalent to $\log_2 85 = x - 3$.

Then $x = \log_2 85 + 3 = \dfrac{\log 85}{\log 2} + 3$.

EXTRA EXAMPLE

Solve $3^{x+4} = 2500$. Give the exact solution and an approximate solution to three decimal places.

$x = \dfrac{\log 2500}{\log 3} - 4 \approx 3.122$

© Houghton Mifflin Harcourt Publishing Company

Name_____ Class_____ Date_____

7-4

Solving Exponential and Logarithmic Equations

COMMON CORE
CC.9-12.A.CED.1*,
CC.9-12.A.REI.11*,
CC.9-12.F.LE.4*

Essential question: *What is the general process for solving exponential and logarithmic equations?*

You know that you can sometimes solve an exponential equation by writing both sides as powers with the same base. When that method is not possible, you can take a logarithm of both sides of the equation. This is justified by the following property.

> **Property of Equality for Logarithmic Equations**
>
> For any positive numbers x, y, and b ($b \neq 1$), $\log_b x = \log_b y$ if and only if $x = y$.

1 EXAMPLE   Taking the Common Logarithm of Both Sides

Solve $2^{x-3} = 85$. Give the exact solution and an approximate solution to three decimal places.

$2^{x-3} = 85$	Original equation
$\log 2^{x-3} = \log 85$	Take the common logarithm of both sides.
$(x-3)\log 2 = \log 85$	Power Property of Logarithms
$\dfrac{(x-3)\log 2}{\log 2} = \dfrac{\log 85}{\log 2}$	Divide both sides by log 2.
$x - 3 = \dfrac{\log 85}{\log 2}$	Simplify.
$x = \dfrac{\log 85}{\log 2} + 3$	Solve for x to find the exact solution.
$x \approx 9.409$	Evaluate. Round to three decimal places.

REFLECT

1a. Why do you use the Power Property of Logarithms?

This moves the variable out of the exponent.

1b. How can you use estimation to check if your answer is reasonable?

Replace x with 9.4 in the original equation. The left side is approximately $2^{6.4}$, which is between 2^6 and 2^7, or between 64 and 128. So it is reasonable that this value is equal to 85.

You can also take the natural logarithm of both sides of an equation. It makes sense to take the natural logarithm, rather than the common logarithm, when the base is *e*.

2 EXAMPLE   Taking the Natural Logarithm of Both Sides

Adam has $500 to invest for 4 years. He wants to double his money during this time. What interest rate does Adam need for this investment, assuming the interest is compounded continuously?

A Write an equation.

The formula for interest compounded continuously is $A = Pe^{rt}$ where A is the amount in the account, P is the principal, r is the annual rate of interest, and t is the time in years.
$P = \underline{500}$ and A is the final amount after $t = 4$ years, so $A = \underline{1000}$.

The equation is $\underline{1000 = 500e^{4r}}$.

B Solve the equation for r.

$1000 = 500\,e^{4r}$	Write the equation.
$2 = e^{4r}$	Divide both sides by 500.
$\ln 2 = \ln e^{4r}$	Take the natural logarithm of both sides.
$\ln 2 = 4r \ln e$	Power Property of Logarithms
$\ln 2 = 4r$	Use the fact that $\ln e = 1$.
$\dfrac{\ln 2}{4} = \dfrac{4r}{4}$	Divide both sides by 4.
$\dfrac{\ln 2}{4} = r$	Solve for r to find the exact answer.
$0.173 \approx r$	Evaluate. Round to three decimal places.

So, Adam needs an interest rate of approximately $\underline{17.3}$ %.

REFLECT

2a. What is the benefit of taking the natural logarithm of both sides of the equation, rather than the common logarithm?

This gives ln e on one side of the equation, and ln e simplifies to 1.

2b. Describe two different ways to use your calculator to check your answer.

(1) Evaluate $500e^{4 \cdot 0.173}$ to check that this value is close to 1000.

(2) Graph $y = 1000$ and $y = 500e^{4x}$ and find the point of intersection. The value of x should be about 0.173.

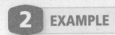

Questioning Strategies

- Why does $\ln e = 1$? $\ln e = \log_e e$ and $e^1 = e.$

- Compare solving an exponential equation using natural logarithms with solving an exponential equation using common logarithms. The methods are identical. The only difference is the type of logarithm used.

EXTRA EXAMPLE

Sonya has $1400 to invest for 5 years. She wants to have $2100 at the end of the 5-year period. What interest rate does she need if the interest is compounded continuously? about 8.1%

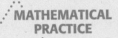

MATHEMATICAL PRACTICE | **Highlighting the Standards**

1 EXAMPLE and **2** EXAMPLE offer an opportunity to address Mathematical Practice Standard 6 (Attend to precision). Discuss how much accuracy is lost or gained by rounding to fewer or greater decimal places. In Reflect Question 1b, substituting 9.4 results in about 84.449, while substituting 9.409 results in about 84.977. In this case, the difference is not very great. Both numbers are close to 85.

In Reflect Question 2b, substituting 0.173 results in $998.85, while substituting 0.2 results in $1112.77. Using two more decimal places to 0.17329 results in $1000.01. Here, the differences in the results are more significant.

3 **EXAMPLE**

Questioning Strategies

- Why is the goal to get a single logarithmic expression on one side of the equation? You can use the definition of a logarithm to solve the equation.

- What is the purpose of using the definition of a logarithm? It results in a linear equation that can be solved easily.

EXTRA EXAMPLE

Solve each logarithmic equation.

A. $\log_4 (2x - 4) = 3$ 34

B. $6 \log (3x + 1) = 12$ 33

Avoid Common Errors

Students often try to use the definition of a logarithm before the logarithmic expression is isolated on one side of the equation. Remind students that the equation must be in the form "logarithm =" before they can solve it.

Teaching Strategy

Tell students that when solving logarithmic equations, it is possible to get extraneous solutions (solutions that do not make the original equation true). It is good practice to always check any answers by substituting them back into the original equation.

4 **EXAMPLE**

Questioning Strategies

- What quadrant or quadrants should your viewing window display? Quadrant I

- In Reflect Question 4c, could you subtract 2.7 as the first step? Why or why not? Yes; it doesn't matter whether you subtract 2.7 first or $4.4 \log x$ first as long as your second step is to subtract the other term.

Teaching Strategy

Have students set their viewing windows so that x-values range from 0 to 2000 and y-values range from 0 to 20. Otherwise, the calculator may not detect the point of intersection.

EXTRA EXAMPLE

Two students performed an experiment involving temperature change and used regression to create equations with natural logarithms. Their equations are shown below. For both equations, x represents elapsed time in minutes and y represents the corresponding temperature in degrees Celsius.

Student A: $y = 10 + 6.9 \ln x$

Student B: $y = 10.2 + 6.7 \ln x$

After how many minutes do the two formulas give the same temperature? about 2.7 minutes

To solve a logarithmic equation in the form $\log_b x = a$, first rewrite the equation in exponential form ($b^a = x$) by using the definition of a logarithm. As you will see in the second part of the following example, you may first need to isolate the logarithmic expression on one side of the equation.

3 EXAMPLE Solving a Logarithmic Equation Algebraically

Solve each logarithmic equation.

A $\log_3(x + 1) = 2$

$3^2 = x + 1$		Definition of logarithm
$9 = x + 1$		Simplify.
$8 = x$		Solve for x.

B $7 + \log_3(5x - 4) = 10$

$\log_3(5x - 4) = 3$		Subtract 7 from both sides.
$3^3 = 5x - 4$		Definition of logarithm
$27 = 5x - 4$		Simplify.
$31 = 5x$		Add 4 to both sides.
$6.2 = x$		Solve for x.

REFLECT

3a. How can you check your solution to part A by substitution?

Substitute 8 for x in the original equation and check that the two sides are equal:

$\log_3(8 + 1) = \log_3 9 = 2$.

3b. Your calculator has keys for evaluating only logarithms with a base of 10 and e. Use the Change of Base Property to rewrite the equation from part A so that the base of the logarithm is 10 or e. Then explain how to use graphing to check your solution.

$\frac{\log(x + 1)}{\log 3} = 2$ or $\frac{\ln(x + 1)}{\ln 3} = 2$. To check the solution, graph $y = \frac{\log(x + 1)}{\log 3}$ and $y = 2$, or $y = \frac{\ln(x + 1)}{\ln 3}$ and $y = 2$, and find the intersection point's x-coordinate.

3c. Explain how you could use graphing to check your solution to part B.

Graph $y = 7 + \frac{\log(5x - 4)}{\log 3}$ and $y = 10$, or $y = 7 + \frac{\ln(5x - 4)}{\ln 3}$ and $y = 10$, and find the intersection point's x-coordinate.

4 EXAMPLE Solving a Logarithmic Equation by Graphing

A telescope's limiting magnitude m is the brightness of the faintest star that can be seen using the telescope. The limiting magnitude depends on the diameter d (in millimeters) of the telescope's objective lens. The table gives two formulas relating m to d. One is a standard formula used in astronomy. The other is a proposed new formula based on data gathered from users of telescopes of various lens diameters.

Formulas for determining limiting magnitude from lens diameter	
Standard formula	$m = 2.7 + 5 \log d$
Proposed formula	$m = 4.5 + 4.4 \log d$

For what lens diameter do the two formulas give the same limiting magnitude?

A Use a graphing calculator. Enter $2.7 + 5 \log x$ as Y_1 and enter $4.5 + 4.4 \log x$ as Y_2.

```
Plot1 Plot2 Plot3
\Y1∎2.7+5log(X)
\Y2∎4.5+4.4log(X
)
\Y3=
\Y4=
\Y5=
\Y6=
```

B Graph the two functions in the same viewing window. Use a window where $0 \le x \le 2000$ with a tick mark every 100 units and $0 \le y \le 20$ with a tick mark every 5 units.

C Press 2nd TRACE and choose **5:intersect** to find the point of intersection of the graphs.

The coordinates of the point of intersection are ___(1000, 17.7)___

So, the two formulas give the same limiting magnitude for a lens diameter of ___1000 mm___

REFLECT

4a. What is the limiting magnitude that corresponds to this lens diameter? How do you know?

17.7; this is the y-coordinate of the point of intersection.

4b. What equation can you write in order to solve the problem algebraically?

$2.7 + 5 \log x = 4.5 + 4.4 \log x$

4c. Show how to solve the equation algebraically. Justify each step. (*Hint:* First get all logarithmic expressions on one side of the equation and all non-logarithmic expressions on the other side of the equation.)

$2.7 + 5 \log x = 4.5 + 4.4 \log x$	(Original equation)
$2.7 + 0.6 \log x = 4.5$	(Subtract $4.4 \log x$ from both sides.)
$0.6 \log x = 1.8$	(Subtract 2.7 from both sides.)
$\log x = \frac{1.8}{0.6} = 3$	(Divide both sides by 0.6.)
$x = 10^3$	(Definition of logarithm)
$x = 1000$	(Evaluate.)

Essential Question

What is the general process for solving exponential and logarithmic equations?

To solve an exponential equation, take either the common logarithm or the natural logarithm of both sides, use the Power Property of Logarithms to remove the variable from the exponent, and then solve for the variable. To solve a logarithmic equation, write the equation in the form $\log_b x = a$ and use the definition of a logarithm to eliminate the logarithmic expression. Then solve the resulting equation for the variable.

Summarize

In their journals, have students list the various ways to solve exponential equations and the various ways to solve logarithmic equations.

Where skills are taught	Where skills are practiced
1 EXAMPLE	EXS. 1–3, 5, 7–9
2 EXAMPLE	EXS. 4, 6, 11
3 EXAMPLE	EXS. 15–20
4 EXAMPLE	EXS. 24, 25

Exercise 10: Students see that a logarithmic equation can have no solution.

Exercise 12: Given the effective rate for interest compounded continuously, students solve an exponential equation to find the annual interest rate by taking the natural logarithm of both sides. Students may need to be reminded to convert the effective rate to a decimal when writing the equation.

Exercise 13: Students solve the equation they created in the previous unit for the population of the United States from 1790 to 1890 to find the number of decades required to reach a given population.

Exercise 14: Students identify and correct an error a student made in solving an exponential equation.

Exercises 21–23: Students use properties of exponents to write sums and differences of logarithmic expressions as single logarithmic expressions so they can use the definition of a logarithm to solve logarithmic equations.

PRACTICE

Solve. Give the exact solution and an approximate solution to three decimal places.

1. $6^x = 15$

$$x = \frac{\log 15}{\log 6}$$

$$x \approx 1.511$$

2. $4^{2x} = 200$

$$x = \frac{\log 200}{2 \log 4}$$

$$x \approx 1.911$$

3. $10^x = 35$

$$x = \log 35$$

$$x \approx 1.544$$

4. $10 + e^{\frac{x}{3}} = 4270$

$$x = 3 \, (\ln 4260)$$

$$x \approx 25.071$$

5. $2^{9-x} + 3 = 62$

$$x = -\frac{\log 59}{\log 2} + 9$$

$$x \approx 3.117$$

6. $e^{6x+1} = 530$

$$x = \frac{\ln 530 - 1}{6}$$

$$x \approx 0.879$$

7. $3^{2x-1} = 14$

$$x = \frac{\log 14}{2 \log 3} + \frac{1}{2}$$

$$x \approx 1.701$$

8. $210 + 4^x = 3 \cdot 4^x$

$$x = \frac{\log 105}{\log 4}$$

$$x \approx 3.357$$

9. $11^{1-x} = 8$

$$x = 1 - \frac{\log 8}{\log 11}$$

$$x \approx 0.133$$

10. What happens if you take the common logarithm of both sides of $5^x = -6$ in order to solve the equation? Why does this happen?

You get $x = \dfrac{\log(-6)}{\log 5}$, which cannot be evaluated because logarithms are not defined

for negative numbers. This happens because the original equation has no solution.

11. Kendra wants to double her investment of $4000. How long will this take if the annual interest rate is 4% compounded continuously? How long will this take if the annual interest rate is 8% compounded continuously? What effect does doubling the interest rate have on the time it takes the investment to double?

About 17.3 years; about 8.7 years; doubling the interest rate halves

the doubling time.

12. Recall that for interest that is compounded continuously, the effective rate R is given by $R = e^r - 1$ where r is the nominal interest rate. What is the nominal interest rate if the effective rate for continuous compounding is 5.625%? Round to the nearest hundredth of a percent.

5.47%

13. The equation $y = 4.1(1.33)^x$ models the population of the U.S., in millions, from 1790 to 1890. In this equation, x is the number of decades since 1790, and y is the population in millions. How many decades after 1790 did the population reach 28 million? Write an expression for the exact answer and give an approximate answer to the nearest tenth.

$\dfrac{\log\left(\frac{28}{4.1}\right)}{\log 1.33}$ decades ≈ 6.7 decades

---

14. **Error Analysis** Identify and correct the error in the student work shown at right.

In the last line, $\dfrac{\ln 20}{\ln 10} \neq \ln 2$. The correct

solution is $\dfrac{\ln 20}{\ln 10} \approx 1.301$.

$$10^x = 20$$
$$\ln 10^x = \ln 20$$
$$x \ln 10 = \ln 20$$
$$x = \frac{\ln 20}{\ln 10} = \ln 2 \approx 0.693$$

Solve each logarithmic equation. Round to three decimal places if necessary.

15. $\log_7 (x - 5) = 2$

54

16. $\log_4 (8x) = 3$

8

17. $\log (7x - 1) = -1$

0.157

18. $\ln(4x - 1) = 9$

2026.021

19. $11 + \log_4 (x + 1) = 15$

255

20. $3 = \ln(3x + 3)$

5.695

Solve by using the Product or Quotient Property of Logarithms so that one side is a single logarithm. Round to three decimal places if necessary.

21. $\log 20 + \log 10x = 5$

500

22. $\ln x - \ln 6 = 3$

120.513

23. $2.4 = \log 7 + \log 3x$

11.961

For Exercises 24 and 25, use graphing to solve.

24. Charles collected data on the atmospheric pressure (ranging from 4 to 15 pounds per square inch) and the corresponding altitude above the surface of Earth (ranging from 1 to 30,000 feet). He used regression to write two functions that give the altitude above the surface of Earth given the atmospheric pressure.

$$f(x) = 66,990 - 24,747 \ln x$$

$$g(x) = -2870x + 40,393$$

a. At what atmospheric pressure(s) do the equations give the same altitude?

approximately 5.6 psi and 12.5 psi

b. At what altitude(s) above Earth do these atmospheric pressures occur?

approximately 24,254 feet and 4415 feet

25. Elena and Paul determined slightly different equations to model the recommended height, in inches, of a tabletop for children x years old.

Elena: $y = 12.2 + 5.45 \ln x$

Paul: $y = 12.5 + 5.2 \ln x$

For what age do the models give the same tabletop height? What is that height?

about 3.3 years; 18.7 inches

FOCUS ON MODELING
Modeling with Logarithmic Functions

Essential question: *How can you model the time it takes a radioactive substance to decay as a function of the percent of the substance remaining?*

© Houghton Mifflin Harcourt Publishing Company

COMMON CORE Standards for Mathematical Content

The following standards are addressed in this lesson. (An asterisk indicates that a standard is also a Modeling standard.) For more detailed information, see each section of the lesson.

Algebra: CC.9-12.A.CED.2*, CC.9-12.A.CED.4*
Functions: CC.9-12.F.IF.2, CC.9-12.F.IF.4*, CC.9-12.F.BF.1*, CC.9-12.F.BF.1a*

Prerequisites
- Exponential decay functions, Lesson 6-3
- Using the definition of a logarithm, Lesson 7-1
- Using properties of logarithms, Lesson 7-3

Math Background
In this lesson, students write and interpret exponential and logarithmic functions that model the half-life of a radioactive isotope. They use their knowledge from previous lessons to model the radioactive decay with an exponential decay function and then convert that function to a logarithmic function. Students then use the Change of Base Property, as well as other properties, to convert the function to one involving a common logarithm that can be analyzed using a graphing calculator.

INTRODUCE

All living things contain carbon-14. When a plant or animal dies, the carbon-14 in it begins to decay, or change to another substance. The process is very slow. It takes 5730 years for just half of it to decay, then another 5730 years for half of the remaining amount to decay, and so on. By using a method similar to the one in this lesson, scientists can determine the amount of carbon-14 in a fossil and can use that amount to determine its age.

TEACH

1 **Model radioactive decay with an exponential function.**

Standards
CC.9-12.A.CED.2 Create equations in two ... variables to represent relationships between quantities ...*

CC.9-12.F.IF.2 Use function notation, evaluate functions for inputs in their domains, and interpret statements that use function notation in terms of a context.

CC.9-12.F.IF.4 For a function that models a relationship between two quantities, interpret key features of ... tables in terms of the quantities, ...*

CC.9-12.F.BF.1 Write a function that describes a relationship between two quantities.*

CC.9-12.F.BF.1a Determine an explicit expression ... from a context.*

Questioning Strategies
- What is the general exponential decay function? $A(t) = a(1 - r)^t$ where a is the initial amount, r is the decay rate, and t is a number of time periods
- Why is 100 used as the initial amount? The function gives the percent remaining after t days. The initial amount on day 0 was 100%.

2 **Convert the exponential decay function to a logarithmic function.**

Standards
CC.9-12.A.CED.4 Rearrange formulas to highlight a quantity of interest, using the same reasoning as in solving equations.*

CC.9-12.F.IF.2 Use function notation, evaluate functions for inputs in their domains, and interpret statements that use function notation in terms of a context.

continued

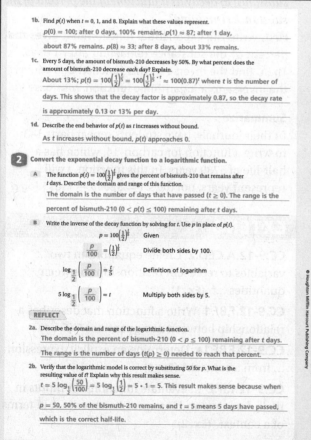

Name_____ Class_____ Date_____

FOCUS ON MODELING

Modeling with Logarithmic Functions

COMMON CORE
CC.9-12.A.CED.2*,
CC.9-12.A.CED.4*,
CC.9-12.F.IF.2,
CC.9-12.F.IF.4*,
CC.9-12.F.BF.1*,
CC.9-12.F.BF.1a*

Essential question: *How can you model the time it takes a radioactive substance to decay as a function of the percent of the substance remaining?*

Radioactive substances decay to other substances over time. The half-life of a radioactive substance is the time it takes for one-half of the substance to decay. How can you determine the length of time it takes a given radioactive substance to decay to a specified percent?

1 Model radioactive decay with an exponential function.

A The isotope bismuth-210 has a half-life of 5 days. Complete the table showing the decay of a sample of bismuth-210.

Number of Half-Lives	Number of Days (t)	Percent of Isotope Remaining (p)
0	0	100
1	5	50
2	10	25
3	15	12.5
4	20	6.25

B Write the decay rate r as a fraction. $r = \frac{1}{2}$

C Write an expression for the number of half-lives in t days. $\frac{t}{5}$

D Write an exponential decay function that models this situation. The function $p(t)$ should give the percent of the isotope remaining after t days.

$$p(t) = 100\left(\frac{1}{2}\right)^{\frac{t}{5}}$$

REFLECT

1a. Show how to check that your model is correct by letting $t = 10$ and comparing the resulting value of $p(t)$ to the value in the table.

When $t = 10$, $p(t) = 100\left(\frac{1}{2}\right)^{\frac{10}{5}} = 100\left(\frac{1}{2}\right)^2 = 100\left(\frac{1}{4}\right) = 25$, which matches the percent in the table.

1b. Find $p(t)$ when $t = 0$, 1, and 8. Explain what these values represent.

$p(0) = 100$; after 0 days, 100% remains. $p(1) \approx 87$; after 1 day, about 87% remains. $p(8) \approx 33$; after 8 days, about 33% remains.

1c. Every 5 days, the amount of bismuth-210 decreases by 50%. By what percent does the amount of bismuth-210 decrease *each day*? Explain.

About 13%; $p(t) = 100\left(\frac{1}{2}\right)^{\frac{t}{5}} = 100\left(\frac{1}{2}\right)^{\frac{1}{5} \cdot t} \approx 100(0.87)^t$ where t is the number of days. This shows that the decay factor is approximately 0.87, so the decay rate is approximately 0.13 or 13% per day.

1d. Describe the end behavior of $p(t)$ as t increases without bound.

As t increases without bound, $p(t)$ approaches 0.

2 Convert the exponential decay function to a logarithmic function.

A The function $p(t) = 100\left(\frac{1}{2}\right)^{\frac{t}{5}}$ gives the percent of bismuth-210 that remains after t days. Describe the domain and range of this function.

The domain is the number of days that have passed ($t \geq 0$). The range is the percent of bismuth-210 ($0 < p(t) \leq 100$) remaining after t days.

B Write the inverse of the decay function by solving for t. Use p in place of $p(t)$.

$p = 100\left(\frac{1}{2}\right)^{\frac{t}{5}}$	Given
$\frac{p}{100} = \left(\frac{1}{2}\right)^{\frac{t}{5}}$	Divide both sides by 100.
$\log_{\frac{1}{2}}\left(\frac{p}{100}\right) = \frac{t}{5}$	Definition of logarithm
$5\log_{\frac{1}{2}}\left(\frac{p}{100}\right) = t$	Multiply both sides by 5.

REFLECT

2a. Describe the domain and range of the logarithmic function.

The domain is the percent of bismuth-210 ($0 < p \leq 100$) remaining after t days.

The range is the number of days ($t(p) \geq 0$) needed to reach that percent.

2b. Verify that the logarithmic model is correct by substituting 50 for p. What is the resulting value of t? Explain why this result makes sense.

$t = 5\log_{\frac{1}{2}}\left(\frac{50}{100}\right) = 5\log_{\frac{1}{2}}\left(\frac{1}{2}\right) = 5 \cdot 1 = 5$. This result makes sense because when $p = 50$, 50% of the bismuth-210 remains, and $t = 5$ means 5 days have passed, which is the correct half-life.

2 continued

4 Compare times to reach certain levels.

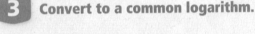

MATHEMATICAL PRACTICE   **Highlighting the Standards**

Steps 1 and 2 address Mathematical Practice Standard 4 (Model with mathematics). When analyzing the table in step 1, discuss why time t is the independent variable and why the remaining percent p is the dependent variable.

When using either the exponential or the logarithmic function, encourage students to estimate the output before evaluating the input and explain why the output is reasonable for the given situation.

Questioning Strategies
- Can p equal 0? Explain. No; the remaining percent gets close to 0 but never reaches it.
- In part A, is the domain a discrete or continuous set? Explain. Continuous; you can find the percent for any number of days, including fractional parts of a day.

3   **Convert to a common logarithm.**

Standards
CC.9-12.A.CED.4 Rearrange formulas ...*

CC.9-12.F.IF.2 Use function notation ...

Questioning Strategies
- What is the benefit of using the common logarithm instead of the natural logarithm? In step 3B, it allows you to evaluate log 100 as 2.
- Without using a calculator, how can you tell that $t = 33.22 - 16.61 \log p$ results in 0 for $p = 100$? log 100 = 2, and 2(−16.61) is −33.22, the opposite of 33.22.

Technology
Have students graph both the exponential and the logarithmic functions from this lesson, as well as the line $y = x$, on their calculators. They should see that the graphs of the functions are reflections across the line, so the functions are inverses of one another.

Standards
CC.9-12.F.IF.2 ... evaluate functions for inputs in their domains, and interpret statements ... in terms of a context.

CC.9-12.F.IF.4 For a function that models a relationship between two quantities, interpret key features of ... tables in terms of the quantities, ...*

Questioning Strategies
- Based only on the rule for the function, should the function's graph rise or fall from left to right? Why? Fall; the function has the form $g(x) = a \log x + k$ where the value of a is negative, so when the graph of the parent function $f(x) = \log x$, which rises, is reflected over the x-axis, the graph falls.
- When you move down the table, how are you moving along the graph? from right to left (toward the y-axis)

CLOSE

Essential Question
How can you model the time it takes a radioactive substance to decay as a function of the percent of the substance remaining?
First, write the exponential function that gives the percent of the substance remaining after t days. Then, find the inverse of this function and convert the inverse to a logarithmic function with base 10.

Summarize
In their journals, have students repeat parts 1–3 to write a function for carbon-14, which has a half-life of 5730 years. In this function, t will represent years, not days. $t = 38069 - 19035 \log p$

EXTEND

CC.9-12.A.CED.2 Create equations in two ... variables to represent relationships between quantities ...* (Ex. 1)

CC.9-12.F.BF.1 Write a function that describes a relationship between two quantities.* (Ex. 1)

CC.9-12.F.BF.1a Determine an explicit expression ... from a context.* (Ex. 1)

CC.9-12.F.IF.2 ... evaluate functions for inputs in their domains, and interpret statements ... in terms of a context. (Ex. 2)

3 Convert to a common logarithm.

A Rewrite your logarithmic function with a common logarithm.

$t = 5 \log_{\frac{1}{2}}\left(\frac{p}{100}\right)$ — Given

$= 5 \cdot \dfrac{\log \frac{p}{100}}{\log \frac{1}{2}}$ — Change of Base Property

$= \dfrac{5}{\log \frac{1}{2}} \cdot \log \frac{p}{100}$ — Write the denominator as part of the first factor.

$= -16.61 \log \frac{p}{100}$ — Evaluate the first factor. Round to two decimal places.

B Write the function without a fraction.

$t = -16.61\left(\log p - \log 100\right)$ — Quotient Property of Logarithms

$= -16.61\left(\log p - 2\right)$ — Evaluate log 100.

$= -16.61 \log p + 33.22$ — Distributive Property

$= 33.22 - 16.61 \log p$ — Commutative Property of Addition

REFLECT

3a. What is the benefit of rewriting the function so that it involves a common logarithm?

It is easier to evaluate the expression for a given value of p using a calculator
when the logarithm is a common logarithm.

3b. The final form of the logarithmic function includes rounded numbers. Check the accuracy of the function by substituting 50 for p and evaluating the expression with your calculator. Do you get the expected result? Explain.

Substituting 50 for p gives $t \approx 5.000108$, which is very close to the exact
value of 5.

3c. Explain how you can find out how long it takes until 5% of the bismuth-210 remains. Round to the nearest tenth of a day.

Substitute 5 for p in the logarithmic function. This gives $t \approx 21.6$, so it takes
about 21.6 days until 5% of the bismuth-210 remains.

3d. To emphasize that t is a function of p, write the equation of the logarithmic function using function notation.

$t(p) = 33.22 - 16.61 \log p$

4 Compare times to reach certain levels.

You can use your calculator, as follows, to compare the amounts of time it takes the percent of bismuth-210 to drop from 100% to 75%, from 75% to 50%, and from 50% to 25%.

A Enter the logarithmic function from step 3 into the equation editor of your graphing calculator.

B Press **2nd** **WINDOW**. Then set the TblStart value at 100 and the △Tbl value to −25.

C Look at the table of values. How many days does it take for the percent to drop from 100% to 75%? from 75% to 50%? from 50% to 25%?

It takes about 2 days to drop from 100% to 75%, about 3 days to drop from
75% to 50%, and 5 days to drop from 50% to 25%.

REFLECT

4a. Why is there an ERROR message in the table in the row corresponding to the value $x = 0$?

In the model, the percent of bismuth-210 that remains never reaches 0.

4b. Make a conjecture about how the amount of time it takes for bismuth-210 to drop from 70% to 60% compares to the amount of time it takes to drop from 20% to 10%. Then check your conjecture using a graphing calculator.

Possible conjecture: The time to drop from 70% to 60% will be shorter than
the time to drop from 20% to 10%. Actual times: about 1.1 days; 5 days.

EXTEND

1. As a sample of bismuth-210 decays, the sample is transformed into a mixture of bismuth-210 and other isotopes in its decay chain. The time needed for the amount of the other isotopes to reach a certain percent of the sample can be obtained from the logarithmic model for bismuth-210 by replacing p in the function's rule. Write a function that gives the time t needed for the amount of the other isotopes to reach p percent of the sample. (*Hint:* Consider how the percent of bismuth-210 and the percent of the other isotopes are related.)

$t = 33.22 - 16.61 \log (100 - p)$

2. Use the function you wrote in Exercise 1 to determine the time needed for the other isotopes to reach 75% of the sample amount. Explain why your result makes sense.

10 days; this makes sense because it takes 10 days for bismuth-210 to decay
to the point where 25% of the isotope is remaining. At that point, the other
isotopes have reached 75% of the sample amount.

Standard	Items
CC.9-12.A.CED.1*	6
CC.9-12.A.CED.2*	7
CC.9-12.A.CED.4*	7
CC.9-12.A.REI.11*	5
CC.9-12.F.IF.2	1
CC.9-12.F.IF.4*	11
CC.9-12.F.IF.7e*	9
CC.9-12.F.BF.1*	7
CC.9-12.F.BF.3	4, 8, 10
CC.9-12.F.BF.5(+)	3, 9
CC.9-12.F.LE.4*	2

TEST PREP DOCTOR ⊕

Multiple Choice: Item 1
- Students who chose **B** remembered that a negative exponent gives the reciprocal of the base, but thought they should also take the reciprocal of the exponent.
- Students who chose **D** may have thought that the base is $\frac{1}{3}$.

Multiple Choice: Item 2
- Students who chose **F** took the square root of 319.
- Students who chose **G** multiplied both sides of the equation by 2 after using the Power Property of Logarithms.
- Students who chose **J** wrote 2 log 10 as log 20.

Multiple Choice: Item 4
- Students who chose **G** or **J** thought that adding a positive value to x translates the graph to the right, when in fact subtracting a positive value from x does so. They may have mixed up the rules for h and k.
- Students who chose **H** or **J** thought that $|a| > 1$ represents a shrink. They may have mixed up the rules for vertical and horizontal shrinks.

Multiple Choice: Item 5
- Students who chose **C** chose the y-coordinate of the ordered pair at the point of intersection.
- Students who chose **D** may have used the common logarithm instead of the natural logarithm.

Multiple Choice: Item 6
- Students who chose **F** or **J** used a logarithmic expression for calculating compound interest instead of an exponential expression.
- Students who chose **H** identified the equation that could be used if the interest was compounded annually rather than continuously.

Free Response: Item 9a
- Students may evaluate $f(\frac{1}{5})$ as -5 thinking only that the answer must be a negative number since x is between 0 and 1.
- Students may evaluate $f(1)$ as 1 thinking they are finding 1^5.

Free Response: Item 10
- Students may answer $g(x) = -\log_{\frac{1}{3}} x - 2$ by counting the number of units between $(3, -1)$ and $(3, -3)$, forgetting that the point was first reflected to $(3, 1)$.

Free Response: Item 11a
- Students who struggle with this problem may be entering the equation into their calculator so that it takes the log of $x + 12$ instead of the log of x. The variable x must be enclosed in parentheses after pressing LOG.

Name _____ Class _____ Date _____

MULTIPLE CHOICE

1. If $f(x) = \log_3 x$, what is $f\left(\frac{1}{9}\right)$?

(A.) -2 C. $\frac{1}{2}$

B. $-\frac{1}{2}$ D. 2

2. Which is the solution of $10^{2x} = 319$?

F. $\log 17.86$ (H.) $\dfrac{\log 319}{2}$

G. $2 \log 319$ J. $\dfrac{\log 319}{\log 20}$

3. Which equation has the same solution as $\log_4 (x + 7) = 5$?

A. $4^{x+7} = 5$ C. $5^{x+7} = 4$

(B.) $4^5 = x + 7$ D. $5^4 = x + 7$

4. The graph of $g(x)$ is the graph of $f(x) = \log x$ translated 6 units to the right and shrunk vertically by a factor of $\frac{1}{4}$. Which is the equation of $g(x)$?

(F.) $g(x) = \frac{1}{4} \log (x - 6)$

G. $g(x) = \frac{1}{4} \log (x + 6)$

H. $g(x) = 4 \log (x - 6)$

J. $g(x) = 4 \log (x + 6)$

5. Miguel and Dee determined slightly different equations to model the recommended chair seat height, in inches, for children x years old.

Miguel: $y = 4.37 \ln x + 5.52$

Dee: $y = 4.52 \ln x + 5.35$

For what age do the two models give the same chair seat height?

(A.) about 3.1 years old

B. about 5.0 years old

C. about 10.5 years old

D. about 12.6 years old

6. Latrell wants to double an investment of $3500 that earns interest at an annual rate of 6% compounded continuously. Which equation can he solve to find the doubling time t for this investment?

F. $7000 = 3500 \ln 0.06t$

(G.) $7000 = 3500e^{0.06t}$

H. $7000 = 3500(1.06)^t$

J. $7000 = 3500 \log_{0.06} t$

7. The half-life of cesium-137 is 30 years. Which equation gives the time t (in years) needed to reach a percent p of remaining radioactive substance?

A. $t = \log_{\frac{1}{2}}\left(\frac{3p}{10}\right)$ C. $t = \dfrac{\log_{\frac{1}{2}}\left(\frac{p}{100}\right)}{30}$

B. $t = \log_{\frac{1}{2}}\left(\frac{10}{3p}\right)$ (D.) $t = 30 \log_{\frac{1}{2}}\left(\frac{p}{100}\right)$

8. The graph of $g(x)$ is a horizontal translation and a vertical stretch of the graph of $f(x) = \log_3 x$. Which is the equation of $g(x)$?

F. $g(x) = 2 \log_3 (x + 2)$

(G.) $g(x) = 2 \log_3 (x - 2)$

H. $g(x) = \frac{1}{2} \log_3 (x + 2)$

J. $g(x) = \frac{1}{2} \log_3 (x - 2)$

© Houghton Mifflin Harcourt Publishing Company

FREE RESPONSE

9. Consider the function $f(x) = \log_5 x$.

a. Complete the table.

x	$f(x)$
$\frac{1}{5}$	-1
1	0
5	1
25	2

b. Sketch the graph of $f(x)$.

c. Give the equation of any asymptote for the graph of $f(x)$.

$x = 0$

d. The function $g(x)$ is the inverse of $f(x)$. Write the equation for $g(x)$.

$g(x) = 5^x$

e. Name three points on the graph of $g(x)$ and tell how you can determine them by looking at the table or graph of $f(x)$.

$\left(-1, \frac{1}{5}\right)$, $(0, 1)$, $(2, 25)$; $g(x)$ and $f(x)$ are inverses, so x- and y-values are switched.

f. The graph of $g(x)$ is the reflection of the graph of $f(x)$ across what line?

$y = x$

10. The graph of $g(x)$ is a reflection in the x-axis and a vertical translation of the graph of $f(x) = \log_{\frac{1}{3}} x$. Write the equation of $g(x)$.

$g(x) = -\log_{\frac{1}{3}} x - 4$

11. The formula $L = 10(\log I + 12)$ gives the sound level L (in decibels) for a sound with intensity I (in watts/m²). You want to know the intensity of a sound whose sound level is 124 decibels.

a. Explain how you can use your calculator's table feature to find the intensity of the sound.

Enter $y = 10(\log x + 12)$ in the equation editor as Y_1. Set up the table so that TblStart $= 0$ and $\triangle$Tbl $= 0.1$. View the table and scroll down until you find a value of Y_1 near 124. The corresponding x-value is the intensity of the sound, ≈ 2.5 watts/m².

b. Explain how you can use your calculator's graphing capabilities to find the intensity of the sound.

Graph $y = 10(\log x + 12)$ and $y = 124$ in the same viewing window. Locate the point of intersection of the two graphs using the intersect feature. The x-coordinate of the point, about 2.5 (watts/m²), is the sound's intensity.

© Houghton Mifflin Harcourt Publishing Company

Trigonometric Functions

UNIT 8

Unit Vocabulary

UNIT 8

Trigonometric Functions

Unit Focus

In this unit, you will learn about the three basic *trigonometric functions*. These functions are related to the trigonometric ratios of angles in right triangles that you learned about in Geometry. Trigonometric functions are defined on a circle centered at the origin with radius 1 unit. You will learn both how the trigonometric functions are derived from the trigonometric ratios and how to evaluate and graph trigonometric functions. You will also use trigonometric functions to model real-world situations.

Unit at a Glance

COMMON CORE

Lesson		Standards for Mathematical Content
8-1	Understanding Radian Measure	CC.9-12.G.C.5
8-2	Angles of Rotation and Radian Measure	CC.9-12.F.TF.1
8-3	The Sine, Cosine, and Tangent Functions	CC.9-12.F.IF.1, CC.9-12.F.TF.2, CC.9-12.F.TF.3(+)
8-4	Evaluating the Trigonometric Functions	CC.9-12.F.TF.8
8-5	Graphing the Sine and Cosine Functions	CC.9-12.F.IF.7*, CC.9-12.F.IF.7e*, CC.9-12.F.TF.4(+)
8-6	Graphing the Tangent Function	CC.9-12.F.IF.7*, CC.9-12.F.IF.7e*, CC.9-12.F.TF.4(+)
8-7	Stretching, Shrinking, and Reflecting Trigonometric Graphs	CC.9-12.F.IF.7*, CC.9-12.F.IF.7e*, CC.9-12.F.BF.3
8-8	Translating Trigonometric Graphs	CC.9-12.F.IF.7*, CC.9-12.F.IF.7e*, CC.9-12.F.BF.3
8-9	Modeling with Trigonometric Functions	CC.9-12.A.CED.2*, CC.9-12.F.IF.2, CC.9-12.F.IF.4*, CC.9-12.F.IF.7e*, CC.9-12.F.BF.1*, CC.9-12.F.TF.5*
	Test Prep	

Unpacking the Common Core State Standards

Use the table to help you understand the Standards for Mathematical Content that are taught in this unit. Refer to the lessons listed after each standard for exploration and practice.

COMMON CORE Standards for Mathematical Content	What It Means For You
CC.9-12.N.Q.1 Use units as a way to understand problems and to guide the solution of multi-step problems; choose and interpret units consistently in formulas; choose and interpret the scale and the origin in graphs and data displays.* Lesson 8-9	When modeling the motion of a Ferris wheel, you will use unit analysis to convert a function based on angle to a function based on time.
CC.9-12.A.CED.2* Create equations in two or more variables to represent relationships between quantities; graph equations on coordinate axes with labels and scales.* Lesson 8-9	You will learn how to write and graph equations of trigonometric functions to model circular motion in real-world situations.
CC.9-12.F.IF.1 Understand that a function from one set (called the domain) to another set (called the range) assigns to each element of the domain exactly one element of the range. If f is a function and x is an element of its domain, then $f(x)$ denotes the output of f corresponding to the input x. The graph of f is the graph of the equation $y = f(x)$. Lesson 8-3	You will learn that the relationship between an angle and its sine, cosine, or tangent value is a function because each trigonometric ratio associated with the angle is unique.
CC.9-12.F.IF.2 Use function notation, evaluate functions for inputs in their domains, and interpret statements that use function notation in terms of a context. Lesson 8-9	You will learn both how to write trigonometric functions using function notation and how to evaluate the functions.
CC.9-12.F.IF.4 For a function that models a relationship between two quantities, interpret key features of graphs and tables in terms of the quantities, and sketch graphs showing key features given a verbal description of the relationship.* Lesson 8-9 (Also 8-8)	When you use a trigonometric function to model circular motion, you can use the function's graph to help you understand the motion in the context of the situation.
CC.9-12.F.IF.7 Graph functions expressed symbolically and show key features of the graph, by hand in simple cases and using technology for more complicated cases.* **CC.9-12.F.IF.7e** Graph exponential and logarithmic functions, showing intercepts and end behavior, and trigonometric functions, showing period, midline, and amplitude.* Lessons 8-5, 8-6, 8-7, 8-8, 8-9	Graphs of sine and cosine functions consist of a repeating wave pattern. You will learn important characteristics of these graphs, such as the length (or period) of a wave and the distance (or amplitude) that a wave's crest rises above and the wave's trough falls below a horizontal line called the midline.

Unpacking the Common Core State Standards

This page lists and explains the Standards for Mathematical Content that are addressed in this unit. For information about the Standards for Mathematical Practice, which are integrated throughout the text, see Teacher Edition pages x–xiii.

UNIT 8

Notes

_____

_____

_____

_____

_____

_____

_____

_____

_____

_____

UNIT 8

Additional Standards in This Unit

CC.9-12.A.REI.4 Solve quadratic equations in one variable. Lesson 8-4

COMMON CORE Standards for Mathematical Content	What It Means For You
CC.9-12.F.BF.1 Write a function that describes a relationship between two quantities.* **CC.9-12.F.BF.1a Determine an explicit expression, a recursive process, or steps for calculation from a context.*** Lesson 8-9	You will learn how to use trigonometric functions to model the motion of a riverboat's paddle wheel and a Ferris wheel.
CC.9-12.F.BF.3 Identify the effect on the graph of replacing $f(x)$ by $f(x) + k$, $k\,f(x)$, $f(kx)$, and $f(x + k)$ for specific values of k (both positive and negative); find the value of k given the graphs. Experiment with cases and illustrate an explanation of the effects on the graph using technology. Lessons 8-7, 8-8, 8-9	You will learn to stretch, shrink, reflect, and translate trigonometric graphs.
CC.9-12.F.TF.1 Understand radian measure of an angle as the length of the arc on the unit circle subtended by the angle. Lesson 8-2	The unit circle is centered at the origin of a coordinate plane and has a radius of 1 unit. An angle with its vertex at the origin can be measured in *radians* using the length of an arc on the unit circle.
CC.9-12.F.TF.2 Explain how the unit circle in the coordinate plane enables the extension of trigonometric functions to all real numbers, interpreted as radian measures of angles traversed counterclockwise around the unit circle. Lesson 8-3	In Geometry, you defined and used the sine, cosine, and tangent of acute angles (measured in degrees) in right triangles. By extending the definitions to angles of rotation whose terminal sides intersect the unit circle, you will be able to define trigonometric functions of any angle (measured in radians, which are real numbers).
CC.9-12.F.TF.3(+) Use special triangles to determine geometrically the values of sine, cosine, tangent for $\frac{\pi}{3}$, $\frac{\pi}{4}$ and $\frac{\pi}{6}$, and use the unit circle to express the values of sine, cosine, and tangent for x, $\pi + x$, and $2\pi - x$ in terms of their values for x, where x is any real number. Lesson 8-3	You will use properties of 30°-60°-90° and 45°-45°-90° triangles to find exact values of the trigonometric functions for $\frac{\pi}{6}$ radians (equivalent to 30°), $\frac{\pi}{4}$ radians (equivalent to 45°), and $\frac{\pi}{3}$ radians (equivalent to 60°). You will also use reflections of angles in Quadrant I to find angles in Quadrants II, III, and IV that have the same or opposite trigonometric values as the angles in Quadrant I.
CC.9-12.F.TF.4(+) Use the unit circle to explain symmetry (odd and even) and periodicity of trigonometric functions. Lessons 8-5, 8-6	Trigonometric functions of angles of rotation repeat their values with each revolution around the unit circle. This repetition is called periodicity. Also, when the direction of rotation is negative, functional values may be the same as the corresponding positive rotations (in which case the function is called even), or they may be the opposite (in which case the function is called odd).

© Houghton Mifflin Harcourt Publishing Company

Notes

© Houghton Mifflin Harcourt Publishing Company

COMMON CORE Standards for Mathematical Content	What It Means For You
CC.9-12.F.TF.5 Choose trigonometric functions to model periodic phenomena with specified amplitude, frequency, and midline.* Lesson 8-9	Trigonometric functions can be used to model real-world situations. You will use trigonometric functions to model the height of a gondola on a Ferris wheel as a function of time.
CC.9-12.F.TF.8 Prove the Pythagorean identity $\sin^2(\theta) + \cos^2(\theta) = 1$ and use it to find $\sin(\theta)$, $\cos(\theta)$, or $\tan(\theta)$ given $\sin(\theta)$, $\cos(\theta)$, or $\tan(\theta)$ and the quadrant of the angle. Lesson 8-4	By applying the Pythagorean Theorem to the unit circle definitions of sine and cosine, you obtain what is called a Pythagorean identity. When the value of only one trigonometric function of a given angle and the quadrant of the angle are known, this identity will allow you to find the values of the other trigonometric functions.
CC.9-12.G.SRT.5 Use congruence and similarity criteria for triangles to solve problems and to prove relationships in geometric figures. Lesson 8-9	When modeling the motion of Ferris wheel, you will recognize and use similar triangles to adjust the model to the radius of the wheel.
CC.9-12.G.C.5 Derive using similarity the fact that the length of the arc intercepted by an angle is proportional to the radius, and define the radian measure of the angle as the constant of proportionality; derive the formula for the area of a sector. Lesson 8-1	For a given angle whose vertex is at the center of concentric circles, the ratio of the length of an intercepted arc to the radius of the corresponding circle is constant. This ratio can be used as the angle's measure, in which case it is called the radian measure of the angle.

UNIT 8

Notes

8-1 Understanding Radian Measure

Essential question: *What is radian measure, and how are radians related to degrees?*

COMMON CORE Standards for Mathematical Content

CC.9-12.G.C.5 Derive using similarity the fact that the length of the arc intercepted by an angle is proportional to the radius, and define the radian measure of the angle as the constant of proportionality ….

Vocabulary

intercepted arcs
radian measure

Prerequisites

Circles, arcs, and angles, Geometry

Math Background

Radians are a unit of angle measure. Radians are different from degrees, but it is possible to convert between degrees and radians. A radian can be defined as the measure of an angle in standard position on a circle of radius r centered at the origin whose terminal side intercepts an arc of length r. This means radians are dimensionless (radians are defined as the ratio of two lengths).

INTRODUCE

Review basic facts about circles. Students should understand the difference between the radius, the diameter, and the circumference of a circle. Remind students that π is the ratio of the circumference to the diameter of any circle. Since the radius is half the diameter, the circumference C is equal to $2\pi r$. Students should also recall that a circle measures 360°.

TEACH

1 EXPLORE

Questioning Strategies

- What happens to the intercepted arc length s as the radius increases? Explain why this is so. It increases. As the radius increases, so does the circumference, which increases the length of the intercepted arc.

- What will be the ratio of arc length to radius for a 60° central angle in a circle of radius 10 feet? for a 60° central angle in a circle of any radius? $\frac{\pi}{3}$; $\frac{\pi}{3}$

2 EXPLORE

Questioning Strategies

- What are the units for a radian? A radian is a dimensionless quantity. It is a ratio of two lengths; therefore, it has no units.

- If you double the diameter of a circle, how does the arc length of a 60° angle change? It doubles.

- If you double the diameter of a circle, how does the radian measure of a 60° angle change? It doesn't change, because the radian measure is a ratio of the arc length to the radius.

- What is the radian measure for a central angle of 180°? π

- If the radian measure is 1, what can you say about the arc length of the angle and the radius of the circle? They are equal.

Avoid Common Errors

Students will perceive that radians are a way of measuring angles and may seek to add a unit symbol or an abbreviation to radian measures. Tell students that although they will sometimes see the abbreviation "rad" used to refer to radians, radian measures do not require a unit symbol or an abbreviation. Degree measures should always have a degree symbol; angle measures without a symbol or unit abbreviation should be assumed to be radians.

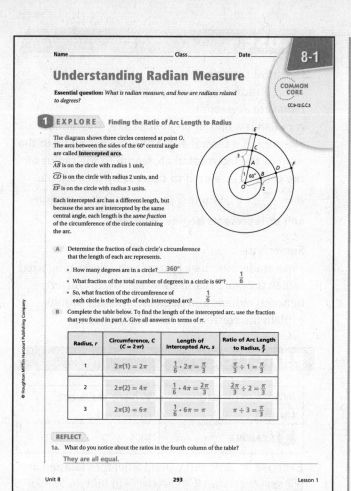

Understanding Radian Measure

8-1

COMMON CORE

CC.9-12.G.C.5

Essential question: *What is radian measure, and how are radians related to degrees?*

1 EXPLORE Finding the Ratio of Arc Length to Radius

The diagram shows three circles centered at point O. The arcs between the sides of the 60° central angle are called **intercepted arcs**.

$\overarc{AB}$ is on the circle with radius 1 unit,

$\overarc{CD}$ is on the circle with radius 2 units, and

$\overarc{EF}$ is on the circle with radius 3 units.

Each intercepted arc has a different length, but because the arcs are intercepted by the same central angle, each length is the *same fraction* of the circumference of the circle containing the arc.

A Determine the fraction of each circle's circumference that the length of each arc represents.

• How many degrees are in a circle? __360°__

• What fraction of the total number of degrees in a circle is 60°? __$\frac{1}{6}$__

• So, what fraction of the circumference of each circle is the length of each intercepted arc? __$\frac{1}{6}$__

B Complete the table below. To find the length of the intercepted arc, use the fraction that you found in part A. Give all answers in terms of π.

Radius, r	Circumference, C ($C = 2\pi r$)	Length of Intercepted Arc, s	Ratio of Arc Length to Radius, $\frac{s}{r}$
1	$2\pi(1) = 2\pi$	$\frac{1}{6} \cdot 2\pi = \frac{\pi}{3}$	$\frac{\pi}{3} \div 1 = \frac{\pi}{3}$
2	$2\pi(2) = 4\pi$	$\frac{1}{6} \cdot 4\pi = \frac{2\pi}{3}$	$\frac{2\pi}{3} \div 2 = \frac{\pi}{3}$
3	$2\pi(3) = 6\pi$	$\frac{1}{6} \cdot 6\pi = \pi$	$\pi \div 3 = \frac{\pi}{3}$

REFLECT

1a. What do you notice about the ratios in the fourth column of the table?

They are all equal.

1b. When the ratio of the values of one variable y to the corresponding values of another variable x is a constant k, y is said to be *proportional* to x, and the constant k is called the *constant of proportionality*. Because $\frac{y}{x} = k$, you can solve for y to get $y = kx$. In the case of arcs intercepted by a 60° central angle, is arc length s proportional to radius r? If so, what is the constant of proportionality, and what equation gives s in terms of r?

Yes; $\frac{\pi}{3}$; $s = \frac{\pi}{3} \cdot r$

1c. Suppose the central angle is 90° instead of 60°. Would arc length s still be proportional to radius r? If so, would the constant of proportionality still be the same? Explain.

Although s is still proportional to r, the constant of proportionality would become $\frac{\pi}{2}$ because a 90° angle represents $\frac{1}{4}$ of a circle, so (for instance) on a circle of radius 2, $s = \frac{1}{4} \cdot 4\pi = \pi$, $r = 2$, and $\frac{s}{r} = \frac{\pi}{2}$.

Radian Measure In the Explore and its Reflect questions, you should have reached the following conclusions:

1. When a central angle intercepts arcs on circles that have a common center, the ratio of each arc length s to radius r is constant.

2. When the degree measure of the central angle changes, the constant also changes.

These facts allow you to create an alternative way of measuring angles.

Instead of degree measure, you can use *radian measure*, defined as follows:

If a central angle in a circle of radius r intercepts an arc of length s, then the angle's **radian measure** is $\theta = \frac{s}{r}$.

2 EXPLORE Relating Radians to Degrees

Let the degree measure of a central angle in a circle with radius r be $d°$, as shown. You can derive formulas that relate the *angle's* degree measure and its radian measure.

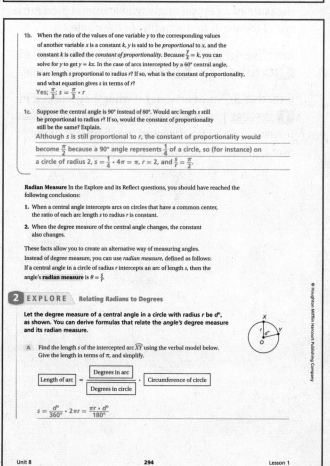

A Find the length s of the intercepted arc $\overarc{XY}$ using the verbal model below. Give the length in terms of π, and simplify.

$$\boxed{\text{Length of arc}} = \frac{\boxed{\text{Degrees in arc}}}{\boxed{\text{Degrees in circle}}} \cdot \boxed{\text{Circumference of circle}}$$

$$s = \frac{d°}{360°} \cdot 2\pi r = \frac{\pi r \cdot d°}{180°}$$

© Houghton Mifflin Harcourt Publishing Company

1 EXPLORE and **2 EXPLORE** include opportunities to address Mathematical Practice Standard 2 (Reason abstractly and quantitatively). Students will explore the relationship between arc length and radius for various intercepted arcs. They will derive the conversion factor between radians and degrees and understand that radians are dimensionless quantities. Students will practice converting between degrees and radians.

3 EXAMPLE

Questioning Strategies

- How can you check that you are using your conversion factor between degrees and radians correctly? **When you convert an angle measure from degrees to radians, the ratio of the degree measure to the radian measure should be about 57.3°.**

- As a quick check of your conversion, you can look at values. If $0° < d° < 180°$, between what values will the corresponding radians be? $0 < \theta < \pi$. If $180° < d° < 360°$, between what values will the corresponding radians be? $\pi < \theta < 2\pi$

EXTRA EXAMPLES

A. Use the formula $\theta = \dfrac{\pi}{180°} \cdot d°$ to convert each degree measure to radian measure. Simplify the result: 10°, 20°, 30°. $\dfrac{\pi}{18}, \dfrac{\pi}{9}, \dfrac{\pi}{6}$

B. Use the formula $d° = \dfrac{180°}{\pi} \cdot \theta$ to convert each radian measure to degree measure. Simplify the result: $\dfrac{7\pi}{6}, \dfrac{4\pi}{3}, \dfrac{3\pi}{2}$. 210°, 240°, 270°

CLOSE

Essential Question
What is radian measure, and how are radians related to degrees?
A radian is a unit of angle measure. The radian measure of a central angle of a circle is equal to the ratio of the intercepted arc length to the radius of the circle. It is related to degrees by the formula $\theta = \dfrac{\pi}{180°} \cdot d°$, where θ represents radian measure and $d°$ represents degree measure.

Summarize
Have students write a journal entry describing what radian measure is and showing how to convert between radians and degrees. Students should explain the conversion formulas in words.

PRACTICE

Where skills are taught	Where skills are practiced
3 EXAMPLE	EXS. 1, 2

Exercise 3: Students extend what they learned in **1 EXPLORE** and **2 EXPLORE** to find the radian measure of a central angle whose intercepted arc is equal in length to the radius of the circle.

Exercise 4: Students extend what they learned in **1 EXPLORE** and **2 EXPLORE** to the unit circle.

Exercise 5: Students extend what they learned in **1 EXPLORE** and **2 EXPLORE** to find the radian measure of a pizza slice and the diameter of the pizza, given an arc length.

B Use the result from part A to write the angle's radian measure θ in terms of d to find a formula for converting degrees to radians.

$$\theta = \frac{s}{r} = \frac{\frac{\pi r \cdot d^\circ}{180^\circ}}{r} = \frac{\pi}{180^\circ} \cdot d^\circ$$

C Solve the equation from part B for d° to find a formula for converting radians to degrees.

$$d^\circ = \frac{180^\circ}{\pi} \cdot \theta$$

REFLECT

2a. What radian measure is equivalent to 360°? Why does this make sense?

2π; 360° is a complete circle, so the arc length is the circumference of the circle, $2\pi r$. The ratio of the arc length to the radius is 2π.

Radian measures are usually written in terms of π, using fractions, such as $\frac{2\pi}{3}$, rather than mixed numbers.

3 EXAMPLE Converting Between Radians and Degrees

A Use the formula $\theta = \frac{\pi}{180^\circ} \cdot d^\circ$ to convert each degree measure to radian measure. Simplify the result.

Degree measure	Radian measure
15°	$\frac{\pi}{180^\circ} \cdot 15^\circ = \frac{\pi}{12}$
45°	$\frac{\pi}{180^\circ} \cdot 45^\circ = \frac{\pi}{4}$
90°	$\frac{\pi}{180^\circ} \cdot 90^\circ = \frac{\pi}{2}$
120°	$\frac{\pi}{180^\circ} \cdot 120^\circ = \frac{2\pi}{3}$
135°	$\frac{\pi}{180^\circ} \cdot 135^\circ = \frac{3\pi}{4}$
165°	$\frac{\pi}{180^\circ} \cdot 165^\circ = \frac{11\pi}{12}$

B Use the formula $d^\circ = \frac{180^\circ}{\pi} \cdot \theta$ to convert each radian measure to degree measure. Simplify the result.

Radian measure	Degree measure
$\frac{\pi}{6}$	$\frac{180^\circ}{\pi} \cdot \frac{\pi}{6} = 30^\circ$
$\frac{\pi}{3}$	$\frac{180^\circ}{\pi} \cdot \frac{\pi}{3} = 60^\circ$
$\frac{5\pi}{12}$	$\frac{180^\circ}{\pi} \cdot \frac{5\pi}{12} = 75^\circ$
$\frac{7\pi}{12}$	$\frac{180^\circ}{\pi} \cdot \frac{7\pi}{12} = 105^\circ$
$\frac{5\pi}{6}$	$\frac{180^\circ}{\pi} \cdot \frac{5\pi}{6} = 150^\circ$
π	$\frac{180^\circ}{\pi} \cdot \pi = 180^\circ$

© Houghton Mifflin Harcourt Publishing Company

REFLECT

3a. Which is greater, 1° or 1 radian? Explain.

1 radian; it is equivalent to $\frac{180^\circ}{\pi} \approx 57^\circ$.

3b. A radian is sometimes called a "dimensionless" quantity. Use unit analysis and the definition of radian to explain why this description makes sense.

A radian is a ratio of two lengths. The units in the numerator and denominator are the same, so they divide out, leaving no units.

PRACTICE

1. Convert each degree measure to radian measure. Simplify the result.

Degree measure	18°	24°	72°	84°	108°	126°	132°
Radian measure	$\frac{\pi}{10}$	$\frac{2\pi}{15}$	$\frac{2\pi}{5}$	$\frac{7\pi}{15}$	$\frac{3\pi}{5}$	$\frac{7\pi}{10}$	$\frac{11\pi}{15}$

2. Convert each radian measure to degree measure. Simplify the result.

Radian measure	$\frac{\pi}{15}$	$\frac{\pi}{5}$	$\frac{4\pi}{15}$	$\frac{3\pi}{10}$	$\frac{8\pi}{15}$	$\frac{13\pi}{15}$	$\frac{9\pi}{10}$
Degree measure	12°	36°	48°	54°	96°	156°	162°

3. When a central angle of a circle intercepts an arc whose length equals the radius of the circle, what is the angle's radian measure? Explain.

1; in the formula $\theta = \frac{s}{r}$, $s = r$, so $\theta = 1$.

4. A *unit circle* has a radius of 1. What is the relationship between the radian measure of a central angle in a unit circle and the length of the arc that it intercepts? Explain.

They are equal; in the formula $\theta = \frac{s}{r}$, $r = 1$, so $\theta = s$.

5. A pizza is cut into 8 equal slices.

a. What is the radian measure of the angle in each slice? $\frac{\pi}{4}$

b. If the length along the outer edge of the crust of one slice is about 7 inches, what is the *diameter* of the pizza to the nearest inch? (Use the formula $\theta = \frac{s}{r}$, but note that it gives you the radius of the pizza.) 18 inches

© Houghton Mifflin Harcourt Publishing Company

Angles of Rotation and Radian Measure

Essential question: What is an angle of rotation, and how is it measured?

COMMON CORE

Standards for Mathematical Content

CC.9-12.F.TF.1 Understand radian measure of an angle as the length of the arc on the unit circle subtended by the angle.

Vocabulary

angle of rotation

standard position

initial side

terminal side

unit circle

coterminal

Prerequisites

Circles, arcs, and angles, Geometry

Radian measure, Lesson 8-1

Math Background

Students are familiar with angles from their study of geometry. However, those angles all measured 180° or less. Students will now be exposed to angles with measures of more than 180°, including angles with measures more than 360°, and to negative angle measures.

The unit circle is a circle with a radius of one unit, centered at the origin. Any point on the circle (x, y) will satisfy the equation $x^2 + y^2 = 1$. This results from the Pythagorean theorem by using the radius of 1 as the hypotenuse. Students will use this Pythagorean relationship to derive the trigonometric identity $\sin^2 \theta + \cos^2 \theta = 1$ later in this unit.

INTRODUCE

In this lesson, students will investigate angles of rotation. These angles are not confined to angles with measures less than 180°, as angles often are in geometry courses. Angles of rotation may measure more than 180° or have negative measures. Remind students that there are 360° in one revolution. Ask them how many degrees there are in two revolutions, in three revolutions, or in one and a half revolutions.

TEACH

1 ENGAGE

Questioning Strategies

- What is the difference between a 180° angle of rotation and a −180° angle of rotation? **They have the same terminal side, but the positive angle has a counterclockwise rotation while the negative angle has a clockwise rotation.**

- What is the difference between a 90° angle of rotation and a −90° angle of rotation? **The positive angle has its terminal side along the positive y-axis. The negative angle has its terminal side along the negative y-axis.**

Teaching Strategy

Introducing students to the unit circle provides an opportunity to further develop students' understanding of units of measure. Point out to students that although the measure of a central angle in a unit circle and the length of its intercepted arc are *numerically* equal, they don't have the same units. Arcs are measured in units of length. Angles are measured in radians, which are unitless.

2 EXAMPLE

Questioning Strategies

- How would the drawing of a 90° angle differ from the drawing in part A? **The arrow for a 90° angle would start at the positive x-axis and end at the positive y-axis. It would not go around in a complete circle.**

- In part B, why does the arrow go clockwise to the terminal side? **to indicate that the angle measure is negative**

continued

© Houghton Mifflin Harcourt Publishing Company

Name_____ Class_____ Date_____

8-2

Angles of Rotation and Radian Measure

COMMON CORE

Essential question: *What is an angle of rotation, and how is it measured?*

CC.9-12.F.TF.1

1 ENGAGE Understanding Angles of Rotation

In trigonometry, an **angle of rotation** is an angle formed by the starting and ending positions of a ray that rotates about its endpoint. The angle is in **standard position** in a coordinate plane when the starting position of the ray, or **initial side** of the angle, is on the positive *x*-axis and has its endpoint at the origin. To show the amount and direction of rotation, a curved arrow is drawn to the ending position of the ray, or **terminal side** of the angle.

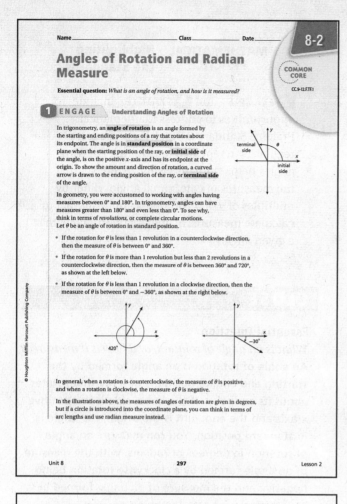

In geometry, you were accustomed to working with angles having measures between 0° and 180°. In trigonometry, angles can have measures greater than 180° and even less than 0°. To see why, think in terms of *revolutions*, or complete circular motions. Let θ be an angle of rotation in standard position.

• If the rotation for θ is less than 1 revolution in a counterclockwise direction, then the measure of θ is between 0° and 360°.

• If the rotation for θ is more than 1 revolution but less than 2 revolutions in a counterclockwise direction, then the measure of θ is between 360° and 720°, as shown at the left below.

• If the rotation for θ is less than 1 revolution in a clockwise direction, then the measure of θ is between 0° and −360°, as shown at the right below.

In general, when a rotation is counterclockwise, the measure of θ is positive, and when a rotation is clockwise, the measure of θ is negative.

In the illustrations above, the measures of angles of rotation are given in degrees, but if a circle is introduced into the coordinate plane, you can think in terms of arc lengths and use radian measure instead.

The **unit circle** is a circle that has a radius of 1 unit and is centered at the origin. Think of θ, an angle of rotation in standard position, as traversing an arc on the unit circle. Recall that radian measure was defined in Lesson 8-1 as $\theta = \frac{s}{r}$ where *s* is the arc length and *r* is the radius of the circle. Since $r = 1$ in this case, the radian measure of θ is simply the arc length: $\theta = s$. (Note: Throughout this unit, the symbol θ will be used to represent both an angle of rotation and its measure. For instance, "angle θ" refers to an angle, while "$\theta = \pi$" refers to an angle's measure.)

REFLECT

1a. The unit circle below shows the measures of angles of rotation that are commonly used in trigonometry. Radian measures appear outside the circle, and equivalent degree measures appear inside the circle. Provide the missing measures.

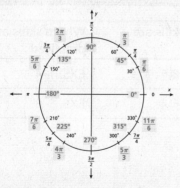

1b. Explain how you can use the diagram above to draw an angle of rotation with a measure of 570°.

   Subtract 360° from 570° to get 210°; the angle represents 1 counterclockwise

   revolution plus 210° more.

EXTRA EXAMPLE

Draw each angle of rotation with the given measure.

A. 720°

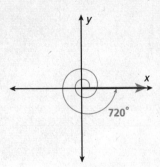

B. $-\dfrac{11\pi}{4}$

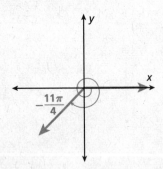

3 EXAMPLE

Questioning Strategies

- How else could you find coterminal angles in parts A and B? **In part A, you could add or subtract any multiple of 360° to or from −30°. In part B, you could add or subtract any multiple of 2π to or from $\dfrac{4\pi}{3}$.**

EXTRA EXAMPLE

Find the measure of a positive angle and a negative angle that are coterminal with each given angle.

A. −45° 315°, −405°

B. $\dfrac{\pi}{3}$ $\dfrac{7\pi}{3}, -\dfrac{5\pi}{3}$

Highlighting the Standards

2 EXAMPLE and 3 EXAMPLE include opportunities to address Mathematical Practice Standard 8 (Look for and express regularity in repeated reasoning). Drawing angles helps students visualize the fact that the measures of coterminal angles differ by multiples of ±360°. Students apply this fact to calculate measures of angles coterminal with a given angle.

CLOSE

Essential Question

What is an angle of rotation, and how is it measured? An angle of rotation is an angle formed by the starting and ending positions of a ray that rotates about its endpoint. If the initial side is the positive *x*-axis and the endpoint is the origin, the angle is in standard position. You can measure an angle of rotation in degrees or radians, with the measure of an angle formed by a clockwise rotation being negative and the measure of an angle formed by a counterclockwise rotation being positive.

Summarize

Have students write a journal entry describing angles of rotation and coterminal angles. They should mention positive and negative angles, as well as radians and degrees.

PRACTICE

Where skills are taught	Where skills are practiced
2 EXAMPLE	EXS. 1–4
3 EXAMPLE	EXS. 5–8

2 EXAMPLE — Drawing Angles of Rotation

Draw each angle of rotation with the given measure.

A 450°

Recognize that 450° represents 1 revolution counterclockwise (360°) plus 90° more. Draw the angle's initial side on the positive x-axis. Then draw a spiraling arrow from the initial side in a counterclockwise direction. The spiral should complete a full circle and then go a quarter of a circle farther. Draw the angle's terminal side where the arrow ends.

B $-\frac{5\pi}{4}$

Recognize that $-\frac{5\pi}{4}$ represents $\frac{1}{2}$ revolution clockwise $(-\pi)$ plus $-\frac{\pi}{4}$ more. Draw the angle's initial side on the positive x-axis. Then draw a spiraling arrow from the initial side in a clockwise direction. The spiral should complete a half circle and then go an eighth of a circle farther. Draw the angle's terminal side where the arrow ends.

REFLECT

2a. Is the measure of an angle of rotation in standard position completely determined by the position of its terminal side? Explain.

No; there are infinitely many angles of rotation that could be drawn in standard position with a given terminal side.

Angles of rotation in standard position that have the same terminal side are called **coterminal**.

3 EXAMPLE — Finding Coterminal Angles

Find the measure of a positive angle and a negative angle that are coterminal with each given angle.

A −30°

For a positive coterminal angle, add 360°: −30° + 360° = 330°

For a negative coterminal angle, subtract 360°: −30° − 360° = −390°

B $\frac{4\pi}{3}$

For a positive coterminal angle, add 2π: $\frac{4\pi}{3} + 2\pi = \frac{10\pi}{3}$

For a negative coterminal angle, subtract 2π: $\frac{4\pi}{3} - 2\pi = \frac{2\pi}{3}$

Unit 8   299   Lesson 2

© Houghton Mifflin Harcourt Publishing Company

REFLECT

3a. Describe a general method for finding the measure of *any* angle that is coterminal with a given angle.

Add or subtract a multiple of 360° or 2π from the given angle's measure.

3b. Find the measure between 720° and 1080° of an angle that is coterminal with an angle that has a measure of −30°. Explain your method.

1050°; 720 and 1080 are consecutive multiples of 360, and −30 + 1080 = 1050

PRACTICE

Draw the angle of rotation with each given measure.

1. −180°

2. 405°

3. $-\frac{2\pi}{3}$

4. $\frac{15\pi}{4}$

Find the measure of a positive angle and a negative angle that are coterminal with each given angle. Answers may vary. Sample answers are given.

5. −10°   350°; −370°

6. 500°   140°; −220°

7. $-\frac{7\pi}{6}$ $\frac{5\pi}{6}$; $\frac{19\pi}{6}$

8. $\frac{11\pi}{4}$ $\frac{3\pi}{4}$; $\frac{5\pi}{4}$

© Houghton Mifflin Harcourt Publishing Company

Unit 8   300   Lesson 2

© Houghton Mifflin Harcourt Publishing Company

The Sine, Cosine, and Tangent Functions

Essential question: *How can the sine, cosine, and tangent functions be defined using the unit circle?*

COMMON CORE **Standards for Mathematical Content**

CC.9-12.F.IF.1 Understand that a function from one set (called the domain) to another set (called the range) assigns to each element of the domain exactly one element of the range. If f is a function and x is an element of its domain, then $f(x)$ denotes the output of f corresponding to the input x. The graph of f is the graph of the equation $y = f(x)$.

CC.9-12.F.TF.2 Explain how the unit circle in the coordinate plane enables the extension of trigonometric functions to all real numbers, interpreted as radian measures of angles traversed counterclockwise around the unit circle.

CC.9-12.F.TF.3(+) Use special triangles to determine geometrically the values of sine, cosine, tangent for $\frac{\pi}{3}$, $\frac{\pi}{4}$, and $\frac{\pi}{6}$, and use the unit circle to express the values of sine, cosine, and tangent for x, $\pi + x$, and $2\pi - x$ in terms of their values for x, where x is any real number.

Vocabulary
reference angle

Prerequisites
Sine, cosine, and tangent, Geometry

Special right triangles, Geometry

Math Background
The sine, cosine, and tangent functions—sometimes called circular functions—are used when modeling periodic motion. Periodic motion is a motion that has a pattern that is repeated at regular intervals. Examples include the swinging of a pendulum and the progress of a wave (light, sound, or ocean waves).

This lesson connects students' past experience with triangle trigonometry to the study of circular trigonometry. Later in the unit, students will investigate real-world applications of trigonometry involving periodic motion.

There are many real-world applications of trigonometric functions. Early trigonometric relationships were used around 200 BCE in describing astronomical observations.

Today these functions are also used in the following fields: acoustics, music, optics, electronics, probability, medical imaging, surveying, architecture, electrical engineering, civil engineering, cartography, and computer game development, to name a few.

INTRODUCE

Ask students to recall the sine, cosine, and tangent ratios from geometry. Then ask them what mnemonics they use to remember these ratios. One popular method is using the alphabet for sine and cosine (cosine goes with adjacent and sine goes with opposite—the earlier letters in the alphabet belong together). Another method is the mnemonic SOHCAHTOA.

Next, have students review the values of the sine, cosine, and tangent for the special angles. Also, have them find the corresponding radian measure for those angles. Gather the information in a table on the board, such as the one below.

Angle	Radians	Sine	Cosine	Tangent
30°	$\frac{\pi}{6}$	$\frac{1}{2}$	$\frac{\sqrt{3}}{2}$	$\frac{\sqrt{3}}{3}$
45°	$\frac{\pi}{4}$	$\frac{\sqrt{2}}{2}$	$\frac{\sqrt{2}}{2}$	1
60°	$\frac{\pi}{3}$	$\frac{\sqrt{3}}{2}$	$\frac{1}{2}$	$\sqrt{3}$

TEACH

1 EXPLORE

Questioning Strategies
- The sine, cosine, and tangent are ratios of the lengths of sides for what type of triangle?
  right triangle

continued

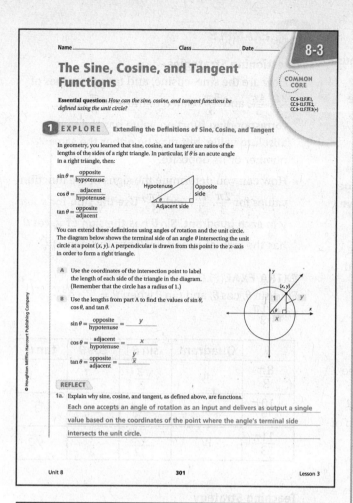

Name_____ Class_____ Date_____

The Sine, Cosine, and Tangent Functions

COMMON CORE

CC.9-12.F.TF.1,
CC.9-12.F.TF.2,
CC.9-12.F.TF.3(+)

Essential question: *How can the sine, cosine, and tangent functions be defined using the unit circle?*

1 EXPLORE Extending the Definitions of Sine, Cosine, and Tangent

In geometry, you learned that sine, cosine, and tangent are ratios of the lengths of the sides of a right triangle. In particular, if θ is an acute angle in a right triangle, then:

$$\sin \theta = \frac{\text{opposite}}{\text{hypotenuse}}$$

$$\cos \theta = \frac{\text{adjacent}}{\text{hypotenuse}}$$

$$\tan \theta = \frac{\text{opposite}}{\text{adjacent}}$$

Hypotenuse Opposite side

θ

Adjacent side

You can extend these definitions using angles of rotation and the unit circle. The diagram below shows the terminal side of an angle θ intersecting the unit circle at a point (x, y). A perpendicular is drawn from this point to the x-axis in order to form a right triangle.

A Use the coordinates of the intersection point to label the length of each side of the triangle in the diagram. (Remember that the circle has a radius of 1.)

B Use the lengths from part A to find the values of $\sin \theta$, $\cos \theta$, and $\tan \theta$.

$$\sin \theta = \frac{\text{opposite}}{\text{hypotenuse}} = \underline{\quad y \quad}$$

$$\cos \theta = \frac{\text{adjacent}}{\text{hypotenuse}} = \underline{\quad x \quad}$$

$$\tan \theta = \frac{\text{opposite}}{\text{adjacent}} = \underline{\quad \frac{y}{x} \quad}$$

REFLECT

1a. Explain why sine, cosine, and tangent, as defined above, are functions.

Each one accepts an angle of rotation as an input and delivers as output a single

value based on the coordinates of the point where the angle's terminal side

intersects the unit circle.

1b. Although you can think of x and y as lengths when the terminal side of θ lies in Quadrant I, you know that the values of x and/or y are negative in other quadrants. Dropping the idea of lengths and simply accepting that $\sin \theta = y$, $\cos \theta = x$, and $\tan \theta = \frac{y}{x}$ no matter where the terminal side of θ lies, complete the table by stating the sign of each function's values in each quadrant.

Trigonometric function	Sign of Function's Values in Quadrant			
	I	II	III	IV
$\sin \theta$	positive	positive	negative	negative
$\cos \theta$	positive	negative	negative	positive
$\tan \theta$	positive	negative	positive	negative

1c. Are the sine, cosine, and tangent functions defined at all points on the unit circle? If not, identify the points where each function is not defined, and state any restrictions on the value of θ.

Sine and cosine are always defined, so there are no restrictions on θ;

tangent is undefined at $(0, 1)$ and $(0, -1)$, so θ cannot equal odd multiples

of $90°$ or $\frac{\pi}{2}$.

1d. What are the maximum and minimum x- and y-coordinates of points on the unit circle? What does this mean for the range of the sine and cosine functions?

The maximum x-coordinate and the maximum y-coordinate are 1, and the

minimum x-coordinate and the minimum y-coordinate are -1; the range of sine is

$\{\sin \theta \mid -1 \le \sin \theta \le 1\}$, and the range of cosine is $\{\cos \theta \mid -1 \le \cos \theta \le 1\}$.

1e. Each table lists several points on the unit circle near $(0, 1)$. If each point is on the terminal side of an angle θ, find the value of $\tan \theta$. Then describe what happens to $\tan \theta$ the closer θ gets to $90°$ or $\frac{\pi}{2}$.

The values of $\tan \theta$ appear to increase and decrease without bound.

Point on terminal side of θ	Value of $\tan \theta$
$\left(\frac{3}{5}, \frac{4}{5}\right)$	$\frac{4}{3}$
$\left(\frac{5}{13}, \frac{12}{13}\right)$	$\frac{12}{5}$
$\left(\frac{7}{25}, \frac{24}{25}\right)$	$\frac{24}{7}$

Point on terminal side of θ	Value of $\tan \theta$
$\left(-\frac{3}{5}, \frac{4}{5}\right)$	$-\frac{4}{3}$
$\left(-\frac{5}{13}, \frac{12}{13}\right)$	$-\frac{12}{5}$
$\left(-\frac{7}{25}, \frac{24}{25}\right)$	$-\frac{24}{7}$

- Why does $\sin\theta = y$ and $\cos\theta = x$? The hypotenuse is 1, so $\sin\theta = \frac{y}{1} = y$ and $\cos\theta = \frac{x}{1} = x$.
- In the table giving the domain and range of the trigonometric functions, why is the range for sine and cosine between −1 and 1 inclusive? The sine and cosine are defined using the unit circle. The greatest value either x or y can have is 1 and the least value is −1. Therefore, the range of both functions is between −1 and 1 inclusive.

Avoid Common Errors

Students are likely to look at the range of the sine function and the range of the cosine function and come to the conclusion that the tangent also has a range of −1 to 1 inclusive. To help them see that this is not the case, have them use string to make right triangles in the first quadrant on the unit circle. As θ increases, they should see that x decreases and y increases. In fact, they should see that x approaches 0 as y approaches 1. Because of this, the ratio of y to x increases rapidly toward infinity. Thus, as θ gets close to 90° or $\frac{\pi}{2}$, the ratio of y to x becomes very large, much greater than 1.

2 EXPLORE

Questioning Strategies

- If you reflect a point (x, y) over the y-axis, what happens to the values of x and y? The value of x becomes the opposite of the original value; the value of y remains the same.
- If you reflect a point (x, y) over the x-axis, what happens to the values of x and y? The value of x remains the same; the value of y becomes the opposite of the original value.
- A ray in the first quadrant that makes an angle θ with the positive x-axis is reflected across the y-axis. What angle does the reflected ray make with the negative x-axis? θ

3 EXAMPLE

Questioning Strategies

- How are the sine, cosine, and tangent values of $\frac{2\pi}{3}$, $\frac{4\pi}{3}$, and $\frac{5\pi}{3}$ related to those of $\frac{\pi}{3}$? Each corresponding function value has the same absolute value, but may be either the same number or its opposite.
- How can you determine the signs of the function values for $\frac{2\pi}{3}$, $\frac{4\pi}{3}$, and $\frac{5\pi}{3}$? Use the sign for x and y in each quadrant. $\sin\theta$ has the sign of y, $\cos\theta$ has the sign of x, and $\tan\theta$ has the sign of $\frac{y}{x}$.

EXTRA EXAMPLE
Find $\sin\theta$, $\cos\theta$, and $\tan\theta$ when $\theta = \frac{8\pi}{3}$, $\frac{10\pi}{3}$, and $\frac{11\pi}{3}$.

θ	Quadrant	$\sin\theta$	$\cos\theta$	$\tan\theta$
$\frac{8\pi}{3}$	II	$\frac{\sqrt{3}}{2}$	$-\frac{1}{2}$	$-\sqrt{3}$
$\frac{10\pi}{3}$	III	$-\frac{\sqrt{3}}{2}$	$-\frac{1}{2}$	$\sqrt{3}$
$\frac{11\pi}{3}$	IV	$-\frac{\sqrt{3}}{2}$	$\frac{1}{2}$	$-\sqrt{3}$

Teaching Strategy
After students write the coordinates of point P in step A, ask them to apply the Pythagorean theorem to the triangle shown on the unit circle in step A. Since the hypotenuse of the triangle for trigonometric functions will always be 1, students can check their values for special angles by confirming that the sum of the squares of the leg lengths is equal to the length of the hypotenuse squared, or 1.

Avoid Common Errors
Later in the unit students will use calculators to evaluate trigonometric functions. Calculators can be set to interpret angles in either degrees or radians. If students assume their calculators are set to degrees when they are actually set to radians, their answers will be wrong. Students should check which mode their calculators are in prior to using them for trigonometry problems. A simple way to check is to type in one of the well-known values, such as sin 30°. If the value given is not 0.5, the calculator is probably in radian mode.

Domain and Range The table below describes the domain and range of each trigonometric function.

Function	Domain	Range
Sine ($\sin\theta = y$)	θ can be any angle of rotation.	$-1 \le \sin\theta \le 1$
Cosine ($\cos\theta = x$)	θ can be any angle of rotation.	$-1 \le \cos\theta \le 1$
Tangent ($\tan\theta = \frac{y}{x}$)	θ cannot be an odd multiple of 90° or $\frac{\pi}{2}$.	All real numbers

2 EXPLORE   Identifying Reference Angles

Let θ' be an angle with a measure between 0 and $\frac{\pi}{2}$, and let (x, y) be the coordinates of the point of intersection of the terminal side of θ' and the unit circle. You can find three other angles related to θ' through reflections in the axes.

A Draw the reflection of the terminal side of θ' in the y-axis. Consider this to be the terminal side of an angle θ with a measure between 0 and 2π. Label the coordinates of the point of intersection of the terminal side of θ and the unit circle.

• In what quadrant is the terminal side of θ?   Q. II

• Due to the reflection, the positive angle that the terminal side of θ makes with the *negative x-axis* is θ'. What is the sum of the measures of θ and θ'? π

• Write θ' in terms of θ. $\theta' = \pi - \theta$

B Draw the reflection of the terminal side of θ' in the x-axis. Consider this to be the terminal side of an angle θ with a measure between 0 and 2π. Label the coordinates of the point of intersection of the terminal side of θ and the unit circle.

• In what quadrant is the terminal side of θ?   Q. IV

• Due to the reflection, the positive angle that the terminal side of θ makes with the *positive x-axis* is θ'. What is the sum of the measures of θ and θ'? 2π

• Write θ' in terms of θ. $\theta' = 2\pi - \theta$

C Draw the reflection of the terminal side of θ' in *both* axes. (First reflect in one axis, then reflect the image in the other axis.) Consider this to be the terminal side of an angle θ with a measure between 0 and 2π. Label the coordinates of the point of intersection of the terminal side of θ and the unit circle.

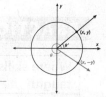

• In what quadrant is the terminal side of θ?   Q. III

• Due to the reflection, the positive angle that the terminal side of θ makes with the *negative x-axis* is θ'. By how much do the measures of θ and θ' differ? π

• Write θ' in terms of θ. $\theta' = \theta - \pi$

REFLECT

2a. The **reference angle** θ' for an angle θ with a measure between 0 and 2π is the acute angle formed by the terminal side of θ and the x-axis.

For θ in Quadrant I, $\theta' = \theta$.

For θ in Quadrant II, $\theta' = \pi - \theta$.

For θ in Quadrant III, $\theta' = \theta - \pi$.

For θ in Quadrant IV, $\theta' = 2\pi - \theta$.

You can use reference angles to find the values of sine, cosine, and tangent of θ if the values are known for θ'. Suppose that $\sin\theta' = y$ and $\cos\theta' = x$ as in the Explore. Complete the table using the coordinates of the intersection points from the Explore.

	Quadrant I $0 < \theta < \frac{\pi}{2}$	Quadrant II $\frac{\pi}{2} < \theta < \pi$	Quadrant III $\pi < \theta < \frac{3\pi}{2}$	Quadrant IV $\frac{3\pi}{2} < \theta < 2\pi$
$\sin\theta$	y	y	$-y$	$-y$
$\cos\theta$	x	$-x$	$-x$	x
$\tan\theta$	$\frac{y}{x}$	$\frac{y}{x}$	$\frac{y}{x}$	$\frac{y}{x}$

2b. Explain how to use the diagram at right to determine the values of $\sin\theta$ and $\cos\theta$ when the values are known for the reference angle θ'.

The absolute value of each function is the same for θ and θ'. The sign of each function depends on the quadrant that contains the terminal side of θ. The sign of the x-coordinate gives the sign of $\cos\theta$, and the sign of the y-coordinate gives the sign of $\sin\theta$.

(−, +)   (+, +)

(−, −)   (+, −)

© Houghton Mifflin Harcourt Publishing Company

This lesson, particularly the use of reference angles in **3** EXAMPLE , includes opportunities to address Mathematical Practice Standard 8 (Look for and express regularity in repeated reasoning). Students apply the patterns they discovered in **1** EXPLORE and **2** EXPLORE about signs of trigonometric functions and reference angles to reason through the values of the trigonometric functions for special angles $\frac{\pi}{3}$, $\frac{2\pi}{3}$, $\frac{4\pi}{3}$, and $\frac{5\pi}{3}$.

CLOSE

Essential Question
How can the sine, cosine, and tangent functions be defined using the unit circle?
The functions can be defined using the unit circle so that the *y*-value of the point where the terminal side of an angle of rotation intersects the unit circle is its sine, the *x*-value is its cosine, and the ratio of *y* to *x* is its tangent.

Summarize
After finishing the Practice exercises students should create a single table in their journals showing the sine, cosine, and tangent values for all the special angles. The angles should be entered in numerical order from 0 radians to $\frac{11\pi}{6}$ radians.

PRACTICE

Where skills are taught	Where skills are practiced
3 EXAMPLE	EX. 1

Exercise 2: Students extend what they learned in **3** EXAMPLE to finding the sine, cosine, and tangent of the quadrantal angles.

Special Angles In geometry, you studied two special right triangles: 30°-60°-90° and 45°-45°-90° triangles. You can use these triangles to find exact values for the trigonometric functions of angles with measure 30°, 45°, and 60° (or, in radians, $\frac{\pi}{6}$, $\frac{\pi}{4}$, and $\frac{\pi}{3}$) or of any angle having one of these angles as a reference angle.

3 EXAMPLE   Finding Sine, Cosine, and Tangent of Special Angles

Find $\sin\theta$, $\cos\theta$, and $\tan\theta$ when $\theta = \frac{\pi}{3}$, $\frac{2\pi}{3}$, $\frac{4\pi}{3}$, and $\frac{5\pi}{3}$.

A The diagram shows an angle of $\frac{\pi}{3}$ and the unit circle.
Use the side-length relationships in a 30°-60°-90° triangle
to label the side lengths of the triangle formed by dropping
a perpendicular from the point P where the angle's terminal
side intersects the unit circle.

What are the coordinates of P? $\left(\frac{1}{2}, \frac{\sqrt{3}}{2}\right)$

B Find each function value.

$\sin\frac{\pi}{3} = \frac{\sqrt{3}}{2}$

$\cos\frac{\pi}{3} = \frac{1}{2}$

$\tan\frac{\pi}{3} = \sqrt{3}$

C Recognize that $\frac{\pi}{3}$ is the reference angle for $\frac{2\pi}{3}$, $\frac{4\pi}{3}$, and $\frac{5\pi}{3}$.
Complete the table, remembering that the quadrant in which the terminal
side of an angle lies determines the signs of the trigonometric functions
of the angle.

θ	Quadrant	$\sin\theta$	$\cos\theta$	$\tan\theta$
$\frac{2\pi}{3}$	II	$\frac{\sqrt{3}}{2}$	$-\frac{1}{2}$	$-\sqrt{3}$
$\frac{4\pi}{3}$	III	$-\frac{\sqrt{3}}{2}$	$-\frac{1}{2}$	$\sqrt{3}$
$\frac{5\pi}{3}$	IV	$-\frac{\sqrt{3}}{2}$	$\frac{1}{2}$	$-\sqrt{3}$

REFLECT

3a. Explain why $\frac{\pi}{3}$ is the reference angle for $\frac{2\pi}{3}$, $\frac{4\pi}{3}$, and $\frac{5\pi}{3}$.
$\frac{2\pi}{3}$ is in Q. II, so subtract $\frac{2\pi}{3}$ from π to get the reference angle: $\pi - \frac{2\pi}{3} = \frac{\pi}{3}$;
$\frac{4\pi}{3}$ is in Q. III, so subtract π from $\frac{4\pi}{3}$ to get the reference angle: $\frac{4\pi}{3} - \pi = \frac{\pi}{3}$;
$\frac{5\pi}{3}$ is in Q. IV, so subtract $\frac{5\pi}{3}$ from 2π to get the reference angle: $2\pi - \frac{5\pi}{3} = \frac{\pi}{3}$.

3b. Explain how to find $\sin\theta$, $\cos\theta$, and $\tan\theta$ when $\theta = \frac{16\pi}{3}$.
Subtract 2 revolutions (4π) from θ to get $\frac{4\pi}{3}$, which is in Q. III; so, $\sin\theta = -\frac{\sqrt{3}}{2}$,
$\cos\theta = -\frac{1}{2}$, and $\tan\theta = \sqrt{3}$.

PRACTICE

1. Each table lists four angles that have the same reference angle. Find the sine,
cosine, and tangent of each angle.

θ	$\sin\theta$	$\cos\theta$	$\tan\theta$
$\frac{\pi}{6}$	$\frac{1}{2}$	$\frac{\sqrt{3}}{2}$	$\frac{\sqrt{3}}{3}$
$\frac{5\pi}{6}$	$\frac{1}{2}$	$\frac{\sqrt{3}}{2}$	$\frac{\sqrt{3}}{3}$
$\frac{7\pi}{6}$	$-\frac{1}{2}$	$\frac{\sqrt{3}}{2}$	$\frac{\sqrt{3}}{3}$
$\frac{11\pi}{6}$	$-\frac{1}{2}$	$\frac{\sqrt{3}}{2}$	$\frac{\sqrt{3}}{3}$

θ	$\sin\theta$	$\cos\theta$	$\tan\theta$
$\frac{\pi}{4}$	$\frac{\sqrt{2}}{2}$	$\frac{\sqrt{2}}{2}$	1
$\frac{3\pi}{4}$	$\frac{\sqrt{2}}{2}$	$\frac{\sqrt{2}}{2}$	-1
$\frac{5\pi}{4}$	$\frac{\sqrt{2}}{2}$	$\frac{\sqrt{2}}{2}$	1
$\frac{7\pi}{4}$	$\frac{\sqrt{2}}{2}$	$\frac{\sqrt{2}}{2}$	-1

2. If the terminal side of an angle falls on one of the axes, the angle is called
a *quadrantal angle*. The table below lists the four quadrantal angles from 0 to
2π (not including 2π). Complete the table by giving the coordinates of the point
where each angle's terminal side intersects the unit circle, and then find the
values of sine, cosine, and tangent.

θ	Intersection point	$\sin\theta$	$\cos\theta$	$\tan\theta$
0	(1, 0)	0	1	0
$\frac{\pi}{2}$	(0, 1)	1	0	Undefined
π	(−1, 0)	0	−1	0
$\frac{3\pi}{2}$	(0, −1)	−1	0	Undefined

Evaluating the Trigonometric Functions

Essential question: *How can you use a given value of one of the trigonometric functions to calculate the values of the other functions?*

© Houghton Mifflin Harcourt Publishing Company

COMMON CORE Standards for Mathematical Content

CC.9-12.F.TF.8 Prove the Pythagorean Identity $\sin^2 \theta + \cos^2 \theta = 1$ and use it to calculate trigonometric ratios.

Also: CC.9-12.A.REI.4, CC.9-12.A.REI.4b

Prerequisites

Pythagorean Theorem, Geometry

The sine, cosine, and tangent functions, Lesson 8-3

Math Background

Students should be familiar with the Pythagorean Theorem from their work in Geometry. Since the sine and cosine functions are defined by using a right triangle with its hypotenuse connecting the origin to the unit circle, the Pythagorean Theorem can be used to generate an identity involving these functions. This identity, $\sin^2 \theta + \cos^2 \theta = 1$, is one of the Pythagorean identities, and it, along with other trigonometric identities, can be used to find the value of one trigonometric function given the value of another.

INTRODUCE

Students are familiar with laws and identities involving exponents and logarithms. Let students know that trigonometric functions have their own set of identities. The first they will study is based on the Pythagorean Theorem. An important fact to remember about identities is that they are relationships that are true for all values of x (or θ).

TEACH

1 EXPLORE

Questioning Strategies

- How do you know the hypotenuse is equal to 1?
  The radius of a unit circle is 1.

- Is $(\cos \theta)^2$ the same as $\cos^2 \theta$? Is $(\sin \theta)^2$ the same as $\sin^2 \theta$? Yes, they are just different ways of writing the same thing.

- Is there a difference between $\sin^2 \theta$ and $\sin 2\theta$? Yes, in the first you take the sine of θ and square it; in the second you are taking the sine of 2θ. For example, $\sin^2 \frac{\pi}{6} = \left(\frac{1}{2}\right)^2 = \frac{1}{4}$ but $\sin 2\left(\frac{\pi}{6}\right) = \sin \frac{\pi}{3} = \frac{\sqrt{3}}{2}$.

2 EXAMPLE

Questioning Strategies

- Is $1 - \sin^2 \theta$ ever negative? Why or why not? No; $-1 \leq \sin \theta \leq 1$, so $0 \leq \sin^2 \theta \leq 1$ and $1 - \sin^2 \theta$ can never be less than 0.

- Do you need to know the precise value of θ to answer part A? Why or why not? No; the Pythagorean identity allows you to find the cosine of θ given the sine of θ without knowing the value of θ itself.

- Do you need to know the quadrant where θ terminates to answer part B? Why or why not? Yes; the sign of the answer varies depending on the quadrant where θ terminates.

EXTRA EXAMPLE

Find the approximate value of each trigonometric function.

A. Given $\sin \theta = -0.544$, where $\frac{3\pi}{2} < \theta < 2\pi$, find $\cos \theta$. **0.839**

B. Given $\cos \theta = -0.123$, where $\frac{\pi}{2} < \theta < \pi$, find $\sin \theta$. **0.992**

continued

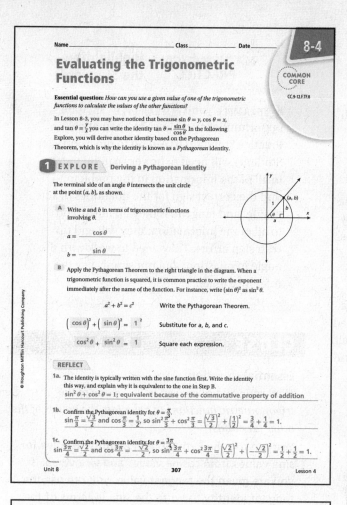

Name_____ Class_____ Date_____

Evaluating the Trigonometric Functions

COMMON CORE

CC.9-12.F.TF.8

Essential question: *How can you use a given value of one of the trigonometric functions to calculate the values of the other functions?*

In Lesson 8-3, you may have noticed that because $\sin\theta = y$, $\cos\theta = x$, and $\tan\theta = \frac{y}{x}$ you can write the identity $\tan\theta = \frac{\sin\theta}{\cos\theta}$. In the following Explore, you will derive another identity based on the Pythagorean Theorem, which is why the identity is known as a *Pythagorean* identity.

1 EXPLORE   Deriving a Pythagorean Identity

The terminal side of an angle θ intersects the unit circle at the point (a, b), as shown.

A Write a and b in terms of trigonometric functions involving θ.

$a = \underline{\quad \cos\theta \quad}$

$b = \underline{\quad \sin\theta \quad}$

B Apply the Pythagorean Theorem to the right triangle in the diagram. When a trigonometric function is squared, it is common practice to write the exponent immediately after the name of the function. For instance, write $(\sin\theta)^2$ as $\sin^2\theta$.

$a^2 + b^2 = c^2$ Write the Pythagorean Theorem.

$\left(\cos\theta\right)^2 + \left(\sin\theta\right)^2 = 1^2$ Substitute for a, b, and c.

$\cos^2\theta + \sin^2\theta = 1$ Square each expression.

REFLECT

1a. The identity is typically written with the sine function first. Write the identity this way, and explain why it is equivalent to the one in Step B.
$\sin^2\theta + \cos^2\theta = 1$; equivalent because of the commutative property of addition

1b. Confirm the Pythagorean identity for $\theta = \frac{\pi}{3}$.
$\sin\frac{\pi}{3} = \frac{\sqrt{3}}{2}$ and $\cos\frac{\pi}{3} = \frac{1}{2}$, so $\sin^2\frac{\pi}{3} + \cos^2\frac{\pi}{3} = \left(\frac{\sqrt{3}}{2}\right)^2 + \left(\frac{1}{2}\right)^2 = \frac{3}{4} + \frac{1}{4} = 1$.

1c. Confirm the Pythagorean identity for $\theta = \frac{3\pi}{4}$.
$\sin\frac{3\pi}{4} = \frac{\sqrt{2}}{2}$ and $\cos\frac{3\pi}{4} = -\frac{\sqrt{2}}{2}$, so $\sin^2\frac{3\pi}{4} + \cos^2\frac{3\pi}{4} = \left(\frac{\sqrt{2}}{2}\right)^2 + \left(-\frac{\sqrt{2}}{2}\right)^2 = \frac{1}{2} + \frac{1}{2} = 1$.

Rewriting the Identity You can rewrite the identity $\sin^2\theta + \cos^2\theta = 1$ to express one trigonometric function in terms of the other. As shown below, each alternate version of the identity involves positive and negative square roots. You determine which sign to use based on knowing the quadrant in which the terminal side of θ lies.

Solve for $\sin\theta$:

$\sin^2\theta + \cos^2\theta = 1$

$\sin^2\theta = 1 - \cos^2\theta$

$\sin\theta = \pm\sqrt{1 - \cos^2\theta}$

Solve for $\cos\theta$:

$\sin^2\theta + \cos^2\theta = 1$

$\cos^2\theta = 1 - \sin^2\theta$

$\cos\theta = \pm\sqrt{1 - \sin^2\theta}$

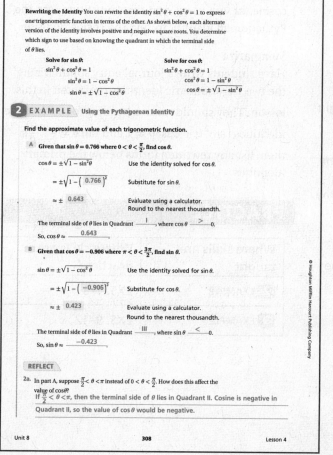

2 EXAMPLE   Using the Pythagorean Identity

Find the approximate value of each trigonometric function.

A Given that $\sin\theta = 0.766$ where $0 < \theta < \frac{\pi}{2}$, find $\cos\theta$.

$\cos\theta = \pm\sqrt{1 - \sin^2\theta}$ Use the identity solved for $\cos\theta$.

$= \pm\sqrt{1 - \left(0.766\right)^2}$ Substitute for $\sin\theta$.

$\approx \pm\ 0.643$ Evaluate using a calculator. Round to the nearest thousandth.

The terminal side of θ lies in Quadrant $\underline{\ I\ }$, where $\cos\theta\ \underline{\ >\ }\ 0$.

So, $\cos\theta \approx \underline{\ 0.643\ }$.

B Given that $\cos\theta = -0.906$ where $\pi < \theta < \frac{3\pi}{2}$, find $\sin\theta$.

$\sin\theta = \pm\sqrt{1 - \cos^2\theta}$ Use the identity solved for $\sin\theta$.

$= \pm\sqrt{1 - \left(-0.906\right)^2}$ Substitute for $\cos\theta$.

$\approx \pm\ 0.423$ Evaluate using a calculator. Round to the nearest thousandth.

The terminal side of θ lies in Quadrant $\underline{\ III\ }$, where $\sin\theta\ \underline{\ <\ }\ 0$.

So, $\sin\theta \approx \underline{\ -0.423\ }$.

REFLECT

2a. In part A, suppose $\frac{\pi}{2} < \theta < \pi$ instead of $0 < \theta < \frac{\pi}{2}$. How does this affect the value of $\cos\theta$?
If $\frac{\pi}{2} < \theta < \pi$, then the terminal side of θ lies in Quadrant II. Cosine is negative in Quadrant II, so the value of $\cos\theta$ would be negative.

Teaching Strategy

Encourage students to make a sketch prior to attempting to solve the problems in **2 EXAMPLE** . The given information should make it clear which quadrant the terminal side of the angle lies in. If students know the values of sine and cosine for 0, $\frac{\pi}{2}$, π, and $\frac{3\pi}{2}$, they can estimate where the terminal side should be. For example, in part B, the angle is in the third quadrant. Since the cosine is very close to -1, the terminal side makes a very small angle with the negative x-axis. In part A, the sine is 0.766, so students will know only that the terminal side is in Quadrant I, but not necessarily its position relative to the other axes. Even if students can only surmise the correct quadrant, a diagram will still be helpful. Once they've sketched the angle, students can write down the signs for all three trigonometric functions in that quadrant and refer to their sketches throughout the problem.

3 EXAMPLE

Questioning Strategies

- Is there another way to begin this problem besides writing $\sin\theta$ in terms of $\cos\theta$? Yes, you can write $\cos\theta$ in terms of $\sin\theta$.

- Write the Pythagorean identity with $\cos\theta$ written in terms of $\sin\theta$. $\sin^2\theta + \left(\dfrac{\sin\theta}{\tan\theta}\right)^2 = 1$

- If you do not remember the two identities from this lesson, how can you derive them? Recall that a point in Quadrant I on the unit circle has coordinates $P(\cos\theta, \sin\theta)$. Draw a right triangle with hypotenuse $\overline{OP}$, where O is the origin. The side lengths of this triangle are $\cos\theta$, $\sin\theta$, and 1. Use the Pythagorean Theorem to arrive at the identity $\sin^2\theta + \cos^2\theta = 1$. Use the definition of the tangent ratio to arrive at the identity $\tan\theta = \dfrac{\sin\theta}{\cos\theta}$.

EXTRA EXAMPLE
Given that $\tan\theta = 1.648$ where $0 < \theta < \dfrac{\pi}{2}$, find the approximate values of $\sin\theta$ and $\cos\theta$.

$\sin\theta = 0.855$; $\cos\theta = 0.519$

© Houghton Mifflin Harcourt Publishing Company

---

2 EXAMPLE and **3 EXAMPLE** include opportunities to address Mathematical Practice Standard 6 (Attend to precision). Students will need to be very careful to take in all of the information in the problem to find the correct sign for the quantities of sine, cosine, and tangent. If they do not attend to all of the information, they will end up with sign errors. They need to work with the angle in question, and not simply use the reference angle.

CLOSE

Essential Question
How can you use a given value of one of the trigonometric functions to calculate the values of the other functions?

You can use the Pythagorean identity to solve for sine values from cosine values and vice versa. If you are given the tangent value, you can use the tangent identity to write the sine in terms of the cosine, or vice versa, and then substitute into the Pythagorean identity to find the cosine and sine.

Summarize
Have students write a journal entry summarizing the two trigonometric identities presented in this lesson. They should make a heading for each of the identities $\left(\sin^2\theta + \cos^2\theta = 1 \text{ and } \tan\theta = \dfrac{\sin\theta}{\cos\theta}\right)$; then, list any rewritten forms below the primary identities.

PRACTICE

Where skills are taught	Where skills are practiced
2 EXAMPLE	EXS. 1–8
3 EXAMPLE	EXS. 9–12

2b. In part B, suppose $\frac{3\pi}{2} < \theta < 2\pi$ rather than $\pi < \theta < \frac{3\pi}{2}$. How does this affect the value of $\sin\theta$?

If $\frac{3\pi}{2} < \theta < 2\pi$, then the terminal side of θ lies in Quadrant IV. Sine is negative in Quadrant IV, so the value of $\sin\theta$ would not change.

2c. In part A, explain how to find the approximate value of $\tan\theta$. Then find it.

Use the identity $\tan\theta = \frac{\sin\theta}{\cos\theta}$; $\tan\theta \approx \frac{0.766}{0.643} \approx 1.191$

Other Identities If you multiply both sides of the identity $\tan\theta = \frac{\sin\theta}{\cos\theta}$ by $\cos\theta$, you get the identity $\sin\theta = \tan\theta\cos\theta$. And if you divide both sides of $\sin\theta = \tan\theta\cos\theta$ by $\tan\theta$, you get the identity $\cos\theta = \frac{\sin\theta}{\tan\theta}$.

3 EXAMPLE Using an Identity That Involves Tangent

Given that $\tan\theta \approx -2.327$ where $\frac{\pi}{2} < \theta < \pi$, find the approximate values of $\sin\theta$ and $\cos\theta$.

A Write $\sin\theta$ in terms of $\cos\theta$.

$\sin\theta = \tan\theta\cos\theta$ Use the identity $\sin\theta = \tan\theta\cos\theta$.

$\approx$ $-2.327\cos\theta$ Substitute the value of $\tan\theta$.

B Use the Pythagorean identity to find $\cos\theta$. Then find $\sin\theta$.

$\sin^2\theta + \cos^2\theta = 1$ Use the Pythagorean identity.

$\left(-2.327\cos\theta\right)^2 + \cos^2\theta = 1$ Substitute for $\sin\theta$.

$5.415\ \cos^2\theta + \cos^2\theta \approx 1$ Square.

$6.415\ \cos^2\theta \approx 1$ Combine like terms.

$\cos^2\theta \approx$ 0.156   Solve for $\cos^2\theta$.

$\cos\theta \approx \pm$ 0.395   Solve for $\cos\theta$.

The terminal side of θ lies in Quadrant II , where $\cos\theta$ < 0.

So, $\cos\theta \approx$ -0.395 , and $\sin\theta \approx -2.327\cos\theta \approx$ 0.919 .

REFLECT

3a. When you multiplied the given value of $\tan\theta$ with the calculated value of $\cos\theta$ in order to find the value of $\sin\theta$, was the product positive or negative? Explain why this is the result you'd expect.

Positive; $\sin\theta$ should be positive in Quadrant II.

3b. If $\tan\theta = 1$ where $0 < \theta < \frac{\pi}{2}$, show that you can solve for $\sin\theta$ and $\cos\theta$ exactly using the Pythagorean identity. Why is this so?

If $\tan\theta = 1$, then $\sin\theta = \cos\theta$, so $\sin^2\theta + \cos^2\theta = 1$ becomes $2\sin^2\theta = 1$, which gives $\sin\theta = \cos\theta = \frac{\sqrt{2}}{2}$; in this case, θ is a special angle: $\frac{\pi}{4}$.

PRACTICE

Find $\sin\theta$ and $\tan\theta$ for each given value of $\cos\theta$.

1. $\cos\theta = 0.596, 0 < \theta < \frac{\pi}{2}$

$\sin\theta \approx$ 0.803 , $\tan\theta \approx$ 1.347

2. $\cos\theta = 0.985, \frac{3\pi}{2} < \theta < 2\pi$

$\sin\theta \approx$ -0.173 , $\tan\theta \approx$ -0.176

3. $\cos\theta = -0.342, \frac{\pi}{2} < \theta < \pi$

$\sin\theta \approx$ 0.940 , $\tan\theta \approx$ -2.749

4. $\cos\theta = -0.819, \pi < \theta < \frac{3\pi}{2}$

$\sin\theta \approx$ -0.574 , $\tan\theta \approx$ 0.701

Find $\cos\theta$ and $\tan\theta$ for each given value of $\sin\theta$.

5. $\sin\theta = 0.186, 0 < \theta < \frac{\pi}{2}$

$\cos\theta \approx$ 0.983 , $\tan\theta \approx$ 0.189

6. $\sin\theta = 0.756, \frac{\pi}{2} < \theta < \pi$

$\cos\theta \approx$ -0.655 , $\tan\theta \approx$ -1.154

7. $\sin\theta = -0.644, \frac{3\pi}{2} < \theta < 2\pi$

$\cos\theta \approx$ 0.765 , $\tan\theta \approx$ -0.842

8. $\sin\theta = -0.328, \pi < \theta < \frac{3\pi}{2}$

$\cos\theta \approx$ -0.945 , $\tan\theta \approx$ 0.347

Find $\sin\theta$ and $\cos\theta$ for each given value of $\tan\theta$.

9. $\tan\theta = 0.301, 0 < \theta < \frac{\pi}{2}$

$\sin\theta \approx$ 0.288 , $\cos\theta \approx$ 0.958

10. $\tan\theta = 2.416, \pi < \theta < \frac{3\pi}{2}$

$\sin\theta \approx$ -0.923 , $\cos\theta \approx$ -0.382

11. $\tan\theta = -0.739, \frac{\pi}{2} < \theta < \pi$

$\sin\theta \approx$ 0.594 , $\cos\theta \approx$ -0.804

12. $\tan\theta = -3.305, \frac{3\pi}{2} < \theta < 2\pi$

$\sin\theta \approx$ -0.958 , $\cos\theta \approx$ 0.290

Graphing the Sine and Cosine Functions

Essential question: *What are the key features of the graphs of the sine and cosine functions?*

COMMON Standards for
CORE Mathematical Content

CC.9-12.F.IF.7 Graph functions expressed symbolically and show key features of the graph ... *

CC.9-12.F.IF.7e Graph ... trigonometric functions, showing period, midline, and amplitude.*

CC.9-12.F.TF.4(+) Use the unit circle to explain ... periodicity of trigonometric functions.

Vocabulary

periodic

period

midline

amplitude

Prerequisites

The sine, cosine, and tangent functions, Lesson 8-3

Math Background

Students will first use function values for special angles to graph the sine and cosine functions over one revolution around the unit circle. Students should notice that the values of the functions are never less than −1 or greater than 1. They will then move on to graph the functions over several revolutions around the unit circle, and will learn about the periodicity of the functions. Students might observe that the graphs of the sine and cosine functions have the same shape, with one being a horizontal translation of the other. This transformation involves a trigonometric identity that is beyond the scope of this course. However, students will explore other transformations of trigonometric functions later in this unit.

INTRODUCE

While this is likely students' first exposure to periodic functions, they should be accustomed to things that repeat at regular intervals. Ask them to name things that repeat at regular intervals, such as a weekly music lesson. Guide them to listing physical phenomena that repeat regularly, such as the height off the ground of a child on a swing. Ask students to imagine graphing the heights as a function of time. Sketching a quick graph, you can show a periodic function.

TEACH

1 EXPLORE

Questioning Strategies

• Is this graph a function? Explain. Yes; each input corresponds to only one output.

• Is the inverse of $f(\theta) = \sin \theta$ a function? Explain. No; the function is not one-to-one. For example, $\sin 0 = 0$, $\sin \pi = 0$ and $\sin 2\pi = 0$.

• What do you think the graph of $f(\theta) = \sin \theta$ would look like if you extended the graph from 2π to 4π? Why? The graph from 2π to 4π would look exactly like the graph from 0 to π because the angles from 2π to 4π have the same sine values as their reference angles from 0 to 2π.

2 EXPLORE

Questioning Strategies

• Compare the ranges for the graphs of $f(\theta) = \sin \theta$ and $f(\theta) = \cos \theta$. The ranges are the same (−1 to 1 for both functions).

• Compare the zeros for the graphs of $f(\theta) = \sin \theta$ and $f(\theta) = \cos \theta$. The zeros for $\sin \theta$ are 0 and π. For $\cos \theta$ they are $\frac{\pi}{2}$ and $\frac{3\pi}{2}$. The zeros differ by $\frac{\pi}{2}$.

© Houghton Mifflin Harcourt Publishing Company

Name_____ Class_____ Date_____

8-5

COMMON CORE
CC.9-12.F.IF.7*,
CC.9-12.F.IF.7e*,
CC.9-12.F.TF.4(+)

Graphing the Sine and Cosine Functions

Essential question: *What are the key features of the graphs of the sine and cosine functions?*

1 EXPLORE Graphing $f(\theta) = \sin \theta$

Graph $f(\theta) = \sin \theta$ for $0 \leq \theta \leq 2\pi$.

A Complete the axis labels on the coordinate plane below. The θ-axis shows angle measures in radians. The $f(\theta)$-axis shows the function values.

B Complete the table of values.

θ	0	$\frac{\pi}{6}$	$\frac{\pi}{2}$	$\frac{5\pi}{6}$	π	$\frac{7\pi}{6}$	$\frac{3\pi}{2}$	$\frac{11\pi}{6}$	2π
$f(\theta) = \sin \theta$	0	0.5	1	0.5	0	−0.5	−1	−0.5	0

C Plot the points from the table and draw a smooth curve through them.

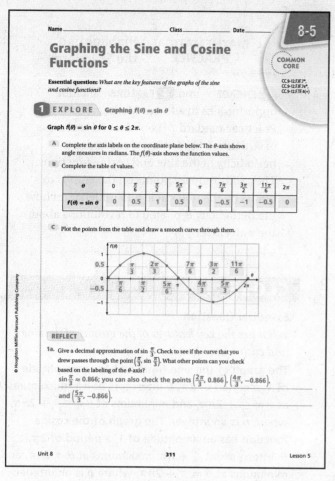

REFLECT

1a. Give a decimal approximation of $\sin \frac{\pi}{3}$. Check to see if the curve that you drew passes through the point $\left(\frac{\pi}{3}, \sin \frac{\pi}{3}\right)$. What other points can you check based on the labeling of the θ-axis?

$\sin \frac{\pi}{3} \approx 0.866$; you can also check the points $\left(\frac{2\pi}{3}, 0.866\right)$, $\left(\frac{4\pi}{3}, -0.866\right)$, and $\left(\frac{5\pi}{3}, -0.866\right)$.

Unit 8   311   Lesson 5

1b. On the interval $0 \leq \theta \leq 2\pi$, where does the sine function have positive values? Where does it have negative values?

$0 < \theta < \pi$; $\pi < \theta < 2\pi$

1c. List the θ-intercepts of the graph of $f(\theta) = \sin \theta$ on the interval $0 \leq \theta \leq 2\pi$. What do you think the next positive θ-intercept will be? Explain.

0, π, 2π; 3π because it is coterminal with π just as 2π is coterminal with 0

1d. What are the minimum and maximum values of $f(\theta) = \sin \theta$ on the interval $0 \leq \theta \leq 2\pi$? Where do the extreme values occur in relation to the θ-intercepts?

The minimum is −1, and the maximum is 1; the extreme values occur exactly halfway between the θ-intercepts.

1e. Describe a rotation that will map the curve onto itself over the interval $0 \leq \theta \leq 2\pi$.

A rotation of 180° clockwise or counterclockwise about the point $(\pi, 0)$ will map the curve onto itself.

2 EXPLORE Graphing $f(\theta) = \cos \theta$

Graph $f(\theta) = \cos \theta$ for $0 \leq \theta \leq 2\pi$.

A Complete the axis labels on the coordinate plane below. The θ-axis shows angle measures in radians. The $f(\theta)$-axis shows the function values.

B Complete the table of values.

θ	0	$\frac{\pi}{3}$	$\frac{\pi}{2}$	$\frac{2\pi}{3}$	π	$\frac{4\pi}{3}$	$\frac{3\pi}{2}$	$\frac{5\pi}{3}$	2π
$f(\theta) = \cos \theta$	1	0.5	0	−0.5	−1	−0.5	0	0.5	1

C Plot the points from the table and draw a smooth curve through them.

Unit 8   312   Lesson 5

© Houghton Mifflin Harcourt Publishing Company

Questioning Strategies

- What does one period of the sine graph or the cosine graph correspond to on the unit circle? one complete revolution of the terminal side around the unit circle

- For $0 \leq \theta \leq 2\pi$, at what value(s) of θ does a crest occur for $\sin \theta$? for $\cos \theta$? $\frac{\pi}{2}$; 0 and 2π

- For $0 \leq \theta \leq 2\pi$, at what value(s) of θ does a trough occur for $\sin \theta$? for $\cos \theta$? $\frac{3\pi}{2}$; π

4 EXPLORE

Questioning Strategies

- Do the graphs of $f(\theta) = \sin \theta$ and $f(\theta) = \cos \theta$ pass the function test for $0 \leq \theta \leq 4\pi$? Explain. Yes; for each input, there is only one output. They pass the vertical line test.

- What is the domain of $f(\theta) = \sin \theta$? all real numbers

- What is the domain of $f(\theta) = \cos \theta$? all real numbers

- The graph of the cosine function can be described as what type of transformation of the graph of the sine function? horizontal translation

Differentiated Instruction

Have students use construction paper to draw the graph of $f(\theta) = \sin \theta$ for $0 \leq \theta \leq 2\pi$. They should cut out the sine wave so they have a physical shape to move around. Students can then set the shape on a set of axes so that it shows the function $f(\theta) = \sin \theta$. They can slide the cutout to the left until it looks like $f(\theta) = \cos \theta$. Students should realize that the graph of the cosine function is a horizontal translation of the graph of the sine function.

MATHEMATICAL PRACTICE | Highlighting the Standards

3 ENGAGE and **4** EXPLORE include opportunities to address Mathematical Practice Standard 7 (Look for and make use of structure). Students will recognize the periodicity of the sine and cosine functions. They will compare points on the graphs to points on the unit circle and understand how the periodicity is related to revolutions about the unit circle.

CLOSE

Essential Question

What are the key features of the graphs of the sine and cosine functions?

The graph of the sine function has an amplitude of 1, a period of 2π, θ-intercepts at $n\pi$, maximums at $\theta = \frac{\pi}{2} + 2n\pi$, and minimums at $\theta = \frac{3\pi}{2} + 2n\pi$, where n is an integer. The graph of the cosine function has an amplitude of 1, a period of 2π, θ-intercepts at $\frac{\pi}{2} + n\pi$, maximums at $\theta = 2n\pi$, and minimums at $\theta = \pi + 2n\pi$, where n is an integer.

Summarize

Have students draw a sine graph and a cosine graph in their journals, one below the other and to the same scale. They should clearly label which is which. They should include labels on the axes, clearly marking the θ-values corresponding to the intercepts and to the maximum and minimum values.

Notes

REFLECT

2a. On the interval $0 \le \theta \le 2\pi$, where does the cosine function have positive values? Where does it have negative values?

$0 < \theta < \frac{\pi}{2}$ and $\frac{3\pi}{2} < \theta < 2\pi$; $\frac{\pi}{2} < \theta < \frac{3\pi}{2}$

2b. List the θ-intercepts of the graph of $f(\theta) = \cos\theta$ on the interval $0 \le \theta \le 2\pi$. What do you think the next positive θ-intercept will be? Explain.

$\frac{\pi}{2}, \frac{3\pi}{2}; \frac{5\pi}{2}$ because $\frac{5\pi}{2}$ is coterminal with $\frac{\pi}{2}$

2c. What are the minimum and maximum values of $f(\theta) = \cos\theta$ on the interval $0 \le \theta \le 2\pi$? Where do the extreme values occur in relation to the θ-intercepts?

The minimum is −1, and the maximum is 1; the extreme values occur exactly halfway between the θ-intercepts.

3 ENGAGE   Understanding the Properties of the Graphs

In the preceding Explores, you graphed the sine and cosine functions over the interval $0 \le \theta \le 2\pi$, which represents all angles of rotation within the first counterclockwise revolution that starts at 0. What you drew are not the complete graphs, however. They are simply one *cycle* of the graph.

As you will see in the next Explore, the graphs of sine and cosine consist of repeated cycles that form a wave-like shape. When a function repeats its values over regular intervals on the horizontal axis as the sine and cosine functions do, the function is called **periodic**, and the length of the interval is called the function's **period**.

The wave-like shape of the sine and cosine functions has a "crest" (where the function's maximum value occurs) and a "trough" (where the function's minimum value occurs). Halfway between the "crest" and the "trough" is the graph's **midline**. The distance that the "crest" rises above the midline or the distance that the "trough" falls below the midline is called the graph's **amplitude**.

REFLECT

3a. Complete the table.

Function	Properties of Function's Graph		
	Period	Midline	Amplitude
$f(\theta) = \sin\theta$	2π	The θ-axis	1
$f(\theta) = \cos\theta$	2π	The θ-axis	1

Unit 8   313   Lesson 5

4 EXPLORE   Extending the Graphs of Sine and Cosine

Use the cycle shown for the first counterclockwise revolution (starting at 0 and ending at 2π) to extend the graphs of the sine and cosine functions to the right (second counterclockwise revolution) and to the left (first clockwise revolution).

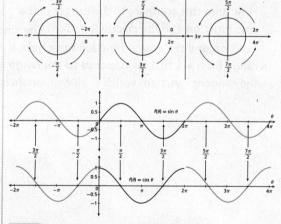

REFLECT

4a. The graphs show that sine and cosine are periodic functions. Explain why this is so by referring to angles of rotation and the unit circle.

One revolution gives all values of the functions. Subsequent revolutions repeat those values.

4b. The graphs show that $\sin(-\theta) = -\sin\theta$ and $\cos(-\theta) = \cos\theta$. Explain why this is so by referring to angles of rotation and the unit circle.

The angles θ and $-\theta$ intersect the unit circle at points that have the same x-coordinate (cosine value) but opposite y-coordinates (sine value).

Unit 8   314   Lesson 5

© Houghton Mifflin Harcourt Publishing Company

Graphing the Tangent Function

Essential question: *What are the key features of the graph of the tangent function?*

COMMON **Standards for**
CORE **Mathematical Content**

CC.9-12.F.IF.7 Graph functions expressed symbolically and show key features of the graph ... *

CC.9-12.F.IF.7e Graph ... trigonometric functions, showing period, midline, and amplitude.*

CC.9-12.F.TF.4(+) Use the unit circle to explain ... periodicity of trigonometric functions.

Prerequisites

The sine, cosine, and tangent functions, Lesson 8-3

Graphing the sine and cosine functions, Lesson 8-5

Math Background

The tangent function is discontinuous. In simple terms, that means that you cannot draw the graph of the function without lifting your pencil point off the paper. A slightly more complex definition for continuous functions is that small changes in the input of a function (in this case, θ) yield small changes in the output. Clearly, as θ passes through $\frac{\pi}{2}$, small changes in the input yield huge changes in the output (from $+\infty$ to $-\infty$). A mathematically rigorous definition of continuous is $\lim_{x \to a} f(x) = f(a)$. In other words, for a continuous function, as θ approaches $\frac{\pi}{2}$ from either side, the function gives the same value. The tangent function does not meet this definition; as θ increases toward $\frac{\pi}{2}$, $f(\theta)$ approaches positive infinity. As θ decreases toward $\frac{\pi}{2}$, $f(\theta)$ approaches negative infinity. Continuity is something students in calculus will be concerned with. But the idea of a discontinuous function can be introduced here, using the simple pencil-on-paper definition.

INTRODUCE

Ask students to explain the difference between the graphs of the sine function and the cosine function. Draw the sine function and draw the cosine function immediately below it. Ask students to define the tangent function in terms of the sine and cosine functions. Explain that the graph of the tangent function will represent the quotient of the two functions shown.

TEACH

1 EXPLORE

Questioning Strategies

- Look at the graph of $f(\theta) = \tan \theta$. Does it meet the requirements to be a function? Explain.
  Yes; each input maps to only one output.

- What is the domain of $f(\theta) = \tan \theta$? all real numbers except odd multiples of $\frac{\pi}{2}$ How does this compare with the domains of the sine function and the cosine function? The domains for the sine and cosine functions are all real numbers.

- What is the range of $f(\theta) = \tan \theta$? all real numbers How does this compare to the ranges of the sine function and the cosine function? The sine function and the cosine function both have a range from -1 to 1, as opposed to the range of the tangent function, which is all real numbers.

continued

Name_____ Class_____ Date_____

Graphing the Tangent Function

Essential question: *What are the key features of the graph of the tangent function?*

1 EXPLORE Graphing $f(\theta) = \tan \theta$

Graph $f(\theta) = \tan \theta$ for $0 \le \theta \le 2\pi$.

A Complete the axis labels on the coordinate plane in part D. The θ-axis shows angle measures in radians. The $f(\theta)$-axis shows the function values.

B Complete the table of values. The dashes that appear as function values for $\theta = \frac{\pi}{2}$ and $\theta = \frac{3\pi}{2}$ indicate that $f(\theta)$ is undefined.

θ	0	$\frac{\pi}{4}$	$\frac{\pi}{2}$	$\frac{3\pi}{4}$	π	$\frac{5\pi}{4}$	$\frac{3\pi}{2}$	$\frac{7\pi}{4}$	2π
$f(\theta) = \tan \theta$	0	1	—	−1	0	1	—	−1	0

C Examine the behavior of the function near $\theta = \frac{\pi}{2}$ and $\theta = \frac{3\pi}{2}$. For each table below, use a calculator set in radian mode to find the approximate values of $\sin \theta$ and $\cos \theta$, then use the fact that $\tan \theta = \frac{\sin \theta}{\cos \theta}$ to find the value of $\tan \theta$. Note that $\frac{\pi}{2} \approx 1.5708$ and $\frac{3\pi}{2} \approx 4.7124$. After examining the values of $\tan \theta$, complete the summary statement below the table.

θ	$\sin \theta$	$\cos \theta$	$\tan \theta$
1.50	0.997	0.071	14.0
1.55	0.9998	0.0208	48.07
1.57	0.9999997	0.0007963	1255.808

θ	$\sin \theta$	$\cos \theta$	$\tan \theta$
1.65	0.997	−0.079	−12.6
1.60	0.9996	−0.0292	−34.23
1.58	0.999958	−0.009204	−108.644

As $\theta \to \frac{\pi}{2}^-$, $\tan \theta \to \underline{+\infty}$.　　　　As $\theta \to \frac{\pi}{2}^+$, $\tan \theta \to \underline{-\infty}$.

θ	$\sin \theta$	$\cos \theta$	$\tan \theta$
4.50	−0.9775	−0.2108	4.637
4.70	−0.99992	−0.01239	80.704
4.71	−0.999997	−0.002389	418.584

θ	$\sin \theta$	$\cos \theta$	$\tan \theta$
5.00	−0.959	0.284	−3.38
4.75	−0.9993	0.0376	−26.58
4.72	−0.99997	0.00761	−131.40

As $\theta \to \frac{3\pi}{2}^-$, $\tan \theta \to \underline{+\infty}$.　　　　As $\theta \to \frac{3\pi}{2}^+$, $\tan \theta \to \underline{-\infty}$.

D Draw the vertical asymptotes found in part C as dashed lines. Then plot the points from part B and draw smooth curves that pass through the plotted points and approach the asymptotes.

REFLECT

1a. What is the relationship between $\frac{\pi}{4}$ and 0.8? Why is 0.8 a good interval to use for the vertical axis?
Sample answer: As a decimal, $\frac{\pi}{4} \approx 0.8$; intervals of 0.8 along the vertical axis produce a graph of the tangent function that is not distorted horizontally or vertically.

1b. On the interval $0 \le \theta \le 2\pi$, where does the tangent function have positive values? Where does it have negative values?
$0 < \theta < \frac{\pi}{2}$ and $\pi < \theta < \frac{3\pi}{2}$; $\frac{\pi}{2} < \theta < \pi$ and $\frac{3\pi}{2} < \theta < 2\pi$

1c. List the θ-intercepts of the graph of $f(\theta) = \tan \theta$ on the interval $0 \le \theta \le 2\pi$. What do you think the next positive θ-intercept will be? Explain.
0, π, 2π; 3π because it is coterminal with π just as 2π is coterminal with 0

1d. How many times does the tangent function run through all of its values on the interval $0 \le \theta \le 2\pi$? What, then, is the function's period?
Twice; π

1e. Does the tangent function have minimum or maximum values? Explain.
No; the value of the tangent function can be any real number, so there is no maximum value or minimum value.

1f. The points where $\tan \theta = \pm 1$ serve as handy reference points when graphing the tangent function. What line lies halfway between them? (Note that this line is called the graph's *midline* even though the tangent function does not have minimum or maximum values.)
The θ-axis

Teaching Strategy

Students might be uncomfortable with the graph of the tangent function due to the multiple vertical asymptotes. However, they are familiar with other functions that have asymptotes. Ask students to make a table for and then a graph of $f(x) = \frac{1}{x}$. Recommend that they create a table showing $x = \pm0.001, \pm0.01, \pm0.1, \pm1, \pm2, \pm3, \pm4, \pm5,$ and ±10. Ask students to describe what happens to $f(x)$ as x gets closer and closer to 0 from the positive side and then from the negative side. Students should realize that the y-axis is an asymptote for this function and that what the function approached from the positive side $(+\infty)$ is different from what it approaches from the negative side $(-\infty)$. Use this as a springboard into the tangent function and its asymptotes.

2 EXPLORE

Questioning Strategies

- What interval between 0 and 2π shows one complete cycle of the tangent function? $\frac{\pi}{2} \leq \theta \leq \frac{3\pi}{2}$

- How does the graph of the tangent function behave as θ increases from $\frac{\pi}{4}$ to $\frac{\pi}{2}$? The graph of the tangent function climbs more steeply as θ increases.

- How can you use the graph of the tangent function from $\frac{\pi}{2}$ to $\frac{3\pi}{2}$ to draw more of the graph of $f(\theta) = \tan\theta$? The graph of each period of $f(\theta) = \tan\theta$ is a horizontal translation of the graph from $\frac{\pi}{2}$ to $\frac{3\pi}{2}$ by a multiple of π. You can keep shifting the original graph left or right by π to get more of the graph.

MATHEMATICAL PRACTICE — Highlighting the Standards

2 EXPLORE includes opportunities to address Mathematical Practice Standard 7 (Look for and make use of structure). Students will recognize the periodicity of the tangent function. They will compare points on the graph with points on the unit circle and understand how the periodicity is related to revolutions about the unit circle.

CLOSE

Essential Question

What are the key features of the graph of the tangent function?

The graph of the tangent function has a period of π, vertical asymptotes at $\theta = \frac{\pi}{2} + n\pi$, and θ-intercepts at $n\pi$, where n is an integer.

Summarize

Have students locate in their journals their summary of the last lesson—drawings of a sine function and a cosine function. Immediately below those, students should draw a tangent function to the same scale. They should include labels on the axes, clearly mark the value of θ for the intercepts, and label the asymptotes. As a final step, students should include the summary table from Reflect question 2g under the graphs.

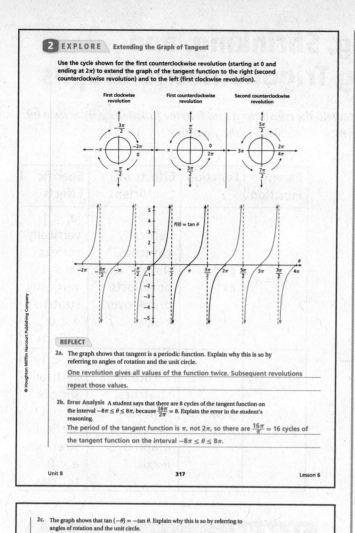

2 EXPLORE Extending the Graph of Tangent

Use the cycle shown for the first counterclockwise revolution (starting at 0 and ending at 2π) to extend the graph of the tangent function to the right (second counterclockwise revolution) and to the left (first clockwise revolution).

REFLECT

2a. The graph shows that tangent is a periodic function. Explain why this is so by referring to angles of rotation and the unit circle.

One revolution gives all values of the function twice. Subsequent revolutions repeat those values.

2b. Error Analysis A student says that there are 8 cycles of the tangent function on the interval $-8\pi \le \theta \le 8\pi$, because $\frac{16\pi}{2\pi} = 8$. Explain the error in the student's reasoning.

The period of the tangent function is π, not 2π, so there are $\frac{16\pi}{\pi} = 16$ cycles of the tangent function on the interval $-8\pi \le \theta \le 8\pi$.

2c. The graph shows that $\tan(-\theta) = -\tan\theta$. Explain why this is so by referring to angles of rotation and the unit circle.

The angles θ and $-\theta$ intersect the unit circle at points that have the same x-coordinate (cosine value) but opposite y-coordinates (sine value), so the ratio of y to x for $-\theta$ is the opposite of the ratio of y to x for θ.

2d. Show that $\tan(-\theta) = -\tan\theta$ using these facts: $\tan\theta = \frac{\sin\theta}{\cos\theta}$ (Lesson 8-4), $\sin(-\theta) = -\sin\theta$ (Lesson 8-5), and $\cos(-\theta) = \cos\theta$ (Lesson 8-5).

$\tan(-\theta) = \frac{\sin(-\theta)}{\cos(-\theta)} = \frac{-\sin\theta}{\cos\theta} = -\frac{\sin\theta}{\cos\theta} = -\tan\theta$

2e. A function is called *even* if $f(-x) = x$ for all x, and it is called *odd* if $f(-x) = -f(x)$ for all x. Which of the trigonometric functions (sine, cosine, and tangent) are even? Which are odd?

cosine; sine and tangent

2f. The graph of $f(\theta) = \tan\theta$ has θ-intercepts at multiples of π and has vertical asymptotes at odd multiples of $\frac{\pi}{2}$. Use the fact that $\tan\theta = \frac{\sin\theta}{\cos\theta}$ to explain how the θ-intercepts and vertical asymptotes of the tangent function are related to the θ-intercepts of the sine and cosine functions.

Tangent's θ-intercepts occur when $\tan\theta = 0$, which is when $\sin\theta = 0$, so tangent has the same θ-intercepts as sine. Tangent's vertical asymptotes occur when $\tan\theta$ is undefined, which is when $\cos\theta = 0$, so tangent has vertical asymptotes where cosine has θ-intercepts.

2g. Complete the table to summarize the properties of the graphs of the sine, cosine, and tangent functions. If a function does not have a property, say so.

Function	Properties of Function's Graph				
	θ-intercepts	Vertical asymptotes	Period	Midline	Amplitude
$f(\theta) = \sin\theta$	Multiples of π	None	2π	The θ-axis	1
$f(\theta) = \cos\theta$	Odd multiples of $\frac{\pi}{2}$	None	2π	The θ-axis	1
$f(\theta) = \tan\theta$	Multiples of π	Odd multiples of $\frac{\pi}{2}$	π	The θ-axis	None

Stretching, Shrinking, and Reflecting Trigonometric Graphs

Essential question: *How do the constants a and b in the functions* $g(\theta) = a\sin b\theta$, $g(\theta) = a\cos b\theta$, *and* $g(\theta) = a\tan b\theta$ *affect their graphs?*

COMMON CORE Standards for Mathematical Content

CC.9-12.F.IF.7 Graph functions expressed symbolically and show key features of the graph . . . *

CC.9-12.F.IF.7e Graph . . . trigonometric functions, showing period, midline, and amplitude.*

CC.9-12.F.BF.3 Identify the effect on the graph of replacing $f(x)$ by . . . , $kf(x)$, $f(kx)$, . . . for specific values of k (both positive and negative); find the value of k given the graphs. . . .

Prerequisites

Graphing the sine and cosine functions, Lesson 8-5

Graphing the tangent function, Lesson 8-6

Math Background

Periodic motion is often modeled using sine and cosine functions. The general form of the sine function is $y = a\sin b(x - h) + k$. (The other trig functions can be written similarly.) The initial conditions describing the real-world situation are incorporated in the constants $a, b, h,$ and k. In this lesson, students will study the effect of different values of a and b. In the next lesson, they will study the effect of different values of h and k and begin to apply trigonometric functions to real-world situations.

INTRODUCE

Ask students to recall the parent quadratic function $f(x) = x^2$. Ask them to recall what effects the coefficient of the x^2-term has on the function. Have students summarize the results in the first row of the table. Have them make predictions for the second row.

Parent Function	Function	Effects of Coefficient	Specific Effects
$f(x) = x^2$	$g(x) = ax^2$	vertically stretches, shrinks, and/or reflects graph over x-axis.	$\|a\| < 1$ vertically shrinks $\|a\| > 1$ vertically stretches $a < 0$ reflects
$f(\theta) = \sin\theta$	$g(\theta) = a\sin\theta$	vertically stretches, shrinks, and/or reflects graph over θ-axis	$\|a\| < 1$ vertically shrinks $\|a\| > 1$ vertically stretches $a < 0$ reflects

TEACH

1 ENGAGE

Questioning Strategies

- Why are the five points indicated on the graphs of the sine and cosine functions key points for these graphs? These points correspond to the minimum, maximum, and zeros for one period of the functions. These are the points that will be transformed to create the graph of the transformed functions.

- Why are the three points and the asymptotes shown key features of the graph of the tangent function? Point *A* is where the value of the tangent is −1, the θ-coordinate of point *B* is the zero of the function, and point *C* is where the value of the tangent is 1. These are the points, along with the vertical asymptotes, that will be transformed to create the graph of the transformed tangent function.

Name_____ Class_____ Date_____

8-7

Stretching, Shrinking, and Reflecting Trigonometric Graphs

COMMON CORE

CC.9-12.F.IF.7*,
CC.9-12.F.IF.7e*,
CC.9-12.F.BF.3

Essential question: *How do the constants a and b in the functions* $g(\theta) = a \sin b\theta$, $g(\theta) = a \cos b\theta$, *and* $g(\theta) = a \tan b\theta$ *affect their graphs?*

1 ENGAGE Recognizing Key Points and Asymptotes on Parent Graphs

In this lesson you will graph functions of the form $g(\theta) = a \sin b\theta$, $g(\theta) = a \cos b\theta$, and $g(\theta) = a \tan b\theta$. You have already seen the graphs of the *parent* functions (when $a = 1$ and $b = 1$) in Lessons 8-5 and 8-6. One cycle of the graph of each parent function is shown below along with five key points or asymptotes from that cycle.

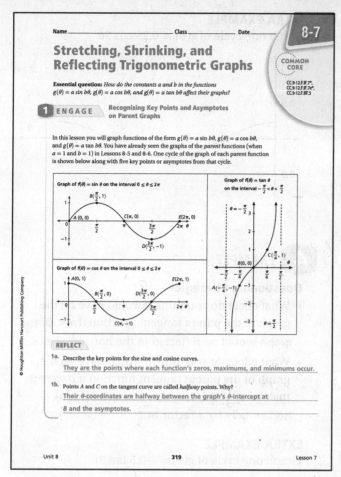

REFLECT

1a. Describe the key points for the sine and cosine curves.

They are the points where each function's zeros, maximums, and minimums occur.

1b. Points A and C on the tangent curve are called *halfway* points. Why?

Their θ-coordinates are halfway between the graph's θ-intercept at

B and the asymptotes.

© Houghton Mifflin Harcourt Publishing Company

2 ENGAGE Understanding Transformations of Trigonometric Graphs

If $f(\theta)$ is one of the three parent trigonometric functions, then the constants a and b in $g(\theta) = af(b\theta)$ alter the graph of $f(\theta)$ in particular ways. Notice that the constant a appears *outside* the function and therefore acts on f's output values, while the constant b appears *inside* the function and therefore acts on f's input values. For instance, consider the function $g(\theta) = 3 \sin 2\theta$ whose parent function is $f(\theta) = \sin \theta$. The mapping diagram below shows what happens when $0, \frac{\pi}{4}, \frac{\pi}{2}, \frac{3\pi}{4},$ and π are used as inputs for g.

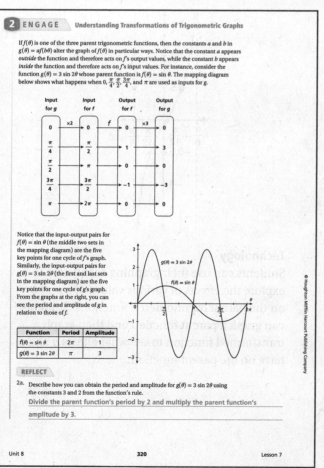

Notice that the input-output pairs for $f(\theta) = \sin \theta$ (the middle two sets in the mapping diagram) are the five key points for one cycle of f's graph. Similarly, the input-output pairs for $g(\theta) = 3 \sin 2\theta$ (the first and last sets in the mapping diagram) are the five key points for one cycle of g's graph. From the graphs at the right, you can see the period and amplitude of g in relation to those of f.

Function	Period	Amplitude
$f(\theta) = \sin \theta$	2π	1
$g(\theta) = 3 \sin 2\theta$	π	3

REFLECT

2a. Describe how you can obtain the period and amplitude for $g(\theta) = 3 \sin 2\theta$ using the constants 3 and 2 from the function's rule.

Divide the parent function's period by 2 and multiply the parent function's

amplitude by 3.

© Houghton Mifflin Harcourt Publishing Company

Questioning Strategies

- What are the values of a and b for $g(\theta)$? $a = 3$; $b = 2$
- What effect does a have on the graph of the parent function in this example? It stretches it vertically.
- What effect would a have on the graph of $g(\theta) = a \sin b\theta$ if $0 < a < 1$? It would shrink the graph vertically.
- What effect does b have on the graph of the parent function in this example? It shrinks it horizontally.
- What effect would b have on the graph of $g(\theta) = a \sin b\theta$ if $0 < b < 1$? It would stretch the graph horizontally.
- How does the constant b affect the graph of $g(\theta) = a \sin b\theta$? It stretches or shrinks the graph horizontally.
- What effects do you think a and b will have on the graph of $g(\theta) = a \cos b\theta$? Why? The same effects as on the sine function; the sine and cosine functions are just horizontal translations of each other, so the effects of a and b would not be any different on cosine as on sine.

3 EXAMPLE

Questioning Strategies

- What are a and b for the function $g(\theta)$? $a = -3$; $b = \frac{1}{2}$
- The value of a for $g(\theta)$ is negative. What effect will this have on the graph of the parent function? A negative value for a will reflect the graph of the parent function over the horizontal axis.
- Knowing that the graph of $f(\theta) = \sin 2\theta$ is shrunk horizontally from the graph of the parent sine function, how do you expect the graph of $g(\theta) = \cos \frac{\theta}{2}$ to look compared with the graph of the parent cosine function? It will be stretched horizontally

EXTRA EXAMPLE
Graph one cycle of $g(\theta) = 0.25 \cos 2\theta$

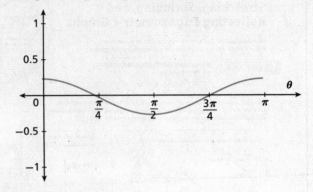

4 EXAMPLE

Questioning Strategies

- What effect do you think a would have on the graph of the parent tangent function if $a < 0$? The graph would be reflected in the horizontal axis.
- What effect do you think b would have on the graph of the parent tangent function if b were 3 instead of $\frac{1}{3}$? The function would be shrunk horizontally by a factor of $\frac{1}{3}$.

EXTRA EXAMPLE
Graph one cycle of $g(\theta) = -0.5 \tan 3\theta$.

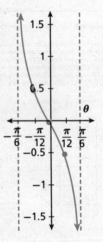

Technology
Students can use their graphing calculators to explore the effects of various values of a and b on the parent trigonometric functions. Students can graph a parent function and then graph a transformed function to see what effects a and b have on the parent function.

2b. In terms of transformations, the change in the period is the result of horizontally shrinking the graph of f by a factor of $\frac{1}{2}$ (since $\pi = \frac{1}{2}(2\pi)$). How would you characterize the change in the amplitude in terms of transformations?

The result of vertically stretching the graph of f by a factor of 3

---

3 EXAMPLE Graphing $g(\theta) = a \cos b\theta$

Graph one cycle of $g(\theta) = -3 \cos \frac{\theta}{2}$.

A Determine the function's period. One cycle of the graph of the parent function, $f(\theta) = \cos \theta$, begins at 0 and ends at 2π. One cycle of the graph of g also begins at 0 but ends when $\frac{\theta}{2} = 2\pi$, or $\theta = 4\pi$.

So, the function's period is $\underline{\quad 4\pi \quad}$.

B Use the period to determine the five key input values for g. Those five values divide the interval $0 \le \theta \le 4\pi$ into four equal parts. So, the first input value is 0, and the second is $\frac{4\pi}{4} = \pi$. These values are entered in the first column of the table at the right. Complete the rest of the first column.

C Determine the output values for the key input values. Remember that g multiplies each output value from the parent function by -3. For instance, when $\theta = 0$, the parent function's output value is 1, but the output value for g is $-3 \cdot 1 = -3$. Complete the second column of the table.

Key input-output pairs	
θ	$g(\theta)$
0	-3
π	0
2π	3
3π	0
4π	-3

D Plot the key points on the coordinate plane shown. Then use them to draw one cycle of the graph of $g(\theta) = -3 \cos \frac{\theta}{2}$. One cycle of the graph of the parent function is shown in gray for comparison.

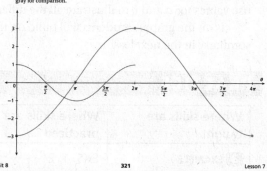

REFLECT

3a. Describe how the graph of f is transformed to obtain the graph of g.

Horizontal stretch by a factor of 2; vertical stretch by a factor of 3; reflection in the θ-axis

3b. Error Analysis A student said that the amplitude of the graph of g is -3. Describe and correct the student's error.

Amplitude is defined as the maximum *distance* that a wave-like curve rises above or falls below its midline, so the amplitude is 3, not -3.

---

4 EXAMPLE Graphing $g(\theta) = a \tan b\theta$

Graph one cycle of $g(\theta) = \frac{1}{2} \tan \frac{\theta}{3}$.

A Determine the graph's asymptotes. The graph of the parent function, $f(\theta) = \tan \theta$, has asymptotes at $\theta = -\frac{\pi}{2}$ and $\theta = \frac{\pi}{2}$. The graph of g has asymptotes at $\frac{\theta}{3} = -\frac{\pi}{2}$, or $\theta = \underline{-\frac{3\pi}{2}}$, and $\frac{\theta}{3} = \frac{\pi}{2}$, or $\theta = \underline{\frac{3\pi}{2}}$.

B Determine the graph's three key points.

* One point is where the graph crosses its midline (the θ-axis). For the parent function, this occurs when $\theta = 0$. For g, this occurs when $\frac{\theta}{3} = 0$, or $\theta = \underline{\quad 0 \quad}$. So, the graph of g crosses its midline at the point $\underline{(0, 0)}$.

* The other two points are the *halfway* points. For the parent function, these points are $\left(-\frac{\pi}{4}, -1\right)$ and $\left(\frac{\pi}{4}, 1\right)$.

For g, the θ-values are $\frac{\theta}{3} = -\frac{\pi}{4}$, or $\theta = \underline{-\frac{3\pi}{4}}$, and $\frac{\theta}{3} = \frac{\pi}{4}$, or $\theta = \underline{\frac{3\pi}{4}}$.

The corresponding $g(\theta)$-values are $\frac{1}{2}(-1) = \underline{-\frac{1}{2}}$ and $\frac{1}{2}(1) = \underline{\frac{1}{2}}$, respectively.

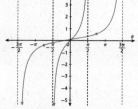

C Use the asymptotes and key points to draw one cycle of the graph of g. One cycle of the parent function's graph is shown in gray.

© Houghton Mifflin Harcourt Publishing Company

Teaching Strategy

Summarize the effects of a and b on the trigonometric functions using the table below. You can put a partially blank table on the board and have students work in pairs to complete it. Then reassemble as a class and ask the pairs to contribute their answers. Discuss the answers and correct any misconceptions. Be sure all students know the correct answers for their charts.

Function	Effects of Coefficient(s)	Specific Effects
$g(\theta) = a\sin b\theta$	a: vertically stretch, shrink, or reflect graph b: stretch or shrink horizontally	$\|a\| < 1$ vertical shrink $\|a\| > 1$ vertical stretch $a < 0$ reflection over θ-axis $b > 1$ horizontal shrink $0 < b < 1$ horizontal stretch
$g(\theta) = a\cos b\theta$	same as above	same as above
$g(\theta) = a\tan b\theta$	same as above	same as above

MATHEMATICAL PRACTICE — Highlighting the Standards

This lesson includes opportunities to address Mathematical Practice Standard 5 (Use appropriate tools strategically). Students should be able to quickly sketch the graphs of the parent functions for sine, cosine, and tangent by hand. They should understand the effects of a and b so they can predict how the graphs of specific equations will look prior to graphing them. If there are discrepancies between their predictions and their graphs, students should be able to resolve the discrepancies and locate any errors. One way to resolve discrepancies is to use a graphing calculator or another graphing technology to graph the transformed function and compare it with what the student has graphed.

CLOSE

Essential Question

How do the constants a and b in the functions $g(\theta) = a\sin b\theta$, $g(\theta) = a\cos b\theta$, and $g(\theta) = a\tan b\theta$ affect their graphs?

For sine and cosine, changing a changes the amplitude. For tangent, changing a stretches or shrinks the graph vertically. For all three functions, changing b changes the period of the function.

Summarize

Students should graph the parent functions of the three trigonometric functions. On the same axes, they should graph equations of the form $g(\theta) = a\sin b\theta$, $g(\theta) = a\cos b\theta$, or $g(\theta) = a\tan b\theta$ for each function. Students should ensure they use values for a and b to illustrate all the different effects on the graphs. Students will build on this summary in the next lesson.

PRACTICE

Where skills are taught	Where skills are practiced
3 EXAMPLE	EXS. 1, 2
4 EXAMPLE	EX. 3

Exercise 4: Students extend what they learned in 1 ENGAGE and 2 ENGAGE to write the rule for a sine function from its graph.

Exercise 5: Students extend what they learned in 2 ENGAGE to express the period and amplitude of the graph of $g(\theta) = a\sin b\theta$ in terms of a and b.

Exercise 6: Students extend what they learned in 4 EXAMPLE to express the period of the graph of $g(\theta) = a\tan b\theta$ and to express the halfway points for one cycle of the graph in terms of a and b.

REFLECT

4a. Describe how the graph of f is transformed to obtain the graph of g.

Horizontal stretch by a factor of 3; vertical shrink by a factor of $\frac{1}{2}$

PRACTICE

For Exercises 1–3, complete each table with the key points or asymptotes for one cycle of the graph of each function, then graph the cycle. (One cycle of the graph of the parent function is shown in gray.)

1. $g(\theta) = -2 \sin 4\theta$

Key input-output pairs	
θ	$g(\theta)$
0	0
$\frac{\pi}{8}$	-2
$\frac{\pi}{4}$	0
$\frac{3\pi}{8}$	2
$\frac{\pi}{2}$	0

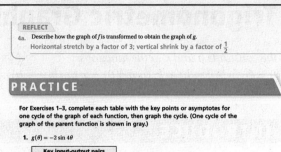

2. $g(\theta) = 0.75 \cos \frac{2\theta}{3}$

Key input-output pairs	
θ	$g(\theta)$
0	0.75
$\frac{3\pi}{4}$	0
$\frac{3\pi}{2}$	-0.75
$\frac{9\pi}{4}$	0
3π	0.75

3. $g(\theta) = -\tan 2\theta$

Key features of graph	
Equation of left asymptote	$\theta = -\frac{\pi}{4}$
Equation of right asymptote	$\theta = \frac{\pi}{4}$
Coordinates of midline crossing	$(0, 0)$
Coordinates of left halfway point	$\left(-\frac{\pi}{8}, 1\right)$
Coordinates of right halfway point	$\left(\frac{\pi}{8}, -1\right)$

4. One cycle of the graph of a sine function is shown along with the five key points for the cycle. Use the points to determine a rule for the function.

$g(\theta) = \underline{\hspace{1cm} 1.5 \sin \frac{4\theta}{3} \hspace{1cm}}$

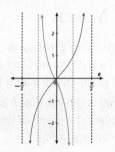

5. What are the period and amplitude of the graph of $g(\theta) = a \sin b\theta$ where $a \neq 0$ and $b > 0$? (Give your answers in terms of a and b.)

Period $= \frac{2\pi}{b}$; amplitude $= |a|$

6. What is the period of the graph of $g(\theta) = a \tan b\theta$ where $a \neq 0$ and $b > 0$? What are the coordinates of the halfway points on one cycle of the graph? (Give your answers in terms of a and b.)

Period $= \frac{\pi}{b}$; halfway points at $\left(-\frac{\pi}{4b}, -a\right)$ and $\left(\frac{\pi}{4b}, a\right)$

Translating Trigonometric Graphs

Essential question: *How do the constants h and k in the functions*
$g(\theta) = a \sin b(\theta - h) + k$, $g(\theta) = a \cos b(\theta - h) + k$, *and* $g(\theta) = a \tan b(\theta - h) + k$
affect their graphs?

COMMON CORE

Standards for Mathematical Content

CC.9-12.F.IF.7 Graph functions expressed symbolically and show key features of the graph ...*

CC.9-12.F.IF.7e Graph ... trigonometric functions, showing period, midline, and amplitude.*

CC.9-12.F.BF.3 Identify the effect on the graph of replacing $f(x)$ by $f(x) + k$, ... and $f(x + k)$ for specific values of k (both positive and negative); ...

Also: CC.9-12.F.IF.4*

Prerequisites

Graphing the sine and cosine functions, Lesson 8-5

Graphing the tangent function, Lesson 8-6

Stretching, shrinking, and reflecting trigonometric graphs, Lesson 8-7

Math Background

In the previous lesson, students learned the effects of the values of a and b on the sine, cosine, and tangent functions of the form $g(\theta) = a \sin b(\theta)$, etc. Students saw that changing the values of these constants had the same effect on these trigonometric functions as on other types of functions. The graphs of the trigonometric functions were shrunk, stretched, and reflected depending on the values of a and b. Students will now study the effects of h and k on trigonometric functions of the form $g(\theta) = a \sin b(\theta - h) + k$, etc., and they will discover that changing these values translates the graphs of the parent functions horizontally or vertically in much the same manner as with previously studied functions. The value of h for trigonometric functions has a special meaning. It indicates the horizontal translation and is called the *phase shift* of the function.

INTRODUCE

Ask students to recall the parent quadratic function $f(x) = x^2$. Ask them what effects the h and k values had on the graph of $g(x) = (x - h)^2 + k$. Have students summarize the results in the first row of the table and make predictions for the second row.

Parent Function	Function	Specific Effects
$f(x) = x^2$	$g(x) = (x - h)^2 + k$	h translates horizontally, and k translates vertically.
$f(\theta) = \sin \theta$	$g(\theta) = \sin(\theta - h) + k$	h translates horizontally, and k translates vertically.

TEACH

1 **ENGAGE**

Questioning Strategies

• What is the value of a in $g(\theta)$ and how does it affect the graph of the parent function? **3; vertical stretch**

• What is the value of b in $g(\theta)$ and how does it affect the graph of the parent function? **2; horizontal shrink**

• What is the value of h in $g(\theta)$ and how does it affect the graph of the parent function? $\frac{\pi}{2}$; **horizontal translation to the right**

• Look at the input column for g (the first column). How were these points chosen? **The period of f is π. So for g, $\theta - \frac{\pi}{2}$ must go from 0 to π to complete a full cycle. To make the initial input for f be 0, the initial input for g must be $\frac{\pi}{2}$ since this makes $\theta - \frac{\pi}{2}$ equal to 0.**

• What happens to the mid-line of this function? Why? **It moves up 1; because $k = 1$**

• What values of k would cause this function to have no real zeros? Why? $k > 3$; $k < -3$; **both values translate the function so that it does not cross the horizontal axis.**

continued

Name_____ Class_____ Date_____

8-8

Translating Trigonometric Graphs

Essential question: *How do the constants h and k in the functions*
$g(\theta) = a \sin b(\theta - h) + k$, $g(\theta) = a \cos b(\theta - h) + k$, *and* $g(\theta) = a \tan b(\theta - h) + k$
affect their graphs?

COMMON CORE

CC-9-12.F.IF.7*,
CC-9-12.F.IF.7e*,
CC-9-12.F.BF.3

1 ENGAGE   Understanding Transformations of
Trigonometric Graphs

In Lesson 8-7 you learned how the constants a and b in the functions $f(\theta) = a \sin b\theta$,
$f(\theta) = a \cos b\theta$, and $f(\theta) = a \tan b\theta$ affect the period and amplitude of their graphs.
In this lesson you will examine how the constants h and k in $g(\theta) = f(\theta - h) + k$ alter
the graph of $f(\theta)$.

Notice that the constant h appears *inside* the function and therefore acts on f's input
values, while the constant k appears *outside* the function and therefore acts on f's output
values. For instance, consider the function $g(\theta) = 3 \sin 2\left(\theta - \frac{\pi}{2}\right) + 1$, the result of
introducing the constants $h = \frac{\pi}{2}$ and $k = 1$ in the function $f(\theta) = 3 \sin 2\theta$. The mapping
diagram below shows what happens when $\frac{\pi}{2}$, $\frac{3\pi}{4}$, π, $\frac{5\pi}{4}$, and $\frac{3\pi}{2}$ are used as inputs for g.

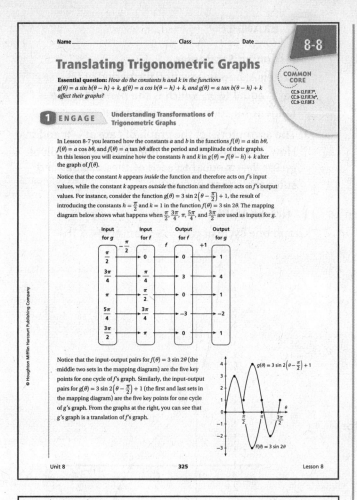

Notice that the input-output pairs for $f(\theta) = 3 \sin 2\theta$ (the
middle two sets in the mapping diagram) are the five key
points in one cycle of f's graph. Similarly, the input-output
pairs for $g(\theta) = 3 \sin 2\left(\theta - \frac{\pi}{2}\right) + 1$ (the first and last sets in
the mapping diagram) are the five key points for one cycle
of g's graph. From the graphs at the right, you can see that
g's graph is a translation of f's graph.

Unit 8   325   Lesson 8

© Houghton Mifflin Harcourt Publishing Company

REFLECT

1a. In terms of the constants $h = \frac{\pi}{2}$ and $k = 1$, describe how the graph of f is translated
to obtain the graph of g.

The graph of f is translated $\frac{\pi}{2}$ units to the right and 1 unit up.

1b. The constants h and k in $g(\theta) = f(\theta - h) + k$ change where a cycle begins and
ends as well as what the maximum and minimum values are, but do the constants
change the period and amplitude? Explain.

No; the length of the cycle (which is the period) and half the difference between

the maximum and minimum values (which is the amplitude) do not change.

2 EXAMPLE   Graphing $g(\theta) = a \cos b(\theta - h) + k$

Graph one cycle of $g(\theta) = 0.5 \cos 3\left(\theta - \frac{\pi}{3}\right) - 1.5$.

A   Think about the related function $f(\theta) = 0.5 \cos 3\theta$.

- What is the period of f? $\frac{2\pi}{3}$

- Use the period to determine the five key input-output pairs for f. Complete the table.

Key input-output pairs for f	θ	0	$\frac{\pi}{6}$	$\frac{\pi}{3}$	$\frac{\pi}{2}$	$\frac{2\pi}{3}$
	$f(\theta)$	0.5	0	−0.5	0	0.5

B   Think about the graph of $g(\theta) = 0.5 \cos 3\left(\theta - \frac{\pi}{3}\right) - 1.5$ in relation to the graph of f.

- How must the graph of f be translated horizontally and vertically to obtain the graph
of g? (Note that $k < 0$ in this case.)

Translate $\frac{\pi}{3}$ units to the right and 1.5 units down.

- Complete the table to show the effect of the horizontal and vertical translations on
the key input-output pairs for f. Remember that a horizontal translation affects only
the input values and a vertical translation affects only the output values.

Key input-output pairs for g	θ	$\frac{\pi}{3}$	$\frac{\pi}{2}$	$\frac{2\pi}{3}$	$\frac{5\pi}{6}$	π
	$g(\theta)$	−1	−1.5	−2	−1.5	−1

Unit 8   326   Lesson 8

© Houghton Mifflin Harcourt Publishing Company

Teaching Strategy

Students may wonder how to determine the key points when graphing a function of the form $g(\theta) = a\sin(\theta - h) + k$. Remind them that for sine (and cosine) the key points are the turning points and the zeros, as they were in the previous lesson. To show students a complete use of key points, you may wish to have students start with the key points for $f(\theta) = \sin\theta$ and use them to generate the key points for $f(\theta) = 3\sin 2\theta$. These key points can then be used to generate the key points for $g(\theta) = 3\sin 2(\theta - \frac{\pi}{2}) + 1$. You may wish to have students perform a similar process for the tangent function that involves key points and asymptotes.

2 EXAMPLE

Questioning Strategies

- In step A, how do you find the period of f?
  Set 3θ equal to 2π. Then, solve for θ.

- How do you find the key input values of θ for g?
  You set $\theta - \frac{\pi}{3}$ equal to each of the key inputs for f and solve each equation for θ.

EXTRA EXAMPLE

Graph one cycle of $g(\theta) = \frac{1}{4}\cos[2(\theta - \pi)] + 2$.

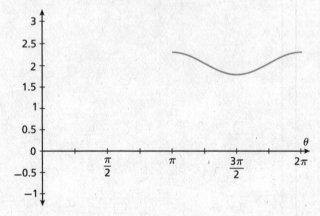

3 EXAMPLE

Questioning Strategies

- In step A, how do you find the period of f?
  Set $\frac{\theta}{2}$ equal to π, which is the period for the tangent function. Then, solve for θ.

- The asymptotes of the graph of f are at $-\pi$ and π. How do you find the asymptotes for the graph of g? Set $\theta + \pi$ equal to each of these values and solve the equation for θ.

EXTRA EXAMPLE

Graph one cycle of $g(\theta) = -2\tan[\frac{1}{2}(\theta - \frac{\pi}{2})] + 1$.

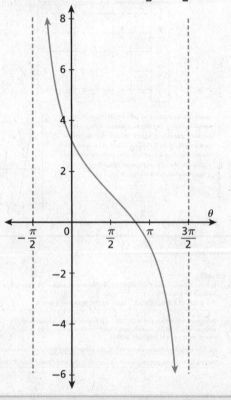

> **MATHEMATICAL PRACTICE** **Highlighting the Standards**
>
> This lesson, particularly **2 EXAMPLE**, includes opportunities to address Mathematical Practice Standard 6 (Attend to precision). Students will need to be very precise about which function (f or g) they are describing. The inputs for f and g are likely to be different, so students will need to clearly state which function they are working with and how the two functions relate. (See the mapping diagram in **1 ENGAGE**.) Insist on clear, concise communication when students are describing the key points and the period of the functions.

continued

C Plot the key points for the graph of g and use them to draw one cycle of the graph. One cycle of the graph of f is shown in gray for comparison.

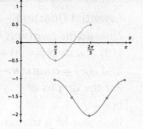

REFLECT

2a. If $g(\theta) = 0.5 \cos 3\left(\theta + \frac{\pi}{3}\right) - 1.5$ instead of $g(\theta) = 0.5 \cos 3\left(\theta - \frac{\pi}{3}\right) - 1.5$, what changes about how the graph of f is translated to obtain the graph of g?

The graph of f is translated to the left $\frac{\pi}{3}$ units rather than to the right $\frac{\pi}{3}$ units.

---

3 EXAMPLE Graphing $g(\theta) = a \tan b(\theta - h) + k$

Graph one cycle of $g(\theta) = 2 \tan \frac{1}{2}(\theta + \pi) + 3$.

A Think about the related function $f(\theta) = 2 \tan \frac{\theta}{2}$.

• What is the period of f? $\underline{2\pi}$

• Use the period to determine the key features of the graph of f. Complete the table.

Key features of the graph of f	Equations of asymptotes	Coordinates of midline crossing	Coordinates of halfway points
	$\theta = -\pi, \theta = \pi$	(0,0)	$\left(-\frac{\pi}{2}, -2\right), \left(\frac{\pi}{2}, 2\right)$

B Think about the graph of $g(\theta) = 2 \tan \frac{1}{2}(\theta + \pi) + 3$ in relation to the graph of f.

• How must the graph of f be translated horizontally and vertically to obtain the graph of g? (Note that $h < 0$ in this case.)

Translate π units to the left and 3 units up.

• Complete the table to show the effect of the horizontal and vertical translations on the key features of the graph of f.

Key features of the graph of f	Equations of asymptotes	Coordinates of midline crossing	Coordinates of halfway points
	$\theta = -2\pi, \theta = 0$	$(-\pi, 3)$	$\left(-\frac{3\pi}{2}, 1\right), \left(-\frac{\pi}{2}, 5\right)$

Unit 8   327   Lesson 8

C Use the key features for the graph of g to draw one cycle of the graph. One cycle of the graph of f is shown in gray for comparison.

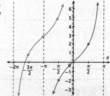

REFLECT

3a. Only one of the constants h and k affects the asymptotes for the graph of a tangent function. Which constant is it, and why?

h; because the asymptotes are vertical, they are affected by shifts left or right, but not shifts up or down.

3b. Only one of the constants h and k affects the midline for the graph of a trigonometric function. Which constant is it, and why?

k; because the midline is horizontal, it is affected by shifts up or down, but not shifts left or right.

---

4 EXAMPLE Modeling the Motion of a Paddle Wheel

A side view of a riverboat's paddle wheel is shown. The paddle wheel has a diameter of 16 feet and rotates at a rate of 1 revolution every 4 seconds. Its lowest point is 2 feet below the water line.

The function $h(t) = 8 \sin \frac{\pi}{2}(t - 1) + 6$ models the motion of the paddle labeled P. The function gives the "height" (which is negative when the paddle is below the water line) at time t (in seconds). Graph the function on the interval $0 \le t \le 6$.

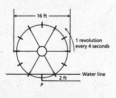

A Complete the table for the related function $f(t) = 8 \sin \frac{\pi}{2}t$.

Key input-output pairs for f	t	0	1	2	3	4
	f(t)	0	8	0	−8	0

Unit 8   328   Lesson 8

Differentiated Instruction

A suggested activity in the previous lesson was to create cutouts of the sine function. Students can use those cutouts to model horizontal and vertical translations. Have students carefully draw axes and label $\frac{\pi}{6}, \frac{\pi}{4}, \frac{\pi}{3}, \frac{\pi}{2}, \frac{2\pi}{3}, \frac{3\pi}{4}, \frac{5\pi}{6}$, and π to match their cutouts. They should label similar intervals from -2π to 2π on the x-axis and label from -5 to 5 on the y-axis. Give students equations with different values of h and k ($a = b = 1$) and have them move their cutouts to show the graph of the equation. Suggested equations include $f(\theta) = \sin(\theta - \frac{\pi}{2})$, $f(\theta) = \sin(\theta - \pi)$, $f(\theta) = \sin(\theta - 2\pi)$, $f(\theta) = \sin(\theta + \frac{\pi}{2})$, and similar variations of the cosine function.

4 EXAMPLE

Questioning Strategies

- How do you know that t goes from 0 to 4? The problem states that the wheel completes a revolution in 4 seconds. So the period of the motion is 4.

- How do you find the key input values for h, given the key inputs for f? Set $t - 1$ equal to each of the key inputs of f and solve for t.

EXTRA EXAMPLE

A different paddle wheel has a diameter of 20 feet, and 3 feet of it dips under the water. It rotates once every 8 seconds. The function that models the motion of the wheel is $h(t) = 10\sin\frac{\pi}{4}(t - 1) + 7$. Graph the function on the interval $0 \le t \le 16$.

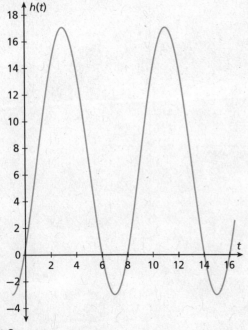

Essential Question

How do the constants h and k in the functions $g(\theta) = a\sin b(\theta - h) + k$, $g(\theta) = a\cos b(\theta - h) + k$, *and* $g(\theta) = a\tan b(\theta - h) + k$ *affect their graphs?* For the graphs of $y = a\sin b(x - h) + k$, $y = a\cos b(x - h) + k$, and $y = a\tan b(x - h) + k$, changing the value of h translates the graph horizontally, and changing the value of k translates the graph vertically.

Summarize

Students should add to their summary from Lesson 8-7. They should graph equations of the form $g(\theta) = a\sin b(\theta - h) + k$, $g(\theta) = a\cos b(\theta - h) + k$, and $g(\theta) = a\tan b(\theta - h) + k$, choosing values for h and k to show different vertical and horizontal translations. (a and b can be 1 since students have already shown the effects of these coefficients in the Lesson 8-7 summary.) The goal is to have the graphs of the parent function, a stretched, shrunk, and/or reflected function, and a translated function next to one another so the effects of the values a, b, h, and k are readily apparent.

PRACTICE

Where skills are taught	Where skills are practiced
2 EXAMPLE	EX. 1
3 EXAMPLE	EX. 2
4 EXAMPLE	EX. 3

B Identify the translations to obtain the graph of h from the graph of f, then complete the table for h.

Amount and direction of horizontal translation: ___1 unit to the right___

Amount and direction of vertical translation: ___6.5 units up___

Key input-output pairs for h	t	1	2	3	4	5
	$h(t)$	6	14	6	−2	6

C Plot the key points for the graph of h and use them to draw one cycle of the graph. One cycle of the graph of f is shown in gray for comparison.

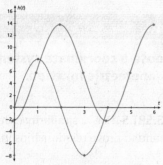

D Extend the graph one quarter of a cycle to the left and to the right in order to show the graph over the interval $0 \le t \le 6$.

REFLECT

4a. What is the significance of the graph's t-intercepts in the context of the situation?

They represent each time paddle P breaks the surface of the water.

4b. What is the significance of the maximum and minimum values of h in the context of the situation?

The maximum represents the height of paddle P when it reaches the top of the wheel, and the minimum represents the "height" of the paddle when it reaches the bottom of the wheel.

PRACTICE

1. Graph one cycle of $g(\theta) = 2 \sin \frac{2}{3}\left(\theta - \frac{\pi}{4}\right) - 1$ by first completing the table of key input-output pairs for the related function $f(\theta) = 2 \sin \frac{2}{3}\theta$, then completing the table for g, and finally using the table for g to graph the cycle.

θ	0	$\frac{3\pi}{4}$	$\frac{3\pi}{2}$	$\frac{9\pi}{4}$	3π
$f(\theta)$	0	2	0	−2	0

θ	$\frac{\pi}{4}$	π	$\frac{7\pi}{4}$	$\frac{5\pi}{2}$	$\frac{13\pi}{4}$
$g(\theta)$	−1	1	−1	−3	−1

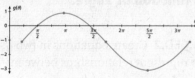

2. Graph one cycle of $g(\theta) = \frac{1}{2} \tan 2\left(\theta + \frac{\pi}{2}\right) + \frac{1}{2}$ by first completing the table of key features for the graph of the related function $f(\theta) = \frac{1}{2} \tan 2\theta$, then completing the table for g, and finally using the table for g to graph the cycle.

	Graph of f	Graph of g
Asymptotes	$\theta = -\frac{\pi}{4}$, $\theta = \frac{\pi}{4}$	$\theta = -\frac{3\pi}{4}$ $\theta = -\frac{\pi}{4}$
Midline crossing	$(0, 0)$	$\left(-\frac{\pi}{2}, \frac{1}{2}\right)$
Halfway points	$\left(-\frac{\pi}{8}, -\frac{1}{2}\right)$, $\left(\frac{\pi}{8}, \frac{1}{2}\right)$	$\left(-\frac{5\pi}{8}, 0\right)$, $\left(-\frac{3\pi}{8}, 1\right)$

3. Suppose a working scale model of a riverboat has a paddle wheel that is 8 inches in diameter, rotates at a rate of 1 revolution every 2 seconds, and dips 0.5 inch below the water line. The function $h(t) = 4 \sin \pi(t - 0.5) + 3.5$ gives the "height" (in inches) of one paddle at time t (in seconds). Graph the function on the interval $0 \le t \le 4$.

FOCUS ON MODELING
Modeling with Trigonometric Functions

Essential question: *How can you model the height of a gondola on a rotating Ferris wheel?*

COMMON CORE   Standards for Mathematical Content

The following standards are addressed in this lesson. (An asterisk indicates that a standard is also a Modeling standard.) For more detailed information, see each section of the lesson.

Number and Quantity: CC.9-12.N.Q.1*

Algebra: CC.9-12.A.CED.2*

Functions: CC.9-12.F.IF.2, CC.9-12.F.IF.4*, CC.9-12.F.IF.7*, CC.9-12.F.IF.7e*, CC.9-12.F.BF.1*, CC.9-12.F.BF.1a*, CC.9-12.F.BF.3, CC.9-12.F.TF.5*

Geometry: CC.9-12.G.SRT.5

Prerequisites

- Angles of rotation and radian measure, Lesson 8-2
- Graphing the sine and cosine functions, Lesson 8-5
- Stretching, shrinking, and reflecting trigonometric graphs, Lesson 8-7
- Translating trigonometric graphs, Lesson 8-8

Math Background

In this lesson, students analyze the motion of a Ferris wheel. Students model the motion using a sine function. They find the values for *a, b, h,* and *k* in $h(t) = a \sin b(t - h) + k$ that describe this particular motion; then, they graph the function.

INTRODUCE

Even though the Ferris wheel is not particularly exciting compared with more modern rides, it is a staple of amusement parks and traveling carnivals. Large wheels with enclosed gondolas, such as the almost-450-foot-tall London Eye, are being erected in tourist areas to give a bird's eye view of the area. It took hundreds of people and seven years to build the London Eye. In this lesson, students will model the height of a gondola on a Ferris wheel as a function of time using a trigonometric function.

TEACH

1 **Choose a coordinate system and a trigonometric function.**

Standards

CC.9-12.G.SRT.5 Use ... similarity criteria to solve problems and to prove relationships in geometric figures.

CC.9-12.F.TF.5 Choose trigonometric functions to model periodic phenomena with specified amplitude, frequency, and midline.*

Questioning Strategies

- What is the radius of the wheel? **6 ft**
- How high off the ground is the bottom of the wheel? **1 ft**
- What is the height above the *x*-axis of point *G*? **0 ft**
- What is the height above the *x*-axis of point *G'*? **6 ft**
- Which function (sine, cosine, or tangent) will give a value of 0 when the terminal side of θ is the positive *x*-axis and a maximum when the terminal side of θ is the positive *y*-axis? **sine**

2 **Write and revise a model for height as a function of angle.**

Standards

CC.9-12. A.CED.2 Create equations in two ... variables to represent relationships between quantities; ... *

CC.9-12.F.IF.2 Use function notation, evaluate functions for inputs in their domains, and interpret statements that use function notation in terms of a context.

CC.9-12.F.BF.1 Write a function that describes a relationship between two quantities.*

CC.9-12.F.BF.1a Determine an explicit expression ... from a context.*

CC.9-12.F.TF.5 Choose trigonometric functions to model periodic phenomena with specified amplitude, frequency, and midline.*

continued

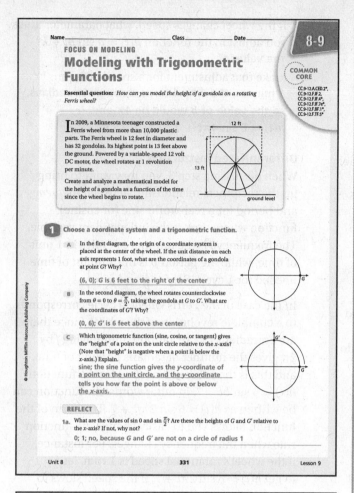

8-9

FOCUS ON MODELING
Modeling with Trigonometric Functions

COMMON CORE

Essential question: *How can you model the height of a gondola on a rotating Ferris wheel?*

In 2009, a Minnesota teenager constructed a Ferris wheel from more than 10,000 plastic parts. The Ferris wheel is 12 feet in diameter and has 32 gondolas. Its highest point is 13 feet above the ground. Powered by a variable-speed 12 volt DC motor, the wheel rotates at 1 revolution per minute.

Create and analyze a mathematical model for the height of a gondola as a function of the time since the wheel begins to rotate.

CC.9-12.A.CED.2*,
CC.9-12.F.IF.2,
CC.9-12.F.IF.4*,
CC.9-12.F.IF.7e*,
CC.9-12.F.BF.1*,
CC.9-12.F.TF.5*

1 Choose a coordinate system and a trigonometric function.

A In the first diagram, the origin of a coordinate system is placed at the center of the wheel. If the unit distance on each axis represents 1 foot, what are the coordinates of a gondola at point G? Why?

(6, 0); G is 6 feet to the right of the center

B In the second diagram, the wheel rotates counterclockwise from $\theta = 0$ to $\theta = \frac{\pi}{2}$, taking the gondola at G to G'. What are the coordinates of G'? Why?

(0, 6); G' is 6 feet above the center

C Which trigonometric function (sine, cosine, or tangent) gives the "height" of a point on the unit circle relative to the x-axis? (Note that "height" is negative when a point is below the x-axis.) Explain.

sine; the sine function gives the y-coordinate of a point on the unit circle, and the y-coordinate tells you how far the point is above or below the x-axis.

REFLECT

1a. What are the values of sin 0 and sin $\frac{\pi}{2}$? Are these the heights of G and G' relative to the x-axis? If not, why not?

0; 1; no, because G and G' are not on a circle of radius 1

Unit 8   331   Lesson 9

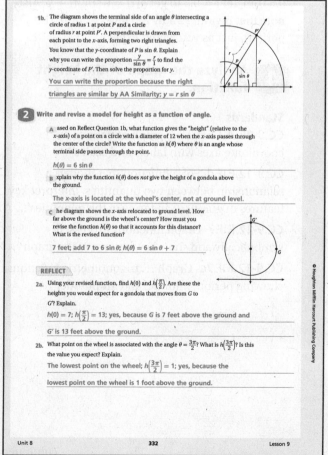

1b. The diagram shows the terminal side of an angle θ intersecting a circle of radius 1 at point P and a circle of radius r at point P'. A perpendicular is drawn from each point to the x-axis, forming two right triangles. You know that the y-coordinate of P is sin θ. Explain why you can write the proportion $\frac{y}{\sin \theta} = \frac{r}{1}$ to find the y-coordinate of P'. Then solve the proportion for y.

You can write the proportion because the right triangles are similar by AA Similarity; y = r sin θ

2 Write and revise a model for height as a function of angle.

A Based on Reflect Question 1b, what function gives the "height" (relative to the x-axis) of a point on a circle with a diameter of 12 when the x-axis passes through the center of the circle? Write the function as $h(\theta)$ where θ is an angle whose terminal side passes through the point.

$h(\theta) = 6 \sin \theta$

B Explain why the function $h(\theta)$ does *not* give the height of a gondola above the ground.

The x-axis is located at the wheel's center, not at ground level.

C The diagram shows the x-axis relocated to ground level. How far above the ground is the wheel's center? How must you revise the function $h(\theta)$ so that it accounts for this distance? What is the revised function?

7 feet; add 7 to 6 sin θ; $h(\theta) = 6 \sin \theta + 7$

REFLECT

2a. Using your revised function, find $h(0)$ and $h\left(\frac{\pi}{2}\right)$. Are these the heights you would expect for a gondola that moves from G to G'? Explain.

$h(0) = 7$; $h\left(\frac{\pi}{2}\right) = 13$; yes, because G is 7 feet above the ground and G' is 13 feet above the ground.

2b. What point on the wheel is associated with the angle $\theta = \frac{3\pi}{2}$? What is $h\left(\frac{3\pi}{2}\right)$? Is this the value you expect? Explain.

The lowest point on the wheel; $h\left(\frac{3\pi}{2}\right) = 1$; yes, because the lowest point on the wheel is 1 foot above the ground.

Unit 8   332   Lesson 9

© Houghton Mifflin Harcourt Publishing Company

2 continued

Questioning Strategies
- What physical characteristic of the Ferris wheel does the value of a in $h(\theta) = a \sin \theta + k$ represent? the radius of the wheel

- What physical characteristic of the Ferris wheel does the value of k in $h(\theta) = a \sin \theta + k$ represent? the height of the center of the wheel above the ground

Teaching Strategy
Another way for students to determine the values for the function $h(\theta) = 6 \sin \theta$ is to ask them to recall the general function $h(\theta) = a \sin b\theta$. Ask them what effect a and b have on the graph. Students should remember that a changes the amplitude and b changes the period. They should recognize the wheel has a maximum "height" of 6 feet and a minimum of -6 feet, so the amplitude of the function's graph must be 6. Hence, the function is $h(\theta) = 6 \sin \theta$.

 Revise the model to make height a function of time.

Standards
CC.9-12.N.Q.1 Use units as a way to understand problems and guide the solution of multi-step problems; ...*

CC.9-12.A.CED.2 Create equations in two ... variables to represent relationships between quantities; ... *

CC.9-12.F.IF.2 Use function notation, evaluate functions for inputs in their domains, ...

CC.9-12.F.BF.1 Write a function that describes a relationship between two quantities.*

CC.9-12.F.BF.1a Determine an explicit expression ... from a context.*

Questioning Strategies
- Have students re-read the initial problem description on the first page of the lesson. What is the rotational speed of the wheel? 1 revolution per minute

- In part C, show the dimensional analysis used to convert from radians per minute to radians.
  $\dfrac{2\pi}{\min} \cdot t \min = 2\pi t$

- To check your answer above, find the angle through which the wheel has turned when $t = 1$ min. 2π

- If the wheel changes speed, what parameter must you adjust in the function $h(t) = a \sin bt + k$? the value of b

  Make that adjustment for a speed of 2 rpm. In 1 minute, the wheel turns through 4π radians, so the value of b would be 4π and $h(t) = 6 \sin 4\pi t + 7$.

Differentiated Instruction
When discussing step 3, you may want to bring up the reciprocal relationship between *frequency* and *period* for a real-world sine (or cosine) function where time is the independent variable. The frequency f is the number of cycles in 1 unit of time, while the period p is the amount of time needed for 1 cycle. So, $f = \dfrac{1}{p}$ and $p = \dfrac{1}{f}$.

In the case of the Ferris wheel, a cycle corresponds to a complete revolution of the wheel. Since there are 2π radians in 1 revolution, multiplying f by 2π gives the number of radians per unit of time, and this is the value of b needed for the function $h(t) = 6 \sin bt + 7$. In other words, the function can be written as $h(t) = 6 \sin 2\pi f t + 7$. This form of the function allows you to easily change the function rule when the frequency changes. For instance, if the wheel's rotational speed is 1 rpm, let $f = 1$ to get $h(t) = 6 \sin 2\pi t + 7$; if the speed slows to 0.5 rpm, let $f = 0.5$ to get $h(t) = 6 \sin \pi t + 7$. Also, note that dividing 2π by $2\pi f$ gives $\dfrac{1}{f}$, or p (the period), just as you would expect.

 Analyze the graph of the height function.

Standards
CC.9-12.A.CED.2 ...; graph equations on coordinate axes with labels and scales.*

CC.9-12.F.IF.4 For a function that models a relationship between two quantities, interpret key features of graphs ... in terms of the quantities ... .*

CC.9-12.F.IF.7 Graph functions expressed symbolically and show key features of the graph ... *

CC.9-12.F.IF.7e Graph ... trigonometric functions, showing period, midline, and amplitude.*

continued

3 Revise the model to make height a function of time.

A The wheel's rotational speed is given in revolutions per minute. The unit analysis below shows that you can convert this rate into another form. Complete the unit analysis.

$$\frac{\text{revolutions}}{\text{minute}} \times \frac{\text{radians}}{\text{revolution}} = \frac{\text{radians}}{\text{minute}}$$

B How many radians are in 1 revolution? What, then, is the wheel's rotational speed in radians per minute?

  2π; 2π radians per minute

C You can use the rotational speed in radians per minute to write angle θ (measured in radians) in terms of time t (measured in minutes). Explain how, and give the result.

  Multiply 2π radians per minute by minutes to get the angle measure; $\theta = 2\pi t$

D Returning to the revised function $h(\theta)$ that you wrote in part C of step 2, you can now replace θ with an expression involving t so that $h(\theta)$ becomes $h(t)$. Write the rule for $h(t)$.

  $h(t) = 6\sin 2\pi t + 7$

REFLECT

3a. When the wheel begins to turn, a gondola at point G moves to points G', G'', G''', and returns to G. Determine the time t (in minutes) that it takes the gondola to reach each point. Then evaluate $h(t)$ to confirm that the model gives the correct heights above the ground.

t	0	$\frac{1}{4}$	$\frac{1}{2}$	$\frac{3}{4}$	1
$h(t)$	7	13	7	1	7

3b. Suppose the speed of the motor that powers the wheel is reduced so that the wheel rotates at a speed of 1 revolution every 2 minutes (or 0.5 revolution per minute). How does the height function change?

  The height function becomes $h(t) = 6\sin \pi t + 7$.

3c. What is the period of the height function in part D? What is the amplitude? Explain your reasoning.

  1 minute; 6 feet; *Sample answer:* the wheel makes one complete revolution, or

  1 complete cycle, in 1 minute. The minimum height is 1 foot and the maximum

  height is 13 feet, so the amplitude is $0.5(13 - 1) = 6$ feet.

4 Analyze the graph of the height function.

A The table in Reflect Question 3a gives the five key points for one cycle of the height function. Use the table to graph the cycle, then repeat the cycle as needed to show the graph over the interval $0 \le t < 5$. Complete the labels and scales on the axes below before graphing.

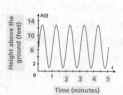

B During any cycle, when is the height function increasing and when is it decreasing? Give your answers in terms of quarters of a cycle, and then explain why your answers make sense in terms of a gondola on a rotating Ferris wheel. (Remember that the gondola starts at the point (6, 7) in the coordinate system from part C of step 2 and that the wheel rotates counterclockwise.)

  The function increases during the first and fourth quarters of a cycle; it

  decreases during the second and third quarters; this makes sense because a

  gondola at (6, 7) rises to (0, 13), then drops to (−6, 7) and continues to drop

  to (0, 1), and finally rises to (6, 7) to complete the cycle.

C During the interval $0 \le t < 5$, how many times is a gondola at a given height between 1 foot and 13 feet above the ground? Explain how you know from the graph and from the context of a gondola on a rotating Ferris wheel.

  10 times; a horizontal line drawn between 1 and 13 on the vertical axis

  intersects the graph 10 times; on each of the 5 rotations, the gondola is at

  the same height once on the way up and once on the way down.

REFLECT

4a. What is the equation of the midline of the height function? Explain your reasoning.

  $h(t) = 7$; the halfway point between the maximum and minimum values is 7 feet.

4b. At which times during the interval $0 \le t < 5$ is the height of the gondola on the midline?

  0 min, 0.5 min, 1 min, 1.5 min, 2 min, 2.5 min, 3 min, 3.5 min, 4 min, and

  4.5 min

4 continued

Questioning Strategies

- How many revolutions does the wheel complete in 5 minutes? **5** How many cycles should appear in the graph of the sine function? **5**

- At what times during the interval $0 \le t < 5$ is the gondola at its highest point? **0.25 min, 1.25 min, 2.25 min, 3.25 min, and 4.25 min**

- At what times during the interval $0 \le t < 5$ is the gondola at its lowest point? **0.75 min, 1.75 min, 2.75 min, 3.75 min, and 4.75 min**

5 **Generalize the height function to any gondola.**

Standards

CC.9-12.A.CED.2 Create equations in two ... variables to represent relationships between quantities; ... *

CC.9-12.F.IF.2 Use function notation, evaluate functions for inputs in their domains, and interpret function notation in terms of a context.

CC.9-12.F.IF.7 Graph functions expressed symbolically and show key features of the graph ...*

CC.9-12.F.IF.7e Graph ... trigonometric functions, showing period, midline, and amplitude.*

CC.9-12.F.BF.1 Write a function that describes a relationship between two quantities.*

CC.9-12.F.BF.1a Determine an explicit expression ... or steps for calculations from a context.*

CC.9-12.F.BF.3 Identify the effect on the graph of replacing $f(x)$ by ... $f(x + k)$ for specific values of k (both positive and negative; ...

Questioning Strategies

- Describe the height function in words. For the gondola that starts at (6, 7), the function gives the gondola's height above the ground at any time t measured in minutes.

- Where on the wheel is the gondola at (0, 1) located? It is at the bottom of the wheel.

- Given the graph of the height function for the gondola that starts at (6, 7), how can the graph of the height function for any other gondola be obtained through a transformation? Explain your reasoning. All gondolas follow the same path around the wheel and therefore run through the same cycle of heights above the ground, but they do so at different times. So, given the graph of the height function for one gondola, you can simply translate the graph horizontally to obtain the graph for any other gondola. The magnitude of the horizontal shift depends on the gondola's position on the wheel relative to the gondola that starts at (6, 7).

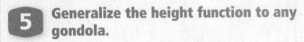

MATHEMATICAL PRACTICE   **Highlighting the Standards**

Modeling circular motion using a trigonometric function supports Mathematical Practice Standard 4 (Model with mathematics). Draw students' attention to how they used the information given in the problem to "customize" the sine function. Each constant in the model can be related to some physical characteristic in the problem situation.

CLOSE

Essential Question

How can you model the height of a gondola on a rotating Ferris wheel?
Use the function $h(t) = a \sin bt + k$ where a is the radius of the wheel, b is 2π times the speed (in revolutions per minute) of the wheel, and k is the height of the center of the wheel above the ground. This function gives the height h at time t of the gondola that starts at (a, k) when the center of the wheel is located at $(0, k)$. For any other gondola, introduce a time shift t' that depends on that gondola's position relative to the gondola at (a, k). Then the height function becomes $h(t) = a \sin b(t + t') + k$.

Summarize

Have students write a one-page summary of how to model circular motion using a trigonometric function.

EXTEND

Standards

CC.9-12.A.CED.2 Create equations in two ... variables to represent relationships between quantities; ... * (Ex. 1)

CC.9-12.F.BF.1 Write a function that describes a relationship between two quantities.* (Ex. 1)

CC.9-12.F.BF.1a Determine an explicit expression ... from a context.* (Ex. 1)

4c. Suppose someone who doesn't know the rotational speed of the wheel is given only the rule for the height function or only the function's graph. Explain how the rotational speed can be determined from each.

The function has the form $h(t) = a \sin bt + k$, and the period of such functions

is $\frac{2\pi}{b}$; since $b = 2\pi$ for $h(t)$, the period is $\frac{2\pi}{2\pi} = 1$, which means that the wheel

completes a revolution in 1 minute; the graph shows that the cycle that starts at

$t = 0$ ends at $t = 1$, so again the wheel completes a revolution in 1 minute.

4d. Suppose the speed of the motor that powers the wheel is reduced so that the wheel rotates at a speed of 1 revolution every 2 minutes (or 0.5 revolution per minute). How does the graph of the height function change? Explain why.

The graph becomes stretched horizontally because each cycle takes twice as long.

5 Generalize the height function to any gondola.

A The height function is based on the gondola at (6, 7) because that point is on the terminal side of angle θ when $\theta = 0$. You can think of the gondolas at other points as either being ahead of the gondola at (6, 7) or being behind it. For instance, consider a gondola at (0, 1). Give an angle θ_1 between 0 and 2π that shows how far ahead the gondola at (0, 1) is relative to the one at (6, 7). Alternatively, give an angle θ_2 between -2π and 0 that shows how far behind it is. How are θ_1 and θ_2 related?

$\theta_1 = \frac{3\pi}{2}$; $\theta_2 = -\frac{\pi}{2}$; they are coterminal angles that differ by 2π.

B The independent variable for the height function is time rather than angle. Convert θ_1 to time t_1 and θ_2 to time t_2 (both times in minutes). By how much do t_1 and t_2 differ? Why does this make sense?

$t_1 = \frac{3}{4}$; $t_2 = -\frac{1}{4}$; they differ by 1 because a cycle lasts 1 minute.

C The height function $h(t)$ based on the gondola at (6, 7) performs several actions to produce an output of height for an input of time. The table lists those actions as well as the results of the actions when $t = 0$ is used as input. Complete the table by providing the missing numerical results. (The unit of measurement for each result is given in parentheses.)

Actions	Results for $h(t)$
Accept a time as input.	0 (minutes)
Convert time to an angle.	0 (radians)
Find "height" relative to wheel's center.	0 (feet)
Output height above ground.	7 (feet)

D A height function based on the gondola at (0, 1) has to perform one more action than $h(t)$ does. This action is a "time shift" that changes the input time $t = 0$ to the time that represents how far ahead or behind the gondola at (0, 1) is relative to the gondola at (6, 7). In the table, the column for $h_1(t)$ uses time t_1 and angle θ_1 from parts A and B of step 5. Complete the column for $h_2(t)$ using time t_2 and angle θ_2.

Actions	Results for $h_1(t)$	Results for $h_2(t)$
Accept a time as input.	0 (minutes)	0 (minutes)
Convert to time ahead or time behind.	$\frac{3}{4}$ (minutes)	$-\frac{1}{4}$ (minutes)
Convert time to an angle.	$\frac{3\pi}{2}$ (radians)	$-\frac{\pi}{2}$ (radians)
Find "height" relative to wheel's center.	-6 (feet)	-6 (feet)
Output height above ground.	1 (feet)	1 (feet)

E Based on the table above, one height function for the gondola at (0, 1) is $h_1(t) = 6\sin 2\pi\left(t + \frac{3}{4}\right) + 7$. Write a rule for the other height function $h_2(t)$.

$h_2(t) = 6\sin 2\pi\left(t - \frac{1}{4}\right) + 7$

REFLECT

5a. The graph of $h_1(t)$ on the interval $0 \le t < 1$ is shown. Using the same coordinate plane, graph $h_2(t)$ on the interval $0 \le t < 1$. What do you notice?

The graphs are identical.

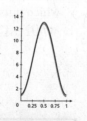

5b. Describe the impact that a "time shift" in the rule for the height function has on the graph of the function. For instance, how is the graph of $h_1(t)$ related to graph of $h(t)$ if both functions have unrestricted domains?

The "time shift" produces a horizontal shift in the graph.

EXTEND

1. Suppose a Ferris wheel has a radius of r feet, rotates counterclockwise at a speed of s revolutions per minute, and has a center whose distance above the ground is c feet (where $c > r$). Relative to the gondola at the rightmost point on the wheel, suppose a gondola has a "time shift" of t_1 minutes. Write a rule for the height h (in feet) of that gondola as a function of the time t (in minutes) since the wheel begins to rotate.

$h(t) = r\sin 2\pi s(t + t_1) + c$

CORRELATION

Standard	Items
CC.9-12.A.CED.2*	13
CC.9-12.F.IF.2	6
CC.9-12.F.IF.4	7, 8, 9, 10, 13
CC.9-12.F.IF.7e*	10, 13
CC.9-12.F.BF.1*	13
CC.9-12.F.TF.1	1
CC.9-12.F.TF.2	11
CC.9-12.F.TF.3(+)	2, 4, 6
CC.9-12.F.TF.4(+)	12
CC.9-12.F.TF.5*	13
CC.9-12.F.TF.8	5
CC.9-12.G.C.5	3

TEST PREP DOCTOR ✚

Multiple Choice: Item 1

- Students who chose **A** used the given ratio of arc length to circumference without multiplying by 2π, the number of radians in a full circle.
- Students who chose **B** multiplied the given ratio of arc length to circumference by π instead of 2π.
- Students who chose **D** did not stay within the constraints stated for θ.

Multiple Choice: Item 3

- Students who chose **A** determined that the arc is $\frac{3}{4}$ of the full circumference, but did not multiply by 2π to obtain the radian measure of the angle.
- Students who chose **B** divided the radius by the arc length instead of dividing the arc length by the radius.
- Students who chose **D** did not stay within the constraints stated for θ.

Multiple Choice: Item 5

- Students who chose **A** or **B** did not recognize that $\sin \theta$ is negative in the fourth quadrant.
- Students who chose **C** did not take the square root when using Pythagorean identity.

Multiple Choice: Item 6

- Students who chose **G** did not use the correct reference angle.
- Students who chose **H** or **J** either did not recognize that the angle is in Quadrant IV or do not know $\sin \theta$ is negative in Quadrant IV.

Free Response: Item 10

- Students who incorrectly identified the amplitude may have used the greatest y-value (7) as the amplitude, or they may have used the vertical distance between highest and lowest points on the graph (6).

Free Response: Item 11

- Students who answered incorrectly may not be able to estimate that 10 radians is between 3π and $\frac{7\pi}{2}$.

Free Response: Item 13

- Students may have difficulty determining the argument of the sine function. Since the wheel rotates twice each second, that is 4π radians per second.

- Students may have difficulty finding that the amplitude is 9 (half the diameter of the circle made by the movement of the reflector).

- Students may not be able to determine that the center of the circle is 13 inches above the ground, which puts the midline of the function's graph at $h(t) = 13$.

UNIT 8 TEST PREP

Name _____ Class _____ Date _____

MULTIPLE CHOICE

1. An angle θ whose vertex is at the center of a unit circle intercepts an arc whose length is $\frac{2}{3}$ of the circle's circumference. What is the radian measure of θ if $0 < \theta < 2\pi$?

A. $\frac{2}{3}$ C. $\frac{4\pi}{3}$

B. $\frac{2\pi}{3}$ D. $-\frac{4\pi}{3}$

2. For which value of θ does $\tan \theta = 1$?

F. $\frac{\pi}{6}$ H. $\frac{\pi}{3}$

G. $\frac{\pi}{4}$ J. $\frac{\pi}{2}$

3. An angle θ whose vertex is at the center of a circle of radius 4 units intercepts an arc whose length is 6π units. What is the radian measure of θ if $0 < \theta < 2\pi$?

A. $\frac{3}{4}$ C. $\frac{3\pi}{2}$

B. $\frac{2}{3\pi}$ D. $-\frac{\pi}{2}$

4. If $0 < \theta < \frac{\pi}{2}$, which of the following is equal to $\sin \theta$?

F. $\sin\left(\frac{\pi}{2} + \theta\right)$

G. $\sin(\pi - \theta)$

H. $\sin(\pi + \theta)$

J. $\sin(2\pi - \theta)$

5. If $\cos \theta = 0.342$ where $\frac{3\pi}{2} < \theta < 2\pi$, what is the approximate value of $\sin \theta$?

A. 0.940

B. 0.883

C. -0.883

D. -0.940

6. If $f(\theta) = \sin \theta$, what is $f\left(\frac{5\pi}{3}\right)$?

F. $-\frac{\sqrt{3}}{2}$

G. $-\frac{1}{2}$

H. $\frac{1}{2}$

J. $\frac{\sqrt{3}}{2}$

Use the following information for Items 7–10.

In the window of a jewelry store, rings are displayed on a rotating turntable. The function

$$d(t) = 3 \sin \pi t + 4$$

models a particular ring's distance (in inches) from the window at time t (in minutes).

7. How fast (in revolutions per minute, or rpm) is the turntable rotating?

A. 1 rpm   C. 3 rpm

B. 2 rpm   D. 4 rpm

8. What is the ring's maximum distance from the window?

F. 1 inch   H. 5 inches

G. 3 inches   J. 7 inches

9. An employee at the jewelry store made a change to the display so that the distance function is now $d(t) = 3 \sin \pi t + 3.5$. Which of the following describes the change?

A. The employee moved the ring closer to the center of the turntable.

B. The employee moved the ring farther from the center of the turntable.

C. The employee moved the turntable closer to the window.

D. The employee moved the turntable farther from the window.

FREE RESPONSE

10. a. Using the original distance function $d(t) = 3 \sin \pi t + 4$ as described on the preceding page, graph the function on the interval $0 \le t \le 6$. Include labels and scales for the axes.

b. Identify the graph's period, amplitude, and midline.

Period = 2; amplitude = 3; midline:

$d(t) = 4$

11. If $\theta = 10$ radians, explain how you know that $\cos \theta < 0$ without using a calculator to find $\cos \theta$.

$3\pi \approx 9.42$ and $\frac{7\pi}{2} \approx 10.99$, so

$3\pi < \theta < \frac{7\pi}{2}$, or $2\pi + \pi < \theta < 2\pi + \frac{3\pi}{2}$.

This means that the terminal side of θ rotates counterclockwise one full revolution plus enough to put it in Quadrant III, where cosine is negative.

12. Use angles of rotation and the unit circle to explain why $\cos(-\theta) = \cos \theta$.

The terminal sides of angles θ and $-\theta$ intersect the unit circle at points that are reflections across the x-axis. These points have the same x-coordinate and opposite y-coordinates. Since cosine outputs the x-coordinate, $\cos \theta$ and $\cos(-\theta)$ are equal.

13. A reflector is attached to a spoke on a bicycle wheel. When the wheel rotates, the reflector is 4 inches above the ground at its lowest point and 22 inches above the ground at its highest point.

a. Write a rule for the function $h(t)$ that gives the height h (in inches) of the reflector at time t (in seconds) when the wheel rotates at a rate of 2 revolutions per second. Assume the following:

- The x-axis is at ground level.
- The y-axis passes through the center of the wheel.
- The reflector starts at the point (9, 13).

Note that the wheel rotates *clockwise*, so angles of rotation must be negative.

$h(t) = 9 \sin(-4\pi t) + 13$

b. Graph $h(t)$ on the interval $0 \le t \le 2$. Include labels and scales for the axes.

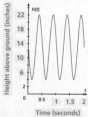

c. Suppose the wheel's rotational speed is increased to 3 revolutions per second. How must you alter the height function's rule? What effect does this change have on the function's graph?

$\sin(-4\pi t)$ becomes $\sin(-6\pi t)$ in the function's rule; the period decreases from $\frac{1}{2}$ to $\frac{1}{3}$ second.

UNIT 9

Sequences and Series

Unit Vocabulary

arithmetic sequence	(9-2)
common difference	(9-2)
common ratio	(9-3)
explicit rule	(9-1)
geometric sequence	(9-3)
geometric series	(9-4)
recursive rule	(9-1)
sequence	(9-1)
series	(9-4)
term	(9-1)

UNIT 9

Sequences and Series

Unit Focus

In this unit you will learn that a sequence is an ordered list of numbers and why every sequence is a function. In an arithmetic sequence, such as 4, 6, 8, 10, the difference between consecutive terms is constant. In a geometric sequence, such as 4, 8, 16, 32, the ratio of consecutive terms is constant. A series is an expression for the sum of the terms of a sequence. For example, the sequence 4, 6, 8, 10 can be used to form the series $4 + 6 + 8 + 10$, whose sum is 28. You will learn rules for finding a given term of a sequence and for finding the sum of a series, and you will model real-world situations using sequences and series, such as the minimum payment needed to pay off a car loan in five years.

Unit at a Glance

COMMON CORE

Lesson		Standards for Mathematical Content
9-1	Sequences	CC.9-12.F.IF.2, CC.9-12.F.IF.3, CC.9-12.F.BF.1*, CC.9-12.F.BF.1a*
9-2	Arithmetic Sequences	CC.9-12.F.BF.1*, CC.9-12.F.BF.1a*, CC.9-12.F.BF.2*, CC.9-12.F.LE.2*
9-3	Geometric Sequences	CC.9-12.F.BF.1*, CC.9-12.F.BF.1a*, CC.9-12.F.BF.2*, CC.9-12.F.LE.2*
9-4	Finite Geometric Series	CC.9-12.A.SSE.1*, CC.9-12.A.SSE.1a*, CC.9-12.A.SSE.1b*, CC.9-12.A.SSE.4
9-5	Modeling with Finite Geometric Series	CC.9-12.A.SSE.1*, CC.9-12.A.SSE.1a*, CC.9-12.A.SSE.1b*, CC.9-12.A.SSE.4, CC.9-12.A.CED.3*
	Test Prep	

UNIT 9

Unit 9   339   Sequences and Series

© Houghton Mifflin Harcourt Publishing Company

© Houghton Mifflin Harcourt Publishing Company

Unpacking the Common Core State Standards

Use the table to help you understand the Standards for Mathematical Content that are taught in this unit. Refer to the lessons listed after each standard for exploration and practice.

COMMON CORE **Standards for Mathematical Content**	**What It Means For You**
CC.9-12.A.SSE.1 Interpret expressions that represent a quantity in terms of its context.* **CC.9-12.A.SSE.1a Interpret parts of an expression, such as terms, factors, and coefficients.*** **CC.9-12.A.SSE.1b Interpret complicated expressions by viewing one or more of their parts as a single entity.*** Lessons 9-4, 9-5	You will write expressions that represent real-world quantities, such as $P(1 + r)^n$. In this expression, P represents the principal, or starting balance, for an account. The quantity $(1 + r)^n$ represents the growth of the account when interest is compounded at a rate r over n compounding periods.
CC.9-12.A.SSE.4 Derive the formula for the sum of a finite geometric series (when the common ratio is not 1), and use the formula to solve problems. Lessons 9-4, 9-5	A finite series expresses the addition of the terms in a finite sequence. You will learn how to develop and apply a formula for the sum of a finite geometric series.
CC.9-12.A.CED.3 Represent constraints by equations or inequalities, and by systems of equations and/or inequalities, and interpret solutions as viable or non-viable options in a modeling context.* Lesson 9-5	You will use a spreadsheet to determine what monthly payment you will have to make to pay off a car loan in a specified amount of time.
CC.9-12.F.IF.2 Use function notation, evaluate functions for inputs in their domains, and interpret statements that use function notation in terms of a context. Lesson 9-1	You will use function notation with sequences. The input is the position number of a term, and the output is the term.
CC.9-12.F.IF.3 Recognize that sequences are functions, sometimes defined recursively, whose domain is a subset of the integers. Lesson 9-1	You will learn about sequences such as the Fibonacci sequence: 1, 1, 2, 3, 5, 8, 13, …. This sequence can be defined recursively by relating terms to preceding terms.
CC.9-12.F.BF.1 Write a function that describes a relationship between two quantities.* **CC.9-12.F.BF.1a Determine an explicit expression, a recursive process, or steps for calculation from a context.*** Lessons 9-1, 9-2, 9-3	By thinking of sequences as functions, you will write both explicit and recursive rules for sequences that model real-world situations.
CC.9-12.F.BF.2 Write arithmetic and geometric sequences both recursively and with an explicit formula, use them to model situations, and translate between the two forms.* Lessons 9-2, 9-3	A recursive rule for a sequence defines each term in relation to previous terms. An explicit rule defines each term by its position in the sequence. You will learn to write and apply both types of rules.
CC.9-12.F.LE.2 Construct linear and exponential functions, including arithmetic and geometric sequences, given a graph, a description of a relationship, or two input-output pairs (include reading these from a table).* Lessons 9-2, 9-3	You will learn that arithmetic sequences are linear functions and geometric sequences are exponential functions. You will apply what you know about linear and exponential functions to your study of sequences.

Unit 9   340   Sequences and Series

Unpacking the Common Core State Standards

This page lists and explains the Standards for Mathematical Content that are addressed in this unit. For information about the Standards for Mathematical Practice, which are integrated throughout the text, see Teacher Edition pages x–xiii.

Notes

Sequences

Essential question: *Why is a sequence a function?*

COMMON CORE

Standards for Mathematical Content

CC.9-12.F.IF.2 Use function notation, evaluate functions for inputs in their domains, and interpret statements that use function notation in terms of a context.

CC.9-12.F.IF.3 Recognize that sequences are functions, sometimes defined recursively, whose domain is a subset of the integers.

CC.9-12.F.BF.1 Write a function that describes a relationship between two quantities.*

CC.9-12.F.BF.1a Determine an explicit expression, a recursive process ... from a context.*

Vocabulary

sequence

term

explicit rule

recursive rule

Prerequisites

Discrete linear functions, Algebra 1

Discrete exponential functions, Algebra 1

Math Background

Students are familiar with the concept of functions and know that a function assigns exactly one output to each input. Students understand that a function has a domain and a range, and they have previously evaluated functions for inputs in their domains. Students have also written functions for real-world situations, and understand the use of function notation to both interpret and express statements in terms of a context.

INTRODUCE

Review the basics of functions by using function notation in all explanations. Make sure that students understand that each input of a function is associated with exactly one output. Review the concepts of domain and range by again focusing on the relationship between input and output values.

Give examples of functions for which the domain is restricted, in particular where the domain is the set of integers, and have students evaluate functions for given values of the domain.

TEACH

1 ENGAGE

Questioning Strategies

- Can a sequence with repeating terms, such as 1, 1, 2, 2, 3, 3, ..., be a function? **Yes, the domain of the function is the set of position numbers, and the set of terms is the range. Values can be repeated in the range of a function.**

- Predict the next term in the sequence $\frac{1}{8}, \frac{1}{4}, \frac{3}{8}, \frac{1}{2}, \frac{5}{8}, ...$ Explain your reasoning. $\frac{3}{4}$; **Each term is $\frac{1}{8}$ more than the previous term, so the next term is $\frac{1}{8}$ more than $\frac{5}{8}$.**

Teaching Strategy

Reinforce the concept that a sequence is a function by emphasizing the domain and range of a sequence. Write the positive integers 1, 2, 3, and so on across the top of the board in front of the class. Explain that, for a sequence, the positive integers correspond to the positions of the terms in the sequence. Then, have students write the terms of the sequence 1, 3, 5, 7, 9, ... directly below the position numbers and draw arrows between each position number and its corresponding term. Identify the position numbers as the domain and the terms as the range; then, ask students to use what they know about relations to explain why this particular relation is a function.

Point out that position numbers can be consecutive integers that start at some number other than 1. A common alternative starting position number is 0. Regardless of what starting position number is used, a sequence is still a function. Students, however, must be careful when using function notation to identify the terms of a sequence. For the sequence 2, 4, 6, 8, ..., for instance, $f(3) = 6$ when the starting position number is 1, but $f(3) = 8$ when the starting position number is 0.

Name_____ Class_____ Date_____

9-1

Sequences

Essential question: *Why is a sequence a function?*

COMMON CORE
CC.9-12.F.IF.2,
CC.9-12.F.IF.3,
CC.9-12.F.BF.1*,
CC.9-12.F.BF.1a*

1 ENGAGE · Understanding Sequences

A **sequence** is an ordered list of numbers or other items. Each element in a sequence is called a **term**. For instance, in the sequence 1, 3, 5, 7, 9, …, the second term is 3.

Each term in a sequence can be paired with a position number, and these pairings establish a function whose domain is the set of position numbers and whose range is the set of terms, as illustrated below. The position numbers are consecutive integers that typically start at either 1 or 0.

Position number	n	1	2	3	4	5	Domain
Term of sequence	$f(n)$	1	3	5	7	9	Range

For the sequence shown in the table, you can write $f(4) = 7$, which can be interpreted as "the fourth term of the sequence is 7."

REFLECT

1a. The domain of the function f defining the sequence 2, 5, 8, 11, 14, … is the set of consecutive integers starting with 0. What is $f(4)$? Explain how you determined your answer.

14; because the domain starts with 0, $f(4)$ is the fifth term of the sequence, which is 14.

1b. How does your answer to Question 1a change if the domain of the function is the set of consecutive integers starting with 1?

Now $f(4)$ represents the fourth term of the sequence, which is 11.

1c. Predict the next term in the sequence 48, 42, 36, 30, 24, …. Explain your reasoning.

Sample answer: 18; each term is 6 less than the previous term, so the next term will be 6 less than 24.

1d. Why is the relationship between the position numbers and the terms of a sequence a function?

Each position number corresponds to exactly one term.

1e. Give an example of a sequence from your everyday life. Explain why your example represents a sequence.

Sample answer: The numbers of my combination lock (24, 8, 44) form a sequence. The numbers are a sequence because their order matters.

Some numerical sequences can be described by using algebraic rules. An **explicit rule** for a sequence defines the nth term as a function of n.

2 EXAMPLE · Using an Explicit Rule to Generate a Sequence

Write the first 4 terms of the sequence $f(n) = n^2 + 1$. Assume that the domain of the function is the set of consecutive integers starting with 1.

n	$n^2 + 1$	$f(n)$
1	$1^2 + 1 = 1 + 1$	2
2	$2^2 + 1 = 4 + 1$	5
3	$3^2 + 1 = 9 + 1$	10
4	$4^2 + 1 = 16 + 1$	17

The first 4 terms are ___2, 5, 10, and 17___

REFLECT

2a. How could you use a graphing calculator to check your answer?

Sample answer: Enter the equation $y = x^2 + 1$ and make a table.

2b. Explain how to find the 20th term of the sequence.

Evaluate $n^2 + 1$ for $n = 20$; $f(20) = 401$.

A **recursive rule** for a sequence defines the nth term by relating it to one or more previous terms.

3 EXAMPLE · Using a Recursive Rule to Generate a Sequence

Write the first 4 terms of the sequence with $f(1) = 3$ and $f(n) = f(n - 1) + 2$ for $n \geq 2$. Assume that the domain of the function is the set of consecutive integers starting with 1.

The first term is given: $f(1) = 3$. Use $f(1)$ to find $f(2)$, $f(2)$ to find $f(3)$, and so on. In general, $f(n - 1)$ refers to the term that precedes $f(n)$.

n	$f(n - 1) + 2$	$f(n)$
2	$f(2 - 1) + 2 = f(1) + 2 = 3 + 2$	5
3	$f(3 - 1) + 2 = f(2) + 2 = 5 + 2$	7
4	$f(4 - 1) + 2 = f(3) + 2 = 7 + 2$	9

The first 4 terms are ___3, 5, 7, and 9___

Questioning Strategies

- What is the fifth term of $f(n) = n^2 + 1$? 26

- What sequence is generated by the rule $f(n) = 3n$ when the domain is the set of consecutive integers starting with 1? Explain your reasoning. **The sequence generated is 3, 6, 9, 12, …; each term is three times the corresponding position number.**

- What is the tenth term of the sequence $f(n) = 3n$ when the domain is the set of consecutive integers starting with 1? Explain how to find it. **30; evaluate $3n$ for $n = 10$.**

Avoid Common Errors

Be sure students pay attention to the domain of the function that defines a sequence. While 1 is typically used as the first number in the domain, some other number (typically 0) can be used instead. A change in the function's inputs will result in a change in the function's outputs, thereby creating a different sequence. For instance, if the domain of $f(n) = n^2 + 1$ is $\{0, 1, 2, 3, …\}$ rather than $\{1, 2, 3, 4, …\}$, then the function generates the sequence 1, 2, 5, 10, … rather than the sequence 2, 5, 10, 17, … .

EXTRA EXAMPLE

Write the first four terms of the sequence $f(n) = n^3 + 1$. Assume that the domain of the function is the set of consecutive integers starting with 1. **The first four terms are 2, 9, 28, and 65.**

3 EXAMPLE

Questioning Strategies

- Is it possible to generate the second term of the sequence $f(n) = f(n-1) + 2$ without knowing that $f(1) = 3$? Explain. **No; since the second term is calculated by using the term before it, it is necessary to know the first term.**

- How is the sequence $f(n) = 3n$ related to the sequence $f(1) = 3$ and $f(n) = f(n-1) + 3$ for $n \geq 2$? **Both rules generate the same sequence: 3, 6, 9, 12, ….**

- If you know only that the rule for the sequence is $f(n) = f(n-1) + 2$ and that $f(4) = 9$, is it possible to determine that $f(1) = 3$? **Yes, if you know that $f(4) = 9$, the recursive rule tells you that adding 2 to $f(3)$ gives $f(4)$, so $f(3)$ is 7. Again, the recursive rule tells you that adding 2 to $f(2)$ gives $f(3)$, so $f(2)$ is 5. Finally, the recursive rule tells you that adding 2 to $f(1)$ gives $f(2)$, so $f(1) = 3$.**

Differentiated Instruction

Visual learners may benefit by drawing diagrams that illustrate how the nth term of a sequence with a recursive rule is generated by the terms that come before it. Students can use arrows to show how previous terms become the inputs to generate the terms that follow.

MATHEMATICAL PRACTICE — Highlighting the Standards

3 EXAMPLE and its Reflect questions offer an opportunity to address Mathematical Practice Standard 7 (Look for and make use of structure). Students explore the concept of a recursive rule as they generate each term of a sequence by referencing a term or terms that came before it. Students must interpret sequence rules expressed using function notation in the context of recursion. As they use a recursive rule to generate a sequence and find a specific term in the sequence, students must understand the structure of a function that is defined in terms of itself.

EXTRA EXAMPLE

Write the first four terms of the sequence with $f(1) = 2$ and $f(n) = f(n-1) + 3$ for $n \geq 2$. Assume that the domain of the function is the set of consecutive integers starting with 1. **The first four terms are 2, 5, 8, and 11.**

REFLECT

3a. Describe how to find the 12th term of the sequence.

Add 2 to the 11th term of the sequence.

3b. Suppose you want to find the 50th term of a sequence. Would you rather use a recursive rule or an explicit rule? Explain your reasoning.

Sample answer: explicit; with an explicit rule, you can calculate the 50th term

directly; with a recursive rule, you have to find the first 49 terms before you

can find the 50th term.

4 EXAMPLE Modeling a Sequence

A male honeybee has one female parent, and a female honeybee has one male and one female parent. In the diagram below, a male honeybee is represented by M in row 1. His parent is represented by F in row 2. Her parents are represented by M and F in row 3, and so on. Write a recursive rule for a sequence that describes the number of bees in each row.

A Extend the diagram to show rows 5, 6, and 7.

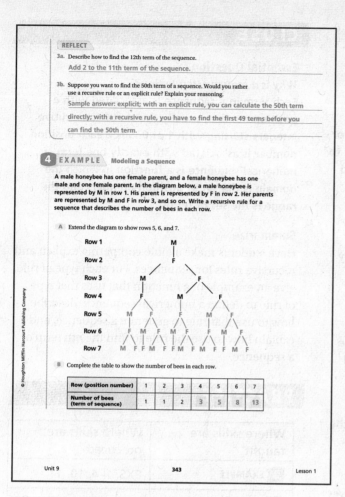

B Complete the table to show the number of bees in each row.

Row (position number)	1	2	3	4	5	6	7
Number of bees (term of sequence)	1	1	2	3	5	8	13

C Write a recursive rule for the sequence in the table. Assume that the domain of the function is the set of consecutive integers starting with 1.

* First, write the rule in words.

The first two terms are both ___1___. Every other term is the ___sum___ of the previous two terms.

* Then, write the rule algebraically.

$f(1) = f(2) =$ __1__ and

$f(n) = f(n - $ __1__ $) + f(n - 2)$ for $n \geq$ __3__

The first and second terms are both 1.

Each successive term is the sum of the preceding two terms.

REFLECT

4a. If you continued the pattern in the diagram, how many bees would be in the 8th row? Explain how you determined your answer.

21; add the numbers of bees in the 7th and 6th rows: 13 + 8 = 21.

4b. The sequence given in the table, 1, 1, 2, 3, 5, 8, 13, ..., is called the Fibonacci sequence. An explicit rule for the Fibonacci sequence is $f(n) = \frac{1}{\sqrt{5}}\left(\frac{1 + \sqrt{5}}{2}\right)^n - \frac{1}{\sqrt{5}}\left(\frac{1 - \sqrt{5}}{2}\right)^n$ where the values of n are consecutive integers starting with 1. Use the explicit rule to show that $f(1) = 1$. Then use a calculator and the explicit rule to find the 9th term of the Fibonacci sequence.

$\frac{1}{\sqrt{5}}\left(\frac{1 + \sqrt{5}}{2}\right) - \frac{1}{\sqrt{5}}\left(\frac{1 - \sqrt{5}}{2}\right) = \frac{1 + \sqrt{5} - (1 - \sqrt{5})}{2\sqrt{5}} = \frac{2\sqrt{5}}{2\sqrt{5}} = 1; 34$

4c. Now use the recursive rule to find the 9th term of the Fibonacci sequence. Does your result agree with the result from the explicit rule?

$f(9) = f(8) + f(7) = 21 + 13 = 34$; yes

4d. Which rule for the Fibonacci sequence would be easier to use if you did not have a calculator? Explain.

Sample answer: recursive; to find terms using the recursive rule, you only need to

add whole numbers, but to find terms using the explicit rule, you have to perform

operations with radical expressions.

4e. The number of petals on many flowers is equal to a *Fibonacci number*, that is, one of the terms in the Fibonacci sequence. Based on this fact, is a flower more likely to have 20 petals or 21 petals? Explain.

21; 21 is a Fibonacci number, but 20 is not.

Questioning Strategies

- Why is the condition $n \geq 3$ imposed on $f(n) = f(n-1) + f(n-2)$ in the rule for generating the Fibonacci sequence? Since the first two terms are given, this part of the rule for generating the Fibonacci sequence is used only to generate the terms for $n \geq 3$, which is the third term and beyond.

- When writing the explicit rule
$f(n) = \frac{1}{\sqrt{5}}\left(\frac{1+\sqrt{5}}{2}\right)^n - \frac{1}{\sqrt{5}}\left(\frac{1-\sqrt{5}}{2}\right)^n$ to generate the Fibonacci sequence, is it necessary to also include $f(1) = 1$ and $f(2) = 1$ as part of the rule? No, when an explicit rule is used to generate a sequence, each term is a function of the position number, not the term before it. So, when using the explicit rule to generate the Fibonacci sequence, $f(1)$ and $f(2)$ are generated by the explicit rule.

Teaching Strategy

Students may be interested to learn more about the Fibonacci sequence. Encourage them to research the origins of Fibonacci numbers and the many ways in which the sequence appears in nature. In addition to bee reproduction and patterns of flower petals, the Fibonacci sequence has also been seen in other natural patterns, such as the branchings of trees, the arrangement of petals, leaves, and seed heads on plants, and the spirals of seashells. Students may be interested to learn that there is an academic journal devoted solely to the study of the Fibonacci sequence.

EXTRA EXAMPLE

The first two terms of a sequence are both 2. Every other term is the sum of the previous two terms. Write a recursive rule for the sequence.
$f(1) = f(2) = 2$ and $f(n) = f(n-1) + f(n-2)$ for $n \geq 3$

CLOSE

Essential Question

Why is a sequence a function?
Each term in a sequence is associated with a position number, usually the set of consecutive integers starting with 1 or 0. Since each position number is associated with exactly one term, a numerical sequence is a function in which the domain is the set of position numbers and the range is the set of terms.

Summarize

Have students make a table comparing explicit and recursive rules for sequences. For each type of rule, give an example of a function that uses that type of rule to define a numerical sequence, describe how to use that rule to generate a sequence, and explain how to use the rule to find the nth term of a sequence.

PRACTICE

Where skills are taught	Where skills are practiced
2 EXAMPLE	EXS. 1–4, 10, 11
3 EXAMPLE	EXS. 5–8
4 EXAMPLE	EXS. 9, 12

Exercises 13–15: Given a table that represents a function, students write an explicit rule for the sequence defined by the function.

Exercises 16–18: Given a table that represents a function, students write a recursive rule for the sequence defined by the function.

PRACTICE

Write the first four terms of each sequence. Assume that the domain of the function is the set of consecutive integers starting with 1.

1. $f(n) = (n-1)^2$

_0, 1, 4, 9_

2. $f(n) = \frac{n+1}{n+3}$

$\frac{1}{2}, \frac{3}{5}, \frac{2}{3}, \frac{5}{7}$

3. $f(n) = 4(0.5)^n$

_2, 1, 0.5, 0.25_

4. $f(n) = \sqrt{n-1}$

0, 1, $\sqrt{2}$, $\sqrt{3}$

5. $f(1) = 2$ and $f(n) = f(n-1) + 10$ for $n \geq 2$ _2, 12, 22, 32_

6. $f(1) = 16$ and $f(n) = \frac{1}{2}f(n-1)$ for $n \geq 2$ _16, 8, 4, 2_

7. $f(1) = 1$ and $f(n) = 2f(n-1) + 1$ for $n \geq 2$ _1, 3, 7, 15_

8. $f(1) = f(2) = 1$ and $f(n) = f(n-2) - f(n-1)$ for $n \geq 3$ _1, 1, 0, -1_

9. Each year for the past 4 years, Donna has gotten a raise equal to 5% of the previous year's salary. Her starting salary was $40,000.

a. Complete the table to show Donna's salary over time.

b. Write a recursive rule for the sequence in the table. Assume that the domain of the function is the set of consecutive integers starting with 0, so the first term of the sequence is $f(0)$.

$f(0) = 40,000$ and $f(n) = 1.05f(n-1)$ for

$n \geq 1$

Year (position number)	Salary ($) (term of sequence)
0	40,000
1	42,000
2	44,100
3	46,305
4	48,620.25

c. What is $f(7)$, rounded to the nearest whole number? What does $f(7)$ represent in this situation?

56,284; Donna's salary 7 years after she began working if she keeps getting the

same raise each year

Write the 12th term of each sequence. Assume that the domain of the function is the set of consecutive integers starting with 1.

10. $f(n) = 3n - 2$ _34_

11. $f(n) = 2n(n+1)$ _312_

---

12. The diagram shows the first four figures in a pattern of dots.

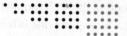

a. Draw the next figure in the pattern.

b. Use the pattern to complete the table.

c. Write an explicit rule for the sequence in the table. Assume that the domain of the function is the set of consecutive integers starting with 1.

_$f(n) = n^2$_

d. How many dots will be in the 10th figure of the pattern?

_100_

Figure (position number)	Number of dots (term of sequence)
1	1
2	4
3	9
4	16
5	25

Write an explicit rule for each sequence. Assume that the domain of the function is the set of consecutive integers starting with 1.

13.

n	f(n)
1	6
2	7
3	8
4	9
5	10

_$f(n) = n + 5$_

14.

n	f(n)
1	3
2	6
3	9
4	12
5	15

_$f(n) = 3n$_

15.

n	f(n)
1	1
2	$\frac{1}{2}$
3	$\frac{1}{3}$
4	$\frac{1}{4}$
5	$\frac{1}{5}$

$f(n) = \frac{1}{n}$

Write a recursive rule for each sequence. Assume that the domain of the function is the set of consecutive integers starting with 1.

16.

n	f(n)
1	8
2	9
3	10
4	11
5	12

$f(1) = 8$ and $f(n) =$

$f(n-1) + 1$ for $n \geq 2$

17.

n	f(n)
1	2
2	4
3	8
4	16
5	32

$f(1) = 2$ and $f(n) =$

$2f(n-1)$ for $n \geq 2$

18.

n	f(n)
1	27
2	24
3	21
4	18
5	15

$f(1) = 27$ and $f(n) =$

$f(n-1) - 3$ for $n \geq 2$

Arithmetic Sequences

Essential question: *How can you write a rule for an arithmetic sequence?*

© Houghton Mifflin Harcourt Publishing Company

:::: COMMON
:::: CORE
Standards for Mathematical Content

CC.9-12.F.BF.1 Write a function that describes a relationship between two quantities.*

CC.9-12.F.BF.1a Determine an explicit expression, a recursive process ... from a context.*

CC.9-12.F.BF.2 Write arithmetic ... sequences both recursively and with an explicit formula, use them to model situations, and translate between the two forms.*

CC.9-12.F.LE.2 Construct linear ... functions, including arithmetic ... sequences, given a graph, a description of a relationship, or two input-output pairs (include reading these from a table).*

Vocabulary

arithmetic sequence

common difference

Prerequisites

Sequences, Lesson 9-1

Math Background

In Lesson 9-1, students became familiar with sequences and learned to use functions to define sequences. Many of the sequences students explored in Lesson 9-1 were arithmetic sequences, although the sequences were not defined as such.

INTRODUCE

Review the basic concepts about sequences that students learned in Lesson 9-1. Remind students that sequences are defined by functions, emphasizing how the domain and range of a function are related to the position numbers and terms of a sequence. Review the distinction between recursive and explicit rules.

TEACH

 EXAMPLE

Questioning Strategies

- What would be the meaning in the context of the situation if $f(1)$ was equal to 20 instead of 60 in the recursive rule? **It would mean that the starting balance was $20.**

- In part C, why does the explicit rule for the sequence involve multiplying the common difference by $n - 1$ and not n? **Month 1 ($n = 1$) represents the initial account balance, $60. A monthly deposit of $20 (the common difference) is made starting with month 2 ($n = 2$). So, the explicit rule must generate the sequence $f(1) = 60 + 0 \cdot 20$, $f(2) = 60 + 1 \cdot 20$, $f(3) = 60 + 2 \cdot 20$, ... The number of 20s added to 60 is always 1 less than the month number.**

- Which rule, the recursive rule or the explicit rule, would be more useful in determining the balance at the end of the 45th month? Explain your reasoning. **The explicit rule is more useful because you can easily evaluate $f(45) = 940$ to find the balance at the end of the 45th month. To use the recursive rule, you would have to start with $f(1)$ and calculate the balance for each successive month up to month 45.**

Differentiated Instruction

Kinesthetic learners may benefit by acting out the situation using counters to represent the money in the account.

EXTRA EXAMPLE

The table shows end-of-month balances in a bank account that does not earn interest. Write a recursive rule and an explicit rule for the arithmetic sequence described by the table.

Month	n	1	2	3	4	5
Account Balance ($)	$f(n)$	50	80	110	140	170

$f(1) = 50$ and $f(n) = f(n - 1) + 30$ for $n \geq 2$;
$f(n) = 50 + 30(n - 1)$

Name_____ Class_____ Date_____

Arithmetic Sequences

Essential question: *How can you write a rule for an arithmetic sequence?*

COMMON
CORE

In an **arithmetic sequence**, the difference between consecutive terms is constant. The constant difference is called the **common difference**, often written as *d*.

CC-9-12.F.BF.1*
CC-9-12.F.BF.1a*
CC-9-12.F.BF.2*
CC-9-12.F.LE.2*

1 EXAMPLE Writing Rules for an Arithmetic Sequence

The table shows end-of-month balances in a bank account that does not earn interest. Write a recursive and an explicit rule for the arithmetic sequence described by the table.

Month	*n*	1	2	3	4	5
Account Balance ($)	*f(n)*	60	80	100	120	140

A Find the common difference by calculating the differences between consecutive terms.

$80 - 60 = 20$

$100 - 80 = 20$

$120 - 100 = 20$

$140 - 120 = 20$

The common difference, *d*, is ___20___.

B Write a recursive rule for the sequence.

$f(1) = 60$ and

The first term is ___60___.

$f(n) = f(n-1) + 20$ for $n \geq 2$

Every other term is the __sum__ of the previous term and the common difference.

C Write an explicit rule for the sequence by writing each term as the sum of the first term and a multiple of the common difference.

n	*f(n)*
1	$60 + 20(0) = 60$
2	$60 + 20(1) = 80$
3	$60 + 20(\boxed{2}) = 100$
4	$60 + 20(\boxed{3}) = 120$
5	$60 + 20(\boxed{4}) = 140$

Generalize the results from the table: $f(n) = \boxed{60} + 20(\boxed{n-1})$

Unit 9   347   Lesson 2

© Houghton Mifflin Harcourt Publishing Company

REFLECT

1a. Explain how you know that the sequence 1, 2, 4, 8, 16, ... is not an arithmetic sequence.

The differences between consecutive terms are not constant.

1b. An arithmetic sequence has a common difference of 3. If you know that the third term of the sequence is 15, how can you find the fourth term?

Add the common difference to the third term to get 18 as the fourth term.

2 EXPLORE Writing General Rules for Arithmetic Sequences

Use the arithmetic sequence 6, 9, 12, 15, 18, ... to help you write a recursive rule and an explicit rule for any arithmetic sequence. For the general rules, the values of *n* are consecutive integers starting with 1.

A Find the common difference.

Numbers

6, 9, 12, 15, 18, ...

Common difference = __3__

Algebra

$f(1), f(2), f(3), \boxed{f(4)}, \boxed{f(5)}, ...$

Common difference = *d*

B Write a recursive rule.

Numbers

$f(1) = \boxed{6}$ and

$f(n) = f(n-1) + \boxed{3}$ for $n \geq 2$

Algebra

Given $f(1)$,

$f(n) = f(n-1) + \boxed{d}$ for $n \geq 2$

C Write an explicit rule.

Numbers

$f(n) = \boxed{6} + \boxed{3}(n-1)$

Algebra

$f(n) = f(1) + \boxed{d}(n-1)$

REFLECT

2a. The first term of an arithmetic sequence is 4 and the common difference is 10. Explain how you can find the 6th term of the sequence.

Evaluate the explicit rule for an arithmetic sequence when *n* = 6:

$f(6) = 4 + 10(6-1) = 54.$

2b. What information do you need to know in order to find the 8th term of an arithmetic sequence by using its recursive rule?

The 7th term and the common difference

2c. What is the recursive rule for the sequence $f(n) = 2 + (-3)(n-1)$?

$f(1) = 2$ and $f(n) = f(n-1) - 3$ for $n \geq 2$

Unit 9   348   Lesson 2

© Houghton Mifflin Harcourt Publishing Company

Questioning Strategies

- What is a recursive rule for an arithmetic sequence with a first term of 10 and a common difference of -4?
  $f(1) = 10$ and $f(n) = f(n-1) - 4$ for $n \geq 2$

- What is an explicit rule for an arithmetic sequence with a first term of $\frac{1}{2}$ and a common difference of $\frac{3}{4}$? $f(n) = \frac{1}{2} + \frac{3}{4}(n-1)$

- If you know the second term and the common difference of an arithmetic sequence, can you write an explicit rule for the sequence? If so, explain how. Yes; you can subtract the common difference from the second term to get the first term. Then, you can substitute the first term and the common difference into the general explicit rule to get the explicit rule for the sequence.

Teaching Strategy

After students have written the general algebraic formulas for recursive and explicit rules for arithmetic sequences, review the process for substituting values for variables in a formula. In both the general recursive and explicit rules, values must be inserted for $f(1)$, the first term in the sequence, and d, the common difference. Remind students that the qualification $n \geq 2$ must be included in the recursive rule and guide students to understand why this is the case. Also, point out that the common difference d is added to $f(n-1)$ in the recursive rule, while d is multiplied by $n-1$ in the explicit rule.

:::
MATHEMATICAL PRACTICE   **Highlighting the Standards**

2 EXPLORE and its Reflect questions address Mathematical Practice Standard 2 (Reason abstractly and quantitatively). Students use a specific arithmetic sequence to help them obtain general rules, both recursive and explicit, for arithmetic sequences. They can then use the general rules to obtain rules for other specific arithmetic sequences and to transform a rule given in one form into the other form (recursive to explicit or explicit to recursive).
:::

Questioning Strategies

- How is the domain of a linear function restricted if the function defines an arithmetic sequence? The domain is restricted to a subset of the set of integers.

- Why is the slope of a linear function that defines an arithmetic sequence equal to the common difference of the arithmetic sequence? The slope of a linear function describes the vertical change for 1 unit of horizontal change in the graph of the function. If 1 unit of horizontal change corresponds to a change of 1 in the position number for the sequence, then the vertical change corresponds to the common difference between two terms.

Differentiated Instruction

Visual learners may benefit by enhancing the graph in **3 EXAMPLE** . For instance, by drawing arrows to identify rise and run, students may be able to more clearly see the relationship between the slope of the linear function and the common difference of the arithmetic sequence.

EXTRA EXAMPLE

If the points plotted on the graph in **3 EXAMPLE** were changed to $(1, 25)$, $(2, 75)$, $(3, 125)$, and $(4, 175)$, what explicit rule would you write for the sequence shown in the graph?
$f(n) = 25 + 50(n-1)$

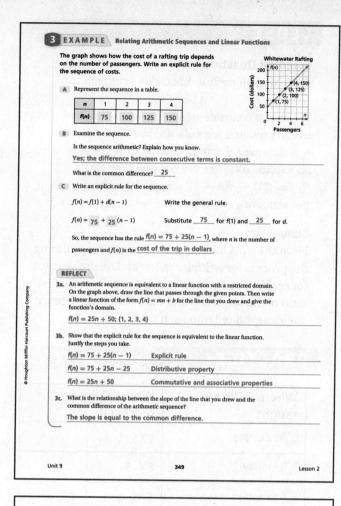

3 EXAMPLE Relating Arithmetic Sequences and Linear Functions

The graph shows how the cost of a rafting trip depends on the number of passengers. Write an explicit rule for the sequence of costs.

A Represent the sequence in a table.

n	1	2	3	4
$f(n)$	75	100	125	150

Whitewater Rafting

(4, 150)
(3, 125)
(2, 100)
(1, 75)

Cost (dollars) vs Passengers

B Examine the sequence.

Is the sequence arithmetic? Explain how you know.

Yes; the difference between consecutive terms is constant.

What is the common difference? __25__

C Write an explicit rule for the sequence.

$f(n) = f(1) + d(n-1)$ Write the general rule.

$f(n) = 75 + 25(n-1)$ Substitute __75__ for $f(1)$ and __25__ for d.

So, the sequence has the rule $f(n) = 75 + 25(n-1)$, where n is the number of passengers and $f(n)$ is the cost of the trip in dollars.

REFLECT

3a. An arithmetic sequence is equivalent to a linear function with a restricted domain. On the graph above, draw the line that passes through the given points. Then write a linear function of the form $f(n) = mn + b$ for the line that you drew and give the function's domain.

$f(n) = 25n + 50; \{1, 2, 3, 4\}$

3b. Show that the explicit rule for the sequence is equivalent to the linear function. Justify the steps you take.

$f(n) = 75 + 25(n-1)$ Explicit rule

$f(n) = 75 + 25n - 25$ Distributive property

$f(n) = 25n + 50$ Commutative and associative properties

3c. What is the relationship between the slope of the line that you drew and the common difference of the arithmetic sequence?

The slope is equal to the common difference.

© Houghton Mifflin Harcourt Publishing Company

Subscript Notation You have used function notation to describe sequences. You can also describe sequences by using subscript notation. In subscript notation, a_n represents the nth term of the sequence. For example, $a_5 = 8$ means that the 5th term of a sequence is 8.

The explicit rule for an arithmetic sequence using subscript notation is $a_n = a_1 + d(n-1)$.

4 EXAMPLE Writing an Arithmetic Sequence Given Two Terms

Each day Xavier waters his plants using water from a rain barrel. On May 6, the barrel held 45 gallons of water, and on May 11, the barrel held 30 gallons of water.

The amount of water in the barrel over time is an arithmetic sequence where a_n is the number of gallons on the nth day in May. Write an explicit rule for the sequence using subscript notation.

A Identify the given terms in the sequence.

$a_6 = 45$ There were 45 gallons in May 6, so the 6th term of the sequence is 45.

$a_{11} = 30$ There were 30 gallons in May 11, so the __11th__ term of the sequence is __30__.

B Find the common difference.

The common difference is equal to the slope of the related linear function.

$m = \frac{y_2 - y_1}{x_2 - x_1}$ Slope formula

$m = \frac{30 - 45}{11 - 6}$ Use (6, 45) for (x_1, y_1) and (11, 30) for (x_2, y_2).

$m = -3$ Simplify.

The common difference is __−3__.

C Find the first term of the sequence.

$a_n = a_1 + d(n-1)$ Write the explicit rule.

$45 = a_1 + -3\left(6 - 1\right)$ Substitute 45 for a_n, 6 for n, and __−3__ for d.

$45 = a_1 + -15$ Simplify.

$60 = a_1$ Solve for a_1.

D Write the explicit rule.

$a_n = a_1 + d(n-1)$ Write the general rule.

$a_n = 60 + -3(n-1)$ Substitute __60__ for a_1 and __−3__ for d.

© Houghton Mifflin Harcourt Publishing Company

Questioning Strategies

- How is an explicit rule for an arithmetic sequence written using function notation related to an explicit rule for an arithmetic sequence written using subscript notation? When position numbers start with 1, the variable n is used in both notations to represent the nth term of the sequence, which in both cases is found by adding the first term to the product of $(n - 1)$ and the common difference.

- How can you determine by what number of gallons the amount of water in the rain barrel increases or decreases each day? Since the common difference is -3, this tells you that the amount of water in the rain barrel decreases by 3 gallons each day.

- How can you find how much water is in the rain barrel on May 13? Evaluate the explicit rule for $n = 13$: $a_{13} = 60 + (-3)(13 - 1) = 24$. There are 24 gallons of water in the rain barrel on May 13.

- What is the recursive rule for the arithmetic sequence that describes the amount of water in the rain barrel over time? $a_1 = 60$ and $a_n = a_{n-1} - 3$ for $n \geq 2$

Avoid Common Errors

Students may use the wrong sign in rules for arithmetic sequences when the common difference is a negative number. Remind students that the common difference is the difference between a term and the one *before* it, and this difference will be negative if a term is less than the one before it.

EXTRA EXAMPLE

What would be the explicit rule for the sequence in **4** EXAMPLE if on May 5 the barrel held 50 gallons of water and on May 15 the barrel held 30 gallons of water? $a_n = 58 + (-2)(n - 1)$

Essential Question

How can you write a rule for an arithmetic sequence?

To write a recursive rule, assume $f(1)$ is given and use the general formula $f(n) = f(n - 1) + d$ for $n \geq 2$, where d is the common difference. To write an explicit rule, use the general formula $f(n) = f(1) + d(n - 1)$, where $f(1)$ is the first term in the sequence and d is the common difference.

Summarize

Have students make a graphic organizer outlining the process for writing explicit and recursive rules for sequences. Include details about how the first term of the sequence and the common difference are incorporated into each rule.

PRACTICE

Where skills are taught	Where skills are practiced
1 EXAMPLE	EXS. 1–4
3 EXAMPLE	EX. 5
4 EXAMPLE	EXS. 6–8

Exercises 9–12: Given a rule for an arithmetic sequence, students write a recursive rule as an explicit rule, or an explicit rule as a recursive rule.

Exercise 13: Students write an explicit rule for an arithmetic sequence to solve a problem that involves finding the nth term of the sequence.

REFLECT

4a. Why does it make sense that the common difference is negative in this situation?

The amount of water decreased from May 6 to May 11. A decrease

indicates that an amount is being subtracted, so the common difference

will be negative.

4b. Explain how you could determine when the rain barrel will be empty (assuming no more water is added to the barrel).

Find n when $f(n) = 0$. Solve the equation $0 = 60 + (-3)(n - 1)$ to get $n = 21$.

The barrel will be empty on May 21.

PRACTICE

Write a recursive rule and an explicit rule for each arithmetic sequence.

1. 3, 7, 11, 15, …

$f(1) = 3$ and $f(n) = f(n - 1) + 4$ for $n \geq 2$; $f(n) = 3 + 4(n - 1)$

2. 19, 9, −1, −11, …

$f(1) = 19$ and $f(n) = f(n - 1) - 10$ for $n \geq 2$; $f(n) = 19 + (-10)(n - 1)$

3. $1, \frac{5}{2}, 4, \frac{11}{2}, \ldots$

$f(1) = 1$ and $f(n) = f(n - 1) + \frac{3}{2}$ for $n \geq 2$; $f(n) = 1 + \frac{3}{2}(n - 1)$

4. Carrie borrowed money interest-free to pay for a car repair. She is repaying the loan in equal monthly payments.

Monthly Payment Number	n	1	2	3	4	5
Loan Balance ($)	$f(n)$	840	720	600	480	360

a. Explain how you know that the sequence of loan balances is arithmetic.

The difference between consecutive loan balances is a constant, −120.

b. Write recursive and explicit rules for the sequence of loan balances.

$f(1) = 840$ and $f(n) = f(n - 1) - 120$ for $n \geq 2$; $f(n) = 840 + (-120)(n - 1)$

c. How many months will it take Carrie to pay off the loan? Explain.

8 months; $f(8) = 0$, so the 8th payment brings the loan balance to 0.

d. How much did Carrie borrow? Explain.

$960; the initial balance is $f(0) = 960$.

5. The graph shows the lengths of the rows formed by various numbers of grocery carts when they are nested together.

a. Write an explicit rule for the sequence of row lengths.

$f(n) = 38 + 12(n - 1)$

b. What is the length of a row of 25 nested carts?

326 inches, or 27 feet 2 inches

Nested Grocery Carts

6. Jen is planting beans on a triangular plot of ground. The numbers of beans in each row form an arithmetic sequence where a_n is the number of beans in row n.

a. She plants 7 beans in the second row and 22 beans in the seventh row. Write an explicit rule for the sequence using subscript notation.

$a_n = 4 + 3(n - 1)$

b. How many beans does she plant in the fifth row? 16

Write an explicit rule for each arithmetic sequence based on the given terms from the sequence.

7. $a_3 = 30$ and $a_9 = 78$

$a_n = 14 + 8(n - 1)$

8. $a_5 = 8.8$ and $a_7 = 8.4$

$a_n = 9.6 + (-0.2)(n - 1)$

Each given rule represents an arithmetic sequence. If the given rule is recursive, write it as an explicit rule. If the given rule is explicit, write it as a recursive rule. Assume that $f(1)$ is the first term of the sequence.

9. $f(n) = 6 + 5(n - 1)$

$f(1) = 6$; $f(n) = f(n - 1) + 5$ for $n \geq 2$

10. $a_n = 2.5 + (-4)(n - 1)$

$a_1 = 2.5$; $a_n = a_{n-1} - 4$ for $n \geq 2$

11. $f(1) = 8$; $f(n) = f(n - 1) - 2$ for $n \geq 2$

$f(n) = 8 + (-2)(n - 1)$

12. $a_1 = -5$; $a_n = a_{n-1} + 7$ for $n \geq 2$

$a_n = -5 + 7(n - 1)$

13. Each stair on a staircase has a height of 7.5 inches.

a. Write an explicit rule for an arithmetic sequence that gives the height (in inches) of the nth stair above the base of the staircase.

$f(n) = 7.5 + 7.5(n - 1)$

b. What is the fourth term of the sequence, and what does it represent in this situation?

30; the fourth stair is 30 inches above the base of the staircase.

Geometric Sequences

Essential question: *How can you write a rule for a geometric sequence?*

COMMON CORE Standards for Mathematical Content

CC.9-12.F.BF.1 Write a function that describes a relationship between two quantities.*

CC.9-12.F.BF.1a Determine an explicit expression, a recursive process ... from a context.*

CC.9-12.F.BF.2 Write ... geometric sequences both recursively and with an explicit formula, use them to model situations, and translate between the two forms.*

CC.9-12.F.LE.2 Construct ... exponential functions, including ... geometric sequences, given a graph, a description of a relationship, or two input-output pairs (include reading these from a table).*

Vocabulary
geometric sequence

common ratio

Prerequisites
Arithmetic sequences, Lesson 9-2

Math Background
In Lesson 9-2, students studied arithmetic sequences and wrote general recursive and explicit rules for them. Students used these rules to solve real-world problems involving arithmetic sequences. In this lesson, they will study the same aspects of geometric sequences.

INTRODUCE

Review what students learned about arithmetic sequences in Lesson 9-2. Make sure that students understand how to use the general recursive and explicit rules for arithmetic sequences to write specific rules, including how recursive rules can be rewritten as explicit rules and vice versa.

TEACH

1 EXAMPLE

Questioning Strategies

• In part C, why does the explicit rule for the sequence involve raising the common ratio to the power $n - 1$ and not n? Fold 1 ($n = 1$) results in 2 layers. The number of layers doubles with fold 2 ($n = 2$) and each subsequent fold. So, the explicit rule must generate the sequence $f(1) = 2 \cdot 2^0$, $f(2) = 2 \cdot 2^1$, $f(3) = 2 \cdot 2^2$, ... The power of 2 that the initial 2 layers is multiplied by is always 1 less than the fold number.

• Which rule, the recursive rule or the explicit rule, would be more useful in determining the number of layers in the sword metal after the 12th fold? Explain you reasoning. The explicit rule is more useful because you can easily evaluate $f(12) = 4,096$ to find the number of layers after the 12th fold. To use the recursive rule, you would have to start with $f(1)$ and calculate the number of layers for each successive fold.

• How would the recursive rule and explicit rule change if the table included a starting value of 1 layer with 0 folds? Recursive rule: $f(0) = 1$ and $f(n) = f(n - 1) \cdot 2$ for $n \geq 1$; explicit rule: $f(n) = 2^n$

Differentiated Instruction
Kinesthetic learners may benefit by acting out the situation by folding sheets of paper to represent the sheets of metal folded by the sword smiths.

EXTRA EXAMPLE

n	1	2	3	4	5
f(n)	5	10	20	40	80

Write a recursive rule and an explicit rule for the geometric sequence described by the table.

$f(1) = 5$ and $f(n) = f(n - 1) \cdot 2$ for $n \geq 2$;
$f(n) = 5 \cdot 2^{n-1}$

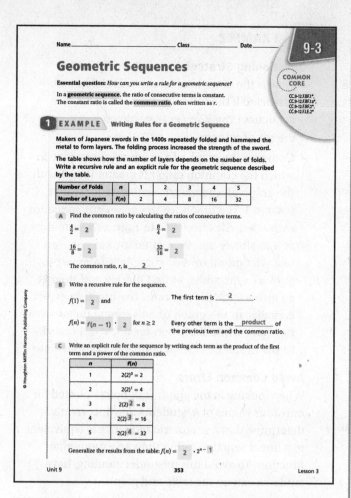

Name _____ **Class** _____ **Date** _____

9-3

COMMON CORE

CC.9-12.F.BF.1*,
CC.9-12.F.BF.1a*,
CC.9-12.F.BF.2*,
CC.9-12.F.LE.2*

Geometric Sequences

Essential question: *How can you write a rule for a geometric sequence?*

In a **geometric sequence**, the ratio of consecutive terms is constant.
The constant ratio is called the **common ratio**, often written as *r*.

1 EXAMPLE   Writing Rules for a Geometric Sequence

Makers of Japanese swords in the 1400s repeatedly folded and hammered the
metal to form layers. The folding process increased the strength of the sword.

The table shows how the number of layers depends on the number of folds.
Write a recursive rule and an explicit rule for the geometric sequence described
by the table.

Number of Folds	*n*	1	2	3	4	5
Number of Layers	*f(n)*	2	4	8	16	32

A Find the common ratio by calculating the ratios of consecutive terms.

$\frac{4}{2} = $ 2 $\frac{8}{4} = $ 2

$\frac{16}{8} = $ 2 $\frac{32}{16} = $ 2

The common ratio, *r*, is ___2___.

B Write a recursive rule for the sequence.

$f(1) = $ 2 and   The first term is ___2___.

$f(n) = $ f(n − 1) · 2 for $n \geq 2$ Every other term is the ___product___ of
the previous term and the common ratio.

C Write an explicit rule for the sequence by writing each term as the product of the first
term and a power of the common ratio.

n	*f(n)*
1	$2(2)^0 = 2$
2	$2(2)^1 = 4$
3	$2(2)^2 = 8$
4	$2(2)^3 = 16$
5	$2(2)^4 = 32$

Generalize the results from the table: $f(n) = $ 2 $\cdot 2^{n-1}$

Unit 9   353   Lesson 3

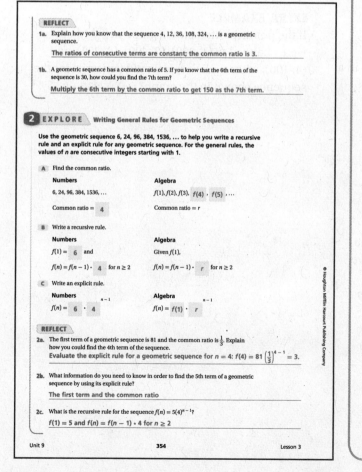

REFLECT

1a. Explain how you know that the sequence 4, 12, 36, 108, 324, ... is a geometric
sequence.

The ratios of consecutive terms are constant; the common ratio is 3.

1b. A geometric sequence has a common ratio of 5. If you know that the 6th term of the
sequence is 30, how could you find the 7th term?

Multiply the 6th term by the common ratio to get 150 as the 7th term.

2 EXPLORE   Writing General Rules for Geometric Sequences

Use the geometric sequence 6, 24, 96, 384, 1536, ... to help you write a recursive
rule and an explicit rule for any geometric sequence. For the general rules, the
values of *n* are consecutive integers starting with 1.

A Find the common ratio.

Numbers   **Algebra**

6, 24, 96, 384, 1536, ... $f(1), f(2), f(3),$ f(4) · f(5) , ...

Common ratio = 4   Common ratio = *r*

B Write a recursive rule.

Numbers   **Algebra**

$f(1) = $ 6 and   Given $f(1)$,

$f(n) = f(n-1) \cdot$ 4 for $n \geq 2$ $f(n) = f(n-1) \cdot$ r for $n \geq 2$

C Write an explicit rule.

Numbers   **Algebra**

$f(n) = $ 6 · 4^{n-1} $f(n) = f(1) \cdot$ r $^{n-1}$

REFLECT

2a. The first term of a geometric sequence is 81 and the common ratio is $\frac{1}{3}$. Explain
how you could find the 4th term of the sequence.

Evaluate the explicit rule for a geometric sequence for $n = 4$: $f(4) = 81\left(\frac{1}{3}\right)^{4-1} = 3$.

2b. What information do you need to know in order to find the 5th term of a geometric
sequence by using its explicit rule?

The first term and the common ratio

2c. What is the recursive rule for the sequence $f(n) = 5(4)^{n-1}$?

$f(1) = 5$ and $f(n) = f(n - 1) \cdot 4$ for $n \geq 2$

Unit 9   354   Lesson 3

Questioning Strategies

- What is a recursive rule for a geometric sequence with a first term of 3 and a common ratio of -2? $f(1) = 3$ and $f(n) = f(n-1) \cdot (-2)$ for $n \geq 2$

- What is an explicit rule for a geometric sequence with a first term of $\frac{5}{6}$ and a common ratio of $\frac{1}{3}$? $f(n) = \frac{5}{6} \cdot \left(\frac{1}{3}\right)^{n-1}$

- If you know the second term and the common ratio of a geometric sequence, can you write an explicit rule for the sequence? If so, explain how. Yes; you can divide the second term by the common ratio to get the first term. Then, you can substitute the first term and the common ratio into the general explicit rule to get the explicit rule for the sequence.

Teaching Strategy

After students have written the general algebraic formulas for recursive and explicit rules for geometric sequences, compare the process for substituting values for the variables in the formulas for geometric sequences with the process for arithmetic sequences. Point out the similarities such as the use of a common difference in arithmetic sequences and the use of a common ratio in geometric sequences. Also, point out the differences such as how the common difference is added in a recursive rule for an arithmetic sequence, while the common ratio is multiplied in a recursive rule for a geometric sequence.

MATHEMATICAL PRACTICE **Highlighting the Standards**

2 EXPLORE and its Reflect questions address Mathematical Practice Standard 2 (Reason abstractly and quantitatively). Students use a specific geometric sequence to help them obtain general rules, both recursive and explicit, for geometric sequences. They can then use the general rules to obtain rules for other specific geometric sequences and to transform a rule given in one form into the other form (recursive to explicit or explicit to recursive).

Questioning Strategies

- How is the domain of an exponential function restricted if the function defines a geometric sequence? The domain is restricted to a subset of the set of integers.

- Compare the graph of a geometric sequence for which the common ratio r is greater than 1 with the graph of a geometric sequence for which $0 < r < 1$. The graph for the geometric sequence with $r > 1$ rises from left to right as x increases, at first slowly and then at an increasingly fast rate. The graph for $0 < r < 1$ falls from left to right as x increases, at first quickly and then at an increasingly slower rate. The graph for $r > 1$ is similar to the graph of an exponential growth function, while the graph for $0 < r < 1$ is similar to the graph of an exponential decay function.

Avoid Common Errors

When looking at the graph with points plotted for only four values of n, students may incorrectly determine that a geometric sequence is equivalent to a linear function rather than an exponential function. To avoid this misunderstanding, have students extend the table and graph.

EXTRA EXAMPLE

If the points plotted on the graph in 3 EXAMPLE were changed to (1, 800), (2, 400), (3, 200), and (4, 100), what explicit rule would you write for the sequence shown in the graph? $f(n) = 800 \cdot 0.5^{n-1}$

3 EXAMPLE Relating Geometric Sequences and Exponential Functions

The graph shows the heights to which a ball bounces after it is dropped. Write an explicit rule for the sequence of bounce heights.

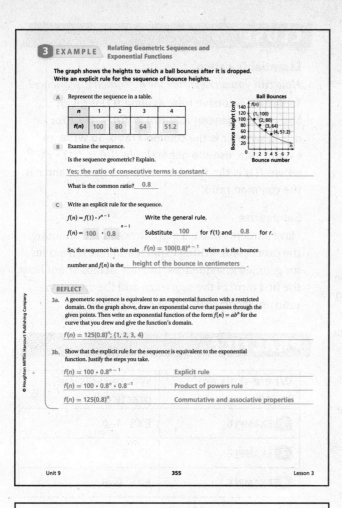

A Represent the sequence in a table.

n	1	2	3	4
$f(n)$	100	80	64	51.2

B Examine the sequence.

Is the sequence geometric? Explain.

Yes; the ratio of consecutive terms is constant.

What is the common ratio? 0.8

C Write an explicit rule for the sequence.

$f(n) = f(1) \cdot r^{n-1}$ Write the general rule.

$f(n) = $ 100 $\cdot$ 0.8 $^{n-1}$ Substitute __100__ for $f(1)$ and __0.8__ for r.

So, the sequence has the rule $f(n) = 100(0.8)^{n-1}$ where n is the bounce number and $f(n)$ is the __height of the bounce in centimeters__ .

REFLECT

3a. A geometric sequence is equivalent to an exponential function with a restricted domain. On the graph above, draw an exponential curve that passes through the given points. Then write an exponential function of the form $f(n) = ab^n$ for the curve that you drew and give the function's domain.

$f(n) = 125(0.8)^n; \{1, 2, 3, 4\}$

3b. Show that the explicit rule for the sequence is equivalent to the exponential function. Justify the steps you take.

$f(n) = 100 \cdot 0.8^{n-1}$ Explicit rule

$f(n) = 100 \cdot 0.8^n \cdot 0.8^{-1}$ Product of powers rule

$f(n) = 125(0.8)^n$ Commutative and associative properties

Unit 9   355   Lesson 3

The explicit and recursive rules for a geometric sequence can also be written in subscript notation.

Explicit: $a_n = a_1 \cdot r^{n-1}$

Recursive: a_1 is given and $a_n = a_{n-1} \cdot r$ for $n \geq 2$

4 EXAMPLE Writing a Geometric Sequence Given Two Terms

The shutter speed settings on a camera form a geometric sequence where a_n is the shutter speed in seconds and n is the setting number. The fifth setting on the camera is $\frac{1}{60}$ second, and the seventh setting on the camera is $\frac{1}{15}$ second. Write an explicit rule for the sequence using subscript notation.

A Identify the given terms in the sequence.

$a_5 = \frac{1}{60}$ The fifth setting is $\frac{1}{60}$ second, so the 5th term of the sequence is $\frac{1}{60}$.

$a_7 = \frac{1}{15}$ The seventh setting is $\frac{1}{15}$ second, so the __7th__ term of the sequence is __$\frac{1}{15}$__ .

B Find the common ratio.

$a_7 = a_6 \cdot r$ Write the recursive rule for a_7.

$a_6 = a_5 \cdot r$ Write the recursive rule for a_6.

$a_7 = a_5 \cdot r \cdot r$ Substitute the expression for a_6 into the rule for a_7.

$\frac{1}{15} = \frac{1}{60} \cdot r^2$ Substitute $\frac{1}{15}$ for a_7 and $\frac{1}{60}$ for a_5.

$4 = r^2$ Multiply both sides by 60.

$2 = r$ Definition of positive square root

C Find the first term of the sequence.

$a_n = a_1 \cdot r^{n-1}$ Write the explicit rule.

$\frac{1}{60} = a_1 \cdot 2^{5-1}$ Substitute $\frac{1}{60}$ for a_n, __2__ for r, and 5 for n.

$\frac{1}{60} = a_1 \cdot 16$ Simplify.

$\frac{1}{960} = a_1$ Divide both sides by 16.

D Write the explicit rule.

$a_n = a_1 \cdot r^{n-1}$ Write the general rule.

$a_n = \frac{1}{960} \cdot 2^{n-1}$ Substitute __$\frac{1}{960}$__ for a_1 and __2__ for r.

Unit 9   356   Lesson 3

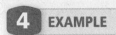

Questioning Strategies

- How is an explicit rule for a geometric sequence written using function notation related to an explicit rule for a geometric sequence written using subscript notation? When the position numbers start with 1, the variable n is used in both notations to represent the nth term of the sequence, which in both cases is found by multiplying the first term by the common ratio raised to the power of $(n − 1)$.

- What is the relationship between the common ratio 2 and the shutter speed of the camera? The time that the shutter takes to open and close is increased by a factor of 2 each time the setting number is increased by 1.

- At what setting is the shutter speed of this camera about 1 second? Explain. setting 11;
$$a_{11} = \frac{1}{960} \cdot 2^{11-1} = \frac{1}{960} \cdot 1024 \approx 1.07$$

- What is the recursive rule for the geometric sequence that describes the shutter speed on the camera in relation to the setting number n?
$$a_1 = \frac{1}{960} \text{ and } a_n = a_{n-1} \cdot 2 \text{ for } n \geq 2$$

Teaching Strategy

Students may be interested in learning more about geometric sequences and photography. Encourage them to explore the relationship between shutter speed and exposure time. Point out that f-stop settings on a camera can also be described by a geometric sequence, with each increasing f-stop corresponding to an aperture, or lens opening, with half the light-gathering area as the previous f-stop.

EXTRA EXAMPLE

What would be the explicit rule for the geometric sequence in **4 EXAMPLE** if the second shutter speed setting was $\frac{1}{500}$ and the fourth shutter speed setting was $\frac{1}{125}$? $a_n = \frac{1}{1000} \cdot 2^{n-1}$

Essential Question

How can you write a rule for a geometric sequence?
To write a recursive rule, assume $f(1)$ is given and use the general rule $f(n) = f(n − 1) \cdot r$ for $n \geq 2$, where r is the common ratio. To write an explicit rule, use the general rule $f(n) = f(1) \cdot r^{n-1}$, where $f(1)$ is the first term in the sequence and r is the common ratio.

Summarize

Have students make a graphic organizer outlining the process for writing explicit and recursive rules for geometric sequences. Include details about how the first term of the sequence and the common ratio are incorporated into each rule.

PRACTICE

Where skills are taught	Where skills are practiced
1 EXAMPLE	EXS. 1–4
3 EXAMPLE	EX. 5
4 EXAMPLE	EXS. 6–8

Exercises 9 and 10: Given a rule for a geometric sequence, students write a recursive rule as an explicit rule, or an explicit rule as a recursive rule.

Exercise 11: Students write an explicit rule for a geometric sequence to solve a problem that involves finding the nth term of the sequence.

REFLECT

4a. When finding the common ratio, why can you ignore the negative square root of 4 when solving the equation $4 = r^2$?

If r were negative, some of the terms of the sequence would be negative.

Negative terms do not make sense in this situation because the terms

represent shutter speeds.

4b. If you graphed the explicit rule for the sequence, what would the graph look like?

The graph would be a set of discrete points showing exponential growth.

PRACTICE

Write a recursive rule and an explicit rule for each geometric sequence.

1. 9, 27, 81, 243, …

$f(1) = 9$ and $f(n) = f(n-1) \cdot 3$, for $n \geq 2$; $f(n) = 9(3)^{n-1}$

2. 5, −5, 5, −5, …

$f(1) = 5$ and $f(n) = f(n-1) \cdot (-1)$, for $n \geq 2$; $f(n) = 5(-1)^{n-1}$

3. 12, 3, $\frac{3}{4}$, $\frac{3}{16}$, …

$f(1) = 12$ and $f(n) = f(n-1) \cdot \frac{1}{4}$, for $n \geq 2$; $f(n) = 12 \cdot \left(\frac{1}{4}\right)^{n-1}$

4. The table shows the beginning-of-month balances, rounded to the nearest cent, in Marla's savings account for the first few months after she made an initial deposit in the account.

Month	n	1	2	3	4
Account Balance ($)	$f(n)$	2010.00	2020.05	2030.15	2040.30

a. Explain how you know that the sequence of account balances is geometric.

The ratio of consecutive account balances is approximately constant (1.005)

b. Write recursive and explicit rules for the sequence of account balances.

$f(1) = 2010$ and $f(n) = f(n-1) \cdot 1.005$, for $n \geq 2$; $f(n) = 2010 \, (1.005)^{n-1}$

c. What amount did Marla deposit initially? Explain.

$2000; the initial amount is $f(0) = 2000$.

---

5. The graph shows the number of players in the first four rounds of the U.S. Open women's singles tennis tournament.

a. Write an explicit rule for the sequence of players in each round.

$f(n) = 128\left(\frac{1}{2}\right)^{n-1}$

b. How many rounds are there in the tournament? (*Hint:* In the last round, only 2 players are left.)

7 rounds

U.S. Open
Women's Singles

(graph: Number of players vs. Round, points (1, 128), (2, 64), (3, 32), (4, 16))

6. The numbers of points that a player must accumulate to reach the next level of a video game form a geometric sequence, where a_n is the number of points needed to complete level n.

a. A player needs 1000 points to complete level 2 and 8,000,000 points to complete level 5. Write an explicit rule for the sequence using subscript notation.

$a_n = 50(20)^{n-1}$

b. How many points are needed for level 7? 3,200,000,000

Write an explicit rule for each geometric sequence based on the given terms from the sequence. Assume that the common ratio r is positive.

7. $a_2 = 12$ and $a_4 = 192$

$a_n = 3 \cdot 4^{n-1}$

8. $a_5 = 0.32$ and $a_7 = 0.0128$

$a_n = 200(0.2)^{n-1}$

Each rule represents a geometric sequence. If the given rule is recursive, write it as an explicit rule. If the given rule is explicit, write it as a recursive rule. Assume that $f(1)$ is the first term of the sequence.

9. $f(n) = 6(3)^{n-1}$

$f(1) = 6$; $f(n) = f(n-1) \cdot 3$ for $n \geq 2$

10. $f(1) = 10$; $f(n) = f(n-1) \cdot 8$ for $n \geq 2$

$f(n) = 10(8)^{n-1}$

11. An economist predicts that the cost of food will increase by 4% per year for the next several years.

a. Use the economist's prediction to write an explicit rule for a geometric sequence that gives the cost in dollars of a box of cereal in year n given that it costs $3.20 in year 1.

$f(n) = 3.20(1.04)^{n-1}$

b. What is the fourth term of the sequence, and what does it represent in this situation?

about 3.60; the cost of the box of cereal is predicted to be about $3.60 in year 4.

Finite Geometric Series

Essential question: *How do you find the sum of a finite geometric series?*

© Houghton Mifflin Harcourt Publishing Company

COMMON CORE Standards for Mathematical Content

CC.9-12.A.SSE.1 Interpret expressions that represent a quantity in terms of its context.*

CC.9-12.A.SSE.1a Interpret parts of an expression, such as terms, factors, and coefficients.*

CC.9-12.A.SSE.1b Interpret complicated expressions by viewing one or more of their parts as a single entity.*

CC.9-12.A.SSE.4 Derive the formula for the sum of a finite geometric series (when the common ratio is not 1), and use the formula to solve problems.

Vocabulary

series

geometric series

Prerequisites

Geometric sequences, Lesson 9-3

Math Background

In Lesson 9-3, students learned to recognize a geometric sequence by seeing that each term was related to the previous term by a common ratio. Students used the general rules for geometric sequences to write both recursive and explicit rules for specific sequences. Students will now learn about geometric series, which are formed by adding the terms of a geometric sequence.

INTRODUCE

Review what students learned about geometric sequences in Lesson 9-3. Make sure that students understand both the general recursive and the general explicit rules for geometric sequences and how to use these rules to write rules for specific sequences. Review the concept of a common ratio and how it is incorporated into a rule for a geometric sequence.

TEACH

1 EXPLORE

Questioning Strategies

- What happens to the total area of the pieces laid down as the number n of stages increases? **As n increases, the total area of the pieces laid down gets closer to 1, the area of the paper.**

- Suppose you take a sheet of paper with an area of 1 square unit and cut it into two pieces with one piece having twice the area of the other. This means that one piece has an area of $\frac{2}{3}$ square unit while the other has an area of $\frac{1}{3}$ square unit. You lay down the larger piece. You cut the remaining piece into two pieces with one piece having twice the area of the other, and you lay down the larger piece. You continue this process of cutting the remaining piece into two pieces having a 2 : 1 ratio of areas and laying down the larger piece. Complete the table.

Stage	Sum of the areas of the pieces that have been laid down	Difference of 1 and the area of the remaining piece
1	$\frac{2}{3}$	$1 - \frac{1}{3} = \frac{2}{3}$
2	$\frac{2}{3} + \frac{2}{3}\left(\frac{1}{3}\right) = \frac{8}{9}$	$1 - \frac{1}{9} = \frac{8}{9}$
3	$\frac{2}{3} + \frac{2}{3}\left(\frac{1}{3}\right) + \frac{2}{3}\left(\frac{1}{9}\right) = \frac{26}{27}$	$1 - \frac{1}{27} = \frac{26}{27}$

- Generalize the second column of the table above: What is the sum of the areas of the pieces that have been laid down at the nth stage? $\frac{2}{3} + \frac{2}{3}\left(\frac{1}{3}\right) + \frac{2}{3}\left(\frac{1}{9}\right) + \cdots + \frac{2}{3}\left(\frac{1}{3}\right)^{n-1}$

- Generalize the third column of the table above: What is the difference of 1 and the area of the remaining piece at the nth stage? $1 - \left(\frac{1}{3}\right)^n$

Name_____ Class_____ Date_____

9-4

COMMON CORE

CC.9-12.A.SSE.1*
CC.9-12.A.SSE.1a*
CC.9-12.A.SSE.1b*
CC.9-12.A.SSE.4

Finite Geometric Series

Essential question: *How do you find the sum of a finite geometric series?*

1 EXPLORE Investigating a Geometric Series

A Start with a rectangular sheet of paper and assume the sheet has an area of 1 square unit. Cut the sheet in half and lay down one of the half-pieces. Then cut the remaining piece in half, and lay down one of the quarter-pieces. Continue the process: At each stage, cut the remaining piece in half, and lay down one of the halves. As you lay pieces down, arrange them to rebuild the original sheet of paper.

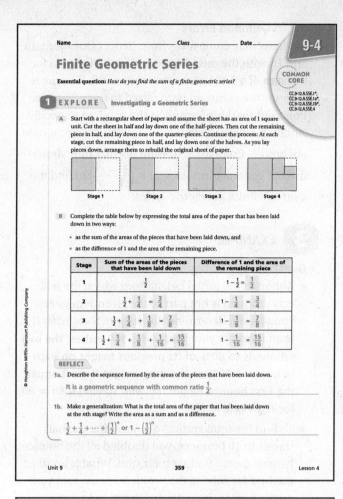

Stage 1   Stage 2   Stage 3   Stage 4

B Complete the table below by expressing the total area of the paper that has been laid down in two ways:

* as the sum of the areas of the pieces that have been laid down, and
* as the difference of 1 and the area of the remaining piece.

Stage	Sum of the areas of the pieces that have been laid down	Difference of 1 and the area of the remaining piece
1	$\frac{1}{2}$	$1 - \frac{1}{2} = \frac{1}{2}$
2	$\frac{1}{2} + \frac{1}{4} = \frac{3}{4}$	$1 - \frac{1}{4} = \frac{3}{4}$
3	$\frac{1}{2} + \frac{1}{4} + \frac{1}{8} = \frac{7}{8}$	$1 - \frac{1}{8} = \frac{7}{8}$
4	$\frac{1}{2} + \frac{1}{4} + \frac{1}{8} + \frac{1}{16} = \frac{15}{16}$	$1 - \frac{1}{16} = \frac{15}{16}$

REFLECT

1a. Describe the sequence formed by the areas of the pieces that have been laid down.

It is a geometric sequence with common ratio $\frac{1}{2}$.

1b. Make a generalization: What is the total area of the paper that has been laid down at the *n*th stage? Write the area as a sum and as a difference.

$\frac{1}{2} + \frac{1}{4} + \cdots + \left(\frac{1}{2}\right)^n$ or $1 - \left(\frac{1}{2}\right)^n$

A **series** is the expression formed by adding the terms of a sequence. A **geometric series** is the expression formed by adding the terms of a geometric sequence. In the Explore, the areas $\frac{1}{2}, \frac{1}{4}, \frac{1}{8},$ and $\frac{1}{16}$ form a geometric sequence. The expression $\frac{1}{2} + \frac{1}{4} + \frac{1}{8} + \frac{1}{16}$ is a geometric series. You can derive a formula for the sum of a geometric series.

2 EXPLORE Deriving a Formula for the Sum of a Geometric Series

Consider the geometric series $a_1 + a_1 r + a_1 r^2 + a_1 r^3 + \cdots + a_1 r^{n-1}$. The series has *n* terms. Let S_n be the sum of the geometric series.

A Find a simplified expression for $S_n - rS_n$.

$S_n = a_1 + a_1 r + a_1 r^2 + a_1 r^3 + \cdots + a_1 r^{n-1}$ Write S_n.

$rS_n = a_1 r + a_1 r^2 + a_1 r^3 + a_1 r^4 + \cdots + a_1 r^n$ Multiply each term of S_n by r.

Align like terms and subtract.

$$S_n = a_1 + a_1 r + a_1 r^2 + a_1 r^3 + \cdots + a_1 r^{n-1}$$
$$rS_n = \quad\ a_1 r + a_1 r^2 + a_1 r^3 + \cdots + a_1 r^{n-1} + a_1 r^n$$
$$S_n - rS_n = a_1 + 0 + 0 + 0 + \cdots + 0 - a_1 r^n$$

So, $S_n - rS_n = a_1 - a_1 r^n$.

B Factor and divide by $1 - r$.

$S_n - rS_n = a_1 - a_1 r^n$ Write the result from part A.

$S_n(1 - r) = a_1\left(1 - r^n\right)$ Factor both sides.

$S_n = a_1\left(\dfrac{1 - r^n}{1 - r}\right)$ Divide both sides by $1 - r$.

REFLECT

2a. In the first Explore, you found that $\frac{1}{2} + \left(\frac{1}{2}\right)^2 + \left(\frac{1}{2}\right)^3 + \cdots + \left(\frac{1}{2}\right)^n = 1 - \left(\frac{1}{2}\right)^n$.

Show that you get the same sum for the geometric series by using the formula you derived above.

$a_1 = \frac{1}{2}$ and $r = \frac{1}{2}$, so $S_n = a_1\left(\dfrac{1 - r^n}{1 - r}\right) = \dfrac{1}{2}\left(\dfrac{1 - \left(\frac{1}{2}\right)^n}{1 - \frac{1}{2}}\right) = \dfrac{1}{2}\left(\dfrac{1 - \left(\frac{1}{2}\right)^n}{\frac{1}{2}}\right) = 1 - \left(\frac{1}{2}\right)^n$

2b. What restrictions are there on the values of *r* that can be used in the formula for the sum of a geometric series?

The value of *r* cannot be 1, because $1 - r$ is in a denominator in the formula for the sum, and division by zero is undefined.

Differentiated Instruction

Learners who have trouble visualizing area may benefit from using a strip of paper instead of a sheet of paper. By starting with a strip of paper whose length is taken to be 1 unit, they can fold it in half, cut at the crease, and lay down one of the halves. By repeating the process and laying down the successive halves end to end, students will still be able to complete the table in part B of the Explore, but they will be focused on length rather than area.

2 EXPLORE

Questioning Strategies

- When cutting paper into pieces having a $2:1$ ratio of areas, you found the sum of the areas of the pieces that have been laid down to be $\frac{2}{3} + \frac{2}{3}\left(\frac{1}{3}\right) + \frac{2}{3}\left(\frac{1}{9}\right) + \cdots + \frac{2}{3}\left(\frac{1}{3}\right)^{n-1}$. Explain why this is a finite geometric series. **The terms form a geometric sequence with $a_1 = \frac{2}{3}$ and $r = \frac{1}{3}$.**

- When cutting paper into pieces having a $2:1$ ratio of areas, you found difference of 1 and the area of the remaining piece to be $1 - \left(\frac{1}{3}\right)^n$. What is true about this difference and the sum of the areas of the pieces laid down? **They are equal.**

- Show that $\frac{2}{3} + \frac{2}{3}\left(\frac{1}{3}\right) + \frac{2}{3}\left(\frac{1}{9}\right) + \cdots + \frac{2}{3}\left(\frac{1}{3}\right)^{n-1} = 1 - \left(\frac{1}{3}\right)^n$ using the formula for the sum of a finite geometric series. $\frac{2}{3} + \frac{2}{3}\left(\frac{1}{3}\right) + \frac{2}{3}\left(\frac{1}{9}\right) + \cdots$

$+ \frac{2}{3}\left(\frac{1}{3}\right)^{n-1} = \frac{2}{3}\left(\dfrac{1 - \left(\frac{1}{3}\right)^n}{1 - \frac{1}{3}}\right) = \frac{2}{3}\left(\dfrac{1 - \left(\frac{1}{3}\right)^n}{\frac{2}{3}}\right) =$

$1 - \left(\frac{1}{3}\right)^n$

Avoid Common Errors

Students may come away from Reflect Questions 1a and 1b with the mistaken idea that the formula for the sum of a finite geometric series with n terms is 1 minus the common ratio raised to the nth power. Point out that this formula is the result of a specific situation where the first term and the common ratio are both $\frac{1}{2}$. Emphasize to students that they should use the general formula $S_n = a_1\left(\dfrac{1 - r^n}{1 - r}\right)$ to find the sum of a finite geometric series.

3 EXAMPLE

Questioning Strategies

- Although the initial height from which the ball was dropped is not part of the given sequence, you can still determine that height. State what it is and explain your reasoning. **100 inches; the ball rebounds to 80% of its previous height on each bounce, so 80% of the drop height h must equal the first bounce height, 80, and solving $0.8h = 80$ for h gives $h = 100$.**

- To find the total vertical distance that the ball travels in 10 bounces, you doubled all the bounce heights before finding their sum. What is another method for solving the problem? Show that your method gives the same answer. **First find the sum of the bounce heights and then double the result:**
$80 + 80(0.8) + \cdots + 80(0.8)^9 = 80\left(\dfrac{1 - 0.8^{10}}{1 - 0.8}\right) \approx$
357 and $2(357) = 714$ inches.

EXTRA EXAMPLE

For the model given in **3 EXAMPLE**, what is the total distance the ball travels in 12 bounces? **about 745 in.**

© Houghton Mifflin Harcourt Publishing Company

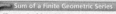

Sum of a Finite Geometric Series

The sum S_n of the geometric series $a_1 + a_1r + a_1r^2 + a_1r^3 + \cdots + a_1r^{n-1}$ is

$$S_n = a_1\left(\frac{1 - r^n}{1 - r}\right)$$

where r is the common ratio, $r \neq 1$, and n is the number of terms.

3 EXAMPLE Finding the Distance Traveled by a Bouncing Ball

The following geometric sequence models n bounce heights of a ball, where the heights are measured in inches. (The initial height from which the ball is dropped before the first bounce is not part of this sequence.)

$$80, \; 80(0.8), \; 80(0.8)^2, \ldots, 80(0.8)^{n-1}$$

Based on the model, what is the total vertical distance that the ball travels in 10 bounces?

A Write a geometric series for the total vertical distance the ball travels.

On the first bounce, the ball travels 80 inches up and 80 inches down. On the second bounce, it travels 64 inches up and 64 inches down. On every bounce, the ball travels twice the bounce height. So, the following geometric sequence models the 10 distances traveled.

$$160, \; \boxed{160} \; (0.8), \; \boxed{160} \; (0.8)^2, \ldots, \; \boxed{160} \; (0.8)^9$$

The following geometric series models the total distance traveled.

$$S_n = 160 + \boxed{160} \; (0.8) + \boxed{160} \; (0.8)^2 + \cdots + \boxed{160} \; (0.8)^9$$

B Use the formula for the sum of a finite geometric series.

In this case, $n = \boxed{10}$, $a_1 = \boxed{160}$, and $r = \boxed{0.8}$.

$$S_n = a_1\left(\frac{1 - r^n}{1 - r}\right) \qquad \text{Write the sum formula.}$$

$$= 160 \left(\frac{1 - 0.8^{\boxed{10}}}{1 - 0.8}\right) \qquad \text{Substitute the values of } n, a_1, \text{ and } r.$$

$$\approx \boxed{714} \qquad \text{Round to the nearest inch.}$$

So, the ball travels approximately $\boxed{714}$ inches in 10 bounces.

REFLECT

3a. Write and simplify an expression for the total distance the ball travels in n bounces. Check that your expression gives the correct result when $n = 10$.

$S_n = 800(1 - (0.8)^n)$; when $n = 10$, $S_{10} = 800(1 - (0.8)^{10}) \approx 714$.

An *annuity* is an account that is increased (or decreased) by equal deposits (or payments) that are made at regular intervals. The *future value* of an annuity is the total amount in the account at some time in the future.

4 EXAMPLE Determining the Future Value of an Annuity

You deposit $1000 into a savings account at the end of each year for 10 years. The account earns 3% interest that is compounded annually. What is the future value of the annuity in 10 years?

A Develop a general formula for the future value of an annuity.

Suppose you deposit P dollars into the account at the end of each year for n years, and the account earns interest compounded annually at a rate i.

At the end of the first year, the total value of the annuity is P. At the end of the second year, interest is applied to the first deposit and there is a new deposit of P dollars, for a total value of $P(1 + i) + P$. Complete the table.

Year	Total Value of Annuity at End of Year
1	P
2	$P(1 + i) + P$
3	$P(1 + i)^2 + P(1 + i) + P$
⋮	⋮
n	$P(1 + i)^{n-1} + P(1 + i)^{n-2} + \cdots + P(1 + i)^2 + P(1 + i) + P$

Complete the equation for the total value A after n years.

$$A = P + P(1 + i) + P(1 + i)^2 + \cdots + P(1 + i)^{\boxed{n-2}} + P(1 + i)^{\boxed{n-1}}$$

This is a geometric series with $a_1 = \boxed{P}$ and $r = \boxed{1 + i}$, so its sum is

$$A = a_1\left(\frac{1 - r^n}{1 - r}\right) = P\left(\frac{1 - (1 + i)^n}{1 - (1 + i)}\right) = P\left(\frac{(1 + i)^n - 1}{(1 + i) - 1}\right) = P\left(\frac{(1 + i)^n - 1}{\boxed{i}}\right).$$

B Use the formula to find the future value of the annuity.

$$A = P\left(\frac{(1 + i)^n - 1}{i}\right) \qquad \text{Write the formula.}$$

$$= 1000 \left(\frac{1.03^{\boxed{10}} - 1}{0.03}\right) \qquad \text{Substitute 1000 for } P, \text{ 0.03 for } i, \text{ and 10 for } n.$$

$$\approx \boxed{11,463.88} \qquad \text{Round to 2 decimal places.}$$

So, the value of the annuity in 10 years is $\boxed{\$11,463.88}$.

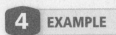 **EXAMPLE**

Questioning Strategies

- How is the given formula for the future value of an annuity related to the formula for the sum of a finite geometric series? **The variable A, which represents the future value of the annuity (the sum of all of the previous deposits and the interest earned on those deposits), corresponds to the variable S_n. Both formulas contain the variable n to represent the number of terms, which is the number of years for the annuity. The expression $i + 1$, which represents the interest rate, corresponds to the common ratio r.**

- What will be the future value of an annuity in 20 years if the annual deposits are $6000 and the interest rate is 4%? Explain how you found the answer. **about $178,668.47; use the formula to find**
$$A = 6000\left(\frac{1.04^{20} - 1}{0.04}\right).$$

```
┄┄┄┄┄┄┄┄┄┄┄
MATHEMATICAL    Highlighting
    PRACTICE     the Standards
┄┄┄┄┄┄┄┄┄┄┄
```

4 **EXAMPLE** and its Reflect questions offer an opportunity to address Mathematical Practice Standard 7 (Look for and make use of structure). Students look at the balance in a savings account earning interest compounded annually over a period of 10 years when the same amount is deposited in the account at the end of each year. Students express this total balance as a sum of the values of the individual deposits, using variables to represent the amount deposited each year and the interest rate. By recognizing that the structure of the sum for the savings account balance is the sum of a finite geometric series, students can then use the formula derived in this lesson to find a general formula for the account balance and then use it to find a specific balance.

EXTRA EXAMPLE
What will be the future value of the annuity in **4** **EXAMPLE** in 20 years? **about $26,870.37**

CLOSE

Essential Question

How do you find the sum of a finite geometric series?
First find a simplified expression for $S_n - rS_n$ where $S_n = a_1 + a_1r + a_1r^2 + \ldots + a_1r^{n-2} + a_1r^{n-1}$; then, factor $S_n - rS_n$ and divide by $1 - r$. The result is $S_n = a_1\left(\frac{1 - r^n}{1 - r}\right)$, which is the formula for the sum of a finite geometric series.

Summarize

Have students make a graphic organizer outlining the process for finding the sum of a geometric series. Include details about how the first term of the series, the number of terms, and the common ratio are incorporated into the formula.

PRACTICE

Where skills are taught	Where skills are practiced
3 EXAMPLE	EXS. 3, 7–9
4 EXAMPLE	EXS. 4, 5

Exercises 1 and 2: Students rewrite a finite geometric series in terms of the first term and the common ratio, and then they find the sum of the series.

Exercise 6: Students use the formula for the future value of an annuity to find the yearly deposit required to reach a certain value after a given number of years.

© Houghton Mifflin Harcourt Publishing Company

> **REFLECT**
>
> **4a.** Does your answer seem reasonable? How do you know?
>
> Yes; the sum of the deposits is $10,000, so it makes sense that the total value of
>
> the annuity is more than $10,000 when the interest is taken into account.
>
> **4b.** The total interest earned on an annuity is the future value minus the sum of the deposits. Write a formula for the total interest I of an annuity after n years with annual deposits of P dollars and interest compounded annually at rate i.
>
> $$I = P\left(\frac{(1 + i)^n - 1}{i}\right) - nP$$

PRACTICE

For each finite geometric series, n indicates the number of terms. Rewrite each series in the form $a_1 + a_1 r + a_1 r^2 + \cdots + a_1 r^{n-1}$. Then find the sum.

1. $4 + 12 + 36 + \cdots + 8748$; $n = 8$

$4 + 4(3) + 4(3)^2 + \cdots + 4(3)^7$;

13,120

2. $10 + 5 + 2.5 + \cdots + 0.000003125$; $n = 6$

$10 + 10(0.5) + 10(0.5)^2 + \cdots + 10(0.5)^5$;

19.6875

3. A ball is dropped from a height of 16 feet and allowed to bounce repeatedly. On the first bounce it rises to a height of 12 feet and then on each subsequent bounce it rises to 75% of its previous height.

a. Write a geometric sequence that models the first n bounce heights, in feet.

$12, 12(0.75), 12(0.75)^2, 12(0.75)^3, \ldots, 12(0.75)^{n-1}$

b. Write a geometric series to model the total vertical distance the ball travels as a result of n bounces. (Exclude the distance traveled before the first bounce.)

$24 + 24(0.75) + 24(0.75)^2 + 24(0.75)^3 + \cdots + 24(0.75)^{n-1}$

c. How far does the ball travel vertically as a result of the first 3 bounces? Show two ways to find the answer—by adding the first three terms of the series and by using a formula.

$24 + 24(0.75) + 24(0.75)^2 = 24 + 18 + 13.5 = 55.5$ feet;

$S_3 = a_1\left(\frac{1 - r^n}{1 - r}\right) = 24\left(\frac{1 - (0.75)^3}{1 - 0.75}\right) = 55.5$ feet

d. How far does the ball travel vertically as a result of the first 9 bounces?

about 88.8 feet

4. Ali deposits $2000 into an account at the end of each year for 4 years. The account earns 5% interest compounded annually.

a. Complete the table to show the value of each deposit as well as the total value of the account at the end of the fourth year. For example, the value of the first deposit is $2000(1.05)^3 = \$2315.25$.

Value of first deposit	$2315.25
Value of second deposit	$2205.00
Value of third deposit	$2100.00
Value of fourth deposit	$2000.00
Total value of account	$8620.25

b. Use the formula for the sum of a finite geometric series to find the total value of the account at the end of the fourth year.

$\$8620.25$; $A = P\left(\frac{(1 + i)^n - 1}{i}\right) = 2000\left(\frac{(1.05)^4 - 1}{0.05}\right) = 8620.25$

5. Mr. Ortiz wants to save money for his grandson's future college costs. He plans to deposit $800 into an account at the end of each year. The account earns 6% interest compounded annually. What will be the value of the account in 18 years? Justify your answer.

about $24,724.52; $A = P\left(\frac{(1 + r)^n - 1}{r}\right) = 800\left(\frac{(1.06)^{18} - 1}{0.06}\right) \approx 24{,}724.52$

6. Ms. Turner wants to accumulate $50,000 for her daughter's future college costs in 12 years. How much does she need to deposit into an account at the end of each year if the account earns 4% interest compounded annually? Explain.

about $3327.61; solve $50{,}000 = P\left(\frac{(1.04)^{12} - 1}{0.04}\right)$ for P.

7. In a single-elimination tournament, a competitor is eliminated after one loss. Suppose a single-elimination tennis tournament has 64 players. In the first round, 32 matches are played. In each subsequent round, the number of matches decreases by one half. How many matches are played in the tournament? Show how to find the answer two ways—by direct calculation and by a formula.

63; $32 + 16 + 8 + 4 + 2 + 1 = 63$; $S_6 = 32\left(\frac{1 - (0.5)^6}{0.5}\right) = 63$

8. Nick works for a cleaning company. It takes him 2 hours 30 minutes to clean an office the first time. If he decreases his time by 5% on each subsequent visit, how much time will he spend cleaning the office during 10 visits? Justify your answer.

about 20.063 hours or 20 hours 4 minutes; $S_{10} = 2.5\left(\frac{1 - (0.95)^{10}}{1 - 0.95}\right) \approx 20.063$

9. Midori earns $850 in her first month at a part time job. If she gets a 1% raise in each subsequent month, how much will she earn in a year? Justify your answer.

about $10,780.13; $S_{12} = 850\left(\frac{1 - (1.01)^{12}}{1 - 1.01}\right) = -85{,}000(1 - (1.01)^{12}) \approx 10{,}780.13$

FOCUS ON MODELING
Modeling with Finite Geometric Series

Essential question: *How can you analyze the balance due on a loan?*

:::: COMMON   Standards for
:::: CORE   Mathematical Content

The following standards are addressed in this lesson. (An asterisk indicates that a standard is also a Modeling standard.) For more detailed information, see each section of the lesson.

Algebra: CC.9-12.A.SSE.1*, CC.9-12.A.SSE.1a*, CC.9-12.A.SSE.1b*, CC.9-12.A.SSE.4, CC.9-12.A.CED.3*

Prerequisites
- Interest compounded monthly, Lesson 6-4
- Geometric sequences, Lesson 9-3
- Finite geometric series, Lesson 9-4

Math Background
Students use what they know about arithmetic and geometric sequences to create a spreadsheet that models monthly payments and balance due on a car loan. Students then extend the model by deriving a formula from the sum of a finite geometric series to calculate the minimum monthly payment required to pay off a car loan for a given principal, interest rate, and number of payments.

INTRODUCE

Begin by asking how many students are interested in learning more about buying a car. Encourage students to discuss cars they would like to buy and have them research how much those cars cost. Explain that in this lesson students will explore getting a car loan and making monthly payments.

TEACH

1   Use a spreadsheet to determine if a given payment will pay off a loan.

Standards
CC.9-12.A.SSE.1 Interpret expressions that represent a quantity in terms of its context.*

CC.9-12.A.SSE.1a Interpret parts of an expression, such as terms, factors, and coefficients.*

CC.9-12.A.SSE.1b Interpret complicated expressions by viewing one or more of their parts as a single entity.*

Questioning Strategies
- How does using the Fill command in step F calculate the balance at the end of each period? When the Fill command is used for a cell that contains a formula, any cell references in that formula are updated relative to the new location. So, for payment period 3, which is located in row 9, the formula in cell B9 becomes =D8*(1+$B$2/12) and now calculates the new balance at the end of period 3 based on the balance after the payment in period 2. The formula in cell D9 is also updated to =B9−C9 to calculate the balance after payment has been made in period 3. This updating process continues through payment period 60.

- What would happen if you omitted the dollar signs in the cell reference $B$2 when you entered the formula =D7*(1+$B$2/12) in cell B8? If a cell reference has dollar signs in a formula, it means that the associated row and/or column will not be updated relative to the new location when the Fill command is used. If $B$2 did not have the dollar signs, the formula in cell B9 would be updated to =D8*(1+B3/12), and the new balance would be calculated using the monthly payment of $350 instead of the annual interest rate of 0.06.

- When you set up cells in step A for values you will change by hand, why do you *not* set up a cell for the number of payment periods? The number of payment periods is not treated as a variable in any calculation in the spreadsheet. The number of payment periods is represented by the number of rows in the table.

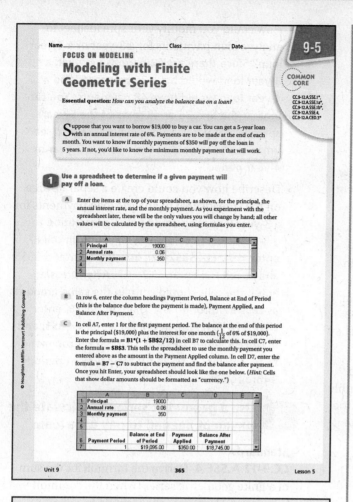

Name_____ Class_____ Date_____

9-5

FOCUS ON MODELING

Modeling with Finite Geometric Series

Essential question: *How can you analyze the balance due on a loan?*

COMMON CORE
CC.9-12.A.SSE.1*,
CC.9-12.A.SSE.1a*,
CC.9-12.A.SSE.1b*,
CC.9-12.A.SSE.4,
CC.9-12.A.CED.3*

Suppose that you want to borrow $19,000 to buy a car. You can get a 5-year loan with an annual interest rate of 6%. Payments are to be made at the end of each month. You want to know if monthly payments of $350 will pay off the loan in 5 years. If not, you'd like to know the minimum monthly payment that will work.

1 Use a spreadsheet to determine if a given payment will pay off a loan.

A Enter the items at the top of your spreadsheet, as shown, for the principal, the annual interest rate, and the monthly payment. As you experiment with the spreadsheet later, these will be the only values you will change by hand; all other values will be calculated by the spreadsheet, using formulas you enter.

	A	B	C	D	E
1	Principal	19000			
2	Annual rate	0.06			
3	Monthly payment	350			
4					
5					

B In row 6, enter the column headings Payment Period, Balance at End of Period (this is the balance due before the payment is made), Payment Applied, and Balance After Payment.

C In cell A7, enter 1 for the first payment period. The balance at the end of this period is the principal ($19,000) plus the interest for one month ($\frac{1}{12}$ of 6% of $19,000). Enter the formula = B1*(1 + $B$2/12) in cell B7 to calculate this. In cell C7, enter the formula = $B$3. This tells the spreadsheet to use the monthly payment you entered above as the amount in the Payment Applied column. In cell D7, enter formula = B7 − C7 to subtract the payment and find the balance after payment. Once you hit Enter, your spreadsheet should look like the one below. (*Hint:* Cells that show dollar amounts should be formatted as "currency.")

	A	B	C	D	E
1	Principal	19000			
2	Annual rate	0.06			
3	Monthly payment	350			
4					
5					
6	Payment Period	Balance at End of Period	Payment Applied	Balance After Payment	
7	1	$19,095.00	$350.00	$18,745.00	

D There are 12 payments per year for 5 years, so there will be 60 payments. Use the Fill command and choose "Series" to enter payment periods 2 through 60 in the Payment Period column.

E In cell B8, enter the formula = D7*(1 + $B$2/12). This calculates the balance at the end of the second month by adding the monthly interest to the balance after payment from the previous period. In cell C8, enter the formula = $B$3. In cell D8, enter the formula = B8 − C8.

F Select cells B8 through D8. Use the Fill command to fill columns B, C, and D for payment periods 3 through 60.

	A	B	C	D	E
1	Principal	19000			
2	Annual rate	0.06			
3	Monthly payment	350			
4					
5					
6	Payment Period	Balance at End of Period	Payment Applied	Balance After Payment	
7	1	$19,095.00	$350.00	$18,745.00	
8	2	$18,838.73	$350.00	$18,488.73	
9	3	$18,581.17	$350.00	$18,231.17	
10	4	$18,322.32	$350.00	$17,972.32	
11	5	$18,062.19	$350.00	$17,712.19	

G According to your spreadsheet, can you pay off the loan in 5 years with monthly payments of $350? How do you know?

No; the balance due after the 60th payment is $1208.64.

REFLECT

1a. Describe what the formula = B1*(1 + $B$2/12) in cell B7 calculates based on what B1 and 1 + $B$2/12 represent in the context of the problem. Include a description of what $B$2/12 represents and how it is obtained.

The formula calculates the principal plus interest at the end of month 1

because B1 represents the principal and 1 + $B$2/12 represents the growth

factor due to the interest. In the growth factor, $B$2/12 represents the

monthly interest rate, which is obtained by dividing the annual rate by 12.

1b. You could have entered the formula = B1 + B1*$B$2/12 in cell B7 instead of = B1*(1 + $B$2/12). What do the terms of this alternate formula represent?

B1 represents the principal; B1*$B$2/12 represents the interest for month 1.

1c. Using monthly payments of $350, how long will it take to pay off the loan? Explain how you can use the spreadsheet to answer this question.

5 years 4 months; Use the Fill command to fill columns B, C, and D

until the amount in column D is zero or less. After payment 64, the

balance due is −$177.54.

© Houghton Mifflin Harcourt Publishing Company

2 Use a spreadsheet to calculate the payment needed to pay off a loan.

Standards
CC.9-12.A.CED.3 ... interpret solutions as viable or non-viable in a modeling context.*

Questioning Strategies

- How could you analyze the effect of getting a loan with a different interest rate? You can enter the new interest rate in cell B2. The spreadsheet will automatically use the new interest rate to recalculate all the amounts for each payment period.

- Will it be possible to pay off the $19,000 loan in 5 years with a monthly payment of $350 if you have a loan with an interest rate of 5%? Explain your reasoning. No; with an interest rate of 5% on the loan there is still a balance due of $581.69 after the 60th payment.

- With what interest rate would it be possible to pay off the $19,000 loan in 5 years with a monthly payment of $350? Explain. You could pay off the $19,000 loan in 5 years with a monthly payment of $350 if you had an interest rate of 4%. If you enter 0.04 into cell B2 and press Enter, the balance due after the 60th payment is −$5.71, meaning the loan has been paid off.

- What if the best interest rate you could get was 5%? Explain how it would be possible to pay off the $19,000 loan in 5 years. If you increase your monthly payment by $9 each month to $359, the balance due after the 60th payment is −$30.37, meaning the loan has been paid off.

- How could you modify your spreadsheet to analyze loan payments for a 3-year or a 4-year loan? Since there are 12 periods per year, a 3-year loan would have 36 payments and a 4-year loan would have 48 payments. You can look at the first 36 or 48 rows of the 5-year spreadsheet you currently have set up to see what has been paid at the end of a 3-year or 4-year period.

- Describe how you could create a separate area on the spreadsheet to analyze loan payments for a 3-year loan. You could enter information for a 3-year loan in columns F, G, and H. In cell F7, enter =B1*(1+$B$2/12); in cell G7, enter =$B$3; and in cell H7, enter =F7−G7. After pressing Enter, the cells should contain the same amounts as cells B7 through D7. Then, in cell F8, enter =H7*(1+$B$2/12); in cell G8, enter =$B$3; and in cell H8, enter =F8−G8. Use the Fill command to fill columns F, G, and H for payment periods 3 through 36.

3 Use a geometric series to calculate the payment needed to pay off a loan.

Standards
CC.9-12.A.SSE.4 Derive the formula for the sum of a finite geometric series (when the common ratio is not 1), and use the formula to solve problems.

Questioning Strategies

- Using the formula derived from the sum of a finite geometric series, what would be the value of r for an annual interest rate of 5%? Explain. The value of r for a 5% annual interest rate would be approximately 0.004. The monthly interest rate is $\frac{1}{12}$ the annual interest rate, so divide 0.05 by 12.

© Houghton Mifflin Harcourt Publishing Company

Continued

2 Use a spreadsheet to calculate the payment needed to pay off a loan.

A Experiment with different monthly payment amounts. To do so, change the value in cell B3. Be sure to keep track of the final balance after payment at the end of the 60th payment period. What is the minimum monthly payment that pays off the loan in 5 years?

$367.33

B What happens when you enter a monthly payment of $95? Explain why this happens.

The balance after payment is $19,000 every month. The interest for the first

month is $95, so a $95 monthly payment pays only the interest and none of

the principal.

C Is it possible to pay off the loan (in any amount of time) with a monthly payment that is less than $95? How do you know?

No; any monthly payment less than $95 will result in a balance due

after the first payment of more than $19,000 and then increasing

subsequent balances due.

REFLECT

2a. Assume you make the monthly payment from part A above. At the end of 5 years, what is the balance due after the last payment? Explain what it means.

−$0.47; You have paid $0.47 too much.

2b. Assume you make the monthly payment from part A above for 59 payments and then $0.47 less than that amount for the 60th payment. At the end of 5 years, what is the total amount of interest you have paid? Explain.

$3039.33; 59 × $367.33 + $366.86 = $22,039.33; $22,039.33 − $19,000 = $3039.33

2c. Explain why the total amount of interest paid at the end of 5 years is not simply 6% of $19,000 multiplied by 5.

6% of $19,000 multiplied by 5 is $1140 · 5 = $5700; this is the simple interest

you would owe if you waited 5 years before repaying the loan all at once, but

you are making monthly payments and interest is compounding monthly.

2d. Suppose you want to make monthly payments of $350 and plan to take a 5-year loan with an annual interest rate of 6%. What is the most expensive loan you can afford? Explain how you found your answer.

$18,103.94; Experiment by changing the principal until the balance due

after the 60th payment is zero or less. In this case, the balance due

after the 60th payment is −$0.01.

---

3 Use a geometric series to calculate the payment needed to pay off a loan.

A You can use what you know about the sum of a finite geometric series to derive a formula that can be used to calculate a monthly loan payment. To begin, set up variables as follows.

P = principal

R = annual interest rate expressed as a decimal

r = monthly interest rate expressed as a decimal

m = monthly payment

Explain how r is related to R.

$r = \frac{R}{12}$ because the monthly interest rate is $\frac{1}{12}$ of the annual interest rate.

B You can use P, r, and m to write an expression for the loan balance B after you make a payment at the end of each month.

At the end of the first month, before the monthly payment is applied, the loan balance is the principal P plus the interest for the month rP, for a total of $P + rP$, or $P(1 + r)$.

At the end of the first month, after the monthly payment is applied, what is the loan balance?

$P(1 + r) − m$

At the end of the second month, before the monthly payment is applied, you owe the balance after payment from the first month plus interest, which is $[P(1 + r) − m](1 + r)$, or $P(1 + r)^2 − m(1 + r)$.

At the end of the second month, after the monthly payment is applied, what is the loan balance?

$P(1 + r)^2 − m(1 + r) − m$

Complete the table.

Period	Balance at End of Period	Balance After Payment (B)
1	$P(1 + r)$	$P(1 + r) − m$
2	$P(1 + r)^2 − m(1 + r)$	$P(1 + r)^2 − m(1 + r) − m$
3	$P(1 + r)^3 − m(1 + r)^2 − m(1 + r)$	$P(1 + r)^3 − m(1 + r)^2 − m(1 + r) − m$
4	$P(1 + r)^4 − m(1 + r)^3 − m(1 + r)^2 − m(1 + r)$	$P(1 + r)^4 − m(1 + r)^3 − m(1 + r)^2 − m(1 + r) − m$

Notes

- How can you use the formula you wrote to calculate the monthly payment to pay off a loan with principal P, monthly interest rate r, and n monthly payments to determine the monthly payment required to pay off the $19,000 loan in 5 years with an annual interest rate of 5%? Substitute 0.004 instead of 0.005 for r in the formula $m = \dfrac{rP(1 + r)^n}{(1 + r)^2 - 1}$:

$m = \dfrac{0.004(19{,}000)(1.004)^{60}}{(1.004)^{60} - 1} \approx 356.82$. So, the required monthly payment would be $356.82.

- How does the minimum monthly payment you found for a 5% annual interest rate using the formula compare with the minimum monthly payment you found for a 5% annual interest rate using the spreadsheet? Explain. Using the spreadsheet, the minimum monthly payment for a 5% annual interest rate was about $359, while using the formula the monthly payment was about $357. The difference is due to a rounding error in the formula when the interest rate 0.05 is divided by 12 to get r. If 0.00417 is substituted for r instead of 0.004, the monthly payment is $358.59, which is just about the same as the spreadsheet result.

- How can you rewrite the formula you wrote in part E to calculate the principal P that you can pay off if you take out a loan with monthly interest rate r, n monthly payments, and a monthly payment of m dollars?

$P = \dfrac{m(1 - (1 + r)^{-n})}{r}$

- How can you use the formula in the previous question to determine the amount of money you could spend on a car if you can get a loan at a 5.4% annual interest rate for 5 years and you can afford a monthly payment of only $250?

$P = \dfrac{250(1 - (1 + 0.0045)^{-60})}{0.0045} \approx 13{,}119.89$; you could spend about $13,000 on a car.

This lesson addresses Mathematical Practice Standard 2 (Reason abstractly and quantitatively). In the first part of the lesson, students experiment with monthly payments to determine what monthly payment results in an ending balance closest to 0. Here, the spreadsheet removes the burden of performing tedious calculations so that students can focus on quantitative reasoning. In the second part of the lesson, students generalize the situation in order to derive a formula that replaces the need for a spreadsheet. Here, students engage in abstract reasoning, and they check the correctness of the formula by comparing what the formula gives as a monthly payment against what they found by trial and error using the spreadsheet.

CLOSE

Essential Question

How can you analyze the balance due on a loan? Use a spreadsheet or derive a formula to calculate a monthly payment. By starting with the formula for the sum of a finite geometric series, you can write a formula to calculate the monthly payment required to pay off any loan with principal P, monthly interest rate r, and n monthly payments.

Summarize

Have students write a one-page summary of how to use a finite geometric series model to write a formula to analyze the balance due on a loan.

EXTEND

Standards

CC.9-12.A.SSE.4 Derive the formula for the sum of a finite geometric series (when the common ratio is not 1), and use the formula to solve problems. (Exs. 1–6)

C Extend the pattern in the Balance After Payment column. Complete the formula for B, the balance after payment at the end of the nth period.

$$B = P(1+r)^n - m(1+r)^{n-1} - m(1+r)^{n-2} - \cdots - m(1+r) - m$$

Simplify the formula by factoring.

$$B = P(1+r)^n - m\left[(1+r)^{n-1} + (1+r)^{n-2} + \cdots + (1+r) + 1\right]$$

The expression $[(1+r)^{n-1} + (1+r)^{n-2} + \cdots + (1+r) + 1]$ is a finite geometric series.

How many terms are in the series? $\underline{\quad n \quad}$

What is the common ratio? $\underline{\quad 1+r \quad}$

D The sum S_n of the finite geometric series $a_1 r^{n-1} + a_1 r^{n-2} + \cdots + a_1 r + a_1$ is $S_n = \dfrac{a_1(1-r^n)}{1-r}$ where r is the common ratio and n is the number of terms.

Replace the finite geometric series $(1+r)^{n-1} + (1+r)^{n-2} + \cdots + (1+r) + 1$ with the expression for its sum, and simplify.

$$B = P(1+r)^n - m \cdot \frac{1(1-(1+r)^n)}{1-(1+r)} = P(1+r)^n - m \cdot \frac{(1+r)^n - 1}{r}$$

E You are interested in knowing what monthly payment will result in a balance B that is equal to 0 after n payments. Set $B = 0$ in the above equation and then solve for m and simplify. This will give you a formula you can use to calculate the monthly payment needed to pay off a loan with principal P, monthly interest rate r, and n monthly payment periods.

$$m = \frac{rP(1+r)^n}{(1+r)^n - 1}$$

F Show how to use the formula to find the minimum monthly payment needed to pay off a 5-year $19,000 loan with an annual interest rate of 6%.

$$m = \frac{rP(1+r)^n}{(1+r)^n - 1} = \frac{0.005(19,000)(1.005)^{60}}{(1.005)^{60} - 1} \approx 367.33$$

REFLECT

3a. How does the minimum monthly payment that you found using the formula compare to the minimum monthly payment that you found using the spreadsheet?

They are the same.

3b. If you could increase the number of monthly payments (say, from 60 to 72), what do you expect would happen to the amount of the monthly payment?

The monthly payment would decrease.

EXTEND

1. Suppose you want to borrow $19,000 and you find a 5-year loan with an annual interest rate of 5%. By how much do you lower your monthly payments by taking this loan instead of the 6% loan? How much do you save over the life of the loan?

$8.78; 60 · $8.78 = $526.80

2. You would like your monthly payments to be no more than $300. Suppose you get a $19,000 loan with an annual interest rate of 6%, but you are able to choose the term (length) of the loan. Enter the formula for the monthly payment m into your calculator as a function of the number of payments, n. Then use the calculator's table feature to find the shortest term for the loan that results in monthly payments of no more than $300.

77 months

3. A friend claims that if you borrow half the amount ($9,500 instead of $19,000), you will cut your monthly payments in half. Is your friend correct? Explain.

Yes; $m = \dfrac{0.005(9500)(1.005)^{60}}{(1.005)^{60} - 1} \approx 183.66$

4. In general, how is the monthly payment affected when the amount borrowed is multiplied by some factor, and the interest rate and number of periods are kept the same? Explain.

The monthly payment is multiplied by the same factor because m is directly proportional to P. m is directly proportional to P because

$$m = \frac{rP(1+r)^n}{(1+r)^n - 1} = \frac{r(1+r)^n}{(1+r)^n - 1} \cdot P, \text{ and } \frac{r(1+r)^n}{(1+r)^n - 1} \text{ is constant.}$$

5. Use the formula $m = \dfrac{rP(1+r)^n}{(1+r)^n - 1}$ to explain why the monthly payment m decreases when the number n of monthly payments increases. Assume that the principal P and interest rate r are constant. (*Hint:* Let $x = (1+r)^n$. Determine what happens to x as n increases. Then determine what happens to $m = rP \cdot \dfrac{x}{x-1}$.)

As n increases, $x = (1+r)^n$ increases because the base $1+r$ is greater than 1.

As x increases, the fraction $\dfrac{x}{x-1}$ decreases (toward 1), so $m = rP \cdot \dfrac{x}{x-1}$ decreases.

6. What alternate form of the formula $m = \dfrac{rP(1+r)^n}{(1+r)^n - 1}$ do you get if you multiply the numerator and denominator by $(1+r)^{-n}$? What is the advantage of using this alternate form when calculating m?

$m = \dfrac{rP}{1 - (1+r)^{-n}}$; there are fewer steps in the calculation process.

Standard	Items
CC.9-12.A.SSE.1*	3, 6, 10
CC.9-12.A.SSE.4	5, 6, 9, 11
CC.9-12.F.IF.2	4, 8, 11
CC.9-12.F.IF.3	1
CC.9-12.F.BF.2*	4, 7, 8, 11
CC.9-12.F.LE.2*	2, 8, 11

TEST PREP DOCTOR ⊕

Multiple Choice: Item 1
- Students who chose **A** did not understand the difference between a recursive and an explicit rule.
- Students who chose **B** did not understand the difference between a recursive and an explicit rule, and they did not understand that the domain of a sequence is a subset of the set of integers.
- Students who chose **D** did not understand that the domain of a sequence is a subset of the set of integers.

Multiple Choice: Item 2
- Students who chose **F** or **G** did not recognize that the pattern in the graph is exponential and used an arithmetic sequence to model the situation rather than a geometric sequence.
- Students who chose **H** used 0.10 for the common ratio r instead of 1.10, not understanding that if $0 < r < 1$, the graph would be falling from left to right instead of rising.

Multiple Choice: Item 4
- Students who chose **F** used n instead of $n - 1$ in the explicit rule $f(n) = 450 - 25(n - 1)$.
- Students who chose **H** or **J** mixed up the first term and the common difference when writing the explicit rule.

Free Response: Item 9
- Students who were unable to calculate total earnings for either job may not have understood how the sum of a finite geometric series can be used here.
- Students who said that job A would pay more may have written the formula for the sum of a finite geometric series incorrectly (such as using 1.05 instead of 1.005), or they may have simply made an error when evaluating the sum.

Free Response: Item 10
- Students who answered part (a) incorrectly may not have understood that position numbers in a sequence can begin with 0 instead of 1.
- Students who calculated the wrong population in part (b) may have made an error when evaluating the rule for the sequence.
- Students who answered part (c) incorrectly did not understand how the common ratio is 1 more than the annual growth rate.

Free Response: Item 11
- Students who wrote a rule for an arithmetic sequence instead of a geometric sequence in part (a) may not have recognized that the terms have a common ratio, not a common difference.
- Students who wrote the rule $f(1) = 100,000$ and $f(n) = f(n - 1) \cdot 0.95$ for $n \geq 2$ in part (a) did not understand the difference between a recursive rule and an explicit rule.
- Students who used a different value for 0.95 in the formula in part (a) did not correctly calculate the common ratio between consecutive terms in the sequence.
- Students who were not able to write a formula in part (b) may not have understood how the sum of a finite geometric series can be used to solve the problem.
- Students who calculated the wrong total in part (b) may have written the formula for the sum of a finite geometric series incorrectly, or they may have simply made an error when evaluating the formula.

Name _____ Class _____ Date _____

MULTIPLE CHOICE

1. Which rule defines a sequence recursively?

 A. $f(n) = 4n + 2$
  domain: $\{0, 1, 2, 3, 4\}$

 B. $f(n) = 4n + 2$
  domain: {all real numbers}

 C. $f(0) = 2, f(n) = f(n-1) + 4$ if $n \geq 1$
  domain: $\{0, 1, 2, 3, 4\}$ ◯

 D. $f(0) = 2, f(n) = f(n-1) + 4$ if $n \geq 1$
  domain: {all real numbers}

2. A college currently has 4990 students. A faculty committee made the following graph to show their plan for recommended enrollments for the next four years.

Which sequence is the best model for the committee's recommendations?

 F. $f(n) = 4990 + 500n$

 G. $f(n) = 4990 + 1.10n$

 H. $f(n) = 4990(0.10)^n$

 J. $f(n) = 4990(1.10)^n$ ◯

3. The sequence $a_n = a_0(1 + r)^n$ can be used to find the value of a car n years after 2005. Which expression represents the value of the car in 2005?

 A. a_0 ◯   **C.** $a_0(1 + r)$

 B. $1 + r$ **D.** $(1 + r)^n$

4. The following rule represents the sequence of balances Hector owes on a loan, where $f(n)$ is the balance he owes in dollars after making n equal payments.

$$f(1) = 450, f(n) = f(n-1) - 25 \text{ if } n \geq 2$$

Which is an explicit rule for the sequence?

 F. $f(n) = 450 - 25n$

 G. $f(n) = 475 - 25n$ ◯

 H. $f(n) = 450n - 25$

 J. $f(n) = 475n - 25$

5. Deon is deriving a formula for S_n, the sum of the finite geometric series $a_1 + a_1r + a_1r^2 + a_1r^3 + \cdots + a_1r^{n-1}$. What is $S_n - rS_n$?

 A. $a_1 + a_1r^n$

 B. $a_1 - a_1r^n$ ◯

 C. $a_1 + a_1 + a_1r + a_1r^2 + \cdots + a_1r^{n-2}$

 D. $a_1 - a_1 - a_1r - a_1r^2 - \cdots - a_1r^{n-2}$

6. Which expression is equal to
$(1 + r)^{n-1} + (1 + r)^{n-2} + \cdots + (1 + r)^2 + (1 + r) + 1?$

 F. $\dfrac{1 - r^n}{1 - r}$ **H.** $\dfrac{1 - (1+r)^n}{r}$

 G. $\dfrac{1 + r^n}{1 + r}$ **J.** $\dfrac{(1+r)^n - 1}{r}$ ◯

7. A sheet of paper is 0.1 mm thick. The paper is folded in half repeatedly, and the sequence of thicknesses (in millimeters) is 0.1, 0.2, 0.4, 0.8, …. What is a rule for this sequence if 0.1 is term 0?

 A. $f(n) = 0.1(0.5)^n$

 B. $f(n) = 0.5(0.1)^n$

 C. $f(n) = 2(0.1)^n$

 D. $f(n) = 0.1(2)^n$ ◯

FREE RESPONSE

8. The table shows the weight of Tom's truck as he loads it with bags of cement.

Bags of Cement n	Truck Weight (lb) $f(n)$
0	2988
1	3068
2	3148
3	3228
4	3308

 a. Write a recursive rule for the sequence of truck weights.

  $f(0) = 2988, f(n) = f(n-1) + 80$

  if $n \geq 1$

 b. Write an explicit rule for the sequence of truck weights.

  $f(n) = 2988 + 80n$

 c. Is the sequence arithmetic, geometric, or neither? Explain.

  Arithmetic; differences are constant.

9. Morgan is considering two job offers. If she takes job A, she will earn $3600 in her first month and then will get a 0.5% raise every month for 2 years. If she takes job B, she will earn $3800 per month to start and will get a 1% raise at the end of every 3-month interval for 2 years. Which job will pay more during the first 2 years? Justify your answer.

 Job B will pay more.

 Job A: Use $S_n = a_1\left(\dfrac{1 - r^n}{1 - r}\right)$ with

 $a_1 = 3600, r = 0.005,$ and $n = 24$:

 $S_{24} = 3600\left(\dfrac{1 - (1.005)^{24}}{1 - 1.005}\right) \approx 91,555$

 Job B: Use $S_n = a_1\left(\dfrac{1 - r^n}{1 - r}\right)$ with

 $a_1 = 3800, r = 0.01,$ and $n = 8,$

 but note that the total pay is 3 times S_8:

 $3 \cdot S_8 = 3 \cdot 3800\left(\dfrac{1 - (1.01)^8}{1 - 1.01}\right) \approx 94,457$

10. The sequence $a_n = 14,000(1.03)^n$ is a model for the population of a town, where n is the number of years after 2010.

 a. What is a_0? What does it represent?

  14,000; the population in 2010,

  based on the model

 b. What is a_4? What does it represent?

  15,757; the population in 2014,

  based on the model

 c. What is the common ratio for the sequence? How can you use the common ratio to find the town's annual growth rate?

  1.03; subtract 1 and express

  the result as a percent to find

  the annual growth rate, 3%.

11. Ms. Hudson donated $100,000 in the year 2000 to establish a scholarship account for her former college. The table shows end-of-year balances in the account over the next several years as scholarships were awarded.

Year	Year-End Balance (Dollars)
2000	100,000.00
2001	95,000.00
2002	90,250.00
2003	85,737.50
2004	81,450.63

 a. Write an explicit formula for the sequence of year-end balances. Let $n = 0$ represent the year 2000.

  $f(n) = 100,000(0.95)^n$

 b. Suppose the balance changed only as a result of awarding scholarships in the years 2001 through 2010 according to the pattern indicated in the table. How much scholarship money was awarded in total during those 10 years? Justify your answer.

  $40,126.31; $S_{10} = \dfrac{5000(1 - (0.95)^{10})}{1 - 0.95}$

  $\approx 40,126.31$

UNIT 10

Statistics

Unit Vocabulary

categorical data (10-1)

census (10-1)

confidence
  interval (10-6)

control group (10-7)

cumulative
  probability (10-3)

data distribution (10-2)

experiment (10-7)

factor (10-7)

individuals (10-1)

interquartile
  range (10-2)

margin of error (10-6)

mean (10-2)

median (10-2)

normal
  distribution (10-2)

null hypothesis (10-8)

numerical data (10-1)

observational
  study (10-7)

parameter (10-1)

permutation test (10-8)

population (10-1)

probability
  distribution (10-3)

proportion (10-1)

random variable (10-3)

randomized
  comparative
  experiment (10-7)

representative (10-1)

resampling (10-8)

sampling (10-1)

sampling
  distribution (10-5)

significant result (10-8)

skewed
  distribution (10-2)

skewed left (10-2)

skewed right (10-2)

standard
  deviation (10-2)

standard error of the
  mean/proportion (10-5)

standard normal
  distribution (10-4)

statistic (10-1)

survey (10-7)

treatment (10-7)

treatment group (10-7)

uniform
  distribution (10-2)

z-score (10-4)

UNIT 10

Statistics

Unit Focus

Statistics are used to summarize and compare sets of data as well as to generalize from a sample taken from a population to the population as a whole. You will learn how to gather data, how to calculate statistics, how to make claims based on statistics, how to describe your degree of certainty about those claims, and how to make decisions based on statistics. A knowledge of statistics is especially useful when evaluating reports in the media about surveys, studies, and experiments.

Unit at a Glance

COMMON CORE

Lesson	Standards for Mathematical Content
10-1 Data-Gathering Techniques	CC.9-12.S.IC.1*
10-2 Data Distributions	CC.9-12.S.ID.1*, CC.9-12.S.ID.3*
10-3 Probability Distributions	CC.9-12.S.ID.1*, CC.9-12.S.IC.2*
10-4 Normal Distributions	CC.9-12.S.ID.4*
10-5 Sampling Distributions	CC.9-12.S.IC.4*
10-6 Confidence Intervals and Margins of Error	CC.9-12.S.IC.4*
10-7 Surveys, Experiments, and Observational Studies	CC.9-12.S.IC.3*, CC.9-12.S.IC.6*
10-8 Determining the Significance of Experimental Results	CC.9-12.S.IC.5*
Test Prep	

Unpacking the Common Core State Standards

Use the table to help you understand the Standards for Mathematical Content that are taught in this unit. Refer to the lessons listed after each standard for exploration and practice.

COMMON CORE Standards for Mathematical Content	What It Means For You
CC.9-12.S.ID.1 Represent data with plots on the real number line (dot plots, histograms, and box plots).* Lessons 10-2, 10-3 (Also 10-4, 10-8)	You will use data displays to see the shapes of data distributions.
CC.9-12.S.ID.3 Interpret differences in shape, center, and spread in the context of the data sets, accounting for possible effects of extreme data points (outliers).* Lesson 10-2	You will summarize a data distribution by describing its shape and identifying its center and spread.
CC.9-12.S.ID.4 Use the mean and standard deviation of a data set to fit it to a normal distribution and to estimate population percentages. Recognize that there are data sets for which such a procedure is not appropriate. Use calculators, spreadsheets, and tables to estimate areas under the normal curve.* Lesson 10-4 (Also 10-8)	A so-called "normal" distribution has a symmetric shape, being mounded in the middle and tapered at the ends. Normal distributions can be represented by bell-shaped curves called normal curves. Questions about the data in a normal distribution can be interpreted as areas under a normal curve.
CC.9-12.S.IC.1 Understand statistics as a process for making inferences about population parameters based on a random sample from that population.* Lesson 10-1	Statistics allow you to draw conclusions about a population from just a sample of the population as long as the sample is representative.
CC.9-12.S.IC.2 Decide if a specified model is consistent with results from a given data-generating process, e.g., using simulation.* Lesson 10-3	Understanding statistics can help you evaluate a model. For instance, a model for flipping a coin may assume that the coin is fair, but when you gather actual coin-flip data, an analysis of the data may suggest that the coin isn't fair.
CC.9-12.S.IC.3 Recognize the purposes of and differences among sample surveys, experiments, and observational studies; explain how randomization relates to each.* Lesson 10-7	You will learn to distinguish among surveys, experiments, and observational studies, and to determine the purpose of each. You will also learn how randomization is used to make each more reliable.
CC.9-12.S.IC.4 Use data from a sample survey to estimate a population mean or proportion; develop a margin of error through the use of simulation models for random sampling.* Lessons 10-5, 10-6	Because a statistic is calculated from a sample of a population, it is an estimate of a characteristic of the population. You will learn to determine a range of values for the statistic that is likely to contain the true value for the population.
CC.9-12.S.IC.5 Use data from a randomized experiment to compare two treatments; use simulations to decide if differences between parameters are significant.* Lesson 10-8	You will learn how to test whether an experimental result is due to chance, or whether the conditions of the experiment are more likely to have caused the result.
CC.9-12.S.IC.6 Evaluate reports based on data.* Lesson 10-7	You will learn how to evaluate statistical claims that you encounter in media reports.

Unpacking the Common Core State Standards

This page lists and explains the Standards for Mathematical Content that are addressed in this unit. For information about the Standards for Mathematical Practice, which are integrated throughout the text, see Teacher Edition pages x–xiii.

Additional Standards in This Unit

CC.9-12.N.Q.1 Use units as a way to understand problems ...* Lesson 10-1

CC.9-12.A.CED.4 Rearrange formulas to highlight a quantity of interest, using the same reasoning as in solving equations.* Lesson 10-6

CC.9-12.S.MD.6(+) Use probabilities to make fair decisions (e.g., drawing by lots, using a random number generator).* Lessons 10-1, 10-3, 10-8

UNIT 10

Notes

_____

_____

_____

_____

_____

_____

_____

_____

_____

_____

_____

_____

Data-Gathering Techniques

Essential question: *What are the different methods for gathering data about a population?*

© Houghton Mifflin Harcourt Publishing Company

COMMON CORE Standards for Mathematical Content

CC.9-12.S.IC.1 Understand statistics as a process for making inferences about population parameters based on a random sample from that population.*

Vocabulary

numerical data, categorical data, population, individuals, census, parameter, sampling, statistic, representative sample, proportion

Prerequisites

Calculating the mean of a data set, Algebra 1

Math Background

Sampling is an important aspect of statistics. It involves making observations of or gathering data from a population, either the entire population (a census) or a part of a population (a sample). Typically, the goal of sampling is to gain knowledge about a population, often to make predictions. Statistics are also used to persuade.

The predictions based on statistics have a certain amount of error associated with them. Error can come about from the sampling method used, whether intentional (sometimes done when using statistics to persuade) or unintentional. *How to Lie with Statistics*, written by Darrell Huff in 1954, outlines how errors can lead to inaccurate conclusions, such as the rather famous but inaccurate prediction of who would win the presidential election in 1948. A frequent source of errors in statistical predictions is bias, which makes it more likely that certain subsets of the population are over-represented in the sample. Sampling methods can affect the statistics gathered, and, therefore, the predictions that are based on them.

INTRODUCE

Ask students to give examples of using statistical surveys. **Answers will vary: Students may mention "4 out of 5 dentists surveyed" or political polls.** Ask students how this information might have been gathered. Prompt them if necessary: Were the data gathered from an online survey? from people on the street? from a poll conducted by telephone? Use this to introduce the idea of a sample.

TEACH

1 ENGAGE

Questioning Strategies

- What is the difference between a parameter and a statistic? **A parameter is based on a census; it represents an entire population. A statistic is based on a sample.**

- Describe how a statistic might be representative of an entire population. **Statistics can result in accurate estimates of parameters. This will happen if the sample is representative of the population.**

- A reporter for a high school paper asked all members of the track team how many miles they run each week. What type of data is the reporter gathering? **numerical** Is this a census or a sample? Why? **It's a census of the track team—unless your intended population is the entire student body, in which case it's a sample.** Will the data be representative of the entire student body? Why or why not? **No; members of the track team most likely run more than members of the entire student body.**

Teaching Strategy

This unit contains a great deal of new vocabulary. Making flash cards will help students learn the language of statistics. They can add to their cards as the unit progresses. In addition to using the cards to study, students can play games with the flash cards, such as one student giving clues to a second who must guess what is on the card.

Name_____ Class_____ Date_____

Data-Gathering Techniques

10-1

COMMON CORE

CC.9-12.S.IC.1*

Essential question: *What are the different methods for gathering data about a population?*

1 ENGAGE — Understanding Data-Gathering Techniques

In the branch of mathematics known as statistics, you work with data. Data can be **numerical**, such as heights or salaries, or **categorical**, such as eye color or political affiliation. You collect data about a **population** by surveying or studying some or all of the **individuals** in the population.

When *all* the individuals in a population are surveyed or studied, the data-gathering technique is called a **census**. A **parameter** is a number that summarizes a characteristic of the population.

When only some of the individuals in a population are surveyed or studied, the data-gathering technique is called **sampling**. A **statistic** is a number that summarizes a characteristic of a sample. Statistics can be used to estimate parameters. Samples that result in accurate estimates are said to be **representative** of the population.

There are a variety of sampling methods, characterized by how the individuals in the sample are chosen. The table below lists a few.

Sampling Method	Description
Random	Each individual in the population has an equal chance of being selected.
Self-selected	Individuals volunteer to be part of the sample.
Convenience	Individuals are selected based on how accessible they are.
Systematic	Members of the sample are chosen according to a rule, such as every *n*th individual in the population.
Stratified	The individuals are organized into groups, and individuals from each group are selected (typically through a random sample within each group).
Cluster	The individuals are organized into groups, and all of the individuals in just some of the groups are selected (typically through a random sample of the groups).

REFLECT

1a. Give an example of numerical data and an example of categorical data other than the examples listed in the first paragraph.

Answers will vary. Sample answer: An example of numerical data is age. An example of categorical data is gender.

1b. Asking your friends is an example of what type of sampling method? Explain.

Convenience sampling, because friends are easily accessible.

1c. Which sampling method do you think is most likely to result in a representative sample? Why?

A random sample is most likely to be representative because the method is unbiased and gives each individual the same chance of being selected.

1d. Which sampling method do you think would be least likely to result in a representative sample? Why?

A self-selected sample is least likely to be representative because the method is biased toward individuals who have a strong interest in the results.

1e. Explain why a researcher might use a sampling method rather than a census to gather information about a population.

A census of all individuals may be too expensive, impractical, or even impossible to obtain.

2 EXPLORE — Finding Statistics Using Various Sampling Methods

The salaries (in thousands of dollars) of all 30 employees at a small company are listed in the table.

Salaries at a Small Company									
21	24	26	28	30	32	33	35	37	41
44	46	47	49	50	51	52	54	55	57
58	62	62	64	64	65	70	71	73	80

Use the table to generate a sample of 6 individuals using each sampling method, and then use the sample to predict the mean of the population.

A Suppose individuals whose salaries are 51, 57, 58, 65, 70, and 73 volunteer to be in the sample. Compute the self-selected sample's mean, rounding to the nearest whole number.

Mean ≈ 62

B Take a convenience sample by choosing the 6 numbers in the first two columns of the table. Record the salaries, and then compute the sample's mean, rounding to the nearest whole number.

21, 24, 44, 46, 58, 62; mean ≈ 43

C Take a systematic sample by choosing every fifth number in the list, reading from left to right in each row. Record the salaries, and then compute the sample's mean, rounding to the nearest whole number.

30, 41, 50, 57, 64, 80; mean ≈ 54

2 EXPLORE

Questioning Strategies

- How are the salaries organized in the table? They are in ascending order, from left to right and top to bottom.

- Explain how taking a convenience sample different from the one described in part B could select all low salaries. Take all of the salaries from the top row. Explain how the convenience sample in part B avoids this issue. It takes salaries from all three rows. Explain why it doesn't avoid the issue completely. It takes salaries from the left side of the table, which are lower than those on the right side.

- With the way the table is organized, the systematic sample is almost as close to the actual mean as the random sample. Why? The data are organized in ascending order. So taking every 5th number gets some low, some medium, and some high salaries.

3 EXAMPLE

Questioning Strategies

- How do you know that the proportion of runners is 50%? There are 5 entries in the table for running out of 10 total entries; $5 \div 10 = 0.5 = 50\%$

- What proportion of the adults who get cardio exercise walk? 20% What proportion swim? 10% What proportion do some other form of cardio exercise? 20% What is the total of all of the proportions, including runners? 100% Is this 100% of all of the people surveyed? Explain. No; it's all of the people who said they get cardio exercise, which is only 40% of the people surveyed.

EXTRA EXAMPLE

A ski area uses the information gained from scanning season ski passes in lift lines to determine how many days out of each season the pass holders ski and how many lift rides they take each day. The table lists the data for a random sample of 15 skiers. Calculate statistics from the sample and use the statistics to make predictions about the ski habits of the approximately 10,000 season pass holders.

Number of Days	Number of Lift Rides
10	12
5	15
2	6
14	18
27	10
3	6
18	15
5	9
4	11
16	13
7	14
12	10
19	8
14	6
25	15

A. What proportion of the skiers ski 10 or more days? Of those, what proportion take 12 or more lift rides in a day? 60%; about 55.5%

B. Use the proportions from part A to predict the total number of skiers who ski 10 or more days in a season and take 12 or more lift rides each time they ski. about 3330

C. Calculate the following two means from the sample data: 1) mean number of days skied and 2) mean number of lift rides taken per day. about 12.1; 11.2

D. Use the means from part C to predict the number of lift rides taken per season by a skier. about 136

© Houghton Mifflin Harcourt Publishing Company

D Take a random sample. Begin by labeling the data in the table with the identifiers 1–10 for the first row, 11–20 for the second row, and 21–30 for the third row. Then use a graphing calculator's random integer generator to generate 6 identifiers between 1 and 30, as shown. (If any identifiers are repeated, simply generate replacements for them until you have 6 unique identifiers.) Record the corresponding salaries, and then compute the sample's mean, rounding to the nearest whole number.

Answers will vary. Sample answer for the
identifiers shown on the calculator screen:
65, 44, 26, 54, 58, 30; mean ≈ 46

REFLECT

2a. Compute the mean of the population. Then list the four samples from best to worst in terms of how well each sample mean estimates the population mean.

Population mean ≈ 49; random, systematic, convenience, self-selected

2b. How do the best and worst sampling methods from your list compare with your answers to Reflect Questions 1c and 1d?

Answers will vary, but students should generally find that random samples
are best and self-selected samples are worst.

Some statistics, such as the mean, apply only to numerical data. For categorical data, an appropriate statistic is a **proportion**, which is the relative frequency of a category.

3 EXAMPLE Making Predictions from a Sample

A community health center surveyed a small random sample of adults in the community about their exercise habits. The survey asked whether the person engages in regular cardio exercise (running, walking, swimming, or other) and, if so, what the duration and frequency of exercise are.

Of the 25 people surveyed, 10 said that they do engage in regular cardio exercise. The table lists the data for those 10 people.

Calculate statistics from the sample, and use the statistics to make predictions about the exercise habits of the approximately 5000 adults living in the community.

Type of exercise	Duration (minutes spent exercising)	Frequency (times per week)
Running	30	4
Walking	20	5
Running	40	3
Running	60	6
Swimming	40	4
Other	90	2
Running	30	3
Walking	20	5
Running	30	4
Other	120	1

A Calculate the following two proportions from the sample data.

Proportion of adults who get regular cardio exercise = $\frac{10}{25}$ = 40 %

Proportion of runners among those who get regular cardio exercise = $\frac{5}{10}$ = 50 %

B Use the proportions from part A and the verbal model below to predict the number of runners among all adults living in the community.

Number of runners in the community	=	Number of adults in the community	×	Proportion of adults who get cardio exercise	×	Proportion of runners among those who get regular cardio exercise

Number of runners in the community = 5000 · 0.4 · 0.5 = 1000

C Calculate the following two means from the sample data.

Mean duration of exercise for those who get regular cardio exercise = 48 min

Mean frequency of exercise for those who get regular cardio exercise = 3.7 times per week

D Use the means from part C to predict, for those who get regular cardio exercise, the number of *hours* spent exercising each week. Show your calculations and include units.

Time spent exercising each week = $\frac{48 \text{ min} \cdot 3.7}{60 \text{ min/h}}$ ≈ 3 hours

REFLECT

3a. One of the *categorical variables* in the survey was regular cardio exercise. That variable had only two possible values: yes or no. What was the other categorical variable, and what were its possible values?

Type of exercise; running, walking, swimming, other

3b. What were the two *numerical variables* in the survey, and what were their possible values?

Duration of exercise, which could be any positive number (though generally a
multiple of 10 less than, say, 240); weekly frequency of exercise, which could be
any counting number from 1 to 7

3c. How much confidence do you have in the predictions made from the results of the survey? Explain your reasoning.

Answers will vary. Students should note that the sample was random, which
makes the results representative of the population, but the sample size was small,
which may not make the results accurate.

1 ENGAGE and **3 EXAMPLE** provide opportunities to address Mathematical Practice Standard 6 (Attend to precision). Students will need to be precise in their communication and their choice of vocabulary. In **3 EXAMPLE**, they will need to be clear and concise about whether they are discussing the population (5000 people), the sample (25 people), those from the sample who are runners (10 people), or their projection of those of the population who are runners (1000 people). This example also provides an opportunity to practice newly learned vocabulary and to clearly state which group of people or proportion thereof they are discussing.

CLOSE

Essential Question
What are the different methods for gathering data about a population?
A census in which information is gathered from every individual in the population can be used. If a census is impractical, a sampling method can be used. Sampling techniques include random, self-selected, convenience, systematic, stratified, and cluster.

Summarize
Have students write a journal entry discussing the different types of sampling—random, self-selected, convenience, systematic, stratified, and cluster. The entry should include a description and an example of each type, a reason why you might use each type, and a statement about how representative of the entire population each type would be.

PRACTICE

Where skills are taught	Where skills are practiced
1 ENGAGE	EXS. 1–10
3 EXAMPLE	EXS. 11–14

PRACTICE

A student council wants to know whether students would like the council to sponsor a mid-winter dance or a mid-winter carnival this year. Classify each sampling method.

1. Survey every tenth student on the school's roster. <u>systematic</u>

2. Survey all freshmen and all juniors. <u>cluster</u>

3. Survey 20 freshmen, 20 sophomores, 20 juniors, and 20 seniors. <u>stratified</u>

4. Survey those who ask the council president for a questionnaire. <u>self-selected</u>

5. Survey those who happen to be in the cafeteria at noon. <u>convenience</u>

Use the following information for Exercises 6–9.

The officers of a neighborhood association want to know whether residents are interested in beautifying the neighborhood and, if so, how much money they are willing to contribute toward the costs involved. The officers are considering the three sampling methods below.

A. Call and survey every tenth resident on the association's roster.

B. Randomly select and survey 10 residents from among those who come to the neighborhood block party.

C. Mail a survey to every resident with instructions to complete and mail the survey back.

6. Identify the population.

<u>all residents of the neighborhood</u>

7. Which sampling method is most likely to result in a representative sample of the population? Explain.

<u>Method A; if method B is used, those who do not attend the block party have</u>

<u>no chance of being represented and if method C is used, only people who feel</u>

<u>strongly are likely to mail their surveys back.</u>

8. Describe another sampling method that is likely to result in a representative sample of the population.

<u>Randomly select names from the association's roster.</u>

9. Describe the categorical and numerical data that the officers of the neighborhood association want to gather through a survey.

<u>Categorical: interest in beautifying neighborhood; numerical: amount willing to</u>

<u>contribute</u>

Use the following information for Exercises 10–14.

A community theater association plans to produce three plays for the upcoming season. The association surveys a random sample of the approximately 7000 households in the community to see if an adult member of the household is interested in attending plays and, if so, what type of plays the person prefers (comedy, drama, or musical), how many members of the household (including the person surveyed) might attend plays, and how many of the three plays those household members might attend.

Of the 50 adults surveyed, 12 indicated an interest in attending plays. The table lists the data for those 12 people.

Preferred type of play	Number of people attending	Number of plays attending
Comedy	2	1
Musical	3	2
Musical	1	2
Drama	2	3
Comedy	3	2
Comedy	2	3
Musical	4	1
Drama	2	3
Comedy	2	2
Musical	2	3
Comedy	5	1
Drama	1	2

10. Describe the categorical and numerical data gathered in the survey.

<u>Categorical: interest in attending plays, preferred type of play;</u>

<u>numerical: number of household members who might attend plays,</u>

<u>how many plays they might attend</u>

11. Calculate the proportion of adults who indicated an interest in attending plays. Then calculate the proportion of those interested in attending plays who prefer dramas.

$\frac{12}{50} = 24\%$; $\frac{3}{12} = 25\%$

12. Approximately 15,000 adults live in the community. Predict the number of adults who prefer plays that are dramas. Show your calculations.

$15{,}000 \cdot 0.24 \cdot 0.25 = 900$

13. For an adult with an interest in attending plays, calculate the mean number of household members who might attend plays. Then calculate the mean number of plays that those household members might attend. Round each mean to the nearest tenth.

mean number attending ≈ 2.4; mean number of plays ≈ 2.1

14. The theater association plans to sells tickets to the plays for $40 each. Predict the amount of revenue from ticket sales. Show your calculations and include units.

<u>Predicted number of households with an adult having an interest in attending</u>

<u>plays = 7000 · 0.24 = 1680; predicted number of tickets sold =</u>

<u>1680 households · $\frac{2.4 \text{ people}}{\text{household}}$ · $\frac{2.1 \text{ tickets}}{\text{person}}$ = 8476.2 tickets;</u>

<u>predicted revenue from ticket sales = 8467.2 tickets · $\frac{\$40}{\text{ticket}}$ = \$338,688</u>

© Houghton Mifflin Harcourt Publishing Company

10-2

Data Distributions

Essential question: *How can you use shape, center, and spread to characterize a data distribution?*

© Houghton Mifflin Harcourt Publishing Company

COMMON CORE Standards for Mathematical Content

CC.9-12.S.ID.1 Represent data with plots on the real number line (dot plots, histograms, and box plots).*

CC.9-12.S.ID.3 Interpret differences in shape, center, and spread in the context of the data sets, accounting for possible effects of extreme data points (outliers).*

Vocabulary

data distribution, uniform distribution, normal distribution, skewed distribution, skewed left, skewed right, mean, median, standard deviation, interquartile range

Prerequisites

Creating line plots, histograms, and box plots, Algebra 1

Math Background

The normal distribution, also called a Gaussian distribution or a bell-shaped curve, is likely the most well-known distribution in statistics. Normal distributions can be completely described by their mean and standard deviation. In normal distributions, 68% of all values fall within one standard deviation of the mean. Similarly, 95% of values fall within two standard deviations, and 99.7% of the values fall within three standard deviations of the mean. Normal distributions are covered in more detail in Lesson 10-4.

The normal distribution can even be used in situations in which the data are not distributed normally (symmetric and with a single hump). The central limit theorem states that the distribution of the means of random samples have a normal distribution for large sample sizes. So, normal distributions can be used to describe the averages of data that do not necessarily have a normal distribution themselves.

INTRODUCE

Ask students which would be most useful to them when researching colleges—a list of all of the college entrance exam scores of last year's freshman class, the average college entrance exam score of last year's freshman class, or a graph showing the college entrance exam scores and the number of students who received each score. Guide them to the understanding that the average score can be useful. They can compare their scores with the average score to see whether they are above or below the average. A graph is also useful. Students can compare their scores with all other scores, not just to the average. They can see where their scores fall in relation to other students' scores. Students should recognize that looking at long lists of numbers is not usually the best way to get an understanding of the data.

TEACH

1 EXPLORE

Questioning Strategies

- What values are on the number lines for line plots, histograms, and box plots? **the data values**

- Interpret the values on the number line for each of the three line plots. **The values on the number line in part A are birth months, with 1 representing January, 2 representing February, and so on. In part B, the values are the birth weights of the babies in kilograms from 3.0 kg to 4.0 kg, with each tick mark representing 0.1 kg. In part C, the values are mothers' ages in years.**

- What does the "height" of each vertical stack of X's in the line plots represent? **the number of times each value occurs**

- How many X's are on each line plot? Why? **There are 20 X's on each line plot because the data came from 20 babies.**

Name_____ Class_____ Date_____

10-2

COMMON CORE

CC.9-12.S.ID.1*,
CC.9-12.S.ID.3*

Data Distributions

Essential question: *How can you use shape, center, and spread to characterize a data distribution?*

A **data distribution** is a set of numerical data that you can graph using a data display that involves a number line, such as a line plot, histogram, or box plot. The graph will reveal the shape of the distribution.

1 EXPLORE Seeing the Shape of a Data Distribution

The table gives data about a random sample of 20 babies born at a hospital.

A Make a line plot for the distribution of birth months.

```
        X         X  X        X  X
X  X  X  X  X  X  X  X  X  X  X  X
1  2  3  4  5  6  7  8  9 10 11 12
         Birth month
```

B Make a line plot for the distribution of birth weights.

```
                   X
              X    X
              X    X
              X    X  X
         X    X    X  X  X
   3.0 3.2 3.4 3.6 3.8 4.0
        Birth weight (kg)
```

C Make a line plot for the distribution of mothers' ages.

```
        X
        X  X
   X    X  X
   X  X X  X  X  X  X                X
27 28 29 30 31 32 33 34 35 36 37 38 39 40
            Mother's age
```

Baby	Birth month	Birth weight (kg)	Mother's age
1	5	3.3	28
2	7	3.6	31
3	11	3.5	33
4	2	3.4	35
5	10	3.7	39
6	3	3.4	30
7	1	3.5	29
8	4	3.2	30
9	7	3.6	31
10	6	3.4	32
11	9	3.6	33
12	10	3.5	30
13	11	3.4	31
14	1	3.7	29
15	6	3.5	34
16	5	3.8	30
17	8	3.5	32
18	9	3.6	30
19	12	3.3	29
20	2	3.5	28

REFLECT

1a. Describe the shape of the distribution of birth months.

The distribution is fairly level; that is, the data are more or less evenly distributed.

1b. Describe the shape of the distribution of birth weights.

The distribution is mounded and symmetric.

1c. Describe the shape of the distribution of mothers' ages.

The distribution is mounded and asymmetric; that is, it trails off more to the right than to the left.

2 ENGAGE Understanding Shape, Center, and Spread

As you saw in the Explore, data distributions can have various shapes. Some of these shapes are given names in statistics.

- A distribution whose shape is basically level (that is, it looks like a rectangle) is called a **uniform distribution**.

- A distribution that is mounded in the middle with symmetric "tails" at each end (that is, it looks bell-shaped) is called a **normal distribution**.

- A distribution that is mounded but not symmetric because one "tail" is much longer than the other is called a **skewed distribution**. When the longer "tail" is on the left, the distribution is called **skewed left**. When the longer "tail" is on the right, the distribution is called **skewed right**.

The figures below show the general shape of normal and skewed distributions.

Skewed left   Symmetric   Skewed right

Shape is one way of characterizing a data distribution. Another way is by identifying the distribution's center and spread. You should already be familiar with the following measures of center and spread:

- The **mean** of n data values is the sum of the data values divided by n. If $x_1, x_2, \ldots, x_n$ are data values from a sample, then the mean $\bar{x}$ is given by:

$$\bar{x} = \frac{x_1 + x_2 + \cdots + x_n}{n}$$

- The **median** of n data values written in ascending order is the middle value if n is odd and is the mean of the two middle values if n is even.

- The **standard deviation** of n data values is the square root of the mean of the squared deviations from the distribution's mean. If $x_1, x_2, \ldots, x_n$ are data values from a sample, then the standard deviation s is given by:

$$s = \sqrt{\frac{(x_1 - \bar{x})^2 + (x_2 - \bar{x})^2 + \cdots + (x_n - \bar{x})^2}{n}}$$

- The **interquartile range**, or IQR, of data values written in ascending order is the difference between the median of the upper half of the data, called the *third quartile* or Q_3, and the median of the lower half of the data, called the *first quartile* or Q_1. So, IQR = $Q_3 - Q_1$.

The first quartile, the median, and the third quartile divide a set of data into four groups that each contain about 25% of the data, so the IQR tells you how spread out the middle 50% (or so) of the data are.

Questioning Strategies

- What information does a data display give you? the shape of the data distribution

- What information do the mean and median give you? the center of the distribution

- What information do the standard deviation and interquartile range give you? the spread of the distribution

Teaching Strategy

Students should add the vocabulary of this lesson to their vocabulary flash cards from the first lesson. Once the flash cards are complete, put students in pairs. Each student shuffles his or her flash cards. One student from each pair lays the cards down with the words up; the other student lays the cards down with the definition up. Students take turns placing a card with a definition on top of a card with the matching word. Students get a point for each correct match. Each turn begins with the student who is about to match cards either accepting or challenging the previous match. If the student correctly challenges a match, that student earns a point and the opponent loses a point. If the challenging student is incorrect, he or she loses both a point and a turn.

Questioning Strategies

- Compare the spread of the birth weights to the spread of the mothers' ages. There is a larger spread in the ages of the mothers than in the birth weights.

- Would your answers to the Reflect questions be different if the birth weights were given in pounds instead of kilograms? Why or why not? No; although the numbers representing the mean, median, standard deviation, and IQR would be different (representing pounds), the overall results would not change. The shape of the birth weight distribution would still be normal, the mean would still equal the median, and the standard deviation and the IQR would still be significantly less than for the skewed distribution.

Avoid Common Errors

When using multiple lists in a calculator, students can confuse them. Students should write down what set of data is in each list to help them avoid any confusion while using the lists.

© Houghton Mifflin Harcourt Publishing Company

To distinguish a population mean from a sample mean, statisticians use the Greek letter mu, written μ, instead of $\bar{x}$. Similarly, they use the Greek letter sigma, written σ, instead of s to distinguish a population standard deviation from a sample standard deviation. Also, for a reason best left to a statistics course, the formula for the sample standard deviation sometimes has $n - 1$ rather than n in the denominator of the radicand. (In this book, n will always be used.)

REFLECT

2a. Describe the shape of each distribution in the Explore using the vocabulary defined on the previous page.

Distribution of birth months is uniform; distribution of baby weights is

normal; distribution of mothers' ages is skewed right.

2b. When the center and spread of a distribution are reported, they are generally given either as the mean and standard deviation or as the median and IQR. Why do these pairings make sense?

Standard deviation depends on the mean; IQR depends on the median.

3 EXPLORE Relating Center and Spread to Shape

Use a graphing calculator to compute the measures of center and the measures of spread for the distribution of baby weights and the distribution of mothers' ages.

A Enter the two sets of data into two lists on a graphing calculator as shown.

B Calculate the "1-Variable Statistics" for the distribution of baby weights. Record the statistics listed below. (Note: Your calculator may report the standard deviation with a denominator of $n - 1$ as "s_x" and the standard deviation with a denominator of n as "σ_x." Use the latter.)

$\bar{x} =$ _____3.5_____   Median = _____3.5_____

$s \approx$ _____0.14_____ $IQR = Q_3 - Q_1 =$ _____0.2_____

C Calculate the "1-Variable Statistics" for the distribution of mothers' ages. Record the statistics listed below.

$\bar{x} =$ _____31.15_____   Median = _____30.5_____

$s \approx$ _____2.6_____ $IQR = Q_3 - Q_1 =$ _____3.5_____

REFLECT

3a. What do you notice about the mean and median for the symmetric distribution (baby weights) as compared with the mean and median for the skewed distribution (mothers' ages)? Explain why this happens.

Mean and median for a symmetric distribution are equal, but mean and median

for a skewed distribution are not. This happens because the mean is pulled toward

the data values in the longer tail, but the median is not.

3b. One way to compare the spread of two distributions is to find the ratio (expressed as a percent) of the standard deviation to the mean for each distribution. Another way is to find the ratio (expressed as a percent) of the IQR to the median. Calculate these ratios, rounding each to the nearest percent if necessary, for the symmetric distribution (baby weights) and the skewed distribution (mothers' ages). What do you observe when you compare the corresponding ratios? Why does this make sense?

The ratio of the standard deviation to the mean is $\frac{0.14}{3.5} = 4\%$ for the symmetric

distribution and $\frac{2.6}{31.15} \approx 8\%$ for the skewed distribution, which indicates that the

skewed distribution has a greater spread. The ratio of the IQR to the median is

$\frac{0.2}{3.5} \approx 6\%$ for the symmetric distribution and $\frac{3.5}{30.5} \approx 11\%$ for the skewed distribution,

which again indicates that the skewed distribution has a greater spread. This makes

sense because the longer tail on a skewed distribution increases the spread.

3c. Which measures of center and spread would you report for the symmetric distribution? For the skewed distribution? Explain your reasoning.

Report either mean and standard deviation or median and IQR for symmetric, but

use only median and IQR for skewed because mean and standard deviation are too

sensitive to the data values in the long tail.

4 EXPLORE Making and Analyzing a Histogram

A Use a graphing calculator to make a histogram for the distribution of baby weights. Begin by turning on a statistics plot, selecting the histogram option, and entering the list where the data are stored.

© Houghton Mifflin Harcourt Publishing Company

4 EXPLORE

Questioning Strategies

- Why were you instructed to set Xmin to 3.15 and Xscl to 0.1? This sets the intervals so that each recorded weight shows as a different bar. By setting the minimum to 3.15 and the increment to 0.1, all weights from 3.15 kilograms to 3.25 kilograms are included in the first bar. Thus, the first bar represents 3.2 kilograms, the second bar represents 3.3 kilograms, and so on.

- How are the shapes of the line plot and the histogram for birth weight related? The shapes are the same; both represent a normal distribution.

- How would a histogram for the mothers' ages be different from the one for birth weights? Its shape would resemble the shape of the line plot for mothers' ages. Its right tail would be longer than its left tail, meaning that it would be skewed right.

5 EXPLORE

Questioning Strategies

- How do you find the interquartile range (IQR)? Calculate $Q_3 - Q_1$, which is the median of the upper half of the data minus the median of the lower half of the data.

- On the box plot, describe what the IQR corresponds to. the width of the box

- How would a box plot for the birth weights be different from the one for mothers' ages? It would be more symmetric. The vertical line that marks the median would be more centered within the box, and the whiskers would be about the same length.

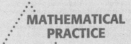

MATHEMATICAL PRACTICE
Highlighting the Standards

The Explores in this lesson provide opportunities to address Mathematical Practice Standard 2 (Reason abstractly and quantitatively). Students review various ways to display data, and they learn to recognize various shapes of data distributions. They also calculate measures of center and spread and relate them to the shapes of the distributions. Finally, they learn that certain measures of center and spread are better statistics for non-normal distributions.

CLOSE

Essential Question
How can you use shape, center, and spread to characterize a data distribution?
The shape of the distribution of a data set can be shown by displaying the data as a line plot, as a histogram, or as a box plot. The measures of center and spread can be used to summarize the distribution. Normal distributions can be summarized using either the mean and standard deviation or the median and IQR, while skewed distributions should be summarized using only the median and IQR.

Summarize
Have students write a journal entry in which they draw a normal distribution and a skewed distribution. Next to the drawings, they should list the measures of center and spread that are used for each type of distribution and explain why.

B Set the viewing window. To obtain a histogram that looks very much like the line plot that you drew for this data set, use the values shown at the right. Xscl determines the width of each bar, so when Xscl = 0.1 and Xmin = 3.15, the first bar covers the interval $3.15 \leq x < 3.25$, which captures the weight of 3.2 kg.

C Draw the histogram by pressing [GRAPH]. You can obtain the heights of the bars by pressing [TRACE] and using the arrow keys.

REFLECT

4a. By examining the histogram, determine the percent of the data that fall within 1 standard deviation ($s = 0.14$) of the mean ($\bar{x} = 3.5$). That is, determine the percent of the data in the interval $3.5 - 0.14 < x < 3.5 + 0.14$, or $3.36 < x < 3.64$. Explain your reasoning.

The bars that are within 1 standard deviation of the mean have heights of 4, 6, and 4, so 14 out of 20, or 70% of the data are in the interval.

4b. Suppose one of the baby weights is chosen at random. By examining the histogram, determine the probability that the weight is more than 1 standard deviation ($s = 0.14$) above the mean ($\bar{x} = 3.5$). That is, determine the probability that the weight is in the interval $x > 3.5 + 0.14$, or $x > 3.64$. Explain your reasoning.

The bars that are more than 1 standard deviation above the mean have heights of 2 and 1, so the probability that the weight is in the interval is $\frac{3}{20} = 0.15$.

4c. Change Xscl from 0.1 to 0.2 and redraw the histogram. Notice that the histogram loses some of its symmetry. Explain why this happens.

The bars are now twice as wide, so weights of 3.2 and 3.3 are combined, weights of 3.4 and 3.5 are combined, and so on. Corresponding bars on each side of the tallest bar no longer have the same height.

4d. To create a histogram for the distribution of mothers' ages, what values of Xscl and Xmin would you use so that the histogram matches the line plot that you drew?

Xscl = 1; Xmin = 27.5

Unit 10   385   Lesson 2

 EXPLORE Making and Analyzing a Box Plot

A Use a graphing calculator to make a box plot for the distribution of mothers' ages. Begin by turning on a statistics plot, selecting the box plot option, and entering the list where the data are stored. (There are two box plot options: one that shows outliers and one that does not. Choose the second of these.)

B Set the viewing window. Use the values shown at the right.

C Draw the box plot by pressing [GRAPH]. The box plot is based on five key values: the minimum data value, the first quartile, the median, the third quartile, and the maximum data value. You can obtain these values by pressing [TRACE] and using the arrow keys.

REFLECT

5a. How does the box plot show that the distribution is skewed right?

The part of the box to the right of the median is wider than the part to the left, and the "whisker" on the right is longer than the one on the left.

5b. Suppose one of the mothers' ages is chosen at random. Based on the box plot and not the original set of data, what can you say is the approximate probability that the age falls between the median, 30.5, and the third quartile, 32.5? Explain your reasoning.

25% or 0.25 because Q_1, the median, and Q_3 divide the data into four almost-equal parts.

5c. A data value x is considered to be an *outlier* if $x < Q_1 - 1.5(IQR)$ or $x > Q_3 + 1.5(IQR)$. Explain why a mother's age of 39 is an outlier for this data set. Redraw the box plot using the option for showing outliers. How does the box plot change?

$Q_3 + 1.5(IQR) = 32.5 + 1.5(3.5) = 37.75$, and $39 > 37.75$, so 39 is an outlier; the right "whisker" now ends at 35 and there is an isolated dot at 39.

Unit 10   386   Lesson 2

Probability Distributions

Essential question: *What is a probability distribution and how is it displayed?*

© Houghton Mifflin Harcourt Publishing Company

COMMON CORE Standards for Mathematical Content

CC.9-12.S.ID.1 Represent data with plots on the real number line (… histograms …).*

CC.9-12.S.IC.2 Decide if a specified model is consistent with results from a given data-generating process, e.g., using simulation.*

Vocabulary

random variable, probability distribution, cumulative probability

Prerequisites

Data gathering techniques, Lesson 10-1

Probability, Grade 7

Math Background

Theoretical probability describes how frequently an event is expected to occur based on analysis of possible outcomes. Experimental probability describes how frequently an event has occurred based on historical data. Both types of probabilities involve forming ratios of "successful" occurrences (the event occurred) to all occurrences (the event did or did not occur). Probabilities, therefore, are numbers (expressed as decimals, fractions, or percents) between and including 0 and 1.

In Lesson 10-2, students graphed data distributions. In this lesson, they will graph probability distributions. While the two distributions are similar, there is one very important difference. For probability distributions, the sum of the areas of the rectangles in the histogram (or the area under the probability curve) is equal to 1 because the events in a probability distribution are mutually exclusive and represent all possibilities.

INTRODUCE

Review with students what probability is and what the characteristics of probabilities are, such as $0 \le P(A) \le 1$ and $P(A) + P(\text{not } A) = 1$ for any event A. Ask students to calculate the following: A spinner is divided into four equal quadrants that are orange, yellow, green, and purple. What is the probability the spinner will land on purple? $\frac{1}{4}$

TEACH

1 ENGAGE

Questioning Strategies

• In the last lesson, you saw histograms for data distributions. In this lesson, you are seeing histograms for probability distributions. Compare the values on the *x*-axis of a histogram for a data distribution and for a probability distribution. **For a data distribution, the *x*-axis shows data values (or groups of data values). For a probability distribution, the *x*-axis shows possible outcomes (that is, the values of the random variable).**

• Compare the values on the *y*-axis of a histogram for a data distribution and for a probability distribution. **For a data distribution, the *y*-axis shows the frequency of each data value (or group of data values). For a probability distribution, the *y*-axis shows the probability of each outcome.**

• If one bar is taller than another in a histogram for a data distribution, what does that tell you? What about a histogram for a probability distribution? **For a data distribution, a taller bar tells you that a data value (or group of data values) has a greater frequency. For a probability distribution, a taller bar tells you that an outcome has a greater probability.**

Name_____ Class_____ Date_____

10-3

Probability Distributions

Essential question: *What is a probability distribution and how is it displayed?*

COMMON CORE
CC.9-12.S.ID.1*,
CC.9-12.S.IC.2*

1 ENGAGE   Introducing Probability Distributions

A **random variable** is a variable whose value is determined by the outcome of a probability experiment. For example, when you roll a number cube, you can use a random variable X to represent the number you roll. The possible values of X are 1, 2, 3, 4, 5, and 6.

A **probability distribution** is a data distribution that gives the probabilities of the values of a random variable. A probability distribution can be represented by a histogram in which the values of the random variable—that is, the possible outcomes—are on the horizontal axis, and probabilities are on the vertical axis. The figure shows the probability distribution for rolling a number cube.

When the values of a random variable are consecutive whole numbers, as is the case for rolling a number cube, a histogram for the probability distribution typically shows bars that each have a width of 1 and is centered on a value of the variable. The area of each bar therefore equals the probability of the corresponding outcome, and the combined areas of the bars is the sum of the probabilities, which is 1.

A **cumulative probability** is the probability that a random variable is less than or equal to a given value. You can find cumulative probabilities from a histogram by adding the areas of the bars for all outcomes less than or equal to the given value.

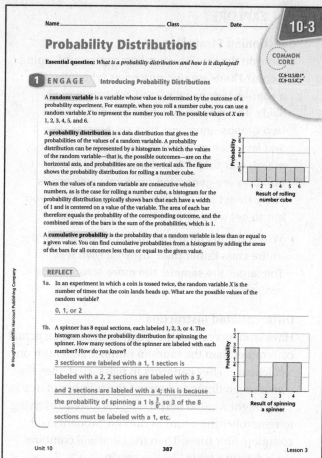

Result of rolling number cube

REFLECT

1a. In an experiment in which a coin is tossed twice, the random variable X is the number of times that the coin lands heads up. What are the possible values of the random variable?

0, 1, or 2

1b. A spinner has 8 equal sections, each labeled 1, 2, 3, or 4. The histogram shows the probability distribution for spinning the spinner. How many sections of the spinner are labeled with each number? How do you know?

3 sections are labeled with a 1, 1 section is

labeled with a 2, 2 sections are labeled with a 3,

and 2 sections are labeled with a 4; this is because

the probability of spinning a 1 is $\frac{3}{8}$, so 3 of the 8

sections must be labeled with a 1, etc.

Result of spinning a spinner

© Houghton Mifflin Harcourt Publishing Company

2 EXAMPLE   Displaying a Probability Distribution

You roll two number cubes at the same time. Let X be a random variable that represents the sum of the numbers rolled. Make a histogram to show the probability distribution for X.

A Complete the frequency table to show the number of ways that you can get each sum in one roll of the number cubes.

Sum	2	3	4	5	6	7	8	9	10	11	12
Frequency	1	2	3	4	5	6	5	4	3	2	1

B Add the frequencies you found in part A to find the total number of possible outcomes.

The total number of possible outcomes is ___36___.

C Divide each frequency by the total number of outcomes to find the probability of each sum. Complete the table.

Sum	2	3	4	5	6	7	8	9	10	11	12
Probability	$\frac{1}{36}$	$\frac{2}{36}$	$\frac{3}{36}$	$\frac{4}{36}$	$\frac{5}{36}$	$\frac{6}{36}$	$\frac{5}{36}$	$\frac{4}{36}$	$\frac{3}{36}$	$\frac{2}{36}$	$\frac{1}{36}$

D Create a histogram with the sums on the horizontal axis and the probabilities on the vertical axis. Complete the histogram below by labeling the axes and drawing a bar to represent the probability of each sum.

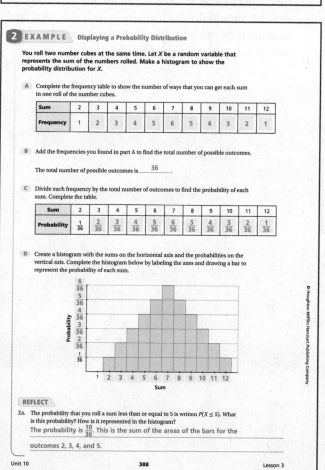

REFLECT

2a. The probability that you roll a sum less than or equal to 5 is written $P(X \leq 5)$. What is this probability? How is it represented in the histogram?

The probability is $\frac{10}{36}$. This is the sum of the areas of the bars for the

outcomes 2, 3, 4, and 5.

© Houghton Mifflin Harcourt Publishing Company

Questioning Strategies

- How many ways can you roll a 2? Describe them.
  Both cubes must land showing a 1, so there is
  one way.

- One number cube is red and the other is blue.
  Describe how many ways you can roll a sum of 3.
  The red cube can show a 1, and the blue cube can
  show a 2, or vice versa, so there are two ways.

- One number cube is red and the other is blue.
  Describe how many ways you can roll a sum of 4.
  The red cube can show a 1, and the blue cube can
  show a 3, or vice versa. The red cube can show a
  2, and the blue cube can show a 2. So, there is
  a total of three ways.

- One number cube is red, and the other is blue.
  Describe how many ways you can roll a sum of 5.
  The red cube can show a 1, and the blue cube can
  show a 4, or vice versa. The red cube can show a
  2, and the blue cube can show a 3, or vice
  versa. So, there is a total of four ways.

- What is the sum of the probabilities in the table
  in part C? Will that always be the case? Explain.
  1; Yes, if all possibilities are accounted for and
  they are mutually exclusive, the sum must be 1.

EXTRA EXAMPLE

A spinner has four equal sections that are labeled
1, 2, 3, and 4. You spin the spinner twice and find
the sum of the two numbers it lands on. Let X be a
random variable that represents the sum of the two
numbers.

A. Complete the table.

Sum	2	3	4	5	6	7	8
Frequency	1	2	3	4	3	2	1
Probability	$\frac{1}{16}$	$\frac{2}{16}$	$\frac{3}{16}$	$\frac{4}{16}$	$\frac{3}{16}$	$\frac{2}{16}$	$\frac{1}{16}$

B. Make a histogram of the probability distribution.

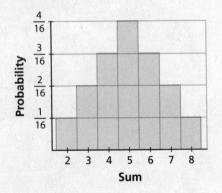

Questioning Strategies

- How do the random numbers represent flipping
  a coin? There are two outcomes when you flip
  a coin—heads or tails—and they are equally
  likely. The random numbers are divided into
  two groups—numbers that are greater than 0
  and less than or equal to 0.5 and numbers that
  are greater than 0.5 and less than 1. Because the
  numbers are generated randomly, you are as
  likely to get a number in the first group as you
  are to get a number in the second group.

- Why did you graph the combined data from the
  entire class rather than just your own results?
  The larger the sample, the more accurate the
  probabilities.

Differentiated Instruction

Have students repeat the simulation using an actual
coin rather than the random number generator on
a calculator. They can work in pairs. First, they flip
a coin seven times and record the number of heads.
They might want to tally the heads instead of trying
to remember the count as they go. Students will
complete four trials. Then the class will combine
their data in a table like the one in part B. Each
student should draw a histogram by hand. As a final
activity, they can compare their actual results with
their randomly generated results.

In the example, you used theoretical probabilities to define a probability distribution. You can also use experimental probabilities to define a probability distribution.

3 EXPLORE Using a Simulation

You flip a coin 7 times in a row. Use a simulation to determine the probability distribution for the number of times the coin lands heads up.

A When you flip a coin, the possible outcomes are heads and tails. You will use your calculator to generate random numbers between 0 and 1, assigning heads to numbers less than or equal to 0.5 and tails to numbers greater than 0.5.

To do the simulation, press **MATH** and then select **PRB**. Choose **1:rand** and press **ENTER**.

Now press **ENTER** 7 times to generate 7 random numbers. This simulates one trial (that is, one set of 7 coin flips). Record the number of heads in the table. For example, on the calculator screen shown here, there are 3 numbers less than or equal to 0.5, so there are 3 heads.

Carry out three more trials and record your results in the table.

Trial	1	2	3	4
Number of Heads				

Answers will vary.

B Report your results to your teacher in order to combine everyone's results. Use the combined class data to complete the table below. To find the relative frequency for an outcome, divide the frequency of the outcome by the total number of trials in the class.

Number of Heads	0	1	2	3	4	5	6	7
Frequency								
Relative Frequency								

Answers will vary.

C Enter the outcomes (0 through 7) into your calculator as list L_1. Enter the relative frequencies as list L_2.

D Make a histogram by turning on a statistics plot, selecting the histogram option, and using L_1 for Xlist and L_2 for Freq. Set the viewing window as shown. Then press **GRAPH**. A sample histogram is shown below.

© Houghton Mifflin Harcourt Publishing Company

REFLECT

3a. Describe the shape of the probability distribution.

The distribution is mounded and roughly symmetric.

3b. Based on the histogram, what is $P(X \leq 3)$? That is, what is the probability of getting 3 or fewer heads when you flip a coin 7 times? Explain.

Answers will vary; the probability should be close to 0.5; this probability is the sum of the areas of the bars for the outcomes 0, 1, 2, and 3.

3c. If you flipped a coin 7 times and got 7 heads, would this cause you to question whether the coin is fair? Why or why not?

Sample answer: Perhaps; the probability of getting 7 heads with a fair coin is about 1%, which is very unlikely.

4 EXAMPLE Analyzing a Probability Distribution

The histogram shows the theoretical probability distribution for the situation in the Explore. Use the distribution to answer each question.

A What is the probability of getting 4 or more heads?

$P(X \geq 4) = P(X = 4) + P(X = 5) + P(X = 6) + P(X = 7)$

So, the probability of getting 4 or more heads is

$\underline{0.273} + \underline{0.164} + \underline{0.055} + \underline{0.008} = \underline{0.5}$.

B What is the probability of getting at least 1 head?

An easy way to calculate this probability is to use the complement of the event. The complement of getting at least 1 head is getting 0 heads. Use the histogram to find $P(X = 0)$ and subtract it from 1.

$P(X = 0) = \underline{0.008}$

So, the probability of getting at least 1 head is

$1 - \underline{0.008} = \underline{0.992}$.

(Histogram: Probability vs. Number of Heads. Bars: 0.008, 0.055, 0.164, 0.273, 0.273, 0.164, 0.055, 0.008 for Number of Heads 0 through 7.)

REFLECT

4a. Why are the probabilities in the histogram you made in the Explore different from the probabilities given in the histogram above?

The histogram in the Explore was based on experimental probabilities, so there is randomness in the results.

© Houghton Mifflin Harcourt Publishing Company

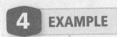

Questioning Strategies

- Describe what information the histogram conveys about the outcome of three heads compared with the outcome of four heads. **The probability of getting three heads is the same as getting four heads—0.273. The probability of either of these events is greater than the probability of getting fewer than three heads or more than four heads.**

- Describe in words what the shape of the histogram shows. **The shape is symmetric with high probabilities in the middle tapering to low probabilities at the ends. So, you are least likely to get no heads or seven heads when flipping a coin seven times. You are slightly more likely to get one head or six heads, and even more likely to get two heads or five heads. You are most likely to get three heads or four heads.**

EXTRA EXAMPLE

You flip a coin 4 times in a row. The histogram shows the theoretical probability distribution for this situation.

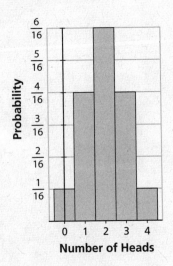

A. What is the probability of getting 3 or more heads? $\frac{5}{16}$

B. What is the probability of getting at most 2 heads? $\frac{11}{16}$

CLOSE

Essential Question

What is a probability distribution and how is it displayed?
A probability distribution is a distribution that shows the likelihood of each outcome of a probability experiment. It can be displayed as a histogram with possible outcomes on the *x*-axis and probabiltities on the *y*-axis.

Summarize

Have students write a journal entry. They should choose between the probability distribution in **2** EXAMPLE and the one in **4** EXAMPLE and summarize it in their entry. Students should include a description of the scenario, a histogram of the probability distribution, and examples of probabilities that can be determined from the histogram.

PRACTICE

Where skills are taught	Where skills are practiced
2 EXAMPLE	EXS. 1, 2
4 EXAMPLE	EXS. 3–6

4b. What do you think would happen to the histogram you made in the Explore if you included data from 1000 additional trials?

The histogram would approach the shape of the histogram that shows the

theoretical probabilities.

4c. Why does it make sense that the histogram that shows the theoretical probabilities is symmetric?

Getting 0 heads means getting 7 tails, but getting 7 tails is just as likely as getting

7 heads, so $P(X = 0) = P(X = 7)$. By similar reasoning, $P(X = 1) = P(X = 6)$,

$P(X = 2) = P(X = 5)$, and $P(X = 3) = P(X = 4)$.

PRACTICE

1. The spinner at right has three equal sections. You spin the spinner twice and find the sum of the two numbers the spinner lands on.

a. Let X be a random variable that represents the sum of the two numbers. What are the possible values of X?

2, 3, 4, 5, and 6

b. Complete the table.

Sum	2	3	4	5	6
Probability	$\frac{1}{9}$	$\frac{2}{9}$	$\frac{1}{3}$	$\frac{2}{9}$	$\frac{1}{9}$

c. Make a histogram of the probability distribution.

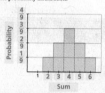

d. What is the probability that the sum is not 2? How is this probability represented in the histogram?

The probability is $\frac{8}{9}$. This is the sum of the areas of the bars for the

outcomes 3, 4, 5, and 6.

2. You roll two number cubes at the same time. Let X be a random variable that represents the absolute value of the difference of the numbers rolled.

a. What are the possible values of X?

0, 1, 2, 3, 4, and 5

b. Complete the table.

Difference	0	1	2	3	4	5
Probability	$\frac{6}{36}$	$\frac{10}{36}$	$\frac{8}{36}$	$\frac{6}{36}$	$\frac{4}{36}$	$\frac{2}{36}$

c. Is this probability distribution symmetric? Why or why not?

No; the probability distribution is skewed right because the histogram

would have its greatest probability for the outcome 1 and would trail

off toward the right.

A trick coin is designed to land heads up with a probability of 80%. You flip the coin 7 times. The histogram shows the probability distribution for the number of times the coin lands heads up. ("0+" means slightly greater than 0.) Use the histogram for Exercises 3–6.

3. What is the probability of getting 6 or 7 heads?

0.577

4. What is the probability of getting 4 or more heads? Explain.

0.967; this is the sum of the areas of the bars corresponding to 4, 5, 6,

and 7 heads

5. Is the probability of getting an even number of heads the same as the probability of getting an odd number of heads? Explain.

No; the probability of getting an even number of heads is about

$0 + 0.004 + 0.115 + 0.367 = 0.486$, while the probability of getting

an odd number of heads is about $0 + 0.029 + 0.275 + 0.210 = 0.514$.

6. Suppose you flip a coin 7 times and get 7 heads. Based on what you know now, would you question whether the coin is fair? Why or why not?

Sample answer: Yes; although it is possible to get 7 heads with a fair coin

(the probability is about 1%), it is much more likely to happen with a trick

coin (the probability of getting 7 heads with the trick coin is 21%).

Normal Distributions

Essential question: *How do you find percents of data and probabilities of events associated with normal distributions?*

COMMON CORE Standards for Mathematical Content

CC.9-12.S.ID.4 Use the mean and standard deviation of a data set to fit it to a normal distribution and to estimate population percentages. Recognize that there are data sets for which such a procedure is not appropriate. Use calculators, … and tables to estimate areas under the normal curve.*

Vocabulary
standard normal distribution, *z*-score

Prerequisites
Probability distributions, Lesson 10-3

Math Background
The general shape of a normal probability distribution is that of a bell. The exact shape of the bell is determined by the distribution's mean and standard deviation. The graph of a normal probability distribution is called a *normal curve* and is given by the equation

$$y = \frac{1}{\sqrt{2\pi\sigma^2}}\, e^{-(x-\mu)^2/2\sigma^2}$$

where μ is the mean and σ is the standard deviation. The mean and standard deviation can be found from the data and the equation for the normal curve can then be written, although students are not asked to do that in this lesson. Students should, however, be able to draw a histogram from data and sketch a smooth, "best-fit" normal curve by hand.

INTRODUCE

Ask students to recall how to find the mean and standard deviation of a set of data. Have them state in words what those statistics describe. Then have them sketch curves representing three normal distributions on the same coordinate plane—each distribution with the same mean, but one with a small standard deviation, the second with a larger standard deviation, and the third with the largest standard deviation.

Students' curves should all be centered at the same location (the mean). One will be narrow and tall (small σ), one will be medium height and broader (medium σ), and the last will be short and wide (large σ). Students are likely to draw the curves all the same height, but with varying widths. This is a good opportunity to discuss the fact that for a normal *probability* distribution, the area under the curve must equal 1, so a normal curve where the standard deviation is greater will not rise as high as a normal curve where the standard deviation is less.

TEACH

1 EXPLORE

Questioning Strategies

- Look at the first table—weight and frequency. How do you know the histogram is symmetric by looking at the table? The frequencies of the highest and lowest weights are the same, the frequencies of the second-highest and second lowest weights are the same, and so on.

- Look at the table in step A. Describe what the relative frequency means with respect to baby weight. It is the percent (in decimal form) of babies with that weight.

- Why is the sum of the relative frequencies 1? because the sum represents the whole sample, or in terms of percent, 100% of the sample

- Why were the adjustments to the heights of the bars made in step B? to make the sum of all the areas of the bars in the histogram 1

- What is the area under the normal curve? 1

- What value does the area under the normal curve between two specific *x*-values represent? the probability the outcome will be between those two *x*-values, in this case the probability a baby's birth weight will be between those two weights

- Why does the normal curve in step E lie directly on top of the histogram? because you used the mean and standard deviation of the baby weights to define the normal curve

© Houghton Mifflin Harcourt Publishing Company

Normal Distributions

10-4

COMMON CORE
CC.9-12.S.ID.4*

Essential question: *How do you find percents of data and probabilities of events associated with normal distributions?*

1 EXPLORE · Substituting a Normal Curve for a Symmetric Histogram

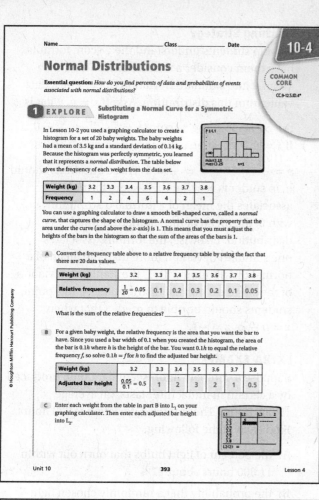

In Lesson 10-2 you used a graphing calculator to create a histogram for a set of 20 baby weights. The baby weights had a mean of 3.5 kg and a standard deviation of 0.14 kg. Because the histogram was perfectly symmetric, you learned that it represents a *normal distribution*. The table below gives the frequency of each weight from the data set.

Weight (kg)	3.2	3.3	3.4	3.5	3.6	3.7	3.8
Frequency	1	2	4	6	4	2	1

You can use a graphing calculator to draw a smooth bell-shaped curve, called a *normal curve*, that captures the shape of the histogram. A normal curve has the property that the area under the curve (and above the *x*-axis) is 1. This means that you must adjust the heights of the bars in the histogram so that the sum of the areas of the bars is 1.

A Convert the frequency table above to a relative frequency table by using the fact that there are 20 data values.

Weight (kg)	3.2	3.3	3.4	3.5	3.6	3.7	3.8
Relative frequency	$\frac{1}{20}$ = 0.05	0.1	0.2	0.3	0.2	0.1	0.05

What is the sum of the relative frequencies? ____1____

B For a given baby weight, the relative frequency is the area that you want the bar to have. Since you used a bar width of 0.1 when you created the histogram, the area of the bar is 0.1*h* where *h* is the height of the bar. You want 0.1*h* to equal the relative frequency *f*, so solve 0.1*h* = *f* for *h* to find the adjusted bar height.

Weight (kg)	3.2	3.3	3.4	3.5	3.6	3.7	3.8
Adjusted bar height	$\frac{0.05}{0.1}$ = 0.5	1	2	3	2	1	0.5

C Enter each weight from the table in part B into L_1 on your graphing calculator. Then enter each adjusted bar height into L_2.

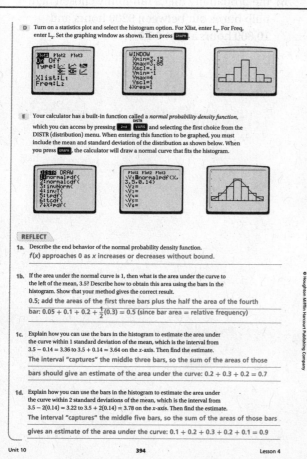

D Turn on a statistics plot and select the histogram option. For Xlist, enter L_1. For Freq, enter L_2. Set the graphing window as shown. Then press **GRAPH**.

E Your calculator has a built-in function called a *normal probability density function*, which you can access by pressing **2nd** **VARS** and selecting the first choice from the DISTR (distribution) menu. When entering this function to be graphed, you must include the mean and standard deviation of the distribution as shown below. When you press **GRAPH**, the calculator will draw a normal curve that fits the histogram.

REFLECT

1a. Describe the end behavior of the normal probability density function.

$f(x)$ approaches 0 as *x* increases or decreases without bound.

1b. If the area under the normal curve is 1, then what is the area under the curve to the left of the mean, 3.5? Describe how to obtain this area using the bars in the histogram. Show that your method gives the correct result.

0.5; add the areas of the first three bars plus the half the area of the fourth bar: $0.05 + 0.1 + 0.2 + \frac{1}{2}(0.3) = 0.5$ (since bar area = relative frequency)

1c. Explain how you can use the bars in the histogram to estimate the area under the curve within 1 standard deviation of the mean, which is the interval from $3.5 - 0.14 = 3.36$ to $3.5 + 0.14 = 3.64$ on the *x*-axis. Then find the estimate.

The interval "captures" the middle three bars, so the sum of the areas of those bars should give an estimate of the area under the curve: $0.2 + 0.3 + 0.2 = 0.7$

1d. Explain how you can use the bars in the histogram to estimate the area under the curve within 2 standard deviations of the mean, which is the interval from $3.5 - 2(0.14) = 3.22$ to $3.5 + 2(0.14) = 3.78$ on the *x*-axis. Then find the estimate.

The interval "captures" the middle five bars, so the sum of the areas of those bars gives an estimate of the area under the curve: $0.1 + 0.2 + 0.3 + 0.2 + 0.1 = 0.9$

2 EXAMPLE

Questioning Strategies

- State your answer to the last question in part A in terms of the context of the problem. 95% of the pennies produced have masses between 2.46 grams and 2.54 grams.

- State your answer to the last question in part B in terms of the context of the problem. What does this mean for the other pennies? 16% of the pennies produced have a mass greater than 2.52 grams. This means that 84% of the pennies produced have a mass less than 2.52 grams.

EXTRA EXAMPLE

Suppose the masses of boxes of Mega Munch cereal coming off an assembly line are normally distributed with a mean of 454.0 grams and a standard deviation of 3.9 grams. Find each of the following.

- **A.** the percent of cereal boxes that have a mass between 446.2 grams and 461.8 grams 95%

- **B.** the probability that a randomly chosen box has a mass greater than 457.9 grams 16%

3 EXAMPLE

Questioning Strategies

- Describe in words how the number 0.4 is determined in part A and what that number means. You find 0.4 by subtracting the mean from the given value of 65 and then dividing that result by the standard deviation. The number 0.4 means that the given value of 65 is 0.4 standard deviation away from the mean.

- How do you find the decimal in the table for the second statement of part A? Read across the "0" row until you intersect the ".4" column.

- What is the meaning of the number read from the standard normal table for a given z-score? The number is the probability that a data value has a z-score less than or equal to the given z-score.

- How do you find the probability that a data value exceeds a given z-score? Subtract the probability obtained from the standard normal table for the given z-score from 1.

Teaching Strategy

To help students understand the z-score formula, have them consider a normal distribution with mean μ and standard deviation σ. Let x be a data value from this distribution. Ask: If $x = \mu$, what is the corresponding z-score? $z = \dfrac{\mu - \mu}{\sigma} = \dfrac{0}{\sigma} = 0$ If $x = \mu + \sigma$, what is the corresponding z-score? $z = \dfrac{(\mu + \sigma) - \mu}{\sigma} = \dfrac{\sigma}{\sigma} = 1$ These questions should help students see that the z-score formula associates the mean of a normal distribution with 0, the mean of the standard normal distribution. Likewise, the formula associates one standard deviation more than the mean of a normal distribution with 1, the standard deviation of the standard normal distribution. At this point, students should be able to predict that when $x = \mu - \sigma$, $z = -1$.

EXTRA EXAMPLE

Suppose a compact fluorescent light bulb produced by a certain manufacturer lasts, on average, 10,000 hours. The standard deviation is 720 hours. Find each of the following.

- **A.** the percent of light bulbs that burn out within 11,000 hours about 92%

- **B.** the probability that a randomly chosen light bulb burns out between 9200 hours and 10,800 hours about 0.73

© Houghton Mifflin Harcourt Publishing Company

Normal Curves All normal curves have the following properties, sometimes collectively called the *68-95-99.7 rule*:

- • 68% of the data fall within 1 standard deviation of the mean.
- • 95% of the data fall within 2 standard deviations of the mean.
- • 99.7% of the data fall within 3 standard deviations of the mean.

The figure at the left below illustrates the 68-95-99.7 rule.

A normal curve's symmetry allows you to separate the area under the curve into eight parts and know the percent of the data in each part, as shown at the right below.

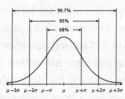 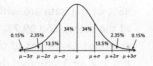

2 EXAMPLE Finding Areas Under a Normal Curve

Suppose the masses (in grams) of pennies minted in the United States after 1982 are normally distributed with a mean of 2.50 g and a standard deviation of 0.02 g. Find each of the following.

A The percent of pennies that have a mass between 2.46 g and 2.54 g

- • How far below the mean is 2.46 g? How many standard deviations is this? _____ 0.04 g; 2 standard deviations
- • How far above the mean is 2.54 g? How many standard deviations is this? _____ 0.04 g; 2 standard deviations
- • What percent of the data in a normal distribution fall within *n* standard deviations of the mean where *n* is the number of standard deviations you found in the preceding questions? _____ 95%

B The probability that a randomly chosen penny has a mass greater than 2.52 g

- • How far above the mean is 2.52 g? How many standard deviations is this? _____ 0.02 g; 1 standard deviation
- • When the area under a normal curve is separated into eight parts as shown above, which of those parts satisfy the condition that the penny's mass be greater than 2.52 g? (Give the percent of data that fall within each part.) _____ 13.5%, 2.35%, 0.15%
- • Find the sum of the percents. Express this probability as a decimal as well. _____ 16%; 0.16

REFLECT

2a. In the second normal curve shown on the previous page, explain how you know that the area under the curve between $\mu + \sigma$ and $\mu + 2\sigma$ represents 13.5% of the data if you know that the percent of the data within 1 standard deviation of the mean is 68% and the percent of the data within 2 standard deviations of the mean is 95%.

The difference between 95% and 68% is 27%; the symmetry of the curve tells you that this difference is split evenly between the interval from $\mu - 2\sigma$ to $\mu - \sigma$ and the interval from $\mu + \sigma$ to $\mu + 2\sigma$, so each interval represents 13.5% of the data.

2b. Another way to approach part B of the Example is to recognize that since the mound in the middle of the distribution (between $\mu - \sigma$ and $\mu + \sigma$) represents 68% of the data, the remainder of the data, $100\% - 68\% = 32\%$, must be in the two tails. Complete the reasoning to obtain the desired probability.

The desired probability is the percent of data in just one tail, which is half of 32%, or 16%.

The Standard Normal Curve The **standard normal distribution** has a mean of 0 and a standard deviation of 1. A data value x from a normal distribution with mean μ and standard deviation σ can be standardized by finding its **z-score** using the formula

$$z = \frac{x - \mu}{\sigma}.$$

Areas under the *standard normal curve* to the left of a given z-score have been computed and appear in the *standard normal table* below. This table allows you to find a greater range of percents and probabilities than you can using μ and multiples of σ as on the previous page. For instance, the intersection of the shaded row and column of the table tells you that the value of $P(z \leq 1.3)$ is 0.9032. (In the table, ".0000+" means slightly more than 0, and "1.0000−" means slightly less than 1.)

					Standard Normal Table					
z	**.0**	**.1**	**.2**	**.3**	**.4**	**.5**	**.6**	**.7**	**.8**	**.9**
−3	.0013	.0010	.0007	.0005	.0003	.0002	.0002	.0001	.0001	.0000+
−2	.0228	.0179	.0139	.0107	.0082	.0062	.0047	.0035	.0026	.0019
−1	.1587	.1357	.1151	.0968	.0808	.0668	.0548	.0446	.0359	.0287
−0	.5000	.4602	.4207	.3821	.3446	.3085	.2743	.2420	.2119	.1841
0	.5000	.5398	.5793	.6179	.6554	.6915	.7257	.7580	.7881	.8159
1	.8413	.8643	.8849	.9032	.9192	.9332	.9452	.9554	.9641	.9713
2	.9772	.9821	.9861	.9893	.9918	.9938	.9953	.9965	.9974	.9981
3	.9987	.9990	.9993	.9995	.9997	.9998	.9998	.9999	.9999	1.000−

© Houghton Mifflin Harcourt Publishing Company

2 EXAMPLE and **3** EXAMPLE include opportunities to address Mathematical Practice Standard 1 (Make sense of problems and persevere in solving them). Students will need to look for entry points into normal distribution problems. First, they will need to confirm the distribution is, indeed, normal. Then they will plan a solution pathway by determining whether the questions are based on integer multiples of the standard deviation, a special case that can be solved quickly, or not. If not, students will need to convert data values to z-scores and use the standard normal table. They will need to determine how to approach the problem—if the answer comes directly from one probability, or if they need to calculate several probabilities and add or subtract them. Finally, students will need to use their knowledge of normal distributions to gain insight into the solution. If they determine their answers don't make sense, they may need to change course and approach the problem differently.

CLOSE

Essential Question
How do you find percents of data and probabilities of events associated with normal distributions?

If a given data value is 1, 2, or 3 standard deviations from the mean, you can use the fact that 68% of the data are within 1 standard deviation of the mean, 95% of the data are within 2 standard deviations of the mean, and 99.7% of the data are within 3 standard deviations of the mean. If the data value is not 1, 2, or 3 standard deviations from the mean, you can calculate z-scores and use the standard normal table.

Summarize
Have students write a journal entry explaining how to use the standard normal table to find the probability of an event, given the mean and standard deviation of a normal distribution.

PRACTICE

Where skills are taught	Where skills are practiced
2 EXAMPLE	EXS. 1–6
4 EXAMPLE	EXS. 7–12

Exercise 13: Students extend what they learned in **1** EXPLORE to explain when normal distributions can be applied to data.

3 EXAMPLE Using the Standard Normal Table

Suppose the heights (in inches) of adult females in the United States are normally distributed with a mean of 63.8 inches and a standard deviation of 2.8 inches. Find each of the following.

A The percent of women who are no more than 65 inches tall

- Convert 65 to a z-score: $z_{65} = \frac{65 - \mu}{\sigma} = \frac{65 - 63.8}{2.8} \approx 0.4$

- Recognize that the phrase "no more than 65 inches" means that $z \leq z_{65}$. Read the decimal from the appropriate row and column of the standard normal table: __0.6554__

- Write the decimal as a percent, rounding to the nearest whole percent: __about 66%__

B The probability that a randomly chosen woman is between 60 inches and 63 inches tall

- Convert 60 to a z-score: $z_{60} = \frac{60 - \mu}{\sigma} = \frac{60 - 63.8}{2.8} \approx -1.4$

- Convert 63 to a z-score: $z_{63} = \frac{63 - \mu}{\sigma} = \frac{63 - 63.8}{2.8} \approx -0.3$

- Because the standard normal table gives areas under the standard normal curve to the left of a given z-score, you find $P(z_{60} \leq z \leq z_{63})$ by subtracting $P(z \leq z_{60})$ from $P(z \leq z_{63})$. Complete the following calculation using the appropriate values from the table:

$P(z_{60} \leq z \leq z_{63}) = P(z \leq z_{63}) - P(z \leq z_{60}) = \underline{0.3821} - \underline{0.0808} = \underline{0.3013}$

- Round the decimal to the nearest hundredth: __about 0.30__

REFLECT

3a. Using the result of part A, you can find the percent of females who are at least 65 inches tall without needing the table. Find the percent and explain your reasoning.

about 34%; the percent of females who are at least 65 inches tall is what's left of the area under the curve (which is 1 or 100%) after you remove the percent of females who are no more than 65 inches tall.

3b. How does the probability that a randomly chosen female has a height between 64.6 inches and 67.6 inches compare with your answer in part B? Why?

The probability is the same because of the symmetry of the curve.

PRACTICE

Suppose the scores on a test given to all juniors in a school district are normally distributed with a mean of 74 and a standard deviation of 8. Find each of the following.

1. The percent of juniors whose score is no more than 90 __97.5%__

2. The percent of juniors whose score is between 58 and 74 __47.5%__

3. The percent of juniors whose score is at least 74 __50%__

4. The probability that a randomly chosen junior has a score above 82 __0.16__

5. The probability that a randomly chosen junior has a score between 66 and 90 __0.815__

6. The probability that a randomly chosen junior has a score below 74 __0.5__

Suppose the heights (in inches) of adult males in the United States are normally distributed with a mean of 69.4 inches and a standard deviation of 3.2 inches. Find each of the following.

7. The percent of men who are no more than 68 inches tall __about 34%__

8. The percent of men who are between 70 and 72 inches tall __about 21%__

9. The percent of men who are at least 66 inches tall __about 86%__

10. The probability that a randomly chosen man is greater than 71 inches tall __about 0.31__

11. The probability that a randomly chosen man is between 63 and 73 inches tall __about 0.84__

12. The probability that a randomly chosen man is less than 76 inches tall __about 0.98__

13. The calculator screen on the left shows the probability distribution when six coins are flipped and the number of heads is counted. The screen on the right shows the probability distribution when six dice are rolled and the number of 1s is counted. For which distribution is it reasonable to use a normal curve as an approximation? Why?

0 1 2 3 4 5 6
Probability of getting
a given number of heads
when 6 coins are flipped

0 1 2 3 4 5 6
Probability of getting
a given number of 1s
when 6 dice are rolled

Use a normal curve for the distribution of heads when 6 coins are flipped because the distribution is symmetric.

© Houghton Mifflin Harcourt Publishing Company

Sampling Distributions

Essential question: *How is the mean of a sampling distribution related to the population mean or proportion?*

COMMON
CORE
Standards for Mathematical Content

CC.9-12.S.IC.4 Use data from a sample survey to estimate a population mean or proportion ...*

Vocabulary

sampling distribution, standard error of the mean, standard error of the proportion

Prerequisites

Data distributions, Lesson 10-2

Probability distributions, Lesson 10-3

Normal distributions, Lesson 10-4

Math Background

This unit began with constructing data distributions for populations or samples. Then students constructed probability distributions, both theoretical (for example, for number cubes) and experimental. Students explored normal distributions in detail, using the 68-95-99.7 rule as well as z-scores and the standard normal table to find percents and probabilities.

In this lesson, students will construct data distributions obtained from different samples of the same population. Students should understand that the mean and standard deviation obtained for a certain characteristic of a sample usually will not match the mean and standard deviation for the entire population, nor will it necessarily match the statistics obtained for a different sample of the same population.

Students will learn in this lesson how to characterize the data obtained from different samples. They will build on this knowledge in the next lesson, where they will use sample statistics to make predictions about population parameters.

INTRODUCE

To introduce students to the idea of a sampling distribution, have students work in groups of equal size to conduct a quick survey. The survey should consist of a single question calling for a numerical response, such as: How long (in minutes) did it take you to get to school today? Each group of students should calculate the sum of the responses within the group as well as the mean of the responses, reporting these results to you. After pointing out that each group represents a sample of the entire class, you can use the reported means to generate a line plot, which represents a sampling distribution. Have students examine the sampling distribution and make a conjecture about what the class mean is. (You may want to have students write down their conjectures so that the most accurate ones can be determined later.) You can then calculate the class mean by adding together the sums that the groups reported to you and dividing by the number of students in the class.

TEACH

Questioning Strategies

- Describe the population parameters in words. The average age of the first 50 people who joined the gym is just over 41. There is a large spread in the data; the standard deviation is 15.3.

- Why isn't the answer in part B the same as in part A? Because the mean of the sample is based on only 5 data values from the population.

- How can you change the way a sample is selected to make the sample mean better match the population mean? Increase the sample size. As the sample size increases, the sample mean approaches the population mean.

continued

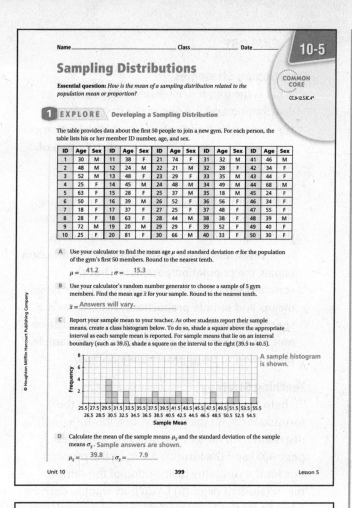

Name _____ Class _____ Date _____

10-5

COMMON CORE
CC.9-12.S.IC.4*

Sampling Distributions

Essential question: *How is the mean of a sampling distribution related to the population mean or proportion?*

1 EXPLORE Developing a Sampling Distribution

The table provides data about the first 50 people to join a new gym. For each person, the table lists his or her member ID number, age, and sex.

ID	Age	Sex	ID	Age	Sex	ID	Age	Sex	ID	Age	Sex	ID	Age	Sex
1	30	M	11	38	F	21	74	F	31	32	M	41	46	M
2	48	M	12	24	M	22	21	M	32	28	F	42	34	F
3	52	M	13	48	F	23	29	F	33	35	M	43	44	F
4	25	F	14	45	M	24	48	M	34	49	M	44	68	M
5	63	F	15	28	F	25	37	M	35	18	M	45	24	F
6	50	F	16	39	M	26	52	F	36	56	F	46	34	F
7	18	F	17	37	F	27	25	F	37	48	F	47	55	F
8	28	F	18	63	F	28	44	M	38	38	F	48	39	M
9	72	M	19	20	M	29	29	F	39	52	F	49	40	F
10	25	F	20	81	F	30	66	M	40	33	F	50	30	F

A Use your calculator to find the mean age μ and standard deviation σ for the population of the gym's first 50 members. Round to the nearest tenth.

$\mu =$ ___41.2___ ; $\sigma =$ ___15.3___

B Use your calculator's random number generator to choose a sample of 5 gym members. Find the mean age $\bar{x}$ for your sample. Round to the nearest tenth.

$\bar{x} =$ ___Answers will vary.___

C Report your sample mean to your teacher. As other students report their sample means, create a class histogram below. To do so, shade a square above the appropriate interval as each sample mean is reported. For sample means that lie on an interval boundary (such as 39.5), shade a square on the interval to the right (39.5 to 40.5).

A sample histogram is shown.

D Calculate the mean of the sample means $\mu_{\bar{x}}$ and the standard deviation of the sample means $\sigma_{\bar{x}}$. Sample answers are shown.

$\mu_{\bar{x}} =$ ___39.8___ ; $\sigma_{\bar{x}} =$ ___7.9___

© Houghton Mifflin Harcourt Publishing Company

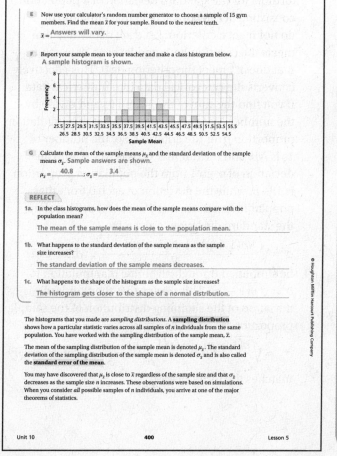

E Now use your calculator's random number generator to choose a sample of 15 gym members. Find the mean $\bar{x}$ for your sample. Round to the nearest tenth.

$\bar{x} =$ ___Answers will vary.___

F Report your sample mean to your teacher and make a class histogram below. A sample histogram is shown.

G Calculate the mean of the sample means $\mu_{\bar{x}}$ and the standard deviation of the sample means $\sigma_{\bar{x}}$. Sample answers are shown.

$\mu_{\bar{x}} =$ ___40.8___ ; $\sigma_{\bar{x}} =$ ___3.4___

REFLECT

1a. In the class histograms, how does the mean of the sample means compare with the population mean?

The mean of the sample means is close to the population mean.

1b. What happens to the standard deviation of the sample means as the sample size increases?

The standard deviation of the sample means decreases.

1c. What happens to the shape of the histogram as the sample size increases?

The histogram gets closer to the shape of a normal distribution.

The histograms that you made are *sampling distributions*. A **sampling distribution** shows how a particular statistic varies across all samples of *n* individuals from the same population. You have worked with the sampling distribution of the sample mean, $\bar{x}$.

The mean of the sampling distribution of the sample mean is denoted $\mu_{\bar{x}}$. The standard deviation of the sampling distribution of the sample mean is denoted $\sigma_{\bar{x}}$ and is also called the **standard error of the mean**.

You may have discovered that $\mu_{\bar{x}}$ is close to $\bar{x}$ regardless of the sample size and that $\sigma_{\bar{x}}$ decreases as the sample size *n* increases. These observations were based on simulations. When you consider *all* possible samples of *n* individuals, you arrive at one of the major theorems of statistics.

© Houghton Mifflin Harcourt Publishing Company

Teaching Strategy

In parts C and F of the Explore, you may want to create a class histogram on the board and have students come up and add their sample means one at a time. You may also want to draw a vertical line on the histogram at the population mean to drive home the point that the sample means are clustering around the population mean.

2 EXAMPLE

Questioning Strategies

- In part A, what would happen to the value of z_{325} if you had chosen a random sample of greater size (such as 100 boxes of cereal)? What would happen to the value of $P(z \leq z_{325})$? Explain your reasoning. The value of z_{325} would increase because increasing n results in a decrease in the denominator of the z-score formula. Increasing the value of z_{325} results in an increase in the value of $P(z \leq z_{325})$ because you are capturing more of the area under the standard normal curve.

- In part B, what interval captures 68% of the means for random samples of 36 boxes? 68% of the means fall between $323 - 3.3 = 319.7$ g and $323 + 3.3 = 326.3$ g.

EXTRA EXAMPLE

The safety placard on an elevator states that up to 8 people (660 kilograms) can ride the elevator at one time. Suppose the mean mass of a group of 8 people is 600 kilograms with a standard deviation of 76 kilograms. You choose a random sample of 16 groups of 8 people.

A. What is the probability that your sample has a mean mass of at most 660 kilograms (the maximum mass the elevator can safely carry)? 99.93%

B. What interval captures 95% of the means for random samples of 16 groups? Describe what this interval means in words. 562 to 638; 95% of the groups of 8 will have a mass between 562 kilograms and 638 kilograms, well within the maximum mass the elevator can safely carry.

3 EXPLORE

Questioning Strategies

- What is the difference between this sampling distribution and the one in the first Explore? The one in the first Explore was a distribution of sample means, while this is a distribution of sample proportions.

- Compare the "Properties of the Sampling Distribution of the Sample Proportion" box with the "Properties of the Sampling Distribution of the Sample Mean" box in the first Explore. In both cases, the mean of the sampling distribution equals the population parameter, but the standard error is calculated differently for sample means and sample proportions. Also, there is a specific mathematical requirement that must be met for the sampling distribution of the sample proportion to be approximately normal.

Teaching Strategy

To help students see the parallel between the formula for $\sigma_{\hat{p}}$ in the property box for the sampling distribution of the sample proportion (student page 403) and the formula for $\sigma_{\bar{x}}$ in the property box for the sampling distribution of the sample mean (student page 401), you may want to derive a formula for the standard deviation of a population consisting of categorical data that either do or do not meet a criterion: Let each data value that meets the criterion be 1, and let each data value that doesn't meet the criterion be 0. This effectively converts the categorical data into numerical data. If you find the sum of the 1s and 0s and divide by the number N of data values, you get the population proportion p for the criterion. So, the number of 1s is Np, and the number of 0s is $N(1 - p)$. The deviation of each 1 from the population proportion is $1 - p$, while the deviation of each 0 from the population proportion is $0 - p$, or $-p$. Therefore, the standard deviation is given by

$$\sigma = \sqrt{\frac{Np(1 - p)^2 + N(1 - p)(-p)^2}{N}},$$ which can be simplified through algebraic manipulation to $\sigma = \sqrt{p(1 - p)}$. This means that the standard deviation of the sampling distribution of the sample proportion is

$$\sigma_{\hat{p}} = \sqrt{\frac{p(1 - p)}{n}} = \frac{\sqrt{p(1 - p)}}{\sqrt{n}} = \frac{\sigma}{\sqrt{n}},$$ which exactly matches the formula for $\sigma_{\bar{x}}$.

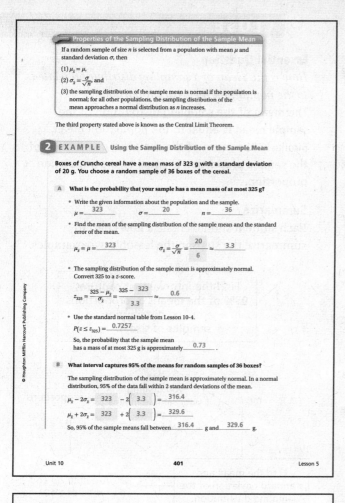

Properties of the Sampling Distribution of the Sample Mean

If a random sample of size n is selected from a population with mean μ and standard deviation σ, then

(1) $\mu_{\bar{x}} = \mu$,

(2) $\sigma_{\bar{x}} = \dfrac{\sigma}{\sqrt{n}}$, and

(3) the sampling distribution of the sample mean is normal if the population is normal; for all other populations, the sampling distribution of the mean approaches a normal distribution as n increases.

The third property stated above is known as the Central Limit Theorem.

2 EXAMPLE Using the Sampling Distribution of the Sample Mean

Boxes of Cruncho cereal have a mean mass of 323 g with a standard deviation of 20 g. You choose a random sample of 36 boxes of the cereal.

A What is the probability that your sample has a mean mass of at most 325 g?

- Write the given information about the population and the sample.

$\mu = \underline{323}$ $\qquad \sigma = \underline{20}$ $\qquad n = \underline{36}$

- Find the mean of the sampling distribution of the sample mean and the standard error of the mean.

$\mu_{\bar{x}} = \mu = \underline{323}$ $\qquad \sigma_{\bar{x}} = \dfrac{\sigma}{\sqrt{n}} = \dfrac{20}{6} \approx \underline{3.3}$

- The sampling distribution of the sample mean is approximately normal. Convert 325 to a z-score.

$z_{325} = \dfrac{325 - \mu_{\bar{x}}}{\sigma_{\bar{x}}} = \dfrac{325 - 323}{3.3} \approx \underline{0.6}$

- Use the standard normal table from Lesson 10-4.

$P(z \le z_{325}) = \underline{0.7257}$

So, the probability that the sample mean has a mass of at most 325 g is approximately $\underline{0.73}$.

B What interval captures 95% of the means for random samples of 36 boxes?

The sampling distribution of the sample mean is approximately normal. In a normal distribution, 95% of the data fall within 2 standard deviations of the mean.

$\mu_{\bar{x}} - 2\sigma_{\bar{x}} = \underline{323} - 2\left(\underline{3.3}\right) = \underline{316.4}$

$\mu_{\bar{x}} + 2\sigma_{\bar{x}} = \underline{323} + 2\left(\underline{3.3}\right) = \underline{329.6}$

So, 95% of the sample means fall between $\underline{316.4}$ g and $\underline{329.6}$ g.

Unit 10 · 401 · Lesson 5

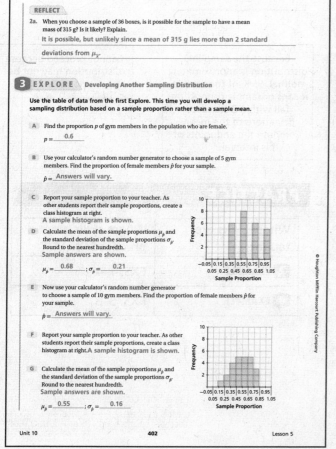

REFLECT

2a. When you choose a sample of 36 boxes, is it possible for the sample to have a mean mass of 315 g? Is it likely? Explain.

It is possible, but unlikely since a mean of 315 g lies more than 2 standard deviations from $\mu_{\bar{x}}$.

3 EXPLORE Developing Another Sampling Distribution

Use the table of data from the first Explore. This time you will develop a sampling distribution based on a sample proportion rather than a sample mean.

A Find the proportion p of gym members in the population who are female.

$p = \underline{0.6}$

B Use your calculator's random number generator to choose a sample of 5 gym members. Find the proportion of female members $\hat{p}$ for your sample.

$\hat{p} = \underline{\text{Answers will vary.}}$

C Report your sample proportion to your teacher. As other students report their sample proportions, create a class histogram at right. A sample histogram is shown.

D Calculate the mean of the sample proportions $\mu_{\hat{p}}$ and the standard deviation of the sample proportions $\sigma_{\hat{p}}$. Round to the nearest hundredth. Sample answers are shown.

$\mu_{\hat{p}} = \underline{0.68}$; $\sigma_{\hat{p}} = \underline{0.21}$

E Now use your calculator's random number generator to choose a sample of 10 gym members. Find the proportion of female members $\hat{p}$ for your sample.

$\hat{p} = \underline{\text{Answers will vary.}}$

F Report your sample proportion to your teacher. As other students report their sample proportions, create a class histogram at right. A sample histogram is shown.

G Calculate the mean of the sample proportions $\mu_{\hat{p}}$ and the standard deviation of the sample proportions $\sigma_{\hat{p}}$. Round to the nearest hundredth. Sample answers are shown.

$\mu_{\hat{p}} = \underline{0.55}$; $\sigma_{\hat{p}} = \underline{0.16}$

Unit 10 · 402 · Lesson 5

© Houghton Mifflin Harcourt Publishing Company

Notes

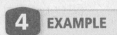

Questioning Strategies

- **How is this example different from** **2** **EXAMPLE** **?** This example involves a proportion rather than a mean

- **How is the solving technique similar to the previous example?** In both cases, you (1) write down facts about the population and the sample, (2) find the mean of the sampling distribution and the standard error, and (3) determine an interval that captures 95% of the means or porportions in the sampling distribution based on the fact that it is approximately normal

- **What is different in this solution from the solution in** **2** **EXAMPLE** **?** part C—checking that the sampling distribution is approximately normal

EXTRA EXAMPLE

About 28% of students at a large school play varsity sports. You choose a random sample of 60 students. What interval captures 68% of the proportions for random samples of 60 students? 68% of the sample proportions lie between 22.2% and 33.8%.

MATHEMATICAL PRACTICE **Highlighting the Standards**

This lesson includes many opportunities to address Mathematical Practice Standard 6 (Attend to precision). Students should know the vocabulary for the unit coming into this lesson. For instance, students will need to distinguish between the population mean and the sampling mean, between the standard deviation and the standard error of the mean, and between sampling distributions of sample means and sampling distributions of sample proportions. Students will need to use precision in their communication and interpret statistical symbols correctly.

CLOSE

Essential Question

How is the mean of a sampling distribution related to the population mean or proportion?
The mean of the sampling distribution of the sample mean is equal to the population mean. Similarly, the mean of the sampling distribution of the sample proportion is equal to the population proportion.

Summarize

Each student should create a flow chart to summarize the steps in the lesson's two examples.

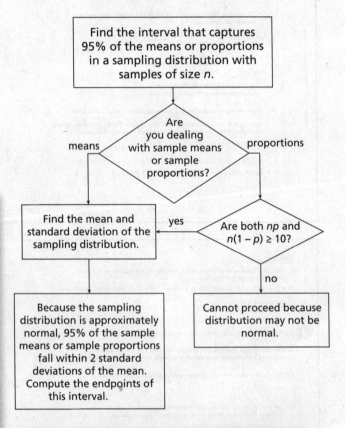

PRACTICE

Where skills are taught	Where skills are practiced
2 EXAMPLE	EXS. 1–4
4 EXAMPLE	EXS. 5–8

REFLECT

3a. In the class histograms, how does the mean of the sample proportions compare with the population proportion?

The mean of the sample proportions is close to the population proportion.

3b. What happens to the standard deviation of the sample proportions as the sample size increases?

The standard deviation of the sample proportions decreases.

When you work with the sampling distribution of a sample proportion, p represents the proportion of individuals in the population that have a particular characteristic (that is, the proportion of "successes") and $\hat{p}$ is the proportion of successes in a sample. The mean of the sampling distribution of the sample proportion is denoted $\mu_{\hat{p}}$. The standard deviation of the sampling distribution of the sample proportion is denoted $\sigma_{\hat{p}}$ and is also called the **standard error of the proportion**.

> **Properties of the Sampling Distribution of the Sample Proportion**
>
> If a random sample of size n is selected from a population with proportion of successes p, then
>
> (1) $\mu_{\hat{p}} = p$,
>
> (2) $\sigma_{\hat{p}} = \sqrt{\dfrac{p(1-p)}{n}}$, and
>
> (3) if both np and $n(1-p)$ are at least 10, then the sampling distribution of the sample proportion is approximately normal.

4 EXAMPLE Using the Sampling Distribution of the Sample Proportion

About 40% of the students at a university live off campus. You choose a random sample of 50 students. What interval captures 95% of the proportions for random samples of 50 students?

A Write the given information about the population and the sample, where a success is a student who lives off campus.

$p = \underline{\ 0.4\ }$ $n = \underline{\ 50\ }$

B Find the mean of the sampling distribution of the sample proportion and the standard error of the proportion.

$\mu_{\hat{p}} = p = \underline{\ 0.4\ }$ $\qquad \sigma_{\hat{p}} = \sqrt{\dfrac{p(1-p)}{n}} = \sqrt{\dfrac{0.4\left(1 - 0.4\right)}{50}} \approx \underline{\ 0.069\ }$

C Check that np and $n(1-p)$ are both at least 10.

$np = \underline{\ 50\ } \cdot \underline{\ 0.4\ } = \underline{\ 20\ }$ $\qquad n(1-p) = \underline{\ 50\ } \cdot \underline{\ 0.6\ } = \underline{\ 30\ }$

Since np and $n(1-p)$ are both greater than 10, the sampling distribution is approximately normal.

D In a normal distribution, 95% of the data fall within 2 standard deviations of the mean.

$\mu_{\hat{p}} - 2\sigma_{\hat{p}} = \underline{\ 0.4\ } - 2\left(\underline{\ 0.069\ }\right) = \underline{\ 0.262\ }$

$\mu_{\hat{p}} + 2\sigma_{\hat{p}} = \underline{\ 0.4\ } + 2\left(\underline{\ 0.069\ }\right) = \underline{\ 0.538\ }$

So, 95% of the sample proportions fall between $\underline{\ 26.2\%\ }$ and $\underline{\ 53.8\%\ }$.

REFLECT

4a. How can you find the interval that captures 99.7% of the sample proportions?

In a normal distribution, 99.7% of the data fall within 3 standard deviations of the mean, so the interval is 19.3% to 60.7%.

4b. How likely is it that a random sample of 50 students includes 31 students who live off campus? Explain.

This is very unlikely since $\dfrac{31}{50} = 62\%$ and this proportion is more than 3 standard deviations from the mean of the sampling distribution.

PRACTICE

The seniors at Fillmore High School have a mean score of 425 on a standardized science test with a standard deviation of 80. You choose a random sample of 30 seniors from the school. Find each of the following.

1. The probability that your sample has a mean score of at most 455 $\underline{\ 0.98\ }$

2. The probability that your sample has a mean score of at most 415 $\underline{\ 0.24\ }$

3. The probability that your sample has a mean score greater than 440 $\underline{\ 0.16\ }$

4. The interval that captures 95% of the means for random samples of 30 seniors

Between 396 and 454

A popcorn manufacturer puts a prize in 25% of its bags of popcorn. A quality control inspector selects a random sample of 40 bags of popcorn at the factory. Find each of the following.

5. The probability that the sample has prizes in at most 30% of the bags $\underline{\ 0.76\ }$

6. The probability that the sample has prizes in at most 9 bags $\underline{\ 0.34\ }$

7. The probability that the sample has prizes in more than 10 bags $\underline{\ 0.5\ }$

8. The interval that captures 95% of the proportions for random samples of 40 bags of popcorn

Between 11.4% and 38.6%

Confidence Intervals and Margins of Error

Essential question: *How do you calculate a confidence interval and a margin of error for a population proportion or mean?*

Standards for Mathematical Content

CC.9-12.S.IC.4 Use data from a sample survey to estimate a population mean or proportion; develop a margin of error through the use of simulation models for random sampling.*

Vocabulary
confidence interval, margin of error

Prerequisites
Data-gathering techniques, Lesson 10-1

Data distributions, Lesson 10-2

Normal distributions, Lesson 10-4

Sampling distributions, Lesson 10-5

Math Background
In the previous lesson, students were introduced to the concept of sampling distributions. They learned that the mean of a sampling distribution equals the population mean (for numerical data) or the population proportion (for categorical data). They also learned that the individual sample means or sample proportions within a sampling distribution vary, forming an approximately normal distribution having a standard deviation that they learned how to calculate.

In the previous lesson, the population parameters (population mean and standard deviation for numerical data and population proportion for categorical data) were known. This lesson extends the study of sampling distributions to populations whose mean or proportion is not known. Students will learn how to determine, with a certain degree of confidence, that the population mean or proportion is within a particular range of values.

INTRODUCE

Point out to students that when they had previously used sampling distributions, the population parameter was already known. Explain that in this lesson, they will use sample statistics to make inferences about population parameters. Review the various types of data distributions, with an emphasis on normal distributions.

TEACH

1 EXPLORE

Questioning Strategies

- Suppose that all numbers in the given situation stay the same. However, you surveyed a random sample of 25 students, not 50 students. What are the reasonably likely values of the sample proportion $\hat{p}$? Explain.

  If $p = 0.3$ and $n = 25$, then $\mu_{\hat{p}} = p = 0.3$ and $\sigma_{\hat{p}} = \sqrt{\dfrac{0.3(1 - 0.3)}{25}} \approx 0.092$. Because reasonably likely values of $\hat{p}$ lie within two standard deviations of $\mu_{\hat{p}}$, you have $\mu_{\hat{p}} - 2\sigma_{\hat{p}} = 0.3 - 2(0.092) \approx 0.12$ and $\mu_{\hat{p}} + 2\sigma_{\hat{p}} = 0.3 + 2(0.092) \approx 0.48$. So, for a random sample of 25 students, the reasonably likely values of the sample proportion $\hat{p}$ lie between 0.12 and 0.48.

- Suppose that all numbers in the given situation stay the same. However, you surveyed a random sample of 100 students, not 50 students. What are the reasonably likely values of the sample proportion $\hat{p}$? Explain.

  If $p = 0.3$ and $n = 100$, then $\mu_{\hat{p}} = p = 0.3$ and $\sigma_{\hat{p}} = \sqrt{\dfrac{0.3(1 - 0.3)}{100}} \approx 0.046$. Because reasonably likely values of $\hat{p}$ lie within two standard deviations of $\mu_{\hat{p}}$, you have $\mu_{\hat{p}} - 2\sigma_{\hat{p}} = 0.3 - 2(0.046) \approx 0.21$ and $\mu_{\hat{p}} + 2\sigma_{\hat{p}} = 0.3 + 2(0.046) \approx 0.39$. So, for a random sample of 100 students, the reasonably likely values of the sample proportion $\hat{p}$ lie between 0.21 and 0.39.

continued

Name_____ Class_____ Date_____

10-6

Confidence Intervals and Margins of Error

COMMON CORE

CC.9-12.S.IC.4*

Essential question: *How do you calculate a confidence interval and a margin of error for a population proportion or mean?*

In Lesson 10-5, you investigated sampling from a population whose parameter of interest (mean or proportion) is known. In many real-world situations, you collect sample data from a population whose parameter of interest is not known. In this lesson, you will learn how to use sample statistics to make inferences about population parameters.

1 EXPLORE Analyzing Likely Population Proportions

You survey a random sample of 50 students at a large high school and find that 40% of the students have attended a school football game. You cannot survey the entire population of students, but you would like to know what population proportions are reasonably likely in this situation.

A Suppose the proportion p of the population that has attended a school football game is 30%. Find the reasonably likely values of the sample proportion $\hat{p}$.

In this case, $p = \underline{\quad 0.3 \quad}$ and $n = \underline{\quad 50 \quad}$.

$\mu_p = p = \underline{\quad 0.3 \quad}$ and $\sigma_p = \sqrt{\dfrac{p(1-p)}{n}} = \sqrt{\dfrac{0.3\left(1-\boxed{0.3}\right)}{\boxed{50}}} \approx \underline{\quad 0.065 \quad}$

The reasonably likely values of $\hat{p}$ fall within 2 standard deviations of μ_p.

$\mu_p - 2\sigma_p = \boxed{0.3} - 2\left(\boxed{0.065}\right) = \underline{\quad 0.17 \quad}$

$\mu_p + 2\sigma_p = \boxed{0.3} + 2\left(\boxed{0.065}\right) = \underline{\quad 0.43 \quad}$

B On the graph, draw a horizontal line segment at the level of 0.3 on the vertical axis to represent the interval of likely values of $\hat{p}$ that you found above.

C Now repeat the process for $p = 0.35, 0.4, 0.45,$ and so on to complete the graph. You may wish to divide up the work with other students and pool your findings.

D Draw a vertical line at 0.4 on the horizontal axis. This represents $\hat{p} = 0.4$. The line segments that this vertical line intersects are the population proportions for which a sample proportion of 0.4 is reasonably likely.

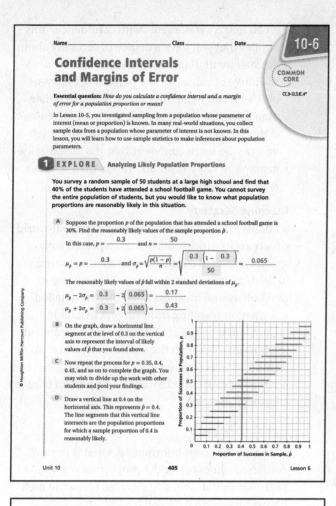

Proportion of Successes in Sample, $\hat{p}$ (horizontal axis)
Proportion of Successes in Population, p (vertical axis)

© Houghton Mifflin Harcourt Publishing Company

Unit 10   405   Lesson 6

REFLECT

1a. Is it possible that 30% of all students at the school have attended a football game? Is it likely? Explain.

It is both possible and likely; in part A of the Explore, you found that for $p = 0.3$, the interval of likely sample proportions (for a sample of 50 students) is 0.17 to 0.43, which includes $\hat{p} = 0.4$.

1b. Is it possible that 60% of all students at the school have attended a football game? Is it likely? Explain.

It is possible, but not likely; for $p = 0.6$, the interval of likely sample proportions (for a sample of 50 students) is 0.46 to 0.74, which does not include $\hat{p} = 0.4$.

1c. Based on your graph, which population proportions do you think are reasonably likely? Why?

30% to 50%; for these population proportions, the intervals of likely sample proportions include $\hat{p} = 0.4$.

A **confidence interval** is an approximate range of values that is likely to include an unknown population parameter. The *level* or *degree* of a confidence interval, such as 95%, gives the probability that the interval includes the true value of the parameter.

Recall that when data are normally distributed, 95% of the values fall within 2 standard deviations of the mean. Using this idea in the Explore, you found a 95% confidence interval for the proportion of all students who have attended a school football game.

To develop a formula for a confidence interval, notice that the vertical bold line segment in the figure, which represents the 95% confidence interval you found in the Explore, is about the same length as the horizontal bold line segment. The horizontal bold line segment has endpoints $\mu_p - 2\sigma_p$ and $\mu_p + 2\sigma_p$ where $\hat{p} = 0.4$. Since the bold line segments intersect at (0.4, 0.4), the vertical bold line segment has these same endpoints.

The above argument shows that you can find the endpoints of the confidence interval by finding the endpoints of the horizontal segment centered at $\hat{p}$. You know how to do this using the formula for the standard error of the sampling distribution of the sample proportion from Lesson 10-5. Putting these ideas together gives the following result.

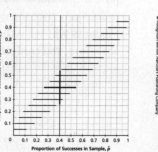

Proportion of Successes in Sample, $\hat{p}$ (horizontal axis)
Proportion of Successes in Population, p (vertical axis)

© Houghton Mifflin Harcourt Publishing Company

Unit 10   406   Lesson 6

- How does the sample size affect the reasonably likely values of the sample proportion $\hat{p}$? Explain. As the sample size increases, the range of the reasonably likely values of the sample proportion $\hat{p}$ decreases.

- In Reflect Question 1c, you drew the conclusion that a population proportion between 30% and 50% would be reasonably likely for the sample size of 50 students. Could you draw this same conclusion if all numbers in the given situation stayed the same except that the sample size was 100 instead of 50? Explain your reasoning. No; a population proportion between 30% and 50% would no longer be reasonably likely. If you drew the graph for a sample size of 100 students, the horizontal line segment at the level of 0.3 would extend from 0.21 to 0.39. A vertical line at $\hat{p} = 0.4$ would not intersect this line segment, which means that with a sample size of 100 students, a population proportion of 30% is not reasonably likely for a sample proportion of 0.4.

Avoid Common Errors

In part A of the Explore, students may want to use 0.4 instead of 0.3 for the value of $\mu_{\hat{p}}$. Remind students that 40% is a *sample* proportion. The value of $\mu_{\hat{p}}$, however, is equal to the *population* proportion, which is unknown. In part A, you *assume* that the population proportion is 30%, and that is the value that you use for $\mu_{\hat{p}}$.

2 EXAMPLE

Questioning Strategies

- Based on the given random sample, one researcher states that between 68% and 84% of four-year-olds in the United States can write their names. Based on the same random sample, another researcher states that between 65% and 87% of four-year-olds in the United States can write their names. If both researchers have made a reasonable statement, what could be the reason for the discrepancy? The first researcher is making the statement with 95% confidence, while the second researcher is making the statement with 99% confidence.

- If you make a statement "with confidence," this implies that you have a degree of certainty about the statement. If this is the case, then why does the range of values for the percent of four-year-olds who can write their name increase rather than decrease as the confidence level increases? If the range of possible values is greater, then you can be more confident that the actual value is going to fall within that range than within a smaller range of values.

Teaching Strategy

Students may benefit from seeing some real-world situations in which statistics are reported with a specified level of confidence. Academic journals in fields ranging from science and medicine to psychology and business often display detailed information resulting from surveys in a table format, often with a confidence level indicated at the bottom. Although the statistics used may go beyond what is covered in this lesson, students can see that level of confidence is a component of many statistical analyses.

EXTRA EXAMPLE

Based on the given information, what is the 90% confidence interval for the proportion p of four-year-olds in the United States who can write their names? between 0.69 and 0.83

3 EXAMPLE

Questioning Strategies

- Suppose the confidence level in the situation is reduced to 95%. Would the confidence interval for the mean test score among all students be wider or narrower than the confidence interval for the mean test score among all students when the confidence level is 99%? Explain your reasoning. The confidence interval for a 95% confidence level will be narrower than the confidence interval for a 99% confidence level. As the confidence interval becomes wider, it is more likely that the mean test score among all students will fall within that confidence interval; therefore, the confidence level increases.

continued

A Confidence Interval for a Population Proportion

A $c\%$ confidence interval for the proportion p of successes in a population is given by

$$\hat{p} - z_c \sqrt{\frac{\hat{p}(1 - \hat{p})}{n}} \leq p \leq \hat{p} + z_c \sqrt{\frac{\hat{p}(1 - \hat{p})}{n}}$$

where $\hat{p}$ is the sample proportion, n is the sample size, and z_c depends upon the desired degree of confidence.

In order for this interval to describe the value of p reasonably accurately, three conditions must be met.

1. There are only two possible outcomes associated with the parameter of interest. The population proportion for one outcome is p, and the proportion for the other outcome is $1 - p$.

2. $n\hat{p}$ and $n(1 - \hat{p})$ must both be at least 10.

3. The size of the population must be at least 10 times the size of the sample, and the sample must be random.

Use the values in the table below for z_c. (Note that for greater accuracy you should use 1.96 rather than 2 for $z_{95\%}$.)

Desired degree of confidence	90%	95%	99%
Value of z_c	1.645	1.96	2.576

2 EXAMPLE Finding a Confidence Interval for a Proportion

In a random sample of 100 four-year-old children in the United States, 76 were able to write their name. Find a 95% confidence interval for the proportion p of four-year-olds in the United States who can write their name.

A Determine the sample size n, the proportion $\hat{p}$ of four-year-olds in the sample who can write their name, and the value of z_c for a 95% confidence interval.

$n = \underline{100}$ $\hat{p} = \underline{0.76}$ $z_c = \underline{1.96}$

B Substitute the values of n, $\hat{p}$, and z_c into the formulas for the endpoints of the confidence interval. Then simplify and round to two decimal places.

$$\hat{p} - z_c \sqrt{\frac{\hat{p}(1 - \hat{p})}{n}} = \underline{0.76} - \underline{1.96} \sqrt{\frac{0.76 \left(1 - \underline{0.76}\right)}{100}} \approx \underline{0.68}$$

$$\hat{p} + z_c \sqrt{\frac{\hat{p}(1 - \hat{p})}{n}} = \underline{0.76} + \underline{1.96} \sqrt{\frac{0.76 \left(1 - \underline{0.76}\right)}{100}} \approx \underline{0.84}$$

So, you can state with 95% confidence that the proportion of all four-year-olds in the United States who can write their name lies between $\underline{0.68}$ and $\underline{0.84}$.

REFLECT

2a. Do the data satisfy the three conditions for using the confidence interval formula? Explain.

Yes; (1) there are only two outcomes associated with the parameter: a child either can or cannot write his or her name; (2) $n\hat{p} = 100(0.76) = 76$ and $n(1 - \hat{p}) = 100(0.24) = 24$, so both are greater than 10; (3) the population of four-year-olds in the United States is far greater than $10n = 10(100) = 1000$.

2b. Find the 99% confidence interval for p and describe how increasing the degree of confidence affects the range of values. Why does this make sense?

$0.65 \leq p \leq 0.87$; as the degree of confidence increases, the range of values gets broader; this makes sense because in order to have a greater degree of confidence in whether the population proportion has been "captured," you have to cast a wider net.

You can use reasoning similar to the argument in the Explore to develop a formula for a confidence interval for a population mean.

A Confidence Interval for a Population Mean

A $c\%$ confidence interval for the mean μ in a normally distributed population is given by

$$\bar{x} - z_c \frac{\sigma}{\sqrt{n}} \leq \mu \leq \bar{x} + z_c \frac{\sigma}{\sqrt{n}}$$

where $\bar{x}$ is the sample mean, n is the sample size, σ is the population standard deviation, and z_c depends upon the desired degree of confidence.

Note that it is assumed that the population is normally distributed and that you know the population standard deviation σ. In a more advanced statistics course, you can develop a confidence interval formula that does not depend upon a normally distributed population or knowing the population standard deviation.

3 EXAMPLE Finding a Confidence Interval for a Mean

In a random sample of 20 students at a large high school, the mean score on a standardized test is 610. Given that the standard deviation of all scores at the school is 120, find a 99% confidence interval for the mean score among all students at the school.

A Determine the sample size n, the sample mean $\bar{x}$, the population standard deviation σ, and the value of z_c for a 99% confidence interval.

$n = \underline{20}$ $\bar{x} = \underline{610}$

$\sigma = \underline{120}$ $z_c = \underline{2.576}$

- You determined in Reflect Question 3b that the formula for a confidence interval given in the example should be used only when the scores are normally distributed. Give an example of a way that scores could be distributed so that the given formula for a confidence interval should *not* be used and explain why. **The distribution of the scores could be uniform, skewed left, or skewed right. For example, two populations could have the same mean and standard deviation, but one could be skewed right with a few very high scores and many relatively low scores, while the other population could be skewed left with a few very low scores and many relatively high scores. When a distribution is skewed, conclusions based on the use of the given formula for a confidence interval are invalid.**

Avoid Common Errors

Remind students that the formula used in this example will produce valid results only when the population is normally distributed.

EXTRA EXAMPLE

For the given situation, what is the 90% confidence interval for the mean score among all students at the school? between 566 and 654

4 EXAMPLE

Questioning Strategies

- In step A, once you solve the margin of error formula for n, on what three variables does the value of n depend? For which of these variables do you know the values? Explain. **The value of n depends on the margin of error E, the z-score z_c that corresponds to a 90% confidence level, and sample proportion $\hat{p}$. You know only the values of E and z_c.**

- In step B, you're told to use 0.5 as the value of $\hat{p}$ because it makes the value of the expression $\hat{p}(1 - \hat{p})$ as large as possible. Consider the function $f(x) = x(1 - x)$. What type of function is this? Explain why it has a maximum, and then find the x-value where the maximum occurs. **The function is a quadratic function. Because you can write the function in standard form as $f(x) = -x^2 + x$, you know that its leading coefficient is negative, so its graph opens down, which means that a maximum occurs at the graph's vertex. The x-coordinate of the vertex is halfway between the x-intercepts, which from the intercept form $f(x) = x(1 - x)$ you know are 0 and 1. So, the maximum occurs at $x = 0.5$.**

....
⋮ **MATHEMATICAL**   **Highlighting**
⋮ **PRACTICE**   **the Standards**
....

3 EXAMPLE and its Reflect questions offer an opportunity to address Mathematical Practice Standard 7 (Look for and make use of structure). In the previous example, students learned to find a confidence interval for a proportion. In this example, students learn to find a confidence interval for a mean. In the previous example, students not only learned the formula for the confidence interval of a proportion, but also came to understand the underlying concepts of how the formula was derived. When students now use the formula for the confidence interval of a mean, they are already familiar with the basic structure of the formula. For example, in both formulas, an amount based on the standard error and the confidence level is both subtracted from and added to either the sample proportion or the sample mean to find the confidence interval.

continued

B Substitute the values of n, $\bar{x}$, σ, and z_c into the formulas for the endpoints of the confidence interval. Then simplify and round to the nearest whole number.

$$\bar{x} - z_c \frac{\sigma}{\sqrt{n}} = 610 - 2.576\frac{120}{\sqrt{20}} \approx 541$$

$$\bar{x} + z_c \frac{\sigma}{\sqrt{n}} = 610 + 2.576\frac{120}{\sqrt{20}} \approx 679$$

So, you can state with 99% confidence that the mean score among all students at the school lies between ___541___ and ___679___.

REFLECT

3a. What is the 99% confidence interval when the sample size increases to 50? Describe how increasing the sample size affects the confidence interval.

$566 \leq \mu \leq 654$; as the sample size increases, the confidence

interval gets narrower.

3b. What do you assume about the test scores of all students at the school in order to use the formula for the confidence interval?

You assume the scores are normally distributed.

In the previous example, you found the 99% confidence interval $541 \leq \mu \leq 679$, which is a range of values centered at $\mu = 610$. You can write the confidence interval as 610 ± 69, where 69 is the *margin of error*. The **margin of error** is half the length of a confidence interval.

> **Margin of Error for a Population Proportion**
>
> The margin of error E for the proportion of successes in a population with sample proportion $\hat{p}$ and sample size n is given by
>
> $$E = z_c\sqrt{\frac{\hat{p}(1-\hat{p})}{n}}$$
>
> where z_c depends on the degree of the confidence interval.
>
> **Margin of Error for a Population Mean**
>
> The margin of error E for the mean in a normally distributed population with standard deviation σ, sample mean $\bar{x}$, and sample size n is given by
>
> $$E = z_c\frac{\sigma}{\sqrt{n}}$$
>
> where z_c depends on the degree of the confidence interval.

From the above formulas, it is clear that the margin of error decreases as the sample size n increases. This suggests using a sample that is as large as possible; however, it is often more practical to determine a margin of error that is acceptable and then calculate the required sample size. The following example shows how to do this.

---

4 EXAMPLE Choosing a Sample Size

A researcher wants to know the percent of teenagers in the United States who have social networking profiles. She is aiming for a 90% confidence interval and a margin of error of 4%. What sample size n should she use?

A Solve the margin of error formula for n.

$$E = z_c\sqrt{\frac{\hat{p}(1-\hat{p})}{n}} \qquad \text{Write the formula.}$$

$$E^2 = z_c^2 \cdot \frac{\hat{p}(1-\hat{p})}{n} \qquad \text{Square both sides.}$$

$$nE^2 = z_c^2 \cdot \hat{p}(1-\hat{p}) \qquad \text{Multiply both sides by } n.$$

$$n = z_c^2 \cdot \frac{\hat{p}(1-\hat{p})}{E^2} \qquad \text{Divide both sides by } E^2.$$

B Estimate the value of $\hat{p}$.

The researcher has not yet conducted the survey and is trying to find $\hat{p}$. So, she must estimate $\hat{p}$ as 0.5, which is the value of $\hat{p}$ that makes the expression $\hat{p}(1-\hat{p})$ as large as possible.

C Determine the values of E and z_c.

E is the margin of error written as a decimal; z_c is the z-score that corresponds to a 90% confidence interval.

So, $E = $ ___0.04___ and $z_c = $ ___1.645___.

D Substitute the values of $\hat{p}$, E, and z_c in the formula from step A.

$$n = z_c^2 \cdot \frac{\hat{p}(1-\hat{p})}{E^2} = 1.645^2 \cdot \frac{0.5\left(1 - 0.5\right)}{0.04^2} \approx 423$$

So, the researcher should survey a random sample of ___423___ teenagers.

REFLECT

4a. Do you expect the sample size to increase or decrease if the researcher decides she wants a margin of error of 3% instead of 4%? Use the margin of error formula to check.

Increase; for $E = 3\%$, the sample size increases to 752.

4b. Do you expect the sample size you calculated in the example to increase or decrease if the researcher decides she wants a margin of error of 4% with a 95% confidence interval? Use the margin of error formula to check.

Increase; in this case, the sample size increases to 600.

- A researcher wants to decrease the margin of error in a study in which he is surveying a random sample of students that represents a much larger population of students. The researcher has determined that, due to cost considerations, the sample size in the study must not be increased. How could the researcher accomplish his goal of decreasing the margin of error while keeping the sample size the same? **The researcher could decrease the confidence level for the results of the survey, which will decrease the margin of error.**

Teaching Strategy

Explain to students that when designing a survey, researchers can use a formula that allows them to calculate the sample size they need to use to obtain a desired margin of error and confidence level. Have students discuss why they may want to use a smaller rather than a larger sample size. Suggest that some reasons may include the cost of the survey, convenience in conducting the survey, and time considerations. Ask students to identify the trade-offs that may result from using a smaller sample size. Encourage them to discuss these trade-offs in terms of the mathematics involved in the formula relating sample size, margin of error, and level of confidence. Have students consider how the advantages of choosing a larger sample size may outweigh the disadvantages, despite the fact that choosing a smaller sample size saves money, effort, and time.

EXTRA EXAMPLE

In the given situation, what is the sample size if the researcher decides she wants a margin of error of 4% with a confidence level of 99%? **1037**

CLOSE

Essential Question

How do you calculate a confidence interval and a margin of error for a population proportion or mean?

To calculate a confidence interval for a population proportion, use the formula

$\hat{p} - z_c \sqrt{\dfrac{\hat{p}(1-\hat{p})}{n}} \le p \le \hat{p} + z_c \sqrt{\dfrac{\hat{p}(1-\hat{p})}{n}}$, where p is the proportion of successes in a population, $\hat{p}$ is the sample proportion, n is the sample size, and z_c is the confidence level. To calculate a confidence interval for a population mean, use the formula

$\bar{x} - z_c \dfrac{\sigma}{\sqrt{n}} \le \mu \le \bar{x} + z_c \dfrac{\sigma}{\sqrt{n}}$, where μ is the mean in a normally distributed population, $\bar{x}$ is the sample mean, n is the sample size, σ is the population standard deviation, and z_c depends on the desired degree of confidence. For both the population proportion and the population mean, the margin of error is half the length of the confidence interval.

Summarize

Have students make a graphic organizer outlining the processes for calculating a confidence interval for a population proportion and a population mean. Include information about calculating the margin of error, as well as steps for choosing a sample size.

PRACTICE

Where skills are taught	Where skills are practiced
2 EXAMPLE	EXS. 1, 2
3 EXAMPLE	EXS. 3–5
4 EXAMPLE	EXS. 6, 7

Exercise 8: Students derive a formula for estimating the margin of error E for the proportion of successes in a population.

Exercise 9: Students derive the confidence interval for the population proportion p.

4c. Suppose the researcher decides to do the same study, but this time restricts the population to teenagers in California. Assuming she still wants a 90% confidence interval and a margin of error of 4%, what sample size n should she use? What do you notice?

423; the sample size does not depend upon the population size.

PRACTICE

1. In a random sample of 100 U.S. households, 37 had a pet dog.

  a. Do the data satisfy the three conditions for the confidence interval formula for a population proportion? Why or why not?

  Yes; (1) there are only two outcomes associated with the parameter: either having a dog or not having a dog; (2) $n\hat{p} = 100(0.37) = 37$ and $n(1 - \hat{p}) = 100(0.63) = 63$, so both are greater than 10; (3) the population of households in the United States is far greater than $10n = 10(100) = 1000$.

  b. Find a 90% confidence interval for the proportion p of U.S. households that have a pet dog.

  $0.29 \le p \le 0.45$

  c. Find a 95% confidence interval for the proportion p of U.S. households that have a pet dog.

  $0.275 \le p \le 0.465$

2. In a quality control study, 200 cars made by a particular company were randomly selected and 13 were found to have defects in the electrical system.

  a. Give a range for the percent p of all cars made by the company that have defective electrical systems, assuming you want to have a 90% degree of confidence.

  $3.6\% \le p \le 9.4\%$

  b. What is the margin or error?

  0.029 or 2.9%

  c. How does the margin of error change if you want to report the range of percents p with a 95% degree of confidence?

  The margin or error increases to 0.034 or 3.4%.

3. The mean number of hours worked per week in a random sample of 1500 employees at a large chain of department stores is 33.9. The standard deviation for the population is 4.5 hours. Find a 90% confidence interval for the mean number μ of hours worked per week among all employees of the chain.

  $33.7 \le \mu \le 34.1$

© Houghton Mifflin Harcourt Publishing Company

---

4. The mean annual salary for a random sample of 300 kindergarten through 12th grade teachers in a particular state is $50,500. The standard deviation among the state's entire population of teachers is $3,700. Find a 95% confidence interval for the mean annual salary μ for all kindergarten through 12th grade teachers in the state.

  $\$50,081 \le \mu \le \$50,919$

5. You survey a random sample of 90 students at a university whose students' grade-point averages (GPAs) have a standard deviation of 0.4. The surveyed students have a mean GPA of 3.1.

  a. How likely is it that the mean GPA among all students at the university is 3.25? Explain.

  This is very unlikely. The 99% confidence interval for μ is $2.99 \le \mu \le 3.21$ and 3.25 lies outside this range.

  b. What are you assuming about the GPAs of all students at the university? Why?

  The GPAs are normally distributed; this assumption is necessary in order to use the formula for the confidence interval for a population mean.

6. A quality control inspector at a factory wants to know the proportion of MP3 players produced by the factory that are defective. He is aiming for a margin of error of 3%. What sample size should he use to attain a 95% degree of confidence?

  1067 MP3 players

7. A phone company wants to conduct a survey to find the percent of teenagers in the United States who send at least 10 text messages per day. The company is aiming for a 2% margin of error in the study.

  a. What sample size should the company use to attain a 95% degree of confidence?

  2401 teenagers

  b. Suppose the company is able to estimate that about 60% of teenagers send at least 10 text messages per day. How does this change the sample size?

  The sample size decreases to 2305 teenagers.

8. The margin of error E for the proportion of successes in a population may be estimated by $\frac{1}{\sqrt{n}}$ where n is the sample size. Explain where this estimate comes from. (*Hint*: Assume a 95% confidence interval.)

  $z_c = 1.96 \approx 2$ and $\hat{p}$ is assumed to be 0.5, so $E = z_c\sqrt{\frac{\hat{p}(1 - \hat{p})}{n}} = 2\sqrt{\frac{0.5(0.5)}{n}}$, which simplifies to $\frac{1}{\sqrt{n}}$.

9. In the Explore, you wrote an interval of the form $\mu_{\hat{p}} - 2\sigma_{\hat{p}} < \hat{p} < \mu_{\hat{p}} + 2\sigma_{\hat{p}}$ that captures 95% of the sample proportions. From Lesson 10-5 you know that $\mu_{\hat{p}} = p$, so you can rewrite the interval as $p - 2\sigma_{\hat{p}} < \hat{p} < p + 2\sigma_{\hat{p}}$. Solve this compound inequality for p. What does this result tell you?

  $\hat{p} - 2\sigma_{\hat{p}} < p < \hat{p} + 2\sigma_{\hat{p}}$; this gives the confidence interval for the population proportion p

© Houghton Mifflin Harcourt Publishing Company

Surveys, Experiments, and Observational Studies

Essential question: *What kinds of statistical research are there, and which ones can establish cause-and-effect relationships between variables?*

© Houghton Mifflin Harcourt Publishing Company

COMMON CORE Standards for Mathematical Content

CC.9-12.S.IC.3 Recognize the purposes of and differences among sample surveys, experiments, and observational studies; explain how randomization relates to each.*

CC.9-12.S.IC.6 Evaluate reports based on data.*

Vocabulary

survey, observational study, factor, experiment, treatment, randomized comparative experiment, treatment group, control group

Prerequisites

Data-gathering techniques, Lesson 10-1

Math Background

Students are familiar with various data-gathering techniques and understand the advantages of using random samples. Students have analyzed examples of surveys and evaluated how well the results represent the population based on the sampling technique used. Students understand that accurate predictions can be made based on data obtained from a sample only if that sample accurately represents the population. However, even if the sample is representative of the population, there are other factors that can prevent a survey or another kind of study from yielding accurate results.

INTRODUCE

Review the various data-gathering techniques students learned in Lesson 10-1. Also, have students look back at some of the surveys in the examples and exercises in that lesson. Ask students to identify possible ways that the results of the surveys could have been influenced by how the survey questions were worded. Guide students to discover other factors that could also affect the accuracy of the data gathered, such as who asks the questions in an interview and whether a survey can be completed anonymously.

TEACH

 EXAMPLE

Questioning Strategies

- Are biased questions in a survey always intentional on the part of the person designing the survey? No, often the bias is completely unintentional, which is why it is a good idea to have someone uninvolved with the survey look at the questions before the survey is administered.

- Many surveys are conducted over the telephone. How could using only landline phones to conduct a survey affect the outcome? People with only cell phones will not be included. Those people may be younger or more urban than people with landline phones and therefore be underrepresented in the survey.

Teaching Strategy

Students may benefit from acting out interview and telephone surveys. Have students design survey questions, including questions that may be biased. Challenge the class to identify potential sources of error for each survey and suggest ways that the accuracy of the survey can be improved.

EXTRA EXAMPLE

Ken, an artist, conducts one-on-one interviews with a random sample of people at the opening night of his latest exhibit to have them rate the quality of his artwork. Explain why the results of this survey are likely to be inaccurate and then suggest a way to improve the accuracy of the survey. Because the person conducting the survey is the artist, people who do not like the artwork may not give their true opinion out of concern for Ken's feelings. A better survey would involve a neutral interviewer or allow people to respond anonymously.

Name_____ Class_____ Date_____

10-7

COMMON CORE

CC.9-12.S.IC.3*,
CC.9-12.S.IC.6*

Surveys, Experiments, and Observational Studies

Essential question: *What kinds of statistical research are there, and which ones can establish cause-and-effect relationships between variables?*

A **survey** measures characteristics of interest about a population using a sample selected from the population. As you saw in Lesson 10-1, a sample needs to be representative of the population in order for the measurements obtained from the sample to be accurate. Random sampling is generally the best way to ensure representation.

Even when random sampling is used for a survey, the survey's results can have errors. Some of the sources of errors are:

- *Biased questions:* The wording of questions in a survey can influence the way people respond to the questions. Survey questions need to be worded in a neutral, unbiased way.

- *Interviewer effect:* If the questions in a survey are being asked by an interviewer, the person being interviewed may give inaccurate responses to avoid being embarrassed. For instance, if the questions involve sensitive issues, the person may not tell the truth, or if the questions involve complex or unfamiliar issues, the person may resort to guessing.

- *Nonresponse:* Some people may be difficult or impossible to contact, or they may simply refuse to participate once contacted. If nonresponse rates are higher for certain subgroups of a population, such as the elderly, then those subgroups will be underrepresented in the survey results.

1 EXAMPLE   Detecting Errors in Surveys

Explain why the results of each survey are likely to be inaccurate and then suggest a way to improve the accuracy of the survey.

A   Mrs. Ruben, the owner of a business, conducts one-on-one interviews with a random sample of employees to have them rate how satisfied they are with different aspects of their jobs.

Because the person conducting the survey is the owner of the business, the
employees may not be completely open about any job dissatisfaction they may
have, since they may feel that their job security is at stake. A better survey would
involve a neutral interviewer or allow the employees to respond anonymously.

B   In a random sample of town residents, a survey asks, "Are you in favor of a special tax levy to renovate the dilapidated town hall?"

The question is biased because the word "dilapidated" suggests that the town hall
is in a complete state of disrepair, which makes it seem that a renovation is urgently
needed. The question could begin with a factual list of repairs that need to be
made, followed by "Are you in favor of a special tax levy to make these repairs?"

REFLECT

1a. Even if the survey question in part B is revised to give a factual list of repairs that need to be made to the town hall, do the people surveyed have enough information to give an informed and accurate response? Explain.

No, because most people responding to the survey will want to know the amount
of the tax levy; without that knowledge, they may be likely to respond negatively
out of fear that their taxes will increase too much.

An **observational study** can be used to determine whether an existing condition, called a **factor**, in a population is related to a characteristic of interest. For instance, an observational study might be used to find the incidence of heart disease among those who smoke. In the study, being a smoker is the factor, and having heart disease is the characteristic of interest.

In an observational study, the condition already exists in the population. In an **experiment**, the condition is created by imposing a **treatment** on the sample. For instance, an experiment might be conducted by having a group of people with eczema take a vitamin E pill daily, and then observing whether their symptoms improve. In the experiment, taking the vitamin E pill is the treatment, and improvement of symptoms is the characteristic of interest.

2 EXAMPLE   Identifying Observational Studies and Experiments

Determine whether each research study is an observational study or an experiment. Identify the factor if it is an observational study or the treatment if it is an experiment. Also identify the characteristic of interest.

A   Researchers measure the cholesterol of 50 subjects who report that they eat fish regularly and 50 subjects who report that they do not eat fish regularly.

Observational study; factor: eating fish regularly; characteristic of interest:
cholesterol level

B   Researchers have 100 subjects with high cholesterol take fish oil pills daily for two months. They monitor the cholesterol of the subjects during that time.

Experiment; treatment: taking fish oil tablets daily; characteristic of interest:
cholesterol level

REFLECT

2a. Suppose the researchers in part A find that considerably more people who eat fish regularly have normal cholesterol levels than those who do not eat fish regularly. Is it reasonable to conclude that eating fish regularly has an effect on cholesterol? Explain.

No; there may be other factors that the people who eat fish regularly have in common,
such as regular exercise, and it may be those factors that have an effect on cholesterol.

Questioning Strategies

- Suppose the researchers in part B find that considerably more subjects who took the fish oil pills had lower cholesterol after two months. Is it reasonable to conclude that taking fish oil pills has an effect of lowering cholesterol? Explain. Yes; if taking the fish oil pills was the only difference between the two groups of subjects, the treatment of taking a fish oil pill could be determined to have an effect of lowering cholesterol.

- What is an example of a situation for which an observational study would be better than an experiment? If the treatment being imposed in an experiment could be harmful, then an observational study would be better. For example, if researchers want to study whether eating fried food every day increases cholesterol, it would be better to conduct an observational study of people who already report that they eat fried food every day rather than ask people to engage in the potentially harmful behavior as a treatment in an experiment.

Avoid Common Errors

Results of observational studies are often incorrectly interpreted as establishing a cause-and-effect relationship. Remind students that observational studies can establish only an association between a factor and a characteristic of interest.

EXTRA EXAMPLE

Researchers measure the bone density of 50 subjects who report that they take a daily multivitamin and 50 subjects who report that they do not take a daily multivitamin. Determine whether the research study is an observational study or an experiment. Identify the factor if it is an observational study or the treatment if it is an experiment. Also, identify the characteristic of interest. observational study; factor: taking a daily multivitamin; characteristic of interest: bone density

Questioning Strategies

- In the research study in part A, how would the experiment be affected if subjects in the control group simply did not take any tablet at all? If subjects in the control group did not take a tablet, then the placebo effect could make it difficult to interpret the results of the experiment. If the treatment group had different outcomes from the control group, researchers could not tell whether the result was actually due to the zinc in the tablet or merely the effect of taking a pill.

- In the research study in part B, could the control group be subjects who did not study for the test? Explain. The focus of the research is the effect of having a classmate involved in the studying process, not the effect of studying itself. If the control group were subjects who did not study for the test, then the focus of the research would be more on the effect of studying versus not studying.

Differentiated Instruction

Visual learners may benefit by thinking of ways to present the results of a randomized comparative experiment. For instance, for the experiment in part A, the results might be presented in a bar graph, with a bar for the treatment group and a bar for the control group. The height of a bar would indicate the mean duration of the colds for the group.

EXTRA EXAMPLE

To see whether honey has an effect on the duration of a sore throat, half the subjects took lozenges containing honey at the onset of a sore throat, and half took lozenges without any honey. The durations of the sore throats were then recorded. Identify the control group and the treatment group in the experiment. Assume all subjects were selected randomly. control group: subjects who took lozenges without honey; treatment group: subjects who took lozenges with honey

© Houghton Mifflin Harcourt Publishing Company

2b. In medical research, subjects sometimes respond to a treatment even if the treatment, called a *placebo*, is designed not to have an effect. (For instance, a placebo may be a pill with no active ingredients.) If the researchers in part B find that taking fish oil pills lowers cholesterol, what should they do to rule out the possibility of a placebo effect?

Give a placebo pill to a second group of subjects to see what happens to
their cholesterol.

Whether a study is observational or experimental, it should be *comparative* in order to establish a connection between the factor or treatment and the characteristic of interest. For instance, determining the rate of car accidents among people who talk on cell phones while driving is pointless unless you compare it with the rate of car accidents among people who don't talk on cell phones while driving and find that it is significantly different.

While a comparative observational study can suggest a relationship between two variables, such as cell phone use while driving and car accidents, it cannot establish a cause-and-effect relationship because there can be *confounding variables* (also called *lurking variables*) that influence the results. For instance, perhaps people who talk on cell phones while driving are more likely to drive aggressively, so it is the aggressive driving (not the cell phone use) that leads to a higher rate of car accidents.

In an experiment, randomization can remove the problem of a confounding variable by distributing the variable among the groups being compared so that its influence on the groups is more or less equal. Therefore, the best way to establish a cause-and-effect relationship between two variables is through a **randomized comparative experiment** where subjects are randomly divided into two groups: the **treatment group**, which is given the treatment, and the **control group**, which is not.

3 EXAMPLE Identifying Control Groups and Treatment Groups

Identify the control group and treatment group in each experiment. Assume all subjects of the research are selected randomly.

A To see whether zinc has an effect on the duration of a cold, half the subjects took tablets containing zinc at the onset of cold symptoms, and half took tablets without any zinc. The durations of the colds were then recorded.

Control group: Subjects who took tablets without zinc

Treatment group: Subjects who took tablets with zinc

B To see whether reviewing for a test with a classmate improves test scores, half the subjects studied with a classmate prior to taking a test, and half studied for the test alone. The test scores were then recorded.

Control group: Subjects who studied for the test alone

Treatment group: Subjects who studied for the test with a classmate

---

REFLECT

3a. How does using a control group help a researcher interpret the results of an experiment? How does using randomization help?

A control group provides a basis for comparison, so the researcher can observe
the magnitude of the effect that the manipulated variable has on the treatment
group. Randomization assures the researcher that any observed difference in effect
between the treatment and control groups is due to the manipulated variable and
not some other variable.

When you encounter media reports of statistical research in your daily life, you should judge any reported conclusions on the basis of how the research was conducted. Among the questions you should consider are:

• Is the research a survey, an observational study, or an experiment? In broad terms, a survey simply measures variables, an observational study attempts to find a relationship between variables, and an experiment attempts to establish a cause-and-effect relationship between variables.

• Was randomization used in conducting the research? As you know, random sampling is considered the best way to obtain a representative sample from a population and therefore get accurate results. Randomization also helps to dilute the effect of confounding variables.

• Does the report include the details of the research, such as sample size, statistics, and margins of error?

4 EXAMPLE Evaluating a Media Report

Evaluate the article about the effect of doctor empathy on the duration and severity of a cold.

A Is this a survey, an observational study, or an experiment? How do you know?

Experiment, because a treatment (standard
or enhanced interaction with a doctor) was
imposed

B Was randomization used in the research? If so, how?

Yes; subjects were randomly assigned to
a control group or one of two treatment
groups.

C Does the report include the details of the research? If not, what information is missing?

The report includes the number of subjects
but no statistics (measures of cold duration/
severity).

> **Caring Doctors Shorten and Ease the Common Cold**
>
> Researchers have found that among patients with colds, those who gave their doctors perfect scores on a questionnaire measuring empathy had colds that did not last as long and were less severe. Empathy on the part of doctors included making patients feel at ease, listening to their concerns, and showing compassion.
>
> A total of 350 subjects who were experiencing the onset of a cold were randomly assigned to one of three groups: no doctor-patient interaction, standard interaction, and enhanced interaction. Only subjects in the third group saw doctors who had been coached on being empathetic.

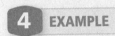

Questioning Strategies

- How could you rewrite the second paragraph of the article if the research involved a survey instead of an experiment? A total of 350 subjects completed a survey that asked them to rate their doctors on level of empathy when subjects interacted with the doctors at the onset of a cold. Subjects also answered questions on how they thought the level of empathy affected the duration of the cold.

- How could you rewrite the second paragraph of the article if the research involved an observational study instead of an experiment? A total of 350 subjects reported the duration of a cold. Subjects also reported whether they had no interaction with a doctor, standard interaction with a doctor, or interaction with a doctor who seemed especially empathetic.

MATHEMATICAL PRACTICE Highlighting the Standards

4 EXAMPLE and its Reflect questions offer an opportunity to address Mathematical Practice Standard 3 (Construct viable arguments and critique the reasoning of others). By looking at media reports about research studies and identifying the type of statistical research based on given information, students can determine whether or not the conclusions in the media report are valid. For example, if the research is an observational study rather than an experiment, students will be able to critique any conclusions that try to establish a cause-and-effect relationship between variables.

Avoid Common Errors

Remind students that the placebo effect can occur even in research where medicine and pills are not involved. When designing experiments, researchers must be aware that a treatment can have an effect simply because the subjects in the treatment group are receiving it.

EXTRA EXAMPLE

A news article says that students who study with classical music playing in the background score higher on math tests than students who study with no music playing. The article reports that 200 students were randomly assigned to one of two groups: 1) studying with classical music playing and 2) studying with no music playing. Subjects in the group with classical music playing had higher scores on the math test. Is this a survey, an observational study, or an experiment? How do you know? Experiment, because a treatment (classical music playing while studying) was imposed

CLOSE

Essential Question

What kinds of statistical research are there, and which ones can establish cause-and-effect relationships between variables?
Statistical research can include surveys, observational studies, and experiments. While surveys measure variables and observational studies may show associations between variables, only experiments can establish cause-and-effect relationships between variables.

Summarize

Have students make a table comparing surveys, observational studies, and experiments. For each type of research, describe how data are gathered and what conclusions can be determined from the results.

PRACTICE

Where skills are taught	Where skills are practiced
1 EXAMPLE	EXS. 1, 2
2 EXAMPLE	EXS. 3, 4
3 EXAMPLE	EX. 5
4 EXAMPLE	EXS. 6, 7

REFLECT

4a. What conclusion do you draw from the report? How much confidence do you place in that conclusion? Why?

A doctor should be empathetic because empathy causes a patient's cold to be

shorter and milder; confidence is fairly high (despite the lack of statistics in the

report) because this was a comparative randomized experiment.

4b. Describe a confounding variable that might have affected the results of the research. How did the researchers deal with such confounding variables?

Answers will vary. Sample answer: Overall health could have been a confounding

variable if healthier subjects happened to see the empathetic doctors and then had

shorter/milder colds; researchers randomly assigned subjects to control and treatment

groups so each group would have subjects in various states of overall health.

PRACTICE

Explain why the results of each survey are likely to be inaccurate and then suggest a way to improve the accuracy of the survey.

1. A store offers its customers a chance to win a cash prize if they call a toll-free number and participate in a survey of customer satisfaction.

   Survey respondents are self-selected and may be inclined to rate their satisfaction

   high in the belief that doing so will increase their chance of winning the cash

   prize; randomly ask customers to complete a quick survey as they are leaving the

   store (regardless of whether they made a purchase).

2. In a random sample of parents in a school district, a survey asks, "Are you willing to pay a small fee for each school sport that your child participates in?"

   The question is biased because of the word "small," which suggests that parents

   should be willing to pay the fee; the question should give the amount of the fee

   so that parents can decide if it's acceptable.

For Exercises 3 and 4, determine whether each research study is an observational study or an experiment. Identify the factor if it is an observational study or the treatment if it is an experiment. Also identify the characteristic of interest.

3. Researchers found that of patients who had been taking a bone-loss drug for more than five years, a high percent also had an uncommon type of fracture in the thigh bone.

   Observational study; factor: taking a bone-loss drug for more than five years;

   characteristic of interest: uncommon type of fracture in the thigh bone

4. Researchers found that when patients with chronic illnesses were randomly divided into two groups, the group that got regular coaching by phone from health professionals to help them manage their illnesses had lower monthly medical costs than the group that did not get the coaching.

   Experiment; treatment: regular coaching by phone from health professionals;

   characteristic of interest: monthly medical costs

5. Is the research study in Exercise 4 a comparative randomized experiment? If so, identify the treatment group and the control group.

   Yes; treatment group: patients who got regular coaching by phone from health

   professionals; control group: patients who did not get coaching

6. Evaluate the article about doctors working when sick.

   a. Is this a survey, an observational study, or an experiment? How do you know?

   Survey; the only variable is doctors who work while sick

   b. Was randomization used in the research? If so, how?

   The article does not say whether random sampling was used.

   c. Does the report include the details of the research? If not, what information is missing?

   Yes; the sample size is given, and sample proportions are reported.

   d. What is your overall evaluation of the report? Why?

   Anonymity allowed honest responses, but the results may not apply to all doctors since only doctors-in-training were surveyed.

   > **Doctors Work When Sick**
   >
   > Doctors know that they can get sick from their patients, but when they are sick themselves, do they stay away from their patients? Researchers asked 537 doctors-in-training to anonymously report whether they had worked while sick during the past year. The researchers found that 58% said they had worked once while sick and 31% said they had worked more than once while sick.

7. Evaluate the article about antibiotic use in infants.

   a. Is this a survey, an observational study, or an experiment? How do you know?

   Observational study; compared two variables (antibiotic use and occurrence of asthma/allergies), but no treatment imposed

   b. Was randomization used in the research? If so, how?

   The article does not say whether subjects were chosen at random.

   c. Does the report include the details of the research? If not, what information is missing?

   Yes; the sample size is given, and the increased risks of developing asthma/allergies are given.

   d. What is your overall evaluation of the report? Why?

   While the study provides reason for caution when doctors give infants antibiotics, it does not establish a cause-and-effect relationship.

   > **Antibiotic Use Tied to Asthma and Allergies**
   >
   > Antibiotic use in infants is linked to asthma and allergies, says a study involving 1401 children. Researchers asked mothers how many doses of antibiotics their children received before 6 months of age as well as whether their children had developed asthma or allergies by age 6. Children who received just one dose of antibiotics were 40% more likely to develop asthma or allergies. The risk jumped to 70% for children who received two doses.

Determining the Significance of Experimental Results

Essential question: *In an experiment, when is the difference between the control group and treatment group likely to be caused by the treatment?*

© Houghton Mifflin Harcourt Publishing Company

COMMON CORE Standards for Mathematical Content

CC.9-12.S.IC.5 Use data from a randomized experiment to compare two treatments; use simulations to decide if differences between parameters are significant.*

Vocabulary
null hypothesis, significant result, resampling, permutation test

Prerequisites
Randomized comparative experiments, Lesson 10-7

Math Background
In Lesson 10-6, students used a sample mean or sample proportion to find an interval that was likely to capture the population mean or population proportion. The statistical reasoning was based on the fact that the sampling distribution was approximately normal and centered on the population parameter. So, if the interval ran from 2 standard deviations below the sample statistic to 2 standard deviations above it, the interval would capture the population parameter 95% of the time. For this reason, the interval was called a 95% confidence interval.

In this lesson, students use similar reasoning to either accept or reject a null hypothesis for a randomized comparative experiment, which says that any result obtained from the experiment is due to chance. Working under the assumption that the null hypothesis is true, students use the data from an experiment to generate a resampling distribution, which is approximately normal. If the experimental result falls somewhere in the middle 90% (or 95% or even 99%) of the resampling distribution, there is no reason to reject the null hypothesis, so the result is not significant. But if the result falls outside the middle (making the result very unusual), the null hypothesis is rejected and the result is called significant. (The level of significance is determined by the probability of getting the result or one that is even more extreme.)

INTRODUCE

Revisit some of the randomized comparative experiments described in Lesson 10-7. Ask students to think about how they could determine whether differences between the control and treatment groups in these experiments were significant (that is, likely to be caused by the treatment and not simply due to chance).

TEACH

 EXAMPLE

Questioning Strategies

- Why does a result have to be rare (that is, have a very low probability of occurrence) for the null hypothesis to be rejected? Why couldn't any result that shows a difference between the treatment and control groups be evidence that the treatment has an effect? There is always going to be some variation within a group and therefore some difference between two groups regardless of whether a treatment has an effect. This is why the null hypothesis says that any difference between the groups is simply due to chance. Only when a difference between the treatment and control groups is rare should the null hypothesis be called into question and the treatment deemed to have an effect.

- When a null hypothesis is rejected, why is it reasonable to accept the alternative hypothesis that the result is due to the *treatment*? Couldn't some factor other than the treatment have produced the effect? The reason that other factors can be ruled out is that the experiment was randomized. That is, subjects were randomly assigned to the treatment and control groups, thereby distributing the effects of other factors between them. The only factor that makes the two groups different is the treatment.

continued

Name_____ Class_____ Date_____

10-8

COMMON CORE

CC.9-12.S.IC.5*

Determining the Significance of Experimental Results

Essential question: *In an experiment, when is a difference between the control group and treatment group likely to be caused by the treatment?*

You can think of every randomized comparative experiment as a test of a *null hypothesis*. The **null hypothesis** states that any difference between the control group and the treatment group is due to chance. In other words, the null hypothesis is the assumption that the treatment has no effect.

In statistics, an experimental result is called **significant** if the likelihood that it occurred by chance alone is very low. A low probability of getting the result by chance is evidence in favor of rejecting the null hypothesis. A significant result, however, does not *prove* that the treatment has an effect; the null hypothesis may still be true, and a rare event may simply have occurred. Nevertheless, standard practice in statistics is to reject the null hypothesis in favor of the *alternative* hypothesis that the result is due to the treatment.

1 EXAMPLE Formulating the Null Hypothesis

For each experiment, state the null hypothesis.

A A potential growth agent is sprayed on the leaves of 12 emerging ferns twice a week for a month. Another 12 emerging ferns are not sprayed with the growth agent. The mean stalk lengths of the two groups of ferns are compared after a month.

   The null hypothesis is that the mean stalk lengths of the two groups of ferns will
   be about the same.

B Ten people with colds are treated with a new formula for an existing brand of cold medicine. Ten other people with colds are treated with the original formula. The mean recovery times for the two groups are compared.

   The null hypothesis is that the mean recovery times for the two groups will be
   about the same.

REFLECT

1a. Suppose in part A that the treated ferns had a mean stalk length that is twice the mean stalk length of the untreated ferns. Should the researcher reject the null hypothesis? Does the experimental result prove that the growth agent works? Explain.

   Yes, the researcher should reject the null hypothesis because the difference

   between the control group and the treatment group is so dramatic. No, the result

   does not prove that the growth agent works; it only provides evidence that

   rejecting the assumption that the growth agent has no effect is reasonable.

© Houghton Mifflin Harcourt Publishing Company

1b. Suppose in part B that the mean recovery time for both groups is 5 days. Should the researcher reject the null hypothesis? Does the experimental result prove that the new formula is no more effective than the original formula? Explain.

   No, the researcher should not reject the null hypothesis because there is no

   difference between the control group and the treatment group. No, the result does

   not prove that the new formula is no more effective than the old; it only supports

   the reasonableness of the assumption that the new formula is no more effective.

1c. In the U.S. legal system, a defendant is assumed innocent until guilt is proved beyond a reasonable doubt. How is this situation like rejecting a null hypothesis?

   A null hypothesis (like innocence) is assumed to be true unless the experimental

   evidence (like evidence of guilt) allows you to reject the null hypothesis

   (innocence).

Suppose a company that offers an SAT prep course wants to demonstrate that its course raises test scores. The company recruits 20 students and randomly assigns half of them to a treatment group, where subjects take the course before taking the SAT, and half to a control group, where subjects do not take the course before taking the SAT. The table below shows the SAT scores of the 10 students in each group. How can you tell whether the course actually improved the scores of the students in the treatment group?

	SAT Scores				
Treatment Group	1440	1610	1430	1700	1690
	1570	1480	1620	1780	2010
Control Group	1150	1500	1050	1600	1460
	1860	1350	1750	1680	1330

One thing you could do is compute the mean SAT score for each group to see if the means are different. Obviously, the company expects the treatment group's mean to be greater than the control group's mean. But even if that is the case, how do you know that the difference in the means can be attributed to the treatment and not to chance? In other words, how do you know if the difference is *significant*?

The null hypothesis for this experiment is that the SAT prep course has no effect on a student's score. Under this assumption, it doesn't matter whether a student is in the treatment group or the control group. Since each group is a sample of the students, the means of the two samples should be about equal. In fact, any random division of the 20 students into two groups of 10 should result in two means whose difference is relatively small and a matter of chance. This technique, called **resampling**, allows you to create a distribution of the differences of means for every possible pairing of groups with 10 students in each. You can *test* the null hypothesis by using this distribution to find the likelihood, given that the null hypothesis is true, of getting a difference of means at least as great as the actual experimental difference. The test is called a **permutation test**.

© Houghton Mifflin Harcourt Publishing Company

Teaching Strategy

Although stating a null hypothesis will probably not be intuitive for students, most students will be very comfortable stating a hypothesis in a more "positive" way. For example, a student will probably have no problem understanding a hypothesis like "Students who stay up late at night have trouble getting up early in the morning." Point out that in an experimental situation, this could be stated as the null hypothesis by saying that "there will be no difference in the number of times students who stay up late and students who do not stay up late have trouble getting up early in the morning." Have students take turns stating hypotheses about their everyday lives; then, have the entire class restate the hypotheses as null hypotheses.

EXTRA EXAMPLE

At a car dealership, 20 identical new cars were given a rust-proofing treatment. Another 20 identical new cars were not given the rust proofing treatment. After three years, the two groups of cars are compared for mean area of rust spots. State the null hypothesis for this experiment. The null hypothesis is that the mean area of rust spots for the two groups of cars will be about the same.

2 EXAMPLE

Questioning Strategies

- In part C, would it be possible to have a simulation in which the mean score difference between Group A and Group B is greater than the mean score difference between the control and treatment groups? Explain. Yes; if the calculator's random integer generator happens to assign the ten highest SAT scores to Group A and the ten lowest SAT scores to Group B, then the difference between the mean scores for Group A and Group B will be greater than the difference between the mean scores for the control and treatment groups.

- Do the results of the three simulations in part C tell you anything about the significance of the difference in mean scores between the control group and the treatment group? Answers will vary depending on the outcomes of the simulations. Students will generally find that the absolute value of the difference between the mean score for Group A and the mean score for Group B is much less than the difference between the control and the treatment groups. However, three simulations are not enough to get an accurate sense of the resampling distribution.

- In part D, suppose your teacher recorded the results of 90 simulations in the frequency table and created a histogram for the 90 simulations. Then suppose your teacher recorded the results of an additional 90 simulations and created a second histogram for all 180 simulations. How would you expect the second histogram to differ from the first histogram? Besides having taller bars, the second histogram would have greater symmetry about the vertical line at 0.

- If 90 simulations were used for the permutation test in parts B through E, how could you use the information given in part F to determine the least difference in mean scores for the control and the treatment groups that would be significant? Explain your reasoning. According to the information given in part F, if $P > 0.10$, then the results are not significant. This means that the difference for which the P-value is equal to 0.10 will be the least difference in mean scores for the control and the treatment groups that is significant. If 90 simulations were used for the permutation test, then to get a P-value of 0.10, you would need $0.10(90) = 9$ results at least as great as the least significant difference. By examining an ordered list of the differences from the 90 simulations, you could count down from the greatest difference to the ninth-greatest difference, which is the least of the significant differences.

continued

© Houghton Mifflin Harcourt Publishing Company

2 EXAMPLE Using a Permutation Test

Use the table of SAT scores on the previous page to construct a resampling distribution for the difference of means, assuming that the null hypothesis is true. Then determine the significance of the actual experimental result.

A State the null hypothesis in terms of the difference of the two group means.

   The difference of the two group means is about 0.

B Calculate the mean score for the treatment group, $\bar{x}_T$, and the mean score for the control group, $\bar{x}_C$. Then find the difference of the means.

   $\bar{x}_T =$ __1633__ $\bar{x}_C =$ __1473__ $\bar{x}_T - \bar{x}_C =$ __160__

C Label the data in the table on the previous page with the identifiers 1 through 20. Then follow these steps to complete each table below:

   • Use a calculator's random integer generator to generate a list of 10 identifiers between 1 and 20 with no identifiers repeated.

   • Record the scores that correspond to those identifiers as the scores for Group A. Record the remaining 10 scores as the scores for Group B.

   • Find $\bar{x}_A$, $\bar{x}_B$, and $\bar{x}_A - \bar{x}_B$, and record them in the table.

   Sample answers appear in each table.

Simulation 1					Means	Difference of means
Group A	1750	1460	1330	1480	1570	$\bar{x}_A = 1536$	
	1610	1700	1350	1430	1680		$\bar{x}_A - \bar{x}_B = -34$
Group B	1440	1690	1620	1780	2010	$\bar{x}_B = 1570$	
	1150	1500	1050	1600	1860		

Simulation 2					Means	Difference of means
Group A	1570	1680	1150	1350	1610	$\bar{x}_A = 1559$	
	1750	1440	2010	1330	1700		$\bar{x}_A - \bar{x}_B = 12$
Group B	1430	1690	1480	1620	1780	$\bar{x}_B = 1547$	
	1500	1050	1600	1460	1860		

Simulation 3					Means	Difference of means
Group A	1600	1860	1460	1330	1350	$\bar{x}_A = 1551$	
	1610	1780	1750	1150	1620		$\bar{x}_A - \bar{x}_B = -4$
Group B	1440	1430	1700	1690	1570	$\bar{x}_B = 1555$	
	1480	2010	1500	1050	1680		

© Houghton Mifflin Harcourt Publishing Company

D Report the differences of means that you found for simulations 1–3 to your teacher so that he or she can create a frequency table and histogram of the class results. You should make your own copy of the frequency table and histogram using the table and the grid below.

Interval	Frequency
$-320 \le x < -240$	1
$-240 \le x < -160$	7
$-160 \le x < -80$	19
$-80 \le x < 0$	26
$0 \le x < 80$	23
$80 \le x < 160$	11
$160 \le x < 240$	2
$240 \le x < 320$	1

Sample results for 90 simulations are shown.

E Explain how you can use the frequency table or the histogram to find the probability that a difference of means is *at least as great* as the difference that you recorded in part B. Then find that probability.

   Divide the sum of the frequencies for the intervals $160 \le x < 240$ and

   $240 \le x < 320$ by the sum of all frequencies (total number of simulations); sample

   answer using the sample frequencies from part D: $(2 + 1)/90 \approx 0.03$.

F The probability that you found in part E is called a *P-value*. The *P*-value determines the significance of the experimental result. Statisticians commonly use the following levels of significance:

   • When $P > 0.10$, the result is *not significant*.
   • When $0.05 < P \le 0.10$, the result is *marginally significant*.
   • When $0.01 < P \le 0.05$, the result is *significant*.
   • When $P \le 0.01$, the result is *highly significant*.

   Using the *P*-value that you obtained in part E, characterize the significance of the experimental result for the SAT scores.

   Answers depend on the class data. For the sample data above, the result is significant.

G State the conclusion that you can draw from the permutation test.

   Reject the null hypothesis that the SAT prep course has no effect in favor of the

   alternative hypothesis that the course has a positive effect.

© Houghton Mifflin Harcourt Publishing Company

- A critic of the experiment pointed out that students taking the SAT prep course spent more time studying for the test, and that the extra time spent studying, not the course itself, was the reason for the observed difference in the mean scores of the treatment and control groups. Do you agree or disagree? Explain. Disagree: The amount of time that a student is willing or able to study for the test is a factor that was randomly distributed between the two groups, so its influence on the results is inconsequential. What distinguished the treatment group from the control group was the course itself. The students taking the course might actually have spent less time, on average, studying for the test than the students not taking the course.

MATHEMATICAL PRACTICE Highlighting the Standards

2 EXAMPLE and its Reflect questions offer an opportunity to address Mathematical Practice Standard 5 (Use appropriate tools strategically). Students use their graphing calculators to generate random numbers that they then use to assign the SAT scores to Group A or Group B in the simulations they run for the permutation test. They can also use their calculators to calculate $\bar{x}_A$, $\bar{x}_B$, and $\bar{x}_A - \bar{x}_B$ for each simulation.

Avoid Common Errors

In part E, when students use the frequency table or histogram in the permutation test to find the probability that a difference of means is at least as great as the difference they recorded for the control and treatment groups in the experiment, they may include only the frequencies for the interval in which the difference occurs. Remind students that they must find the sum of frequencies for all the intervals including and above the difference.

EXTRA EXAMPLE

In another experiment for the same company that offers the SAT prep course, $\bar{x}_T = 1652$ and $\bar{x}_C = 1370$. Based on the result in **2 EXAMPLE**, predict whether or not the null hypothesis can be rejected for this experiment. Explain your reasoning. The null hypothesis is quite likely to be rejected. In **2 EXAMPLE**, $\bar{x}_T - \bar{x}_C = 160$. In this experiment, $\bar{x}_T - \bar{x}_C = 282$. Since the difference is much greater in this experiment, the difference will probably be significant.

CLOSE

Essential Question

In an experiment, when is the difference between the control group and treatment group likely to be caused by the treatment?
In an experiment, the null hypothesis states that any difference between the control group and the treatment group is due to chance. If the difference between the control group and the treatment group has a very low probability of occurring by chance alone, then the null hypothesis is rejected, and the standard practice in statistics is to attribute the cause of the difference to the treatment. You can use a permutation test to determine whether a difference between means in the control group and treatment group is significant.

Summarize

Have students make a graphic organizer outlining the steps for formulating a null hypothesis and using a permutation test to determine whether experimental results are significant.

PRACTICE

Where skills are taught	Where skills are practiced
1 EXAMPLE	EXS. 1, 2
2 EXAMPLE	EXS. 3, 4

REFLECT

2a. The reason that the test is called a *permutation* test is that the process of resampling assigns different permutations of the labels "treatment" and "control" to the 20 SAT scores. Although the number of permutations of *n* distinct objects is *n*!, the objects in this case are 10 "treatment" labels and 10 "control" labels, so the 20 labels are not distinct. When a set of *n* objects contains n_1 copies of the first object, n_2 copies of the second object, . . . , and n_L copies of the last object, then the

formula for the number of permutations of the *n* objects becomes $\dfrac{n!}{n_1! \cdot n_2! \cdot \cdots \cdot n_L!}$.

Use this formula to find the number of permutations of the labels for the SAT scores. Did your class generate all possible resamples?

$\dfrac{20!}{10! \cdot 10!} = 184{,}756$; no

2b. Suppose your class had generated all possible resamples. Explain why the distribution would be perfectly symmetric and centered on 0.

For every treatment group and control group for which a difference of means

equals *x*, you can switch the labels on the two groups and obtain a difference

of means that equals −*x*. The sum of all possible differences of means is 0, so

the mean of the differences is 0.

2c. Explain why it makes sense to call the test of significance in part F a *one-tailed* test?

The *P*-value is calculated using only one tail of the resampling distribution.

PRACTICE

1. King County, Washington, recently required all restaurant chains to post Calorie counts for menu items. Researchers gathered data on the average Calories per transaction at a Mexican restaurant chain both before and after the regulation went into effect.

a. State the null hypothesis in terms of the difference in the average Calories per transaction before and after Calorie counts were posted.

The difference in the average Calories per transaction before and after

Calorie counts were posted is about 0.

b. The researchers found a slight increase in the average Calories per transaction once the regulation went into effect, but the result was not statistically different from 0. What does this result mean in terms of accepting or rejecting the null hypothesis?

The null hypothesis should not be rejected, because the result shows no

evidence that posting Calorie counts affects people's menu choices.

For Exercises 2–4, use the following information.

A textbook company has created an electronic version of one of its books and wants to know what effect, if any, using the e-book has on student learning. With the permission of the school district, a teacher who has two classes that already use the textbook agrees to participate in a research study. One of the classes uses the e-book for the next unit of instruction while the other class continues to use the print version of the book. After teaching the unit, the teacher gives the same test to both classes. The mean score for the class using the e-book is 82.3, while the mean score for the class using the print book is 78.2.

2. State the null hypothesis in terms of the difference of the mean test scores.

The difference of the mean test scores using the e-book and the print

book is about 0.

3. Identify the treatment group and its mean test score, $\bar{x}_T$, as well as the control group and its mean test score, $\bar{x}_C$. Then find $\bar{x}_T - \bar{x}_C$.

Treatment group: class using e-book; $\bar{x}_T = 82.3$; control group: class using

print book; $\bar{x}_C = 78.2$; $\bar{x}_T - \bar{x}_C = 4.1$

4. The resampling distribution for the difference of mean test scores, given that the null hypothesis is true, is normal with a mean of 0 and a standard error of 2. The distribution is shown at the right.

a. Describe how the resampling distribution is obtained from the students' test scores.

Determine all possible permutations of the labels

"e-book" and "print" for the individual test scores from both classes. For each

permutation, calculate the mean test score for each group and find the difference

of the means. The resampling distribution consists of all differences of means.

b. Write an interval that captures the middle 95% of the differences of means in the resampling distribution. If the experimental result falls within this interval, the result is not significant; if it falls outside the interval, the result is significant. Which is the case?

$-4 \le x \le 4$; the experimental result is significant.

c. Explain why the test of significance in part b is called a *two-tailed* test.

A result that falls in either tail (outside the middle 95%) is significant.

d. Should the null hypothesis be accepted or rejected? What does acceptance or rejection mean in this situation?

Reject the null hypothesis, which means that there is enough evidence to reject

the assumption that the e-book had no effect on student learning in favor of

the assumption that it had an effect.

© Houghton Mifflin Harcourt Publishing Company

COMMON CORE CORRELATION

Standard	Items
CC.9-12.S.ID.1*	6
CC.9-12.S.ID.3*	2
CC.9-12.S.ID.4*	5, 8, 10, 11
CC.9-12.S.IC.1*	3, 8
CC.9-12.S.IC.2*	4
CC.9-12.S.IC.3*	1, 9
CC.9-12.S.IC.4*	7, 8
CC.9-12.S.IC.5*	6, 10
CC.9-12.S.IC.6*	7

TEST PREP DOCTOR ⊕

Multiple Choice: Item 1

- Students who chose **A** may have thought that because 50 people were involved in the research and something was measured, the research was an experiment.

- Students who chose **C** may have overlooked the fact that only people with colds were recruited for the research.

- Students who chose **D** may not have understood the concept of statistical research.

Multiple Choice: Item 2

- Students who chose **F** did not recognize that a normal distribution would be symmetric.

- Students who chose **G** probably confused the concepts of a distribution's being skewed left and skewed right.

- Students who chose **J** may not have known what a uniform distribution is.

Free Response: Item 9

- Students who incorrectly answered in part (a) that the research was an experiment did not understand that an experiment would have to involve a treatment, such as having one group exercise 5 hours per week while having another group do no exercise.

- Students who incorrectly answered in part (a) that the research was a survey did not understand that, since the research included a factor and a characteristic of interest, it was an observational study.

- Students who incorrectly determined in part (b) that the researcher could conclude that exercise causes people to eat high-fat foods less frequently did not understand that cause-and-effect relationships between variables can be established only by experiments.

Free Response: Item 10

- Students who stated the null hypothesis incorrectly in part (a) may not have understood that the form of a null hypothesis is that the treatment will have no effect and that any difference between the control group and the treatment group is due to chance.

- Students who stated the interval as $-0.14 \leq x \leq 0.14$ found the interval for the middle 68%, not the middle 95%. Students who stated the interval as $-0.42 \leq x \leq 0.42$ found the interval for the middle 99.7%, not the middle 95%. These students did not understand that the interval that captures the middle 95% of the differences of the means is the mean plus or minus two standard deviations, not one or three standard deviations.

- Students who said that the null hypothesis should not be rejected may not have understood that the mean difference in hair growth between the control and treatment groups was 0.3 inches, which falls outside of the range of $-0.28 \leq x \leq 0.28$. These students may not have understood that because the mean difference falls outside this range, the null hypothesis that any difference was due to chance was very unlikely to be true.

Name _____ Class _____ Date _____

MULTIPLE CHOICE

1. What type of research, described below, is being conducted?

   A researcher recruits 50 people with colds and measures the level of stress they were under during the week prior to the start of the cold.

   A. Experiment

   (B.) Observational study

   C. Survey

   D. None of these

2. Identify the word or phrase that completes this statement: The mean of the data in the distribution shown is greater than the median because the distribution is __?__.

   F. normal   (H.) skewed right

   G. skewed left   J. uniform

3. You want to estimate a population mean by taking a sample from the population and finding the sample's mean. Which sampling technique gives the best estimate?

   A. Convenience sampling

   (B.) Random sampling

   C. Self-selected sampling

   D. Systematic sampling

4. Suppose you roll a die repeatedly and make a histogram of the results (number of 1s, number of 2s, and so on). If the die is fair, which shape will the histogram have?

   F. Normal   H. Skewed right

   G. Skewed left   (J.) Uniform

5. A normal distribution has a mean of 10 and a standard deviation of 1.5. In which interval does the middle 95% of the data fall?

   A. $-3 \leq x \leq 3$ (C.) $7 \leq x \leq 13$

   B. $8.5 \leq x \leq 11.5$ D. $5.5 \leq x \leq 14.5$

6. A researcher recorded the heights of 5 plants grown in soil treated with a fertilizer and 5 plants grown in soil not treated with the fertilizer. The mean height of the treatment group was 24 cm, while the mean height of the control group was 22 cm. A histogram of the differences of means for 50 resamples of the data under the assumption that the fertilizer had no effect on the plants' growth is shown.

   Based on the histogram, what is the probability that a difference of means is *at least as great* as the experimental result?

   F. 0.01   H. 0.1

   (G.) 0.02   J. 0.2

7. A newspaper reports on a survey of likely voters in an upcoming local election. The survey showed that 57% support candidate Robertson with a margin of error of 4%. Which statement about all voters in the election is most likely to be accurate?

   A. Between 55% and 59% favor Robertson.

   (B.) Between 53% and 61% favor Robertson.

   C. Between 53% and 57% favor Robertson.

   D. Between 57% and 61% favor Robertson.

FREE RESPONSE

8. Researchers plan to use a survey to find the percent of workers who are employed full-time in a state. The researchers are aiming for a 3% margin of error at a 95% confidence level. Can they attain this result by polling 1000 randomly selected workers? Justify your answer.

   No; to find the minimum sample size, you must solve the margin-of-error formula $E = z_c \cdot \sqrt{\frac{\hat{p}(1 - \hat{p})}{n}}$ for n and then substitute 0.03 for E, 1.96 for z_c, and 0.5 as an estimate for $\hat{p}$. Doing so gives $n \approx 1067.1$, so to get a 3% margin of error at a 95% confidence level, the researchers would have to poll at least 1068 people.

9. A researcher finds that people who exercise for at least 5 hours per week eat high-fat foods less often than people who exercise less than 5 hours per week.

   a. What type of research is this? Explain how you know.

   Observational study; the researcher starts with an existing condition (amount of exercise) and checks for a characteristic of interest (consumption of high-fat foods).

   b. Can the researcher conclude that exercise causes people to eat high-fat foods less frequently? Explain.

   No; although the study may show an association between exercise and consumption of high-fat foods, it cannot establish a cause-and-effect relationship. There are likely other factors at work, such as overall health-consciousness.

10. In a randomized comparative experiment, 100 people used a hair growth agent for two months and 100 people did not. The mean hair growth among people who used the agent was 1.3 inches, and the mean hair growth among people who did not use it was 1.0 inch.

    a. State the null hypothesis for this experiment in terms of the effect of the treatment and in terms of the difference of the means.

    The treatment has no effect on hair growth; the difference of the means is about 0.

    b. Given that the null hypothesis is true, the resampling distribution for the difference of means is normal with a mean of 0 inches and a standard deviation of 0.14 inch. State the interval that captures the middle 95% of the differences of the means.

    $2(-0.14) \leq x \leq 2(0.14)$, or $-0.28 \leq x \leq 0.28$

    c. Should the null hypothesis be rejected? Explain why or why not.

    Yes; because the observed result falls outside the middle 95% of the differences of means, it is a very unlikely result.

11. Suppose the upper arm length (in centimeters) of adult males in the United States is normally distributed with a mean of 39.4 cm and a standard deviation of 2.3 cm.

    a. What percent of adult males have an upper arm length no greater than 41.7 cm? Explain how you know.

    84%; 41.7 cm is 1 standard deviation above the mean; in a normal distribution, the percent of data less than the mean is 50%, and the percent of data between the mean and 1 standard deviation above the mean is 34%.

    b. What is the probability that a randomly chosen adult male has an upper arm length greater than 44 cm? Explain how you know.

    0.025; 44 cm is 2 standard deviations above the mean; in a normal distribution, the percent of data between 2 and 3 standard deviations above the mean is 2.35%, and the percent of data greater than 3 standard deviations above the mean is 0.15%.

COMMON CORE **Correlations**

Correlation of *On Core Mathematics* to the Common Core State Standards

Standards	Algebra 1	Geometry	Algebra 2
Number and Quantity			
The Real Number System			
CC.9-12.N.RN.1 Explain how the definition of the meaning of rational exponents follows from extending the properties of integer exponents to those values, allowing for a notation for radicals in terms of rational exponents.			Lesson 1-2
CC.9-12.N.RN.2 Rewrite expressions involving radicals and rational exponents using the properties of exponents.			Lesson 1-2
CC.9-12.N.RN.3 Explain why the sum or product of two rational numbers is rational; that the sum of a rational number and an irrational number is irrational; and that the product of a nonzero rational number and an irrational number is irrational.			Lesson 1-1
Quantities			
CC.9-12.N.Q.1 Use units as a way to understand problems and to guide the solution of multi-step problems; choose and interpret units consistently in formulas; choose and interpret the scale and the origin in graphs and data displays.*	Lessons 1-1, 1-2, 1-3, 1-5, 1-6, 2-3, 2-8, 3-6, 4-2, 4-3, 7-6		Lesson 2-6
CC.9-12.N.Q.2 Define appropriate quantities for the purpose of descriptive modeling.*	Lessons 1-3, 1-4, 2-3, 2-8, 3-6, 7-6		
CC.9-12.N.Q.3 Choose a level of accuracy appropriate to limitations on measurement when reporting quantities.*		Lesson 9-1	
The Complex Number System			
CC.9-12.N.CN.1 Know there is a complex number i such that $i^2 = -1$, and every complex number has the form $a + bi$ with a and b real.			Lesson 1-3
CC.9-12.N.CN.2 Use the relation $i^2 = -1$ and the commutative, associative, and distributive properties to add, subtract, and multiply complex numbers.			Lesson 1-3
CC.9-12.N.CN.3(+) Find the conjugate of a complex number; use conjugates to find moduli and quotients of complex numbers.			Lesson 1-4

(+) Advanced   * = Also a Modeling Standard

© Houghton Mifflin Harcourt Publishing Company

Standards	Algebra 1	Geometry	Algebra 2
CC.9-12.N.CN.7 Solve quadratic equations with real coefficients that have complex solutions.			Lesson 1-5
CC.9-12.N.CN.9(+) Know the Fundamental Theorem of Algebra; show that it is true for quadratic polynomials.			Lesson 3-10
Algebra			
Seeing Structure in Expressions			
CC.9-12.A.SSE.1 Interpret expressions that represent a quantity in terms of its context.* **a.** Interpret parts of an expression, such as terms, factors, and coefficients. **b.** Interpret complicated expressions by viewing one or more of their parts as a single entity.	Lessons 1-1, 1-2, 1-3, 2-8		Lessons 2-6, 3-5, 3-11, 4-4, 4-5, 9-4, 9-5
CC.9-12.A.SSE.2 Use the structure of an expression to identify ways to rewrite it.	Lessons 1-2, 1-3, 2-1, 2-2, 8-1		Lessons 3-9, 3-10
CC.9-12.A.SSE.3 Choose and produce an equivalent form of an expression to reveal and explain properties of the quantity represented by the expression. **a.** Factor a quadratic expression to reveal the zeros of the function it defines. **b.** Complete the square in a quadratic expression to reveal the maximum or minimum value of the function it defines. **c.** Use the properties of exponents to transform expressions for exponential functions.	Lessons 8-2, 8-3, 8-10		Lessons 2-4, 2-5, 6-4, 6-6
CC.9-12.A.SSE.4 Derive the formula for the sum of a finite geometric series (when the common ratio is not 1), and use the formula to solve problems.			Lessons 9-4, 9-5
Arithmetic with Polynomials and Rational Expressions			
CC.9-12.A.APR.1 Understand that polynomials form a system analogous to the integers, namely, they are closed under the operations of addition, subtraction, and multiplication; add, subtract, and multiply polynomials.	Lessons 4-6, 8-1		Lessons 3-5, 3-6, 3-7, 3-8
CC.9-12.A.APR.2 Know and apply the Remainder Theorem: For a polynomial $p(x)$ and a number a, the remainder on division by $x - a$ is $p(a)$, so $p(a) = 0$ if and only if $(x - a)$ is a factor of $p(x)$.			Lesson 3-8
CC.9-12.A.APR.3 Identify zeros of polynomials when suitable factorizations are available, and use the zeros to construct a rough graph of the function defined by the polynomial.			Lesson 3-9
CC.9-12.A.APR.4 Prove polynomial identities and use them to describe numerical relationships.			Lesson 3-6

(+) Advanced   * = Also a Modeling Standard

Standards	Algebra 1	Geometry	Algebra 2
CC.9-12.A.APR.5(+) Know and apply the Binomial Theorem for the expansion of $(x + y)^n$ in powers of x and y for a positive integer n, where x and y are any numbers, with coefficients determined for example by Pascal's Triangle. (The Binomial Theorem can be proved by mathematical induction or by a combinatorial argument.)			Lesson 3-7
CC.9-12.A.APR.6 Rewrite simple rational expressions in different forms; write $a(x)/b(x)$ in the form $q(x) + r(x)/b(x)$, where $a(x)$, $b(x)$, $q(x)$, and $r(x)$ are polynomials with the degree of $r(x)$ less than the degree of $b(x)$, using inspection, long division, or, for the more complicated examples, a computer algebra system.			Lesson 4-3
CC.9-12.A.APR.7(+) Understand that rational expressions form a system analogous to the rational numbers, closed under addition, subtraction, multiplication, and division by a nonzero rational expression; add, subtract, multiply, and divide rational expressions.			Lessons 4-4, 4-5
Creating Equations			
CC.9-12.A.CED.1 Create equations and inequalities in one variable and use them to solve problems.*	Lessons 1-4, 2-3, 5-5, 6-5, 7-4, 7-5, 8-3, 8-7		Lessons 3-11, 4-6, 6-7, 7-4
CC.9-12.A.CED.2 Create equations in two or more variables to represent relationships between quantities; graph equations on coordinate axes with labels and scales.*	Lessons 2-3, 2-5, 2-8, 3-6, 4-2, 4-3, 4-5, 4-6, 5-1, 5-5, 5-6, 5-8, 6-1, 6-2, 6-3, 6-4, 6-5, 6-6, 7-1, 7-2, 7-3, 7-4, 7-6, 8-9, 8-10		Lessons 2-3, 2-4, 2-5, 2-6, 3-9, 3-11, 4-1, 4-2, 4-3, 4-7, 5-1, 5-2, 5-3, 5-5, 5-6, 6-2, 6-3, 6-4, 6-5, 6-6, 7-5, 8-9
CC.9-12.A.CED.3 Represent constraints by equations or inequalities, and by systems of equations and/or inequalities, and interpret solutions as viable or nonviable options in a modeling context.*	Lessons 1-4, 2-3, 2-8, 3-6		Lessons 2-6, 3-11, 9-5
CC.9-12.A.CED.4 Rearrange formulas to highlight a quantity of interest, using the same reasoning as in solving equations.*	Lesson 2-5		Lesson 7-5
Reasoning with Equations and Inequalities			
CC.9-12.A.REI.1. Explain each step in solving a simple equation as following from the equality of numbers asserted at the previous step, starting from the assumption that the original equation has a solution. Construct a viable argument to justify a solution method.	Lessons 2-1, 2-2, 2-4		
CC.9-12.A.REI.2 Solve simple rational and radical equations in one variable, and give examples showing how extraneous solutions may arise.			Lessons 4-6, 5-7
CC.9-12.A.REI.3 Solve linear equations and inequalities in one variable, including equations with coefficients represented by letters.	Lessons 2-1, 2-2, 2-3, 2-4		

(+) Advanced   * = Also a Modeling Standard

© Houghton Mifflin Harcourt Publishing Company

Standards	Algebra 1	Geometry	Algebra 2
CC.9-12.A.REI.4 Solve quadratic equations in one variable. a. Use the method of completing the square to transform any quadratic equation in x into an equation of the form $(x - p)^2 = q$ that has the same solutions. Derive the quadratic formula from this form. b. Solve quadratic equations by inspection (e.g., for $x^2 = 49$), taking square roots, completing the square, the quadratic formula and factoring, as appropriate to the initial form of the equation. Recognize when the quadratic formula gives complex solutions and write them as $a \pm bi$ for real numbers a and b.	Lessons 7-5, 8-2, 8-3, 8-4, 8-5, 8-6, 8-7, 8-9, 8-10		Lesson 1-5
CC.9-12.A.REI.5 Prove that, given a system of two equations in two variables, replacing one equation by the sum of that equation and a multiple of the other produces a system with the same solutions.	Lesson 3-4		
CC.9-12.A.REI.6 Solve systems of linear equations exactly and approximately (e.g., with graphs), focusing on pairs of linear equations in two variables.	Lessons 3-1, 3-2, 3-3, 3-4, 3-6		
CC.9-12.A.REI.7 Solve a simple system consisting of a linear equation and a quadratic equation in two variables algebraically and graphically.	Lesson 8-9	Lesson 8-7	
CC.9-12.A.REI.10 Understand that the graph of an equation in two variables is the set of all its solutions plotted in the coordinate plane, often forming a curve (which could be a line).	Lessons 2-6, 2-7		
CC.9-12.A.REI.11 Explain why the x-coordinates of the points where the graphs of the equations $y = f(x)$ and $y = g(x)$ intersect are the solutions of the equation $f(x) = g(x)$; find the solutions approximately, e.g., using technology to graph the functions, make tables of values, or find successive approximations. Include cases where $f(x)$ and/or $g(x)$ are linear, polynomial, rational, absolute value, exponential, and logarithmic functions.*	Lessons 4-5, 5-5, 5-8, 6-5, 7-4		Lessons 4-6, 5-7, 6-7, 7-4
CC.9-12.A.REI.12 Graph the solutions to a linear inequality in two variables as a half-plane (excluding the boundary in the case of a strict inequality), and graph the solution set to a system of linear inequalities in two variables as the intersection of the corresponding half-planes.	Lessons 2-6, 2-7, 3-5, 3-6		
Functions			
Interpreting Functions			
CC.9-12.F.IF.1 Understand that a function from one set (called the domain) to another set (called the range) assigns to each element of the domain exactly one element of the range. If f is a function and x is an element of its domain, then $f(x)$ denotes the output of f corresponding to the input x. The graph of f is the graph of the equation $y = f(x)$.	Lessons 1-5, 1-6, 4-2, 4-7, 5-2		Lesson 8-3

(+) Advanced   * = Also a Modeling Standard

On Core Mathematics Algebra 2

Common Core Correlations

Standards	Algebra 1	Geometry	Algebra 2
CC.9-12.F.IF.2 Use function notation, evaluate functions for inputs in their domains, and interpret statements that use function notation in terms of a context.	Lessons 1-5, 1-6, 4-1, 4-2, 4-7, 5-1, 6-1, 6-2, 6-3, 6-4, 6-6, 7-1, 7-2, 7-3, 7-6, 8-10		**Lessons 2-1, 2-2, 2-3, 2-4, 2-5, 2-6, 3-4, 4-1, 4-2, 4-3, 4-7, 5-1, 5-2, 5-3, 5-5, 5-6, 6-1, 6-2, 6-3, 6-4, 6-5, 7-1, 7-5, 8-9, 9-1**
CC.9-12.F.IF.3 Recognize that sequences are functions, sometimes defined recursively, whose domain is a subset of the integers.	Lessons 4-1, 5-1		**Lesson 9-1**
CC.9-12.F.IF.4 For a function that models a relationship between two quantities, interpret key features of graphs and tables in terms of the quantities, and sketch graphs showing key features given a verbal description of the relationship.*	Lessons 4-3, 4-4, 4-5, 5-3, 5-4, 6-1, 6-6, 7-1, 7-2, 7-3, 7-6, 8-8, 8-9, 8-10		**Lessons 2-6, 3-11, 4-1, 4-2, 4-3, 4-7, 5-5, 5-6, 6-2, 6-3, 6-6, 7-5, 8-9**
CC.9-12.F.IF.5 Relate the domain of a function to its graph and, where applicable, to the quantitative relationship it describes.*	Lessons 1-5, 1-6, 4-1, 4-2, 5-1, 5-2, 5-8, 6-1, 6-6, 7-1, 8-8		**Lessons 2-6, 3-11**
CC.9-12.F.IF.6 Calculate and interpret the average rate of change of a function (presented symbolically or as a table) over a specified interval. Estimate the rate of change from a graph.*	Lessons 4-3, 4-5, 8-10		**Lessons 2-6**
CC.9-12.F.IF.7 Graph functions expressed symbolically and show key features of the graph, by hand in simple cases and using technology for more complicated cases.* **a.** Graph linear and quadratic functions and show intercepts, maxima, and minima. **b.** Graph square root, cube root, and piecewise-defined functions, including step functions and absolute value functions. **c.** Graph polynomial functions, identifying zeros when suitable factorizations are available, and showing end behavior. **d.** (+) Graph rational functions, identifying zeros and asymptotes when suitable factorizations are available, and showing end behavior. **e.** Graph exponential and logarithmic functions, showing intercepts and end behavior, and trigonometric functions, showing period, midline, and amplitude.	Lessons 4-1, 4-3, 4-5, 5-1, 5-2, 5-3, 5-8, 6-1, 6-2, 6-3, 6-4, 6-6, 7-1, 7-2, 7-3, 8-8		**Lessons 2-1, 2-2, 2-3, 2-4, 2-5, 2-6, 3-1, 3-2, 3-3, 3-4, 3-9, 3-11, 4-1, 4-2, 4-3, 4-7, 5-1, 5-2, 5-3, 5-4, 5-5, 5-6, 6-1, 6-2, 6-3, 6-4, 6-5, 6-6, 6-7, 7-1, 7-2, 8-5, 8-6, 8-7, 8-8, 8-9**
CC.9-12.F.IF.8 Write a function defined by an expression in different but equivalent forms to reveal and explain different properties of the function. **a.** Use the process of factoring and completing the square in a quadratic function to show zeros, extreme values, and symmetry of the graph, and interpret these in terms of a context. **b.** Use the properties of exponents to interpret expressions for exponential functions.	Lessons 8-2, 8-3, 8-8, 8-10		**Lessons 2-4, 2-5, 6-4, 6-6**
CC.9-12.F.IF.9 Compare properties of two functions each represented in a different way (algebraically, graphically, numerically in tables, or by verbal descriptions).	Lessons 4-2, 8-10		**Lesson 4-7**

(+) Advanced   * = Also a Modeling Standard

Standards	Algebra 1	Geometry	Algebra 2
Building Functions			
CC.9-12.F.BF.1 Write a function that describes a relationship between two quantities.* **a.** Determine an explicit expression, a recursive process, or steps for calculation from a context. **b.** Combine standard function types using arithmetic operations. **c.** (+) Compose functions.	Lessons 1-6, 2-3, 2-8, 4-5, 4-6, 4-9, 5-5, 5-6, 5-8, 6-1, 6-2, 6-3, 6-4, 6-6, 7-1, 7-2, 7-3, 7-6, 8-3, 8-8, 8-10		Lessons 2-6, 3-5, 3-11, 4-1, 4-2, 4-3, 4-4, 4-5, 4-7, 5-5, 5-6, 6-2, 6-3, 6-4, 6-6, 7-5, 8-9, 9-1, 9-2, 9-3
CC.9-12.F.BF.2 Write arithmetic and geometric sequences both recursively and with an explicit formula, use them to model situations, and translate between the two forms.*	Lesson 4-1		Lessons 9-2, 9-3
CC.9-12.F.BF.3 Identify the effect on the graph of replacing $f(x)$ by $f(x) + k$, $kf(x)$, $f(kx)$, and $f(x + k)$ for specific values of k (both positive and negative); find the value of k given the graphs. Experiment with cases and illustrate an explanation of the effects on the graph using technology.	Lessons 4-4, 5-4, 6-2, 6-3, 6-4, 7-1, 7-2, 7-3		Lessons 2-1, 2-2, 2-3, 3-1, 3-2, 3-3, 4-1, 4-2, 5-4, 6-2, 6-3, 6-4, 6-5, 7-2, 8-7, 8-8, 8-9
CC.9-12.F.BF.4 Find inverse functions. **a.** Solve an equation of the form $f(x) = c$ for a simple function f that has an inverse and write an expression for the inverse. **b.** (+) Verify by composition that one function is the inverse of another. **c.** (+) Read values of an inverse function from a graph or a table, given that the function has an inverse. **d.** (+) Produce an invertible function from a non-invertible function by restricting the domain.	Lesson 4-7		Lessons 5-1, 5-2, 5-3, 5-5, 5-6
CC.9-12.F.BF.5(+) Understand the inverse relationship between exponents and logarithms and use this relationship to solve problems involving logarithms and exponents.			Lessons 7-1, 7-3
Linear, Quadratic, and Exponential Models			
CC.9-12.F.LE.1 Distinguish between situations that can be modeled with linear functions and with exponential functions.* **a.** Prove that linear functions grow by equal differences over equal intervals, and that exponential functions grow by equal factors over equal intervals. **b.** Recognize situations in which one quantity changes at a constant rate per unit interval relative to another. **c.** Recognize situations in which a quantity grows or decays by a constant percent rate per unit interval relative to another.	Lessons 5-2, 5-3, 5-6, 5-7, 5-8		
CC.9-12.F.LE.2 Construct linear and exponential functions, including arithmetic and geometric sequences, given a graph, a description of a relationship, or two input-output pairs (include reading these from a table).*	Lessons 4-5, 4-6, 5-1, 5-2, 5-3, 5-5, 5-8		Lessons 6-2, 6-3, 6-4, 6-5, 9-2, 9-3

(+) Advanced   * = Also a Modeling Standard

Standards	Algebra 1	Geometry	Algebra 2
CC.9-12.F.LE.3 Observe using graphs and tables that a quantity increasing exponentially eventually exceeds a quantity increasing linearly, quadratically, or (more generally) as a polynomial function.*	Lesson 5-7		Lessons 6-1, 6-6
CC.9-12.F.LE.4 For exponential models, express as a logarithm the solution to $ab^{ct} = d$ where a, c, and d are numbers and the base b is 2, 10, or e; evaluate the logarithm using technology.*			Lesson 7-4
CC.9-12.F.LE.5 Interpret the parameters in a linear or exponential function in terms of a context.*	Lessons 4-4, 4-5, 4-6, 4-9, 4-10, 5-2, 5-3, 5-6, 5-8		Lessons 6-4, 6-5
Trigonometric Functions			
CC.9-12.F.TF.1 Understand radian measure of an angle as the length of the arc on the unit circle subtended by the angle.			Lesson 8-2
CC.9-12.F.TF.2 Explain how the unit circle in the coordinate plane enables the extension of trigonometric functions to all real numbers, interpreted as radian measures of angles traversed counterclockwise around the unit circle.			Lesson 8-3
CC.9-12.F.TF.3(+) Use special triangles to determine geometrically the values of sine, cosine, tangent for $\pi/3$, $\pi/4$ and $\pi/6$, and use the unit circle to express the values of sine, cosines, and tangent for x, $\pi + x$, and $2\pi - x$ in terms of their values for x, where x is any real number.			Lesson 8-3
CC.9-12.F.TF.4(+) Use the unit circle to explain symmetry (odd and even) and periodicity of trigonometric functions.			Lessons 8-5, 8-6
CC.9-12.F.TF.5 Choose trigonometric functions to model periodic phenomena with specified amplitude, frequency, and midline.*			Lesson 8-9
CC.9-12.F.TF.8 Prove the Pythagorean identity $\sin^2(\theta) + \cos^2(\theta) = 1$ and use it to calculate trigonometric ratios.			Lesson 8-4
Geometry			
Congruence			
CC.9-12.G.CO.1 Know precise definitions of angle, circle, perpendicular line, parallel line, and line segment, based on the undefined notions of point, line, distance along a line, and distance around a circular arc.		Lessons 1-1, 1-4, 1-5, 9-4	
CC.9-12.G.CO.2 Represent transformations in the plane using, e.g., transparencies and geometry software; describe transformations as functions that take points in the plane as inputs and give other points as outputs. Compare transformations that preserve distance and angle to those that do not (e.g., translation versus horizontal stretch).		Lessons 2-1, 2-2, 2-3, 2-4, 2-5, 2-6, 5-1, 5-2	

(+) Advanced   * = Also a Modeling Standard

Standards	Algebra 1	Geometry	Algebra 2
CC.9-12.G.CO.3 Given a rectangle, parallelogram, trapezoid, or regular polygon, describe the rotations and reflections that carry it onto itself.		Lesson 4-1	
CC.9-12.G.CO.4 Develop definitions of rotations, reflections, and translations in terms of angles, circles, perpendicular lines, parallel lines, and line segments.		Lessons 2-2, 2-5, 2-6	
CC.9-12.G.CO.5 Given a geometric figure and a rotation, reflection, or translation, draw the transformed figure using, e.g., graph paper, tracing paper, or geometry software. Specify a sequence of transformations that will carry a given figure onto another.		Lessons 2-2, 2-5, 2-6, 3-1	
CC.9-12.G.CO.6 Use geometric descriptions of rigid motions to transform figures and to predict the effect of a given rigid motion on a given figure; given two figures, use the definition of congruence in terms of rigid motions to decide if they are congruent.		Lessons 2-2, 2-5, 2-6, 3-1	
CC.9-12.G.CO.7 Use the definition of congruence in terms of rigid motions to show that two triangles are congruent if and only if corresponding pairs of sides and corresponding pairs of angles are congruent.		Lessons 3-2, 3-3	
CC.9-12.G.CO.8 Explain how the criteria for triangle congruence (ASA, SAS, and SSS) follow from the definition of congruence in terms of rigid motions.		Lesson 3-3	
CC.9-12.G.CO.9 Prove geometric theorems about lines and angles.		Lessons 1-6, 1-7, 2-3, 2-4	
CC.9-12.G.CO.10 Prove theorems about triangles.		Lessons 3-5, 3-6, 3-7, 3-8, 3-9	
CC.9-12.G.CO.11 Prove theorems about parallelograms.		Lessons 4-2, 4-3, 4-4, 4-5	
CC.9-12.G.CO.12 Make formal geometric constructions with a variety of tools and methods (compass and straightedge, string, reflective devices, paper folding, dynamic geometry software, etc.).		Lessons 1-1, 1-4, 1-5	
CC.9-12.G.CO.13 Construct an equilateral triangle, a square, and a regular hexagon inscribed in a circle.		Lesson 7-3	
Similarity, Right Triangles, and Trigonometry			
CC.9-12.G.SRT.1 Verify experimentally the properties of dilations given by a center and a scale factor: **a.** A dilation takes a line not passing through the center of the dilation to a parallel line, and leaves a line passing through the center unchanged. **b.** The dilation of a line segment is longer or shorter in the ratio given by the scale factor.		Lesson 5-1	

(+) Advanced   * = Also a Modeling Standard

Standards	Algebra 1	Geometry	Algebra 2
CC.9-12.G.SRT.2 Given two figures, use the definition of similarity in terms of similarity transformations to decide if they are similar; explain using similarity transformations the meaning of similarity for triangles as the equality of all corresponding angles and the proportionality of all corresponding pairs of sides.		Lessons 5-3, 5-4	
CC.9-12.G.SRT.3 Use the properties of similarity transformations to establish the AA criterion for two triangles to be similar.		Lesson 5-4	
CC.9-12.G.SRT.4 Prove theorems about triangles.		Lessons 5-6, 5-7	
CC.9-12.G.SRT.5 Use congruence and similarity criteria for triangles to solve problems and prove relationships in geometric figures.		Lessons 3-4, 4-2, 4-3, 4-4, 4-5, 5-5, 5-6, 5-7	
CC.9-12.G.SRT.6 Understand that by similarity, side ratios in right triangles are properties of the angles in the triangle, leading to definitions of trigonometric ratios for acute angles.		Lessons 6-1, 6-2, 6-3	
CC.9-12.G.SRT.7 Explain and use the relationship between the sine and cosine of complementary angles.		Lessons 6-2, 6-3	
CC.9-12.G.SRT.8 Use trigonometric ratios and the Pythagorean Theorem to solve right triangles in applied problems.		Lesson 6-4	
CC.9-12.G.SRT.9(+) Derive the formula $A = 1/2\ ab\ \sin(C)$ for the area of a triangle by drawing an auxiliary line from a vertex perpendicular to the opposite side.		Lesson 6-5	
CC.9-12.G.SRT.10(+) Prove the Laws of Sines and Cosines and use them to solve problems.		Lessons 6-6, 6-7	
CC.9-12.G.SRT.11(+) Understand and apply the Law of Sines and the Law of Cosines to find unknown measurements in right and non-right triangles (e.g., surveying problems, resultant forces).		Lessons 6-6, 6-7	
Circles			
CC.9-12.G.C.1 Prove that all circles are similar.		Lesson 5-3	
CC.9-12.G.C.2 Identify and describe relationships among inscribed angles, radii, and chords.		Lessons 7-1, 7-5	
CC.9-12.G.C.3 Construct the inscribed and circumscribed circles of a triangle, and prove properties of angles for a quadrilateral inscribed in a circle.		Lessons 7-2, 7-4, 7-6	
CC.9-12.G.C.4(+) Construct a tangent line from a point outside a given circle to the circle.		Lesson 7-5	

(+) Advanced   * = Also a Modeling Standard

© Houghton Mifflin Harcourt Publishing Company

Standards	Algebra 1	Geometry	Algebra 2
CC.9-12.G.C.5 Derive using similarity the fact that the length of the arc intercepted by an angle is proportional to the radius, and define the radian measure of the angle as the constant of proportionality; derive the formula for the area of a sector.		Lessons 9-4, 9-5	Lesson 8-1
Expressing Geometric Properties with Equations			
CC.9-12.G.GPE.1 Derive the equation of a circle of given center and radius using the Pythagorean Theorem; complete the square to find the center and radius of a circle given by an equation.		Lesson 8-1	
CC.9-12.G.GPE.2 Derive the equation of a parabola given a focus and directrix.		Lesson 8-2	
CC.9-12.G.GPE.4 Use coordinates to prove simple geometric theorems algebraically.		Lessons 1-2, 1-3, 3-7, 3-8, 3-9, 8-1, 8-6	
CC.9-12.G.GPE.5 Prove the slope criteria for parallel and perpendicular lines and use them to solve geometric problems (e.g., find the equation of line parallel or perpendicular to a given line that passes through a given point).		Lessons 8-4, 8-5	
CC.9-12.G.GPE.6 Find the point on a directed line segment between two given points that partitions the segment in a given ratio.		Lesson 8-3	
CC.9-12.G.GPE.7 Use coordinates to compute perimeters of polygons and areas of triangles and rectangles, e.g., using the distance formula.*		Lesson 9-2	
Geometric Measurement and Dimension			
CC.9-12.G.GMD.1 Give an informal argument for the formulas for the circumference of a circle, area of a circle, volume of a cylinder, pyramid, and cone.		Lessons 9-3, 9-5, 10-2, 10-3, 10-4	
CC.9-12.G.GMD.2(+) Give an informal argument using Cavalieri's principle for the formulas for the volume of a sphere and other solid figures.		Lessons 10-2, 10-5	
CC.9-12.G.GMD.3 Use volume formulas for cylinders, pyramids, cones, and spheres to solve problems.*		Lessons 10-2, 10-3, 10-4, 10-5, 10-6	
CC.9-12.G.GMD.4 Identify the shapes of two-dimensional cross-sections of three-dimensional objects, and identify three-dimensional objects generated by rotations of two-dimensional objects.		Lesson 10-1	

(+) Advanced   * = Also a Modeling Standard

© Houghton Mifflin Harcourt Publishing Company

Standards	Algebra 1	Geometry	Algebra 2
Modeling with Geometry			
CC.9-12.G.MG.1 Use geometric shapes, their measures, and their properties to describe objects (e.g., modeling a tree trunk or a human torso as a cylinder).*		Lessons 9-2, 9-3, 10-2	
CC.9-12.G.MG.2 Apply concepts of density based on area and volume in modeling situations (e.g., persons per square mile, BTUs per cubic foot).*		Lessons 9-2, 10-2, 10-5	
CC.9-12.G.MG.3 Apply geometric methods to solve design problems (e.g., designing an object or structure to satisfy physical constraints or minimize cost; working with typographic grid systems based on ratios).*		Lessons 5-5, 10-6	
Statistics and Probability			
Interpreting Categorical and Quantitative Data			
CC.9-12.S.ID.1 Represent data with plots on the real number line (dot plots, histograms, and box plots).*	Lessons 9-2, 9-3, 9-4		**Lessons 10-2, 10-3**
CC.9-12.S.ID.2 Use statistics appropriate to the shape of the data distribution to compare center (median, mean) and spread (interquartile range, standard deviation) of two or more different data sets.*	Lessons 9-1, 9-2, 9-3, 9-4		
CC.9-12.S.ID.3 Interpret differences in shape, center, and spread in the context of the data sets, accounting for possible effects of extreme data points (outliers).*	Lesson 9-2		**Lesson 10-2**
CC.9-12.S.ID.4 Use the mean and standard deviation of a data set to fit it to a normal distribution and to estimate population percentages. Recognize that there are data sets for which such a procedure is not appropriate. Use calculators, spreadsheets, and tables to estimate areas under the normal curve.*			**Lesson 10-4**
CC.9-12.S.ID.5 Summarize categorical data for two categories in two-way frequency tables. Interpret relative frequencies in the context of the data (including joint, marginal, and conditional relative frequencies). Recognize possible associations and trends in the data.*	Lesson 9-5		
CC.9-12.S.ID.6 Represent data on two quantitative variables on a scatter plot, and describe how the variables are related.* **a.** Fit a function to the data; use functions fitted to data to solve problems in the context of the data. **b.** Informally assess the fit of a function by plotting and analyzing residuals. **c.** Fit a linear function for a scatter plot that suggests a linear association.	Lessons 4-9, 4-10, 5-6, 5-8		**Lessons 5-5, 5-6, 6-6**

(+) Advanced   * = Also a Modeling Standard

© Houghton Mifflin Harcourt Publishing Company

Standards	Algebra 1	Geometry	Algebra 2
CC.9-12.S.ID.7 Interpret the slope (rate of change) and the intercept (constant term) of a linear model in the context of the data.*	Lessons 4-9, 4-10		
CC.9-12.S.ID.8 Compute (using technology) and interpret the correlation coefficient of a linear fit.*	Lessons 4-8, 4-10		
CC.9-12.S.ID.9 Distinguish between correlation and causation.*	Lesson 4-8		
Making Inferences and Justifying Conclusions			
CC.9-12.S.IC.1 Understand statistics as a process for making inferences about population parameters based on a random sample from that population.*			Lesson 10-1
CC.9-12.S.IC.2 Decide if a specified model is consistent with results from a given data-generating process, e.g., using simulation.*			Lesson 10-3
CC.9-12.S.IC.3 Recognize the purposes of and differences among sample surveys, experiments, and observational studies; explain how randomization relates to each.*			Lesson 10-7
CC.9-12.S.IC.4 Use data from a sample survey to estimate a population mean or proportion; develop a margin of error through the use of simulation models for random sampling.*			Lessons 10-5, 10-6
CC.9-12.S.IC.5 Use data from a randomized experiment to compare two treatments; use simulations to decide if differences between parameters are significant.*			Lesson 10-8
CC.9-12.S.IC.6 Evaluate reports based on data.*	Lesson 4-8		Lesson 10-7
Conditional Probability and the Rules of Probability			
CC.9-12.S.CP.1 Describe events as subsets of a sample space (the set of outcomes) using characteristics (or categories) of the outcomes, or as unions, intersections, or complements of other events ("or," "and," "not").*		Lesson 11-1	
CC.9-12.S.CP.2 Understand that two events A and B are independent if the probability of A and B occurring together is the product of their probabilities, and use this characterization to determine if they are independent.*		Lesson 11-7	
CC.9-12.S.CP.3 Understand the conditional probability of A given B as $P(A$ and $B)/P(B)$, and interpret independence of A and B as saying that the conditional probability of A given B is the same as the probability of A, and the conditional probability of B given A is the same as the probability of B.*		Lessons 11-6, 11-7	

(+) Advanced   * = Also a Modeling Standard

On Core Mathematics Algebra 2

Common Core Correlations

Standards	Algebra 1	Geometry	Algebra 2
CC.9-12.S.CP.4 Construct and interpret two-way frequency tables of data when two categories are associated with each object being classified. Use the two-way table as a sample space to decide if events are independent and to approximate conditional probabilities.*		Lessons 11-6, 11-7, 11-10	
CC.9-12.S.CP.5 Recognize and explain the concepts of conditional probability and independence in everyday language and everyday situations.*		Lessons 11-6, 11-7	
CC.9-12.S.CP.6 Find the conditional probability of A given B as the fraction of B's outcomes that also belong to A, and interpret the answer in terms of the model.*		Lesson 11-6	
CC.9-12.S.CP.7 Apply the Addition Rule, $P(A \text{ or } B) = P(A) + P(B) - P(A \text{ and } B)$, and interpret the answer in terms of the model.*		Lesson 11-5	
CC.9-12.S.CP.8(+) Apply the general Multiplication Rule in a uniform probability model, $P(A \text{ and } B) = P(A)P(B|A) = P(B)P(A|B)$, and interpret the answer in terms of the model.*		Lesson 11-8	
CC.9-12.S.CP.9(+) Use permutations and combinations to compute probabilities of compound events and solve problems.*		Lessons 11-3, 11-4	
Using Probability to Make Decisions			
CC.9-12.S.MD.6(+) Use probabilities to make fair decisions (e.g., drawing by lots, using a random number generator).*		Lessons 11-2, 11-9	
CC.9-12.S.MD.7(+) Analyze decisions and strategies using probability concepts (e.g., product testing, medical testing, pulling a hockey goalie at the end of a game).*		Lesson 11-10	

(+) Advanced   * = Also a Modeling Standard